THE KITCHEN REVOLUTION

Change the way you cook
and eat forever – and save
time, effort, money and food
****
Rosie Sykes,
Polly Russell
&
Zoe Heron

EBURY
PRESS

1 3 5 7 9 10 8 6 4 2

Published in 2008 by Ebury Press, an imprint of
Ebury Publishing
Ebury Publishing is a division of the Random
House Group

Text © Rosie Sykes, Polly Russell and Zoe Heron 2008

Rosie Sykes, Polly Russell and Zoe Heron have
asserted their right to be identified as the authors
of this Work in accordance with the Copyright,
Designs and Patents Act 1988

The Random House Group Limited Reg. No. 954009

Addresses for companies within the Random House
Group can be found at www.randomhouse.co.uk

A CIP catalogue record for this book is available
from the British Library

The Random House Group makes every effort to
ensure that the papers used in our books are made
from trees that have been legally sourced from
well-managed and credibly certified forests.
Our paper procurement policy can be found on
www.randomhouse.co.uk

Design: objectif
Typesetter: Seagull Design
Editor: Jane Bamforth

Printed and bound in China by Midas
ISBN: 9780091913731

To buy books by your favourite authors and
register for offers visit www.rbooks.co.uk

RS: For Rob who never fails to make me smile, for
my mum and my sisters Annabel and Camilla who
have been there despite and still

In memory of Chris and Richard Sykes, both fine
cooks who inspired my own
culinary ways

Special thanks to: Imo for her kindness,
inspiration and hours of testing. Annabel and
Camilla for all their help and endless
testing. Other willing testers: Sarah Allen and her
family and all their enthusiasm, Caroline Howard
and Rebecca Hurley. For help, encouragement
and support Chris, Agnes and Rose-Helene, Leila
McAlister, Gerard Baker, Bob Granleese, Thomas
Blythe, Tim Dillon, Kevin Mcfadden, Sue Lewis,
Andy Tyrell, Martin Cohen, Robert Bradshaw, Colette
and Giles Webster, all at Rochelle Canteen, Artur
Kodjak, all at Leila's, Mary Sykes, Nicky Napier.
For the splendid produce: Mckanna meats, Ben Fish,
Vernon at Secretts. The great and the good:
Joyce Molyneux, Shaun Hill and Juliet Peston.

PR: For Steve, Millie and Angus

Special thanks to the following people who helped
with all manner of things:
Jane and Robert Savage, Dick, Mandy, Felix and
Ellie-May Russell, David and Brenda Rose, Clare
Birchall and Robert Smith, Kara and Nick Lawson,
Paul Myerscough, Sam Edenborough, Ben Olins,
Linda Sandino, NJ Stevenson, Jenny Linford, Richard
Vine , Mela Freidman, Kasia Janda, Julia Walsh,
Jeremy Hayward, Huw Morgan, Sophie Smallhorn,
Peter Jackson, Kate Hathway, Matthew Russell,
Polly and Mark Anderson, Vicky Price, Jo and
Pepita Pecorelli, Andrew Mallison, Mark Ranson,
Jill Norman, Matthew Herbert, Sue Bradley,Robyn
Pierce, Lucy Pope, Anna Lobbenburg and Sladja.

ZH: For Tom, Cecilia and Edward

Special thanks to my family for all their love
and support and everyone who helped with the
testing: Tom Clifford who cooked alongside me,
Jill Wilkinson, Joan and Peter Clifford, Anna and
Tim Standley, Rachel Baldwin, Sunshine Jackson,
Tracey Banks, Torica Back, Lorna Kelly and Noel
Dixon and also Helen Thomazin, Rebecca Andrew,
Victoria Dowd, Alice Smellie and Kate Warwick.
Finally to all the willing guinea pigs who ate,
advised and made it a thoroughly enjoyable year.

From Us All: Special thanks to Victoria Hobbs for
her patience, advice and support and also to Sara
Fisher and Euan Thorneycroft. Thanks also to Sarah
Lavelle, Carey Smith, Ed Griffiths, Judith Hannam
and Jane Bamforth.

How THE KITCHEN REVOLUTION started

Despite searching high and low, we couldn't find a cookbook to help with the most basic culinary need: cooking day in and day out. There are books with systems for raising babies, for deciding what clothes to wear, for designing gardens and for decorating houses – but no book with a system for the most basic need of all: how to put good food on the table every day economically, simply and, most importantly, deliciously.

There are, of course, thousands of fantastic cookbooks. But between juggling work, family and social life who has time to plan different meals five, six or seven nights every week? Even if you've got Nigella, Delia and Jamie on your shelves, who hasn't faced the weekly shop thinking what on earth can I do this time? Many of us find ourselves cooking the same recipes over and over. These might be excellent, but even the best meals get repetitive and dull. Alternatively, we end up spending a huge amount of time and money cooking different one-off recipes only to open the fridge the next day and find it's bare. For many, the tyranny of daily cooking can be relentless.

And that's not all. On the one hand, we're constantly being told about the health, economic and social benefits of fresh, home-cooked meals, free from the additives and high fat and high salt content of most ready-made food. On the other hand, with people working longer hours, and with pre-prepared food getting tastier and more tempting, more of us are eating ready meals. This isn't really surprising when the reality of producing home-cooked food day in and day out can feel like an exhausting slog.

The trouble is, many of us are stuck without the necessary knowledge – the old skill of 'housekeeping', of managing a kitchen, seems to be dying out. According to recent reports, up to a third of household food in the United Kingdom is wasted. Yet all too often the fridge and store cupboard are empty, even though you have recently done a shop that nearly broke the bank as well as your back.

This book aims to help solve these culinary conundrums with a system that provides recipes for every day of the week. You don't need to spend a fortune shopping three times a week – or spend hours every night cooking huge meals from scratch. It's possible to feed an entire household, whether two, four or five people, without being either superhuman or a kitchen drudge. It just takes a bit of planning, housekeeping and some cunning recipes.

That's where this book comes in. The recipes have been created by professional chef, Rosie Sykes and enthusiastic home cook, Polly Russell; and thoroughly road-tested by working mother, former kitchen sceptic and non-cook, Zoe Heron. Together we've devised a system to make organising a week's worth of cooking simple and manageable – with the system you do not have to start shopping, preparing and cooking from scratch every day and you utilise the tastiest (and cheapest) seasonal ingredients. There are shopping lists for every week, and recipes for every day of the week throughout the year – recipes that build on each other and logically fit together to reduce your shopping bill and your workload.

We have been testing the system and recipes as we go along and it works. The recipes taste great and the costs can be surprisingly low. In each week there are four recipes that take, on average, about half an hour so these are good for midweek cooking. The remaining two meals every week take longer and are intended for slower, more leisurely weekend cooking. The quantities for one of these meals includes sufficient to leave surplus ingredients for using later in the week. The other makes enough to serve eight so that half can be frozen for when cooking is just not an option.

This book is for anyone who cares about the food they eat and wants to cook well. It's for anyone setting up home – people who are buying their first flat, or moving in with their partner or friends, getting married or starting a family. If you want to learn to manage your kitchen, then this is the book for you.

Kitchen Revolution will make cooking and shopping for balanced and delicious meals easier and cheaper – helping you to plan good food and ensure that you and the people you cook for eat well every day. It's about how to reduce the cost of your weekly shop by buying food strategically and making the most of ingredients that are in season.

And *Kitchen Revolution* is for anyone who wants to make good food, but is worried about the effort of planning to cook every night. It offers a system and shows how easy it can be. If you're not a natural kitchen whizz it may just revolutionise your life.

The system

We all need to eat three times a day. Most of us, however, have just one big meal – either at lunch time or, more commonly, in the evening. In any week there are some days when we may feel like cooking at a leisurely pace, others when we frankly can't be bothered. So we've come up with a weekly system – a way to plan the week's meals to allow for lazy days as well as cooking days, to cut down on work in the kitchen and to make the most of seasonal food.

The system gives you a tasty meal every day of the week, organises your shopping and minimises the amount of food you waste. It aims to put the pleasure back into everyday cooking and eating – this is food you can proudly share with friends and family.

The idea is simple. Once a week you cook a large meal, a roast or something similar, which then provides, through leftovers, the ingredients for recipes for at least two other days. In addition, there are recipes for two other midweek meals that will take between 20 and 40 minutes – one based on fresh, seasonal ingredients, the other using ingredients from the store cupboard or freezer. The final recipe every week is one that is cooked in double quantities so that half can be frozen for those days when you can't be bothered to cook.

The idea of the system may sound prescriptive, but it's designed to be used flexibly. We don't expect you to cook every night – and we don't imagine people will do the recipes slavishly. After all, everyone likes to eat beans on toast occasionally! The idea is for you to make the recipes your own, and to make your life easier. Some of them may seem adventurous, and it's good to be nudged out of a rut sometimes – but if they don't appeal, then leave them out.

Before we describe the system in more detail, these are the broad principles on which it is based:

1   Use your ingredients to the fullest
The secret of shopping and cooking efficiently is to make the most of your ingredients. A few ingredients make a delicious meal and this meal then begets another – cook a joint of beef and a Thai beef salad is waiting for you the next day. A good housekeeper won't cook from scratch every night and won't need to shop endlessly for new ingredients. Use what you've got, use it well and you can create dishes that taste good – and cost little in time, energy and money.

2   Make the most of your fridge, freezer and store cupboard
The kitchen is as much a place to store food as it is a place to cook food. If you get the storing component of the kitchen right, time spent shopping and cooking is significantly reduced. The fridge, freezer and store cupboard are all essential tools and when these three work together you have an efficient kitchen. You do not need a huge freezer to make our system work – even a fridge-freezer can store a small quantity of stock and a couple of frozen meals and still leave room for the ice tray and frozen peas.

It may seem obvious, but having essentials like stock in the freezer and canned pulses in the store cupboard provides a culinary safety net and saves endless treks to the shops as well as time at the stove. Doubling up your quantities when you cook a casserole and putting half in the freezer is like having savings in the bank – something to fall back on when you really don't have the time or inclination to cook. At least once a week (if not more) we suggest you grab something from the freezer and have a night without cooking. You should not be a slave to your kitchen – your kitchen should be a slave to you. Make it work well and hard and your cooking life is dramatically improved.

3   Seasonal foods are the best
It makes sense to buy and use ingredients that are in season – they're usually tastier, often fresher and almost certainly cheaper. Moreover, seasonal food tends to support local agriculture and burns up fewer transport miles. It is good for your conscience, taste buds and wallet. Knowing what is in season, and when, is the key to successful seasonal planning and cooking, so the recipes for each month are designed to help you take advantage of seasonal produce.

4 Recipes should be easy and interesting

Our aim is to provide recipes that are delicious, easy and interesting. As well as the comforting old favourites – roast beef, lasagne, fish pie and the like – we have tried to include recipes that are innovative and unusual.

But writing a book for everyday cooking by people with busy lives time has been as important as offering appealing, original recipes. Making the recipes as easy as possible, while making them varied and tasty, has involved months of discussion, debate, testing and refinement. We've tried to cut down on unnecessary faff as much as possible and recipes often highlight shortcuts that can be taken if time is really tight. Most of the midweek recipes will take around half an hour to make. All the recipes have been discussed, simplified, reversioned and retested many times, so you can be certain that if a complex one is still in the book it's because it tastes good and it's worth it.

The two 'weekend' meals – the Big meal from scratch and the Two for one – take longer but they produce food for later in the week so there is an economy of time at work, even though they can't be made in a flash.

Some recipes have ingredients that are not run of the mill – venison, preserved lemons or smoked mussels, for instance. Where these might be hard to get hold of, are expensive or may not appeal, the recipe gives suggestions for different options and substitutions.

5 Cooking for four (or two, or six, or eight)

There's no doubt that cooking for a household of one or two is very different to cooking for five or six. To give the maximum flexibility, the recipes are written to feed four as this makes it relatively easy to multiply the ingredients up or divide them down.

The system explained

Day 1 (preferably on a weekend)

Our system gives you recipes for seven meals each week and provides you with a complete shopping list to cover all the ingredients required.

Day 2 & 3

We've divided the meals so that every week you cook:

One meal called: **Big meal from scratch.** This is usually the most labour-intensive meal you will cook every week, but it will provide ingredients to form the basis of two or more suppers.

Day 4

Two meals called: **Something for nothing.** Using leftovers in an appetising and interesting way is the essence of good housekeeping. A few anchovies, capers, herbs and leftover rice are stuffed into peppers and baked. Roast parsnips are tossed in spices and roasted again as an interesting accompaniment to fish. Keep life simple – use your leftovers.

Day 5

Day 6 (preferably on a weekend)

One meal called: **Seasonal supper.** A quick, simple supper made from fresh, seasonal ingredients.

One meal called: **Larder feast.** For those days when your fridge is bare – a meal made primarily from store cupboard ingredients.

Day 7

One meal called: **Two for one.** A comforting and dependable meal that freezes well. The recipe provides enough for double quantities so you can eat half immediately and bank half in the freezer.

One meal called: **Lazy day supper.** For which there is no recipe – you just defrost a previous Two for one meal that is already in the freezer.

Apart from the 'weekend' recipes – the Big meal from scratch and the Two for one – all the others are designed for midweek cooking when time is likely to be tight.

The Something for nothing recipes are, in theory, reliant on the Big meal from scratch – but it's not a disaster if the big meal hasn't been cooked. There are instructions with every Something for nothing recipe for cooking from scratch.

The order the recipes are cooked in isn't rigid. Be led by the amount of time you have spare on different days and the sell-by dates of the food. As the Larder feast recipes don't rely on many fresh ingredients, these tend to be good for later on in the week when the fridge is getting bare.

Living the system – Zoe's experience

To test all the recipes, Zoe spent a year 'living the system' and it has, without any hesitation of a doubt, transformed her life in the kitchen. It's been an amazing lesson in inventive cooking – giving her the most extraordinary repertoire of delicious recipes.

Probably the biggest, and unexpected, benefit has been being able to rustle up a good meal for friends and family with minimum stress and at no great cost. With the system there's no fear in inviting friends and family to stay for lunch or supper at the last minute – you've got all the ingredients you need, the recipe will be good and interesting, and, if it's designed for midweek, will take only 30–40 minutes. The Big meal from scratch and Two for one recipes have provided lots of opportunities for more planned entertaining. So it's been a very social year, despite holding down a job and having another baby.

The recipes are designed to feed four but cooking for more or less has been surprisingly easy. Many recipes can be halved, or multiplied. The Two for ones already serve eight, so are good suppers to make if there are lots of people coming over. And as they freeze, they can be cooked well in advance. Quantities in the midweek suppers tend to be easy to halve – and if not, the leftovers are usually good to eat the following day.

The other unexpected benefit has been providing food and leftovers for toddlers and babies. The majority of the recipes have been tested on Zoe's young children and have gone down really well.

Shopping no longer involves the repetitive tedium of staring at the supermarket shelves while desperately scrabbling for ideas about what to cook. On average Zoe has spent about £50–£60 a week buying largely organic meat and vegetables and cooking for four people for seven nights.

How you use the system is up to you. We all use it differently. Since Zoe has stopped testing she does about two weeks a month – only cooking every other night or so. Polly tends to make the Big meals from scratch and the Something for nothings rather than following the whole system proper. Rosie dips in and out, with many of the recipes finding their way onto her menus. What we've all done, however, is stock up on Larder feast ingredients so that it's always possible to make a good meal, even when the fridge is bare.

How the book is structured

Basics
In the next section there are suggestions for equipment and store cupboard ingredients as well as basic tips on managing the kitchen, storing leftovers and making the most of the freezer.

Month by month
Each month starts with a brief introduction to the sorts of food that come into season, to give a sense of what to expect to find in the recipes.

Introductions to weeks
At the start of every week there is an outline of the proposed recipes. This gives guidance on recipe timings for the week to help you plan your cooking.

Shopping list
Each week begins with a list of every ingredient that's required for the six recipes that follow. The list is organised into different sections – meat and fish or fruit and vegetables – for example. The lists can look daunting at first because they are often quite long, but many of the ingredients are likely to be products you keep all the time – oil, vinegar or dried spices for instance – so they will not need to be purchased every single week. With the shopping list already compiled it's just a question of checking it and crossing off anything that's already in stock.

Introductions to recipes
Every recipe has an introduction. Sometimes these are just a couple of sentences, but at other times they include details on how to source specific ingredients or explain how a recipe is structured.

Get ahead preparation
Most of the recipes include a 'get ahead preparation' section. This is there so that if you want to cook in advance of eating, or if you have a few moments to spare, you know what can be done. It isn't strictly necessary, but it's useful if you have free time and would like to get the meal under way.

Puddings
At the end of each month there are recipes for four seasonal puddings. These stand outside the system, but come in handy for special meals or when you need a treat.

Recipe ingredients and instructions
The recipes have been written so that the steps are included in the instructions rather than being hidden in the ingredients lists. In other words, if an onion needs chopping this is written into the recipe instead of appearing in the ingredients as 'onion, chopped', with the result that the recipes, though often simple, can look wordy. It also, however, that there are no surprise tasks or added labour.

The basics

This chapter covers the essential skills of managing the kitchen – from equipment, to supplies for your store cupboard, shopping tips and what to do with leftovers.

Equipment
There's no getting away from the fact that if you are going to cook reasonably often, having the right equipment will make your life immeasurably better. Trying to cook with blunt knives or thin, cheap pans is like going camping in a leaky tent – it's miserable. We don't expect you to spend hundreds of pounds on top-of-the-range pans – there are some perfectly good inexpensive versions. All you need to be sure of is that the bottoms of the pans are thick and heavy – this allows the heat to distribute slowly and evenly, so avoids burning. Another good outlay is a hand blender – it has multiple attachments and can be used as a blender, whisk and food processor all in one.

Here is a list of essential kitchen equipment:

* Three good heavy-based saucepans ranging in size from a small milk pan to a large 10.5-litre pan; one large heavy-based frying pan; one 10.5 litre casserole with a heavy base and a lid
* One large roasting tin; one large baking sheet or tray; one shallow ovenproof dish about 30 x 20 cm (suitable for making lasagne); one soufflé dish about 20 cm in diameter
* Two chopping boards (one for raw meat or fish and one for vegetables and fruit); three sharp knives: a small vegetable knife, a big 'cooks knife' (about 15-cm blade) and a serrated bread knife
* Food processor or hand blender (ideally with whisk attachment); scales
* Peeler; cheese grater; two wooden spoons and two spatulas; potato masher; corkscrew; can opener; tablespoons; big metal slotted spoon; garlic crusher; balloon whisk
* Sieve and colander; lemon squeezer; measuring jug; pestle and mortar
* Large and small mixing bowls; range of airtight containers (or old takeaway boxes); foil loaf tins for freezing; labels for freezer

Store cupboard
As with equipment, if you're going to cook reasonably often it's worth having some basic ingredients in your store cupboard – oils, vinegars and spices that are used time and time again and will store well for months. We don't expect (and wouldn't advise) you to go out and buy all these in advance as it would be quite expensive – but as you follow the book your store cupboard will grow as you buy the necessary bits and pieces.

In the shopping list each week we include a section on store cupboard ingredients, so you can check what you've got in stock and what you need to pick up. We make a distinction between 'store cupboard' ingredients like spices, which once bought are unlikely to run out for a while, and goods like canned tomatoes, pasta, rice, etc., which store well but which will need to be restocked on a regular basis. We hope this will help.

Below is a list of what we've ended up with in our store cupboards having lived the system.
* Vegetable bouillon powder (Marigold or Kallo), plain flour, sugar
* Extra virgin olive oil, groundnut or grapeseed oil
* White wine vinegar, red wine vinegar, balsamic vinegar, sherry vinegar
* Mustard powder, Dijon mustard, wholegrain mustard, capers, clear honey
* Salt, whole black peppercorns and a pepper grinder
* Ground allspice, cloves, ground cumin and cumin seeds, ground coriander and coriander seeds, paprika (including smoked), turmeric, garam masala, mace blades, nutmegs, cinnamon sticks and ground cinnamon, ground ginger, cardamom pods, saffron, chilli powder, cayenne pepper
* Bay leaves, dried thyme
* Tomato ketchup, Worcestershire sauce, soy sauce, sweet chilli sauce, Tabasco or other chilli sauce, tahini, Thai fish sauce
* Foil, cling film, greaseproof paper, baking parchment

Throughout the book recipes call for either olive oil or groundnut or grapeseed oil. The latter are our preferred flavourless oils and are readily available in supermarkets. They have the advantage of cooking at high temperatures without burning, and without affecting the flavour of the food.

For olive oil, extra virgin has the best flavour – but as it's fairly expensive you might want to save extra virgin for dressings and use a more standard and less pricey olive oil for cooking.

Shopping

The shopping lists make the weekly shop easier, in as much as you don't have to think about what to buy, but how you do the shopping is completely up to you. Polly, Rosie and Zoe shop in completely different ways.

Zoe does all her shopping online with one of the supermarkets. It's quick, easy and if you've got a list you can just type in the ingredients and know immediately whether the shop has them or not (otherwise you can end up trailing up and down aisles, which is hellish). Supermarket online menus often don't have the more adventurous ingredients, but our recipes are designed to offer alternatives. Only occasionally do you have to visit a shop in person. If shopping online, however, watch the sell-by dates – occasionally a supermarket will send meat or fish on its use-by – in which case it either has to be cooked immediately or stored in the freezer.

Living in an area with a large Somali, Nigerian and Indian community means that Polly has access to small specialist stores that sell fruits and vegetables, grains, nuts, herbs, spices and pickles at bargain prices. As much as possible she shops at independent shops and at her local farmers' market, partly because she enjoys it and partly because she likes to support local businesses. However, shopping like this is time consuming and not always compatible with a busy life, so Polly also uses the local supermarket and a vegetable-box delivery scheme.

As Rosie has worked in restaurants for many years she has a fantastic range of suppliers that she can call on, so she tends to visit her butcher or speak to her fishmonger as well as using small shops and markets close to her home.

Storing leftovers

'Leftovers' is not the most appetising of words but we're hoping to reclaim it and give it a new lease of life. So we should start by setting out the basic rules governing the storing of food in the fridge.

The first advice is to store any leftover food in airtight containers. We use cheap plastic ones – often old takeaway containers. This prevents 'fridge taint' (where the butter starts smelling of onions, for example), and helps to preserve food longer.

Some foods like fish and cooked rice have a definite, short shelf life. Fish should be eaten as near to the day of purchase as possible or stored in the freezer until required. Rice often contains bacteria that aren't killed by cooking – in fact, they only starts to grow once the rice is cooked and has cooled down. This doesn't mean that all cooked rice is going to make you ill – 99.9 per cent is perfectly safe – but it's advisable not to keep cooked rice for more than 24 hours. A few Something for Nothing recipes involve leftover rice, and we suggest that you do these within 24 hours of cooking the rice for the Big Meal from Scratch. For most ingredients there are no such rigid rules. Cooked fish has a more limited shelf life than meat and should be used within a couple of days of being cooked. Cooked meat, particularly in a casserole, is usually fine for five days.

But generally there are no hard and fast rules, and using your judgement is what's required. It's a judgement our grandparents' generation was perfectly happy to make but one that scares many of us. We're so used to getting our food neatly packaged with a label saying 'eat by this date', that we have forgotten how to trust our own senses of smell, sight and taste. Until Polly and Rosie stopped her, Zoe routinely threw away vegetables that were past their 'use by date', even though they looked and smelt fine.

So the rule is this: if it looks OK and smells OK, then it is OK. If looks or smells a little dodgy – then it is a little dodgy and is best avoided. Our sense of smell has evolved over millennia to help us avoid food that will make us ill – so trust your nose.

Making the most of your freezer

The freezer is a great resource, and if used well can make life immeasurably easier. It is useful for storing raw ingredients, stocks and pastry but it comes into its own when it holds one or two complete home-cooked meals. At the end of a tiring day, or when there hasn't been time to cook, pulling a casserole, bake or braise out of the freezer can be a lifesaver. All the Two for One recipes are designed to freeze well, so there should be no difference in eating quality between the fresh and defrosted versions.

Freezing is one of the safest ways to store food, but there is one basic rule: only freeze food once in any one state. If raw meat or fish has been frozen and defrosted you shouldn't freeze it again while it is raw. But, once it's been cooked it's perfectly safe to freeze it again. By the same measure, a cooked meal from the freezer cannot be defrosted and then refrozen.

As a storage place for basic ingredients the freezer is fantastic – not just for frozen peas and the like, but for fresh herbs, fresh chillies and fresh ginger. Ginger can be grated while it's frozen so there's no need to thaw it. The texture of fresh chillies changes when they are frozen, but not their flavour, and it's useful to have them to hand. Herbs can be washed and chopped then frozen (ice-cube trays are good for this) or can even be frozen in bunches. Either way, having 'fresh' coriander, parsley, thyme and basil in the freezer as a back-up is reassuring.

As stock plays such an important part in many recipes, it's well worth having supplies of concentrated chicken, fish and perhaps beef stock in the freezer. To concentrate fresh stock for the freezer, boil it rapidly in a pan and reduce it by a third or a half. Then cool it and freeze it in ice-cube trays or 100–200 ml portions. The concentrate can be diluted when required. Making stock is not always convenient, but if you keep a supply of chicken carcasses and bones in a bag in the freezer there's a ready supply ready when you have time. These don't need to be defrosted – they can be whacked straight into the stockpot and cooked as normal.

One of the most important aspects of freezing is good labelling. There's nothing more annoying than rooting about in the freezer trying to distinguish chicken from fish stock or a beef from a lamb casserole.

Defrosting food

The basic rule with defrosting is to ensure that any food is completely thawed before it is heated if necessary, or eaten. This is especially important with raw meat or fish – if a frozen chicken breast is not completely defrosted when cooked, there's a chance the middle will never reach a safe temperature.

How long something will take to defrost is dependent on temperature and time. As a rule of thumb, a casserole for four will probably take about 8 hours at cool to normal room temperature and about 24 hours in a fridge. Of course, the exact time will depend on the volume and density of whatever's being defrosted so it's not an exact science. Once defrosted food should be eaten, or cooked and eaten, within a day as it deteriorates faster than fresh food.

There are certain dishes that can be cooked from frozen – lasagnes and casseroles, for example. These have to be warmed slowly at first, then heated to a high temperature when they are completely defrosted to ensure that they are completely warmed through.

With all the Two for one recipes there are instructions for freezing and defrosting.

There is extra information on shopping, ingredients and basic methods scattered throughout the book:

JANUARY

January is not often a month associated with gastronomic pleasures. Many people will be dieting after the excesses of Christmas, yet it's cold outdoors and our bodies crave warming, wintry food. So, our recipes for January include some that are light and flavourful, such as Five-Spice Steamed Fish with Chinese Greens, and some hearty dishes, too – Beef (or Venison) Stew with Walnuts and Prunes. Purple sprouting broccoli appears at this time of year, and its tender stems and delicate florets offer a welcome diversion from the root vegetables that are abundant all winter long. We combine it with almonds, garlic and cream in a gratin to accompany grilled lamb chops. January also sees the arrival of Seville oranges from Spain. These are traditionally used to make marmalade, but their astringent flesh and aromatic rind can also add flavour to savoury dishes. Towards the end of the month, we use them for a contemporary version of the 1970s classic, Duck à l'orange, and they also feature in a steamed pudding. If a Marmalade Steamed Pudding sounds good but too wicked for the season, the Pomegranate and Pink Grapefruit Jellies are as beautiful to look at as they are lovely to eat.

January	Week 1	Week 2	Week 3	Week 4
Big meal from scratch	Caramelised vegetable tart with baked celery and broccoli	Roast chicken with fruit and nut stuffing, mujaddara and lemon carrots	Five-spice steamed fish with Chinese greens and seaweed rice	Roast duck with Seville oranges, celeriac mash and watercress
Something for nothing 1	Warm bacon, egg and beetroot salad	Baked butternut squashes with ricotta and chicory and little gem salad	Fish and potato bake	Cheat's cassoulet
Something for nothing 2	Lamb chops with broccoli and celery gratin	Upside-down chicken pie	Spinach tian	Celeriac and goats' cheese bake
Seasonal supper	Rolled fish fillets with apple stuffing and creamed chicory	Roast root vegetables with pearl barley	Sausages with crisp roast vegetables and caraway-flavoured cabbage	Italian cauliflower farfalle
Larder feast	Spiced chickpea stew with rice and yoghurt	Soupe au pistou	Pasta with green vegetables	Saffron rice with prawns
2 for 1	Beef (or venison) stew with walnuts and prunes	Fish with a shallot and bacon topping	Lamb harira with coriander paste	Braised pork with artichokes and mushrooms
Puddings	Marmalade steamed pudding	Prune and nut fool	Pomegranate and pink grapefruit jellies	Ginger and apricot cake

January Week 1 – Overview

The main dish in the Big Meal from Scratch recipe is a Caramelised Beetroot and Chicory Tart Tartin. This is rich and colourful and includes a large proportion of seasonal vegetables. If you would rather not cook beetroot from scratch, it can be bought ready cooked just so long as it's not been pickled in vinegar.

For midweek, Warm Bacon, Egg and Beetroot Salad – quick, simple and full of flavour – is a perfect antidote to the January blues and uses the beetroot from the big meal. A gratin with lamb chops is made from the surplus. It requires minimal preparation and makes a substantial and gratifying supper. The vegetables will last 3–4 days in the fridge, so plan to use them midweek.

The Seasonal Supper of stuffed fish uses a technique that is well worth remembering. Fillets of flat fish are spread with a mixture of breadcrumbs, apple and herbs then rolled and baked. The result is delicious and, as a lucky bonus, low fat. The fish should be cooked soon after it is purchased or else should be stored or frozen until required. Spiced Chickpea Stew with Rice and Yoghurt uses store cupboard ingredients to create an Indian-inspired, meal in half an hour.

Finally, as January is likely to be cold, an intense, meaty stew such as Beef with Prunes and Walnuts. Pickled walnuts are an old fashioned ingredient that add depth to a stew. They can be found at most supermarkets. As with most casseroles it takes a couple of hours from start to finish, with about half an hour of preparation and an hour and a half of cooking – a recipe well worth making at leisure.

January Week 1	Recipe	Time
Big meal from scratch	Caramelised vegetable tart with baked celery and broccoli Added extra – Celery Soup	1½ hours
Something for nothing 1	Warm bacon, egg and beetroot salad	20 mins
Something for nothing 2	Lamb chops with broccoli and celery gratin	30 mins
Seasonal supper	Rolled fish fillets with apple stuffing and creamed chicory	35 mins
Larder feast	Spiced chickpea stew with rice and yoghurt	30 mins
2 for 1	Beef (or venison) stew with walnuts and prunes	2–3 hours

All recipes serve 4 apart from the 2 for 1 recipe which makes 8 portions

SHOPPING LIST (for 4 people)

Meat and fish
4-8 lamb loin chops (depending on their size)
1.2 kg braising beef (shin, chuck or flank) or venison shoulder, off the bone, cut into small, even-sized chunks
200-250 g rindless free-range smoked streaky bacon
4 skinned, double fillets of flat fish (sole or dab for choice), approx. 800 g

Dairy
240 g (approx.) butter
4 free-range eggs
150 g Parmesan
200 ml crème fraîche
200 g natural yoghurt

Fruit and vegetables
800 g (approx.) waxy potatoes (large new potatoes, such as Charlotte, if possible)
1.2 kg uncooked beetroot (each beet no bigger than a tennis ball) or 1 kg cooked beetroot (not pickled in vinegar)
2 medium carrots, approx. 200 g
1 kg purple sprouting broccoli or 1.4 kg if the broccoli comes with long, thick stalks that will need removing
3 heads celery
7 heads chicory, approx. 700 g
150 g (approx.) watercress, about 2 bunches
½ cucumber
4 medium onions, approx. 480 g
4 medium red onions, approx. 480 g
4 large or banana shallots, approx. 120 g
8 garlic cloves
1 bunch fresh flatleaf parsley
8 sprigs fresh thyme
1 sprig fresh sage
1 small bunch chives
large handful of fresh coriander
2 cooking apples, approx. 150 g each
3 lemons

Basics
370 ml (approx.) olive oil
60 ml groundnut or grapeseed oil
200 g basmati rice
100 g brown breadcrumbs or 2-3 slices bread suitable for crumbing
290 g plain flour
1 tbsp tomato purée
1 bay leaf
salt and pepper
400 ml beef stock (fresh or made from a stock cube)
1 litre chicken stock (fresh or made from a stock cube)

Store cupboard
55 ml sherry vinegar
2 tsp caraway seeds
½ tsp celery seeds
1 level tsp ground cumin
2 tsp ground coriander
½ tsp turmeric
1-2 pinches of cayenne pepper (depending on taste)
½ tsp dried thyme (optional)
2 × 400 g cans chickpeas
1 × 400 g can chopped tomatoes or 500 g passata
200 g roasted red peppers from a can or jar
4-8 anchovy fillets in olive oil
100 g no-soak dried prunes
200 g (drained weight) pickled walnuts
60 g flaked almonds
250 ml white wine
300 ml red wine

Serving suggestions
Potatoes for boiling or baking (Lamb Chops with Broccoli and Celery Gratin)
Potatoes for mashing or white beans or soft polenta, and greens (Beef/Venison Atew with Walnuts and Prunes)

To download or print out this shopping list, please visit www.thekitchenrevolution.co.uk/January/Week1

Caramelised Vegetable Tart with Baked Celery and Broccoli

The main dish in this recipe is a savoury tarte Tatin with a beetroot, chicory and sweet onion filling. Hot-water crust pastry provides a deliciously crisp crust.

To accompany the tart there is broccoli and baked celery hearts. Celery makes an excellent hot vegetable. The hearts are the pale centres of a celery head that has been trimmed right back, and are usually about 15 cm in length. You can also buy these ready prepared in some supermarkets. Use the leftovers to make Celery Soup (see page 19). The quantities here include extra beetroot for the Warm Egg and Beetroot Salad (see page 20) and extra broccoli for the Lamb Chops with Broccoli and Celery Gratin (p.21)

Caramelised vegetable tart
1.2 kg uncooked beetroot or 1 kg cooked beetroot (not pickled); includes approx. 600 g extra for the Warm Bacon, Egg and Beetroot Salad
4 medium red onions, approx. 480 g
3 heads chicory, approx. 100 g each
40 g (approx.) butter
groundnut or grapeseed oil
2 tsp sherry vinegar
small handful of fresh flatleaf parsley
230 g plain flour, plus extra for dusting
2 tsp caraway seeds
100 ml olive oil
salt and pepper

Baked celery
3 large celery hearts; includes 1 heart for the broccoli and celery gratin
2 large or banana shallots or 4 small shallots, approx. 60 g
4-8 anchovy fillets in olive oil
3 tbsp olive oil
½ lemon
4 sprigs fresh thyme

Broccoli
1 kg purple sprouting broccoli or 1.4kg if the broccoli comes with long, thick stalks that will need removing; includes approx. 500 g extra for the Broccoli and Celery Gratin

GET AHEAD PREPARATION (optional)

The tart can be made 2 days in advance and warmed gently when required. If you have only a little time:
* Cook the beetroot.
* Make the pastry, roll out and leave to rest.
* Soften the onions.
* Brown the chicory with the onions.
* Make the dressing for the celery.

1½ hours before you want to eat cook the tart filling

* If using raw beetroot, wash them and place, unpeeled, in a large pan. Cover with water. Place over a medium heat and simmer gently until cooked (about 30 minutes).
* Peel and finely slice the onions. Melt half the butter and a glug of the oil in a pan, over a medium heat, and add the onions. After a couple of minutes reduce the heat and cook, covered, for about 20 minutes until slightly brown and soft. Stir occasionally.
* While the onions are cooking, prepare the chicory. Pare away any brown or tough parts but keep the heads intact. Cut each head into quarters lengthways, with the root attached so that the leaves stay together.
* Heat the remaining butter and a splash of oil in a large frying pan, when the butter is foaming, add the chicory and cook until golden brown. Add the vinegar and let it evaporate.
* While the chicory browns, prepare the celery. Remove any tough outer stalks and set them aside for use later in the week with the beef stew. Cut away any brown or tough edges from the stalk ends but keep the hearts intact. Cut the celery hearts into quarters lengthways.
* Lightly oil a 25 cm diameter, 5–7 cm deep pie or flan dish with groundnut or grapeseed oil. When the chicory is brown and the vinegar has evaporated, season well then tip into the prepared dish. Arrange the heads like the spokes of a wheel. Set aside until the onions are ready. Rinse the frying pan and start cooking the celery.

1 hour before you want to eat prepare the celery

* Heat 1 tablespoon of olive oil in a frying pan over a medium heat and brown the celery, turning occasionally, for 5 minutes.
* While the celery is cooking, peel and halve the shallots. Add the shallots to the celery and cook for a further 5 minutes. When they are lightly browned, tip them into a shallow baking dish.
* Preheat the oven to 200°C/400°F/Gas Mark 6.
* By now the onions should have melted down to a sweet mass. If there is a lot of liquid, remove the lid, turn the heat up and simmer for a few minutes.

* Now make the dressing. Place 2 tablespoons of olive oil in another frying pan over a medium heat. Add the anchovies and mash them with a fork until they dissolve in the oil. Strip off the thyme leaves and mix them in with the anchovies, a squeeze of lemon juice and a good grinding of pepper.

* Pour the dressing over the celery and shallots and stir well. Cover the dish with foil and put it in the bottom of the oven. Cook for 45 minutes.

* Roughly chop the parsley, stir it into the onions and season to taste. Spread the onions over the chicory, filling in any gaps.

* Drain the cooked beetroot (a knife should pass easily through the beetroot centre) and run cold water over them to cool. Put half the beetroot aside for later in the week. Peel the remaining beetroot and cut them into 5 mm slices. Lay the slices over the onion mixture and season thoroughly.

45 minutes before you want to eat make the pastry and cook the tart

* Sift the flour and salt into a bowl with the caraway seeds. Heat the olive oil with 4 tablespoons water until just boiling and slowly pour it onto the dry ingredients. Stir with a wooden spoon until a dough starts to form, then knead for a couple of minutes. Immediately roll the pastry out. It must be big enough to generously cover the tart filling. Place the pastry on top of the filling and tuck the edges neatly inside the dish.

* Put the tart on the top shelf of the oven and cook for 30 minutes until the pastry is browned.

15 minutes before you want to eat cook the broccoli

* Trim the broccoli. Bring a large pan of salted water to the boil and add the broccoli. Bring back to the boil, reduce the heat and simmer for 3–4 minutes.

* Take the tart out of the oven and turn the oven off. Leave the celery in the oven.

* Allow the tart to stand for a couple of minutes, then cover it with a large plate and, holding the flan or pie dish firmly, invert it. After a few minutes lift the dish off.

* Drain the broccoli, season, and tip two-thirds into a serving dish. Set the remaining aside for later in the week.

* Set four quarters of celery hearts aside for later in the week. Serve the remaining eight quarters.

* Slice the tart to serve.

Afterwards

Put the remaining cooled vegetables (ideally 500 g beetroot, 500 g purple sprouting broccoli and four celery quarters) into separate containers, cover and refrigerate for later in the week.

Added extra

Celery Soup

1 medium onion
60 g butter
300–500 g approx. celery (use surplus celery from the Big Meal from Scratch)
2 large potatoes, approx. 300 g

½ tsp celery seeds (optional)
strip of lemon zest
1 litre chicken or vegetable stock
salt and pepper

* Peel and chop the onion. Melt the butter in a pan and fry the onion over a gentle heat for about 10 minutes. Trim, wash and slice the celery. Peel and roughly chop the potatoes. Add the celery to the onion and cook for 5 minutes. Add the celery seeds, lemon zest and potatoes. Stir for a couple of minutes before covering with the stock. Simmer gently for 20 minutes. Season and remove the lemon zest. Blend until smooth.

**Something
for nothing 1**

Warm Bacon, Egg and Beetroot Salad

Bacon, egg and potato is a classic combination. Combined with some beetroot and watercress, this salad this makes a quick, easy and delicious meal.

800 g waxy potatoes (Charlotte if
   possible or large 'new
   potatoes')
200–250 g rindless, free-range
   smoked streaky bacon
4 free-range eggs
500 g cooked beetroot left over
   from the Big Meal from Scratch
   or 500 g bought beetroot (not
   pickled in vinegar)
1 large or banana shallot,
   approx. 30 g
3 tbsp sherry vinegar
6 tbsp olive oil
150 g (approx.) watercress
salt and pepper

*20 minutes before
you want to eat*

* Peel the potatoes and cut them into 2-cm cubes. Place them in a pan of salted water and bring to the boil. Turn down the heat and simmer for about 5–6 minutes or until the potatoes are just cooked.
* While the potatoes are cooking, heat a frying pan over a medium heat and add the bacon rashers. Cook until the edges are crispy then place on kitchen paper to remove any excess fat and set aside. Use scissors or a knife to cut the bacon into 1-cm lengths.
* Meanwhile, cook the eggs in boiling water for 8 minutes. Once cooked, run cold water over them until they are cool enough to handle, then peel.
* Cut the beetroot into 1-cm cubes. When the potatoes are a couple of minutes from being cooked, add the beetroot and allow it to warm through while the potatoes finish cooking, then drain the potatoes and beetroot well. Keep them warm in the pan with the lid on.
* Finally, make the dressing. Peel and slice the shallot and mix with the vinegar and oil. Mix well and taste for seasoning.
* Now mix everything together. Put the hot potatoes, beetroot and bacon in a bowl. Add the watercress and dressing, season and toss together gently. Halve the eggs.
* To serve, divide between four plates and put two egg halves on top of each.

**Something
for nothing 2**

Lamb Chops with Broccoli and Celery Gratin

This is a simple but excellent meal. The sweet and juicy flavour of lamb chops works
well with a garlicky gratin. The addition of almonds to the gratin adds an interesting
texture and a delicate nutty flavour. If you don't have any leftover celery it's possible to
replace it with extra broccoli.

Lamb chops
4–8 loin chops (depending on
    their size)
salt and pepper

Broccoli and celery gratin
3 garlic cloves
4 quarters of celery hearts left
    over from the Big Meal from
    Scratch or 1 celery heart halved
    lengthways and braised in
    vegetable stock for about 30–
    40 minutes until soft

1–2 tbsp olive oil
60 g flaked almonds
zest and juice of ½ lemon
250 ml white wine
4 tbsp crème fraîche
100 g Parmesan
500 g cooked purple sprouting
    broccoli left over from the Big
    Meal from Scratch
salt and pepper

To serve
boiled or baked potatoes

GET AHEAD PREPARATION (optional)

The gratin can be prepared a
couple of hours in advance, and
put under the grill 10 minutes
before you want to eat. If you
have only a little time:
* Peel and slice the garlic.
* Cut up the celery.
* Make the sauce.

*30 minutes before
you want to eat*

* Preheat the grill to medium.
* Season the lamb chops on both sides with generous amounts of salt and pepper, place
  on a grill rack and leave at room temperature while you prepare the ingredients for
  the gratin.
* Peel the garlic and cut it into thin slices.
* Heat the oil over a medium heat in a pan large enough to hold all the ingredients. Add
  the garlic and cook for a minute or so until soft, then add the almonds and cook for 2–
  3 minutes until they are starting to brown. Add the lemon zest and juice and the wine,
  bring to the boil and reduce by a third. Then add the crème fraîche, and stir to a
  smooth sauce-like consistency. Grate half the Parmesan into the sauce and add a little
  water if it seems too thick.
* Separate the celery sticks and cut into 5-cm lengths.
* Add the broccoli and celery to the sauce, season the lot with salt and pepper and warm
  through gently while you cook the chops.
* Place the chops under the grill and cook for 3–4 minutes on each side, assuming your
  chops are about 2–3 cm thick. Cook for longer if you prefer your meat well done or if
  the chops are particularly thick.
* While the chops are cooking, grate the rest of the Parmesan. Once you have turned the
  chops over, tip the celery and broccoli mixture into a shallow, ovenproof dish. Season
  with lots of pepper and scatter the Parmesan over the top.
* When the chops are ready, remove them from the grill and leave to rest in a warm
  place while you put the gratin under the grill.
* Grill the broccoli and celery for about 10 minutes or until the cheese is melted and
  bubbling.
* Serve the chops with a helping of the gratin

Seasonal supper

Rolled Fish Fillets with Apple Stuffing and Creamed Chicory

Rolling fillets of flat fish keeps the fish moist and full of flavour and the end result tastes and looks wonderful. The apple in the stuffing has a slight sharpness that works well with fish. It's worth buying the fillets ready skinned – any fishmonger will skin them for you and most supermarkets sell skinless fish fillets. Sole or dab work very well with this recipe, but whiting is a good value alternative as the fillets are thin like those of a flat fish.

Rolled fish fillets with apple stuffing
- ½ tbsp groundnut or grapeseed oil, plus extra for greasing
- 30 g butter
- 1 large or banana shallot, approx. 30 g
- 2 garlic cloves
- 2 cooking apples, approx. 150 g each
- 100 g brown breadcrumbs or 2-3 slices of bread suitable for crumbing
- ½ lemon
- 1 sprig fresh sage

- small handful of fresh flatleaf parsley
- 4 skinned double fillets of flat fish (sole or dab for choice), approx. 800 g
- salt and pepper

Creamed chicory
- 4 heads chicory, approx. 400 g
- ½ lemon
- 60 g butter
- 4 tbsp crème fraîche
- 1 small bunch chives

GET AHEAD PREPARATION (optional)

The stuffing can be made up to a day in advance. If you have only a little time:
* Peel and finely slice the shallot.
* Peel and crush the garlic.
* Zest the half lemon.
* Chop the herbs.
* Make the breadcrumbs.

35 minutes before you want to eat

* First make the stuffing. Heat the oil and butter in a small pan over a low heat. Peel and finely slice the shallot and add it to the pan to soften for about 5 minutes. Peel and crush the garlic. Peel and coarsely grate the apples.
* When the shallot has started to soften, increase the heat and add the apple and garlic. Cook until the apple is beginning to fluff up. While the apple is cooking, grate the zest from the half lemon, roughly chop the sage and parsley and, if necessary, finely chop the bread or whizz it in a food processor.
* When the apple has broken down, add the zest, breadcrumbs and herbs and stir thoroughly. The mixture needs to be dry, so turn the heat up and cook off any excess liquid, stirring constantly. When the stuffing is dry, season and spread it on a flat tray to cool.
* Preheat the oven to 200°C/400°F/Gas Mark 6.
* Next make the creamed chicory. Trim the heads of chicory and halve them lengthways. Cut out the thick core at bottom of each one then finely slice the halves into half-moon pieces.
* Heat the butter in a pan, add the chicory and cook over a high heat, stirring often, until it starts to soften.
* When the chicory has wilted a little, add the lemon juice and an equal quantity of water. Bring to a simmer and cook until everything is soft and nearly all the liquid has evaporated.
* Now cook the fish. Oil an ovenproof dish big enough to hold four rolled-up fish fillets. Lay the fillets out skinned sides up. Season each fillet then spread the filling mixture over its surface. Roll each fillet up.
* Put the fillets into the oiled dish with the seams at the bottom, pour over the lemon juice and season. Cover the dish with foil and bake for 15 minutes.
* Make sure all the liquid has evaporated from the chicory and add the crème fraîche. Bring the crème fraîche to the boil and simmer well until it is just coating the chicory. Snip the chives, with scissors, into the chicory, season to taste and keep warm.
* Put a fish fillet on each plate, with any cooking juices, and plenty of creamed chicory.

Larder feast

Spiced Chickpea Stew with Rice and Yoghurt

Chickpeas are an invaluable store cupboard staple, adding a deep nutty flavour and crunchy texture wherever they are used. For this meal a spicy chickpea stew is tempered by a refreshing yoghurt raita. We have suggested levels of spice but do adjust to suit your palate if you like things milder or more powerful. This recipe requires less than 15 minutes assembling and chopping, and 15 minutes cooking.

Chickpea stew
200 g basmati rice
1 medium onion, approx. 120 g
1 tbsp olive oil
2 garlic cloves
200 g roasted red peppers from a
  can or jar
½ tsp ground cumin
2 tsp ground coriander
½ tsp turmeric
1-2 pinches of cayenne pepper
  (depending on taste)

1 × 400 g can chopped tomatoes
  or 500 g passata
1 tbsp tomato purée
2 × 400 g cans chickpeas
large handful of fresh coriander
salt and pepper

Raita
200 g natural yoghurt
1 clove garlic
½ tsp ground cumin
½ lemon
½ cucumber

GET AHEAD PREPARATION (optional)

The chickpea stew can be made 2 days in advance and warmed gently when required. If you have only a little time:
* Peel and slice the onion and garlic.
* Slice the peppers.
* Peel, deseed and slice the cucumber.

*30 minutes before
you want to eat*

* Wash the rice under cold running water until it runs clear then put it in a large pan and cook according to the manufacturer's instructions. Keep warm.
* While the rice is cooking, peel and slice the onion. Heat the oil in a heavy-based pan and cook the onion over a medium to high heat until it is lightly browned. This will take about 5 minutes and you will need to stir at regular intervals.
* While the onion is cooking, peel and thinly slice two cloves of garlic and slice the red peppers into 1 cm strips.
* When the onion is soft and starting to brown, add the sliced garlic, the cumin, ground coriander, turmeric and cayenne. Cook the spices for 2 minutes then stir in the tomatoes or passata, tomato purée, red peppers and chickpeas. Roughly chop the fresh coriander and add half to the chickpea mixture. Season with ½ teaspoon salt and simmer for about 15 minutes with the lid off. Stir now and then.
* Next, make the raita. Peel and crush the remaining clove of garlic. Mix the yoghurt with all but one tablespoon of the remaining fresh coriander, the cumin, the crushed garlic, a couple of generous pinches of salt and pepper and a squeeze of lemon juice. Peel and deseed the cucumber and chop it into 1-cm chunks. Add the chunks to the yoghurt mixture, stir well and set aside.
* Taste the chickpeas for seasoning and adjust as necessary. The mixture should not be very wet, so if it is, turn up the heat and boil rapidly until the chickpeas are sitting in a thick tomato liquid.
* Divide the rice between four bowls and pile the chickpea mixture on top. Scatter with the rest of the chopped coriander, put a generous spoonful of the raita on the side and serve.

Two for one

Beef (or Venison) Stew with Walnuts and Prunes

This rich stew is perfect for winter weekend cooking. You can prepare it at leisure and then leave it to cook while you venture out into the cold or laze in front of the telly for an hour or two.

Pickled walnuts became popular in Britain in the eighteenth century and have remained part of the classic British repertoire ever since. Within the last few decades they have ceased to be commonplace, though they are still stocked by most supermarkets. Walnuts for pickling are collected before their shells form in early June. They turn black and are grey-brown inside once pickled, and have a mild spiced and sweet flavour which works especially well with meat. If they prove impossible to find, the recipe works fine without them.

Beef stew
4 tbsp plain flour
1.2 kg braising beef (chuck or blade) or venison shoulder, off the bone, cut into small, even-sized chunks
groundnut or grapeseed oil
50 g (approx.) butter
2 medium carrots, approx. 200 g
2 medium onions, approx. 240 g
3 celery sticks
300 ml red wine
200 g (drained weight) pickled walnuts
100 g no-soak dried prunes
400 ml beef stock (fresh or made from a stock cube or vegetable bouillon powder)
4 sprigs fresh thyme or ½ tsp dried thyme
1 bay leaf
salt and pepper

To serve
mashed potatoes, mashed white beans or soft polenta and buttered, steamed greens

GET AHEAD PREPARATION (optional)

The entire dish can be prepared 2 days in advance and gently reheated. If you have only a little time:
* Brown the meat.
* Peel and chop the carrots.
* Peel and slice the onions.
* Trim and slice the celery.

2–3 hours before you want to eat

* First prepare the meat. Put the flour in a large bowl, add 1teaspoon salt and 1 teaspoon pepper and mix well. Pat the meat dry with kitchen paper and drop it, a few pieces at a time, into the flour. Turn each piece so that it's lightly coated.
* Meanwhile, put a large casserole dish over a medium heat, splash in some oil and half the butter and melt until the butter is foaming. Lift the meat from the flour and drop it into the hot fat to brown all over. As the pieces brown, remove from the dish and put to one side. Browning all the meat will take about 15 minutes – resist the urge to constantly turn the meat, as this will only slow things down.
* While the meat is browning peel the carrots, slice them in half lengthways then chop finely. Peel the onions, trim the celery and slice both finely.
* It is a good idea to deglaze the dish when you have browned half the meat. Pour in half the red wine, bring it to the boil, stirring to scape the flavours from the bottom, and let it simmer for a minute before tipping it over the browned meat. Now wipe out the dish, and melt the rest of the butter with 1–2 tablespoons of oil to brown the remaining meat. When all the meat is browned, deglaze as above then wipe the dish.
* Return the clean casserole to the heat, add 1–2 tablespoons of oil and throw in the carrots, celery and onions. Cook over a medium-high heat for 5–7 minutes, until they are beginning to soften and lightly brown, stirring from time to time.
* While the vegetables are browning, drain the pickled walnuts. Cut them and the prunes in half.
* When the vegetables are browned, tip the meat and its liquid back into the casserole dish and add the stock, prunes, walnuts, the leaves of the fresh thyme or the dried thyme, and the bay leaf.

* Stir once or twice to mix, cover with a lid and leave to just simmer over a very low heat until the meat is tender – this will take about 2 hours. Stir the dish every now and again and check the meat after 1½ hours.
* When the meat is tender, check the sauce for seasoning.
* Spoon half into a freezerproof airtight container or strong freezer bag and leave to cool. When it is completely cold, cover and freeze.
* Serve the remaining stew with mash or soft polenta, and perhaps some greens.

Lazy day supper – reheating instructions

Defrost the stew completely before reheating. Transfer to a casserole dish with a couple of tablespoons of water and bring gently to simmering point over a medium heat. Simmer for 15 minutes to ensure that the meat is warmed through, then serve as above.

January Week 2 – Overview

Roast chicken would be a serious contender in any culinary popularity contest. It doesn't really matter what herbs or spices are rubbed on the skin and in the cavity, it's likely to be loved. The roast chicken recipe, this week's Big Meal from Scratch, takes its inspiration from Morocco and is stuffed with nuts, dried fruit and spices. If you can buy a large 3 kg chicken, but as they're not always available we suggest roasting two smaller birds side by side. This quantity should leave you with enough to make a chicken pie later in the week.

Accompanying the roast chicken is a lentil and bulghar wheat recipe called Mujaddara, which is a staple dish in much of the Middle East. The extra Mujaddara is used to make ricotta-and-herb-stuffed butternut squashes. Though the preparation for the squashes takes less than 10 minutes, they do require baking for 30–40 minutes so this will need to factored into any planning.

For a Seasonal Supper, root vegetables are chopped into small pieces then roasted until sweet, soft, crisp and caramelised, and served with pearl barley. The recipe is easy to execute but the vegetables take some time to chop so don't embark on this when you're in a hurry or are especially weary.

Soupe au Pistou – the Larder Feast – is packed with vegetables and a scattering of pasta, enhanced by a garlic, basil and Parmesan paste that is stirred in at the end. This soup is very much a movable feast; the ingredients do not need to be followed slavishly, so add or subtract vegetables depending on what's available. We have made it a store cupboard fallback for those days when there is very little in the fridge, but if you do happen to have any of the ingredients fresh, use them.

The Two for One this week – Fish with a Bacon and Shallot Topping – is quick, easy and freezes really well. This takes just 20–25 minutes to prepare and 20 minutes to cook and it makes a useful frozen 'ready meal' because it can be cooked from frozen in about 20 minutes. As with all fish, remember to cook it within two days of purchase or freeze it until required.

January Week 2	Recipe	Time
Big meal from scratch	Roast chicken with fruit and nut stuffing, mujaddara and lemon carrots	2¼ hours
Something for nothing 1	Baked butternut squash with ricotta and chicory and little gem salad	40 mins
Something for nothing 2	Upside-down chicken pie	30 mins
Seasonal supper	Roast root vegetables with pearl barley	45 mins
Larder feast	Soupe au pistou	30 mins
2 for 1	Fish with a shallot and bacon topping	45 mins

All recipes serve 4 apart from the 2 for 1 recipe which makes 8 portions

SHOPPING LIST (for 4 people)

Meat and fish
2 × 1.5 kg free-range chickens
600 g rindless free-range smoked streaky
  bacon
8 x portion sized (120-160 g) pieces of
  salmon or any firm white fish, such as
  coley, cod or haddock

Dairy
75 g (approx.) butter
1 free-range egg
200 g ricotta
splash of milk
100 ml double cream

Fruit and vegetables
400-500 g baby carrots
5 carrots, approx. 500 g
2 butternut squashes, approx. 800 g each
4 small parsnips, approx. 400 g
½ medium swede, approx. 250 g
1 small turnip, approx. 100 g
4-5 small leeks, approx. 450 g
2 medium heads chicory, approx. 100 g each
1 little gem lettuce
8 medium onions, approx. 1 kg
4 medium red onions, approx. 500 g
4 large or banana shallots, approx. 120 g
11 garlic cloves
1 very large bunch fresh flatleaf parsley
1 medium bunch fresh coriander
1 small bunch of chives
1 sprig fresh rosemary
5 sprigs fresh thyme
100 g frozen peas
4 lemons

Basics
300 ml olive oil
2 slices bread
500 g chilled ready-made puff pastry
2 pinches of sugar
5-8 tsp Dijon mustard
300ml chicken stock (fresh or made from a
  stock cube)
3 vegetable stock cubes or 5 tsp vegetable
  bouillon powder
30 g (approx.) plain flour
salt and pepper

Store cupboard
250 g dried brown lentils
200 g bulghar wheat (ideally coarse grain)
300 g pearl barley
75 g small pasta, such as tubetti, stelleti or
  even broken-up pieces of spaghetti
1 × 400 g can green beans (haricot verts are
  good) or fresh beans if you prefer
1 × 400 can flageolet or haricot beans

1 × 400 g can chopped tomatoes
1 × 300 g can potatoes
1 × 190 g jar pesto
75 g no-soak apricots, about 10
50 g (approx.) flaked almonds (toasted if
  possible)
50 g shelled walnut pieces
75 g raisins
1 tsp turmeric
½ tsp ground cinnamon
1 tsp paprika
1-2 pinches of ground cumin
1 tsp dried thyme (optional)
a few poppy seeds
splash of sherry vinegar
300 ml white wine

Serving suggestions
spinach (Upside-down Chicken Pie)
halloumi, rosemary and olive oil (Roast Root
  Vegetables with Pearl Barley)
frozen peas or another other green vegetable
  and potatoes of your choice (Fish with a
  Shallot and Bacon Topping)

To download or print out this shopping list,
please visit www.thekitchenrevolution.co.uk/
January/Week2

Roast Chicken with Fruit and Nut Stuffing, Mujaddara and Lemon Carrots

There's nothing quite like roast chicken with stuffing. In this case the stuffing is Middle Eastern in inspiration, made with spiced almonds, walnuts, apricots, raisins and coriander. Accompanying it is a dish called Mujaddara, commonly found throughout the Middle East. It is made from a mixture of lentils, bulghar or rice and caramelised onions and is delicious hot or cold. Frying onions until they are caramelised takes a while, so it's worth making a larger quantity of Mujaddara than is required for one meal. The extra Mujaddara is used to stuff butternut squash later in the week and the surplus chicken is turned into chicken pie.

Roast chicken with fruit and nut stuffing

2 × 1.5 kg free-range chickens includes 1 × 1.5 kg chicken or 800 g chicken joints (from the 3 kg chicken) for the chicken pie
2 medium onions, approx. 240 g
3 tbsp (approx.) olive oil
2 garlic cloves
50 g flaked almonds (toasted if possible)
50 g walnut pieces
75 g raisins
75 g no-soak apricots, approx. 10
½ lemon
1 small bunch fresh coriander
1 small bunch fresh flatleaf parsley
2 slices bread
½ tsp ground cinnamon
1 tsp paprika
1 tsp turmeric
1–2 pinches of ground cumin

2 tbsp sherry vinegar
300 ml chicken stock (fresh or made from a stock cube)
salt and pepper

Mujaddara
6 medium onions, approx. 750 g; includes 1 onion extra for the baked butternut squashes
3 tbsp olive oil
250 g dried brown lentils, washed; includes 50 g extra for the baked butternut squashes
1 vegetable stock cube or 1 tsp vegetable bouillon powder
200 g coarse cracked wheat (bulghar); includes 40 g extra for the baked butternut squahes
salt and pepper

Lemon carrots
400–500 g baby carrots
pinch of sugar
½ lemon
25 g butter

GET AHEAD PREPARATION (optional)

The mujaddara can be made up to a day in advance. The chickens could be stuffed and prepared prior to going in the oven (up to 24 hours in advance if the stuffing is cold). If you have only a little time:
* Prepare the onions.
* Caramelise the onions for the mujaddara.
* Make the stuffing for the chicken.
* Make the dressing to rub over the chicken.
* Scrape the carrots.

2¼ hours before you want to eat prepare the chicken and caramelise the onions

* Take the chickens out of the fridge so they come to room temperature.
* Peel and thinly slice all the onions for the stuffing and the mujaddara. Take two heavy-based pans – a large one for the mujaddara and a smaller one for the stuffing. Heat 3 tablespoons oil in the large pan, and 1 tablespoon oil in the small pan over a medium heat. Add one-quarter of the onions to the small pan and put the rest into the large pan. Soften over a medium heat, stirring every now and then, for about 10 minutes.
* Meanwhile, peel and thinly slice the garlic. Add this to the small pan and cook, making sure it doesn't burn.
* Put the almonds, walnuts and raisins in a big bowl. Chop the apricots into small pieces and add to the bowl. Grate the zest of the half lemon and add this. Wash, dry and roughly chop the coriander and parsley and add half to the bowl with a generous pinch of salt and pepper. Finely chop the bread and leave to one side.
* Heat the oven to 190°C/375°F/Gas Mark 5.
* When the onions have been cooking for 10 minutes, turn the heat down very low under the large pan and continue cooking. These onions need to be completely caramelised and soft. This will take a further 30–40 minutes gentle cooking with occasional stirring and the lid off.
* Add the breadcrumbs with half the cinnamon, paprika, turmeric and a pinch of ground cumin to the small pan and stir for a minute.
* Now tip the spiced bread and onion mixture into the fruit and nuts. Season and stir well.

* Mix all but about 1 tablespoon of the remaining parsley and coriander, and the remaining cinnamon, paprika, turmeric and cumin with the remaining 2 tablespoons oil, the juice of the half lemon and 1 teaspoon each of salt and pepper.
* Place the chickens side by side on a rack in a roasting tin and stuff the cavities with the fruit and nut stuffing.
* Rub the chickens with the herb mixture. Carefully prise the skin away from the breast bone and push some of the mixture under the skin.
* Place the chickens in the oven and roast for 1½ hours.
* When the onions for the mujaddara are brown, sweet and very, very soft, take them off the heat.

40 minutes before you want to eat cook the mujaddara and the carrots

* Wash the lentils in cold running water and place in a heavy-based pan. Cover them with water, add the stock cube or bouillon powder and a pinch of salt and bring to the boil. Cook for about 30 minutes.
* While the lentils are cooking, prepare the bulghar. Put a kettle on to boil and wash the bulghar in cold running water. Put the washed bulghar into a large pan and cover with the boiled water. Add ½ teaspoon salt, cover, place over a gentle heat and simmer for about 10 minutes.
* Peel or scrape the carrots. Place in a pan and add 1 cm water, ½ teaspoon salt, the sugar, the grated zest of the lemon half and the butter. Cover, and simmer over a medium heat for 10 minutes.
* When the lentils are cooked drain well and add to the caramelised onions. Check on the bulghar – it should retain a little bite – then drain it. Add to the pan containing the onions and lentils.
* Mix the bulghar, lentils and caramelised onions together and season to taste. Set one-third of the mujaddara mixture aside. Put the rest into a serving dish and leave covered with buttered foil to keep warm.

10 minutes before you want to eat make the gravy

* Check that the chickens are cooked by piercing a thigh and if the juices run clear remove from the oven, place on a carving board, cover with foil and leave to rest.
* Remove the lid from the carrot pan and cook the carrots uncovered for the final 5 minutes.
* Pour any fat from the roasting tin then place the tin over a low heat. Add the vinegar and reduce, stirring constantly with a wooden spoon. Squeeze in the juice of the half lemon and add the chicken stock. Stir well, then leave to simmer while the chickens are carved.
* Put the carrots in a serving dish, carve the chickens and serve with a spoonful of the nut and fruit stuffing and the mujaddara.
* Add the remaining chopped herbs to the gravy, season to taste, then pour into a jug to serve.

Afterwards

Strip the chicken of any remaining meat (ideally 400-500 g) and place in a covered container in the fridge. Put any leftover mujaddara (ideally 500 g) into an airtight container and refrigerate. The carcases will make a good stock (see page 495).

Something for nothing 1

Baked Butternut Squash with Ricotta and Chicory and Little Gem Salad

Butternut squash has a delicate, sweet flavour that is enhanced through baking. Stuffing them transforms them from a good vegetable into a delicious meal. Here squashes are filled with ricotta, herbs and Mujaddara (lentils, bulghar and caramelised onions). For extra sweetness, add any fruit and nut stuffing left over from the roast chicken. The squashes are great served with a chicory and little gem salad. If there is no leftover Mujaddara replace it with 1 large onion slowly cooked until caramelised in 1 tablespoon olive oil, then mixed with 1 x 400 g can drained brown lentils.

Baked butternut squash with ricotta
2 butternut squashes, approx. 800 g each
500 g (approx.) mujaddara left over from the Big Meal from Scratch or see above
generous handful of fresh flatleaf parsley
1 small bunch chives
½ lemon
200 g ricotta cheese
olive oil, for rubbing
salt and pepper

Chicory and little gem salad
1 little gem lettuce
2 medium heads chicory, approx. 100 g each
2 tsp Dijon mustard
½ lemon
generous pinch of sugar
2 tbsp olive oil

GET AHEAD PREPARATION (optional)

The squashes can be steamed and stuffed a day in advance if kept covered in the fridge. Add 10 minutes to the baking time if cooking from cold. If you have only a little time:
* Steam the prepared squashes until soft.
* Mix the stuffing mixture together.

40 minutes before you want to eat

* Preheat the oven to 220°C/425°F/Gas Mark 7.
* First, prepare the squashes. Cut each in half lengthways. Use a teaspoon to scrape out the seeds and use a knife to remove a shallow rectangular wedge from the neck so that there is space in the seed cavity and also in the neck to fill with stuffing. Place the squashes, flesh sides down, in a roasting tin with 3 cm boiling water. Cover with foil to make an airtight seal, and cook in the oven for 10–15 minutes until they soften.
* While the squashes are cooking, make the stuffing. Put the mujaddara in a mixing bowl. Wash and drain the parsley and chives, chop finely and add to the bowl. Zest and juice the half lemon and add to the bowl along with the ricotta. Mix the whole lot together well using a fork to break up the ricotta. Season to taste and set aside.
* Once soft, take the squashes out of the oven and drain thoroughly. Dry the roasting tin and place the squashes, skin sides down, in it. Season the flesh with salt and pepper, and rub with a little oil. Spoon the stuffing mixture into the squash cavities, piling it quite high. Turn the oven to 200°C/400°F/Gas Mark 6 then return the squashes to the oven and bake for 20 minutes or until soft.
* While the squashes are baking, make the salad. Wash and drain the lettuce and chicory leaves and tear into bite-sized pieces. In a large salad bowl mix the mustard and the juice of the half lemon. Add about ¼ teaspoon each of salt and pepper and the sugar. Add the oil and mix well.
* When the squashes are cooked, add the salad to the dressing, toss well.

Something
for nothing 2

Upside-down Chicken Pie

A home-made chicken pie is very cheering but can be time consuming to make. This recipe adapts the method for the much-loved classic into a quicker, less complicated process – it involves cooking a puff pastry rectangle and pie filling separately, then assembling them when both are cooked. If you have no left over chicken, use two large poached chicken breasts.

Of course, if you prefer an old-fashioned pie, make the filling below, tip it into an ovenproof dish, cover with pastry and bake for about 20 minutes at 180°C/350°F/Gas Mark 4.

30 g plain flour, plus extra for
    dusting
500 g chilled ready-made puff
    pastry
4-5 small leeks, approx. 450 g
50 g butter
1 egg
splash of milk
poppy seeds, to scatter
300 ml white wine

100 ml double cream
small handful of fresh flatleaf
    parsley
400-500 g cooked chicken left
    over from the Big Meal from
    Scratch or see above

To serve
steamed spinach

GET AHEAD PREPARATION (optional)

The chicken and leek filling can
be made up to 2 days in advance
and reheated gently when
required. If you have only a
little time:
* Wash and slice the leeks.

*30 minutes before
you want to eat*

* Preheat the oven to 220°C/425°F/Gas Mark 7 and preheat a large baking sheet.
* Roll the pastry out on a lightly floured work surface until it is 1.5 cm thick and about 25 x 35 cm. Cut into four squares and leave to rest.
* While the pastry is resting, wash and finely slice the leeks. Melt the butter in a pan over a medium heat, add the leeks and stir for a couple of minutes. Put a lid on the pan and leave the leeks to cook for 5 minutes until soft.
* In the meantime, beat the egg with the milk then take the preheated baking tray from the oven and place the pastry squares on top. Brush the pastry with the egg, scatter over some poppy seeds and put the pastry in the hot oven to puff up. It will take about 10–15 minutes to become crisp and golden.
* When the leeks are soft, take the lid off the pan and add the flour. Stir until the flour is well blended then cook for a couple of minutes. Splash in the wine and stir vigorously to form a smooth sauce. Bring up to a simmer, turn the heat down and leave the sauce to bubble away very gently.
* By now the pastry squares should be crisp and well puffed up. Take them out of the oven and carefully cut them in half horizontally so that each one is divided into a top and a bottom. If the insides of the squares are slightly doughy you can return them to the oven to dry out for 3–5 minutes.
* Stir the cream into the sauce and bring back to a simmer. Roughly chop the parsley and shred the chicken. Add both to the sauce. Let the chicken heat through for a couple of minutes and season the sauce very well with salt and pepper. Put a lid on the pan and leave over a very low heat
* Put the crisp squares without the poppy seeds on top on four warmed plates, and divide the chicken and leek filling between them. Top with the reamining squares (with the poppy seeds) and serve with steamed spinach.

Seasonal supper

Roast Root Vegetables with Pearl Barley

This wholesome supper dish is great for relaxed entertaining because all the vegetables are cooked together, requiring little or no attention, and can be served warm or at room temperature. You can change the quantities of root vegetables depending on your personal preference. We think this makes a complete meal, but, if you like, it would go well with a few slices of fried halloumi. If possible, marinate the halloumi in roughly chopped rosemary leaves and olive oil prior to cooking.

300 g pearl barley
½ medium swede, approx. 250 g
1 small turnip, approx. 100 g
4 large carrots, approx. 400 g
4 small parsnips, approx. 400 g
2 medium red onions, approx.
　210 g
2 garlic cloves
1 sprig fresh rosemary
2 sprigs fresh thyme
6 tbsp olive oil
small handful of fresh flatleaf
　parsley, roughly chopped
juice and zest of 1 lemon
splash of sherry vinegar
salt and pepper

To serve
halloumi marinated in rosemary
　leaves and olive oil (see
　above)

GET AHEAD PREPARATION (optional)

The entire meal could be cooked in advance and served at room temperature – make sure you take it out of the fridge at least 40 minutes before you want to eat. If you have only a little time:
* Peel, chop and parboil all the vegetables.
* Peel and slice the onion.
* Crush the garlic.
* Cook the pearl barley.
* Roughly chop the herbs.

45 minutes before you want to eat

* Put the pearl barley in a bowl and cover with water.
* Preheat the oven to 200°C/400°F/Gas Mark 6 and preheat a large roasting tin. Fill a large pan with hot or boiling water and bring to the boil.
* Peel and chop the root vegetables into a 2–3-cm dice and add to the boiling water in the following order: swede, turnips, carrots and parsnips. Let the water come back to the boil after adding each vegetable. When they have all been added, cook for another 3–4 minutes.
* While the vegetables are cooking, peel the onions and cut them into sixths, then peel and crush the garlic. Strip the rosemary and thyme leaves from their stalks and roughly chop them.
* Drain the parboiled vegetables well and tip into the preheated roasting tin along with the onions.
* Add the onion wedges, crushed garlic, 3 tablespoons of the oil and the rosemary and thyme. Mix well to make sure all the vegetables have a good coating of oil. Sprinkle with salt and a good grinding of pepper and cook in the oven on a high shelf for 30 minutes or until cooked through.

30 minutes before you want to eat

* Drain the pearl barley, put it into a large pan and cover with plenty of water. Add a generous pinch of salt and bring to the boil – boil vigorously for 25 minutes, adding more water during cooking if necessary.
* While the barley is cooking make a dressing by mixing the parsley, lemon zest and juice, the remaining oil and salt and pepper.
* Once the barley is cooked, strain off any water and refresh under cold running water. Drain well, tip into a large serving dish and sprinkle with a little vinegar.
* When the vegetables are ready – completely cooked through and starting to caramelise at the edges – stir them through the barley while pouring in the dressing. Serve immediately or at room temperature.

Larder feast

Soupe au Pistou

Traditionally soupe au Pistou is a Provençal vegetable soup enriched with the French equivalent of pesto. Using store cupboard ingredients, this version is very much a cheat's version that's nevertheless very good. Canned beans and tomatoes, dried pasta, frozen peas, and pesto provide the core of the soup. The quantities of the other ingredients can contract and expand depending on what you have to hand.

Pistou is traditionally made with garlic, basil, olive oil and salt. Unlike pesto, it doesn't contain pine nuts. To save time we've suggested using bought Italian pesto, but you could make some pistou yourself by blending a handful of basil, 2 garlic cloves and 75 ml olive oil in a food processor.

2 medium red onions, approx. 240 g
2 tbsp olive oil
2 garlic cloves
1 × 300 g can potatoes
1 large carrot, approx.100 g or 2 celery sticks or 1 × 400 g can carrots
4 tsp vegetable bouillon powder or 2 vegetable stock cubes
1 × 400 g can chopped tomatoes
3 sprigs fresh thyme or 1 tsp dried thyme

1 × 400 g can flageolet or haricot beans
1 × 400 g can green beans (haricot verts are good) or fresh beans if you have them
100 g frozen peas
75 g small pasta, such as tubetti, stelleti or broken-up pieces of spaghetti
1 × 190 g jar pesto
salt and pepper

GET AHEAD PREPARATION (optional)

The soup can be made a day in advance, up until the point that the pasta is added. If you have only a little time:
* Peel and slice the onions.
* Chop the garlic.
* Open the cans of potatoes and beans and drain and rinse the contents.
* Slice the potatoes and cover with water until required.

30 minutes before you want to eat

* Peel and finely slice the onions. Heat the oil in a pan and cook the onions over a gentle heat for about 7 minutes.
* Meanwhile, peel and roughly chop the garlic and drain the potatoes and slice them into 1-cm thick slices. When the onions have softened, add the garlic and after a minute turn the heat up and add the potatoes. Cook, stirring occasionally, for a few minutes while you peel and slice the carrot or celery. Add the carrot or celery to the pan and cook for a minute or so.
* Dissolve the vegetable bouillon powder or stock cube in 1 litre of hot water then add the stock to the vegetables and bring to simmer. When simmering, add the tomatoes, thyme and season well with salt and pepper.
* Let this come to a simmer while draining and rinsing the flageolet or haricot beans and the green beans. Add them to the simmering soup.
* Bring the mixture to a simmer again and add the peas and pasta.
* Stir well, bring to the boil and simmer gently for about 10 minutes until the pasta is cooked — you may need to add a little hot water as it will thicken. You can leave it to simmer for longer if you have time.
* Once the soup is ready, ladle it into big bowls with a generous teaspoon of pesto or pistou on top.

Two for one

Fish with a Shallot and Bacon Topping

Topping fish fillets with a mixture of bacon and softened shallots ensures they stay moist when baked in the oven. The portions destined for the freezer are frozen raw and can be cooked in 30 minutes without defrosting when required.

The recipe was given to Rosie by her friend Jon Birchall, who usually makes the dish with salmon. Fillets of firm white fish would work just as well.

4 large or banana shallots,
    approx. 120 g
3 tbsp (approx.) olive oil
600 g rindless free-range
    smoked streaky bacon
5 garlic cloves
a few sprigs fresh parsley
a few sprigs fresh coriander
8 × portion-sized (120-160 g)
    skin-on pieces of salmon or
    any firm white fish, such as
    coley, cod or haddock
1-2 tbsp Dijon mustard
1 lemon
salt and pepper

To serve
green vegetable (frozen peas go
    particularly well with the
    bacon topping) and potatoes of
    your choice

GET AHEAD PREPARATION (optional)

The topping can be made a day in advance and once cold pressed onto the raw fillets if kept in the fridge. If you have only a little time:
* Cook the baccon and soften the onion.
* Peel and cook the garlic.

45 minutes before you want to eat

* Preheat the oven to 200°C/400°F/Gas Mark 6. Place a baking sheet, large enough to hold an ovenproof dish containing four fish pieces in a single layer, in the oven to heat.
* Next make the topping. Peel and finely slice the shallots then heat a splash of oil in a pan over a high heat and, using a pair of scissors, snip the bacon into the pan. When the fat from the bacon starts to run, add the shallots. If there is not very much fat in the pan add a little more oil. Put a lid on the pan and let the shallots soften over a low heat for about 10 minutes.
* Meanwhile, peel and crush the garlic, chop the parsley and coriander and set aside.
* When the shallots are soft, add the garlic and stir for a couple of minutes. There may be quite a lot of liquid in the pan, so turn the heat up to dry the mixture off.
* Oil an ovenproof dish large enough to hold four fish pieces in a single layer. Season the skin sides of all the fish pieces with salt and pepper. Place four of them skin-side down in the dish and the other four in a freezerproof box. Season the flesh of all the fish pieces and smear the tops with the Dijon mustard.
* By now the shallot and bacon mixture should be ready. Stir in the herbs and season the mixture to taste.
* Carefully cover the tops of the four fish pieces intended for the oven with half the shallot and bacon mixture. Place the dish in the oven on the hot baking sheet (the bottom heat should help crisp up the skin). Cook for about 15-20 minutes depending on the thickness of the fish.
* When the fish is cooked, drizzle with a squeeze of lemon juice and serve with a green vegetable and some potatoes.
* When the rest of the topping is completely cold, use to cover the tops of the remaining four pieces of fish. Cover and put in the freezer.

Lazy day supper – cooking instructions

The fish cooks very well from frozen. Preheat the oven to 200°C/400°F/Gas Mark 6. Oil a baking sheet and place in the oven to heat. Put the fish straight on to the baking sheet and bake for 25-30 minutes until the fish is cooked through. Serve as above.

Buying fish

In recent years the problems associated with plummeting fish stocks, fish farming and the environmental damage caused by modern fishing techniques have made eating fish an ethical minefield. The days when it was simply a question of recognising whether it was fresh or not are long gone. Quality doesn't just mean bright red gills and shiny bright eyes any more. It also refers to how the fish was caught, whether it comes from sustainable stocks and how much environmental damage catching or farming it produced. But as information about fish and fishing changes from year to year it's very difficult to know what, when or where to buy it. For those of us who love eating fish this can be very disheartening.

However, there are some general rules and guidelines that can be followed. First, buy fish from either a reputable retailer or a fishmonger who knows exactly where and how the fish is sourced. Second, in general fish that's line-caught is likely to be better quality than fish that's been trawler-caught and, as an added bonus, line fishing tends to be less environmentally damaging and to support small fishing communities. Third, discover the website www.fishonline.org which is produced by the Marine Conservation Website and gives clear, up-to-the-minute information on individual fish species, what fish to avoid and what species to eat. Fourth, look for the Marine Stewardship Council logo (MSC approved) when buying fish as this means it has come from well-managed fisheries that are sustainable. For more on buying salmon see page 393, and page 147 for more on buying cod, haddock or other white fish.

In almost every fish recipe that specifies a species we give two or three alternatives so that you can make a decision based on what's available and what's most desirable.

January Week 3 – Overview

This week's Big Meal from Scratch, Five-Spice Steamed Fish with Chinese Greens and Seaweed Rice, is delicately flavoured. It is an easy meal to make but it does depend on very fresh fish so this recipe is best made the day the fish is purchased. See pages 35 and 147 for more on buying white fish.

The recipe for Spinach Tian, a layered rice dish with onions, garlic and spinach, is made using extra rice from the big meal. As it is preferable to use rice within a day, it will need to be made soon after the Big Meal from Scratch. The extra fish from the big meal will keep well in the fridge and is used for a simple Fish and Potato Bake; it takes 20 minutes to prepare and 15 minutes cooking in the oven.

The Seasonal Supper is a homely meal of Sausages and Roast Vegetables. Coating the vegetables with polenta guarantees they turn crispy in the oven. When buying sausages, choose the best quality your budget will allow – you do get what you pay for.

The Pasta with Vegetables relies entirely on larder ingredients like frozen peas and beans, pasta and wine, so it's a good recipe to remember when you need to rustle up a meal with little warning.

Lamb Harira, a Moroccan soup, is traditionally eaten after fasting and is filling, nutritious and very satisfying. From start to finish the recipe takes 1¾ hours but much of this is cooking time rather than cook's labour.

January Week 3	Recipe	Time
Big meal from scratch	Five-spice steamed fish with Chinese greens and seaweed rice	1½ hours
Something for nothing 1	Fish and potato bake	35 mins
Something for nothing 2	Spinach tian	35 mins
Seasonal supper	Sausages with crisp roast vegetables and caraway-flavoured cabbage	40 mins
Larder feast	Pasta with green vegetables	30 mins
2 for 1	Lamb harira with coriander relish	1¾ hours

All recipes serve 4 apart from the 2 for 1 recipe which makes 8 portions

SHOPPING LIST (for 4 people)

Meat and fish
1.2 kg neck of lamb fillets
8 good quality free-range sausages
1.2 kg fillets of firm white fish, such as cod or other white fish, skinned (if buying from a fishmonger ask to keep the bones for the stock)

Dairy
6 free-range eggs
100 g Gruyère
20 g butter

Fruit and vegetables
800 g waxy maincrop potatoes such as Desirée
400 g floury potatoes, such as Maris Piper or baking potatoes
2 large carrots, approx. 240 g
3 parsnips, approx. 500 g
500 g large leaf spinach or 300 g baby leaf spinach
600 g dark Chinese greens, such as pak choi
1 small white cabbage, approx. 500 g
2 red peppers, approx. 300 g
8 medium onions, approx. 1 kg
3 medium red onions, approx. 360 g
8 small or 4 large or banana shallots, approx. 120 g
1 bunch spring onions, approx. 8
19 garlic cloves (approx. 2 heads)
14 cm (approx.) piece of fresh root ginger
2 stalks lemon grass
1 small red chilli
2 bunches fresh coriander
1 bunch fresh flatleaf parsley
1 bunch chives
4 lemons
300 g frozen broad beans
200 g frozen petit pois peas

Basics
150 ml olive oil
75 ml groundnut or grapeseed oil
75 g fresh (white or brown) breadcrumbs or 2-3 slices bread suitable for crumbing
400 ml fish stock (fresh or made with 400 g fish bones, a stock cube or vegetable bouillion powder)
salt and pepper

Store cupboard
450 g jasmine rice
30 g long grain rice
300 g dried brown lentils
1 tbsp polenta or semolina
400 g pasta, such as penne or fusilli
2 x 50 g cans anchovy fillets in olive oil
2 x 400 g cans chopped tomatoes
1 x 400 g can chickpeas
1 x 400 g can (200 g drained weight) artichoke hearts
1 x 11 g pack sushi nori (dried seaweed) or 1 x 55 g packet crispy seaweed
250 g (approx.) precooked and peeled chestnuts (optional for Sausages with Crisp Roast Vegetables and Caraway-Flavoured Cabbage)
1 tsp toasted sesame oil
2 tbsp rice vinegar
3 tbsp oyster sauce
4 tbsp dark soy sauce
1 x 8-10 g sachet dashi (optional for Five-spice Steamed Fish with Chinese Greens and Seaweed Rice)
4 dried kaffir lime leaves
pinch of five-spice powder
1 tsp caraway seeds
1 heaped tsp ground cinnamon
1½ tsp ground coriander
1 heaped tsp cumin
1 tsp cayenne pepper
1 tsp turmeric
250 ml white wine
1 vegetable stock cube or 1 tsp vegetable bouillon powder

Serving suggestions
crusty bread and little gem lettuces, olive oil, lemon juice, Dijon mustard and seasoning (Spinach Tian)
green vegetable (Fish and Potato Bake)
Parmesan (Pasta with Green Vegetables)
flatbreads (Lamb Harira with Coriander Relish)

To download or print out this shopping list, please visit www.thekitchenrevolution.co.uk/January/Week3

**Big meal
from scratch**

Five-spice Steamed Fish with Chinese Greens and Seaweed Rice

Light but with intense flavours, this Big Meal from Scratch will appeal to gastronomes and dieters alike – a definite crowd pleaser. Fish is steamed in the oven in a delicate broth then served with ribbons of carrots, soy-seasoned Chinese greens and sweet, seaweed-flavoured rice. Ideally the broth will be made using dashi, a Japanese fish stock which has a subtle, slightly smoky flavour. If the dashi proves elusive the recipe is fine without it. The quantities here include extra for the Fish and Potato Bake and for the Spinach Tian.

Five-spice steamed fish
400 ml fish stock (fresh, or made
    with a stock cube or vegetable
    bouillon powder or 400 g fish
    bones)
6 cm piece of fresh root ginger
2 stalks lemon grass
1 small bunch fresh coriander,
    preferably with stalks
1 small red chilli
4 kaffir lime leaves
1 x 8-10 g sachet dashi
    (optional, but well worth it)
1 bunch spring onions, approx. 8
1.2 kg fillet of firm white fish
    (cod, pollack or haddock or
    other white fish; if buying from
    a fishmonger ask to keep the
    bones), skinned; includes
    approx. 600 g extra for the fish
    and potato bake
pinch of five-spice powder
1 tsp toasted sesame oil

2 large carrots, approx. 240 g
3 tbsp soy sauce
½ lemon (optional)

Chinese greens
600 g dark Chinese greens, such
    as pak choi
3 garlic cloves
1 tbsp dark soy sauce
3 tbsp oyster sauce
½ lemon

Seaweed rice
1 bunch chives
1 x 11 g packet sushi nori (dried
    seaweed) or 1 x 55 g packet
    crispy seaweed
400 g jasmine rice; includes
    150-200 g extra for the spinach
    tian
2 tbsp rice vinegar
salt and pepper

GET AHEAD PREPARATION (optional)

The broth can be made up to a day in advance and kept in the fridge. If you have only a little time:
* Peel and slice the ginger.
* Roughly chop the lemon grass and coriander.
* Trim the spring onions.
* Make the carrot ribbons and keep in water until required.

*1½ hours before
you want to eat
prepare the broth,
fish and vegetables*

* First make the broth. If you have some fish bones, wash and chop them so they fit in a large pan and cover with about 700 ml water. If using fish stock put it in a pan or if using a cube put in a pan with 500 ml water.
* Peel the ginger and cut into thin circles and roughly chop the lemon grass and coriander stalks. Add to the stock, along with the whole chilli, lime leaves and the dashi. Trim the tough green ends from the spring onions (keeping the bulbs for later) and add these to the pan. Place over a high heat, bring up to a simmer and skim away any foam or scum from the top. Turn the heat to very low, cover and leave to infuse for about 45 minutes.
* While the broth is infusing, remove any fins from the fish and pick out any little bones or sinew. Throw any trimmings into the broth. Cut the fillet into seven even-sized pieces. Rub four of the pieces with the five-spice powder and sprinkle with the sesame oil. Place all seven pieces in a shallow ovenproof dish large enough to hold them in a single layer and set aside until you are ready to cook them.
* Peel the carrots and, if they are very long, cut them in half. Using a potato peeler, peel ribbons from the carrots and place in cold water until required. The centres of the carrots will be hard to peel so slice this part as thinly as possible and add any leftover pieces to the infusing broth.
* Now finely chop the spring onion bulbs, roughly chop the coriander leaves and mix together. Put these to one side to add to the broth later.
* Prepare the Chinese greens. Trim any brown bottoms from the greens and discard any tough outer leaves. Quarter the greens and put them in a pan with a few centimetres of water. Peel and finely slice the garlic, and mix it with the soy and oyster sauces together with a squeeze of lemon juice. This is will dress the greens once they are cooked.

* Prepare the ingredients for the seaweed rice. Chop the chives, shred the sushi nori or dried seaweed into strips and mix them together.

20–30 minutes before you want to eat cook the the fish, rice and greens

* Preheat the oven to 180°C/350°F/Gas Mark 4.
* Cook the rice according to the instructions on the packet (usually 10 minutes in boiling water).
* Strain the fish stock by pouring it through a fine sieve and into a bowl or jug. Rinse the stock pan and return the stock to the pan. Bring the stock to the boil over a high heat then pour enough over the fish to come halfway up the overproof dish. Cover the dish with foil and place in the oven to steam for 15 minutes until the fish is cooked and firm.
* Put the greens on to steam over a high heat; once the water is simmering they will only take 3–5 minutes.
* When the rice is cooked, drain thoroughly and put half (about 500 g) aside for use later in the week. Return the remaining rice to the pan and stir in the rice vinegar, seaweed and chives and season to taste with salt and pepper. Place in a warmed serving dish and cover to keep warm.
* When the greens are soft, remove them from their pan and dress them with the soy and oyster sauce mixture, then tip them into a warmed covered serving dish.
* After about 15 minutes in the oven the fish will be cooked. Turn off the oven and remove the fish. Strain the cooking liquor from the oven dish into the pan containing the rest of the stock and place on a medium heat. (Keep the fish covered and warm in the oven.) Put soup plates in the oven to warm.
* When the stock is simmering add the ribboned carrots, soy sauce and spring onions and coriander. Taste and add a squeeze of lemon juice if you think it necessary. The carrots should retain their crunch and hardly be cooked.
* To serve, use a slotted spoon to lift a pile of ribboned carrots into each of four soup plates. Place the fish pieces that have been rubbed with five-spice powder on top and pour over the hot stock. Serve the rice and greens separately.

Afterwards

Allow the leftover rice to cool thoroughly and put it in the fridge in an airtight container – it will not keep for longer than a day so aim to make the Spinach Tian soon after. Flake the three remaining pieces of fish and place in an airtight container in the fridge for use later in the week. Ideally there will be about 500 g fish and 500 g rice, but don't worry if you have more or less.

Something for nothing 1

Fish and Potato Bake

This is good, filling food that's very simple to make – parboil some potatoes, soften some onions and mix these together with cooked fish. The dish takes 15 minutes to prepare and about 20 minutes to cook in the oven. Served with a softly boiled egg on top, and perhaps some green vegetables, it is perfect.

Margot Henderson, who runs the Rochelle School Canteen where Rosie sometimes works, makes a similar dish with salt cod or anchovies and it is a favourite with everyone. This is Rosie's speedy version.

800 g waxy, maincrop potatoes
   such as Desirée
2 medium onions, approx. 240 g
olive oil
4 garlic cloves
2 × 50 g cans anchovy fillets in
   olive oil
500 g (approx.) cooked white fish
   left over from the Big Meal
   from Scratch, flaked, or 550 g
   pollack, cod or haddock fillet,
   gently poached until cooked,
   then flaked
handful of fresh flatleaf parsley
½ lemon
4 free-range eggs
salt and pepper
To serve
green vegetable of your choice

GET AHEAD PREPARATION (optional)

The whole dish can be made a day in advance, prior to being baked. If you only have a little time:
* Prepare the potatoes.
* Peel and slice the onionsß and crush the garlic.
* Roughly chop the parsley.

35 minutes before you want to eat

* Preheat the oven to 200°C/400°F/Gas Mark 6.
* First, peel the potatoes and slice them as thinly as possible. Place in a pan of salted water and bring to the boil. Simmer the potatoes until they are just cooked. This will take 5–7 minutes; keep an an eye on them as you don't want them to collapse.
* In the meantime, heat a generous splash of oil in a large casserole dish. Peel and finely slice the onions and add them to the dish. Soften for 7–10 minutes while you peel and crush the garlic.
* While the onion is cooking, prepare the fish. Roughly chop the parsley and mix it with the flaked fish and a squeeze of lemon juice.
* When the potatoes come to the boil, drain and return them to the pan. Add the fish and parsley mixture to the drained potatoes, fold together and season well with salt and pepper.
* When the onions are soft, add the garlic to the casserole dish. Cook for a couple of minutes before adding the anchovies and their oil. Let the anchovies soften and melt into the onions – this will take about 5 minutes.
* When the anchovies have broken down completely, add the potato and fish mixture to the dish and fold together thoroughly. The mixture should be glistening with oil so add a little more if it isn't and season to taste.
* Place the casserole dish in the oven for 15 minutes until the top is golden and the potatoes are completely soft.
* While the potato bake is cooking, soft-boil the eggs by lowering them into a pan of boiling water and simmering for 7 minutes. When they are cooked, run cold water over them until they are cool enough to peel.
* Serve piles of the potato bake with a soft-boiled egg on top of each and, if you like, a green vegetable on the side.

Spinach Tian

Tian refers to a vegetable gratin topped with breadcrumbs and perhaps cheese. The resulting dish is comforting and very moreish. In this recipe spinach is mixed with softened onions and rice, then baked with a cheese and breadcrumb top. A Tian can be made with any greens or, in summer, fennel or grated courgettes – so this is a useful recipe to have up your sleeve. It's important to season the mixture well before it is baked in the oven, so taste it at this point to make sure it's packing enough punch.

5 medium onions, approx. 600 g
2 tbsp olive oil
4 garlic cloves
500 g large leaf spinach or 300 g
    baby leaf spinach
100 g Gruyère
500 g (approx.) cooked Thai
    jasmine rice left over from the
    Big Meal from Scratch or 180 g
    long grain rice cooked
    according to the
    manufacturer's instructions
2 free-range eggs
½ lemon
75 g breadcrumbs or 2–3 slices
    breads suitable for crumbing

salt and pepper

To serve
crusty bread and a salad made
    with little gem lettuces and a
    dressing of olive oil, lemon
    juice, Dijon mustard and
    seasoning

GET AHEAD PREPARATION (optional)

The entire dish can be made a day in advance up to the point of warming in the oven. If you only have a little time:
* Peel and slice the onions and garlic.
* Prepare the spinach.
* Grate the cheese.

*35 minutes before
you want to eat*

* Heat the oven to 180°C/350°F/Gas Mark 4.
* Peel and finely slice the onions. Heat the oil in a large frying pan over a medium heat. Add the onion and cook, stirring every now and then, for 10–12 minutes or until the onions are soft.
* While the onions are cooking, peel and finely slice the garlic and wash the spinach well. Once washed, remove any large, thick stalks then slice the spinach into 2–3-cm wide strips. Grate the cheese and put to one side.
* When the onions are soft add the garlic, stir for a minute then pile the spinach on top. Allow time for the strips nearest the heat to wilt, then turn them over and cook the rest.
* Remove from the heat, tip into a colander and, using a large spoon or the base of a cup, press out any excess liquid.
* Tip the squeezed spinach and onion mixture back into the pan and mix in the rice. Beat the eggs together, season with 1 level teaspoon each of salt and pepper and add the juice of the half lemon. Tip into the rice and spinach and mix very well.
* Taste for seasoning, then place the mixture in an ovenproof dish about 5 cm in depth. Mix the breadcrumbs and cheese together and sprinkle evenly over the onion, rice and spinach mixture.
* Place in the oven and cook for 20 minutes or until the bake is hot and the top has browned.
* Serve with crusty bread and a salad.

Seasonal supper

Sausages with Crisp Roast Vegetables and Caraway-Flavoured Cabbage

The vegetables for this recipe are crunchy and sweet and served with chestnuts and caramalised shallots – a perfect accompaniment to good quality sausages.

Cooked, peeled chestnuts are usually found in big supermarkets – either vacuum packed, in the freezer section or in tins. But don't worry if you can't find them – the recipe works perfectly well without them.

Sausages
8 good quality free-range
  sausages
groundnut or grapeseed oil

Crisp roast vegetables
3 tbsp groundnut or grapeseed
  oil
400 g floury potatoes, such as
  Maris Piper or baking potatoes
3 parsnips, approx. 500 g
1 tbsp polenta
8 small or 4 banana shallots
250 g cooked, peeled chestnuts
  (optional)

handful fresh flatleaf parsley
salt and pepper

Caraway-flavoured cabbage
500 g (approx.) white cabbage
small knob of butter
1 tsp caraway seeds
½ lemon

GET AHEAD PREPARATION (optional)

If you have a little time:
* Prepare the potatoes and cover
  them with water until required.
* Prepare the parsnips.
* Prepare the shallots.
* Drain the chestnuts.
* Shred and wash the cabbage.

40 minutes before you want to eat

* Preheat the oven to 220°C/425°F/Gas Mark 7. Put 2 tablespoons oil in a roasting tin, and place in the oven.
* Peel the potatoes and cut into 2 cm dice. Put into a large pan of salted water and bring to the boil. Meanwhile, peel the parsnips and cut into 2 cm dice. When the water with the potatoes is just about boiling, add the parsnips and bring back to the boil, drain well and tip the potatoes and parsnips back into the pan.
* Sprinkle the parboiled potatoes and parsnips with the polenta and shake well to distribute evenly. Tip the vegetables into the roasting tin, season well and stir. Put the tin back in the oven for about 30 minutes.
* Peel the shallots, cut off the roots and if they are large, slice in half lengthways. Heat 1 tablespoon oil in a heavy-based pan over a high heat. When the oil is hot add the shallots and cook until evenly browned all over, about 10 minutes. Drain the chestnuts. When the shallots have been cooking for 5 minutes, and are starting to colour, add the chestnuts and brown these too.
* Put the sausages into a roasting tin and into the oven for 15–20 minutes.
* Prepare the cabbage. Shred the cabbage into strips about 1 cm wide and 5 cm long. Wash in cold water then drain well.
* When the chestnuts and shallots have browned add them to the potatoes and parsnips after they have been in the oven for 20 minutes. Mix well and cook together for 10 minutes.
* Meanwhile, put the cabbage in the pan you cooked the chestnuts and shallots. Add the butter and ½ teaspoon each of salt and pepper. Cover and cook over a medium heat for 10 minutes. Check that the cabbage is cooked, sprinkle with the caraway seeds and squeeze over some lemon juice. Mix well and cook for a couple of minutes uncovered so that any excess liquid evaporates.
* Check that the roast vegetables are cooked and remove them from the oven. Line a bowl with kitchen paper and spoon in the roast vegetables. Pat with another piece of kitchen paper to absorb any excess fat, and sprinkle with the chopped parsley.
* Put two sausages on each of four warmed plates, with caraway-flavoured cabbage and the roast vegetables.

Larder feast

Pasta with Green Vegetables

Healthy, low-fat and packed with flavour, this pasta sauce is comforting without being guilt inducing. The vegetables are cooked in a light, winey broth which allows the sweet flavours of the artichokes, beans and peas to shine through.

300 g frozen broad beans
200 g frozen petit pois peas
2 tbsp olive oil
1 medium onion
2 garlic cloves
400 g pasta, such as penne or fusilli
1 x 400 g can (200 g drained weight) artichoke hearts
250 ml white wine

150 ml vegetable stock (made from a stock cube or 1 tsp vegetable bouillon powder)
small handful of fresh flatleaf parsley (optional)
salt and pepper

To serve
freshly grated Parmesan

GET AHEAD PREPARATION (optional)

The pasta sauce can be made a day in advance and warmed prior to serving. If you only have a little time:
* Defrost the peas and beans.
* Peel and slice the onion and garlic.
* Drain and quarter the artichoke hearts.

30 minutes before you want to eat

* First take the chill off the frozen peas and beans – tip them into a pan with some water and bring to the boil, then drain immediately.
* Next, heat the oil in a heavy-based pan over a medium to low heat. Peel and slice the onion, add it to the pan and soften gently for about 10 minutes, stirring now and then. Meanwhile, peel and thinly slice the garlic. When the onion has been cooking for about 5 minutes add the garlic.
* While the onion and garlic are cooking, put the pasta on to cook according to the manufacturer's instructions (usually about 10 minutes in boiling water).
* Next, drain the artichoke hearts and slice into quarters lengthways.
* Once the onion and garlic are soft, add the beans, peas and artichokes to the pan. Turn the heat up, stir for a minute or two then add the wine. Boil vigorously for about 2 minutes, then add the stock. Season with salt and pepper and simmer until the liquid reduces by about half.
* Meanwhile, wash, drain and roughly chop the parsley if you are using it. Add this to the pan and stir once or twice.
* Drain the pasta when it is cooked. Taste the sauce for seasoning then add it to the pasta and toss well.
* Serve in warmed large bowls with Parmesan on the side.

Two for one

Lamb Harira with Coriander Relish

Harira is a traditional Morrocan soup which is usually eaten to break the fasting day during Ramadan. It is a very filling dish with plenty of carbohydrates to keep the body going. Generally the meat ratio is low – we have upped it a little but feel free to increase the quantities of other ingredients and decrease the meat. Once tried, this dish is likely to become a firm favourite.

The recipe is based on one given to Rosie by her great friend and mentor the chef Juliet Peston. Juliet also makes this dish with chicken legs, or prawns and scallops which she fries and adds just before serving.

Lamb harira
1.2 kg neck of lamb fillets
4 tbsp olive oil
3 medium red onions, approx. 360 g
6 garlic cloves
2 red peppers, approx. 300 g
1 heaped tsp ground cinnamon
1½ tsp ground coriander
1 heaped tsp cumin
1 tsp cayenne pepper
1 tsp turmeric

300 g dried brown lentils
2 × 400 g cans chopped tomatoes
1 × 400 g can chickpeas
30 g long grain rice
salt and pepper

Coriander relish
1 large bunch fresh coriander
8 cm piece of fresh root ginger
1 lemon
splash of olive oil

To serve
warm flatbreads

GET AHEAD PREPARATION (optional)

The entire dish can be cooked a day in advance. If you only have a little time:
* Peel and slice the onions and garlic.
* Deseed and slice the red peppers.
* Make the coriander relish.
* Drain the chestnuts.

1 hour 45 minutes before you want to eat
* First brown the lamb. Cut the fillets into 3-cm chunks and season well with salt and pepper. Heat half the oil in a large, heavy-based flameproof casserole dish and brown the lamb in batches until the chunks are an even colour all over. (If the pan base gets very brown during the process, you could pause to clean and dry it.)
* While the meat is browning, peel and slice the onions and garlic, and deseed and finely slice the red peppers.
* After the final batch of meat has browned, add the remaining oil to the casserole dish and add the onions. Cook for about 5 minutes until the onions are soft.
* When the onions are soft, add the spices and garlic. Stir for a few minutes then add the peppers. Let them soften for a few minutes.
* When the peppers have softened a little, add the lentils and tomatoes. You can use the liquid in the tomatoes to scrape the spices from the bottom of the casserole. Then return the meat to the dish and add enough water to just cover the contents. Bring to a simmer and leave to cook for 30 minutes until the lentils are just cooked.

45 minutes before you want to eat
* When the lentils are just cooked, add the chickpeas and simmer for another 30–45 minutes until the lamb is very tender.

15 minutes before you want to eat
* When the lamb is meltingly soft, spoon half of the harira out and set it aside to cool, ready for freezing.
* Rinse the rice and throw it into the casserole, with a good dose of seasoning and a little more water as the rice will absorb quite a bit of liquid – you want a soupy consistency. Cook the rice for 10 minutes.
* Meanwhile, warm some flatbreads and make the coriander paste. Wash the coriander and remove its large stalks, and peel and coarsely chop the ginger. Put both in a food processor with the juice of the lemon, a splash of oil and a pinch of salt and pepper and whizz until smooth. If you do not have a processsor use a pestle and mortar or chop the coriander and ginger as finely as possible before mixing with the lemon juice, oil and seasoning.
* To serve, ladle the harira into warmed large soup bowls and top each serving with a heaped teaspoonful of the coriander paste. To eat, stir the paste into the harira before eating the soup with flatbreads.

Afterwards
Freeze the harira and leftover coriander relish separately.

Lazy day supper – reheating instructions

Allow the harira and coriander paste to defrost completely before reheating. Transfer the harira to a pan and bring up to a simmer. At this point add 30 g washed long grain rice, a good dose of seasoning and a little more water as the rice will absorb quite a bit of liquid – the harira should have a soupy consistency. Simmer gently for 10–15 minutes, until the rice is cooked, while you warm some flatbreads. Serve as above.

Cutting onions

You're going to cut up a lot of onions if you follow this book, so it's worth knowing how to do so quickly and safely. Most of the time we suggest you cut them (into thin, semicircular slices), but occasionally the recipe calls for chopped onions (small dice). There are quick and safe ways to do both, which, if you master them will make your life much easier.

First, whether slicing or chopping, cut the peeled onion in half lengthways. Lie the two onion halves down, skin-side up, then cut off the sprouting end – but keep the root end so that it holds the onion intact. To slice the onion, hold it firmly with your fingertips curled under so they can't be cut, and, starting from the sprouting end, cut downwards to create thin half-moon slices. To chop the onion, cut a series of slices lengthways towards the root (keeping the root intact so that the half onion is held together), then turn the halves and cut them as above, so that the diced onion falls on to the chopping board.

January Week 4 – Overview

For this week's Big Meal from Scratch, the sharp astringency of Seville oranges provides a perfect contrast to the richness of duck. The end result is something well worth sharing with friends, but be warned – there is surprisingly little meat on a duck and even a big bird will only feed four. If there are more people to be fed, buy two birds and cook them side by side. To ensure there are leftovers for making a Cassoulet later in the week, we suggest roasting a couple of duck legs alongside the duck. Seville oranges are in season in January but if they prove difficult to find they can be replaced with any other small, juicy oranges.

Our Cheat's Cassoulet, made using surplus duck meat and the duck legs, takes a while to assemble but the end result is well worth it.

Any surplus celeriac mash from the Big Meal from Scratch is used to make a Celeriac and Goats' Cheese Bake that's ideal after a long day at work. It takes 20 minutes to prepare and 20 minutes to bake.

Cauliflower is very good at this time of year, so for a Seasonal Supper there is a recipe for Italian Cauliflower Farfalle. The combination of cauliflower and pasta may not seem an obvious marriage but it works very well. Aside from tasting good the recipe is quick and the dish takes only 30 minutes to make.

The Larder Feast of Saffron Rice with Prawns is a distant cousin to paella. The recipe takes 45 minutes in total so bear this in mind when planning the week's cooking.

To end the week the Two for One is Braised Pork with Artichokes and Mushrooms – it takes a couple of hours in total but will not disappoint.

January Week 4	Recipe	Time
Big meal from scratch	Roast duck with Seville oranges, celeriac mash and watercress	2¼ hours
Something for nothing 1	Cheat's cassoulet	1 hour
Something for nothing 2	Celeriac and goats' cheese bake	40 mins
Seasonal supper	Italian cauliflower farfalle	30 mins
Larder feast	Saffron rice with prawns	45 mins
2 for 1	Braised pork with artichokes and mushrooms	2 hours

All recipes serve 4 apart from the 2 for 1 recipe which makes 8 portions

SHOPPING LIST (for 4 people)

Meat and fish
1 medium-large duck, approx. 1.75 kg
2-3 duck legs
1.5 kg free-range boned pork shoulder
4-6 coarse thick pork sausages (Toulouse if you can get them)
200 g cubed smoked pancetta or bacon lardons
200 g frozen cooked peeled prawns

Dairy
135 g butter
4 free-range eggs
250 g soft rindless goats' cheese
25 g Parmesan
200 ml crème fraîche

Fruit and vegetables
3 carrots, approx. 300 g
2 leeks, approx. 300 g
2.5-3 kg celeriac (ideally 3-4 small celeriac, not much bigger than cricket balls)
1 cauliflower, approx 400g
150 g mushrooms (chestnut if possible)
3 celery sticks
125-150 g watercress, approx. 2 bunches
2 medium red onions, approx. 240 g
7 medium onions, approx. 840 g
4 large or banana shallots, approx. 120 g
11-13 garlic cloves
10 sprigs fresh thyme
2 sprigs fresh sage
1 small sprig fresh rosemary
1 large bunch fresh flatleaf parsley
6 Seville oranges or other small juicy oranges
1 lemon

Basics
120 ml olive oil
3 tbsp groundnut or grapeseed oil
85 g breadcrumbs or 2-3 slices bread suitable for crumbing
100 g stale bread
300 ml fish stock (fresh or made from a stock cube)
300 ml vegetable stock (made from a stock cube or bouillon powder)
salt and pepper

Store cupboard
400 g paella rice (such as Calasparra)
400 g farfalle pasta
2 × 400 g cans haricot beans
1 × 400 g can chopped tomatoes
4-5 piquillo peppers, or other red peppers preserved in oil, from a can or jar
1 × 100 g can clams or mussels in oil (*not* in brine) or 100 g tuna in oil
2 × 390 g cans artichoke hearts
60 g chopped walnuts
65 g pine nuts (buy them toasted if you like)
60 g raisins
180 ml white wine vinegar
pinch of nutmeg (ground or freshly grated)
3 bay leaves
pinch of saffron threads
1 tsp paprika
75 ml brandy (optional for the Cheat's Cassoulet)
300 ml red wine
1.2 litres white wine

Serving suggestions
crusty bread and lamb's lettuce, olive oil and lemon juice (for Celeriac and Goats' Cheese Bake)
crusty bread and salad ingredients (Saffron Rice with Prawns)
tagliatelle or potatoes for mashing (for Braised Pork with Artichokes and Mushrooms)

To download or print out this shopping list, please visit www.thekitchenrevolution.co.uk/January/Week4

Roast Duck with Seville Oranges, Celeriac Mash and Watercress

Duck has succulent, rich meat that makes a simple roast seem rather special. For this meal we roast the duck on a bed of Seville oranges, then use the oranges to make a gravy that is citrussy and tangy.

Duck à l'orange was a regular feature of menus in the 1970s and 1980s, but its association with formal, old-fashioned dining means it's fallen out of favour in more recent years. This is a shame because the richness of duck and the sweet but sharp flavour of oranges complement one another wonderfully. Seville oranges have a sharp and slightly bitter flavour when compared to other varieties. Using them to accompany roast duck is a modern twist on an old classic.

The intense mineral taste of celeriac works as a good contrast to the richness and sweetness of the duck and oranges. Steamed or boiled celeriac absorbs a huge quantity of water and this dilutes the taste when the vegetable is mashed. To overcome this problem Polly uses a method she learnt from a friend and inspired cook, Huw Morgan. The celeriac here is wrapped tightly in foil, baked until completely soft then mashed with butter. Creamy essence of celeriac is the end result.

It's worth pricking the skin of a duck prior to cooking to extract excess fat, thereby encouraging a crisp skin. For a 1.75 kg bird the total cooking time, including 20 minutes at 220°C/425°F/Gas Mark 7, will be 1 hour and 10 minutes. For different sized birds cook for 45 mins per kilo.

The extra duck meat is used to make a Cheat's Cassoulet and the extra celeriac mash makes a Celeriac and Goat's Cheese Bake.

Roast duck with Seville oranges	Celeriac mash	Watercress
1 medium-large duck, approx. 1.75 kg	2.5-3 kg celeriac (ideally 3-4 small celeriac not much larger than cricket balls); includes approx. 800 g extra for the Celeriac and Goats' Cheese Bake	125-150 g watercress, approx. 2 bunches
2-3 duck legs (for the Cheat's Cassoulet)		
3 medium onions, approx. 660 g		GET AHEAD PREPARATION (optional)
6 Seville oranges or other small juicy oranges	85 g butter	* Cut the celeriac into quarters or halves.
2 sprigs fresh sage	pinch of nutmeg (ground or freshly grated)	* Peel and quarter one of the onions and slice the remaining ones.
2 sprigs fresh thyme		
salt and pepper		

2¼ hours before you want to eat

* Preheat the oven to 220°C/425°F/Gas Mark 7.
* Now prepare the celeriac. If using larger ones, cut into quarters or halves (unpeeled) and wrap each piece in foil with some salt and pepper. If using small celeriac, keep whole and wrap individually in foil. Place the celeriac on a baking sheet on the bottom of the oven; don't worry about whether it has come up to temperature.
* Prepare the duck by pricking the fatty areas of skin, particularly where the legs and the breast meet, with a small skewer. Season the duck and the duck legs thoroughly, especially with salt as this will help to render the fat and crisp the skin.
* Peel one of the onions and cut into quarters. Cut one of the oranges into quarters, and stuff this and the onion inside the duck cavity with a few torn-up sage leaves.
* Place the duck in a roasting tin. Lie the duck legs skin sides up alongside. Place in the preheated oven and roast for 20 minutes. (For guinea fowl cooking times see above.)
* Peel and slice the remaining onions into 1.5-cm thick slices. Cut two of the five remaining oranges into slices of a similar thickness and squeeze the juice from the other three.

1½ hours before you want to eat

* After the initial 30 minutes, remove the duck from the oven and lift the bird and the legs out of the roasting tin. Turn the oven down to 180°C/350°F/Gas Mark 4.
* Drain the fat from the tin and chill. When it solidifies there will be a layer of cooking juices underneath which you should reserve for gravy. Keep the fat for the cassoulet later in the week or, if not, for roasting potatoes. Arrange the sliced oranges and onions

in the tin and scatter the thyme over. Return the duck and legs to the tin. Cook for a
further 30 minutes.

1 hour before you
want to eat

* Take the duck and duck legs out of the oven and lift them from the tin. Set the legs
aside to cool for the cassoulet later in the week. Drain off any fat again and stir the
oranges and onions before adding half the orange juice.
* Return the duck to the tin and cook for a final 20 minutes until the juices run clear
when the thighs are pierced with a knife or a skewer.

30 minutes before
you want to eat
mash the celeriac
and make the
gravy

* Check the celeriac is ready – when pierced with a knife there should be no resistance.
Remove from the oven, unwrap and leave to cool for a moment.
* When the duck has been cooked for a total of about 1 hour and 20 minutes, remove
from the oven and rest for 20 minutes or so. Turn the oven off and put some plates and
serving dishes in it to warm.
* Meanwhile, make the gravy. Pour off as much fat as you can from the roasting tin and
place the tin on the hob (you may need to use two rings). Add enough water to just
cover the orange and onion slices. Bring to the boil and stir very thoroughly to scrape
the flavours from the bottom of the tin. Add any cooking juices from under the duck
fat and the reserved orange juice and allow the gravy to simmer very gently until it
reduces to a pouring consistency.
* Meanwhile make the celeriac mash. Melt the butter in a large pan over a gentle heat.
Pull the skins off the celeriac and add the flesh to the melted butter. Mash or purée the
celeriac with a hand blender. Add a good pinch of nutmeg and season to taste. Cover
with a lid and leave over a low heat, stirring occasionally to avoid sticking.
* Chop the remaining sage leaves then strain the gravy into a jug and stir in the sage.
* Reserve 400 g of the celeriac mash and put the remainder in a warmed serving dish.
Place the watercress in a bowl.
* Carve the duck and serve with lashings of gravy on top, and the celeriac mash and
watercress on the side.

Afterwards

* Place the reserved 400 g mash and the meat and skin from the cold duck legs (ideally
300 g meat) in separate containers, cover and refrigerate for use later in the week.
* The duck carcass and leg bones will make rich stock – you could make it now (see page
495), or put the carcass and bones in the freezer to make it at a later date.

Something for nothing 1

Cheat's Cassoulet

Cassoulet originates in the Languedoc region of France and is traditionally made over about three days with haricot beans, sausages, pork fat, pork and goose or mutton, layered up and cooked slowly to form a wickedly rich and intensely flavoured casserole. For the recipe below we've adapted a traditional recipe so that something similar can be made in just 1 hour. This involves assembling layers of duck and tomato sauce, beans and sausages and baking in the oven.

4-6 coarse thick pork sausages
2 × 400 g cans haricot beans
300 ml vegetable stock (made from a stock cube or bouillon powder(
a few sprigs fresh thyme
1 bay leaf
1 generous tbsp duck fat (left over from the roast duck) or 1 tbsp ground nut or grapeseed oil
200 g cubed smoked pancetta or lardons

6 garlic cloves
2 onions, approx. 240 g
3 carrots, approx. 300 g
75 ml brandy (optional)
300 ml red wine
1 × 400 g can chopped tomatoes
300 g duck left over from the Big Meal from Scratch
handful of fresh parsley
85 g breadcrumbs or 2-3 slices bread suitable for crumbing
salt and pepper

GET AHEAD PREPARATION (optional)
The cassoulet can be prepared up to a day in advance up to the point of being heated in the oven. If you only have a little time:
* Peel and roughly chop the garlic.
* Peel and slice the onions.
* Peel and slice the carrots.
* Cook the beans.
* Make the tomato sauce.
* Brown the sausages.

1 hour before you want to eat

* Preheat the oven to 200°C/400°F/Gas Mark 6.
* Place the sausages in a roasting tin, brown them in the oven for 10–15 minutes.
* Next prepare the bean mixture. Drain and rinse the beans, tip them into a heavy-based large casserole dish. Add the stock, thyme and bay leaf, place over a medium-high heat and bring to a simmer.
* Heat a nut of duck fat in a frying pan over a medium heat and add the pancetta or lardons. Peel and roughly chop the garlic and peel and finely slice the onions. When the pancetta or lardons have started to release their fat add the garlic and shake the pan for a minute or so. Now remove from the pan with a slotted spoon and add to the beans.
* Add the onions to the frying pan and let them soften for 5–7 minutes. Peel and slice the carrots. When the onions have softened, lift about two-thirds from the frying pan and put them into another pan (for the tomato sauce).
* Add the carrots to the onions in the frying pan with a little more duck fat, and let them soften for 5 minutes. When soft add to the beans and leave to simmer.
* Add the remaining duck fat to the onions for the tomato sauce, put the pan on a high heat and brown the onions for 1 minute. Add the brandy and let it evaporate, then add the wine and bring back to the boil for 2 minutes. Add the tomatoes to the wine and onion mix and season well. Bring the mixture to a simmer and let it bubble for about 10 minutes, stirring occasionally.
* Remove the sausages from the oven.
* Slice the sausages into 2-cm pieces and shred the duck meat. Roughly chop the parsley and add half to the breadcrumbs.
* Add the duck and the remaining parsley to the tomato sauce, heat through and season.
* Check the beans for seasoning and use a slotted spoon to lift out two-thirds and set them aside. Spoon half the tomato mixture on to the beans in the casserole, cover with half the sausages and add another layer of beans. Continue with a layer of tomato, then sausages and finally with a layer of beans. Top with breadcrumbs and season.
* Cook in the oven until the top becomes crisp and the cassoulet is piping hot. It will be ready to eat in 15–20 minutes, but if you can leave it for up to an hour you will get the full unctuous softness of cassoulet.

**Something
for nothing 2**

Celeriac and Goats' Cheese Bake

This recipe turns leftover celariac mash into a light, quick supper. The leeks, celery, walnuts and bread add texture and the goats' cheese some sharpness. At this time of year lamb's lettuce should be in good supply, so serve this dish with a simply dressed salad and some crusty bread.

2 leeks, approx. 300g
generous nut of butter
olive oil
3 celery sticks
4 free-range eggs
5 tbsp crème fraîche
400 g leftover celeriac mash
   from the Big Meal from
   Scrathc, or 400g floury
   potatoes, cooked and mashed
250 g soft rindless goats' cheese
60 g chopped walnuts
1 small sprig fresh rosemary
100 g stale bread
salt and pepper

To serve
crusty bread
lamb's lettuce salad, dressed
   with olive oil and lemon juice

GET AHEAD PREPARATION (optional)

The entire bake can be assembled a day in advance up to the point where it goes into the oven. If you only have a little time:
* Clean and slice the leeks and celery.
* Make the leek and celery base for the bake.
* Mix together the eggs, crème fraîche, goats' cheese and one third of the walnuts.

*40 minutes before
you want to eat*

* Preheat the oven to 190°C/375°F/Gas Mark 5
* Clean and slice the leeks, then heat the butter and a splash of oil in a small pan over a medium heat. When the butter is foaming, add the leeks and cook gently with the lid on until they are soft. This should take 5–7 minutes – and you will need to stir them from time to time.
* While the leeks are cooking, clean and slice the celery. Break the eggs into a large bowl and whisk with the crème fraîche. Add the celeriac mash and whisk together thoroughly. Add half the cheese and one-third of the walnuts. Mix well and season to taste with salt and pepper.
* When the leeks are soft, take the lid off the pan, turn up the heat and add the celery and some salt and pepper. Cook the celery and leeks for a couple of minutes so that the celery starts to soften and the leeks lose a little of their excess liquid.
* Next, assemble the bake. Place the celery and leeks on the base of an ovenproof dish and tip the celeriac mixture over the top. Crumble over the rest of the cheese. Strip the rosemary leaves from their stalks and chop them finely. Chop the bread into small cubes, toss in a little oil with the chopped rosemary and the remaining walnuts. Sprinkle the bread and walnuts over the top and bake in the oven for about 20 minutes until the mixture is set.
* If the top isn't golden after 20 minutes, turn the oven up to 200°C/400°F/Gas Mark 6 and return the dish for a few minutes.
* Serve with crusty bread and a lamb's lettuce salad.

Seasonal supper

Italian Cauliflower Farfalle

Cauliflower, pasta and raisins may, to the uninitiated, sound rather dubious, but beleive us, it works.

Cauliflower is available these days throughout the year but its proper season runs from December through until March.

This dish is a meal in itself but serve it with a simple salad if you feel so inclined.

1 cauliflower, approx. 400g	2 tbsp white wine vinegar	GET AHEAD PREPARATION (optional)
1 lemon	150 ml white wine	
4 tbsp olive oil	400 g farfalle pasta	* Roast the cauliflower.
65 g pine nuts (buy them toasted if you like)	60 g raisins	* Peel and slice the onions.
	small handful of fresh flatleaf parsley	* Peel and crush the garlic.
2 medium red onions, approx. 240 g	25g Parmesan	* Roughly chop the parsley.
2-3 garlic cloves	salt and pepper	

30 minutes before you want to eat

* Preheat oven to 200°C/400°F/Gas Mark 6 to roast the cauliflower.
* Cut the cauliflower into florets and put them in a single layer in an ovenproof dish. Squeeze the lemon over the florets, drizzle with a very generous glug of oil and season thoroughly with salt and pepper. Put the cauliflower in the oven and roast for about 20–25 minutes while you get everything else ready.
* While the cauliflower is in the oven, put the pine nuts (if they're not already toasted) on a baking sheet in one layer and toast them in the oven for about 5 minutes until they are golden. Watch them carefully as they have a tendency to burn.
* Next, heat a good splash of oil in a pan with a lid and peel and finely slice the onions. Add the onions and let them soften over a medium heat with the lid on for 7–10 minutes while you peel and crush the garlic.
* When the onions are soft, add the garlic to the pan and turn the heat up so that the onions get some colour. Next, add the vinegar and let it boil until it disappears. Now add the wine and reduce the liquid by half.
* While the wine is simmering away, cook the farfalle according to the manufacturer's instructions (usually 8–10 minutes in boiling water).
* When the wine has reduced, add the raisins and allow to simmer while you check on the cauliflower.
* When the cauliflower is tender, bring it out of the oven and mix with the softened onions and garlic. Roughly chop the parsley and add it to the pan with a little more oil.
* Once cooked, drain the farfalle and toss with the cauliflower. Season to taste and add the pine nuts.
* To serve, pile into warmed bowls and grate some Parmesan over the top.

Larder feast

Saffron Rice with Prawns

Saffron-yellow paella cooked in shallow wide pans is synonymous with Spanish cooking, but the popularity of rice in Spain means that the typical 'holiday paella', is just one dish among many. Although recipes vary, the classic way to cook Spanish rice is in a large, shallow pan or earthenware dish on the top of the stove.

Here we raid the larder to make a saffron-infused seafood rice. Short grain rice, ideally Spanish paella (Calasparra) rice, is the most important ingredient in this recipe. Once cooked, Spanish rice is fat and succulent. Short grain pearl rice grown in California will also do. Unlike long grain or basmati rice, you do not need to prewash these short grains because any residual starch will help create a creamy, rich texture. Peppers in cans and jars are now widely available and the best of these are piquillo peppers. If you can't find them buy piquante red peppers, which pack a bit more of a punch than piquillos but do the job just as well.

200 g frozen, cooked peeled prawns
2 medium onions, approx. 240 g
2 tbsp olive oil
3-4 garlic cloves
4-5 piquillo, or other peppers in oil, from a can or jar
generous handful of fresh flatleaf parsley
300 ml white wine
pinch of saffron threads
1 tsp paprika

400 g paella rice (Calasparra)
300 ml fish stock (fresh or made from a stock cube)
1 ×100 g can clams or mussels (approx. 75 g drained weight), in oil *not* brine, or 100 g tuna in oil
salt and pepper

To serve
crusty bread and salad

GET AHEAD PREPARATION (optional)

* Defrost the prawns.
* Peel and slice the onion.
* Peel and crush the garlic.
* Drain and slice the peppers.
* Roughly chop the parsley.
* Drain the clams or mussels.

45 minutes before you want to eat

* Put the frozen prawns in a large basin of cold water so that they start to defrost.
* Peel and finely slice the onion, then heat the oil in a large, wide flameproof dish or casserole over a medium heat. Cook gently for 5–7 minutes. Meanwhile, peel and crush the garlic then drain the peppers and slice them into 1-cm wide strips.
* When the onions are soft, add the garlic and cook for 2 minutes, stirring all the while to prevent it burning.
* Roughly chop the parsley and add half to the onions along with the wine and peppers. Bring to a gentle simmer.
* Preheat the oven to 200°C/400°F/Gas Mark 6.
* Add the saffron, paprika and rice, stirring so that everything is well coated with liquid. Pour over the stock and cook over a medium heat for 10 minutes, stirring now and then to prevent sticking.
* When the rice is still wet but not covered with liquid, season to taste with salt and pepper and transfer to the oven. Cook, uncovered, for 15 minutes.
* Remove the rice from the oven when all the liquid has evaporated. Drain the prawns and clams or mussels or tuna then add to the rice, cover with foil and allow to stand for 5 minutes so that the rice continues to cook and the flavours intensify.
* Serve with the remaining parsley, crusty bread and a salad.

Two for one

Braised Pork with Artichokes and Mushrooms

The combination of artichokes, mushrooms, pork and wine in this Two for One recipe is powerful without being heavy. Like most casseroles and braises, it requires some initial preparation and assembly, but then takes care of itself in the oven for 1½ hours. Reducing the sauce and adding crème fraîche at the very end of cooking is a good but not essential step. This adds about 10 minutes, but if time is of the essence miss it out and dive straight in. This dish is excellent served with creamy mash or tagliatelle.

1.5 kg free-range boned pork shoulder, trimmed and cut into 2.5-cm (approx.) cubes
3 tbs groundnut or grapeseed oil
30 g (approx.) butter
4 large or banana shallots, approx. 120 g
150 g mushrooms (chestnut if possible)
750 ml white wine
150 ml white wine vinegar

4 sprigs fresh thyme or ½ tsp dried thyme
2 × 390 g cans artichoke hearts
2 tbsp crème fraîche
2 bay leaves
salt and pepper

To serve
Mash or tagliatelle

GET AHEAD PREPARATION (optional)

The entire dish can be cooked 2 days in advance and heated up when required. If you only have a little time:
* Brown the meat (and return it to the fridge or a cool place).
* Prepare and brown the shallots.
* Halve the mushrooms.

2 hours before you want to eat

* Heat the oven to 170°C/325°F/Gas Mark 3.
* First, brown the meat. Heat half the oil and half the butter over a medium heat in a large, heavy-based flameproof casserole dish with a lid. While they are heating, pat the meat dry with kitchen paper and season with salt and pepper. Add the meat to the oil and butter in batches and brown – you don't have to make every single side equally brown but most of the meat should have a nice colour. As the meat browns transfer it on to a plate. While the meat is browning, peel the shallots and cut them in half.
* Once the meat has browned, add the rest of the oil and butter to the empty pan. When hot, add the peeled shallots to the casserole dish and cook until caramelised all over. While the shallots are cooking, cut the mushrooms in half.
* When the shallots are browned, add the mushrooms to the dish and let these start to colour.
* Next add the wine and vinegar and stir well, scraping the base and sides of the dish. If you are using fresh thyme, strip the leaves from the stalks. Drain the artichokes, cut them in half and add them to the mushrooms and shallots along with the thyme leaves or dried thyme. Add the meat, stir once or twice and bring to a gentle simmer.
* Once the meat is simmering, cover with a lid, and transfer to the oven. Cook for a total of 1½ hours – 45 minutes with the lid on and 45 minutes with the lid off.

10 minutes before you want to eat

* After cooking in the oven for 1½ hours the meat will be tender and the sauce will have reduced. Turn off the oven and remove the casserole dish. Lift the meat, artichokes and shallots from the dish using a slotted spoon. Put half in a serving dish, cover with foil and place in the oven to keep warm. Set the other half aside to cool for freezing.
* Put the casserole dish over a high heat and bring to the boil so that the liquid reduces by a third. When the liquid has reduced, tip half on to the pork and vegetable mixture intended for freezing. Continue to heat the remaining liquid and whisk in the crème fraîche to make a creamy sauce. Taste for seasoning and pour over the pork and vegetables in the serving dish.
* Serve with creamy mash or tagliatelle.

Lazy day supper – reheating instructions

Defrost the pork completely before reheating. Tip it into a large casserole dish and place over a gentle heat for 25 minutes, stirring now and then. Once the pork is nearly at simmering point, stir 2 tablespoons crème fraîche into the sauce. Serve with tagliatelle or mash.

Buying meat

There are various considerations that come into play when deciding what meat to buy and where to buy it. Many people have to balance tight household budgets and seek out inexpensive cuts and special offers; other people may have concerns about the ethics of meat production and avoid buying intensively reared animals. Some people might worry about the environmental damage caused by conventional meat production and look for organic products; others may worry about food miles and only buy meat from local butchers or farmers' markets. Many of us juggle with all these concerns and this book doesn't want to tell anyone definitively how or what they should buy. There are, however, a few principles that we adhere to when purchasing meat.

First, Zoe, Polly and Rosie all enjoy meat but we don't believe it's necessary to have it every single day in order to eat very well. Meat production is responsible for much environmental damage because animals have to be fed large amounts of food to produce relatively small amounts of meat or dairy. To produce 1 kg animal protein requires around 6 kg plant protein, so feeding animals is a very inefficient way of converting plants into human food. Consuming meat every single day might not be a desirable thing to do on the grounds of the environment and health. Eating meat, and ideally good quality, well-farmed meat, every now and then and in balanced portions is probably more sensible.

Second, although intensive farming drives down the cost of meat it doesn't improve its quality or taste. By and large, free-range and organic meat tastes superior and it is better value for money, bite for bite, than the insipid and often bland products produced through intensive methods. Intensive farming, moreover, raises questions about animal welfare and causes significant environmental damage.

Finally, for more information about meat we direct you to Hugh Fearnley-Whittingstall's excellent *The River Cottage Meat Book*. It is comprehensive, opinionated, sensible and utterly readable.

Marmalade Steamed Pudding

This recipe might not be diet food, but we're convinced that any damage to your waistline is compensated for by the pleasure that inevitably follows each bite of this light and moist steamed pudding. The recipe is not complicated but it does take a long time to cook because the pudding has to sit simmering away in a pan of water for 2 hours. If you want to replace the marmalade with lemon curd, raspberry jam or golden syrup that is absolutely fine. This will generously serve 4, adequately serve 6.

90 g butter, plus extra for
  greasing
4 tbsp marmalade
1 orange
90 g caster sugar
3 small free-range eggs

100 g self-raising flour
1 tsp baking powder

To serve
cream and custard

2½ hours before you want to eat

* Butter the inside of a 1-litre pudding basin. Put the basin in a pan deep enough for a lid to fit it when the basin is sitting in the pan. Fill the pan with enough water to come halfway up the basin, then remove the basin and bring the water up to simmering point.
* Cut out a circle of greaseproof paper the same size as the bottom of the basin. Put this in the basin then spoon the marmalade over the top.
* Grate the zest from the orange and add it to the butter. Cream the butter and sugar together in a large bowl until pale and fluffy. You can use a hand beater to do this if you have one.
* Squeeze the juice from the orange and whisk it with the eggs. Mix the eggs, a little at a time, into the butter and sugar mixture.
* Add the flour and baking powder and fold together gently.
* Pour the mixture into the pudding basin.
* Make a square of foil big enough to cover the pudding and make a 3–4-cm tuck in the middle; this will allow for the expansion of the pudding. Put the foil over the bowl and secure it very firmly around the rim so that no water can get into the pudding – secure the foil with string or an elastic band. You can also make a rudimentary string handle for lifting the pudding from the water at the end of cooking. Wind the string around the basin at least twice and tie a double knot, making sure you have two long ends. Pass the ends loosely across the diameter of the basin and secure them on the other side.
* Place the basin in the pan of simmering water then cover with a lid and simmer for about 2 hours. You must remember to top up the water once or twice.
* After 2 hours remove the basin from the pan and allow the pudding to sit for 10 minutes before removing the foil. Invert the pudding on to a plate and serve with wicked amounts of cream and custard.

Prune and Nut Fool

Polly's granny used to make this pudding with swirly streaks of yoghurt and dried fruit purée. Years and many food fashions later it still tastes excellent and is a good household standby. No-soak pitted prunes or canned prunes can be used to make the fruit puree with minimum fuss. If you have ordinary dried prunes these will need softening overnight in water. You can make this pudding an hour or two before you want to eat. It's delicious with brandy snaps.

75 g no-soak pitted prunes or
    290g (approx) canned prunes
30 g unsalted, shelled pistachio
    nuts
30 g chopped almonds
100 g whipping or double cream
350 g Greek yoghurt
3 tsp dark brown sugar

To serve
brandy snaps

At least 45 minutes before you want to eat

* If you are using no-soak prunes put them in a pan with about 3 tablespoons water, bring to the boil then simmer and cook for about 10 minutes until very soft.
* Drain the boiled or canned prunes and remove any stones.
* Whizz the prunes in a food processor to form a purée. If the purée is warm allow it to cool to room temperature then place in the fridge to chill.
* Roughly chop the pistachios, mix with the almonds and set to one side.
* Whip the cream in a large bowl until it is thick but not stiff.
* Strain any excess liquid from the yoghurt and fold into the cream.
* Add the cold fruit purée and the sugar, and gently stir so that the mixture remains streaky. Spoon into a serving bowl or individual dishes.
* Sprinkle with the nuts, cover and place in the fridge for at least 20 minutes.
* Serve with brandy snaps.

January puddings

Pomegranate and Pink Grapefruit Jellies

These pink jellies with grapefruit segments and pomegranate seeds suspended in them look like jewels. We prefer the jelly to be only just set rather than stiff with gelatine – the finished product should have a melting and just-off-runny texture. This recipe makes enough for six people and the jelly can be set in individual glasses or in one large glass bowl. If you want to make a jelly to turn out add a couple more leaves of gelatine. The jelly is relatively quick to assemble but will take a few hours to set.

4 pink grapefruit
1 pomegranate
500 ml (approx.) pomegranate
    juice
5 leaves (approx. 8 g) gelatine

To serve
Greek yoghurt

3½ hours before you want to eat

* Start by squeezing the juice from two of the grapefruit into a measuring jug.
* Next, slice a cap from the top and bottom of each of the remaining grapefruit so that they will stand easily. Then, with the fruit standing on a chopping board and using a very sharp knife, cut the peel and pith away in strips with a downward action so that you are left with the flesh only.
* Hold each grapefruit over a bowl and use the knife to cut on either side of the membrane that divides the individual grapefruit segments, releasing the segments and leaving behind any membrane. The segments should fall into the bowl as you cut them out. When you have finished segmenting each grapefruit, squeeze the leftover membrane in the measuring jug to capture any additional juice. You should now have a bowl of segments and a jug of juice.
* Next, roll the pomegranate around on a flat surface under your hand to loosen the seeds. Cut the pomegranate in half and sit the two halves, seed sides down, on a board. Hold the red dome of each half fruit with one hand while tapping it with a rolling pin or small heavy pan. The skin will start to break as the seeds fall away from their membrane compartments. Collect the seeds, taking off any membrane that hasn't already come away, and add them to the bowl of grapefruit segments.
* When you've collected all the pomegranate seeds, tip them and the grapefruit segments into a sieve over the jug of juice to drain any juice. Return the fruit to its bowl and put it in the fridge.
* In total you need 750 ml liquid so add enough pomegranate juice to the measuring jug to make up this amount.
* Pour about one-third of the juice into a bowl and add the gelatine leaves. Push the leaves under the liquid and allow to soak for about 10 minutes until completely softened.
* When the gelatine has been soaking for nearly 10 minutes, pour another third of the juice into a pan and bring to simmering point. Remove from the heat.
* Use your hands to pick up the gelatine and give it a good squeeze to remove any excess liquid. Set the liquid it was soaking in to one side.
* Stir the softened gelatine into the hot juice until it has completely dissolved, then tip this into the soaking liquid. Stir well to incorporate and pour into six individual glasses or one large glass bowl. Cover and refrigerate.
* After 2 hours add the pomegranate seeds and grapefruit segments to the jellies, then return to the fridge for at least another hour.
* Serve with Greek yoghurt.

Ginger and Apricot Cake

This is classic sticky gingerbread with the addition of canned apricots. You can make it in a buttered ovenproof dish and serve it hot from the oven, or in a loaf tin, as here, and turn it out and eat warm. It also reheats well in the oven, wrapped in foil. Canned apricots are a fantastic standby ingredient. Here they melt into soft nuggets of fruit nestling in the sticky gingerbread.

This recipe was suggested to Rosie by her great friend Imo.

50 g butter, plus extra for greasing
1 generous tbsp black treacle, approx. 50 g
1 generous tbsp golden syrup, 50 g
65 g light muscovado sugar
110 g plain flour
1 tsp mixed spice
2 tsp ground ginger

½ tsp bicarbonate of soda
pinch of salt
1 medium free-range egg
140 ml milk
1 × 300 g can apricot halves in juice

To serve
cream or crème fraîche

1 hour before you want to eat

* Preheat the oven to 180°C/350°F/Gas Mark 4.
* Grease a 500 g loaf tin with butter.
* Put the butter, treacle, golden syrup and sugar into a pan and warm them over a low heat, stirring from time to time, until the butter has melted.
* While the butter is melting, sift the dry ingredients together in a bowl and whisk the milk and egg together. Drain the apricots and cut each one in half.
* When the butter has melted, pour the butter mixture into the flour followed by the egg and milk, and beat vigorously.
* Tip one-third of the cake mixture into the tin and cover with half the apricots – they will sink, but don't worry. Cover with another third of the cake mixture then scatter over the rest of the apricots. Again, don't worry if they sink. Cover with the last of the cake mixture.
* Place in the middle of the oven and cook for 25 minutes
* Cover the tin with foil and bake for 25 minutes more. The gingerbread is ready when a skewer or cocktail stick inserted into it comes out completely clean.
* Turn the cake out of its tin once it has cooled down.
* Slice into slabs and serve with dollops of whipped cream or crème fraîche.

FEBRUARY

February is when the need for substantial and sustaining food becomes most acute. Happily, this is the month for Jerusalem artichokes, celeriac, leeks and brassicas – all of which are especially good in casseroles, gratins and soups. Each of them features in this month's recipes – a creamy Scallop and Jerusalem Artichoke Bake, an intensely flavoured celeriac and mushroom gratin, and seasonal greens in a colourful and spicy pork stir-fry. There are some crowd pleasers this month, too: bubble and squeak, Thai Beef Casserole and a South African variation on shepherd's pie. Crumble fans will love the Ginger and Forced Rhubarb Pudding, and *Torrijas*,the Spanish version of French toast will bring cheer to the darkest and coldest of days.

February	Week 1	Week 2	Week 3	Week 4
Big meal from scratch	Fish in Parma ham with red wine leeks and mustard mash	Roast guinea fowl (or chicken) with chicory and bacon, and roast carrots and parsnips	Roast Lamb with anchovies, rosemary potatoes and winter greens	Chicken (or partridge) with mushrooms, mash and greens
Something for nothing 1	Cock-a-leekie	Chicory and bacon pasta	Purple sprouting broccoli with chilli and anchovy sauce and pasta	Pork chops with bubble and squeak
Something for nothing 2	Cheese and onion potato bread pizza with rocket, pear and walnut salad	Guinea fowl (or chicken) pie	Bobotie – South African shepherd's pie	Celeriac and mushroom bake
Seasonal supper	Stir-fry pork with seasonal greens	Scallop and Jerusalem artichoke (or fish and potato) bake	Chicken (or pheasant) wrapped in bacon with Jerusalem artichokes	Root vegetable tagine with couscous
Larder feast	Grown-up baked beans – butter beans, anchovies and rosemary	Artichoke and pesto tart	Polenta with gorgonzola and garlic spinach	Thai fishcakes
2 for 1	Meatloaf	Thai beef casserole with stir-fried pak choi	Layered crab (or smoked salmon) and celeriac	Bacon and spinach pancakes
Puddings	Caramelised blood oranges with Grand Marnier	*Torrijas* – Spanish eggy bread	Baked banana and Greek yoghurt pudding	Rhubarb and ginger crumb pudding

February Week 1 – Overview

The Big Meal from Scratch this week, Fish in Parma Ham with Red Wine Leeks and Mustard Mash, is a simple but very effective way to cook fish. Though the fish takes just 30 minutes, the leeks take longer to cook, so you should start the meal an hour before you want to eat. Remember to use fish a day or two after purchasing or put it in the freezer until required.

Surplus leeks from the big meal are used as the basis for a Scottish chicken broth, Cock-a-Leekie. With the leeks ready to go, the meal is ready in half an hour. The remaining mash from the Big Meal from Scratch gets transformed into a pizza base that is topped with red onions and blue cheese. This recipe takes about 40 minutes from start to finish but will become a firm favourite once you've tried it out. It is especially fun to make with children.

This week the Seasonal Supper is Stir-Fry Pork with Seasonal Greens which, once all the vegetables are prepared, takes minutes to cook. Even quicker is the Larder Feast – a great 'standby' supper of Grown–Up Baked Beans.

The home-made Meatloaf is well seasoned and full of flavour, and will revise any preconceptions about this much maligned dish.

February Week 1	Recipe	Time
Big meal from scratch	Fish in Parma ham with red wine leeks and mustard mash	1 hour
Something for nothing 1	Cock-a-leekie	30 mins
Something for nothing 2	Cheese and onion potato bread pizza with rocket, pear and walnut salad	40 mins
Seasonal supper	Stir-fry pork with seasonal greens	35 mins
Larder feast	Grown-up baked beans – butter beans, anchovies and rosemary	20 mins
2 for 1	Meatloaf	1½ hours

All recipes serve 4 apart from the 2 for 1 recipe which makes 8 portions

SHOPPING LIST (for 4 people)

Meat and fish
1 kg free-range chicken drumsticks and
  thighs, bone-in
500 g minced beef
400 g minced pork
400 g free-range pork tenderloin or fillet
8 slices Parma ham
750-850 g pollack, haddock or cod fillet
  (in 1 piece)

Dairy
80 g butter
250-75 ml milk
2 free-range eggs
150-200 g soft blue cheese (Roquefort is
  good)

Fruit and vegetables
1.5 kg floury potatoes such as Desiréeor
  baking potatoes
9 leeks approx. 1.2 kg
200-300 g purple sprouting broccoli
200-300 g spring greens or 1 small Savoy
  cabbage
80-120 g rocket
8 medium red onions, approx. 960 g
4 spring onions
8-9 garlic cloves
6 cm (approx.) piece of fresh ginger
1 small red chilli
1 large bunch fresh flatleaf parsley
6 sprigs fresh sage
1 small bunch fresh coriander
2 small sprigs and 1 large sprig fresh
  rosemary
4 sprigs fresh thyme
2 lemons
2 firm pears

Basics
1 loaf rustic bread, such as pain de
  campagne, ciabatta or Pugliese
150 g bread or 4 slices bread
90 ml olive oil
3 tbsp groundnut or grapeseed oil
150 g self-raising flour
1 tbsp Worcestershire sauce
1 heaped tbsp wholegrain mustard
2 tsp mustard powder
generous pinch of cayenne pepper
2 tsp sugar (light brown or unrefined golden
  if possible)
1 litre chicken stock (fresh or made with a
  stock cube)
150 ml vegetable stock (fresh or made from a
  stock cube or bouillon powder)
salt and pepper

Store cupboard
300 g or 4 slabs dried egg noodles
3 × 420 g cans butter beans
2 × 50 g cans anchovy fillets in olive oil,
  or about 20 fillets
60 g no-soak prunes or dried prunes (soaked
  for 3 hours)
50 g shelled walnuts
4 tbsp toasted sesame oil
1 tbsp balsamic vinegar
90 ml dark soy sauce
generous pinch of ground mace
5 black peppercorns
105 ml dry sherry or sake
400 ml red wine
200 ml cider

Serving suggestions
crusty bread (Cock-a-Leekie)
broccoli or purple sprouting broccoli (Grown-
  up Baked Beans - Butter Beans, Anchovies
  and Rosemary)
baking potatoes, green salad ingredients
  and a selection of chutneys and pickles
  (Meatloaf)

To download or print out this shopping list,
please visit www.thekitchenrevolution.co.uk/
February/Week1

Big meal from scratch

Fish in Parma Ham with Red Wine Leeks and Mustard Mash

Wrapping fish in a generous slice of Parma ham helps keep it moist when cooking. The leeks in red wine that accompany this are slightly sweet and sour, and would also go well with poultry or game birds, so this is a recipe worth bearing in mind for other occasions.

It is often surprisingly difficult to find good fish. In a supermarket the best advice is buy what looks freshest. It is not always easy to check for freshness with fish that has been filleted, cut into pieces and packaged in plastic but the flesh should look moist and healthy; discolouration is a bad sign and escaped liquid is a tell-tale indication of age. If you can get hold of it, Cornish pollack would work well with this recipe. It has a similar flavour and texture to cod and is considerably less expensive.

The quantities here allow for extra leeks and extra mash, one for Cock-a-leekie (see page 66) and the other for Cheese and Onion Potato Bread Pizza (see page 67).

Fish in Parma ham
750-850 g pollack, haddock, coley or cod fillet (in 1 piece and skinned)
olive oil
8 slices Parma ham
8 sage leaves, approx. 2 sprigs
salt and pepper

Red wine leeks
8 leeks, approx.1 kg; includes approx. 500 g for the cock-a-leekie
30 g butter
1 tbsp balsamic vinegar
1 tsp sugar (light brown or unrefined golden if possible)

400 ml red wine
150 ml vegetable stock (made with a stock cube or bouillon powder)

Mustard mash
1.5 kg floury potatoes such as Maris Piper or baking potatoes; includes 600 g for the cheese and onion potato bread pizza
100 ml milk or 75 ml milk and 2 tbsp double cream
50 g butter
1 heaped tablespoon wholegrain mustard

GET AHEAD PREPARATION (optional)

* Wash and slice the leeks.
* Prepare the fish and refrigerate until required.
* Peel and chop the potatoes and cover with cold water

1 hour before you want to eat cook the leeks

* Cut the leeks into 1-cm thick slices and wash them very well. Heat the butter over a medium heat in a heavy-based pan with a lid and, when foaming, add the leeks, stirring them around so they are well coated in the butter. Let the leeks soften over a low heat for 5–7 minutes.
* When the leeks are soft, turn the heat up, splash in the balsamic vinegar and reduce it down completely.
* Now add the sugar and wine. Let the wine reduce by half , then add the stock, salt and pepper. Leave the leeks to cook over a low heat with a lid on while you cook the potatoes and fish – the leeks will happily bubble away until you are ready to eat.

40 minutes before you want to eat cook the potatoes

* Preheat the oven to 220°C/425°F/Gas Mark 7.
* Peel the potatoes, cut them into large, even-sized chunks and put them in a pan of water with a good pinch of salt. Bring to the boil and simmer gently until they are just cooked – this will take 20–25 minutes, depending on their size.

30 minutes before you want to eat cook the fish

* Check the fish fillet for small bones and season well on both sides.
* Oil a large baking sheet. Place the Parma ham along it so that the slices are just overlapping and place the sage leaves in a line along the middle. Put the fish on top, drizzle with oil and wrap the ham around the fish. Turn the fish over so that the join on the ham is on the bottom.
* Put the fish in the oven and cook for 15–25 minutes, depending on the thickness of the fillet.

10 minutes before you want to eat mash the potatoes

* When the potatoes are cooked, tip them into a colander and drain well.
* Put the milk, or milk and cream, and the butter in the potato pan over a low heat to allow the butter to melt and the milk to warm. Place the colander over the pan to help steam-dry the potatoes.

* When the milk is hot, add the mustard and then the potatoes. Mash well with a traditional masher or, for a really smooth texture, pass the potatoes through a mouli-legumes or potato ricer. Taste and season as necessary, and add more mustard if you want a stronger flavour.
* Take the fish out of the oven – the Parma ham coat should be crisp and the fish inside should feel firm to the touch. Turn off the oven and put plates and serving dishes into it to warm.
* Once the leeks are very soft, take the lid off, turn the heat to high and reduce the liquid so that it just comes to the level of the leeks. Taste and season.
* Serve the fish in slices with some leeks and a good helping of mash.

Afterwards Put the leftover mash and leeks in separate containers, cover and refrigerate for use later in the week. Ideally there will be approx. 500 g leeks and 400 g leftover mash.

Choosing white fish
About ten of our recipes call for cod, yet cod is often the species cited as being overfished and unsustainable. This is true for the North Sea, but over 80 per cent of the cod sold in the United Kingdom comes from Icelandic waters that are generally well managed and felt to be sustainable. It is true, however, that we eat vast amounts of cod and put huge demands on the species so there's good reason for seeking out alternatives. Haddock is an obvious contender but that, too, is under pressure so consider using pollack or coley as an alternative.

Pollack has white firm flesh and a similar flavour to cod. As a good example of the craziness of the modern food system, much of the pollack caught in Alaska is sent to China to be processed and then transported back to Europe where it is used to make breaded fish products. Pollack is also landed by a small Cornish fishery and is worth seeking out.

Coley has a stronger flavour than cod, haddock or pollack but this is often an advantage in recipes where the flavours are powerful. Raw coley has a slightly greyish tinge but it turns white once cooked.

Cock-a-Leekie

This is a speedy version of the famous Scottish soup made with chicken, leeks and prunes – a hot broth for cold, dark nights.

Traditionally cock-a-leekie involves a whole boiling fowl (an egg-laying bird at the end of its laying life) which is simmered very gently for a long time before being stripped off the bones and served along with the prunes in a leeky broth. Given midweek time constraints and the near impossibility of sourcing a free-range boiling fowl, the recipe here is written for chicken thighs and drumsticks, and uses the surplus red wine leeks from the Big Meal from Scratch.

This is very good served with warm crusty bread or, if you would prefer a more substantial soup, add a few small potatoes during cooking.

1 kg free-range chicken
    drumsticks and thighs
1 litre chicken stock (fresh or
    made with a stock cube)
5 black peppercorns
400–500 g leeks left over from
    the Big Meal from Scratch or
    500 g leeks, finely sliced and
    washed thoroughly
60 g no-soak prunes or dried
    prunes soaked for 3 hours
generous handful of fresh flatleaf
    parsley
salt and pepper

To serve
crusty bread, warmed in the oven

GET AHEAD PREPARATION (optional)

The entire recipe can be made up
to a day in advance up to the
point of adding the prunes.

*30 minutes before
you want to eat*

* Remove any skin from the chicken by using a tea towel or dry, clean cloth to keep your grip as you pull the skin from the meat. Season the chicken well all over with salt and pepper.
* Put the stock in a large pan and add the chicken, peppercorns and ½ teaspoon salt.
* If cooking leeks from scratch, add the washed slices to the simmering pan at the same time as the chicken.
* Slowly bring the stock and chicken to the boil, skimming off any scum that rises to the surface, and simmer very gently for 20 minutes or until the chicken is cooked and the flesh comes away from the bones. Cooking the chicken gently ensures the meat stays tender.
* When the thighs and drumsticks are cooked, lift them out. Add the leftover leeks, if using, to the pan and warm them through while you strip the chicken meat from the bones – this is most easily done with a knife and fork.
* Now return the shredded chicken to the pan, add the prunes and continue to simmer for another 3 minutes.
* Roughly chop the parsley and throw it in at the end. Serve in warmed big bowls with crusty bread.

Something for nothing 2

Cheese and Onion Potato Bread Pizza with Rocket, Pear and Walnut Salad

This is an innovative way of turning surplus mash into a very tasty supper. The mash is mixed with flour and an egg to form a potato-bread pizza base. This is topped with red onions, blue cheese and rosemary and served alongside a salad of rocket, pears and walnuts. The sharpness of the cheese is especially lovely with the sweetness of the pears. If, however, you are not a big blue cheese fan, replace it with a cheese of your choice.

Cheese and onion potato bread pizza
500 g mashed potatoes left over from the Big Meal from Scratch or 600 g potatoes peeled, boiled then mashed
5 medium red onions, approx. 600 g
1 tbsp olive oil
1 free-range egg
150 g self-raising flour
milk, if needed

150-200 g soft blue cheese (Roquefort is good)
2 small sprigs fresh rosemary
salt and pepper

Rocket, pear and walnut salad
50 g shelled walnuts
juice of 1 lemon
1 tbsp olive oil
2 firm pears
80-120 g rocket

GET AHEAD PREPARATION (optional)
* Prepare and cook the onions.
* Make the potato bread and roll it out. It is best kept in the fridge, but transfer to a hot tray before it goes in the oven.
* Prepare the pears and toss them in oil and lemon.

40 minutes before you want to eat

* Take the mash out of the fridge and let it come to room temperature.
* Peel and finely slice the onions. Heat a generous splash of oil over a medium heat in a pan with a lid and add the onions. Stir them about so that they are all coated with oil, then turn the heat down and cook with the lid on for 15–20 minutes until soft and sweet.
* Preheat the oven to 200°C/400°F/Gas Mark 6.
* While the oven is warming, put the walnuts in a roasting tin and place them in the oven to toast – watch carefully as they will burn quickly.
* While the onions are cooking, make the potato bread base. Place the mash in a bowl and break it up until it is in manageable pieces. Beat the egg, add it to the mash and mix to a soft paste. Sift in the flour and mix to a soft dough. If it's too dry add a little milk, if too wet use more flour. Dust a large baking sheet with flour and roll the dough out on it to a thickness of 1 cm.
* After the onions have been cooking for 15–20 minutes and when they are soft, remove the pan lid and turn up the heat for a few minutes to cook off any excess liquid. Taste the onions and season well.
* Spread the onions over the potato base and crumble the cheese over them. Strip the rosemary leaves from their stalks and scatter over the top with a little salt and pepper. Place at the top of the oven and cook for about 15–20 minutes until the bread is firm and has puffed up a bit, and the cheese has melted.
* While the pizza is cooking, make the salad. Roughly chop the toasted walnuts. Pour the lemon juice into a bowl and whisk in the oil and some salt and pepper. Peel the pears, quarter and core them. Toss the pear quarters in the lemon juice and oil dressing. Trim the rocket if necessary, then wash and dry it.
* Toss the walnuts and rocket with the dressed pears and serve with slices of pizza.

Seasonal supper

Stir-fry Pork with Seasonal Greens

The stir-fry is a favourite kitchen standby – it's quick to cook and is an excellent vehicle for delivering punchy tastes and interesting textures. The bulk of the work for a stir fry lies in the washing, peeling and chopping of vegetables. Once you have done this everything else comes together relatively quickly. Never start cooking a stir-fry until everything is 'prepped'. Aside from preparation, speed and heat are two other key ingredients for success – anything else results in limp and soggy vegetables.

<u>Stir-fry pork</u>
400 g free-range pork tenderloin
    or fillet
3 cm piece of fresh root ginger
4 tbsp soy sauce
1 tbsp toasted sesame oil
1 tsp brown sugar (ideally dark
    brown soft)
3 tbsp dry sherry or sake

<u>Noodles</u>
300 g or 4 slabs dried egg
    noodles

<u>Stir-fry vegetables</u>
1 large garlic clove
3 cm piece of fresh root ginger
1 small red chilli
1 small bunch fresh coriander
4 spring onions
200–300 g purple sprouting
    broccoli
200–300 g spring greens or 1
    small Savoy cabbage
1 leek, approx. 150 g
2 tbsp soy sauce
1 tsp brown sugar (ideally dark
    brown soft)
4 tbsp dry sherry or sake
1 tbsp groundnut or grapeseed oil
1 tsp toasted sesame oil

<u>GET AHEAD PREPARATION (optional)</u>

* Make the marinade.
* Marinade the pork.
* Prepare the ingredients for the
    stir-fry.
* Mix the soy sauce, sugar and
    sherry or sake for the
    vegetables with 4 tbsp water.

35 minutes before you want to eat

* Cut the pork tenderloin into 1-cm slices and place in a bowl. Peel and chop the ginger for the marinade and mix with the remaining marinade ingredients. Add 1 tablespoon of water and pour over the meat. Set aside until needed.
* Peel the garlic and ginger and slice into matchsticks, deseed and finely chop the chilli and roughly chop the coriander.
* Trim the vegetables and cut the spring onions into 1-cm thick slices, the broccoli into bite-sized florets, the greens or cabbage into thin shreds and the leeks into 1-cm thick diagonal slices.
* Mix the soy sauce, sugar and sherry or sake for the vegetables with 4 tablespoons water and set aside.
* When the meat has been marinating for at least 20 minutes, cook the noodles according to the manufacturer's instructions.
* Preheat the oven to a low temperature; put a wok over a high heat and add half the groundnut or grapeseed oil and the sesame oil. When the oil is very hot, lift the pork from the marinade and add to the wok. Stir once or twice until evenly browned and crisp on the edges, then set aside and keep warm.
* Add the remaining oil and heat over a high heat. Add the garlic and ginger, and fry for a few seconds. Add the leek and toss about for a minute or two. Now add the broccoli and chilli and cook over a high heat for another minute, stirring constantly. Then add the spring onions and greens or cabbage and cook for a further minute, tossing constantly. Add the soy sauce mixture and cook for about 3 minutes. Add the coriander and stir through.
* Drain the noodles and place the vegetables and pork on top. Pour any juices from the pan over the meat and serve.

Larder feast

Grown-up Baked Beans – Butter Beans, Anchovies and Rosemary

This is baked beans on toast for adults and just about as easy. Garlic, rosemary and anchovies are a winning combination and here they are added to fat butter beans and served with bruschetta for a crowd-pleaser supper.

The ideal bread for bruschetta is dense in texture and chewy rather than light and airy. This is not essential – an everyday baguette will do the job – but a French country loaf would be better.

½ tbsp olive oil
5 garlic cloves
2 × 50 g cans anchovy fillets in olive oil, approx. 20 fillets
1 large sprig fresh rosemary
handful of fresh flatleaf parsley
juice of 1 lemon
3 × 420 g cans butter beans
1 loaf rustic bread, such as pain de campagne or pugliese
salt and pepper

To serve
steamed broccoli or purple sprouting broccoli drizzled with olive oil

GET AHEAD PREPARATION (optional)

The baked bean mixture can be prepared a day in advance and reheated prior to serving.

20 minutes before you want to eat

* If you don't have a toaster that can cope with 2–3-cm thick slices, turn on the grill so that it is hot when you come to make the bruschetta.
* Heat the oil in a heavy-based pan over a gentle heat. Peel and finely slice or grate the garlic cloves and add to the oil. Cook for a few minutes until the garlic starts to soften – do not allow it to burn.
* Add half the anchovies and a generous splash of their oil to the pan and stir until they start to melt into the oil.
* Strip the rosemary leaves from their stalks, add them to the pan and stir for about 3 minutes. While the rosemary and anchovies are cooking, roughly chop the parsley.
* Drain and rinse the beans, then add to the pan and heat, stirring gently, for a few minutes.
* When the beans have warmed through, stir in the lemon juice, the remaining anchovies and the parsley and season to taste with salt and pepper. Set aside while you make the bruschetta.
* Cut the bread into 2–3-cm thick slices and toast until browned, then rub one side of each slice with the remaining garlic clove.
* Check the butter bean mixture for seasoning and pile on top of the bruschetta.
* Serve immediately with some steamed broccoli drizzled with olive oil.

Two for one

Meatloaf

A good meatloaf is rich, moist and packed with flavour and it is a shame it's gone out of fashion in recent years. This version is quick to make and works well hot or cold. It is particularly compatible with a sharp tomato chutney or pickle.

groundnut or grapeseed oil
150 g bread or 4 slices bread
   (any kind will do)
125 ml milk
1 free-range egg
200 ml cider
4 sprigs fresh thyme
4 sprigs fresh sage
small handful of flatleaf parsley
3 red onions, approx. 360 g
2 garlic cloves
2 tsp mustard powder
1 tbsp Worcestershire sauce

generous pinch of cayenne pepper
generous pinch of ground mace
500 g minced beef
400 g minced pork
salt and pepper

To serve
baked potatoes, green salad and
   a selection of chutneys and
   pickles

GET AHEAD PREPARATION (optional)

The meatloaf mixture can be made up to a day in advance, kept in the fridge and cooked when required. But if you only have a little time:
* Prepare the onions, garlic and herbs.

1¼ hours before you want to eat

* Preheat the oven to 180°C/350°F/Gas Mark 4.
* Thoroughly oil two loaf tins, approx. 500 g capacity – foil ones are good, especially for freezing.
* Break up the bread, put it in a bowl and pour in the milk. Leave to one side so the bread absorbs all the milk.
* Meanwhile, break the egg into a large mixing bowl and whisk it with the cider. Strip the thyme leaves from their stalks and roughly chop the sage and parsley. Peel and finely chop the onions and garlic, and add these to the bowl with the thyme, sage and parsley and, finally, the mustard powder, Worcestershire sauce, cayenne and mace.
* Tip in the meat and the softened bread and mix together very, very well. Season very generously with salt and pepper. You can, if you want, see if it is sufficiently seasoned and spiced by heating a little oil in a small pan and cooking a teaspoonful of the meat mixture. Otherwise season by instinct.
* Pack the meatloaf into the loaf tins, smooth the tops down and cover the tins with a layer of greaseproof paper and then one of foil, twisting the corners to make a tight lid. Put one meatloaf in the freezer.
* Boil the kettle, place the other meatloaf in a roasting tin and pour in boiling water to come halfway up the sides of the tin. Place in the oven and cook for 40 minutes.
* After 40 minutes take the foil and greaseproof paper off the meatloaf, turn the oven up to 200°C/400°F/Gas Mark 6 and cook for 10 minutes so that you have a nice brown, crisp top. Then turn the oven off and let the meatloaf sit for 10–15 minutes before serving it with baked potatoes, a crisp green salad and chutneys and pickles.

Lazy day supper – cooking instructions

Allow the meatloaf to defrost thoroughly, then cook according to the instructions above. Make sure you let it rest for 10–15 minutes before serving as suggested above.

Buying fresh fruit and vegetables

If you want to shop ethically, buying fruit and vegetables can be a minefield. Is it better to support a local fruit and vegetable market selling good quality conventionally farmed produce or buy organic fruit, sold in a plastic box and airfreighted from Italy, at a supermarket?

Is it better to buy from a local grocer or support an organic-box delivery scheme? There are no clear answers but, again, there are some general principles we try to adhere to.

As much as possible we try to buy produce that's in season. It usually tastes better, it is less expensive and it hasn't been shipped round the world.

Good grocers, farmers' markets, and fruit and vegetable markets often sell great quality produce at reasonable prices. Moreover, it isn't overly packaged and hasn't been dragged around the country as part of a supermarket distribution scheme. If we have the time we support these local businesses.

As for organic or non-organic produce, ideally we choose organic though the cost can sometimes be prohibitive and it's not always the best option. Faced with an organic pear from Italy or a standard British pear we'd probably support British agriculture and as a consequence contribute to less transport pollution. If purse strings can stretch to it, buying Fairtrade products, particularly bananas and pineapples, seems like a good idea.

Fixed rules can be limiting, so we encourage you to make decisions about buying based on individual circumstances – but with the proviso that seasonal is likely to be better, packaging is usually unnecessary and closer to home is mostly good news.

February Week 2 – Overview

The end of this week is Valentine's Day, and even if you don't embrace the concept, it can be an excuse to cook a favourite meal for someone you love. This week of recipes includes a few that might be suitable, including a Roast Guinea Fowl or Chicken with Chicory and Bacon, the Artichoke and Pesto Tart or the Thai Beef Casserole. Scallops are supposed to be an aphrodisiac and they feature this week; but be warned – they are twinned with Jerusalem artichokes. These seasonal root vegetables can induce the most terrible wind, so if cooked as a prelude to a night of passion expect explosive results.

Guinea fowl are generally available at supermarkets and have a firm texture and subtle game flavour. They can be substituted with chickens if necessary, but it's worth using guinea fowl if at all possible. In this recipe they are roasted on a bed of chicory and bacon – total preparation and cooking takes about 2 hours. The cooked chicory and bacon mixture is used as the basis for an almost instant pasta recipe later in the week, so the time spent browning and softening the chicory pays dividends in the end.

The Big Meal from Scratch recipe calls for two 1½ kg birds, leaving enough surplus meat to make a pie. If you end up eating into the second bird, whatever meat is lacking for the pie can be made up with extra mushrooms. The pie takes 20 minutes to prepare and 20 to cook – comfort food that's well worth waiting for.

If Jerusalem artichokes prove difficult to find, the bake can be made using potatoes, though the distinctive nutty flavour of the artichokes will be lacking. Altogether this Seasonal Supper takes 40 minutes – about 20 minutes preparation and 20 minutes in the oven.

This week's Larder Feast is a tart with artichokes and pesto that looks impressive and is easy to put together. Most of the cooking time is spent softening onions then the tart is assembled and baked for 15 minutes in the oven. Feel free to add to the toppings if there are spare ingredients available – some ham or goat's cheese would be a good addition.

In the Two for One recipe, Thai Beef Casserole, the meat doesn't have to be browned, so once the spices and curry paste have been roasted the meat is added and the whole lot is cooked for a couple of hours. It's great weekend food – very simple with excellent results.

February Week 2	Recipe	Time
Big meal from scratch	Roast guinea fowl (or chicken) with chicory and bacon, and roast carrots and parsnips	2 hours
Something for nothing 1	Chicory and bacon pasta	15 mins
Something for nothing 2	Guinea fowl (or chicken) pie	40 mins
Seasonal supper	Scallop and Jerusalem artichoke (or fish and potato) bake	40 mins
Larder feast	Artichoke and pesto tart	35 mins
2 for 1	Thai beef casserole with stir-fried pak choi	2–3 hours

All recipes serve 4 apart from the 2 for 1 recipe which makes 8 portions

SHOPPING LIST (for 4 people)

Meat and fish
2 × 1.5 kg guinea fowl or free-range chickens
1.5 kg stewing beef or braising steak
250-300 g rindless free-range smoked
   streaky bacon
8 large scallops off the shell, approx. 200 g,
   or 200 g skinless fillet of white-fleshed fish
   cut into 4-cm chunks
5-6 slices Parma or Serrano ham (optional)

Dairy
90 g butter
30 g Parmesan
250 ml milk
350 ml crème fraîche
150g goats' cheese (optional)

Fruit and vegetables
500 g waxy new potatoes (ideally the size of
   small eggs), such as Charlotte, Nadine or
   Pink Fir Apple
6 medium carrots, approx. 600 g
4 medium parsnips, approx. 600 g
300 g Jerusalem artichokes or new potatoes
2 leeks, approx. 200 g
6-8 mixed heads red and white chicory,
   approx. 600-800 g
200 g pak choi or other oriental greens
400 g - 600 g mixed mushrooms (whatever
   you can get, though field flats and
   chestnuts add a lot of flavour and oyster
   mushrooms add texture)
5 medium red onions, approx. 600 g
8 large or banana shallots, approx. 240 g
3 spring onions
2 garlic cloves
3-4 cm piece of fresh root ginger
1 bunch fresh flatleaf parsley
3 sprigs fresh tarragon
8-9 sprigs fresh thyme
1 sprig fresh sage
3 sprigs fresh basil
2 lemons
1 juicy lime

Basics
75 g dried breadcrumbs or matzo meal
approx. 800 g chilled ready-made puff pastry
60 ml olive oil
120 ml groundnut or grapeseed oil
2 bay leaves
30 g plain flour, plus extra for dusting
400 ml chicken stock (fresh or made from a
   stock cube or bouillon powder)
salt and pepper

Store cupboard
300 g Thai jasmine rice
500 g fusilli pasta
1 × 280-300 g jar artichoke hearts in olive
   oil (the chargrilled ones are good if you
   can get them) or 1 × 390 g can artichoke
   hearts
100 g pitted black olives (ideally but not
   necessarily marinated in oil with herbs)
3 tbsp pesto
4 tbsp passata or 50 g canned chopped
   tomatoes
1 tbsp sherry vinegar
2 × 400 ml cans coconut milk
15 g-25 g dried ceps (porcini) or other dried
   mushrooms (depending on how much you
   like their distinctive, savoury flavour)
3 tbsp Thai fish sauce
2 tsp soy sauce
3 tbsp (approx.) Thai red curry paste
400 ml dry white wine

Serving suggestions
watercress, lemon juice and olive oil
   (Chicory and Bacon Pasta)
frozen peas or spring greens (Guinea fowl/
   chicken) pie)
spinach and crusty bread (Scallop and
   Jerusalem Artichoke/Fish and Potato) Bake)
150-200 g rocket, olive oil and dressing

To download or print out this shopping list,
please visit www.thekitchenrevolution.co.uk/
February/Week2

**Big meal
from scratch**

Roast Guinea Fowl (or Chicken) with Chicory and Bacon, and Roast Carrots and Parsnips

Roast guinea fowl is a good alternative to the more usual roast chicken. It has a slightly stronger flavour and firmer texture than chicken, and is now generally available. Some supermarkets sell free-range guinea fowl and these are the birds to go for as intensively reared ones are disappointing. If in doubt, it's better to buy a good free-range chicken. Guinea fowl aren't large birds, so cooking two will provide leftovers to make Guinea Fowl Pie.

Chicory is a winter salad leaf that has a savoury, slightly bitter taste. It has white leaves that are tinged with green at the edges, and is pale because it's grown in the dark. It can be eaten raw or cooked. In this recipe the chicory is cooked underneath the guinea fowl and so absorbs all the meat juices.

The quantities here allow for extra chicory and guina fowl, for the Chicory and Bacon Pasta, and for the Guinea Fowl Pie.

Roast guinea fowl (or chicken)
8 large or banana shallots, approx. 240 g
6-8 mixed heads red and white chicory, approx. 100 g each; includes 3-4 extra heads for the chicory and bacon pasta
3-4 tbsp groundnut or grapeseed oil
150 g- 200 g rindless free-range smoked streaky bacon rashers; includes 2-3 extra rashers for the chicory and bacon pasta
50 g butter
1 tbsp sherry vinegar
250 ml dry white wine

2 x 1.5 kg guinea fowl or chickens; includes 1 × 1.5 kg bird extra for the guinea fowl pie
1 lemon
3 sprigs fresh tarragon
2 bay leaves
4 sprigs fresh thyme
1 tablespoon (approx.) olive oil
400 ml chicken stock (fresh or made with a stock cube or bouillon powder)
salt and pepper

Roast carrots and parsnips
6 medium carrots, approx. 600 g

4 medium parsnips, approx. 600 g
generous splash of groundnut or grapeseed oil
4-5 sprigs fresh thyme

GET AHEAD PREPARATION (optional)

* Prepare the carrots and parsnips and cover with cold water.
* Peel the shallots.
* Cut the chicory into quarters.
* Brown the bacon, shallots and chicory.

2 hours before you want to eat prepare the chicory and bacon

* Peel the shallots, keeping them whole. Trim any dry, brown areas from the base of the chicory and cut the heads into quarters lengthways.
* Heat 1 tablespoon of the groundnut or grapeseed oil in a heavy-based frying pan over a medium heat. Cut the bacon into 2-3-cm pieces and cook for a couple of minutes. When the bacon has started to colour, remove with a slotted spoon and place in a roasting tin.
* Next, add the shallots to the pan and brown well all over – you may need to add a splash of oil. Shake the pan regularly to get a nice even colour. This will take a few minutes. When the shallots are golden brown, remove them with a slotted spoon and add to the bacon.
* Now add about 20 g of the butter and a splash of oil to the pan, heat until it foams and then add the chicory. Cook it in a single layer – you may need to do two batches. Each batch will take about 3-4 minutes. Turn the pieces of chicory once or twice, and when they are browned add them to the bacon and shallots.
* Add the rest of the butter to the pan and when it has melted splash in the vinegar. Let the vinegar reduce to almost nothing, then add the wine. Bring the wine to the boil and give it a good stir to scrape any flavours from the bottom of the pan, then pour this liquor onto the chicory and bacon mixture.
* Now prepare the guinea fowl. Halve the lemon, strip the tarragon leaves from their stalks and set aside. Season the guinea fowl or chickens inside and out with salt and pepper, and place a lemon half, 1 bay leaf, 2 thyme sprigs and half the tarragon stalks inside each cavity. Rub each bird with a glug of oil (about ½ tablespoon) and place on top of the chicory and bacon mixture.
* Next, get the carrots and parsnips ready. Peel the carrots and cut them into 2-3-cm chunks. Peel the parsnips and cut them into quarters lengthways, removing the thick core if there is one.

1¼ hours before you want to eat roast the vegetables and the birds

* Preheat the oven to 220°C/425°/Gas Mark 7 or its nearest setting.
* Splash the groundnut or grapeseed oil into another roasting tin and put in the oven to heat.
* When the oil has been in the oven for about 10 minutes, add the carrots. Add some seasoning, give the carrots a good shake and put the tin near the bottom of the oven.
* Put the birds in the top of the oven for 20 minutes.
* After 20 minutes, turn the oven down to 180°C/350°F/Gas Mark 4. Add the parsnips to the carrots, season again, add the thyme leaves and mix well. Return the tin to the lower part of the oven and leave to cook for another 40 minutes, by which time the carrots and parsnips should be soft and golden.
* Next, add the stock to the tin containing the guinea fowl or chickens and leave the birds to cook at the top of the oven for another 40–50 minutes (depending on the size of your bird). Check on them every so often and baste with the juices in the tin; give the carrots and parsnips a stir at the same time.

10 minutes before you want to eat thicken the sauce

* After 50 minutes at 180°C/350°F/Gas Mark 4, test the birds with a skewer. If the juices run clear in the thickest part of the thigh they are ready. If this isn't the case, return them to the oven for another 15 minutes. When they are cooked, turn the oven off – you can leave the carrots and parsnips in it to keep warm. Put some plates and serving dishes in the oven to warm.
* Lift the birds from their chicory bed and leave them to rest on a carving board in a warm place.
* Put the roasting tin with the chicory and all the delicious juices on to a high heat. Let the liquid reduce by a third, checking on it how it tastes from time to time.
* Roughly chop the tarragon leaves and sprinkle them over the chicory mixture. Put half the chicory mixture to one side for use later in the week.
* Carve the birds and serve slices on top of the chicory with some of the delicious juices over the top. Place the carrots and parsnips in a warmed serving bowl and pass around separately.

Afterwards

Place the extra chicory and bacon mixture (ideally 300-400 g), and remaining meat (ideally 400-600 g) from the guinea fowl or chickens, in separate containers, cover and refrigerate for use later in the week. If possible, use the bird carcasses to make a stock (see page 495).

Something for nothing 1

Chicory and Bacon Pasta

This recipes uses the chicory and bacon mixture remaining from the Big Meal from Scratch to make a creamy, lemony pasta that can be on the table and ready to go in about 15 minutes. If you haven't got any leftovers, it's easy to make up a fresh batch of the chicory and bacon mixture – just cook up three or four rashers of bacon, two large shallots and three or four chicory heads, following the method in the previous recipe. But rather than baking this mixture in the oven, add the vinegar, wine and stock and cook on the hob until the chicory is cooked through.

1 garlic clove
30 g Parmesan
½ lemon
1 sprig fresh sage
500 g fusilli pasta
1 tbsp olive oil
300-400 g chicory and bacon
  mixture left over from the Big
  Meal from Scratch or see above
100 ml crème fraîche
salt and pepper

To serve
watercress dressed with lemon
  juice and olive oil

15 minutes before you want to eat

* Peel and finely chop the garlic and grate the Parmesan. Grate the zest from the half lemon and squeeze out all the juice, then strip the sage leaves from their stalks and chop finely.
* Put the fusilli in boiling water and cook for 8–10 minutes or according to the packet instructions.
* Heat the oil in a large, heavy-based frying pan or saucepan over a low heat and cook the garlic for a few minutes, moving it constantly to avoid browning.
* Add the chicory and bacon mixture to the pan, stir well, add the lemon zest and juice to taste and cook for a few minutes to let the chicory heat through.
* Stir in the crème fraîche, bring to the boil and season to taste with salt and pepper. Simmer for a couple of minutes so that the sauce develops a good coating consistency then add the sage leaves.
* Strain the fusilli well and toss with the chicory mixture. Sprinkle with the grated Parmesan and serve.

Something
for nothing 2

Guinea Fowl (or Chicken) Pie

A hot, savoury pie makes for a warming winter supper and this one has the benefit of being quick to make. We have been rather vague with quantities for the guinea fowl or chicken and the leeks – this is because the ingredients can happily shrink or expand depending on what you have to hand. Add extra leeks, mushrooms or meat as suits. If you have no left over chicken poach two large breasts until cooked.

15-25 g dried ceps (porcini) or other dried mushrooms (depending on how much you like their distinctive, savoury flavour)
400 g chilled, ready-made puff pastry
plain flour, for dusting
2 leeks, approx. 200 g
30 g butter
1 tbsp groundnut or grapeseed oil
400-600 g mixed fresh mushrooms (whatever you can get, though field flats and chestnuts add a lot of flavour and oyster mushrooms add texture)

30 g plain flour
150 ml white wine
250 ml milk, plus extra for brushing
small handful of fresh flatleaf parsley
100 ml crème fraîche
400-600 g cooked guinea fowl or chicken meat left over from the Big Meal from Scratch, shredded or see above
salt and pepper

To serve
cooked peas or steamed spring greens

GET AHEAD PREPARATION (optional)

The pie filling can be made up to 2 days in advance. The pie can be assembled up to the point of baking a day in advance. If you have only a little time:
* Roll out the pastry and rest in the fridge.
* Soak the ceps.
* Prepare the leeks, mushrooms and parsley.

40 minutes before you want to eat

* Preheat the oven to 200°C/400°F/Gas Mark 6.
* Place the ceps in a bowl and cover with boiling water. If using unrolled pastry, roll it out on a board so that it's about 1 cm larger than the circumference of a 1.2–1.5-litre pie dish. Cover with cling film and place in the fridge.
* Slice the leeks and wash well. Heat the butter and oil in a heavy-based pan over a medium heat and cook the leeks gently for about 5 minutes.
* Meanwhile clean the fresh mushrooms and slice them into bite-sized pieces.
* When the leeks are soft, turn the heat up, add the mushrooms and fry them until they soften.
* Lift the ceps from their soaking liquid, leaving any grit or mud behind (reserve the soaking liquid). Add the ceps to the mushrooms in the pan, turn the heat down and allow them a couple of minutes of cooking.
* Add the flour to the pan and stir over a medium heat for a few minutes, then add the wine and milk, stirring constantly to remove any lumps. Sieve the cep soaking liquid into the pan and bring everything to the boil, stirring constantly. Simmer over a gentle heat until the juices thicken into a sauce, stirring occasionally.
* Roughly chop the parsley and add it to the sauce with the crème fraîche. Add the meat and season to taste.
* Put an egg cup or pie raiser in the middle of a pie dish and pile the filling around it.
* Wet the rim of the dish with water then place the pastry on top of the pie dish and press it down well around the edges. Trim any excess pastry, brush with a little milk and make a cross in the middle.
* Cook the pie in the oven for 15–20 minutes, until the pastry is golden.
* Serve with peas or well-seasoned, buttered greens.

Seasonal supper

Scallop and Jerusalem Artichoke (or Fish and Potato) Bake

This recipe is certainly suitable for a family supper, and is a good way of encouraging kids to eat fish, but it will also work well for casual entertaining. The method is not complicated – once assembled the whole dish is baked in a hot oven. This is very good served with spinach and crusty bread. If either scallops or Jerusalem artichokes are not available they can be replaced with firm white fish or potatoes respectively.

30 g butter
500 g waxy new potatoes (ideally the size of small eggs), such as Charlotte, Nadine or Pink Fir Apple
300 g Jerusalem artichokes
4–6 rashers rindless free-range smoked, streaky bacon, approx. 100–150 g
8 large scallops off the shell, approx. 200 g, or 200 g skinless, fillet of white-fleshed fish cut into 4-cm chunks

½ lemon
handful of fresh flatleaf parsley
150 ml crème fraîche
75 g dried breadcrumbs or matzo meal
salt and pepper

To serve
pan-fried spinach and crusty bread

GET AHEAD PREPARATION (optional)

* Wash and slice the potatoes and cover them with water until required.
* Peel and slice the artichokes and cover them with water and a little lemon juice until required.
* Grate the lemon zest.
* Roughly chop the parsley.

40 minutes before you want to eat

* Preheat the oven to 200°C/400°F/Gas Mark 6 and grease the inside of an ovenproof dish large enough to hold all the ingredients.
* Wash the potatoes if necessary. Cut them into slices the thickness of a pound coin, and place in a large pan of salted water. Bring to the boil over a high heat, then simmer on a medium heat while you prepare the artichokes.
* While the potatoes are cooking, peel the artichokes. These can be a real fiddle so don't worry too much about getting into every crevice. If there is a particularly small protuberance, lop it off rather than spend ages trying to peel it. Cut the artichokes into similar-size pieces to the potatoes.
* When the potatoes have been simmering for about 5 minutes, add the artichokes. Bring the water back to the boil, then turn down the heat and simmer for another 5 minutes or until both the potatoes and artichokes are just cooked.
* While the artichokes and potatoes are simmering, cook the bacon. Melt half the remaining butter in a frying pan over a medium heat and, using scissors, cut bite-sized lengths of the bacon into the butter. Fry for a few minutes until starting to crisp, then set aside. In the meantime, trim the scallops of any membrane or anything that looks undesirable – they sometimes have a greyish muscle – pat them dry and set them aside. Melt the remaining butter in the pan over a high heat and when foaming sear the scallops for 1 minute on each side until just starting to brown. If using fish skip this stage.
* Once the potatoes and artichokes are cooked, drain well. Grate the zest from the half lemon and roughly chop the parsley. Put the sliced potatoes and artichokes in a bowl with the zest and parsley. Add the crème fraîche and bacon, season well with salt and pepper and gently fold together, trying not to break up the potatoes and artichokes.
* Next, build your bake. Put half the artichoke and potato mixture on the bottom of the ovenproof dish and distribute the scallops (or pieces of fish) evenly on top. Season generously with salt and pepper then add the remaining potato and artichoke mixture. Sprinkle the breadcrumbs or matzo meal over the top.
* Place in the oven and bake for 25 minutes until piping hot and browned on top.
* Serve with pan-fried spinach and crusty bread.

Larder feast

Artichoke and Pesto Tart

Ready-made puff pastry is a quick base for a tart and has an infinite number of possible toppings. Here we suggest spreading pesto on the base then smothering it with sweet red onions and artichoke hearts. For added luxury, add slices of Parma ham or goats' cheese.

5 medium red onions, approx. 600 g
3 tbsp olive oil
1 × 280-300 g jar artichoke hearts in olive oil (chargrilled ones are good if you can get them) or 1 × 390 g can artichoke hearts in olive oil
400 g (approx.) chilled ready-made puff pastry
plain flour, for dusting
100 g pitted black olives (ideally but not necessarily marinated

in oil with herbs)
3 tbsp pesto
150-200 g rocket, dressed with olive oil and lemon juice (optional)
4-6 slices Parma or Serrano ham or 150 g goats' cheese (optional)
salt and pepper

To serve
rocket

<u>GET AHEAD PREPARATION (optional)</u>

The onions can be cooked a few days in advance. If you have only a little time:
* Prepare and soften the onions.
* Roll out the pastry and rest in the fridge.
* Prepare the olives and artichokes.

40 minutes before you want to eat

* If using frozen pastry, remove from the freezer to defrost.
* Preheat the oven to 220°C/425°F/Gas Mark 7 and preheat a baking tray (approx. 35 x 25 cm).
* Peel the onions and slice them as finely as possible. Heat the oil in a heavy-based pan over a medium heat and add the onions. Stir them well, put a lid on the pan and cook slowly until they are soft and starting to brown. This will take about 20 minutes. Stir from time to time and remove the lid for the last 5-7 minutes so any excess liquid evaporates.
* Drain the artichoke hearts and reserve the marinating oil. Slice each heart into bite-sized pieces and cut the olives in half.
* Roll out the pastry on a lightly floured work surface to a rectangle that is just under 1 cm thick. It needs to be approximately 35 x 25 cm. With a knife, draw a border evenly round the rectangle about 2 cm from the edge and without cutting through the pastry. Make sure the piece of pastry moves easily, as it has to be lifted on to the hot baking sheet.
* When the onions are ready, season to taste and tip them into a sieve – too much liquid will make the pastry soggy. Spread the pesto evenly over the pastry square inside the frame.
* Take the hot baking sheet from the oven and lift the pastry on to it. Spread the onions out evenly over the pastry, inside the frame. Scatter the artichokes, olives, Parma ham and goat's cheese (if using) over the top, sprinkle with some of the marinating oil from the artichokes and season well.
* Place the tart at the top of the oven and cook for 10–15 minutes or until the pastry is brown and crisp and the border has risen a little.
* Remove the tart from the oven. Then cut into even slices and serve with dressed rocket.

Two for one

Thai Beef Casserole with Stir-fried Pak Choi

This is the very essence of comfort food: it's easy to make and packed with flavour. Just what's needed to counteract Sunday night blues after a big weekend, or ideal for pulling out from the freezer when it's cold and you really cannot face cooking. If you can arrange life so that this is made a day before it is eaten all the better – the flavours will intensify and develop over time. The batch you put in the freezer will be just as good, if not better, than the one you eat immediately.

Thai curry paste is ubiquitous in almost all supermarkets – certainly worth having in the larder if the thought of grinding lemon grass, ginger, galangal, garlic and chilli into a paste just seems too exhausting for words. Before buying, it's worth checking the ingredients lists carefully – some brands contain all sorts of weird and unnecessary chemicals but there are two or three that include nothing but recognisable foodstuffs.

When buying meat to braise or stew it's worth sticking to just one cut and even dicing it yourself. Packets of unidentified stewing or braising steak can often be a mixture and can cook unevenly. Cuts that will work well in this dish are chuck or blade steak, skirt or thick flank. If you are confined to shopping from a supermarket go for a cut of meat that has a good marbling of fat.

Thai beef casserole
1 juicy lime
3–4 cm piece of fresh root ginger
1.5 kg stewing beef (see above), cut into small, even-sized chunks
1–2 tbsp groundnut or grapeseed oil
3 tbsp Thai red curry paste (add less or more, depending on taste)
4 tbsp passata or 50 g canned chopped tomatoes

2 × 400 ml cans coconut milk
3 tbsp Thai fish sauce
3 spring onions
3 sprigs fresh basil
300 g Thai jasmine rice
salt and pepper

Stir-fried pak choi
200 g pak choi or other oriental greens
1 garlic clove
2 tsp soy sauce
1 tbsp groundnut or grapeseed oil

GET AHEAD PREPARATION (optional)

The entire meal can be made a day in advance. If you have only a little time:
* Zest the lime.
* Prepare the ginger and spring onions.

2–3 hours before you want to eat cook the casserole

* Before starting to cook, zest the lime and peel and grate the ginger. Season the meat with salt and pepper.
* Heat the oil in a large flameproof casserole dish over a medium heat. When the oil is hot fry the curry paste, ginger and lime zest for approximately 1 minute, stirring constantly to prevent any burning. Add the passata or tomatoes and allow to simmer down for
2 minutes, again stirring constantly.
* Add the beef, coconut milk and fish sauce and stir well to ensure all the ingredients are well covered and mixed together. Cover and simmer very gently on the lowest heat for at least 1½ hours and up to 2 hours, until the meat is very tender.
* While the beef is cooking slowly, you can get everything else ready for the meal. First of all, trim the spring onions and chop them, using as much of the green part as you can. Next, strip the basil leaves from their stalks; they will go into the curry at the end.
* Prepare the pak choi or other oriental greens for stir-frying. Trim any tired leaves and cut each head into quarters or sixths lengthwise, depending on size. Peel and crush the garlic. Mix the soy sauce with 2 tablespoons water and the juice of half the lime.

25 minutes before you want to eat cook the rice

* When the meat is tender, take the casserole dish off the heat, throw in the spring onions and tear in the basil leaves. Set half aside to freeze and allow the remaining half to stand with a lid on.
* Fill a pan with the water and when it is at a rolling boil stir in the jasmine rice and a generous pinch of salt. Let it come back to the boil and cook for 10 minutes or according to the instructions on the packet.

5 minutes before you want to eat cook the pak choi

* While the rice is cooking, heat the oil in a wok or large frying pan over a medium heat and add the garlic. Stir for a minute, without letting the garlic colour as this will make it taste bitter. Then add the greens and gently stir-fry for 2–3 minutes until they start to wilt.
* Turn up the heat, add the soy sauce mixture and carry on stir-frying for 1–2 minutes while the liquid evaporates. Give the beeef a good stir before serving it on a pile of rice with greens on the side.

Lazy day supper – reheating instructions

Defrost the casserole entirely before reheating, then tip it into large pan and gently warm over a medium heat until it is simmering. When it is piping hot, cook the rice and greens as above. You can add some fresh basil leaves and some chopped spring onions to the casserole if you wish.

February Week 3 – Overview

The powerful flavours of this week's Big Meal from Scratch, Roast Lamb with Anchovies, Rosemary Potatoes and Winter Greens, promise to ward off the season's colds and chills. In all, the recipe takes nearly 3 hours, though not all of this involves physical labour, so make sure there is plenty of time available before starting.

Extra anchovy and garlic butter made for the big meal is used later in the week to make Spaghetti with Chilli and Purple Sprouting Broccoli that takes just 15 minutes. Surplus lamb is turned into a South African version of shepherd's pie called Bobotie. This takes 20 minutes to prepare but 30 minutes to cook, so factor that in when planning the week.

Jerusalem artichokes feature again in a Seasonal Supper, but this time they are partnered with Chicken or Pheasant Wrapped in Bacon. If you can't find Jerusalem artichokes, replace them with celeriac – another root vegetable that goes well with game and bacon. The Larder Feast of Polenta with Blue Cheese and Spinach should be made with quick-to-cook polenta, but if you are very pushed for time, ready-made slices of polenta can be used.

The two layered crab and celeriac bakes – one for the freezer and one to eat immediately – take about 10 minutes to assemble then 40 minutes to cook. Fresh crab can be tricky to find (and it does need to be seriously fresh), so replace this with smoked salmon if necessary.

February Week 3	Recipe	Time
Big meal from scratch	Roast Lamb with anchovies, rosemary potatoes and winter greens	2¾ hours
Something for nothing 1	Purple sprouting broccoli with chilli and anchovy sauce and pasta	15 mins
Something for nothing 2	Bobotie – South African shepherd's pie	50 mins
Seasonal supper	Chicken (or pheasant) wrapped in bacon with Jerusalem artichokes	35 mins
Larder feast	Polenta with gorgonzola and garlic spinach	30 mins
2 for 1	Layered crab (or smoked salmon) and celeriac	50 mins

All recipes serve 4 apart from the 2 for 1 recipe which makes 8 portions

SHOPPING LIST (for 4 people)

Meat and fish

1 × 2 kg leg of English lamb or hogget

4 small free-range chicken (or large pheasant) breasts, approx. 150 g each, with wing bones if possible

400 g rindlss free-range smoked streaky bacon rashers

500 g fresh crab meat (a mixture of brown and white) or 300 g smoked salmon (hot-smoked if possible)

Dairy

225 g butter

2 free-range eggs

150-180 g Gorgonzola or other blue cheese such as Roquefort

500 ml soured cream

600-800 ml milk

Fruit and vegetables

900 g new potatoes

3 baking potatoes, approx. 900 g

2 carrots, approx. 200 g

600 g Jerusalem artichokes or 1 × 750 g celeriac, plus 1 sprig fresh thyme

2 celeriac, approx. 750 g each

500 g winter greens or sprout tops

600 g purple sprouting broccoli

2 medium red onions, approx. 240 g

2 large onions, approx. 350 g

8 spring onions

10 garlic cloves

2 generous sprigs fresh rosemary

1 bunch flatleaf parsley

a few sprigs fresh dill

4 lemons

650 g frozen spinach

Basics

200 g bread, 4-6 slices

120 ml olive oil

75 ml groundnut or grapeseed oil

salt and pepper

Store cupboard

300 g polenta or 500 g ready-cooked polenta

400 g spaghetti

80-100 g anchovy fillets in olive oil

¼-½ tsp crushed dried chillies

2-3 tsp garam masala

pinch of ground cinnamon

pinch of nutmeg (ground or freshly grated)

450 ml white wine

Serving suggestions

Parmesan (Purple Sprouting Broccoli with Chilli and Anchovy Sauce and Pasta)

purple sprouting broccoli or another green vegetable (Layered Crab or Smoked Salmon and Celeriac)

frozen peas (Chicken or Pheasant Wrapped in Bacon with Jerusalem Artichokes)

To download or print out this shopping list, please visit www.thekitchenrevolution.co.uk/February/Week3

**Big meal
from scratch**

Roast Lamb with Anchovies, Rosemary Potatoes and Winter Greens

It may seem perverse, but stuffing anchovies into the flesh of lamb adds a subtle salty note that complements the sweetness of the meat. At this time of year lamb is fully flavoured and can easily accommodate the intensity of the anchovies. This recipe would also work beautifully with hogget, an 18-month-old lamb with darker and more strongly flavoured meat. Hogget is not widely available, but a good butcher can supply it.

The anchovy and garlic butter will keep well in the fridge for a couple of weeks and is very useful for tossing with pasta or vegetables for a simple and delicious supper, or to serve with grilled steak or a piece of fish. We suggest using the leftover butter and any remaining greens for Purple Sprouting Broccoli with Chilli and Anchovy Sauce and Pasta. The leftover lamb is transformed into Bobotie – South African Shepherd's Pie.

Roast lamb with anchovies
150 g butter; includes 75 g extra
    for the purple sprouting
    broccoli with chilli and
    anchovy sauce and pasta
6 garlic cloves
80-100 g anchovy fillets in olive
    oil
1 × 2 kg leg of English lamb or
    hogget; includes 600 g for the
    bobotie
squeeze of lemon juice
250 ml white wine
salt and pepper

Rosemary potatoes
2 medium red onions, approx.
    240 g
900 g new potatoes
2 generous sprigs fresh rosemary
3 tbsp olive oil

Winter greens
500 g winter greens or sprout
    tops
small nut of butter
pinch of nutmeg (ground or
    freshly grated)

GET AHEAD PREPARATION (optional)

* The anchovy butter can be
    made in 2 days in advance and
    the lamb prepared a few hours
    in advance up to the point of
    going in the oven. If you only
    have a little time:
* Peel the garlic.
* Scrub the potatoes.
* Wash and trim the greens.

2¼ hours before you want to eat prepare the leeks

* Preheat the oven to 220°C/425°F/Gas Mark 7.
* Place the butter somewhere warm or in the microwave for a few seconds to soften.
* Peel the garlic, slice three cloves into thickish pieces and crush the other three. Cut about nine anchovies in half and mash the rest to a paste in a bowl using a fork. Mix with the crushed garlic and put to one side.
* Place the lamb on a rack in a roasting tin. Make several deep incisions into the thick side of the leg. When making an incision twist the knife from side to side so that there is a pocket large enough to stuff a slice of garlic and half an anchovy into each hole. A cocktail stick is useful for pushing them in.
* Mix the garlic and anchovy paste with the butter – this can be done in a food processor if preferred. Season with a little pepper. Rub half the butter over the lamb, squeeze over a little lemon juice and grind over a little more pepper. The rest of the anchovy butter will be used later in the week.
* When the oven is hot, place the lamb as near to the top as possible and allow it to cook for 30 minutes at a high temperature.

1¾ hours before you want to eat prepare the potatoes

* Peel the onions and cut in half lengthways, then cut each half into four lengthways so that you have a total of 16 wedge-shaped pieces.
* Scrub the potatoes, pat dry and tip into a large roasting tin. Strip the rosemary leaves from their stalks. Add the onions, rosemary leaves, oil and salt and pepper to the potatoes and toss well.

1½ hours before you want to eat

* Once the lamb has been in the oven for 30 minutes, reduce the temperature to 160°C/325°F/Gas Mark 3 and add the wine to the roasting tin. Cook the lamb for another 50 minutes, basting once halfway through with the pan juices. If you like lamb more well done, cook it for the 40 minutes per 1 kg as opposed to our suggestion of 25 minutes per 1 kg.

1¼ hours before you want to eat	❊ Place the potatoes in the oven. Give them a shake every time you baste the lamb. ❊ Wash the greens and remove any tough stalks.
30 minutes before you want to eat cook the greens and the gravy	❊ After 1 hour at the lower temperature the lamb should be pink in the middle and ready to eat. Place on a carving board and leave to rest for about 20 minutes. ❊ Turn the oven up to 220°C/425°F/Gas Mark 7 and move the potatoes to a higher shelf for the next 15 minutes or so they have a chance to turn crisp and golden. ❊ Fill a large pan with a lid with about 3–5 cm salted water and bring to the boil. Add the greens, cover with the lid and cook for about 5 minutes. ❊ Now make the gravy. Put the roasting tin over a low to medium heat – you may have to use two rings. Let the juices come to the boil and whisk vigorously to bring all the flavours together; add water from the greens to thin out the gravy if you prefer. ❊ Drain the greens well and toss with a little butter and a good pinch of nutmeg. ❊ Carve the lamb and serve with the potatoes, greens and gravy.
Afterwards	❊ Keep any leftover greens as they can be added to the pasta and broccoli dish later in the week. Carve the remaining meat from the bone and either chop it roughly or pulse it a couple of time in a food processor. Place the lamb and the remaining anchovy butter in containers, cover and refrigerate for use later in the week. ❊ Ideally there will be 75 g anchovy butter and 450 g lamb left over.

Purple Sprouting Broccoli with Chilli and Anchovy Sauce and Pasta

This is based on a classic Italian dish and is quick to make. Purple sprouting broccoli is such a seasonal treat that it's good to find different ways to use it. Supermarkets tend to sell it ready trimmed, but if buying from a greengrocer or farmers' market any thick, woody stems have to be removed so all that remains is the small stems, delicate leaves and tender florets. You can serve this with Parmesan, depending on your taste for salty, rich food. If there is no remaining anchovy butter replace it with or 4–8 anchovies mashed with 2 crushed garlic cloves and mixed with a little pepper and 65 g butter.

600 g purple sprouting broccoli (perhaps a little less if you are using greens left over from the Big Meal from Scratch)
400 g spaghetti
small handful of fresh flatleaf parsley
1 tbsp olive oil

¼–½ tsp crushed dried chillies (depending on how spicy you like your food)
75 g (approx.) anchovy and garlic butter left over from the Big Meal from Scratch or see above
juice of ½ lemon
salt and pepper

To serve
grated Parmesan (optional)

GET AHEAD PREPARATION (optional)

* Prepare and cook the broccoli.
* Roughly chop the parsley.

* Bring two large pans of well-salted water to the boil.
* Cut the broccoli into bite-sized florets, chopping off any woody stalks or dried ends. Steam the broccoli or drop it into one of the pans of boiling water for about 3 minutes – until tender but not soft.
* Add the pasta to the second pan and cook for about 10 minutes or according to the manufacturer's instructions.
* Meanwhile roughly chop the parsley and put to one side.
* Heat the oil in a heavy-based pan over a medium heat. Add the chillies and stir, taking care they don't burn, for a couple of minutes.
* Drain the broccoli (and leftover greens from the roast lamb on pae 84 if you have any) and add to the chillies with the anchovy butter. Toss until the butter has melted and coated the broccoli, then add generous amounts of pepper.
* Add the lemon juice and shake the pan vigorously to encourage the butter and other pan juices to come together into a sauce. Cook for a couple of minutes.
* Drain the pasta and toss with the broccoli mixture. Add the parsley and taste for salt, pepper and lemon juice.
* Serve in warmed big bowls with grated Parmesan, if desired.

Something
for nothing 2

Bobotie – South African Shepherd's Pie

In South Africa, Bobotie has been popular for centuries and the term covers a range of baked curry dishes, usually topped with an egg and milk sauce. The recipe below is an original way of transforming leftover lamb. It does take a while to cook in the oven, but once assembled you will be freed from the kitchen. If you don't have any leftover lamb, use fresh minced lamb and brown it in a pan with some seasoning.

The recipe was given to Rosie by her great friend Sonja Edridge. She suggests you serve it with rice cooked with turmeric (with optional sultanas and raisins), bowls of chutney, sliced banana and coconut.

450 g (approx.) cooked lamb left
   over from the Big Meal from
   Scratch or 600 g minced lamb,
   seasoned and browned
2 large onions, approx. 350 g
1 tbsp groundnut or grapeseed oil
200 g stale bread, 4–6 slices
300 ml milk
3 garlic cloves
2 carrots, approx. 200 g

2–3 tsp garam masala
pinch of ground cinnamon
2 free-range eggs
8 rashers rindless free-range
   smoked streaky bacon (approx.
   200 g)
salt and pepper

GET AHEAD PREPARATION (optional)

The entire dish can be prepared a day in advance prior to going into the oven. If you only have a little time:
* Chop the lamb.
* Prepare the onions, garlic and
   carrots.

50 minutes before you want to eat

* Preheat the oven to 200°C/400°F/Gas Mark 6.
* Start by preparing the leftover lamb. Either roughly chop it into small chunks using a sharp knife or put in a food processor and chop. If using a processor, pulse two or three times and make sure the meat doesn't become completely pulverised.
* Next, peel and finely slice the onions, and heat the oil in a casserole over a medium heat. When the oil is hot, add the onions and let them cook for 5 minutes to soften.
* While the onion is softening, soak the bread in the milk, peel and crush the garlic, and peel and coarsley grate the carrots.
* When the onions are soft, add the garlic to the casserole dish, stir about for a couple of minutes then add the garam masala and cinnamon and let these cook for 1–2 minutes.
* When the spices have toasted, add the lamb and grated carrot. Turn the heat up and stir continuously for 3 minutes then remove from the heat.
* Next, beat one of the eggs in a small bowl, squeeze the bread to get rid of excess milk, reserving the milk, and stir the bread into the egg. Thoroughly mix the egg and bread into the lamb and season to taste with salt and pepper. Lay the rashers of bacon over the lamb then whisk the remaining egg into the reserved milk, and pour this over the bacon.
* Cook the bobotie in the oven for 30 minutes.

Seasonal supper

Chicken (or Pheasant) Wrapped in Bacon with Jerusalem Artichokes

Jerusalem artichokes are in season throughout the winter and add a distinctive element to any dish. Here we suggest serving them cooked in white wine to accompany chicken or pheasant breasts wrapped in bacon.

Jerusalem artichokes taste bitter until cooked when they become sweet and characteristically nutty. They are often covered in small bumps and knobbles, so when peeling them just cut away all the pieces that are impossible to deal with – this will save time and aggro. They discolour quickly, so if preparing them in advance drop them straight into cold water sharpened with lemon juice or vinegar. Jerusalem artichokes contain a substance called inulin, which can lead to excessive wind – so moderation is advisable.

If you are not able to find Jerusalem artichokes they can be replaced with a 750 g celeriac – peeled, cut into 2-cm cubes and cooked as below except with thyme instead of parsley. The resulting taste will be significantly different but just as good.

Chicken (or pheasant) wrapped in bacon
4 small free-range chicken (or large pheasant) breasts (approx. 150 g each), with wing bones if possible
8 rashers (approx. 200 g) rindless free-range smoked streaky bacon
groundnut or grapeseed oil, for oiling
salt and pepper

Jerusalem artichokes
600 g Jerusalem artichokes
splash of groundnut or grapeseed oil
60 g butter
200 ml white wine
small handful of fresh flatleaf parsley

To serve
cooked peas

GET AHEAD PREPARATION (optional)
* Peel the artichokes and put in water with a few squeezes of lemon juice until required.
* Chop the parsley.

35 minutes before you want to eat

* Preheat the oven to 200°C/400°F/Gas Mark 6.
* While the oven is heating, prepare the meat. Season the chicken or pheasant breasts thoroughly all over with salt and pepper and wrap each breast in two rashers of bacon so that all the meat is covered and, if there is a bone, it is sticking out. If the bacon is very thick it might be hard to wrap, so use the back of a knife to stretch it out a bit.
* Oil a baking sheet, then place the breasts on it, skin side up, and cook in the oven for 15–25 minutes, depending on their size. They will be ready when the bacon is crisp and the breast underneath firm.
* While the chicken is cooking, prepare the artichokes. Peel them, using a small knife to slice off all the knobbles and a peeler to remove the skin. Cut into circles the thickness of a pound coin.
* Place a frying pan on a high heat with a splash of oil and half the butter and add the artichokes. Cook for about 5 minutes, moving them about, until they get a little bit brown. Now splash in half the wine and keep stirring them for a further 5 minutes, still on a high heat, by which time the wine should have evaporated. Then add the rest of the wine, 200 ml water and the rest of the butter. Carry on cooking the artichokes on a high heat until all the liquid evaporates, by which time they should be just soft and golden. They will happily sit like this, with a splash of more water and covered with a lid, over a low heat until you are ready to serve.
* Now chop the parsley, and stir it into the artichokes just before serving.
* When the chicken or pheasant breasts are cooked, take them out of the oven and serve on a pile of artichokes. Perfect accompanied with peas.

Larder feast

Polenta with Gorgonzola and Garlic Spinach

Polenta is a staple food in north Italy and its subtle taste and ability to soak up a tasty sauce make it a versatile kitchen ingredient. It can be served either soft and almost runny, or in firm slices that have been grilled or baked. This recipe uses quick-cook polenta which is added to boiling water then left to set. Once set the polenta is cut into wedges, grilled and served with garlic spinach. If the only polenta available is ready-cooked, this can be layered and baked in the oven with cheese crumbled in between the layers.

1.2 litres hot or boiling water
300 g polenta or 500 g ready-
    cooked polenta
4 tbsp olive oil
150–180 g Gorgonzola
650 g frozen spinach
1 garlic clove
1 lemon
salt and pepper

GET AHEAD PREPARATION (optional)

* The polenta can be prepared to the point of grilling up to 2 days in advance. If you only have a little time:
* Defrost the spinach.
* Prepare the garlic.
* Zest and juice the lemon.

30 minutes before you want to eat

* If using quick to cook polenta put 1 litre of the hot or boiling water into a large pan and add 1 teaspoon salt. Let the water come back to the boil, pour the polenta into it in a slow stream and whisk well as the mixture thickens. When it gets too thick to whisk, turn the heat down and use a wooden spoon to stir as it carries on thickening. Add another 200 ml hot or boiling water and stir until the polenta is thick and starts coming away from the sides of the pan.
* Once the polenta has thickened, stir in 1 tablespoon of the oil, crumble in two-thirds of the cheese and stir well.
* Oil a wide shallow roasting tin or dish and pour in the polenta. Smooth out the top, set aside and allow to cool and firm for 15 minutes. Meanwhile preheat the grill to its highest setting.
* If you are using ready-cooked polenta, preheat the oven to 200°C/400°F/Gas Mark 6. Cut the polenta into 2.5-cm thick slices. Oil an ovenproof dish and put half the slices on the base of the dish, crumble over two-thirds of the cheese and cover with the rest of the polenta. Crumble the rest of the cheese and sprinkle it over. Put the dish in the oven and bake for 20 minutes until the polenta is crisp on top and the cheese has melted.
* While the polenta is setting or baking, prepare the spinach. Defrost the spinach according to the instructions on the packet, and peel and crush the garlic. Grate the zest from half the lemon and squeeze out all the juice.
* Heat 1 tablespoon of the remaining oil in a heavy-based pan and add the spinach, then the garlic and cook for a couple of minutes. Add the lemon zest and juice and seasoning to the spinach and toss for a couple of minutes. Cover and leave to keep warm.
* When the quick-to-cook polenta is cool and feels firm to the touch, cut into wedges, remove from the roasting tin or dish and brush with a little oil. Place the wedges of polenta on a grill rack and grill to heat through and brown without burning. Crumble the remaining cheese. Turn the polenta over when one side is brown and sprinkle the second side with the cheese.
* Serve the polenta with the spinach.

Two for one

Layered Crab (or Smoked Salmon) and Celeriac

This recipe makes a layered bake with potato and celeriac, crab or smoked salmon, dill and spring onions, soured cream and plenty of lemon.

Celeriac is at its best through the winter months. It is, at first sight, a rather unwieldy looking vegetable, yet its bumpy skin and hairy roots hide a soft, velvety flesh that has the creaminess of potato and the added flavour of celery. To prepare celeriac remove the roots from the base – don't be alarmed by how far up they go, just slice them off. Next, peel the skin and don't be timid – a celeriac is not a carrot or potato, it's fine to remove a thick layer to reveal the smooth creamy-white flesh. Celeriac can be steamed or boiled and is excellent roasted; try baking it in its skin, wrapped in foil, then peeling and mashing. It is also delicious raw in a salad, cut into matchstick strips or coarsely grated and served with a creamy dressing.

The quantities in the recipe below are enough to make two dishes – the idea is to freeze one for a later date.

8 spring onions
a few sprigs fresh dill
2 lemons
500 g fresh crab meat (a mixture of brown and white) or 300 g smoked salmon (hot smoked if possible)
3 baking potatoes, approx. 900 g
2 celeriac, approx. 750 g each
500 ml soured cream
300-500 ml milk
butter, for greasing
salt and pepper

To serve
steamed purple sprouting broccoli or another green vegetable

GET AHEAD PREPARATION (optional)

The entire dish can be prepared a few hours in advance then cooked at the last minute. If you have only a little time:
* Prepare the spring onions.
* Mix the crab meat or cut the salmon.
* Prepare the potatoes and cover with water.
* Peel and slice the celeriac and toss in lemon juice.
* Mix the soured cream and milk.

50 minutes before you want to eat

* Preheat the oven to 200°C/400°F/Gas Mark 6.
* First, prepare the spring onion layer. Trim and finely slice the spring onions, using as much of the green part as you can. Roughly chop the dill and grate the zest of one lemon and add to the onions.
* Next, mix together the brown and white crabmeat or cut the salmon into small squares. Season well with salt and pepper and set aside.
* Then, prepare the potatoes and celeriac. Peel and thinly slice the potatoes into 5-mm thick rounds. Peel the celeriac, cut in quarters and thinly cut each quarter into 5-mm thick slices. Put the potato and celeriac slices in a large bowl, add the juice of the lemons and season well.
* Finally, mix the soured cream with the milk in a measuring jug – whisk well to incorporate them.
* Now, assemble the bake. Grease two ovenproof dishes, each one approximately 25 x 25 cm square and 5 cm deep, with butter– one is for freezing so a foil container would be ideal. Place a layer of potato and celeriac on the bottom of each – use about a third of the potato in total. Now divide half the crab or smoked salmon between the two dishes, sprinkle with the dill and spring onion mixture, and pour over one-third of the cream and milk. Continue layering the bakes, finishing with a final layer of celeriac and potato and the last of the soured cream mixture.
* Season well, cover the dishes with foil and bake both of them for 20 minutes. After 20 minutes remove the foil and bake for another 20 minutes. By now the potato and celeriac should be cooked. Insert a knife and if it meets no resistance the bake is ready. Leave one bake to sit while you cook a green vegetable. Set the other one aside to get completely cold for freezing.

Lazy day supper – reheating instructions

Defrost the bake thoroughly before reheating. Cover with foil, preheat the oven to 180°C/350°F/Gas Mark 4 and cook the bake for 30 minutes until it is heated right through.

Buying and preparing fresh crab

A couple of our recipes call for fresh crab. Brown crab is the species caught in British water particularly in Devon, Orkney and Norfolk, using low-impact crab traps. Whole crabs are sold cooked and contain a tasty combination of rich and creamy brown meat in the back shell and delicate flaky white meat in the legs and claws. Dressed crab, where the ready cooked crab has been removed from the shell and returned to the cleaned body shell is also available from major supermarkets.

If you buy a whole cooked crab to remove the meat, lay the crab on its back and remove the large front claws and then the legs by twisting them sharply. Hold the crab firmly and use your thumbs to press the body out of the back shell. Remove and discard the feathery gills (known as dead man's fingers) and any other attachments. Place the body on a chopping board, cut it into four and remove all the white meat from the little channels using a small, sharp knife and a skewer, or a crab pick if you have one. Scoop out the brown meat from the back shell and reserve. Crack the thick shell of the claws using a mallet, hammer or a heavy weight, and remove the meat, discarding the thin piece of bone concealed within the meat of the pincers. Break the thinner shell of the legs with nutcrackers and hook out the meat with a skewer or crab pick.

April to December is the season for fresh crab in Britain and at other times of the year the meat is sold having been frozen. Frozen crab is perfectly adequate but nothing beats the flavour of fresh.

February Week 4 – Overview

Pancake Day, or Shrove Tuesday, moves around each year depending on the date for Easter but it's usually towards the end of February or at the beginning of March. For this reason, this week includes a savoury Two for One pancake recipe. As with all Two for Ones, the quantities will serve a total of eight so if you're feeling sociable they can be eaten at one sitting rather than half going into the freezer. Pancakes are fun to make, but if you're really pushed for time they could be bought ready-made –just omit the relevant ingredients from your shopping list – see Quick Option (page 93).

The Big Meal from Scratch recipe is for a Chicken or Partridge Casserole with Mushrooms, Mash and Buttery Greens. Making extra mash and greens provides the ingredients for a bubble and squeak Something for Nothing recipe on another day. The mushroom sauce used to braise the chicken or partridge has an intense flavour and this is put to good use as the basis for a Celeriac and Mushroom gratin. Both the Something for Nothing recipes are ready in around half an hour.

For a Seasonal Supper, a Root Vegetable Tagine is richly flavoured with cumin, coriander, cinnamon and a hot North African chilli paste called harissa. The tagine takes about 40 minutes to make, as a fair amount of vegetable-chopping is required.

Canned salmon is used in the Larder Feast for delicious Thai Fishcakes that are easy to make and ready in just 30 minutes.

February Week 4	Recipe	Time
Big meal from scratch	Chicken (or partridge) with mushrooms, mash and greens	1½ hours
Something for nothing 1	Pork chops with bubble and squeak	30 mins
Something for nothing 2	Celeriac and mushroom bake	35 mins
Seasonal supper	Root vegetable tagine with couscous	40 mins
Larder feast	Thai fishcakes	30 mins
2 for 1	Bacon and spinach pancakes	50 mins

All recipes serve 4 apart from the 2 for 1 recipe which makes 8 portions

SHOPPING LIST (for 4 people)

Meat and fish
1.5 kg free-range chicken, jointed (see page 183) or 1.5 kg free-range chicken thighs and drumsticks or 4 partridges
4 free-range pork loin chops
400 g rindless free-range smoked back bacon

Dairy
170-180 g butter
650-700 ml milk
230-245 ml double cream
300 g garlic and herb cream cheese
300 g cottage cheese
40 g Parmesan
3 large free-range eggs

Fruit and vegetables
1.7 kg floury potatoes, such as Maris Piper or baking potatoes
200g waxy maincrop potatoes, such as Desirée
1 large celeriac, approx. 1.7-1.9 kg
1 small swede, approx. 500 g
3 parsnips, approx. 300 g
600 g-700 g winter greens or loose cabbage such as hispy (500 g if ready sliced)
500 g baby leaf spinach
500 g mushrooms (ideally chestnut)
4 celery sticks
2 medium red onions, approx. 240 g
8-10 shallots, approx. 300 g
2 bunches spring onions
8 garlic cloves
5 cm piece of fresh root ginger
a few sprigs fresh thyme
1 large bunch fresh flatleaf parsley
1 large bunch fresh coriander
2 lemons
2 limes
250 g frozen spinach
120 g frozen peas

Basics
50 ml olive oil
200 ml groundnut or grapeseed oil
350 ml chicken stock (fresh or made with a stock cube or bouillon powder)
500 ml vegetable stock (made from a stock cube or bouillon powder)
270 g plain flour
salt and pepper

Store cupboard
300 g basmati or Thai jasmine rice
400 g couscous
6 tbsp fine matzo meal or dry breadcrumbs
50 g dried mushrooms (a selection is good)
600 g canned salmon
20 g no-soak pitted prunes
20 g no-soak apricots
20 g large green olives
2 tbsp (approx.) dessicated coconut
30 g ground almonds, approx. 1 heaped tbsp
1½ tbsp sesame seeds
2 tbsp toasted sesame oil
3 tbsp sweet chilli sauce
4 tsp soy sauce
4 tsp Thai fish sauce
2 tbsp Thai green curry paste
1 heaped tbsp harissa paste or unsweetened chilli sauce, plus extra to serve
1 tsp ground cumin
1 tsp ground ginger
1 tsp ground coriander
1 small cinnamon stick
3 bay leaves
pinch of saffron threads
pinch of nutmeg (ground or freshly grated)
750 ml white wine

Quick option (Bacon and spinach pancakes)
16 ready-made pancakes,; remove 270 g plain flour, 3 eggs and 430 ml milk from the shopping list

Serving suggestions
mustard (Pork Chops with Bubble and Squeak)
rocket, Parmesan (Celeriac and Mushroom Bake)
frozen soya beans (Thai Fishcakes)
little gem lettuce, celery, carrots, apple, walnuts or mixed salad leaves (Bacon and Spinach Pancakes)

To download or print out this shopping list, please visit www.thekitchenrevolution.co.uk/February/Week4

**Big meal
from scratch**

Chicken (or Partridge) with Mushrooms, Mash and Greens

This chicken or partridge casserole, flavoured with wild mushrooms and plenty of
wine, is ideal for cold, dark winter days. Although the recipe works very well with
chicken, the more robust flavour of partridge makes an otherwise good meal
something very special. If you do use partridge keep them whole and serve one per
person. The quantities given here allow for extra mushroom sauce, greens and mash
for the Celeriac and Mushroom Bake and the Pork Chops with Bubble and Squeak.

Chicken (or partridge) with wild
mushrooms
50 g dried mushrooms (a
    selection is good)
1.5 kg free-range chicken,
    jointed (see page 183) or 1.5 kg
    free-range chicken thighs and
    drumsticks or 4 whole
    partridges
2–3 tbsp groundnut or grapeseed
    oil
8–10 shallots, approx. 300 g
750 ml white wine
200 g mushrooms (ideally
    chestnut); with the dried
    mushrooms, allows for 150 g
    mushroom sauce for the
    celeriac and mushroom bake
350 ml chicken stock (fresh or
    made from a stock cube or
    bouillon powder)

a few sprigs fresh thyme
2 bay leaves
Small handful parsley
salt and pepper

Mash
2 kg floury potatoes, such as
    Maris Piper or baking potatoes;
    includes 1 kg extra for the
    bubble and squeak
200 ml milk or 150 ml milk and
    2–3 tbsp double cream
50 g butter

Greens
600–700 g winter greens or loose
    cabbage such as hispy;
    includes approx. 250 g for the
    bubble and squeak
40 g butter

GET AHEAD PREPARATION (optional)

You can cook the shallots and
mushrooms, and brown the meat
a couple of hours in advance, so
that the casserole is ready to
cook. If you only have a little
time:
* Peel and chop the shallots.
* Clean and halve the fresh
    mushrooms.

*1½ hours before
you want to eat
make the casserole*

* Pour enough boiling water over the dried mushrooms so that they are just covered.
  Leave them to soften.
* Next, brown the chicken joints or partridges. Heat a generous glug of oil in a casserole
  dish over a medium heat. Season the joints or partridges thoroughly on both sides and
  brown in the hot oil until deep golden in colour – you may have to do this in batches.
  Once each batch is browned, lift it out and set it aside.
* While the meat is browning, peel and roughly chop the shallots.
* When all the meat has browned, remove the final batch from the casserole dish. As
  long as the dish isn't burnt on the bottom, return to the heat and splash in a large
  glass of the wine. Let the wine bubble away for a while, stirring occasionally, then pour
  the wine over the browned chicken or partridges and wipe the dish dry.
* Now, return the dish to the heat with another glug of oil. Add the shallots and cook
  over a medium heat until starting to brown. Meanwhile, clean the fresh mushrooms
  and cut them in half.
* After 10 minutes, the shallots should be quite soft. Turn the heat up under the
  casserole dish, add a splash more oil and the fresh mushrooms and let the mushrooms
  soften and brown with the shallots for 5 minutes, stirring regularly. Then lift the dried
  mushrooms out of their soaking liquid (keep this liquor as you will add it to the
  casserole later) and add them to the dish. Turn the heat down and cook gently for a
  further 5 minutes.
* Once the mushrooms are cooked, add the remaining wine and bring to the boil. Let
  this simmer for a minute, then pour in all but the last teaspoon of the mushroom
  soaking liquor, which might be a bit gritty. Add the stock, thyme and bay leaves and
  turn up the heat to bring everything to the boil.
* Once boiling, reduce the heat to a low simmer, return all the chicken legs and thighs
  or the partridges, to the pan and leave to cook very gently, uncovered, for about
  45 minutes.

30 minutes before you want to eat cook the potatoes

* Peel the potatoes and cut them into even-sized chunks. Put them into a pan of water with a good pinch of salt. Bring them to the boil, then simmer gently until they are just cooked – this will take about 20 minutes depending on the size of the chunks.
* While the potatoes are cooking, wash and trim the greens – remove any hard stalks or ribs from the leaves and the cut into ribbons about 2 cm wide. Roughly chop the parsley.

10–15 minutes before you want to eat cook the chicken breasts and the greens

* Put the oven on its lowest setting to warm plates and serving dishes.
* After 45 minutes cooking, check the contents of the casserole dish. If you are cooking partridges, check whether a leg comes away easily or, with chicken joints, that the flesh comes easily off the bones. If this is the case they are ready; if not, let them simmer gently for a little longer before testing again.
* If you are cooking chicken joints and they are tender, put the breasts on top and leave them to cook for 10 –15 minutes with a lid on.
* If you are cooking partridges and they are finished, scatter over the parsley, put a lid on the casserole and leave to keep warm in the oven.
* Now put the greens in a pan with a lid and add about 1 cm water, a little salt and the butter. Cook over a medium heat for about 10 minutes. Once the greens are cooked, drain them and check for seasoning before turning them into a warmed serving dish.
* When the potatoes are cooked, make the mash. Drain the potatoes well and keep in the colander. Put the milk, or milk and cream, and the butter into the empty potato pan over a low heat, so that the butter melts and the milk heats up. While this is happening, place the potatoes in the colander over the pan to make sure they are very dry and you don't get a sloppy mash.
* When the milk is hot and the butter has melted, add the potatoes and mash well with a traditional masher or, for a really smooth texture, pass the potatoes through a mouli-legumes or potato ricer. Taste and season as necessary. Turn the mash into a warmed serving dish and keep warm in the oven, covered with a little butter paper or foil.
* To serve, give each person 1–2 chicken joints (or one partridge), with a good spoonful of the mushroom and shallot sauce on top and pass the mash and greens separately.

Afterwards

While the leftover mushroom and shallot sauce is still warm, strain out the liquid and store the mushroom mixture and the liquid in separate airtight containers in the fridge – you will use some of the liquid with the bubble and squeak, and the rest of the mushrooms and liquid in the celeriac bake. Put the leftover mash and greens in separate containers, cover and refrigerate for use later in the week.

Ideally, there will be 150 g mushroom mixture, 400 ml cooking liquid, 600–800 g mash and approx. 200g greens.

**Something
for nothing 1**

Pork Chops with Bubble and Squeak

This is a comforting and very quick supper – perfect when you are tired and feeling the winter blues. The secret to golden and crispy (rather than burnt and bitter) bubble and squeak is cooking over a relatively gentle heat, rather than frantic frying. Luckily, it is the same for pork chops – these are also ruined if they are cooked too quickly.

30-40 g butter
groundnut or grapeseed oil
600-800 g mash left over from
    the Big Meal from Scratch or
    800 g potatoes, cooked and
    mashed
4 free-range pork loin chops
approx. 200 g greens left over
    from the Big Meal from Scratch
    or 250 g greens, shredded and
    steamed

200 ml cooking liquid left over
    from the Big Meal from Scratch
    (optional)

To serve
mustard

*30 minutes before
you want to eat*

* Melt about three-quarters of the butter with a splash of oil in a heavy-based frying pan (non-stick if possible) over a medium heat. When the fat is foaming, add the mash and flatten to cover the bottom of the pan. Cook on a medium to low heat for about 5–8 minutes without touching. You want the mash to get crispy and golden.
* Once the mash has crisped up, scrape the bottom of the pan and turn the mash – you don't want to flip it like a pancake, but rather incorporate the crisp parts within the softer parts. Leave it to cook for about another 10-15 minutes, turning once or twice (resist the temptation to turn the mash too often).
* Meanwhile, start cooking the chops. Heat a splash of of oil and the remaining butter in a heavy-based frying pan, season the chops and add them to the pan. Fry over a medium to high heat for approximately 5–6 minutes on each side; you want the chops to have a nice golden exterior, so turn the heat down if you think they are cooking too fast.
* When you've turned the chops, gently mix the greens into the mash and continue cooking, turning once or twice before the chops are ready.
* When the chops are cooked, lift them from the pan and tip away the excess fat. Leave the chops to rest for 5 minutes, and if you have any cooking liquid left from the Big Meal from Scratch pour it into the chops pan and heat it. Turn the bubble and squeak one last time. Let the gravy come to a simmer and give it a good stir.
* The bubble and squeak is ready when about half the mash is golden and crunchy.
* Serve the chops with the bubble and squeak on the side, the hot gravy and a little mustard.

Something
for nothing 2

Celeriac and Mushroom Bake

This is rich and flavoursome – perfect for a cold February night. If you don't have any mushroom mixture left over from the Big Meal from Scratch, peel and slice 2 large shallots, cook them in a little butter until soft and add 15 g dried mushrooms soaked for 10 minutes in boiling water. Cook the shallots and mushrooms for a further 10 minutes until the mushrooms are soft.

250 g frozen spinach
200 ml cooking liquid left over
   from the Big Meal from Scratch
   or 200 ml chicken or vegetable
   stock (fresh or made from a
   stock cube or bouillon powder)
200 ml double cream
milk, if needed
1 bay leaf
pinch of nutmeg (ground or
   freshly grated)
4 garlic cloves
1 large celeriac, approx. 1.7–
   1.9 kg
30 g butter
1 tbsp groundnut or grapeseed oil
300 g mushrooms (ideally
   chestnut)
150 g cooked mushroom mixture
   left over from the Big Meal

from Scratch) or see above
salt and pepper

To serve
rocket and Parmesan salad

GET AHEAD PREPARATION (optional)

The whole dish can be made up
to a day in advance and
reheated. If you only have a
little time:
* Prepare the celeriac and leave
in water with a little lemon juice
until required.
* Defrost the spinach.
* Prepare the mushrooms.

*35 minutes before
you want to eat*

* Preheat the oven to 220°C/425°F/Gas Mark 7.
* First, defrost the spinach according to the instructions on the packet (either in the microwave or pour boiling water over the top).
* While the spinach is defrosting, make the creamy sauce. Put the cooking liquid (or stock) into a measuring jug and add the cream. You need 450 ml of liquid so top the mixture up with milk if you need to. Squash the garlic cloves and take them out of their skins.
* Now pour the liquid into a large pan and add the bay leaf, a pinch of nutmeg and the garlic cloves (they will be strained out later so don't worry too much). Bring the liquid quickly to the boil, then turn it right down and leave it on the lowest possible heat to allow the flavours to infuse.
* Meanwhile peel, quarter and thinly slice the celeriac. Add these slices to the liquid in the pan and let them soften, with a lid on, until you are ready to assemble the dish.
* Now make the mushroom and spinach mixture. Put the butter and the oil in a large frying pan on a medium-high heat, while it warms, clean and slice the mushrooms. Cook them in the butter for a few minutes until they are soft. Then add the spinach and the mushroom mixture from the Big Meal from Scratch and stir until everything is amalgamated. Season to taste with salt and pepper.
* Now assemble the dish. Lift about half of the sliced celeriac out of the pan and spread it in an even layer over the base of a deep ovenproof dish. Season this layer and tip the mushroom mix on top, spread it out evenly, then cover with the rest of celeriac.
* Strain over the remaining liquid, season the top and bake for 15–20 minutes.
* The gratin is done when it offers no resistance to the tip of a knife and is brown on the top.
* Serve with a rocket and Parmesan salad.

Seasonal supper

Root Vegetable Tagine with Couscous

Tagine is a Moroccan word for stew – typically vegetables, meat, chicken or fish cooked very slowly with spices and herbs (and sometimes preserved lemons). At this time of year, swedes and parsnips are at their best and widely available so here they are used to make a rich, spicy, root vegetable tagine – served with couscous. Tagine also refers to the earthenware dish with a distinctive pointed lid in which the stews are cooked, but they can just as easily be cooked in a large heavy-based pan or a casserole dish. The recipe is sserved with harissa, a north African chilli paste made with chille and cumin. Harissa is widely available in supermarkets but if you can't find any use a plain chilli sauce and increase the cumin in the recipe.

Root vegetable tagine
2 medium red onions, approx.
    240 g
2 tbsp olive oil
4 celery sticks
2 garlic cloves
1 small swede, approx. 500 g
3 parsnips, approx. 300 g
200 g waxy maincrop potatoes,
    such as Desirée
1 tsp ground cumin
1 tsp ground ginger
1 tsp ground coriander
pinch of saffron threads
1 lemon
500 ml stock (fresh or made from
    a stock cube or bouillon
    powder)

1 small cinnamon stick
120 g frozen peas
1 heaped tbsp harissa paste
30 g ground almonds, approx.
    1 heaped tbsp
20 g large green olives
20 g no-soak pitted prunes
20 g no-soak apricots

Couscous
400 g couscous
juice of 1 lemon
small handful of fresh flatleaf
    parsley
small handful of fresh coriander
1 tbsp olive oil
salt and pepper

GET AHEAD PREPARATION (optional)

The entire tagine can be made up to 2 days in advance and reheated when needed – the flavours will improve with time. If you only have a little time:
* Prepare the onions, celery and garlic.
* Peel and cut the swede, parsnips and potatoes and cover with cold water until required.
* Chop the parsley and coriander.

40 minutes before you want to eat

* Peel and slice the onions, then heat a good splash of oil in a large heavy-based pan over a low heat and cook the onions for 5 minutes.
* Wash and slice the celery sticks, then add them to the pan and cook for another 5–7 minutes until they are soft. Meanwhile peel and crush the garlic and peel or wash and cut swede, parsnips and potatoes into bite-sized chunks.
* Next, add the garlic, cumin, ginger and ground coriander to the pan and let them roast for a couple of minutes, stirring to prevent burning.
* Turn the heat up under the pan and splash in another generous glug of oil. Now add the swede, parsnips and potatoes and stir thoroughly for a couple of minutes until they are well coated with the spiced onions and start to brown. Grate the lemon zest.
* Add the saffron, cook for a minute then add the stock, lemon zest and cinnamon stick. Bring to the boil, season to taste and simmer for about 20 minutes.
* Pour in enough boiling water to just cover the couscous, then cover tightly with cling film and leave for 15 minutes. Finely chop the parsley and coriander.
* Use a fork to fluff up the softened couscous and stir in the oil, lemon juice and herbs. Season to taste, cover and leave in a warm place.
* When the vegetables are just soft, add the peas. Lift out a ladleful of the tagine liquid, mix it in a cup with the harissa and ground almonds and stir the mixture back into the tagine. Now add the olives, prunes and apricots to the tagine, and heat through for 2 minutes.
* Serve the tagine on the couscous with extra harissa or chilli sauce to taste.

Larder feast

Thai Fishcakes

These fishcakes have a real kick to them, flavoured as they are with ginger, curry paste and garlic. Canned salmon has a strong enough flavour to withstand these tastes without being overpowered. Serve with rice, a dipping sauce and perhaps some steamed soya beans. These are found frozen in most big supermarkets and are very moreish.

Thai fishcakes
300 g basmati or Thai jasmine
  rice
5 cm piece of fresh root ginger
2 garlic cloves
2 tbsp Thai green curry paste
2 tsp Thai fish sauce
juice of 1 lime
2 tbsp sweet chilli sauce
600 g canned salmon
2 tbsp (approx.) dessicated
  coconut
6 tbsp fine matzo meal or dry
  breadcrumbs
1 tbsp toasted sesame oil
1 tbsp groundnut or grapeseed oil
salt

For the dipping sauce
1½ tbsp sesame seeds
1 tbsp toasted sesame oil
2 tsp soy sauce
1 tbs sweet chilli sauce
2 tsp Thai fish sauce
juice of 1 lime
1 small bunch fresh coriander
  (optional)

To serve
steamed soya beans

GET AHEAD PREPARATION (optional)

The fishcakes can be made a day in advance and kept in the fridge and then fried when required. The dipping sauce can also be made a day in advance (but omit the sesame seeds and coriander until ready to serve). If you only have a little time:
* Peel the ginger and garlic.
* Make the paste for the fishcakes.
* Toast the sesame seeds.

30 minutes before you want to eat

* Wash the rice under cold running water then cook according to the instructions on the packet and keep hot until ready to serve.
* While the rice is cooking start the fishcakes. Peel the ginger and garlic and put in a food processor or grate very finely. Blend along with the curry paste, fish sauce, lime juice and sweet chilli sauce. Drain the salmon very thoroughly and add to the paste along with the coconut, matzo meal or breadcrumbs and a little salt. Mix together well or pulse a couple of times in a food processor.
* Form the salmon mixture into eight cakes. Cover and keep refrigerated while you toast the sesame seeds for the dipping sauce.
* Preheat the oven to low to keep the fishcakes warm.
* Heat the sesame seeds in a frying pan until browned – keep an eye on them as they will burn very quickly. Remove from the heat and leave to cool.
* Now cook the fishcakes. Heat half the sesame oil and groundnut or grapeseed oil in a frying pan over a high heat. When the oil is hot, add the fishcakes. Turn after about 5 minutes on each side, then remove them from the oil and drain on kitchen paper. You will need cook the fishcakes in two batches. Keep the first batch warm in the oven while you add the remaining oil to the pan and cook the second batch.
* In the meantime, make the dipping sauce. Mix together the sesame oil, soy sauce, chilli sauce, fish sauce and lime juice. Add the sesame seeds, stir well and put in a dish suitable for serving.
* Roughly chop the fresh coriander, if using, add half to the dipping sauce and use the rest to sprinkle over the fishcakes and rice.
* Serve with the rice and soya beans, with the dipping sauce on the side.

Two for one

Bacon and Spinach Pancakes

This recipe is inspired by Italian crespelle – light pancakes filled with stuffing then baked with tomato sauce and lashings of Parmesan. Here bacon, spinach and cheese are rolled into the pancakes and covered with cheese. The tomato sauce is omitted for the sake of speed, but could easily be added if time or inclination allowed.

Pancakes are quick and easy to make once you get the hang of them – your main ally is a very good, non-stick frying pan. If you are very tight for time, however, you can buy ready-made pancakes (look for ones with little or no sugar); you will need 16. Staffordshire oat pancakes are particularly good stuffed with the mixture below.

The batter makes a few more than 16 pancakes, which leaves room for trial and error and even a special breakfast treat. The batter will keep in the fridge for a couple of days.

Pancakes
270 g plain flour
3 large free-range eggs
400 ml milk
200 ml water
groundnut or grapeseed oil
salt

Bacon and spinach filling
groundnut or grapeseed oil
400 g rindless smoked back
  bacon, approx 12 rashers
2 bunches spring onions

500 g baby leaf spinach
40 g Parmesan
300 g garlic and herb cream
  cheese
300 g cottage cheese
20 g butter
salt and pepper

To serve
salad of little gem lettuce,
  celery, carrots, apple and
  walnuts, or just salad leaves

GET AHEAD PREPARATION (optional)

The whole dish, and either element (filling or pancakes), can be made a day in advance. If you only have a little time
* Make the pancake batter
* Prepare the spring onions and spinach.

50 minutes before you want to eat

* First of all, make the pancake batter. Sift the flour and salt into a large bowl, make a well in the centre and add the eggs and milk and water in a slow stream, stirring well, until you have a smooth batter.
* Now make the filling. Heat a splash of oil in a large pan with a lid over a medium heat. When the oil is hot, snip the bacon into small pieces with a pair of scissors, add it to the pan and let it cook for a few minutes while you trim and slice the spring onions, using as much green as you can.
* Now throw the spring onions into the pan. Shake the pan once or twice then cover with a lid. Leave the onions to soften while you wash the spinach.
* Wash and thoroughly drain the spinach. Remove the lid from the pan, turn the heat up and add the spinach.
* Once the spinach starts to wilt, lower the heat a little and stir until it turns into a soft mass.
* At this point, increase the heat under the pan and let the cooking liquid reduce. When the mixture is almost dry, taste, and season with salt and pepper.
* In the meantime, roughly grate the Parmesan and put all but 1 tablespoon into a mixing bowl. Add the soft cheeses to the bowl, season, mix well and return to the fridge until required.
* When the spinach mixture has dried, tip it on to a plate and flatten it out to cool down quickly. Leave the spinach cooling while you cook the pancakes.
* Preheat the oven to 200°C/400°F/Gas Mark 6.
* Heat a flat, non-stick frying pan over a medium heat and add a splash of oil.
* When the oil is hot, pour enough batter into the frying pan to just cover the base, swirling it all the time to create a very thin layer.
* Turn the pancake when it has set and can be easily lifted at the edges – loosen it round the edges and carefully turn it over – you want the final result be soft and golden on both sides. You may find the temperature needs adjusting every now and then.
* Make seven more pancakes in the same way – the first one is always the most tricky, and you may find you have to give that one up to trial and error. Be sure to add a little oil to the pan between pancakes.

* Stack the pancakes on top of each other on a large plate with a piece of greaseproof paper or foil between each one so they don't stick together.
* When you have eight pancakes ready, put a large ovenproof dish in the oven with a small nut of butter to melt. Mix the cool spinach mixture with the cheese in the bowl and season to taste.
* Place a generous tablespoon or two of the filling across the length of one end of each pancake then roll the pancake up. The filling should be ample for 16, so bear this in mind when you are filling the pancakes.
* When eight pancakes have been filled and rolled, take the dish from the oven and swirl the butter around. Lay the pancakes side by side in the dish and scatter the remaining Parmesan over the top.
* Bake the pancakes in the oven for 15–20 minutes.
* While they are in the oven, cook another eight pancakes and fill them with the remaining filling. Wrap them individually in foil and set them aside to freeze when they are completely cold.
* Make a simply dressed, crunchy salad of little gem lettuce, carrots, celery, apple and walnuts.

Lazy day supper – reheating instructions

* If possible, defrost the pancakes thoroughly before reheating. Then scatter with Parmesan and bake in a buttered dish as above.
* You can also cook the pancakes from frozen. Preheat the oven to 160°C/325°F/Gas Mark 3. Butter an ovenproof dish and grate a little Parmesan. Unwrap the pancakes from the foil and lay them in the buttered dish. Dot with butter, sprinkle with the Parmesan and bake for 45 minutes until heated right through. Put under a hot grill for a couple of minutes at the end to crisp them up and serve as above.

February
puddings

Caramelised Blood Oranges with Grand Marnier

They may be a sweet-trolley favourite, but good caramelised oranges are refreshing, beautiful and hard to beat at the end of a big meal. Here we suggest using blood oranges which, when sliced and suspended in the boozy syrup, look like jewels. They can be made a day or two before they are needed.

8 blood oranges
175 g caster sugar
juice of ½ lemon
5 tbsp Grand Marnier

To serve
ice cream or sorbet

At least 1 hour and up to 24 hours before you want to eat

* Peel and pith the oranges using a knife in the following way. Slice the top and bottom of each orange so that it stands easily on a chopping board, then slice downwards, following the curve of the orange. The trick is to remove the skin and pith without wasting too much flesh.
* Cut the oranges into rounds just over 5 mm thick and remove any pips.
* Place in a serving dish, ideally a glass bowl.
* Take five or six lengths of peel, slice away any pith and cut into fine matchsticks.
* Place the shredded peel in a pan, cover with water, bring to the boil and then drain.
* Cover the peel with water once more and bring to the boil again. Cook for about 20 minutes or until the peel is tender and sweet.
* While the peel is cooking place the sugar in a heavy-based pan and stir over a medium heat until the sugar has melted and is just starting to turn brown and caramelise.
* Remove from the heat and add 125 ml water. It will bubble furiously so take care not to get splashed.
* When the bubbling stops return the pan to the heat and stir until the caramel has dissolved and a syrup forms. Add the drained shredded peel to the pan and boil for 2–3 minutes.
* Remove from the heat and add the lemon juice and Grand Marnier.
* Spoon the peel and syrup over the oranges and allow to cool, basting the oranges with the syrup every now and then.
* Once cool, place the oranges in the fridge until you want to eat.
* Serve with ice cream or sorbet.

Torrijas – Spanish Eggy Bread

Torrijas are the Spanish equivalent of eggy bread but are more grown up than the nursery staple as the egg is mixed with sherry before coating the bread. *Torrijas* have the same comforting texture as pancakes but involve half the work. Like pancakes, they can be served with stewed fruit, fruit purée, jam or honey, or ice cream.

2 free-range eggs
2 tbsp sherry
1 tbsp (approx.) icing sugar
groundnut or grapeseed oil
30 g (approx.) butter
4 slices brioche or other
  enriched bread or fruit bread
2 tbsp milk
pinch of salt

To serve
stewed fruit, fruit purée, jam or
  clear honey
ice cream

25 minutes before you want to eat

* Whisk the eggs with the milk, sherry, a pinch of salt and the icing sugar. Add a little more icing sugar if the mixture doesn't seem very sweet – bear in mind that if you are using a fruit or sweet bread you may not need too much. Put the mixture into a shallow dish.
* Preheat the oven to its lowest setting.
* Heat a splash of oil and a nut of butter in a large heavy-based frying pan. Dip a slice of bread in the egg mixture; make sure it is well coated but don't let it get so soaked that it falls apart.
* When the butter has melted, add the bread and brown it well on both sides.
* Keep it warm while you fry the other slices, adding more oil and butter as needed.
* Cut each slice of bread into two triangles and pile them on a plate. Serve with the accompaniment of your choice.

February
puddings

Baked Banana and Greek Yoghurt Pudding

Yoghurt becomes much firmer, almost solid, once it is baked and bananas sweeten to almost caramel. This pudding can be served hot or cold. It was given to Rosie by her friend and colleague Toby Hughes.

4 ripe bananas, approx. 600 g
juice of 1 lemon
3 tbsp soft brown muscovado
   sugar
500 g Greek yoghurt

To serve
clear honey

25 minutes before you want to eat

* Preheat the oven to 180°C/350°F/Gas Mark 4.
* Peel the bananas, mash with the lemon juice and sugar, stir into the yoghurt then pour the mixture into an ovenproof dish approximately 5 cm deep.
* Place in the oven and leave to cook for 15 minutes until the pudding is firm to touch.
* Take the pudding out of the oven and leave to sit for a few minutes before serving with honey drizzled over the top.

February
puddings

Rhubarb and Ginger Crumb Pudding

When rhubarb is in season it's tempting to make a crumble every week – this recipe stays within the realms of crumble but adds something different.

60 g butter
1 tsp ground ginger
200 g soft breadcrumbs or 8
  slices bread suitable for
  crumbing
500 g rhubarb
2 oranges
60 g crystallized stem ginger in
  syrup, plus 2 tbsp ginger syrup
  from the jar
85 g soft light brown sugar
1 lemon

To serve
custard or cream

45 minutes before you want to eat

* Preheat the oven to 200°C/400°F/Gas Mark 6.
* Melt the butter in a heavy-based pan over a gentle heat and add the ground ginger and breadcrumbs, stirring and shaking all the while. Cover the base of an ovenproof dish with a third of this mixture.
* Trim the rhubarb and cut it into 3–4-cm pieces. Grate the zest of the oranges. Coarsely grate the crystallized ginger into a bowl, mix with the sugar and orange zest and toss the rhubarb through it.
* Put a layer of rhubarb on top of the buttery crumbs, follow with more crumbs and then continue the layers until the dish is full. Finish with a layer of crumbs.
* Put the ginger syrup, orange and lemon juices and 2 tbsp water in a bowl and mix together well. Pour this over the pudding, then bake for 20–30 minutes until the rhubarb feels tender and the pudding has become golden and crisp.
* Serve with custard or cream.

MARCH

March is between times – neither winter nor spring. Root vegetables and game are on the wane and spring salad leaves and vegetables have yet to make their mark. What's needed is a little clarity: strong flavours, interesting combinations and reliable favourites. We have two contrasting large meals in the middle of the month: a delicately flavoured Fillet of Beef Stuffed with Spinach and Walnuts and a rustic Italian-inspired 'Bollito Misto' – a whole chicken poached with sausages and served with lentils. In the middle off the month we have a meal guaranteed to get the taste buds going: Persian-Flavoured Mackerel served with Cumin and Coriander carrots. In the same week a recipe for Rich Beef Stew with a bread and mustard crust is warming and familiar. To clear away colds and get the taste buds salivating, a pudding of Marinated and Grilled Pineapple is the one to go for, but if it's straightforward comfort that's required the Treacle Tart is ideal.

March	Week 1	Week 2	Week 3	Week 4
Big meal from scratch	Roast pork with stuffed baked apples, roast potatoes, parsnip and swede mash and greens	Persian mackerel, spiced rice and cumin and coriander carrots	Bollito misto – poached chicken and sausages with lentils and green sauce	Stuffed fillet of beef, dauphinoise potatoes and beetroot with horseradish
Something for nothing 1	Pork and red cabbage bake	Teriyaki mackerel with cucumber salad	Toad in the hole with onion gravy	Spinach, walnut and Roquefort soufflé
Something for nothing 2	Root vegetable cakes with spinach and fried eggs	Egg fried rice with pak choi or Chinese lettuce	Herb, leek and lemon risotto	Red flannel hash with fried eggs
Seasonal supper	Caldo verde – Portuguese vegetable soup with goats' cheese toasts	Chicken tortillas with avocado and pomegranate salsa	Spring onion chicken noodle soup	Cabbage in ham with mustard potatoes
Larder feast	Flageolet bean crumble	Tapenade and goats' cheese spaghetti	Grown-up fish fingers and baked beans	Couscous with pomegranate molasses
2 for 1	Vegetable cobbler	Rich beef stew with a French bread and mustard crust	Caribbean macaroni cheese	Fish rarebit
Puddings	Treacle tart	Chocolate cardamom pots with oranges	Grilled marinated pineapple	Honey cake

March Week 1 – Overview

Roast pork is classically served with apple sauce, but for the Big Meal from Scratch this week tradition is altered a little and instead the apples are stuffed and baked alongside the pork.

Extra pork from the big meal is turned into a bake with red cabbage. Juniper berries add a spicy, aromatic flavour but are not absolutely essential if they can't be found in the spice section of a delicatessen or supermarket. The parsnip and swede mash accompanying the roast pork is made in generous quantities so that it can be transformed another day into crispy fried Vegetable Cakes served with Spinach and Fried Eggs. This makes a very homely supper that can be ready in half an hour.

Spring greens are excellent at this time of year and these are celebrated in a Seasonal Supper of a Portuguese soup, Caldo Verde.

The Larder Feast turns a gutsy tomato and bean stew into a bean crumble by topping it with herbed stuffing. In all, the recipe takes just 35 minutes including about 15 minutes preparation and time at the stove.

A Two for One Vegetable Cobbler is filled with sweet root vegetables and finished with a light, cheesy scone topping. It takes some time to chop the vegetables, make the scone mixture and bake it, so make the recipe when you're not in a hurry.

March Week 1	Recipe	Time
Big meal from scratch	Roast pork with stuffed baked apples, roast potatoes, parsnip and swede mash and greens	2½ hours
Something for nothing 1	Pork and red cabbage bake	45 mins
Something for nothing 2	Root vegetable cakes with spinach and fried eggs	30 mins
Seasonal supper	Caldo verde – Portuguese vegetable soup with goats' cheese toasts	35 mins
Larder feast	Flageolet bean crumble	35 mins
2 for 1	Vegetable cobbler	1½ hours

All recipes serve 4 apart from the 2 for 1 recipe which makes 8 portions

SHOPPING LIST (for 4 people)

Meat and fish
- 1.5 kg boned shoulder or boned rolled loin of free-range pork (ask the butcher to score the skin)
- 4 rashers rindless free-range smoked streaky bacon (optional for Flageolet Bean Crumble)
- 3 tbsp duck, goose or beef fat (optional)

Dairy
- 120-160 g goats' cheese, rind on (harder rather than very soft)
- 10 free-range eggs
- 320 g butter
- 300 g Cheddar
- 60 g Cheddar or Parmesan
- 140 ml soured cream
- 60 ml milk

Fruit and vegetables
- 2.4 kg floury potatoes, such as Maris Piper or baking potatoes
- 1 small butternut or other squash, approx. 400 g
- 9 parsnips, approx. 1.1 kg
- 6 carrots, approx. 600 g
- 1-2 swedes, approx. 700 g
- 1 red cabbage, approx. 750 g
- 400-500 g spinach
- 500 g winter greens (250 g if presliced)
- 300 g Brussel tops, curly kale, chard or Savoy cabbage
- 200 g curly kale
- 5 medium leeks, approx. 600 g
- 3 medium onions, approx. 360 g
- 2 large red onions, approx. 400 g
- 12 garlic cloves
- 2 sprigs fresh sage
- handful fresh parsley
- 10 sprigs fresh thyme
- 4 sweet apples, such as Cox or Braeburn
- ½ lemon
- 4 sticks celery (optional for Flageolet Bean Casserole)

Basics
- 400 g self-raising flour, plus extra for dusting
- 4 slices bread
- 100g breadcrumbs or 2-3 slices bread suitable for crumbing
- 100 g dried breadcrumbs or 50 g stuffing mix (preferably with herbs)
- 50 g medium oatmeal or porridge oats
- 75 g wholemeal flour
- 155 ml groundnut or grapeseed oil
- 140ml olive oil
- 1½ tbsp wholegrain mustard
- 2 tsp Dijon mustard
- 1 tbsp soft brown sugar
- 3 tbsp plain flour
- 1 bay leaf
- 1 tbsp herbes de Provence (not necessary if you use stuffing mix)
- 150 ml vegetable stock (made from a stock cube or bouillon powder)
- salt and pepper

Store cupboard
- 25 g raisins
- 80 g no-soak dried apricots
- 1 × 400 g can celery hearts (optional for Flageolet Bean Casserole)
- 2 × 350-400 g cans flageolet beans
- 1 × 400 g can chopped tomatoes
- 1 tbsp red wine or cider vinegar
- pinch of nutmeg (ground or freshly grated)
- generous pinch of garam masala
- pinch of paprika (smoked or plain)
- 1 tbsp dry sherry (optional)
- 150 ml white wine
- 200 ml red wine
- 200 ml cider
- 75 ml Calvados or white vermouth or 120 ml white wine

Serving suggestions
- green salad ingredients (Flageolet Bean Crumble)

To download or print out this shopping list, please visit www.thekitchenrevolution.co.uk/March/Week1

**Big meal
from scratch**

Roast Pork with Stuffed Baked Apples, Roast Potatoes, Parsnip and Swede Mash and Greens

Apple sauce is a traditional accompaniment for roast pork, but here we suggest you stuff apples with a spiced breadcrumb mixture and bake them alongside the meat.

With pork there's no doubt that the better the meat, the better the roast. Free-range or organic meat nearly always tastes superior to intensively reared meat, which tends to be watery and flavourless. To get a good crackling the rind needs to be dry and well scored. To score pork, either ask a butcher or use a sharp knife to make lines across the joint through the rind and fat, but not all the way into the meat. To dry the rind, it helps to leave the meat uncovered in the fridge for 12 hours prior to cooking.

If your pork is a different weight to the one specified, cook for 20–25 mins per 500 g at 180°C/350°F/Gas Mark 4 after an initial 20 minutes at 220°C/425°F/Gas Mark 7.

Extra pork and potatoes are used for the Pork and Cabbage Bake and the extra parsnip and swede mash is turned into Roast Vegetable Cakes.

Roast pork
1 medium onion, approx. 120 g
1.5 kg boned shoulder or boned rolled loin of free-range pork; includes 600g extra for the pork and red cabbage bake
1 tbsp groundnut oil
1 small sprig fresh sage
5 sprigs fresh thyme
75 ml Calvados or white vermouth or 120 ml white wine
2 tbsp plain flour
salt and pepper

Stuffed baked apples
1 medium onion, approx. 120 g
1 garlic clove
80 g no-soak dried apricots
½ lemon
100 g breadcrumbs or 2-3 slices bread suitable for crumbing
4 sweet apples, such as Cox or Braeburn

30 g (approx.) butter
1 large sage leaf

Roast potatoes
1.5 kg floury potatoes, such as Desirée or baking potatoes; includes 600 g for the pork and red cabbage bake
plain flour, for dusting
3 tbsp duck, goose or beef fat or groundnut or grapeseed oil

Parsnip and swede mash
1 or 2 swedes, approx. 700 g; includes 350 g extra for the root vegetable cakes
6 medium parsnips, approx. 700 g; includes 350 g extra for the root vegetable cakes
50 g butter

Greens
500 g winter greens (250 g if presliced)

GET AHEAD PREPARATION (optional)

* Score and season the pork.
* Stuff the apples.
* Peel the root vegetables.
* Peel and chop the potatoes and place in cold water.
* Prepare the greens.

2¼ hours before you want to eat cook the por

* Preheat the oven to 220°C/425°F/Gas Mark 7.
* Peel and slice the onion. Make sure the pork rind is well scored and dried, then rub with plenty of oil and liberal amounts of salt, and season the flesh with both salt and pepper. Put the onion, thyme and sage in a large roasting tin, put the pork on top, skin side up, and place in the oven. Roast for 20 minutes then turn the oven down to 180°C/350°F/Gas Mark 4 and roast for 1 hour 20 minutes (see above for cooking different weights).

2 hours before you want to eat prepare the apples and potatoes

* To make the stuffing, peel and finely chop the onion, peel and crush the garlic and put into a mixing bowl. Chop the apricots into small pieces, shred the sage leaf finely, grate the lemon zest and add to the bowl. Add the breadcrumbs, season well with salt and pepper and mix together.
* Remove and discard the apple cores. Scoop out a good tablespoon from each apple without destroying the 'shell' so that you have a big hole for the stuffing in the centre. Roughly chop the scooped-out flesh into small chunks and add to the breadcrumb mixture. Fill the apple cavities with the stuffing, cramming in as much as possible. Dot the stuffing in each apple with butter. The apples will be baked around the pork so set them aside until you are ready.

* Peel the potatoes, chop them into large chunks and place in a pan of salted water. Bring to the boil, turn the heat down and simmer for 5–7 minutes. Drain and shake the potatoes so their edges get bashed and roughed. Sprinkle the potatoes with flour and shake them well.

1¼ hours before you want to eat cook the apples and potatoes

* When the pork has been cooking for 45 minutes in total remove it from the oven. Use a spoon to scoop any pork fat from under the pork into another roasting tin for the potatoes. Add the fat or oil, to the pork fat. Put the apples around the outside of the pork. Return the pork and the tin for the potatoes to the oven.
* After about 15 minutes the fat in the potato tin will be hot enough to roast the potatoes. Take the tin from the oven and add the parboiled potatoes. Return to the oven quickly and roast for 45 minutes to 1 hour, turning once or twice.

50 minutes before you want to eat cook the mash

* Peel the swede, cut it into 3–4-cm pieces and place in a pan of salted water over a high heat. While the swede is cooking, peel the parsnips and cut into pieces of similar size to the swede. Once the swede water is boiling turn the heat down to a simmer and cook for a few minutes, then add the parsnips. Bring back to the boil and turn the heat down to simmer for about 10 minutes or until both vegetables are just tender.
* Drain the vegetables, season and mash with butter. Cover to keep warm.

20 minutes before you want to eat cook the greens and the gravy

* Remove the pork from the oven, place on a carving board and allow to rest, covered with foil, for at least 20 minutes.
* Check the potatoes are well roasted and the apples softened. If either need more cooking increase the oven temperature to 220°C/425°F/Gas Mark 7 and allow to cook while you finish the greens and gravy. Otherwise turn the oven off. Put the baked apples, roast potatoes and mash in serving dishes in the oven and keep warm while the pork rests and you cook the greens and make the gravy.
* Bring a few centimetres of water to boil in a large steamer or pan and when it is boiling add a little salt and the greens. Cook the greens until they are tender – about 5–7 minutes.
* In the meantime, lift the onion slices from the roasting tin and discard them. Place the tin on the heat, add the Calvados, vermouth or wine and simmer while stirring until the liquid has almost evaporated.
* Next, sprinkle in the flour, stir it in and let it cook for a couple of minutes. When the flour is incorporated, the greens should be ready. Drain them well, and pour about 250 ml of their water into the gravy. Stir well and bring to the boil. Turn down the heat and simmer gently, stirring now and then, while you carve the pork. Taste and season the gravy before serving.

Afterwards

Place the leftover pork (approx. 500 g), roast potatoes (approx. 600 g), parsnip and swede mash (approx. 700 g) and gravy (approx. 150 ml) in separate containers, cover and refrigerate for use later in the week.

Something for nothing 1

Pork and Red Cabbage Bake

When red cabbage is cooked slowly it becomes sweet but with a sharpness that is great with pork. This recipe is for an all-in-one dish that is homely and intensely flavoured.

1 large red onion, approx. 200 g
2 tbsp groundnut or grapeseed oil
30 g butter
2 garlic cloves
1 red cabbage, approx. 750 g
500 g cooked pork left over from the Big Meal from Scratch or 600 g pork fillet seasoned and pan-fried in a little butter and oil
Handful fresh parsley
1 tbsp wholegrain mustard
1 tbsp red wine or cider vinegar
200 ml red wine
2-3 juniper berries (optional)

1 tbsp light brown soft sugar
25 g raisins
150 ml gravy left over from the Big Meal from Scratch or stock made with vegetable bouillon powder
600 g roast potatoes left over from the Big Meal from Scratch or 600 g peeled potatoes cut into small dice, boiled, well drained and tossed in a small nut of butter
3 sprigs fresh thyme
salt and pepper

GET AHEAD PREPARATION (optional)

The entire dish can be prepared in advance and warmed through in the oven when required. If you only have a little time:
* Prepare the onion, garlic and cabbage.
* Cut the potatoes and cover with water until required.

45 minutes before you want to eat

* Peel and finely slice the onion. Heat a splash of of oil and a generous nut of butter in a large, heavy-based pan over a medium heat. Add the onion and fry, stirring gently from time to time. Meanwhile peel and crush or grate the garlic and halve, decore and finely slice the cabbage.
* After about 10 minutes, when the onion has softened, add the garlic and stir for about 3 minutes.
* Next, turn the heat up, add the rest of the butter and when it has melted add the cabbage and stir so that it gets a good coating of butter. Cover the pan and let the cabbage wilt down for 5 minutes.
* While the cabbage is softening, cut the pork into 3-cm thick chunks and roughly chop the parsley. Mix the pork, mustard and parsley together.
* Once the cabbage has softened a little, add the vinegar, wine, lightly crushed juniper berries (if using), sugar and raisins to the pan and bring back to a simmer.
* Preheat the oven to 200°C/400°F/Gas Mark 6.
* Now add the gravy or stock to the pan, increase the heat and bring to the boil.
* Cover the pan again and let the cabbage simmer for 10–12 minutes until soft.
* In the meantime, cut the potatoes into rough chunks and strip the thyme leaves from their thick stalks. Toss the potatoes with the remaining oil and thyme leaves, and season with salt and pepper.
* Now assemble the dish to go into the oven. Put half the cabbage on the bottom of an ovenproof dish, layer the pork on top and cover with the remaining cabbage. Add all the cooking liquor and finally finish with a layer of potatoes.
* Put the dish in the oven and bake until the pork has heated through and the potatoes are crisp and golden – this will take no more than 15 minutes.

Root Vegetable Cakes with Spinach and Fried Eggs

These root vegetable cakes go very well with fried eggs and spinach, but could also be served with sausages, chops or bacon.

2 leeks (approx. 240 g with their green tops)
60 g butter
80 ml groundnut or grapeseed oil
50 g medium oatmeal or porridge oats (whizz the porridge oats in a food processor or with a hand blender until fine)
700 g swede and parsnip mash left over from the Big Meal from Scratch or 800 g parsnip and swede peeled, chopped and boiled until soft enough to mash well
pinch of nutmeg (ground or freshly grated)
generous pinch of garam masala
5 free-range eggs
75 g wholemeal flour
400-500 g spinach
salt and pepper

GET AHEAD PREPARATION (optional)

The vegetable cakes can be assembled and left covered in the fridge up to a day in advance until you are ready to start frying. If you only have a little time:
* Slice and wash the leeks.

30 minutes before you want to eat

* Preheat the oven to 150°C/300°F/Gas Mark 2.
* Slice the leeks finely, wash them well and drain. Melt half the butter with a splash of oil in a small pan, add the leeks and cook on a medium heat with a lid on until they are soft – this will take about 5 minutes. After 5 minutes take the lid off, turn the heat up and reduce any liquid in the pan.
* Place the oatmeal or porridge oats in a bowl with the leftover mash, a generous pinch of nutmeg and the garam masala. Tip in the cooked leeks and mix the whole lot together. Beat one of the eggs and gradually add it to the mixture until you have a thick consistency that you can shape into cakes. If the mixture is too moist, add a little of the flour.
* Shape the mixture into eight cakes and toss them in the flour. Leave them to set for a few minutes while you destalk and wash the spinach.
* Heat 3 tablespoons of the oil in a large frying pan, add a couple of cakes and brown them very well on each side. Keep them warm in the oven while you cook the rest.
* Place plates in the oven to warm while you cook the spinach and fry the four remaining eggs.
* Next cook the spinach. Heat a good splash of oil in a large pan with a lid and pile in the spinach and a pinch of salt. Pop the lid on and leave to cook down for 3–5 minutes until tender. Take the lid off once the spinach is soft and add a little butter.
* Meanwhile, wipe the frying pan with kitchen paper, add the remaining butter and oil, and put over a medium heat. When the butter is melted and the oil is hot, crack in the eggs and fry gently.
* When you have fried the eggs, place two cakes on each warmed plate with a pile of spinach and a fried egg on top.

Seasonal supper

Caldo Verde – Portuguese Vegetable Soup with Goats' Cheese Toasts

Caldo Verde is a thick Portuguese soup that turns the most basic combination of potatoes and greens into something surprisingly scrumptious and comforting. We have added some squash to this recipe to give it some colour. Feel free to add slices of chorizo to the soup when the greens are cooked.

1 medium onion
3 garlic cloves
1 small butternut or other squash, approx. 400 g
600 g floury potatoes, such as Maris Piper or baking potatoes
4 tbsp olive oil
300 g greens (Brussel tops, curly kale, chard or Savoy cabbage)
salt and pepper

Goats' cheese toasts
4 slices bread (stale is perfectly acceptable)
1 free-range egg
1 tbsp dry sherry (optional)
pinch of paprika
120-160 g hard goats' cheese, rind on

GET AHEAD PREPARATION (optional)

The soup, up until the point of adding the greens, can be made in advance and reheated when required. If you only have a little time:
* Prepare the onion, garlic and greens.
* Prepare the squash and potatoes and cover with cold water until required.
* Make the goats' cheese mixture.
* Toast the bread.

35 minutes before you want to eat

* Preheat the grill.
* Peel and slice the onion, peel and crush the garlic, and peel the squash and potatoes and cut them into 4-cm chunks.
* Put the garlic, onion, squash and potatoes in a pan and just cover with water. Add a pinch of salt and 1 tablespoon of the oil and bring to the boil. Reduce the heat to low and simmer for 15–20 minutes until the potatoes and squash are just cooked.
* Meanwhile remove any thick stalks from the greens, roll up the leaves and shred them into fine ribbons 1–2 cm wide.
* Next prepare the goats' cheese toasts. Toast the bread lightly. Beat the egg in a bowl with 1 tablespoon of the oil, the sherry, if using, paprika, and salt and pepper. Crumble or grate the cheese and mix it into the egg. Place the toast on a baking sheet and spread with the cheese mixture, then set aside.
* Once the potatoes and squash are cooked, they have to be mashed a little to thicken the soup. A hand blender is great for this job; just pulse it a few times in the pan and you should achieve the thickness you want without losing all the texture. Alternatively, take a large cup of the potatoes, squash and their cooking liquid out of the pan and whizz in a food processor or push through a sieve. Whichever method you choose, be sure to leave a good few pieces of potato and squash so that the soup has a chunky texture. If you feel it is too thick, add some hot water to the purée.
* Bring the soup to the boil over a medium heat, add the greens and some seasoning then turn the heat down and simmer. Stir the greens into the soup and cook gently for a few minutes until they are wilted and the soup has wonderful flecks of green.
* Put the goats' cheese toasts under the grill until golden.
* Ladle the soup into warmed bowls and dowse generously with the remaining oil. Pop a golden toast on top of each serving and push into soup (cut the toast in half if necessary).

Larder feast

Flageolet Bean Crumble

A supply of olive oil, canned flageolet beans, canned tomatoes, some garlic, seasoning and an onion is really all that's required for a very tasty and satisfying meal. Moreover, this crumble can very well accommodate whatever other vegetables you might have lurking about, so don't worry about sticking religiously to the recipe – use it as a guide. It could be adapted to include more meat – browned sausages, cooked chicken or ham, for instance.

3 tbsp olive oil
4 rashers rindless smoked
   streaky bacon (optional)
1 large red onion, approx. 200 g
2 carrots, approx. 200 g
   (optional)
100 g dried breadcrumbs or 50 g
   stuffing mix (preferably with
   herbs)
1 × 400 g can celery hearts or
   4 sticks fresh celery
2 × 350-400 g cans flageolet
   beans
2 garlic cloves
200 ml cider
1 × 400 g can chopped tomatoes
60 g Cheddar or Parmesan (or
   any other hard cheese you
   have)

40 g butter
1 tbsp herbes de Provence (you
   won't need them if you're using
   stuffing mix)
1 bay leaf
salt and pepper

To serve
green salad (optional)

GET AHEAD PREPARATION (optional)

The dish can be made up to the stage where the topping is added a day in advance, and then reheated and grilled prior to eating. If you only have a little time:
* Prepare the onion, garlic and celery.
* Make the topping.

35 minutes before you want to eat

* Heat the oil in a casserole dish and, using a pair of scissors, snip the bacon (if using) into the oil and cook for a couple of minutes.
* In the meantime, peel and slice the onion and then add it to the bacon. Peel and slice the carrots (if using), add them to the onion and leave to soften for 7–10 minutes.
* While the onion and carrots are softening, make the stuffing, if using, according to the instructions on the packet. Drain and rinse the celery hearts and flageolet beans and chop the celery into smallish chunks. Finally, peel and finely slice the garlic. If using fresh celery chop and add to the onions.
* After 7–10 minutes, turn the heat up and add the garlic. Stir it about for a minute then throw in the celery and beans.
* Preheat the grill to its highest setting.
* Next, add the cider and let it bubble it until it has reduced by a third, then add the tomatoes, bay leaf and a good dose of salt and pepper. Let the whole lot bubble rapidly for about 5 minutes while you make the topping. Stir now and then.
* Grate the cheese and cut the butter into little cubes. Stir the cheese and butter into the stuffing or toss them through the breadcrumbs with the herbes de Provence.
* When the topping is ready, sprinkle the stewed vegetables with half the crumbs or stuffing and put the dish under the grill until the top is crisp. This will probably take about 5 minutes. Remove the casserole from under the grill, stir the crispy crust through the vegetables and top them with the remaining mixture. Put under the grill for another 5 minutes until the crust is crisp.
* Serve immediately with a simple green salad.

Two for one

Vegetable Cobbler

This Vegetable Cobbler has a delicious cheese scone topping and a root vegetable filling. The combination manages to be homely without being boring. Making the cobbler top and preparing all the vegetables for the filling takes most of the time.

If push comes to shove, the cobbler topping could be made with ready-made scone mix or it could be replaced with frozen pastry.

3 medium leeks, approx. 400 g
3 medium parsnips,
   approx. 400 g
4 medium carrots, approx. 400 g
300 g potatoes, such as King
   Edwards
200 g curly kale
60 g butter
4 garlic cloves
1 tbsp wholegrain mustard
1 heaped tbsp plain flour
150 ml white wine
150 ml vegetable stock (made
   from a stock cube or bouillon
   powder)
small handful of fresh flatleaf
   parsley
140 ml soured cream
salt

For the cheese scone topping
400 g self-raising flour, plus
   extra for dusting
50 g cold butter
3 sprigs fresh thyme
300 g Cheddar
4 free-range eggs
2 tsp Dijon mustard
4 tbsp milk

GET AHEAD PREPARATION (optional)

* Make the scone topping and
   refridgerate until required.
* Grate the cheese.
* Prepare the leeks and kale.
* Prepare the parsnips, carrots
   and potatoes, cut them into
   chunks and cover with water
   until required.

1½ hours before you want to eat

* Preheat the oven to 200°C/400°F/Gas Mark 6.
* Start by making the cheese scone dough. Sift the flour and a pinch of salt into a mixing bowl. Cut the butter into small pieces or grate it, then rub into the flour until you have a breadcrumb consistency. You can do this in a food processor but be careful not to overwork it as the final result will be tough.
* Strip the thyme leaves from their stalks and grate the cheese. Add the thyme leaves and three-quarters of the cheese to the butter and flour.
* Beat the eggs and mustard into the milk and fold the liquid into the dry ingredients. Bring the mixture together until it has a rough pastry-like texture.
* Use your hands to bring the mixture together into a ball, cover with cling film and set aside while you make the cobbler filling.
* Trim, slice and wash the leeks.
* Peel the parsnips, carrots and potatoes. Cut them into roughly bite-sized chunks. Remove any tough stalks from the kale and shred it. Bring a large pan of water to the boil over a medium heat. Add ½ teaspoon salt and the carrots and potatoes. Bring the water back to the boil, turn the heat down and simmer for 3–4 minutes then add the parsnips. Bring back to the boil and simmer for another 3 minutes before adding the kale. When the water is boiling again, simmer for a couple more minutes until the vegetables are all just cooked. Drain very well and set aside.
* When the vegetables are drained, melt the butter in the large pan over a medium heat. When the butter is foaming, add the leeks and cook for about 5 minutes until soft. While they are cooking, peel and crush the garlic. Once the leeks have softened, add the garlic and cook it for a couple of minutes.
* Then stir in the mustard and flour. Mix until smooth and let the flour cook for a couple of minutes then add the wine and stock. Bring to the boil, stirring all the time to remove any lumps, and let the sauce thicken. Stirring with a whisk will help remove any lumps. At this point, roughly chop the parsley.
* When the liquid has thickened sufficiently to just coat the back of a wooden spoon, add the vegetables and parsley and stir in the cream. Remove from the heat and stir well so that everything is evenly coated in the sauce. Season to taste with salt and pepper, then tip half the filling into a pie dish or casserole. Set the other half aside to cool ready for freezing in a plastic box or bag.

* Take the cobbler dough from the fridge. Dust a worktop with flour, then roll out the dough to a thickness of about 2 cm. Using a large cutter or cup, cut it into several rounds – enough to cover the pie dish or casserole twice. You can re-roll any trimmings to make more rounds.
* Cover the vegetable mixture with half the rounds and sprinkle with half the remaining cheese. Sprinkle the rest of the cheese over the remaining rounds and layer them up in a plastic container to freeze with foil between to prevent them sticking.
* Bake the vegetable cobbler in the oven for 20–25 minutes until the scones on top are golden brown and puffed up.
* Freeze the remaining vegetable mixture and topping separately.

Lazy day supper – cooking instructions

* The vegetable filling must be thoroughly defrosted prior to cooking, but the scone topping can be cooked from frozen.
* Preheat the oven to 190°C/375°F/Gas Mark 5. Place the vegetable mixture in a dish and put the scones on top, straight from the freezer. Put in the oven and bake for 30–40 minutes until the top is golden and crisp. Check on the scones about halfway through – if they are getting too brown, cover the dish with foil and continue cooking.

March Week 2 – Overview

To start this week we have a recipe for baked mackerel stuffed with Persian spices and served with cumin and coriander carrots and spiced rice. It only takes about 1¼ hours to prepare and cook, so this Big Meal from Scratch isn't too demanding.

As with all big meals, there are leftovers to utilise later in the week. On this occasion extra rice is turned into Egg Fried Rice and leftover mackerel is smothered in teriyaki sauce and served with noodles. Both recipes take 30 minutes and 25 minutes respectively, so they are good midweek options. Of the two, the egg fried rice ought to be made first as rice only keeps for a day or so once cooked. If you are really pushed for time, the teriyaki sauce can be bought ready-made (see Quick Option, page 000).

A recipe for pomegranate and avocado salsa with marinated chicken breasts and tortilla wraps is a fresh and spicy Seasonal Supper that is ready in 20 minutes. For a Larder Feast that uses some of the best store cupboard ingredients available, spaghetti with an olive tapenade and marinated goats' cheese is hard to beat. This takes about 30 minutes from start to finish.

Beef stew is a reliable favourite, but adding a crust made from mustard-smeared French bread adds a new dimension. As with most stews and casseroles, this is perfectly suited to freezing, but slow cooking is essential so in total the recipe will take 2 hours.

March Week 2	Recipe	Time
Big meal from scratch	Persian mackerel, spiced rice and cumin and coriander carrots	1¼ hours
Something for nothing 1	Teriyaki mackerel with cucumber salad	25 mins
Something for nothing 2	Egg fried rice with pak choi or Chinese lettuce	30 mins
Seasonal supper	Chicken tortillas with avocado and pomegranate salsa	20 mins
Larder feast	Tapenade and goats' cheese spaghetti	30 mins
2 for 1	Rich beef stew with a French bread and mustard crust	2½ hours

All recipes serve 4 apart from the 2 for 1 recipe which makes 8 portions

SHOPPING LIST (for 4 people)

Meat and fish
6 × 400 g (approx.) mackerel (ask the fishmonger to gut them for you)
4 free-range chicken breasts, skinless
200 g cooked peeled Atlantic prawns
150 g good quality ham
1.2-1.6 kg braising beef (ask the butcher to cut into small even-sized chunks)

Dairy
80 g butter
200 ml soured cream or crème fraîche
200 g (approx.) goats' cheese, rind on (a piece big enough to cut into 4 rounds)
2 free-range eggs

Fruit and vegetables
10 carrots, approx. 1 kg
1 cucumber
4 ripe avocados
500 g (approx.) pak choi or Chinese lettuce
100 g (approx.) button mushrooms
2 celery sticks
2 bunches spring onions
5 medium onions, approx. 600 g
1 small red onion or 2 large banana shallots, approx. 60 g
8 garlic cloves
4-cm piece of fresh root ginger
1 large bunch fresh coriander
1 small bunch fresh parsley
4 sprigs fresh thyme
10-cm sprig of fresh rosemary
handful of fresh basil leaves
2 sprigs fresh dill
1 pomegranate
2 lemons
2 limes
150 g (approx.) frozen peas

Basics
150 ml olive oil
105 ml groundnut or grapeseed oil
1 baguette
2 tbsp plain flour
1 bay leaf
3 tbsp Dijon mustard
2 tsp mustard powder
1½ tbsp sugar
500 ml beef or chicken stock (fresh or made from a stock cube or bouillon powder)
salt and pepper

Store cupboard
600 g long grain rice
500 g spaghetti
400 g soba noodles or egg noodles
1-2 packets soft flour tortillas

200 g pitted large black olives (Kalamata would be ideal)
3 tbsp capers
5-8 anchovy fillets in olive oil
100 g pine nuts (toasted if possible)
60 g raisins
4 tbsp sake
4 tbsp mirin
2 tbsp Thai fish sauce
20 ml balsamic vinegar
5 tbsp soy sauce
1 tbsp oyster sauce
½ tbsp sweet chilli sauce
½ tsp chilli sauce (such as Tabasco)
2 heaped tsp coriander seeds
2 tsp cumin seeds
1-2 pinches of five-spice powder (optional for the Egg Fried Rice with Pak Choi or Chinese Lettuce)
generous pinch of ground cinnamon
generous pinch of nutmeg (ground or freshly grated)
pinch of ground allspice
pinch of ground cloves
1 tsp paprika (smoked if possible)
1 tbsp sesame seeds
300 ml red wine

Quick option, Teriyaki Mackerel with Cucumber Salad
6 tbsp ready-made teriyaki sauce; remove soy sauce, sake, mirin and sugar from the shopping list

Quick option, Tapanade and Goats' Cheese Spaghetti
3 tbsp ready made tapanade: remove olives, anchovies and capers

Serving suggestions
lemon wedges (Persian Mackerel, Spiced Rice and Cumin and Coriander Carrots)
greens (Rich Beef Stew with a French Bread and Mustard Crust)

To download or print out this shopping list, please visit www.thekitchenrevolution.co.uk/March/Week2

Persian Mackerel, Spiced Rice and Cumin and Coriander Carrots

The flesh of mackerel is succulent and its strong flavour works well with spices and dried fruits. In this recipe these are used as the basis for a richly flavoured stuffing. The recipe is based on a complicated Turkish dish where a whole fish is taken out of its skin and stuffed – we have opted for the far less complicated plan of stuffing the cleaned cavities. Do not be put off by the long list of ingredients – the recipe is straightforward, involving roasting carrots, stuffing and roasting the fish and making a simple rice pilaf. The mackerel is cooked with lots of powerful flavours so the rice and carrot dishes that accompany it are relatively simple.

The recipe includes extra mackerel for the Teriyaki Mackerel and extra rice for the Egg Fried Rice.

Persian mackerel
75 g pine nuts (toasted if possible)
2 medium onions, approx. 240 g
3 tbsp olive oil
generous pinch of ground cinnamon
generous pinch of grated nutmeg
pinch of ground allspice
pinch of ground cloves
handful of fresh parsley
2 sprigs fresh dill
60 g raisins
6 × 400 g (approx.) mackerel (ask the fishmonger to gut them otherwise you'll need to do it when you get home); includes 2 extra mackerel for the teriyaki mackerel
½ lemon

salt and pepper
Spiced rice
1 medium onion, approx. 120 g
2 garlic cloves
50 g butter
olive oil
600 g long grain rice; includes 150 g rice for the egg fried rice
small handful of fresh parsley

Cumin and coriander carrots
900 g-1 kg carrots
2 heaped tsp coriander seeds
2 level tsp cumin seeds
2 tbsp olive oil
½ lemon
1 small bunch fresh coriander

To serve
lemon wedges (optional)

GET AHEAD PREPARATION (optional)

* Make the stuffing.
* Gut and clean the mackerel, if necessary
* Prepare the onions, garlic and carrots.

1¼ hours before you want to eat prepare the rice and carrots

* Preheat the oven to 200°C/400°F/Gas Mark 6.
* If the pine nuts aren't ready toasted, place them on a baking sheet in the oven as it heats up and toast for 5 minutes.
* Peel and slice the onions for the stuffing and the rice. Peel and slice the garlic for the rice.
* Next, start preparing the rice dish. Heat the butter and a splash of oil in a large heavy-based pan over a medium heat and add the garlic and one-third of the onions. Stir until they are well coated with butter then turn the heat down to low. Put a lid on the pan and leave them to sweat for 10 minutes or so, then remove them from the heat and set aside – the rice gets added later.
* While the onions and garlic are sweating, start preparing the carrots. Peel and chop them into 3–5-cm chunks. Lightly crush the coriander and cumin seeds in a pestle and mortar or with a rolling pin.
* Put the carrots in a roasting tin or ovenproof dish, add the oil, the crushed cumin and coriander, some salt and pepper and toss together. Shake the tin or dish so that the carrots form an even layer, then put the carrots into the oven to roast until they are tender. This will take about 30–40 minutes.

55 minutes before you want to eat prepare the fish

* Heat a generous splash of oil in a second heavy-based pan and add the remaining sliced onions. Cook over a medium heat for 5 minutes so that they soften and start to colour slightly, then add the cinnamon, nutmeg, allspice and cloves and let them cook for a couple of minutes before removing the pan from the heat.
* Roughly chop the pine nuts, parsley and dill. Add two-thirds of the parsley, all the dill and pine nuts, the raisins and a slug more oil to the onions. Mix the stuffing together well and taste and season as necessary with salt and pepper.

* If the mackerel have not already been gutted, make a slit down the length of their stomachs and pull out all the innards. Wash the stomach cavities to remove any trace of blood.
* Season the cavities and fill four of the mackerel with the stuffing. Grease a roasting tin with oil. Place all the fish in the roasting tin and drizzle 1 tablespoon oil over the top, followed by some salt and pepper. When the carrots have about 20 minutes left to cook, put the mackerel on the top shelf of the oven and cook for 20 minutes.
* Give the carrots a shake when you put the fish in.

35 minutes before you want to eat cook the rice

* Put the rice in a sieve and rinse it in cold running water – this helps to remove any starchy dust that might make the cooked rice less fluffy.
* Meanwhile, put the pan of sweated onions over a medium heat and cook until they get a little of colour – this will take a few minutes. Once they start to colour add the washed rice and stir so that it is well coated in butter.
* Add an equal volume of water to the rice; the rice should then be covered by about 1 cm water. Season with salt and stir once. Bring to the boil, then cover with a lid, turn the heat down to its lowest setting and simmer for about 15 minutes. Don't take the lid off during this time and keep the heat very low. After 15 minutes the water should be completely absorbed and the rice cooked. If the rice requires additional cooking, add a little more water, replace the lid and steam for another for another 5 minutes.
* If the rice is cooked, take it off the heat and leave it to stand with the lid on until you are ready to serve.

5 minutes before you want to eat

* After 20 minutes in the oven the mackerel should have crispy skins and their fins should come out easily if pulled. This is a good indication that they are cooked; if the fins don't pull loose easily return the fish to the oven.
* When the mackerel are ready, squeeze the juice of half a lemon liberally over all six of them.
* Take the carrots out of the oven, squeeze the juice of the half lemon over them. Roughly chop the coriander and stir in.
* Stir the remaining parsley into the rice and season if needed.
* Serve each mackerel on a bed of rice with some carrots. Hand round lemon wedges if you think it necessary.

Afterwards

When the surplus rice (about 400–500 g) is cold put it in the fridge. Place the two remaining mackerel in an airtight container and put into the fridge. Any extra carrots can be served later in the week as a cold salad with a drop more olive oil and lemon juice, and a sprinkling of poppy seeds.

Egg Fried Rice with Pak Choi or Chinese Lettuce

A good egg fried rice is likely to be popular with everyone, even fussy kids. When done properly it bursts with flavour and different textures. The quantities for ingredients are approximate. Don't worry about following them exactly as they can contract or expand depending on what's available – and some can be left out entirely if you are feeding fussy eaters.

Egg fried rice
2-cm piece of fresh root ginger
100 g (approx.) button
  mushrooms
150 g piece good quality ham
1 bunch spring onions, approx. 8
2 free-range eggs
2 tbsp (approx.) groundnut or
  grapeseed oil
200 g cooked peeled Atlantic
  prawns
150 g (approx.) frozen peas
1-2 pinches of five-spice powder
  (optional)
400-500 g (approx.) cooked rice
  left over from the Big Meal
  from Scratch or 150 g rice
  cooked according to the
  instructions on the packet
salt and pepper

Pak choi or Chinese lettuce
500 g (approx.) pak choi or
  Chinese lettuce
1 garlic clove
1 tbsp (approx.) groundnut or
  grapeseed oil
1 tsp soy sauce
1 tbsp oyster sauce

GET AHEAD PREPARATION (optional)

* Prepare the ginger,
  mushrooms, ham, spring
  onions and pak choi.
* Make the egg strips.

*30 minutes before
you want to eat*

* First prepare all the ingredients. Peel and finely chop the ginger. Cut the mushrooms into slices about 5 mm thick. Chop the ham into rough 1 cm squares. Trim the spring onions and slice. Break the eggs into a bowl and beat together well. Remove the roots from the pak choi or Chinese lettuce and cut any particularly large leaves into about 10-cm lengths. Peel the garlic and slice finely.
* Now cook the egg fried rice. Heat 1 tablespoon of the oil in a wok or frying pan over a high heat. Add the ginger, cook for a minute then add the prawns (these can be added frozen). Cook stirring all the while, until the prawns have warmed through then add the peas and mushrooms. Continue to stir for 2–3 minutes then add the ham. Stir together for a minute or two then tip into a bowl and set aside.
* Next, make the egg strips. Turn down the heat under the pan, add a drop more oil then pour in the beaten eggs. Swirl the pan to create a thin pancake and cook until the eggs are no longer runny. Lift the egg pancake out of the pan and shred into strips about 1 cm wide and 3 cm long.
* Return the pan to the heat, add another splash of oil and then the spring onions. Fry over a high heat for 1 minute so that they start to colour, then add the five-spice powder (if using). Stir once or twice, then tip in the rice. Allow to fry for a few minutes, stirring every now and then so that the rice does not stick. Then add the prawn, pea, mushroom and ham mixture and the egg strips and stir well. Season and reduce the heat so the mixture heats through while you cook the pak choi or Chinese lettuce.
* Heat the remaining oil in another pan over a high heat. When it is hot, add the garlic and the pak choi or Chinese lettuce. Stir for a few minutes until the greens start to wilt, then add the soy sauce and oyster sauce. Allow to cook, stirring constantly so that the soy and oyster sauces reduce and coat the greens.
* Divide the egg fried rice between four warmed plates and pile the greens on top. Serve immediately.

**Something
for nothing 2**

Teriyaki Mackerel with Cucumber Salad

The sticky sweetness of Japanese teriyaki sauce works particularly well with the savoury flavour of mackerel. Here cooked mackerel fillets are basted in a teryaki-style marinade before being grilled under a high heat, to create a crisp skin covered in caramelised, sticky sauce. As it is an oily fish, mackerel can be heated twice without drying out. The intense flavour of the mackerel contrasts with the cool sweetness of the cucumber salad and dressing and the plain noodles.

If you do not have time to make the teriyaki sauce you could replace the soy soy sauce, sake, mirin and sugar in the recipe with 180ml of a ready-made version and add the ginger as per the instructions.

Teriyaki mackerel
- 4 tbsp soy sauce
- 4 tbsp sake
- 4 tbsp mirin
- 1½ tbsp sugar
- 2cm piece of fresh root ginger
- 400 g soba noodles or egg noodles
- groundnut or grapeseed oil
- 2 cooked mackerel left over from the Big Meal from Scratch

Cucmber salad
- 1 cucumber
- handful of fresh coriander
- 2 spring onions
- ½ tbsp sweet chilli sauce
- 2 tbsp Thai fish sauce
- ¼ tbsp soy sauce
- juice of 1 lime
- 1 tbsp sesame seeds

GET AHEAD PREPARATION (optional)
- Make the teriyaki sauce.
- Peel and chop the cucumber.
- Roughly chop the coriander.
- Trim and chop the spring onions.
- Toast the sesame seeds.

25 minutes before you want to eat

- Heat the grill to it highest temperature.
- Put the soy sauce, sake, mirin and sugar in a pan and bring to boil over a medium heat. Allow to simmer gently for about 10 minutes, or until the mixture is syrupy. Meanwhile peel and then grate the ginger and set aside.
- While the sauce is cooking, prepare the cucumber for the salad. Peel it and slice it into quarters lengthways, then deseed it and cut it into pieces about the thickness of a pound coin.
- Roughly chop the coriander and trim and finely chop the spring onions, using as much of the green parts as you can. Mix together in a bowl with the cucumber.
- Next, make the dressing for the cucumber salad. Mix together the sweet chilli sauce, fish sauce, soy sauce, sesame seeds and the lime juice. Toss the cucumber salad with the dressing.
- When the teriyaki sauce is syrupy, add the grated ginger and stir well.
- Cook the noodles according to the instructions on the packet.
- Lightly oil some foil and place it on a baking sheet, oiled side uppermost. Place the mackerel on the foil and brush them with about half the teriyaki and ginger sauce, then put them under grill for about 2 minutes, or until the marinade starts to brown and caramelise. Turn the mackerel over and repeat on the other side.
- Put the sesame seeds in a small pan and toast over a medium heat until browned – this will take 2–3 minutes.
- Divide the noodles between four warmed large bowls. Spoon the cucumber salad over them.
- Remove the mackerel from under the grill and, using a knife or spatula, separate the four fillets from the bones. Place one fillet on top of each bowl of noodles and salad.
- Drizzle with any remaining teriyaki sauce and serve.

Seasonal supper

Chicken Tortillas with Avocado and Pomegranate Salsa

Other than having to extract the pink, jewel-like seeds from the middle of a pomegranate, this meal is very straightforward. Kids will enjoy building their own wraps and adults will appreciate the fresh, healthy flavours.

Pomegranates have a sharp-sweet taste that is ever so slightly astringent. This complements avocado in much the same way as lime and lemon do. Avocados in season are not expensive but they still feel like a luxury, so it's good to make the most of them when they are abundant. There are many different varieties but the bumpy-skinned Hass avocados are the most creamy and rich. Whatever variety you choose, make sure they are ripe and yield slightly when gently squeezed.

Chicken tortillas
2 garlic cloves
1 tsp paprika (smoked if possible)
2 tbsp olive oil
juice of 1 lemon
½ tsp chilli sauce (such as Tabasco)
4 free-range chicken breasts, skinless
1-2 packets soft flour tortillas
1 tbsp groundnut or grapeseed oil
200 ml soured cream or crème fraîche
salt and pepper

Avocado and pomegranate salsa
1 pomegranate
4 ripe avocados
1 small red onion or 2 shallots, approx. 60 g
juice of 1 lime
1 small bunch fresh coriander

GET AHEAD PREPARATION (optional)

* Prepare the marinade.
* Prepare the chicken and add to the marinade.
* Roughly chop the coriander.
* Prepare the onions or shallots.

20 minutes before you want to eat

* Preheat the oven to 140°C/275°F/Gas Mark 1.
* First marinate the chicken. Peel and crush the garlic and place it in a large bowl with the paprika, oil, lemon juice, chilli sauce and a generous pinch of salt and pepper. Cut the chicken breasts into 1-cm thick strips and add them to the marinade, turning them over a couple of times so that each strip is well coated.
* Next make the salsa. Roll the whole pomegranate around on a flat surface under your hand to loosen the seeds. Cut the pomegranate in half and sit the two halves seed sides down on a chopping board. Hold the red dome of the one of the halves with one hand while tapping the fruit with a rolling pin or small, heavy pan – the skin will start to break as the seeds fall away from their membrane compartments. Collect them and place in a bowl.
* Now halve the avocados and remove the stones. Scoop out the flesh and add it to the pomegranate seeds. Peel the onion or shallots, chop them as finely as possible and add to the bowl. Add the lime juice and, with the back of fork, mash and mix well. Chop the coriander, stir in a small handful and season to taste.
* Now heat the tortillas according to the instructions on the packet (either in the oven, microwave, under a grill or in a frying pan) while you cook the chicken.
* Heat the groundnut or grapeseed oil in a frying pan over a medium heat. When the oil is hot, add the strips of chicken and cook for about 3 minutes on each side or until the meat is cooked and starting to caramelise on the edges.
* Place the chicken, salsa, soured cream or crème fraîche, remaining coriander and pile of tortillas on the table. Lay a tortilla out, fill with strips of chicken, spoons of salsa and soured cream or crème fraîche and sprinkle with the remaining coriander, then roll up the tortillas and eat straight away.

Larder feast

Tapenade and Goats' Cheese Spaghetti

Tapenade is an intense olive, caper and anchovy paste that is usually spread thinly on bruschetta. It is an excellent stand-by recipe because it relies almost entirely on ingredients from the store cupboard. Pasta is not the usual partner for tapenade but it works well. The recipe suggests adding pine nuts to the tapenade to give the mixture more of a creamy, rich texture. Goats' cheese is slightly dry and has a sharp flavour that combines well with the olive, caper and anchovies – it makes a luxurious addition.

It is possible to buy tapenade, so if you are in a very big hurry use this and stir some chopped pine nuts into it.

500 g spaghetti
1 garlic clove
5-8 anchovy fillets in olive oil
200 g pitted large black olives
   (Kalamata would be ideal)
3 tbsp capers
3 tbsp pine nuts
½ lemon
4 tbsp olive oil, plus extra for

greasing
200 g (approx.) goats' cheese,
   rind on (a piece big enough to
   cut into 4 rounds)
handful of basil leaves
   (optional)
salt and pepper

GET AHEAD PREPARATION (optional)

Aside from cooking the pasta you can do all the preparation for this recipe well ahead of time. The tapenade will keep covered in the fridge for 2 weeks. If you only have a little time:
* Peel the garlic.

30 minutes before you want to eat

* Preheat the grill to its highest setting.
* Put a large pan of salted water on to boil.
* Meanwhile, make the tapenade. Peel and crush the garlic. Whizz a small squeeze of lemon juice, the garlic, anchovies, olives, capers and pine nuts in a food processor or with a hand blender until you have a coarse purée. Then add the oil, pulsing with the processor or whizzing with the blender until it is well blended.
* When the water is boiling cook the pasta according to the instructions on the packet.
* Slice the cheese into four rounds. Lightly grease a baking sheet or flat, ovenproof dish with oil and lay the rounds on top. Place under the grill and cook until the cheese is melted, browning and bubbling. When it is cooked peel away any rind.
* To serve, toss the tapenade through the cooked spaghetti and top with a goats' cheese round. Tear some basil leaves over the dish and add a generous grinding of pepper.

Two for one

Rich Beef Stew with a French Bread and Mustard Crust

This dish is perfect for a cold, rainy March night. Although it takes relatively little time to prepare and freezes very well, it does need at least an hour and ideally longer in the oven to ensure the beef is melt-in-the-mouth tender. The crust is not, as one might expect, a pastry crust, but slices of bread that have been spread with mustard. The recipe calls for braising beef – this covers a multitude of cuts such as topside, silverside or chuck steak. This is a substantial dish but, if it's very cold and everyone is starving, jacket potatoes would go well and could be cooked alongside the meat in the oven. The stew is also excellent served with buttered greens.

The quantities below are for eight – half for eating today, the other half for freezing. The crust cannot be frozen.

2 tbsp plain flour
2 tsp mustard powder
1.2–1.6 kg braising beef(ask the butcher to cut it into small even-sized chunks)
4 tbsp groundnut or grapeseed oil
300 ml red wine
2 medium onions, approx. 240 g
2 garlic cloves
2 celery sticks
2 carrots, approx. 200 g
500 ml beef or chicken stock (fresh or made from a stock cube or bouillon powder)
good slug of balsamic vinegar

4 sprigs fresh thyme
10-cm sprig fresh rosemary
1 bay leaf
1 baguette
3 tbsp Dijon mustard
30g butter
salt and pepper

To serve
steamed spring greens

GET AHEAD PREPARATION (optional)

The entire dish can be cooked, up to the point of adding the bread crust, 2 days in advance. If you only have a little time:
* Prepare the onion, garlic, celery and carrots.
* Season the flour.

2½ hours before you want to eat

* Preheat the oven to 160°C/325°F/Gas Mark 3.
* Mix the flour, mustard powder and a good dose of salt and pepper in a plastic bag. Add the meat and shake well until it's coated in flour.
* Heat 1 tablespoon of the oil in a large, heavy-based frying pan over a medium-high heat and fiercely brown one-third of the meat all over. When this is nicely browned, put it into an ovenproof dish with a lid and repeat with the remaining batches.
* It is a good idea to deglaze the pan between batches. Do this by splashing in one-third of the wine and stirring it about to remove any of the tasty flavours from browning the meat. Wipe the pan with kitchen paper before returning it to the heat.
* While the meat is browning, peel and slice the onions and garlic and clean and chop the celery. Peel the carrots and slice them into 5 mm-thick rounds.
* Once all the meat is browned, wipe the pan out and return it to the heat. Heat the remaining oil over a medium-high heat, add the vegetables and garlic and brown them all over. Add the stock to the frying pan, bring to the boil and give it a good stir.
* Pour the vinegar and remaining wine into the frying pan and bring to the boil. Once boiling, add this liquid to the meat and vegetables and mix everything together well. Strip the leaves from 2 sprigs of thyme and set aside. Put the remaining sprigs, bay leaf and rosemary on top of the meat. Cover with a well-fitting lid or two layers of foil.
* Cook in the oven until the meat is tender – this will take 1½–2 hours. Stir from time to time to check how it's getting along.
* About 10 minutes before the meat is due to come out of the oven, slice the baguette and spread a good layer of mustard on enough pieces to cover the top of the dish.
* When the meat feels very tender take it out of the oven and turn the oven up to 220°C/425°F/Gas Mark 7 or its nearest setting. Remove the bay leaf and the thyme and rosemary sprigs.
* At this point take out half the beef and put it in a container suitable for freezing. Set it to one side to cool, then freeze.

* Cover the remaining beef with slices of mustard-smeared baguette – put them mustard side downwards. Dot the top of the bread with a little butter, sprinkle with the reserved thyme leaves and return the dish to the oven. About 10 minutes later the bread will be crisp and golden and the dish is ready to serve. Serve with steamed greens.

Lazy day supper – reheating instructions

* Defrost the meat completely before reheating.
* Preheat the oven to 160°C/325°F/Gas Mark 3, and place the beef in an ovenproof dish with a lid. Cook for about 30 minutes, by which time the meat should be thoroughly heated through.
* When the casserole is hot, top it with some mustard-smeared slices of bread, laying them mustard-side down. Turn the oven up to 220°C/425°F/Gas Mark 7.
* Dot the top of the bread with butter and sprinkle with fresh thyme leaves. Return the dish to the oven for about 10 minutes until the top is golden. Serve as above.

March Week 3 – Overview

Much of the food in this week's recipes could be described as being comforting and homely but without being dull. To start off there is a Big Meal from Scratch based on Bollito Misto, an Italian recipe in which a whole chicken is gently poached with sausages. This is accompanied by lentils and a herb sauce. This meal provides the basis of up to three meals later in the week. As an added extra, lentils can be turned into a simple rustic soup with olives. Two Something for Nothings include leftover sausages made into Toad in the Hole served with a caramelised onion gravy, and a flavourful Herb, Leek and Lemon Risotto made using the poaching liquid from the Bollito Misto.

Fish fingers are loved by children and guiltily enjoyed by adults too. The Larder Feast this week is a 30-minute recipe for home-made Fish Fingers and Baked Beans. Spring onions are very good in March and they are also very good in our chicken Noodle Soup Seasonal Supper. This fragrant soup combines chilli with the sweet crunch of caramelised garlic and shallots and the slippery voluptuousness of noodles – a meal in one bowl.

A Two for One recipe for Caribbean Macaroni Cheese is an interesting version of the family favourite which will be as popular with children as with grown-up kids.

March Week 3	Recipe	Time
Big meal from scratch	Bollito misto – poached chicken and sausages with lentils and green sauce Added extras – Lentil and vegetable soup Green sauce	1¼ hours
Something for nothing 1	Toad in the hole with onion gravy	45 mins
Something for nothing 2	Herb, leek and lemon risotto	40 mins
Seasonal supper	Spring onion chicken noodle soup	40 mins
Larder feast	Grown-up fish fingers and baked beans	30 mins
2 for 1	Caribbean macaroni cheese	40 mins

All recipes serve 4 apart from the 2 for 1 recipe which makes 8 portions

SHOPPING LIST (for 4 people)

Meat and fish
1.75 kg (approx.) free-range chicken
12-14 good quality pork sausages
2 free-range chicken breasts, part boned, skin on
4 frozen skinless, boneless coley or other white fish

Dairy
6 free-range eggs
750 ml milk
150 g butter
60-100 g Parmesan
300 g mature Cheddar

Fruit and vegetables
3 large carrots, approx. 350 g
250 g sweet potatoes
2 celery sticks
200 g pak choi or other Chinese greens
200-250 g baby corn or any other vegetable that will add crunch and sweetness
4 onions, approx. 460 g
2 large leeks, approx. 240 g
10 large or banana shallots, approx. 300 g
4 bunches spring onions
7 garlic cloves
5 sprigs fresh mint
6 sprigs fresh basil
4 sprigs fresh tarragon
1 large bunch fresh parsley
1 small bunch chives
a few sprigs fresh thyme
8-cm piece of fresh root ginger
1 small red chilli
2 lemons

Basics
280 ml olive oil
150 ml groundnut or grapeseed oil
2 slices bread for breadcrumbs (optional)
125 g plain flour
2 tsp light brown soft sugar
5 tsp Dijon mustard
a few black peppercorns
1 bay leaf
500 ml chicken or ham stock (fresh or made from a stock cube)
salt and pepper

Store cupboard
500 g macaroni
400 g risotto rice
300 g green or brown lentils (puy for preference)
350-400 g fat rice noodles or egg noodles
200 g polenta
3 × 400 g cans chopped tomatoes
2 × 400 g cans borlotti beans

2 tbsp capers
6 anchovy fillets in olive oil
75 ml soy sauce
1 tbsp balsamic vinegar
3 tbsp HP Sauce
2-3 tsp sweet chilli sauce
5-10 drops chilli sauce, such as Tabasco (according to taste)
generous pinch of herbes de Provence
generous pinch of paprika
175 ml red wine
400 ml white wine
2 tbsp sherry (fino or amontillado)
100 g tofu (smoked is good), optional for Spring Onion Chicken Noodle Soup

Serving suggestions
cabbage or greens (Toad in the Hole with Onion Gravy)
green salad ingredients (Herb, Leek and Lemon Risotto)
16 cooked peeled tiger prawns (Spring Onion Chicken Noodle Soup)
green salad ingredients or green vegetable (Grown-up Fish Fingers with Baked Beans)
salad leaves, olive oil and lemon juice (Caribbean Macaroni Cheese)

To download or print out this shopping list, please visit www.thekitchenrevolution.co.uk/March/Week3

**Big meal
from scratch**

Bollito Misto – Poached Chicken and Sausages with Lentils and Green Sauce

Poaching concentrates flavours and ensures nothing becomes dry. The idea for this recipe is based on a Bollito Misto, a north Italian dish involving a mixture of boiled meats. An authentic version, which is delicious, should include beef, veal, chicken, tongue, sausage and a calf's head. We have simplified this by just poaching a whole chicken and some sausages. Don't be worried by the idea of poached sausages – poaching is a very good way to let the true flavour and texture of a good pork sausage stand out.

Lentils are served with the meats along with a fresh, zingy accompanying sauce that contains herbs, mustard and lemon. There are lots of herbs here – use any leftover in the risotto later in the week or freeze them (see page 137).

The recipe includes extra sausages for Toad in the Hole, and surplus broth to make the Herb, Leek and Lemon Risotto.

Poached chicken and sausages
2 celery sticks
3 large carrots, approx. 350 g
3 medium onions, approx. 300 g
1 × 1.75 kg (approx.) free-range chicken
a few sprigs fresh thyme
1 bay leaf
generous strip lemon zest
a few black peppercorns
12–14 good quality pork sausages; includes 8 extra sausages for the toad in the hole
salt and pepper

Lentils
1 large leek, approx. 120 g

2 large or banana shallots, approx. 120g
2 tbsp olive oil
300 g green or brown lentils (puy for preference)

Green sauce
5 sprigs fresh mint
2 sprigs fresh basil
2 sprigs fresh tarragon
1 large bunch fresh parsley
1 small bunch chives
2 garlic cloves
2 tbsp capers
6 anchovy fillets in olive oil
juice of 1 lemon
1 tbsp Dijon mustard
150 ml olive oil

GET AHEAD PREPARATION (optional)

The lentils can be made 2 days in advance and reheated when required. The green sauce can be made a day in advance, but the herbs will lose their colour after a while. If you only have a little time:
* Prepare the celery, carrots, shallots, leek and onions.
* Prepare the herbs.

1¼ hours before you want to eat cook the chicken

* Clean the celery sticks, peel the carrots and keep them whole. Peel the onions and cut them in half. Strip the mint, basil and tarragon leaves from their stalks, set the leaves aside and keep the stalks to flavour the poaching chicken. Remove any stalks from the bunch of parsley and keep to flavour the chicken. Season the chicken inside and out.
* Place the chicken in your largest pan. Add the carrots, celery, onions, herb stalks, thyme, bay leaf, lemon peel and peppercorns and cover with water. Bring to the boil and skim off any residue that collects on top. Cover, turn down the heat to the lowest setting and simmer very, very gently for 50 minutes.

50 minutes before you want to eat cook the lentils

* Trim and thoroughly wash the leek, peel the shallots and chop both finely. Put the oil in a heavy-based pan over a medium heat. Add the shallots and leek and cook gently with a lid on for 10–15 minutes until they are soft and melting.
* While the shallots are softening, wash the lentils in cold running water. When the leeks and shallots have been cooking for 10 minutes, add the lentils and stir them about so they are well coated with the oil, shallots and leeks. Cover with water and simmer gently for 30 minutes. After 30 minutes the lentils should have absorbed all the liquid and be soft. If all the water is absorbed before the lentils have softened, add more. Taste the lentils and season. Cover and keep warm.

30 minutes before you want to eat cook the sausages and make the green sauce

* After 30 minutes of the chicken poaching, add all the sausages. If there's not enough room in the pan, poach the sausages in a separate pan of water, adding some of the vegetables from the chicken pan. Cook the sausages very gently for 20 minutes until they are firm and cooked.
* Now make the green sauce. Roughly chop the reserved mint, basil, tarragon and parsley leaves and chives. Peel and crush the garlic and roughly chop the capers and

anchovies Place the lemon juice, mustard and garlic in a food processor and blend for a minute. Throw in the anchovies, herbs and capers and slowly start to add the oil. When all the oil has been added season to taste. Place in a serving bowl.

10 minutes before you want to eat

* Lift out the sausages, carrots and celery. Leave the chicken to rest in the cooking liquor for 10 minutes. While the chicken is resting, cut the carrots and celery and four to six of the sausages in half and keep warm. If preferred, the sausages can be sliced and stirred into the lentils.
* Lift the chicken out of the pan (reserve all the cooking liquor), carve and serve on a warmed plate with the sausages and vegetables.
* Pass round the hot lentils. Serve the meat and vegetables with the green sauce and some hot stock.

Afterwards

* Put the eight remaining sausages in an airtight container in the fridge. Strain the chicken cooking liquor (about 1.7 litres), lift out the onions and discard any pieces of herb. Put the onions in an airtight container in the fridge. Store the liquor in the fridge. If you cooked the sausages separately don't save the liquor but do keep the onions.
* Use the chicken carcass to make stock (see page 495). Any leftover lentils and vegetables can be used for soup (see below) and any extra green sauce will go well with pasta (see below).

Added extras

Lentil and Vegetable Soup

* Chop up any leftover vegetables and a couple of tablespoons of pitted olives, add them to the lentils with some of the chicken cooking liquor and you have an instant soup to which you can add any leftover herbs. Blend a cupful for a thicker result. This soup freezes well.

Green Sauce

* The green sauce can be kept in a jam jar in the fridge for up to two weeks (though it may discolour a little). It is good with simply cooked vegetables, grilled fish or meat or stirred through rice or pasta.

**Something
for nothing 1**

Toad in the Hole with Onion Gravy

This is a good old-fashioned comfort supper that is completed by a rich onion gravy. The 'toad' batter has to be cooked in very, very hot oil in a hot oven. Anything less than searing heat will prevent the batter puffing up. Using sausages that are already cooked saves about 20 minutes of cooking time.

Toad in the hole
3 tbsp groundnut or grapeseed oil or fat from the surface of the chicken cooking liquor left over from the Big Meal from Scratch
8 cooked sausages left over from the Big Meal from Scratch or 8 sausages, cooked
125 g plain flour
2 free-range eggs
250 ml milk
2 tsp Dijon mustard
salt

Onion gravy
3 cooked onions from the Big Meal from Scratch or 3 onions, peeled, finely sliced and sweated gently for 20-30 minutes until meltingly soft
30 g butter
1 tsp light brown soft sugar
1 tbsp balsamic vinegar
175 ml red wine
300-400 ml chicken cooking liquor left over from the Big Meal from Scratch or good quality chicken or beef stock

To serve
steamed cabbage or greens

GET AHEAD PREPARATION (optional)
* Make the gravy - the longer it simmers the richer it will be.
* Brown the sausages.

*45 minutes before
you want to eat*

* Preheat the oven to 220°C/425°F/Gas Mark 7. Put the oil or fat for the toad in the hole in an ovenproof dish or roasting tin that measures about 25 x 20 cm and place in the oven so that the fat starts heating.
* Cut the onions into thin slices, put them into a large, heavy-based pan with the butter and sugar and cook over a medium to high heat until they start to caramelise. When they are golden brown, splash in the vinegar, shortly followed by the wine. Bring the wine back to the boil and simmer for 10 minutes or until it has reduced by two-thirds.
* When the oven has reached the required temperature the fat will be hot. Add the sausages and return the dish to the oven for a few minutes to let them brown. Turn them after a couple of minutes so that they brown more evenly.
* While the sausages are browning make the batter. Put the flour, eggs, milk, mustard and ½ teaspoon salt and mustard into a food processor with 50 ml water and pulse for 10 seconds at a time until you have a smooth batter – do not work the batter for longer than is necessary to create a smooth consistency. Once finished, remove the processor lid so that the batter gets plenty of air.
* Once the sausages are browned, take the dish out of the oven, give the batter a vigorous stir and pour it around the sausages. Return the dish to the oven and leave the batter to puff up and cook for 20–25 minutes.

*20 minutes before
you want to eat*

* By now the wine should have reduced, so add the cooking liquor or stock. Bring it to the boil then reduce the heat to medium and let the whole lot simmer away to form a sweet onion gravy. Once it develops the depth of flavour you like, leave it on the lowest heat to tick away until you are ready to serve.
* When the toad in the hole has been in the oven for 20–25 minutes it should be golden and firm.
* Serve straight away with lashings of gravy and steamed cabbage or greens.

**Something
for nothing 2**

Herb, Leek and Lemon Risotto

The combination of fresh herbs, lemon and a generous amount of Parmesan makes
for a risotto that's far from ordinary. This has become a favourite in Zoe's household.

Risotto is not difficult to cook, but it does require patience. Hot stock needs to be
stirred into the rice in stages so that the grains cook evenly. It's not necessary to stir
non-stop, but you do need to stir regularly to prevent sticking and to keep the liquid
well distributed. In all, this risotto will take about 35–40 minutes to make, depending
on which rice you use. There are three grades of risotto rice – arborio is the most
common and carnaroli is considered to be superior, but the king of risotto rice is
vialone nano. This takes less time to cook, so if you are in a hurry it is probably worth
the little extra financial investment.

2 large or banana shallots,
   approx 120g
1 leek, approx. 120 g
80 g butter
1 litre chicken cooking liquor left
   over from the Big Meal from
   Scratch (top up with water or
   stock if you don't have enough)
2 handfuls (approx.) of mixed
   basil, tarragon, chives and
   parsley (combined as you
   wish, but more parsley and
   chives than the rest)
60–100 g Parmesan

1 lemon
400 g risotto rice (see above)
150 ml white wine
salt and pepper

To serve
green salad

GET AHEAD PREPARATION (optional)

* Prepare the shallots and leek.
* Prepare the herbs.
* Zest the lemon.
* Grate the Parmesan.

*40 minutes before
you want to eat*

* Peel and finely chop the shallots and trim, finely slice and wash the leek. Melt two-
thirds of the butter in a large, heavy-based pan over a medium heat. Add the shallots
and leek to the butter, cover with a lid, turn the heat down low and cook gently until
they are melted and very soft. This will take about 10–15 minutes. Stir regularly to
prevent them colouring or burning. Meanwhile, bring the cooking liquor or stock to
the boil in another pan.
* Strip the basil and tarragon leaves from their stalks. Use scissors to cut the chives into
5-mm lengths, then finely chop the parsley and tear the basil and tarragon leaves into
small pieces. Mix all the herbs together and set aside. Grate the Parmesan and zest the
lemon and set aside.
* When the leeks and shallots are soft, add the rice and turn up the heat. Stir the rice so
that it is coated in the buttery leek and shallot mixture, then add the wine and let it
evaporate entirely, stirring all the while.
* Add 3 ladlefuls of the hot cooking liquor and turn the heat down so that it is
simmering and the rice is gently absorbing the liquid.
* As soon as the rice has absorbed almost all the cooking liquor, add another 3 ladles.
Stir from time to time to prevent sticking and so that the rice absorbs the liquid
evenly. Continue this process until the rice is soft to the bite and the risotto has a thick
and creamy consistency.
* When it has reached this stage, stir in the rest of the butter, all but 1 tablespoon of the
Parmesan, the lemon zest and the herbs. Season well, then cover the pan, remove it
from the heat and let the risotto sit for 5 minutes.
* Stir once again before spooning the risotto into warmed bowls with a final sprinkling
of Parmesan. Serve with a green salad.

Seasonal supper

Spring Onion Chicken Noodle Soup

This Chicken Noodle Soup is brimming with different textures and flavours. To start, chicken breasts are cooked in a broth. This is used as the basis for the soup which is served with prawns, a hot chilli relish and crispy fried shallots and garlic. We love this meal's simplicity and the fact that when you come to eat, every diner gets to pick and choose which sauce or seasoning they want to add to their soup. This added element of autonomy makes this recipe excellent for children and fussy eaters.

The recipe is based on a dish Rosie has eaten many times at her friend Imo's home. Imo's mum is a fantastic cook and has always been a culinary inspiration to Rosie.

2 free-range chicken breasts, part-boned, skin on
500 ml chicken or ham stock (fresh or made with a stock cube)
2 tbsp sherry (fino or amontillado)
350–400 g dried fat rice noodles or egg noodles
6 large or banana shallots, approx. 360g
3 garlic cloves
100 ml groundnut or grapeseed oil
1 small red chilli

8 cm piece of fresh root ginger
75 ml soy sauce
12 spring onions
100 g tofu (smoked is good), optional
200 g pak choi or other Chinese greens
200–250 g baby corn or beansprouts (or any vegetable you have that will add a bit of crunch and some sweetness)

To serve
16 cooked, peeled tiger prawns

GET AHEAD PREPARATION (optional)

The chicken broth, noodles, fried shallots and garlic and chilli dip can all be made in advance.
* Prepare the shallots and garlic.
* Deseed and chop the chillies.
* Prepare the ginger.
* Prepare the greens.

40 minutes before you want to eat

* Place the chicken breasts in a pan with the stock, sherry and 250 ml water. Bring to the boil, skim and simmer very gently until the chicken breasts are just cooked. This should take 10–12 minutes. Once they are cooked, remove from the pan from the heat and lift chicken from the hot liquid. Set the hot liquid in the pan to one side as this forms the basis of the soup.
* Meanwhile, cook the noodles according to the manufacturers instructions, drain and refresh under cold running water.
* While the noodles and chicken are cooking, peel and finely chop the shallots and garlic. Heat the oil and deep-fry the garlic and shallots on a high heat until they turn a light golden brown. Strain through a sieve and put the crispy shallot and garlic pieces into a small serving dish.
* Make the chilli relish by deseeding and finely chopping the chilli and peeling the ginger. Place the chopped chilli in a small dish with a little grating of the ginger and cover with the soy sauce.
* Finely shred or grate the remaining ginger, trim and finely slice the spring onions and cut the tofu into bite-sized cubes. Wash and break up the pak choi or other greens.
* When the chicken breasts are cool enough to handle, peel off the skins and cut the meat into 5-mm thick slices, on a slight diagonal.
* Throw the ginger into the reserved chicken cooking liquid and bring to a simmer. Add the baby corn or beansprouts and tofu and simmer for 4 minutes. Next add the pak choi or greens, spring onions and noodles and allow to heat through for a further 3 minutes.
* Serve the noodle soup in large bowls with the chicken and prawns on a separate plate in the middle of the table, so you can pick at them and dip them into the crispy garlic and shallots and/or the chilli relish. Alternatively add the chicken and prawns to the broth and sprinkle the garlic, shallot and chilli relish on top.

Larder feast

Grown-up Fish Fingers and Baked Beans

This is an adult version of that old store cupboard favourite, frozen fish fingers and canned baked beans. The recipe uses polenta as a crust for the fish, to make a sort of home-made fish finger. Canned borlotti beans, canned tomatoes and some dried herbs are a simple take on baked beans.

Coley is a much under-rated fish in the United Kingdom, yet it has a flavour and texture similar to cod. Although its flesh is slightly grey when raw, it turns white on cooking. It can be found in the freezer section of most supermarkets, is economical and can be cooked from frozen.

Fish fingers
4 frozen skinless, boneless
  fillets of coley or other white
  fish
200 g polenta
1 free-range egg
5 tbsp olive oil

Baked beans
3 tbsp olive oil
1 large onion, approx. 160g
2 garlic cloves
generous pinch of dried herbes

de Provence
generous pinch of paprika
250 ml white wine
1½ × 400 g cans borlotti beans
1 × 400 g can chopped tomatoes
1 tsp light brown soft sugar

To serve
green salad or vegetable of
  choice

GET AHEAD PREPARATION (optional)

The baked beans can be made up to 2 days in advance. If you only have a little time:
* Prepare the onion and garlic.

30 minutes before you want to eat

* Take the fish out of the freezer (there is no need to defrost it in advance as it will cook from frozen).
* Next cook the beans. Heat a very generous slug of oil in a heavy-based pan over a medium heat. Peel and finely slice the onion, add it to the oil and gently sweat it while you peel and crush the garlic. Add the garlic to the pan and stir it about for a couple of minutes before you add the herbs de Provence and paprika.
* Cook over a medium to high heat for 5 more minutes, then turn the heat up, add the wine and bring to the boil. Add the borlotti beans, tomatoes and sugar. Allow to boil then reduce the heat to a simmer and leave to cook while you cook the fish.
* Preheat the oven to 200°C/400°F/Gas Mark 6.
* In a shallow dish, beat the egg with 2 tablespoons water and a tablespoon of oil, and season well with salt and pepper. Put the polenta into another shallow dish and season it thoroughly.
* Pat the fish dry and dip the fillets into the polenta to give them a thin coating. Now drop them into the egg, then once again into the polenta – keep one hand for egg dipping and one for dry dipping then you won't end up with polenta-covered fingers!
* To cook the fish, heat about 2 tablespoons of the oil in a large frying pan over a high heat until the oil is smoking. Fry the fillets until they are crisp and golden on both sides, then lift them out of the pan and on to a baking sheet. Cook the fish in the oven for 10 minutes until an inserted skewer or small sharp knife meets no resistance
* Check on the beans and season them to taste. When the fish is ready, put a good pile of beans on each plate with a piece of fish on top.

Two for one

Caribbean Macaroni Cheese

This is macaroni cheese with a twist – and it's fantastically easy to make as you don't have to faff around making a cheese sauce. This is the sort of food kids absolutely love and that big kids will enjoy too. Nothing flash or pretentious – just good and simple.

This recipe makes enough for eight servings, half of which are intended to be frozen. It's possible to freeze the spare macaroni cheese in the dish it's baked in, but if you are short of space in the freezer you could cut it into four pieces once it has cooled and wrap them separately in foil.

This recipe is adapted from one by Lindsay Bareham.

500 g macaroni
250 g sweet potatoes
3 free-range eggs
500 ml milk
3 tbsp HP Sauce
2–3 tsp sweet chilli sauce
5–10 drops chilli sauce, such as
  Tabasco (according to taste)
2 × 400 g cans chopped tomatoes
2 bunches spring onions
300 g mature Cheddar
40 g (approx.) butter

2 slices bread for breadcrumbs
  (optional)
handful of fresh parsley
salt and pepper

To serve
salad leaves of choice dressed
  with olive oil and lemon juice

GET AHEAD PREPARATION (optional)

This dish can be prepared in advance up to the point where it goes into the oven, but if there are only a few spare moments any of the following would be helpful:
* Cook the macaroni.
* Peel, cut up and cook the sweet potatoes.
* Slice the spring onions.
* Grate the Cheddar.

40 minutes before you want to eat

* Preheat the oven to 200°C/400°F/Gas Mark 6.
* First cook the macaroni according to the instructions on the packet. Once cooked, drain and set to one side.
* While the macaroni is cooking, peel the sweet potatoes then cut them into 1–2-cm chunks. Place the potatoes in a pan, cover with water, season with a pinch or two of salt and bring to the boil. Once boiling, allow to simmer for about 5 minutes until the sweet potatoes are almost cooked – be careful not to overcook them or they will turn mushy and fall apart. Once cooked, drain and set aside.
* Meanwhile, make the sauce. Break the eggs into a arge bowl. Add the milk, HP sauce, sweet chilli sauce, Tabasco and tomatoes. Whisk together well. Trim the spring onions, chop them finely using as much of the green as you can and add them to the mix. Grate the Cheddar cheese and stir half into the sauce. Season generously with salt and pepper and stir well.
* Add the macaroni and sweet potatoes to the sauce and fold everything together so that it is well mixed.
* Butter two ovenproof dishes (or, if you prefer, one ovenproof dish and one foil container suitable for the freezer). Divide the macaroni mixture between the two dishes.
* If using, process or grate the bread into crumbs and sprinkle over the tops of both dishes.
* Finely chop the parsley and sprinkle it over the tops of both dishes along with the rest of the cheese. Dot the tops with butter, then bake in the oven for about 20 minutes or until the tops are brown and the macaroni mixture has set.
* Remove the dishes from the oven, put one aside to cool and freeze and serve the other with salad leaves of your choice.

**Lazy day supper
– reheating
instructions**

* If you can, defrost the macaroni cheese thoroughly before reheating it. Cover with foil and heat in the oven for 30–45 minutes at 180°C/350°F/Gas Mark 4. Remove the foil for the last 10 minutes of cooking.
* You can cook this dish from frozen but it will take about an hour. Place in a hot oven (180°C/350°F/Gas Mark 4), on a preheated baking sheet to get maximum heat into the base. Cook uncovered for the first 15 minutes to get some heat into the macaroni cheese, then cover with foil for the last 45 minutes.

KITCHEN REVOLUTION EXTRA

Herbs
Fresh herbs can make the difference between an ordinary dish and one that's extraordinary. Bought from a supermarket they can seem very expensive. If a recipe calls for a few sprigs of a herb and you end up buying a whole packet, put the leftover sprigs in the freezer (see page 13) rather than wasting them. In city centres huge bunches of coriander, mint, dill and parsley can be bought from Middle Eastern, Indian and Arabic shops at literally half the price of the mean packets sold in supermarkets. Not everyone has access to these shops, however, so another option is to grow your own. Even a pot on a window sill can produce sufficient quantities of thyme, rosemary, sage, chives or mint to keep a busy kitchen going.

March Week 4 – Overview

Fillet is the most tender and expensive cut of beef and something worth saving for a very special treat. It is best cooked hot and fast to prevent it drying out or toughening and in this recipe a spinach and walnut stuffing also helps ensure this special cut is served at its best. Altogether the recipe takes 2 hours, but most of this time is spent preparing the accompanying stuffing and Dauphinoise potatoes – the fillet cooks for as little as 20 minutes. When buying the meat for this recipe it's best to use a piece from the middle fillet as the end is thinner and harder to stuff.

The spinach mixture used to stuff the fillet is also used to make a Spinach, Walnut and Roquefort Soufflé later in the week. Soufflés have a reputation for requiring excessive culinary skill – they require care but if the steps of the recipe are followed in sequence they are not particularly tricky. They do, however, call for a little time. The preparation for a soufflé takes around 25 minutes and then it has to cook in a hot oven for about 35 minutes, so this Something for Nothing may be best made at a weekend, when there is a little more time.

The other Something for Nothing recipe is a Beetroot Hash served with Fried Eggs. Using the excess beetroot from the Big Meal from Scratch, this crimson fry-up can be on the table in 25 minutes.

Twenty minutes preparation and 20 minutes cooking produces a meal of cabbage Wrapped in Ham served with wholegrain mustard potatoes. This Seasonal Supper especially suits a relaxed midweek meal.

This week's Larder Feast is Vegetable Couscous with a Pomegranate Molasses dressing. The molasses are stocked by some supermarkets and most Middle Eastern food stores, but it can be replaced with a mixture of lemon juice, sugar and mustard.

For the Two for One this week a traditional recipe for Welsh rarebit is used as the topping for baked fish fillets – the combination of fish and melted cheese is rich but kept in check by leeks, mustard and plenty of Worcestershire sauce. The recipe takes just 35 minutes and produces enough to feed eight, with half intended for the freezer.

March Week 4	Recipe	Time
Big meal from scratch	Stuffed fillet of beef, Dauphinoise potatoes and beetroot with horseradish Added Extra – The best beef sandwich	2 hours
Something for nothing 1	Spinach, walnut and Roquefort soufflé	1 hour
Something for nothing 2	Red flannel hash with fried eggs	25 mins
Seasonal supper	Cabbage in ham with mustard potatoes	40 mins
Larder feast	Couscous with pomegranate molasses	30 mins
2 for 1	Fish rarebit	35 mins

All recipes serve 4 apart from the 2 for 1 recipe which makes 8 portions

SHOPPING LIST (for 4 people)

Meat and fish

750 g fillet of beef, taken from the middle or thicker end of the fillet

8 × portion-sized (120-160 g) skinless fillets of pollack or other white fish, such as coley, cod or haddock

8 slices good quality ham, approx. 15 cm long

Dairy

150 g Roquefort

350 g mature Cheddar or Double Gloucester

200 g (drained weight) feta marinated in olive oil or 200 g chilled feta

280 ml double cream

200 ml crème fraîche

500 ml milk

280 g butter

12 free-range eggs

Fruit and vegetables

1 kg waxy maincrop potatoes, such as Desirée

1.3 kg floury potatoes, such as Maris Piper or baking potatoes

750 g small to medium uncooked beetroot or 600-700 g cooked beetroot (not pickled in vinegar)

1 small Savoy cabbage, approx. 400 g

1.25 kg large leaf spinach or 600-700 g baby leaf spinach or 750 g frozen spinach

3 leeks, approx. 500 g

2 small onions, approx 180g

1 medium onion, approx. 120 g

4-6 spring onions

4 garlic cloves

2 small bunches of chives

1 bunch fresh parsley

handful of fresh coriander (optional)

handful of fresh mint (optional)

Basics

100 g breadcrumbs or 4 slices of bread suitable for crumbing

600 ml (approx.) chicken or vegetable stock (fresh or made from a stock cube or bouillon powder)

60 ml groundnut or grapeseed oil

50 g plain flour

½-1 tbsp wholegrain mustard, depending on taste

1½ tbsp mustard powder

salt and pepper

Store cupboard

300 g couscous

1 × 400 g can palm hearts

1-2 tbsp pomegranate molasses

1 heaped tbsp grated horseradish or 2 heaped tbsp horseradish sauce

85 g shelled walnuts

2 tbsp toasted pine nuts

1 tbsp sherry vinegar

2-3 tsp coriander seeds (optional)

½ tsp cayenne pepper

2 tsp Worcestershire sauce

2 pinches of nutmeg

75 ml bitter or ale (optional for Fish Rarebit)

1 tsp dried mint (optional)

Serving suggestions

crusty bread and salad ingredients (Spinach, Walnut and Roquefort soufflé)

watercress and/or rocket (Red Flannel Hash with Fried Eggs)

frozen peas (Cabbage in Ham with Mustard Potatoes)

new potatoes, butter, sage, watercress (Fish Rarebit)

To download or print out this shopping list, please visit www.thekitchenrevolution.co.uk/March/Week4

Stuffed Fillet of Beef, Dauphinoise Potatoes and Beetroot with Horseradish

This meal creates impact visually and gastronomically, and is ideal for a special occasion. The recipe is adapted from a Jane Grigson recipe. The Dauphinoise potatoes (potatoes cooked slowly with cream and nutmeg) can, once assembled, be left to their own devices, and the beetroot, once cooked, is simply tossed with a warmed dressing flavoured with horseradish.

The stuffing for the fillet involves minimal fuss and the beef itself, once stuffed, is browned in a fiercely hot roasting tin, then roasted for a short while in the oven. Nothing requires last-minute attention so the whole meal can be brought together at a fairly gentle pace.

The recipe includes extra quantities of spinach for the Spinach, Walnut and Roquefort Soufflé, and extra beetroot for the Red Flannel Hash with Fried Eggs.

Stuffed fillet of beef

1.25 kg large leaf spinach or 600-750 g baby leaf spinach or 750 g frozen spinach; includes 250 g for the spinach, Walnut and Roquefort Soufflé
30 g butter
2 small onions
3 garlic cloves
2 tbsp groundnut or grapeseed oil
85 g shelled walnuts
small handful of fresh flatleaf parsley
pinch of nutmeg (ground or freshly grated)
1 free-range egg
750 g fillet of beef, taken from the middle or thicker end of the fillet
salt and pepper

Dauphinoise potatoes

1 kg waxy maincrop potatoes, such as Desirée
200 ml milk
280 ml double cream
pinch of nutmeg (ground or freshly grated)

Beetroot with horseradish

750 g small to medium uncooked beetroot or 600-700 g cooked beetroot (not pickled in vinegar); includes 250 g for the red flannel hash with fried eggs
1 tbsp sherry vinegar
50 g butter
groundnut or grapeseed oil
1 heaped tbsp grated horseradish or 2 heaped tbsp horseradish sauce
1 small bunch chives

GET AHEAD PREPARATION (optional)

The beef can be stuffed and the potatoes prepared to the point of cooking in the oven. If the beef is stuffed beforehand remove it from the fridge a couple of hours before cooking to bring it to room temperature. If you only have a little time:
* Prepare the onions and garlic.
* Cook the beetroot.
* Peel the potatoes and leave covered in water until required.
* Prepare the spinach.

*2 hours before
you want to eat
prepare the
beetroot and the
potatoes*

* If using raw beetroot, place them uncooked in a large pan with half the vinegar, season, cover with water and simmer gently for 30-40 minutes until tender.
* Peel and thickly slice the potatoes. Pour the milk and cream into a large pan. Add generous amounts of grated nutmeg and seasoning, and bring to the boil. Add the sliced potatoes and stir around for a couple of minutes. Let the cream come back to the boil then simmer for 10-15 minutes, stirring occasionally. Transfer to an ovenproof dish large enough to hold the potatoes and creamy liquid.

*1¼ hours before
you want to eat
make the stuffing*

* If using large leaf spinach, destalk it and wash it thoroughly in cold water, then leave to drain in a colander. If you are using baby spinach, wash it in cold water then drain it in a colander.
* To cook the fresh spinach, heat the butter in a very large pan, add the spinach and cover. Let it wilt until it is just soft. You may have to do this in a few batches. Tip the spinach into a colander and place under running cold water. Put the colander over a bowl, then to squeeze out the excess liquid cover the spinach with a small plate and weigh this down using a couple of cans.
* If you are using frozen spinach, defrost and cook it according to the pack instructions. Drain it in a sieve and weight it as above.
* Preheat the oven to 180°C/350°F/Gas Mark 4.
* Peel and finely chop the onions and peel and crush the garlic. Heat a generous splash of oil in a small heavy-based pan and add the onions and garlic. Cover and cook gently over a low heat for about 15 minutes until very soft, stirring occasionally.

* Place the walnuts in the hot oven for 5 minutes. Use a clean tea towel to rub off any skins that come away easily, then roughly chop the nuts.
* When the onion and garlic mixture is soft, tip it out into a large mixing bowl.
* Chop the parsley and drained spinach and add to the bowl. Throw in the walnuts and season well with salt, pepper and grated nutmeg. Season very generously and mix well.
* Place half the mixture in a covered container and keep in the fridge for use later in the week.
* Beat the egg, add it to the remaining stuffing and mix thoroughly.

1¼ hours before you want to eat stuff the beef and cook the potatoes

* Trim any fat or sinew from the fillet. Insert a thin knife along the length of the meat to create a small passage through its core. Open up the passage into a 2.5-3-cm wide cavity using a wooden spoon handle. Fill the cavity with as much stuffing as possible. Allow the meat to rest, at room temperature, for 20-30 minutes.
* Put any excess stuffing into an ovenproof dish and cover with foil or buttered paper.
* Put the potatoes on the lowest shelf of the oven and cook for about 50 minutes. If they begin to brown before they are cooked cover them with foil.
* Drain the beetroot and leave to cool.

1 hour before you want to eat cook the beef

* Turn the oven up to 220°C/425°F/Gas Mark 7 and place a roasting tin on the top shelf.
* Thoroughly rub the outside of the fillet with oil and season well.
* Place the meat in the hot roasting tin and roast it on the top oven shelf for about 8 minutes, then turn it over and cook it for another 8 minutes for rare, 15 minutes for medium or 20-25 minutes for well done.
* If you have a larger piece of meat, use these timings as your guide: 10 minutes per 500 g for rare, 15 minutes per 500 g for medium and 20 minutes per 500 g for well done.
* While the beef is in the oven, peel the beetroot (if necessary) and cut them into 2-cm chunks and put them in a bowl.

15 minutes before you want to eat finish the beetroot

* When the meat is cooked, remove it from the oven, and leave it to rest for 10-20 minutes in a warm place. Turn the oven down to 160°C/325°F/Gas Mark 3 and place any surplus stuffing in the oven to cook for 15 minutes. Put plates and dishes in the oven to warm.
* Melt the butter with a dash of oil in a large pan and add the beetroot. Cook, covered, over a medium heat, stirring occasionally, until the beetroot is heated through.
* Increase the heat, splash in the remaining vinegar, add the horseradish and mix together. Cook for a couple of minutes, reduce the heat and snip the chives into the beetroot and season.
* Slice the beef and serve with the vegetables.

Afterwards

Put the remaining spinach and walnut stuffing (200 g), leftover beetroot (150-250 g), and any remaining beef, in the fridge.

Added extra

The Best Beef Sandwich

If you have any beef left over, slice thickly and slap between two chunky pieces of white bread. Spread generously with butter and either horseradish or mustard. Add salad, season well and savour every last mouthful.

Spinach, Walnut and Roquefort Soufflé

The word soufflé means 'puffed up', which is exactly what you will feel when you bring this risen, wobbly feat to the table. Soufflés have a reputation for being difficult to master but they are remarkably quick and simple to make. You just need to follow three basic steps: make a flavoured sauce; fold in stiffly whisked egg whites; place in a hot oven – and *do* not be tempted to open the oven before the cooking time is complete to check the soufflé's progress. This soufflé is especially simple because you are using the extra spinach stuffing from the Big Meal from Scratch as the basis for the soufflé flavouring. If you don't have any, use 250 g raw spinach cooked for 2 minutes, drained well and mixed with 1 tablespoon chopped walnuts and generous amounts of salt and pepper.

This soufflé is best made in straight-sided 1.4-litre soufflé dish, 20 cm in diameter, but a casserole dish of the same capacity will also work. It makes a good meal for four when accompanied by bread and salad. If you want to increase the quantities add a third to all the ingredients, use 6–7 egg whites and a 2-litre dish and add 5–10 minutes to the cooking time.

50 g butter, plus extra for
  greasing
50 g plain flour
300 ml milk
4 large free-range eggs plus 1
  egg white
200 g spinach and walnut
  stuffing left over from the Big
  Meal from Scratch or see above

150 g Roquefort
salt and pepper

To serve
crusty bread and salad

GET AHEAD PREPARATION (optional)

The sauce can be made and the
egg yolks and the stuffing and
cheese mixture can be added to
it up to a day in advance.

*1 hour before you
want to eat*

* Preheat the oven to 200°C/400°F/Gas Mark 6 and grease a 1.4-litre ovenproof dish with butter.
* Start by making the sauce. Melt the butter in a heavy-based pan and stir in the flour. Add the milk, using a whisk or fork to mix well. Stir continuously over a gentle heat until the sauce thickens to coat the back of a spoon.
* Once the sauce has thickened, remove it from the heat and allow it to cool for a few moments. Separate the four eggs. Crumble the Roquefort and mix with the spinach amd walnut stuffing. Beat the egg yolks into the sauce, one at a time, and when they are incorporated add the spinach and cheese mixture. Season very well with salt and pepper.
* Whisk all the egg whites until they form soft peaks.
* Once the whites are whisked, add 1 tablespoon to the egg and cheese sauce and fold in gently. This helps incorporate the rest of the whites.
* Fold in the remaining whites and pour the mixture into the prepared dish. It should come about two-thirds up the dish, allowing plenty of room for rising.
* Place in the middle of the oven for 35–40 minutes until the soufflé has risen and the top is brown.

**Something
for nothing 2**

Red Flannel Hash with Fried Eggs

Polly first tried this combination during a sunny brunch in San Francisco and at the time, some 15 years ago, it seemed like the very essence of Californian food – irreverent, flavourful and surprisingly simple. In a sense, although brunch takes place in the morning rather than the evening, it serves a similar function to our notion of supper – a casual meal prepared without excessive labour and eaten at leisure, ideally in convivial company.

Use the beetroot left over from the Big Meal from Scratch and this will require minimal effort. If you don't have any beetroot you can omit it altogether and simply double the potato quantities. Needless to say, the finished dish will not be a brilliant pink colour or have the earthy rich flavour of the beetroot. But it will still taste good.

500 g floury potatoes, such as
  Maris Piper or baking potatoes
1 medium onion
60 g butter
1 tbsp groundnut or grapeseed oil
150-250 g cooked beetroot left
  over from the Big Meal from
  Scratch
  (or see above)

2 tbsp crème fraîche
4 free-range eggs
handful of chives
salt and pepper

To serve
Watercress and/or rocket

GET AHEAD PREPARATION (optional)

* Prepare the potatoes.
* Peel and slice the the onion.

*25 minutes before
you want to eat*

* Preheat the oven to 140°C/275°F/Gas Mark 1 and put a large serving dish in to warm.
* Peel the potatoes and cut them into 2–3-cm dice. Place potatoes in a large pan of salted water and bring to the boil, then simmer gently for approximately 5 minutes. Drain when the potatoes are just cooked.
* Meanwhile, peel and slice the onion. Heat just over half the butter and oil in a frying pan. Add the onion and allow to cook over a gentle heat for 5–10 minutes or until it is soft and starting to brown.
* Add the potatoes and press down to slightly flatten and crush them. Cook over a medium heat until they start to crisp and brown, then turn them. You want the potato hash to have lots of brown crispy bits so resist the urge to keep turning before the edges or underside start browning. This will take about 15 minutes.
* Once the potatoes have delicious crisp edges, add the beetroot and crème fraîche. Fold together gently, allow to cook for about 5 minutes and season with salt and pepper to taste.
* Tip the beetroot hash into the warmed serving dish, cover and keep warm in the oven while you fry the eggs.
* Wipe the frying pan with kitchen paper, add the remaining butter and oil and put over a medium heat. When the butter has melted and the oil is hot crack the eggs and fry them gently.
* When the eggs are cooked, season them and place on top of the hash. Use scissors to snip the chives over them and serve with a simply dressed watercress or rocket salad.

Seasonal supper

Cabbage in Ham with Mustard Potatoes

This simple and unusual bake should convert even the most unenthusiastic cabbage sceptic. Here, crescents of Savoy cabbage, with its brilliant green, crinkly leaves, are wrapped in ham and baked with mustardy potatoes.

4 medium floury potatoes, approx. 800 g, such as Maris Piper or baking potatoes
1 small Savoy cabbage, approx. 400 g
60 g (approx.) butter, plus extra for greasing
4–6 spring onions
175 ml crème fraîche
½–1 tbsp wholegrain mustard, depending on taste
8 slices (approx. 15 cm long) good quality ham
handful of fresh parsley
salt and pepper

To serve
peas

GET AHEAD PREPARATION (optional)

The whole dish can be prepared in advance up to going into the oven, but if there are only a few spar. If you only have a little time:
*Prepare and boil the potatoes.
* Prepare and cook the cabbage.
* Mix the prepared spring onions with the crème fraîche and mustard.

40 minutes before you want to eat

* Put a large pan of water on to boil. Peel the potatoes and cut them into 2 cm chunks, then put them in a large pan of salted water. Bring to the boil then simmer for about 5–6 minutes, or until the potatoes are just cooked.
* While the potatoes are cooking, trim any coarse outer leaves from the cabbage but keep the root intact. Cut the cabbage in half lengthways, then cut each half lengthways again into eight – so that you have a total of 16 crescent-shaped slices, still attached by the root.
* Check on the potatoes and, if cooked, drain them well and set aside.
* Cook the cabbage in a large pan of boiling salted water for about 8–10 minutes until just soft.
* Preheat the oven to 200°C/400°F/Gas Mark 6.
* While the cabbage is cooking, grease an ovenproof dish large enough to hold all the ingredients with butter. Trim and finely slice the spring onions, roughly chop the parsley and put them in the dish and mix with the crème fraîche and mustard. Toss the potatoes with this mixture and add a good dose of salt and pepper.
* Now melt the butter in a small pan or in the microwave.
* Once the cabbage is cooked, drain and rinse under cold running water for a minute or two. Season the cabbage pieces, brush with butter and wrap a piece of ham around each piece.
* Lay the ham and cabbage rolls on top of the potatoes in the dish (they can overlap a little if you can't fit them in flat). Dot with the remaining butter, cover with foil and bake in the oven for 15 minutes or until hot.
* Serve with peas.

Larder feast

Couscous with Pomegranate Molasses

This recipe strays a little further into the wilds of hard-to-get foods than we would normally suggest, but once you've introduced your taste buds to pomegranate molasses you'll forgive us the hassle taken to locate it. Some supermarkets stock it in their cryptically named 'speciality' sections or in 'Mediterranean' sections, but it's pretty ubiquitous in Turkish and Greek grocery stores and most Indian food shops seem to sell it too. Pomegranate molasses is made from sour pomegranates boiled down to a thick brown liquid, not dissimilar in viscosity and colour from treacle. It is delicious served as it is with vanilla ice cream and also works well as a marinade for lamb or an accompaniment for fish. Here we use it as the basis for a dressing to accompany warm couscous. In the event that the molasses proves elusive, replace it with 1 tablespoon lemon juice mixed with half a teaspoon of sugar and half a tablespoon of Dijon mustard.

350 ml (approx.) chicken or vegetable stock (fresh or made from a stock cube or bouillon powder)
300 g couscous
1 × 400 g can palm hearts
handful of fresh coriander or 2–3 tsp coriander seeds
handful of fresh mint or 1 tsp dried mint

200 g (drained weight) feta marinated in olive oil or 200 g chilled feta plus 4 tbsp olive oil
1 garlic clove
1 2 tbsp pomegranate molasses (or see above)
2 tbsp toasted pine nuts
salt and pepper

GET AHEAD PREPARATION (optional)

* Cook the couscous and reheat it in the microwave or in a bowl over a pan of simmering water.
* Make the pomegranate molasses dressing.
* Roughly chop the fresh coriander and mint, if using.

30 minutes before you want to eat

* Bring the stock to the boil. Place the couscous in a heatproof bowl, pour the stock over the couscous until it is just covered. Cover the bowl with clingfilm and leave to stand for 10–15 minutes so that all the liquid is absorbed into the grains.
* Meanwhile, drain the palm hearts and slice them rounds about 1 cm thick. If using fresh herbs, roughly chop the coriander and mint. Drain the marinated feta and keep 4 tablespoons of the oil for the dressing. Chop the feta into small cubes if necessary.
* Make the dressing by peeling and crushing the garlic and whisking it with 1 tablespoon of the pomegranate molasses, 1 tablespoon water, the reserved oil from the marinated feta or the 4 tablespoons oil if you are using chilled feta, and salt and pepper. Taste and add more pomegranate molasses if you like. The dressing is meant to be very intense as a contrast to the other ingredients.
* When the couscous has been standing for about 20 minutes take the lid off and check to see whether it's ready. If there is any liquid left, drain well and then fluff up the grains with a fork. Fold in the feta, the fresh coriander or coriander seeds, the fresh or dried mint, and the palm hearts.
* Divide the couscous mixture between four bowls and pour the dressing over the top. Sprinkle with the pine nuts and serve.

Two for one

Fish Rarebit

Welsh rarebit or, as it was originally called, Welsh rabbit, is cheese on toast, only with a difference. The cheese is mixed with a little beer, mustard and lashings of Worcestershire sauce before being grilled. The origins of this peculiarly named cheese toast are not clear but it has a strong association with the early part of last century when dining clubs and grand restaurants had extensive menus of 'savouries'. The recipe below is a Welsh rarebit only in that it includes a beery-cheesy mixture. Rather than accompanying toast, this is used as the topping for fish and leeks. The combination of flavours works very well, the dish is quick to assemble and, like all Two for Ones, has the advantage that half can be frozen.

3 leeks, approx. 500 g
30 g butter
2 free-range eggs
1½ tbsp mustard powder
½ tsp cayenne pepper
350 g mature Cheddar or Double
   Gloucester
2 tsp Worcestershire sauce
75 ml bitter or ale (optional)
100 g breadcrumbs or 4 slices
   bread suitable for crumbing

groundnut or grapeseed oil, for
   oiling
8 × portion-sized (120-160 g)
   skinless fillets of pollack or
   other white fish, such as coley,
   cod or haddock
salt and pepper

To serve
new potatoes with butter and
   sage
watercress with lemon

GET AHEAD PREPARATION (optional)

The rarebit mix can be made
2-3 days in advance. If you only
have a little time:
* Trim, slice and wash the leeks,
   then cook them.

35 minutes before
you want to eat

* Start by preparing the leeks. Trim, finely slice, wash and drain the leeks. Melt the butter in a heavy-based pan with a lid and add the leeks. Cover with the lid and sweat gently for 5–7 minutes.
* Meanwhile, make the rarebit topping. Break the eggs into a large bowl, add the mustard and cayenne pepper and beat them all together. Grate the cheese (there is quite a lot of it so you might want to use a food processor) and add this, along with the Worcestershire sauce, to the egg mixture. Stir in the beer, if using, and the breadcrumbs. You should have a consistency that drops slowly off the spoon. Season to taste with salt and pepper and set aside.
* By now the leeks should be soft, so remove the lid from the pan and turn the heat up to evaporate any surplus liquid. Season the leeks according to taste and turn them on to a large plate or flat tray to cool a little.
* Preheat the oven to 180°C/350°F/Gas Mark 4 and heat the grill to its highest temperature.
* Oil an ovenproof dish large enough to hold four fillets of fish in a single layer. Place four fillets on the dish and season the fish. Mix the leeks into the cheese mixture and cover each of the four fillets with the leek mixture, making sure to use no more than half the total amount.
* Place the dish under the grill and leave the rarebit topping to get brown and set. It will probably slip off the sides a little but that does not matter. When the rarebit topping is brown and crisp (which will probably only take 3–5 minutes), place the fish in the oven to cook through for another 7–10 minutes.
* When the fish is cooked and the top melted and brown, serve immediately with boiled new potatoes tossed with butter and sage, and watercress dressed with lemon juice to cut through the richness of the cheese topping.
* To freeze the remaining four fish fillets, place them in one layer in a suitable container (plastic, foil or ovenproof dish). Season the fish and cover with the remaining leek and rarebit topping. Cover well and freeze.

Lazy day supper
– cooking
instructions

Defrost the fish completely then cook as above.

Cod, haddock, pollack and coley

There are about ten recipes in this book that call for cod, yet it is often the species cited as being over fished and unsustainable. This is true for the North Sea, but over 80 per cent of the cod sold in the UK comes from Icelandic waters that are generally well managed and felt to be sustainable. Nevertheless, we eat vast amounts of cod and put huge demands on the species, so there's good reason for seeking out alternatives. Haddock is perhaps the most obvious contender, but that, too, is under pressure, so consider using pollack or coley as an alternative. Pollack has white, firm flesh and a similar flavour to cod. As a good example of the craziness of the modern food industry, much of the pollack caught in Alaska is sent to China to be processed, and then transported back to Europe to be made into breaded fish products. Pollack is also landed by a small Cornish fishery and this is a product worth seeking out. Coley has a stronger flavour than cod, haddock or pollack, but this is often an advantage in recipes where flavours are powerful. When raw, coley has a slightly greyish tinge, but it turns white once cooked.

March puddings   # Treacle Tart

Treacle tart is sticky, rich, sweet and very moreish. For this reason we've given quantities to serve six rather than four – no one is going to complain if there is leftover tart to snack on. We have given the recipe for a very easy sweet pastry. You can use ready-made sweet pastry if you don't have the time to make your own – if you do, the total time for making the tart will be 45 minutes instead of 1 hour 20 minutes. Putting a layer of rolled oats over the bottom of the pastry before adding the filling helps to prevent it becoming soggy and removes the need for blind baking. You will need a 30-cm flan tin or pie dish.

Filling
60 g butter
12 tbsp golden syrup
1 lemon
150 g breadcrumbs (you will
    need approx. 6 slices bread,
    crusts removed)
2 tbsp double cream
1 heaped tbsp rolled oats

Pastry
300 g plain flour, plus extra for
    dusting
60 g icing sugar
200 g cold unsalted butter
cold water to bind
1 egg

To serve
cream (clotted cream would be
    particularly good)

GET AHEAD PREPARATION (optional)

* Make the pastry.
* Prepare the breadcrumbs.

1 hour 20 minutes before you want to eat

* Sift the flour and sugar into a large bowl and mix well.
* Grate the butter into the bowl, then, using the tips of your fingers, rub it into the flour and sugar to form a breadcrumb texture.
* Add the egg and use a knife to cut and blend the mixture. Add as much water as needed to bind the mixture together. Do not add too much or the pastry will be tough – 2 tablespoons should be about right.
* Bring the pastry together with your hands, trying not to be too heavy-handed. Press it out on a lightly floured surface into a rough round around 15–20 cm in diameter, wrap in cling film and place in the fridge for at least 20 minutes. Use the butter paper to grease 30cm loose-bottomed flan tin and set aside.

45 minutes before you want to eat

* When the pastry has rested for at least 20 minutes roll it out into a round sufficient to line the flan tin or pie dish. It should be no more than 5 mm thick. Press the pastry into the buttered flan tin, making sure you get it right into the sides. Prick it lightly all over. Trim the edges of the pastry.
* Heat the oven to 180°C/350°F/Gas Mark 4.
* Now make the tart filling. Melt the butter and golden syrup together in a pan over a medium heat. Grate the zest of the lemon and squeeze its juice. Make the breadcrumbs by whizzing the bread in a food processor.
* When the butter has melted, stir in the cream, lemon zest and juice and finally the breadcrumbs. The mixture should fall thickly from the spoon.
* Now scatter the oats over the bottom of the pastry case and pour in the filling mixture.
* Bake in the oven for 30 minutes.
* Remove from the oven, allow to cool for about 10 minutes and serve with plenty of cream.

March puddings

Chocolate Pots with Orange and Cardamom

Orange and cardamom make this a chocolate pudding with a difference. Although the fruit and spice cut through the richness of the chocolate and cream, it is nonetheless rich and luxurious – a little goes a long way. The quantities here will make enough for six generous or eight small servings. The pudding is quick to make but takes a few hours to set.

8 cardamom pods
100 ml milk
200 g good quality plain
  chocolate
1 orange
2 free-range eggs
250 ml double cream

GET AHEAD PREPARATION (optional)

The chocolate pots will keep in the fridge for up to 2 days.

2 hours before you want to eat (30 minutes preparation, 1½ hours chilling)

* Slit the cardamom pods open and prise out the seeds. Crush the seeds a little with the back of a spoon or in a pestle and mortar, and put in a small pan with the milk. Slowly bring to boiling point, then remove from the heat and leave to infuse while preparing the other ingredients.
* Break the chocolate into a bowl, cover with cling film and place over a pan of boiling water – try not to let the water touch the bottom of the bowl as this will make the chocolate lumpy. Leave the chocolate to melt.
* While the chocolate is melting grate the zest of the orange and squeeze out its juice.
* Separate the eggs then use a whisk the beat the egg yolks until they turn thick.
* When the chocolate has melted stir in the egg yolks, zest and juice, and strain in the milk.
* Whisk the egg whites until they form soft peaks and fold them into the chocolate mixture using a large metal spoon.
* Whisk the cream until it forms soft peaks and, using the metal spoon again, fold it into the other ingredients.
* Pour the chocolate into a large dish or distribute it between six or eight small ramekins or pots (espresso coffee cups will do). Cover with cling film and refrigerate for a couple of hours or overnight until set.

March puddings

Honey Cake with Citrus Syrup

This cake is as light as a cloud. It can be eaten straight from the oven with a warm citrus syrup poured over the top, or cold and split into two and filled with Greek yoghurt or whipped cream and passion fruit.

Honey cake
butter, for greasing
1 lemon
150 ml (approx.) milk
5 free-range eggs
½ tsp baking powder
125 g semolina
125 g ground almonds
7 tbsp clear honey
pinch of salt

Citrus syrup
2 passion fruit
100 g unrefined golden sugar
juice of 1 lemon

To serve
Greek yoghurt

1 hour before you want to eat

* Preheat the oven to 180°C/350°F/Gas Mark 4.
* Lightly grease a 18–20 cm round cake tin approximately 10 cm deep with butter. Grate the zest of the lemon and squeeze out its juice. Put the juice in a jug and add milk to make up 150 ml liquid. Next, separate the eggs and sift the baking powder into a bowl with the semolina and almonds.
* Whisk the egg yolks with the lemon zest and honey until light and fluffy. Carefully clean and dry the whisk, then whisk the whites with the salt until they form soft peaks.
* Now stir the baking powder, semolina and almond mixture into the yolk mixture and, when it starts to get difficult, add the milk and blend until smooth.
* Add a big spoonful of the egg whites to the yolk mixture – this will make folding in the rest of the whites easier. Gently fold the remaining whites into the yolk mixture, trying to keep in as much air as possible. Pour this mixture into the cake tin and bake for 40 minutes, until firm.
* While the cake is in the oven, make the syrup. Halve the passion fruit and scoop out the pulp. Dissolve the sugar in 250 ml water over a medium heat. Once the sugar has dissolved, turn the heat up and simmer rapidly for a few minutes until the liquid becomes syrupy. Add the lemon juice and passion fruit pulp and leave to cool until the cake is ready.
* Once the cake is out of the oven, pierce a few holes in the top with a cocktail stick, then pour the syrup over it. Let it sit for 10 minutes while the syrup soaks in.
* Take the cake out of the tin and slice it while it is still warm. Serve with Greek yoghurt.

March puddings   # Roast pineapple

At this time of the year, when British fruit is on the wane, there are usually a lot of sweet juicy pineapples about. These can easily be turned into delicious and interesting puddings. The best part of this recipe is that you don't need to peel the pineapple!

1 medium pineapple, approx.
  450 g
2 star anise
pinch of freshly ground black
  pepper
pinch of ground nutmeg
50 g butter
200 ml rum or orange juice

To serve
lime or coconut sorbet

25 minutes before you want to eat

* Preheat the oven to 220°C/425°F/Gas Mark 7 and preheat a roasting tin.
* Top and tail the pineapple and cut it in half lengthways, then cut each half into quarters so that you are left with eight boat-shaped slices. Remove the woody pineapple core by cutting straight down the flesh.
* Crush the star anise either in a pestle and mortar or under a clean tea towel with a rolling pin. Mix the star anise with the pepper and nutmeg. Lay all the pieces of pineapple in a line and sprinkle half the spice mixture over them.
* Heat half the butter in a frying pan over a medium heat and when it is foaming add four pieces of pineapple, spiced sides down, and leave them to brown – this will take about 3 minutes. While these pieces are browning, sprinkle their top sides with a quarter of the remaining spice mixture.
* Once the pieces are browned, turn them over and after frying for a minute put them into the roasting tin in the oven, flesh sides up, with all the pan juices.
* Melt the rest of the butter in the frying pan and repeat the process with the remaining four pieces of pineapple, then add them to the roasting tin. Cook in the oven until the pineapple pieces are soft and golden all over – this will take about 5–10 minutes.
* Return the frying pan to the heat, pour in the rum or orange juice and bring to the boil. Remove from the heat until the pineapple pieces are ready.
* Once the pineapple pieces are ready, turn the oven off, lift the pieces on to a plate and return them to the oven to keep warm while you make a sauce.
* Pour any juices from the tin into the frying pan with the rum or orange juice and place over a high heat. Bring to a simmer and let the sauce bubble away, swirling the pan all the time. Add a little water if it seems thick – you want a thick pouring consistency.
* Take the pineapple out of the oven and serve it with the sauce and a scoop of sorbet; we would favour lime or coconut.

APRIL

April is when spring really arrives, and early lettuces, sorrel, radishes, wild garlic and watercress are signs that summer is around the corner. We begin the month with an Easter dish of Roast Lamb Stuffed with Green Olives and Anchovies, served with Garlic Beans and Spring Vegetables and, later in the week, Poached Eggs with Spinach and Cream. Sorrel and wild garlic are hard to find in shops, but we include each of them because they grow abundantly at this time of year and also because sorrel can easily be replaced by spinach with lemon juice and the wild garlic by the cultivated variety. Rhubarb and Almond Tart is simple to make and will be popular with marzipan lovers and our spicy sponge with little Easter eggs baked into it makes a good alternative to the traditional Simnel cake.

April	Week 1	Week 2	Week 3	Week 4
Big meal from scratch	Olive and anchovy stuffed lamb with garlic flageolet beans and spring vegetables	Spanish chicken casserole with wild rice and spring greens	Smoked haddock, peas and bacon with jacket potatoes and mustard cabbage	Pork chops, leeks and prunes in cider with mash and broccoli
Something for nothing 1	Moussaka	French onion soup	Fish pie	Greek butter bean and broccoli salad
Something for nothing 2	Pasta ribbons with tomato flageolet beans	Wild rice, mushroom and spinach loaf	Stuffed baked potatoes	Smoked salmon, potato pancakes and beetroot salad
Seasonal supper	Roast duck breasts with radish and potato salad	Wild garlic and bacon pasta	Goats' cheese bruschetta with beetroot and rocket salad	Baked omelette with butternut squash and sorrel
Larder feast	Spring eggs	Sardine and tomato tart	Spicy sweetcorn with sesame seeds and tomatoes	Japanese miso noodle soup
2 for 1	Chowder	Chinese pork dumplings	Rabbit (or chicken) with almonds, pine nuts and garlic	Italian sausage and bean casserole
Puddings	Bread pudding	Koliva – Serbian sweet wheat pudding	Rhubarb and almond tart	Alternative Easter cake

April Week 1 – Overview

Though the date for Easter changes year by year, it's often around late March or early April, and this week's recipes, particularly the Big Meal from Scratch and the Two for One, might be useful if hoards of people require feeding.

It's traditional to eat lamb at Easter, so the big meal is boned Lamb Stuffed with Olives and Anchovies, accompanied by Garlicky Flageolet Beans and Spring Vegetables. Don't worry if you're cooking for anchovy sceptics as the flavour softens and melts into the lamb. Altogether this meal takes 2½ hours to cook, so leave yourself plenty of time. The Chowder – the Two for One – can be ready in about 40 minutes, expands quite easily to accommodate more guests, and reheats very well. Served with hunks of buttered warm bread, it is intensely flavoured and filling.

Leftovers from the Big Meal from Scratch make two meals later in the week. Any extra lamb is used for Moussaka, and the garlic beans form the basis for a pasta bake.

The appearance of the season's radishes prompts a Seasonal Supper recipe for Roast Duck Breasts with Radish and Potato Salad. Also quick is a Larder Feast recipe for eggs poached in a delicious broth with seasoned spinach and peas.

April Week 1	Recipe	Time
Big meal from scratch	Olive and anchovy stuffed lamb with garlic flageolet beans and spring vegetables	2½ hours
Something for nothing 1	Moussaka	45 mins
Something for nothing 2	Pasta ribbons with tomato flageolet beans	40 mins
Seasonal supper	Roast duck breasts with radish and potato salad	25 mins
Larder feast	Spring eggs	25 mins
2 for 1	Chowder	40 mins

All recipes serve 4 apart from the 2 for 1 recipe which makes 8 portions

SHOPPING LIST (for 4 people)

Meat and fish
1 × 1.6-1.8 kg boned shoulder of lamb
4 duck breasts
200-250 g rashers rindless free-range
  smoked streaky bacon
350 g skinned smoked pollack or haddock
  fillets
450 g skinned unsmoked pollack or haddock
  fillets

Dairy
1.2 litres milk
450 g Greek yoghurt
80 ml single cream
300 g feta
50 g (approx.) Parmesan or Gruyère
8 large free-range eggs
115-25 g butter

Fruit and vegetables
2 aubergines, approx. 400 g
1 kg large, floury potatoes, such as Marish
  Piper or baking potatoes
400-500 g small new potatoes
300 g carrots (baby ones if possible)
400 g spring greens
5 celery sticks
2-3 bunches radishes (with leaves if
  possible)
6 medium onions, approx. 720 g
4 medium red onions, approx. 500 g
1 large or banana shallot, approx. 30 g
26 garlic cloves
1 small bunch fresh parsley
6 sprigs fresh mint
4 sprigs thyme
2 sprigs fresh rosemary, approx. 10 cm long
2 sprigs fresh dill (optional for Pasta
  Ribbons with Tomato Fageolet Beans)
 5 sprigs fresh or 1 tsp dried oregano or
  marjoram
1 lemon
500 g frozen spinach
300 g frozen or canned petit pois peas

Basics
160 ml olive oil
30 ml groundnut or grapeseed oil
75 g breadcrumbs or 3 slices bread suitable
  for crumbing
30-40 g plain flour
½ tbsp Dijon mustard
2-3 black peppercorns
3 bay leaves
500 ml vegetable stock (made from a stock
  cube or bouillon powder)
200 ml vegetable or chicken stock (made
  from a stock cube or bouillon powder)
salt and pepper

Store cupboard
300-400 g fettucine pasta (green if you can
  get it)
3 × 400 g cans flageolet beans or 500 g dried
  beans
1 × 400 g can chopped tomatoes
1 × 200 g can chopped tomatoes
150 g (approx.) pitted green olives in brine
50 g olives stuffed with anchovies
5-6 anchovy fillets in olive oil
2 tsp capers
1½ tbsp sherry vinegar
1 tsp ground cinnamon
1 tsp paprika
¼ tsp ground mace
pinch of saffron threads
1 bottle white wine
75 ml red wine
2 tsp dried dill (optional for Lamb and
  Spring Vegetables)
1 tsp dried oregano or marjoram (optional for
  Pasta Ribbons with Tomato Flageolet Beans)

Serving suggestions
rocket or salad leaves (Pasta Ribbons with
  Tomato Flageolet Beans)
bread or new potatoes (Spring Eggs)
crusty bread and a green vegetable (Chowder)

To download or print out this shopping list,
please visit www.thekitchenrevolution.co.uk/April/
Week1

**Big meal
from scratch**

Olive and Anchovy Stuffed Lamb with Garlic Flageolet Beans and Spring Vegetables

The week starts with a recipe for lamb stuffed with garlic, rosemary, anchovies and olives that is typically Mediterranean. To the uninitiated, anchovies may not seem like an obvious partner for lamb, but they lose their distinctive taste in the cooking and combine meltingly with the meat.

As far as timing goes, the first thing to do is make the stuffing, prepare the lamb and get it in the oven. When the lamb has been cooking for a while the flageolet beans are laid underneath so that they cook gently and absorb any juices that seep out. You will therefore need a rack to sit the lamb on, and a roasting tin that is deep enough to hold all the beans. This recipe calls for a lot of garlic – an easy way to peel the cloves is to soak them in hot water for ten minutes beforehand.

The recipe includes extra ingredients for the Moussaka and extra flageolet beans for the Pasta Ribbons with Tomato Flageolet Beans.

<u>Olive and anchovy stuffed lamb</u>
2 garlic cloves
50 g olives stuffed with
 anchovies
150 g (approx.) pitted green
 olives in brine
5-6 anchovy fillets in olive oil
2 tsp capers
1 lemon
½ tbsp Dijon mustard
1 sprig rosemary, approx. 10 cm
 long
75-100 ml olive oil
1 × 1.6-1.8 kg boned shoulder of
 lamb; includes 600 g extra for
 the moussaka
salt and pepper

<u>Garlic flageolet beans</u>
olive oil
2 medium red onions, approx.
 240 g
20 garlic cloves
10 cm sprig rosemary
4 sprigs thyme
1 bay leaf
1 bottle white wine
3 × 400 g cans flageolet beans or
 500 g dried beans soaked
 overnight and cooked for 1 hour
 in vegetable stock; includes
 600 g canned beans or 300 g
 dried beans for the tomato
 flageolet beans
500 ml vegetable stock (made
 from a stock cube or bouillon
 powder)

<u>Spring vegetables</u>
300 g carrots (baby ones,
 if possible)
60 g butter
400 g spring greens
3 sprigs fresh mint

<u>GET AHEAD PREPARATION (optional)</u>

The tapenade, stuffing and beans can be made and the lamb can be stuffed a few hours in advance. If you only have a little time:
* Prepare all the garlic.
* Peel and slice the onions.
* Prepare the carrots and greens.

*2¼ hours before
you want to eat
stuff the lamb*

* Peel the garlic and put it in a food processor. Drain the olives stuffed with anchovies and add these to the processor. Tip the pitted green olives, anchovies and capers into a sieve and rinse well under cold running water. Add these to the processor. Grate the zest from half the lemon and add it, along with the mustard, to the other ingredients. Strip the leaves from the rosemary sprig, chop them finely and throw them into the processor. Add about ½ teaspoon pepper and a generous squeeze of lemon juice. Then pulverise the mixture while slowly adding the oil. Taste and adjust the seasoning as necessary. The mixture should have the same consistency as pesto.
* Preheat the oven to 220°C/425°F/Gas Mark 7.
* If the lamb has been rolled already, unroll it. If the lamb has been held together by a net, keep this to tie the lamb up again once it is filled with stuffing. Place the lamb skin side down on a chopping board, season and spread the olive and anchovy stuffing in the middle.
* Roll up the lamb, tucking any stray pieces of meat well inside. Either ease the rolled meat back into its net, or fasten it securely with string and/or skewers.
* Place the lamb on a rack over a large roasting tin with the seam of the meat facing down. Season the joint well and roast for about 20 minutes, before reducing the heat to 180°C/350°F/Gas Mark 4 and cooking it for another 1¼ hours. If you like your lamb rare or well done, once the heat is reduced follow these timings per 500g
10 minutes for rare, 15 minutes for medium and 20 minutes for well done.

*1½ hours before
you want to eat
prepare the beans*

* Heat a good splash of oil in a heavy-based pan over a medium heat and peel the onions and slice them thinly. Add the onions to the pan, cover and leave over a low heat for 10 minutes or so. In the meantime, peel and roughly chop the garlic. When the onions are

soft add the garlic and turn the heat up so they both get a golden tinge, stirring to avoid any burning or sticking.

* Add the herbs and wine to the pan. Bring to the boil, simmer for 1–2 minutes then add the drained beans. Stir well and add enough stock to just cover the beans. Season well and bring back to a simmer.

1 hour before you want to eat

* Take the lamb and roasting tin out of the oven and carefully lift off the rack with the lamb. Pour the beans into the tin, stir and pop the lamb and its rack back on top. Return the tin to the oven.
* After 20 minutes give the beans a stir and baste the lamb with liquid from the tin.

30 minutes before you want to eat

* If using, wash and scrape baby carrots. Peel large carrots and cut them into 3 cm chunks. Put the carrots into a large pan, add some salt, all the butter, and enough water to come halfway up, then leave until ready to cook.
* Trim the greens, tear the leaves into halves or quarters and set aside.
* After 1 hour at 180°C/350°F/Gas Mark 4, remove the lamb from the oven, place it on a carving board, cover with foil and allow to rest for at least 20 minutes. Turn the oven off and leave the beans inside to keep warm. Add serving dishes and plates as well.
* If the beans have a lot of liquid place them on the hob and reduce.

15 minutes before you want to eat cook the carrots and greens

* Bring the carrots to the boil and simmer for 7 minutes until they are starting to soften.
* After 7 minutes throw the greens on top of the carrots, cover with a lid and let them steam for 5 minutes until soft, by which time the carrots will be tender too. While the greens and carrots are cooking, roughly chop the mint.
* Remove the lid from the pan for 1–2 minutes to reduce the liquid, stir in the mint and season to taste.
* When the carrots and greens are cooked, tip them into a serving dish.
* Check the beans for seasoning and turn them into a serving dish.
* Remove the foil from the lamb and carve. Pour any juices from the lamb into the flageolet bean mixture.
* Serve slices of lamb on top of a generous spoonful of beans and pass the carrot and greens round separately.

Afterwards

Put the leftover lamb (450-500 g) and remaining beans (600 g) in separate containers, cover and refrigerate for use later in the week.

Moussaka

Moussaka is a classic Greek dish of lamb layered with aubergines. It is a great way to use cooked lamb and this recipe has the added bonus of replacing a traditional white sauce with a mixture of Greek yoghurt, feta, eggs and herbs. This has the advantage of being lighter as well as being a time saver. If you have no lamb left over from the Big Meal from Scratch, add 500 g lamb mince when you brown the onions in the recipe.

2 aubergines, approx. 400 g
3 tbsp olive oil
2 large potatoes (King Edward, if possible), approx. 300 g
2 medium onions, approx. 240 g
2 garlic cloves
450–550 g cooked lamb left over from the Big Meal from Scratch
1 tsp ground cinnamon
1 tsp paprika
1 bay leaf
75 ml red wine
1 × 200 g can chopped tomatoes

2 sprigs fresh dill or 2 tsp dried dill
salt and black pepper

For the topping
3 large free-range eggs
3 sprigs fresh mint
a few sprigs fresh parsley
300 g feta
450 g Greek yoghurt

GET AHEAD PREPARATION (optional)

The moussaka can be cooked up to 2 days in advance and reheated, covered in foil, in a gentle oven. If you only have a little time:
* Slice and roast the aubergines.
* Prepare the onions and garlic.
* Prepare and cook the potatoes
* Make the lamb and tomato sauce.
* Make the egg and feta topping.

45 minutes before you want to eat

* Preheat the oven to 200°C/400°F/Gas Mark 6. Cut the aubergines into 1-cm slices, place on a baking sheet and toss with 2 tablespoons of the oil. Place in the oven so that they soften and turn slightly brown – this will take about 20 minutes.
* Wash and peel the potatoes and cut them into 1 cm slices. Put them into a pan, cover with water, add a pinch of salt and bring to the boil, then simmer for 10 minutes until just cooked.
* Peel and slice the onions, then heat the rest of the oil in a heavy-based pan over a medium heat, add the onions and cook gently for about 10 minutes.
* Peel and crush the garlic and finely chop the lamb or pulse it a couple of times in a food processor – take care not to overprocess the meat.
* Now turn the heat up under the onions, add the garlic, cinnamon and paprika and stir for a couple minutes. Then add the lamb, mix together well and, keeping the pan on a high heat, brown the meat for a couple of minutes.
* Finally, add the bay leaf, wine and tomatoes and bring to a simmer. Reduce the liquid by one-third – this will take about 5 minutes.
* Break the eggs into a large bowl and whisk. Chop the mint and parsley. Crumble the feta into very small pieces and stir it into the eggs along with the yoghurt, chopped herbs and seasoning.
* Roughly chop the fresh dill. Add the fresh or dried dill to the lamb mixture and season to taste.
* By now the aubergines will be ready. Remove them from the oven and reduce the temperature to 190°C/375°F/Gas Mark 5.
* To assemble the moussaka, put about half the potatoes on the base of an ovenproof dish in an even layer, followed by a layer of half the meat mixture, then half the aubergines and a thin layer of the topping.
* Now repeat the process with the remaining potatoes, meat and aubergines and, finally, the rest of the topping.
* Place the moussaka in the oven and cook for 20–25 minutes until the top is set and golden brown.

Pasta Ribbons with Tomato Flageolet Beans

This baked pasta is comforting and homely. Flageolet beans in a rich tomato sauce are layered with pasta ribbons and baked with a cheese and breadcrumb topping.

2 tbsp olive oil
2 medium red onions, approx.
    240 g
300–400 g fettucine (green if you
    can get it)
50 g (approx.) Parmesan or
    Gruyère
75 g breadcrumbs or 3 slices
    bread suitable for crumbing
5 sprigs fresh or 1 tsp dried
    oregano or marjoram
1 × 400 g can chopped tomatoes
600 g (approx.) garlic flageolet
    bean mixture left over from the
    Big Meal from Scratch or 2 ×
    400 g cans flageolet beans
    cooked with onion and garlic
    until full of flavour
salt and pepper

To serve
Rocket or salad leaves

GET AHEAD PREPARATION (optional)

* Peel and slice the onions.
* Grate the cheese.
* Chop, grate or whizz the bread
  into breadcrumbs, if
  necessary.

*40 minutes before
you want to eat*

* Preheat the oven to 200°C/400°F/Gas Mark 6.
* Make the tomato sauce first. Heat a generous splash of oil in a large, heavy-based pan. While the oil is heating, peel and slice the onions then add them to the pan and cook gently for 7–10 minutes.
* While the onions are softening, cook the fettucine according to the instructions on the packet. Grate the cheese and, if necessary, chop, grate or whizz the bread into breadcrumbs.
* When the onions are soft, strip the leaves from the fresh oregano or marjoram stalks straight into the pan, or add the dried herbs, stir once or twice then add the tomatoes and bring to a simmer. Let the sauce bubble away for 5 minutes over a medium heat, then add the beans and let them warm through.
* By now the fettucine should be ready, drain and toss with a little oil and plenty of salt and pepper.
* Now assemble the dish. Layer one-third of the fettucine on the bottom of a large ovenproof dish. Pile a layer of half the beans on top and then another layer of one-third of the fettucine. Make another layer with the remaining beans, and end with a layer of the remaining fettucine.
* Cover the top layer with the grated cheese and the breadcrumbs.
* Place in the oven and bake for 15 minutes, until the top is crisp and golden.

Seasonal supper

Roast Duck Breasts with Radish and Potato Salad

This is a simple but satisfying meal of pan-fried duck breasts served with a warm potato and radish salad.

Radishes are related to the horseradish root and contain a chemical similar to that found in mustard, hence their fiery kick. Radishes respond well to cooking and their crispness complements the richness of duck. This recipe is especially good if you can find radishes with their leaves on. This is an indication that they are very fresh. If they aren't available, replace the leaves with a handful of rocket. The radish and potato salad also goes well with lamb chops.

400–500 g small new potatoes
4 duck breasts
1 large or banana shallot,
    approx. 30 g
1½ tbsp sherry vinegar
2–3 bunches radishes with their
    leaves or, if they are leafless,
    add a handful of rocket
salt and pepper

GET AHEAD PREPARATION (optional)

* Wash and trim the radishes.
* Peel and chop the shallot.
* Wash the new potatoes.

25 minutes before you want to eat

* Preheat the oven to 200°C/400°F/Gas Mark 6 and place a roasting tin or ovenproof dish inside.
* Wash the potatoes, cut them in half and put them in a pan of well-salted water. Bring to the boil then simmer until the potatoes are cooked. This should take about 15–20 minutes.
* Put a large heavy-based frying pan on a medium heat. While it heats up, season the duck breasts very well, making sure to rub a good amount of salt into their skins. When the pan is hot, put the breasts in, skin sides down, and leave them to cook over a medium heat for 5 minutes. Pour off any excess fat into a heatproof dish. You may need some for the radishes. Removing the fat will also encourage the skins to crisp up.
* Peel and finely chop the shallot and place it in a serving bowl with the vinegar and some seasoning.
* After about 5 minutes turn the duck breasts over and brown them for a minute. Then remove them from the pan and place them in the preheated roasting tin or ovenproof dish, skin sides up, and roast for 5 minutes.
* Return the frying pan to the heat and, if necessary, add a little of the reserved duck fat. Trim the tops off the radishes (keeping the leaves if you have them) and wash and dry both parts separately – keep the radishes whole. When the fat is hot, add the radishes and brown them for a couple of minutes. Then add a splash of water and cook for 5 more minutes, shaking or stirring occasionally.
* While the radishes are cooking, check on the duck. Once the breasts have been cooking for 5 minutes they will be pink. For well done meat, leave in the oven for another 5–10 minutes. When the duck breasts are cooked ,leave them to rest in a warm place for 5 minutes.
* Drain the potatoes and place in the bowl with the shallot and vinegar.
* When the radishes have been cooking in water for 5 minutes, add the radish leaves or rocket to the pan along with some seasoning and toss for a minute or so. Add the radishes to the potatoes and combine.
* Place a pile of radish and potato salad on each plate, slice the duck breasts and serve with any juices that have collected.

Larder feast

Spring Eggs

This dish of eggs, spinach and peas is simple and delicious. The peas and spinach are simmered in stock with saffron and mace, then eggs are added and gently poached before being covered in cream and put under the grill to set. If you have time you can add peeled potatoes when cooking the peas and spinach; if you do, the mixture will have to simmer for longer before you add the eggs.

This is a combination of two recipes, one from Elizabeth David's *Book of Mediterranean Food* and one from Jane Grigson's *Good Things*.

2 tbsp groundnut or grapeseed
   oil
generous nut of butter
1 medium onion, approx. 120 g
2 garlic cloves
500 g frozen spinach
¼ tsp ground mace
pinch of saffron threads
300 g frozen or canned petit pois
   peas

200 ml vegetable or chicken
   stock (made from a stock cube
   or bouillon powder)
5 large free-range eggs
80 ml single cream
salt and black pepper

To serve
garlic bread or new potatoes

GET AHEAD PREPARATION (optional)

* Peel and slice the onion and
  garlic.
* Defrost the spinach.

25 minutes before you want to eat

* Put the oil and butter in a large heavy-based frying pan (one that will fit under the grill and whose handles will cope with the heat and has a lid) on a medium heat. While the fat is heating, peel and finely slice the onion then add it to the pan and leave to cook gently for 5–7 minutes. Meanwhile, peel and finely slice the garlic, and defrost the frozen spinach according to the instructions on the packet (usually in a microwave or in boiling water).
* When the onion is soft, add the garlic and stir for a minute or so. Next, add the mace and saffron and a very generous grinding of pepper. Add the peas and stir them about so they get a good buttery coating, then add the spinach and stock. Bring to a simmer, cover with a lid and allow to bubble gently for 5 minutes.
* Preheat the grill to high.
* One at a time, break four of the eggs into a small cup and gently slide them into the pan, in different corners. Replace the lid and simmer for 3–5 minutes so that the eggs set.
* Meanwhile, whisk the remaining egg with the cream and plenty of salt and pepper. When the poached eggs are just set, pour the cream and mixture over the top.
* Place the pan under the grill and leave the cream to set and brown for 2–3 minutes.
* Serve immediately with garlic bread or new potatoes. We would favour hot garlic bread.

Two for one

Chowder

Chowder is a potato-thickened fish soup from New England. It is substantial enough to count as a casserole, and it will certainly warm you up on a chilly day. This is an ideal recipe if you are expecting family or friends as it is relatively quick to cook and will serve, and most likely please, large numbers.

There are as many variations of chowder as there are cooks and you can be led by your instinct. By all means add corn, or more or less bacon, as you see fit or as suits your supplies at the time of cooking.

40–50 g butter
200–250 g rindlessfree-range
   smoked streaky bacon
5 celery sticks
3 medium onions, approx. 360 g
1.2 litres milk
1 bay leaf
2–3 black peppercorns
350 g skinned smoked pollack or
   haddock fillets
450 g skinned unsmoked pollack
   or haddock fillets

30–40 g plain flour
700 g large, floury potatoes,
   such as Maris Piper or baking
   potatoes
handful of fresh parsley
salt and pepper

To serve
crusty bread

GET AHEAD PREPARATION (optional)

The chowder can be made up to 2 days ahead and heated when required. If you only have a little time:
* Prepare the bacon, celery and onion.
* Peel the potatoes, cut them into dice and cover with water until required.

40 minutes before you want to eat

* Put a large heavy-based pan over a medium heat and melt the butter. When the butter is foaming, use scissors to cut the bacon into small pieces and add to the pan. Cook the bacon until it starts to brown.
* While the bacon is browning, dice the celery and peel the onions and chop them as finely as possible.
* When the bacon has browned, add the onions and celery to the pan and cook for about 10 minutes or until the onions are soft.
* Meanwhile, put the milk, bay leaf and peppercorns into another pan and place over a low to medium heat. Cut each of the fish fillets into three or four pieces so that they will fit in the pan and add to the milk. Bring the milk to simmering point then remove the pan from the heat and allow to stand for a few minutes.
* When the onions and celery have been cooking for about 10 minutes and are translucent and soft, add the flour. Stir well over a medium heat for a couple of minutes then turn down the heat to very low and add the milk, straining it through a sieve to catch the fish, peppercorns and bay leaf. Throw the bay leaf and peppercorns away and put the fish to one side, taking care not to break them up.
* Allow the milk to simmer very gently while you peel the potatoes and cut them into 1–2 cm dice. Add the potatoes to the simmering milk along with a generous pinch of of salt and a couple of grinds of pepper. Bring back to the boil, then reduce the heat and allow to simmer gently for about 10 minutes or until the potatoes are soft and cooked. While the potatoes are cooking roughly chop the parsley.
* When the potatoes are soft, lift out about 5 tablespoons of potato and put them in a sieve over the pan. Push the potatoes through the sieve to slightly thicken the broth (don't worry if there are bits of bacon and vegetables – just return them to the pan). Stir well to incorporate the sieved potatoes then add the fish, using your hands to gently break the fillets into bite-sized pieces.
* Gently stir the parsley into the soup. Warm through gently and taste for seasoning. Add more salt and pepper if necessary.
* Put half the soup in a container suitable for freezing and divide the rest between four bowls.
* Serve with crusty bread.

**Lazy day supper
– reheating
instructions**

Allow the soup to defrost thoroughly, then tip into a pan and reheat gently. Add more parsley and serve as above.

KITCHEN REVOLUTION EXTRA

Softening (or sweating) onions

When onions are cooked the starch in them turns to sugars, so the sharp bite of the raw onion becomes sweet and pleasant. This flavour forms the basis of a huge number of European recipes – many of the recipes in the book start with 'soften the onions'.

To soften a sliced or chopped onion it has to be cooked in a little fat (butter or oil), in a heavy-based pan over a low to medium heat for at least 7 minutes, and up to 15 minutes if possible. It's important to cook it slowly in order to extract the maximum sweetness. If you rush the cooking by turning up the heat, the outside will brown and burn before the onion is properly soft – so you'll get a bitter taste without the sweetness.

April Week 2 – Overview

Spain is the inspiration for the first recipe this week – a casserole of chicken gently cooked in softened onions and sherry and served with wild rice and spring greens. The total time for this Big Meal from Scratch is about 1½ hours, but most of the work is concentrated in the first 30 minutes. Slicing the onions is the most onerous task and they provide the basis for both the chicken casserole and then, later in the week, a cheat's French Onion Soup – warming, rich and ready in just 15 minutes. Though this can be made using stock cubes or bouillon powder, it would really benefit from good, fresh chicken stock if at all possible.

Wild rice takes longer to cook than most other varieties so it's worth doubling up the batch for the big meal and using the extra to make a Wild Rice, Mushroom and Spinach Loaf. It takes 45 minutes to cook, a little longer than most mid-week recipes, but half this time is spent assembling the loaf and it is in the oven for the other half. Rice only keeps a day or two in the fridge so it should be cooked soon after the big meal.

Wild garlic comes into season in April and grows abundantly in shady woodland areas. This week it's used to make a simple Seasonal Supper of pasta with wilted wild garlic and bacon. Not everyone lives near a wood or has time to forage, so the wild garlic can be replaced with spinach and a generous bunch of chives if necessary.

The Sardine and Tomato Tart is based on a simple principle that can be adapted to suit the contents of your larder or fridge. It works well with the rich oiliness of sardines but would also be good with ham, or bacon, or mushrooms, or a combination of all three.

Chinese Pork Dumplings, this week's Two for One, freeze very well but are so moreish and delicious they are unlikely to remain frozen for long. The excellent taste hopefully goes some way to compensate for the rather involved amount of preparation. The dumplings take an hour from start to finish so this isn't a recipe for the tired or harassed.

April Week 2	Recipe	Time
Big meal from scratch	Spanish chicken casserole with wild rice and spring greens	1½ hours
Something for nothing 1	French onion soup	15 mins
Something for nothing 2	Wild rice, mushroom and spinach loaf	45 mins
Seasonal supper	Wild garlic and bacon pasta	20 mins
Larder feast	Sardine and tomato tart	35 mins
2 for 1	Chinese pork dumplings	1 hour

All recipes serve 4 apart from the 2 for 1 recipe which makes 8 portions

SHOPPING LIST (for 4 people)

Meat and fish
1-1.5 kg free-range chicken legs, thighs and drumsticks
8 rashers rindless free-range smoked back bacon, approx. 250 g, or 250 g pancetta
800 g minced pork

Dairy
50 g butter
6 free-range eggs
100 ml milk
80 ml crème fraîche
125 g Gruyère or other strong cheese
60-80 g Parmesan

Fruit and vegetables
18 garlic cloves
8 medium onions, approx. 1 kg
2 green peppers, approx. 300 g
1 bunch fresh flatleaf parsley
5-6 sprigs fresh mint
4 sprigs fresh thyme
4 sprigs fresh basil (optional for the Sardine and Tomato Tart)
small handful of fresh coriander
200 g wild garlic or 200 g baby leaf spinach and 1 large bunch chives
8-cm piece of fresh root ginger
3 small red chillies
400 g baby spinach
400 g spring greens
300 g mushrooms
15 spring onions, approx. 2 bunches
1 lemon
1 Chinese cabbage or other greens, approx. 400 g

Basics
plain flour, for dusting
100 ml olive oil
40 ml groundnut or grapeseed oil
350-400 g chilled ready-made shortcrust pastry
½ tsp soft brown sugar
1 bay leaf
½ loaf of crusty French bread for croûtons
2.8 litres chicken stock (fresh or made from a stock cube or bouillon powder)
salt and pepper

Store cupboard
240 g sardines canned in olive oil
1 x 400 g can chopped tomatoes
2-3 red peppers or pimientoes from a can or jar
1 × 225g can sliced bamboo shoots
2-3 tbsp pitted black olives
2 tbsp hoisin plum sauce
50 g pine nuts (toasted if possible)
50 g sultanas
450 g wild and basmati rice mix
225 g easy cook long grain rice
400 g dried orecchiette or farfalle pasta
2 tbsp sherry vinegar
100 ml soy sauce
60 ml rice vinegar
pinch of nutmeg (ground or freshly grated)
1 piece of star anise or 1 tsp five-spice powder
465 ml sherry (oloroso or fino if possible)
100 ml white wine
60 ml brandy (optional for French Onion Soup)

Serving suggestions
rocket, Parmesan, olive oil and lemon juice (Wild Rice, Mushroom and Spinach Loaf)
chicory, avocado, walnuts (Wild Garlic and Bacon Pasta)
little gem and cos lettuces, sherry vinegar and olive oil (Sardine and Tomato Tart)

To download or print out this shopping list, please visit www.thekitchenrevolution.co.uk/April/Week2

**Big meal
from scratch**

Spanish Chicken Casserole with Wild Rice and Spring Greens

This is a straightforward but delicious meal. Chicken legs and thighs, the most succulent cuts, are braised with sherry and onions until the meat is falling off the bone. Wild rice has a nutty taste and is good for mopping up the richly flavoured sauce.

The extra onions used to braise the chicken form the basis of the French Onion Soup (see page 000) later in the week. As wild rice takes longer to cook than ordinary white rice it's worth making double quantities so that the leftovers can be used to make a Wild Rice, Mushroom and Spinach Loaf (see page 000).

Spanish chicken casserole
olive oil
1–1.5 kg free-range chicken legs, thighs, drumsticks
7 medium onions, approx. 850 g; includes 3 onions for the French onion soup
2 green peppers, approx. 300 g
8 garlic cloves; includes 2 garlic cloves for the onion soup
375 ml sherry (oloroso or fino if possible)
2 tbsp sherry vinegar
500 ml chicken stock (fresh or made from a stock cube or bouillon powder)
1 bay leaf
50 g pine nuts (toasted, if possible)
50 g sultanas

Wild rice
450 g wild and basmati rice mix; includes approx. 150 g for the wild rice, mushroom and spinach loaf
small handful of fresh parsley
5–6 sprigs fresh mint
generous 1–2 nuts of butter

Spring greens
400 g spring greens
butter
pinch of nutmeg (ground or freshly grated)

GET AHEAD PREPARATION (optional)

* Prepare the onions and garlic.
* Core and deseed the peppers and cut them into strips.
* Toast the pine nuts.
* Trim the greens.

1½ hours before you want to eat prepare the casserole

* Put a generous slug of oil into a large casserole and place over a medium heat. While the oil is heating, season the chicken all over with salt and pepper. Add the chicken pieces to the hot oil in batches and cook until they are deep golden in colour. As they turn golden, lift them from the pan and set aside on a plate. As you fry the batches tip any excess fat into a small container and set aside to use for frying the onions and peppers later.
* While the chicken is cooking, peel and finely slice the onions, then core and deseed the peppers and slice them into 1-cm strips. Peel and crush the garlic. Be sure to follow this order as the onions go into the pan 5 minutes before everything else.
* Once all the chicken pieces are golden and the onions are sliced, add a large wine glass of the sherry to the casserole. Let the alcohol bubble away, and scrape and stir the casserole with a wooden spoon. Pour this cooking liquor over the chicken.
* Wipe the casserole dry and return it to the heat with the fat you set aside earlier. If there isn't very much, add another tablespoon or so of oil – you need 2–3 tablespoons fat altogether.
* When the fat is hot, add the onions and sauté gently for 7–10 minutes. While the onions are cooking, finish preparing the peppers and garlic if necessary. Once the onions have been frying for about 10 minutes, add the peppers and fry gently for another 5–7 minutes. Finally, add the garlic, stir once or twice and cook for about 2 minutes.
* Next, turn the heat up, add the vinegar and let it bubble away for 1 minute. Now add the rest of the sherry and simmer for a few minutes. Add the stock and return the chicken pieces to the pan along with the bay leaf. Season well, bring to the boil then turn the heat right down and simmer very gently until the chicken is tender – this will take about 45 minutes.

45 minutes before you want to eat cook the rice

* Rinse the rice and place it in a pan. Cover with water and cook according to the instructions on the packet – this should take 30–45 minutes.
* Roughly chop the parsley and mint, and, if you haven't bought ready-toasted pine nuts, toast the pine nuts in a frying pan over a very low heat. Keep an eye on them because they will burn easily if forgotten.
* Once you have prepared the rice, herbs and nuts, wash and trim the spring greens, so that they are ready to be steamed.

15 minutes before you want to eat cook the greens, finish the rice and casserole

* Put the oven on its lowest setting and warm up some serving dishes and plates.
* Check the chicken – the meat should by now be very tender and falling off the bone. Remove the chicken from the casserole, put the pieces in a dish, cover with foil and place in the oven.
* Remove half the onions and cooking liquor from the casserole with a ladle and put aside in a plastic container for later in the week.
* Return the casserole to the heat, skim off any excess oil if you can and allow the sauce to bubble and reduce a little over a high heat.
* Steam the spring greens for 5–7 minutes so that they are tender but not completely soft.
* Check that the rice is cooked and tip it into a sieve to strain off any excess liquid. Return the rice to the pan and, over a low heat, stir in the butter and the parsley and mint, and season to taste. Tip into a warmed serving dish.
* Add all but a small handful of the pine nuts and sultanas to the sauce in the casserole, taste it for seasoning and pour the lot over the chicken pieces.
* When the greens are cooked, shake off any excess water, toss them in a little butter with a pinch of nutmeg and a good dose of seasoning, and pile them into a warmed serving dish. Sprinkle the remaining pine nuts and sultanas on top of the chicken and serve.

Afterwards

* Tip any leftover sherry and onion sauce from the meal into the onions and cooking liquor you put to one side earlier. You should have about 450 ml.
* Let any leftover rice cool as quickly as possible, then place it in a plastic container and refrigerate for use in the next day or so. You should have about 450 g.

**Something
for nothing 1**

French Onion Soup

French Onion Soup usually takes an hour or so to make, but using the extra sherry onion sauce from the Big Meal from Scratch you can replicate this classic in just 15 minutes.

If you haven't got any remaining sherry and onion sauce you can still make this excellent soup but it will just take much longer. You will need to slice 3 medium onions and slowly soften them in some butter and oil for 15–20 minutes. Then add 2 crushed garlic cloves and a pinch of sugar. After a couple of minutes stirring over a high heat to get a little colour, add 250 ml white wine and let this bubble away for a couple of minutes before adding 1 litre strong chicken stock. Then proceed as below.

400 ml (approx.) leftover sherry
　　and onion sauce from the Big
　　Meal from Scratch or see above
100 ml white wine
½ tsp light brown soft sugar
800 ml strong chicken stock
　　(ideally fresh or can be made
　　with a stock cube)
4 sprigs fresh thyme
½ loaf of crusty French bread
1 large garlic clove
125 g Gruyère or other strong
　　cheese
60 ml brandy, such as Cognac or
　　Armagnac (optional but very
　　tasty)
salt and pepper

GET AHEAD PREPARATION (optional)

The soup can be made a day in advance up to the point of adding the croûtons and melting the cheese. If you only have a little time:
* Prepare the garlic.
* Grate the cheese.
* Make the croûtons and rub them with garlic.

*15 minutes before
you want to eat*

* Preheat the grill to its highest setting.
* While the sherry and onion sauce is cold use a teaspoon to scrape as much of the fat off the top as you can – the fat isn't good for much so it's probably best to throw it away.
* Place the wine and sugar in a large pan and bring to the boil. Strip the thyme leaves from their stalks. Add the sherry and onion sauce and let it heat through before adding the stock and the thyme leaves.
* Bring this lot up to the boil, then turn the heat down to low and simmer while you make the croûtons.
* Depending on whether your bread is a thin or fat baton, cut one or two 3-cm thick slices of bread per person. Place them on a baking sheet and put them under the grill for a couple of minutes on either side until they are golden and crisp. While the bread is toasting, peel the garlic and chop it in half and grate the cheese. When the toasts are ready, rub them vigorously on one side with the cut sides of the garlic.
* Now taste the onion soup for seasoning and adjust as necessary. Add the brandy if you are feeling decadent and it's a particularly cold night.
* Ladle the soup into four deep bowls and put the croûtons on top. Sprinkle the cheese on to the croûtons – it doesn't matter if some of the cheese falls into the soup.
* Place the bowls, two at a time, under the grill until the cheese melts and turns golden. Remove from the grill with care as the bowls will be very hot.
* If you're feeling lazy just you can forego the grill and just ladle some soup over the cheese to melt it.

Something
for nothing 2

Wild Rice, Mushroom and Spinach Loaf

The wild rice in this recipe adds a nutty flavour to spinach, mushrooms and parsley. The combined result is light and flavourful and would be as good served piping hot as at room temperature. This is the time of year for St George's mushrooms which have creamy white-caps and white gills. You might be lucky enough to find these when shopping but, if not, large field mushrooms also work very well.

200 g (approx.) baby leaf
  spinach
groundnut or grapeseed oil
30 g butter
4 spring onions
300 g mushrooms (see above)
450 g cooked wild and basmati
  rice mix left over from the Big
  Meal from Scratch or 150 g raw
  weight cooked according to
  manufacturer's instructions
large handful of fresh flatleaf
  parsley
½ lemon
3 free-range eggs
100 ml milk
80 ml crème fraîche
salt and pepper

To serve
rocket and Parmesan

GET AHEAD PREPARATION (optional)

The loaf can be made a day in
advance and either served at
room temperature or gently
warmed in the oven. If you only
have a little time:
* Prepare the spinach, spring
  onions and mushrooms.
* Chop the parsley.
* Mix the eggs, milk, crème
  fraîche and seasoning.

*45 minutes before
you want to eat*

* Preheat the oven to 190°C/375°F/Gas Mark 5.
* Heat a splash of oil and half the butter in a pan over a medium heat. While the fat is heating, trim and finely slice the spring onions, including all but the tough parts of the green stalks. Add these to the pan and let them soften over a low heat while you clean and slice the mushrooms.
* Add the mushrooms to the spring onions along with a spot more butter and cook over a medium to high heat until they start to soften. This will take a few minutes. Wash the spinach if necessary.
* When the mushrooms are soft, add the spinach and toss it about for a few minutes. When the spinach has wilted, turn up the heat to evaporate any liquid and season to taste with salt and pepper.
* While the mushrooms and spinach are cooking, prepare the rice and egg mixture. Tip the cold, cooked rice into a large bowl. Roughly chop the parsley and grate the zest of the half lemon and add them to the rice. Mix together and check for seasoning.
* Crack the eggs into a jug, add the milk and crème fraîche and plenty of seasoning and whisk. Pour half the mixture into the rice and combine thoroughly. Season to taste.
* Oil a 900 g loaf tin or 1-litre ovenproof dish and spoon in one-third of the rice mixture. Cover with half the mushroom mixture and follow with one-third of the rice, the remaining mushroom mixture and then the remaining rice. Now pour the remaining egg mixture over the loaf and tap the tin or dish on a work surface so that the liquid distributes itself evenly.
* Grease some foil with the remaining butter. Cover the loaf tin or dish with the foil and put in a roasting tin. Add boiling water to come half way up sides of the tin or dish.
* Bake in the oven for 20–25 minutes until the loaf is firm to the touch and feels piping hot when you insert a skewer into the middle for 10 seconds and test it on your inner wrist.
* Take the loaf out of the oven and let it sit for a few minutes, then turn it out and serve cut into slices with a salad – we suggest rocket and Parmesan dressed with olive oil and lemon juice.

Seasonal supper

Wild Garlic and Bacon Pasta

Wild garlic grows abundantly in shaded glades throughout Britain at this time of year. It has dark green, delicate leaves not unlike tulip leaves in shape. It is not often available from supermarkets or grocers, but it's such an excellent seasonal treat that we have included it anyway. If you are hunting it out, be led by your nose as it has a pungent garlic-onion scent.

If you don't have a nearby wood in which to forage, or the time to do so, we suggest you replace the garlic leaves with baby leaf spinach and a generous quantity of chives.

This dish takes very little time to prepare and cook so if you are serving it with a salad (we suggest chicory, avocado and walnuts dressed in a little olive or walnut oil and lemon juice) it's a good idea to get the salad ready before you start to cook.

400 g dried orecchiette or
  farfalle pasta
8 rashers rindless free-range
  smoked back bacon, approx.
  250 g or 250 g pancetta
½ tbsp groundnut or grapeseed
  oil
60-80 g Parmesan
200 g wild garlic or 200 g baby
  leaf spinach and 1 large bunch
  chives
200 g baby leaf spinach
4 tbsp olive oil
juice of ½ lemon
salt and pepper

To serve
chicory, avocado and walnut
  salad

GET AHEAD PREPARATION (optional)

* Cut and fry the bacon.
* Prepare the wild garlic or
  spinach leaves.
* Grate the Parmesan.

20 minutes before you want to eat

* First put the orecchiette or farfalle on to cook in boiling water according to the instructions on the packet.
* Next cut the bacon into 2–3 cm lengths and fry in a heavy-based frying pan over a medium heat. Fry until crisp around the edges. Lift the bacon or pancetta from the pan and place on kitchen paper.
* While the bacon or pancetta is cooking, grate the Parmesan and set it aside in a bowl.
* Next prepare the wild garlic and spinach. If using wild garlic, remove any long, thick stalks and tear the leaves into pieces about the same size as the baby spinach leaves. Wash the leaves and dry them using a salad spinner or tea towel. Cut the chives, if using, into 1-cm lengths with scissors. Set aside.
* When the pasta is cooked, drain well. Add all but a drizzle of the olive oil and mix. Cover with a lid and set aside for 1–2 minutes.
* Add the remaining olive oil to the frying pan, set over a medium-high heat and allow to get hot. Throw in the garlic and spinach leaves and cook them, turning and tossing them, for 1–2 minutes until they start to wilt. Remove from the heat, add the chives, if using, and sprinkle with the lemon juice. Mix in a couple of generous pinches of salt and pepper and toss once more.
* Tip the leaves into the pasta along with the bacon or pancetta and the Parmesan. Toss well and season to taste; be generous with the pepper.
* Serve with a chicory, avocado and walnut salad.

Larder feast

Sardine and Tomato Tart

Compared to other fish, sardines, whether fresh or canned, are extraordinarily inexpensive. They are also high in omega 3s, so get a tick for being healthy. Most importantly, they are very, very tasty. It's well worth having a can or two at the ready at all times.

This recipe takes its ingredients from the larder and its inspiration from Spanish sardine empanadas. These are pastries filled with fresh or canned sardines, olive oil, garlic and sometimes tomatoes. This tart is open but is similar in its flavours and simplicity.

If you use ready-made pastry it should take no more than 35 minutes to prepare and cook the tart from scratch. The tart is assembled on a cold baking sheet, but if this is put on a solid oven shelf or a large baking sheet that has been preheated in the oven it will encourage the base of the pastry to crisp immediately and will speed up the overall cooking time.

2 tbsp olive oil, plus extra for drizzling
1 medium onion, approx. 120 g
2 garlic cloves
2-3 red peppers or pimientoes from a can or jar
1 × 400 g can chopped tomatoes
plain flour, for dusting
350-400 g chilled ready-made shortcrust pastry
handful of fresh basil leaves (optional)

240 g (approx. 160 g drained weight) sardines canned in olive oil
2-3 tbsp pitted black olives
salt and black pepper

To serve
little gem and cos lettuce salad dressed with a sherry vinegar and olive oil

GET AHEAD PREPARATION (optional)

The tart can be made a few hours in advance and either served at room temperature or gently warmed in the oven. If you only have a little time:
* Prepare the onion, garlic and pimientoes.
* Roll out the pastry and leave to rest in the fridge.

35 minutes before you want to eat

* Preheat the oven to 200°C/400°F/Gas Mark 6 and preheat a large baking sheet.
* Heat the oil in a heavy-based pan over a medium heat. While the oil is heating, thinly slice the onion then add it to pan and cook until soft, taking care that it doesn't burn. This will take about 7 minutes.
* Peel and thinly slice the garlic. When the onion has been cooking for about 2 minutes add the garlic and cook slowly for about 5 minutes.
* Next, slice the peppers or pimientoes into thin strips and add them, along with the tomatoes, to the onion and garlic. Season with a little salt and a generous amount of black pepper, and cook, bubbling vigourously, for 10 minutes without a lid to evaporate excess liquid. Stir from time to time to prevent sticking.
* While the sauce is cooking lightly flour a work surface and roll the pastry into a rectangle about 25 x 30 cm and 5 mm thick. Grease a baking sheet with a drizzle of oil and place the pastry on top. Pinch of the edges of the pastry all the way round to form a small lip.
* When the sauce is thick enough to leave a line when it is parted in the pan, smooth it over the base of the pastry.
* Roughly tear the basil leaves, if using, and arrange half of them over the sauce.
* Drain the sardines of any oil and arrange in a pattern to your liking over the tomato sauce and basil. Scatter with the olives, season with pepper and scatter with the remaining basil.
* Bake in the oven for approximately 15 minutes or until the edge of the pastry is browned.
* Drizzle with oil and serve with a little gem and cos lettuce salad.

Two for one

Chinese Pork Dumplings

Once you've cooked this, you may never need to order a takeaway again (or almost never). The recipe does take some effort and time, but when cooked there's sufficient to store in the freezer and save for a lazy night.

Pork dumplings
225 g long grain rice
8-cm piece of fresh root ginger
4 garlic cloves
8 spring onions
2 free-range eggs
2 tbsp hoisin plum sauce
4 tbsp soy sauce
2 tbsp sherry
800 g minced pork
salt

Broth
3 small red chillies
1 tbsp groundnut or grapeseed oil
3 spring onions
3 garlic cloves
225g can sliced bamboo shoots
4 tbsp rice vinegar
4 tbsp sherry
3 tbsp soy sauce
1.5 litres chicken stock (fresh or made with a stock cube)
1 Chinese cabbage or other greens, approx. 400 g
small handful of fresh coriander
1 piece of star anise or 1 tsp five-spice powder
pepper

GET AHEAD PREPARATION (optional)

The broth and dumplings can be made up to 2 days in advance, up to the point of being put together. If you only have a little time:
* Brown and whizz the rice.
* Prepare the ginger, garlic, shallots and spring onions.
* Deseed and chop the chillies.
* Prepare the Chinese cabbage.
* Chop the coriander.

1 hour before you want to eat make the meatballs

* Rinse the rice and heat a large frying pan or wok. Add the rice to the pan and let it dry out over a low heat for 10–15 minutes, stirring from time to time.
* In the meantime peel and finely slice the ginger and garlic, and trim and chop the spring onions. Reserve a small pile of ginger to go into the broth and put the rest into a food processor with the garlic and spring onions and whizz to a paste.
* Tip the spring onion and garlic mixture into a bowl, add the eggs, hoisin and plum sauce, soy sauce and sherry and mix together.
* By now the rice should be very slightly browned and dried out. Tip it into a food processor and whizz to a coarse powder. Add this to the bowl containing the ginger and spring onion mixture and mix well.
* Add the pork and some salt and work the mixture together well. (If you like, test it for flavour: heat a splash of oil in a small frying pan and cook a little piece, then taste it and adjust the rest of the mixture, if necessary.)
* Shape the mixture into dumplings about the size of a ping pong ball. At this point set half of them aside to cool.

30 minutes before you want to eat make the broth

* Deseed and finely chop the chillies. Heat a generous splash of oil in a large pan and add the chillies. Brown them, without burning, for 1 minute then lift them out with a slotted spoon – you can keep them and scatter them on the final dish if you like.
* Add the spring onions and garlic to the chilli oil and cook gently for a couple of minutes, then add the bamboo shoots and the reserved ginger. Turn up the heat and brown a little before adding the rice vinegar, sherry and soy sauce. Let these boil for a minute or so, then add the star anise or 5 spice powder and stock and bring back to the boil. The broth is now ready to poach the dumplings. Ladle out half of the broth and set aside to cool.
* Add the dumplings you are planning to eat to the remaining broth and poach them gently, with a lid on, for 20 minutes. Meanwhile, trim and slice the Chinese cabbage or greens.
* After 20 minutes add the cabbage or greens to the pan, put the lid back on and cook for another 5–7 minutes. In the meantime, roughly chop the coriander.
* To serve, taste the broth and season it if necessary. Add the coriander and ladle the dumplings and broth into bowls.

Afterwards

Freeze the reserved dumplings and stock separately.

**Lazy day supper
– reheating
instructions**

* Remove the broth and dumplings from the freezer the day before you plan to serve them. Make sure they are completely defrosted.
To reheat, put the stock in a pan and bring it to the boil, then add the dumplings and simmer with a lid on for 20 minutes while you shred about 400 g greens and wash and roughly chop a small handful of fresh coriander. Add the greens and cook for another 5–7 minutes before adding the coriander.
To cook the dish from frozen, first defrost the broth by putting it into a pan with a lid on and letting it melt over a low heat. This will probably take 15 minutes.
* When the stock is liquid and hot, add the frozen dumplings and poach them very gently for about 30 minutes with a lid on. In the meantime, trim and slice about 400 g greens and wash and roughly chop a small handful of fresh coriander. Add the greens and proceed as above.

April Week 3 – Overview

There is nothing showy or complicated about the Big Meal from Scratch this week, but there is something very restorative and pleasing about the combination of Smoked Haddock, Bacon, Peas and Jacket Potatoes. In terms of organisation, the fish cooks quickly but the potatoes need to bake in the oven for 1–1½ hours. As with all fish, eat the haddock within a day or so of buying, or freeze immediately after purchase.

Three further meals can potentially be made from the big meal extras. The smoked haddock is cooked in a creamy, bacon sauce and if there is any surplus this will make a quick and very tasty pasta dish. Baking extra potatoes means that stuffed potatoes can be made with minimal preparation. It's difficult to imagine improving on the standard baked potato served with salt, pepper and plenty of butter but stuffing the potatoes with a cheese and spinach filling and baking them again is certainly a contender. The surplus smoked haddock from the big meal is turned into a pastry-topped Fish Pie that is easy to assemble and takes about 20 minutes in a hot oven. The cooked smoked haddock will keep for about three days in the fridge if covered, so this needs to be factored into any weekly cooking plan.

A Seasonal Supper of Goats' Cheese Bruschetta with a Beetroot and Rocket Salad is, in essence, smart cheese on toast. If the beetroot are cooked from raw it will take 30–40 minutes but if you use ready-cooked beetroot everything can be ready in 10 minutes.

Large soft flour tortillas make ideal vehicles for wrapping a spicy mixture of sweetcorn, tomato and potato for the Larder Feast, which takes 25 minutes to cook.

The Spanish recipe for Rabbit with Almonds and Garlic – this week's Two for One – is not very labour intensive, but because it's a casserole it does take 1½ hours to cook so is best tackled when there's plenty of time, perhaps over the weekend. Rabbit is usually available at good butchers, but the casserole also works well with chicken legs, thighs or drumsticks, or a whole jointed chicken (see page 183 for instructions on how to joint a chicken or ask the butcher to joint one for you).

April Week 3	Recipe	Time
Big meal from scratch	Smoked haddock, peas and bacon with jacket potatoes and mustard cabbage Added Extra – Bacon, pea and Parmesan pasta	1½ hours
Something for nothing 1	Fish pie	40 mins
Something for nothing 2	Stuffed baked potatoes	30 mins
Seasonal supper	Goats' cheese bruschetta with beetroot and rocket salad	30 mins
Larder feast	Spicy sweetcorn with sesame seeds and tomatoes	25 mins
2 for 1	Rabbit (or chicken) with almonds, pine nuts and garlics	1½–2 hours

All recipes serve 4 apart from the 2 for 1 recipe which makes 8 portions

SHOPPING LIST (for 4 people)

Meat and fish
1.2–1.5 kg skinned smoked haddock fillet, cut into 8 portion-sized pieces
2–3 rabbits, 1.8 kg total weight, jointed or 1.8 kg free-range chicken pieces (on the bone)
150 g (approx.) rindless free-range smoked streaky bacon
200 g rindless free-range smoked streaky bacon or ham (optional for Stuffed Baked Potatoes)

Dairy
340 ml milk
60 ml double cream
4 tbsp crème fraîche
100 g cream cheese or 100 ml crème fraîche
150 g butter
5 large free-range eggs
120 g strong Cheddar or blue cheese (or any cheese you have to hand)
350 g soft goats' cheese, rindless
200 g Greek yoghurt

Fruit and vegetables
8 large or 16 small potatoes suitable for baking
750 g uncooked beetroot (ideally each beet about the size of a golf ball) or 600 g cooked beetroot (not pickled in vinegar)
3 leeks, approx. 600 g
1 small Savoy cabbage, approx. 400–600 g
80–100 g rocket
1 medium green pepper, approx. 150 g
5 medium onions, approx. 600 g
4 spring onions
5 garlic cloves
1 green chilli (optional for Spicy Sweetcorn with Sesame Seeds and Tomatoes)
1 large bunch fresh flatleaf parsley
handful of coriander
2 sprigs fresh thyme or 1 tsp dried thyme
2 sprigs fresh rosemary
5 sprigs fresh mint
½ lemon
350 g (approx.) frozen petit pois peas
400 g frozen spinach

Basics
150 ml olive oil
30 ml groundnut or grapeseed oil
8 large slices bread (a crusty country bread would work well)
300 g chilled ready-made puff pastry
90 g plain flour
2 tsp wholegrain mustard
3 bay leaves
100 ml fish or vegetable stock (fresh or made from a stock cube or bouillon powder)

salt and pepper

Store cupboard
600 g canned sweetcorn, drained weight
300g canned new potatoes, drained weight
1 × 400 g can chopped tomatoes or 250 ml passata
80 g shelled walnuts
2 tbsp sesame seeds
60 g pine nuts
3 tbsp slivered almonds
1 packet (approx. 8) tortillas
1 tsp walnut oil (optional for Goats' Cheese Bruschetta with Beetroot and Rocket Salad)
1 tbsp sherry vinegar or white wine vinegar
1 tbsp white wine vinegar
¼ tsp cumin seeds
½ tsp brown or yellow mustard seeds
1 tsp caraway seeds (optional for Goats' Cheese Bruschetta with Beetroot and Rocket Salad)
½ tsp garam masala
¼ tsp turmeric
½ tsp ground cumin
½ tsp ground coriander
1 tsp paprika
1 litre dry white wine
½ tsp chilli sauce, ideally green (optional for Spicy Sweetcorn with Sesame Seeds and Tomatoes)

Serving suggestions
greens (Fish Pie)
salad leaves, olive oil and lemon juice, and chutney or relish (Stuffed Baked Potatoes)
green beans, garlic and butter, and rice (Rabbit or Chicken with Almonds, Pine Nuts and Garlic)

To download or print out this shopping list, please visit www.thekitchenrevolution.co.uk/April/Week3

Smoked Haddock, Peas and Bacon
with Jacket Potatoes and Mustard Cabbage

This Big Meal from Scratch is simple, comforting and very tasty. In a sense, you could think of this recipe as a reconstructed chowder – it combines the flavours of bacon and smoked haddock in a creamy sauce, with potatoes to mop up and counter the intense flavours. The peas add colour and a touch of sweetness.

Smoked haddock comes dyed and undyed – the former bright yellow, the latter a pale cream. Either will work for this recipe, though our inclination would be for undyed as the dye adds nothing in flavour and the finished recipe doesn't require prettying up.

The recipe includes extra smoked haddock to use in Fish Pie (see page 178) and jacket potatoes for Stuffed Baked Potatoes (see page 179) later in the week.

Smoked haddock, peas and
bacon
40 g butter
150 g (approx.) free-range
  rindless smoked streaky bacon
1 medium onion
1 tbsp white wine vinegar
250 ml white wine
350 g (approx.) frozen petit pois
100 ml fish or vegetable stock
  (fresh or made with a stock
  cube or bouillon powder)
handful of fresh parsley
1.2–1.5 kg skinned smoked
  haddock fillet, cut into 8
  portion-sized pieces; includes
  approx. 500 g extra for the
  Fish Pie

4 tbsp crème fraîche
salt and pepper

Jacket potatoes
8 large or 16 small potatoes
  suitable for baking; includes 4
  large or 8 small extra potatoes
  for the stuffed baked potatoes
1 tbsp olive oil

Mustard cabbage
1 small Savoy cabbage, approx.
  600–800 g
50 g butter
boiling water
2 tsp wholegrain mustard

GET AHEAD PREPARATION (optional)

* Prepare the potatoes, onion
  and parsley.
* Trim and finely shred the
  cabbage.

*1½ hours before
you want to eat
cook the potatoes*

* Preheat the oven to 180°C/350°F/Gas Mark 4.
* Wash the potatoes, dry them thoroughly and prick each one with a fork or skewer two or three times. Pour a little oil into your hand and rub this all over the potatoes. Repeat the process with a generous amount of salt. Place the oiled and salted potatoes on a large baking sheet and place in the oven for at least 1 hour and up to 1½ hours.

*40 minutes before
you want to eat
prepare the
haddock*

* Put half the butter in a heavy-based pan, ideally large enough to hold all the haddock pieces in a single layer. Place over a medium heat. When the butter is foaming, use a pair of scissors to cut the bacon into 2–3-cm pieces straight into the pan and fry them for 3–5 minutes, turning and stirring to ensure the pieces are evenly cooked. While the bacon is sizzling, peel and finely dice the onion.
* When the bacon is cooked, add the rest of the butter and the onion and fry gently for 7–10 minutes or until the onion is soft. Stir from time to time to prevent burning.
* Once the onion is soft, turn up the heat, add the vinegar and allow the liquid to evaporate. This will only take seconds, and when the vinegar has reduced add the wine and bring to a gentle simmer. Allow the wine to simmer for about 5 minutes or until the liquid has reduced to half.
* Now add the peas to the pan and cover with the stock. Bring to the boil then simmer for 5 minutes.
* While the peas are cooking, roughly chop the parsley and place a serving dish (large enough to hold four of the haddock pieces in their pea and bacon sauce) in the oven to warm.
* Now turn the heat down low and add the haddock to the pan, ensuring that each piece is submerged, though not necessarily covered, in the liquid. Season with lots of pepper, add half the parsley, cover and allow to gently steam and poach for about 5 minutes. If your pan is small you can cook the haddock in two batches, keeping the cooked pieces warm in the oven.

<table>
<tr><td>15 minutes before
you want to eat
cook the cabbage</td><td>

* Discard any coarse outer leaves from the cabbage. Cut out any thick parts of stem on the remaining leaves and shred into 2-cm slices.
* Heat the butter for the cabbage in a large pan with a lid and, when it has melted, add the cabbage. Stir the leaves until they are coated with butter and add a generous splash of boiling water (no more than 3 tablespoons). Season with salt and pepper, cover with a lid and let the cabbage wilt down for 7–10 minutes.
* When the haddock is cooked remove it from the pan using a slotted spoon and place four of the pieces in the warmed serving dish. Cover with foil and set aside. Put the remaining haddock in a suitable container and allow to cool.
* Now make the sauce. Increase the heat under the pan and bring the pea and bacon mixture to a rolling boil. The sauce is supposed to be of a thin pouring consistency so don't worry too much about thickening it. Add the crème fraîche and stir well. Taste the sauce and season it accordingly. Pour the sauce and peas over the four haddock pieces in the serving dish, add the remaining parsley and cover with foil to keep warm.
* Check on the cabbage – it should have softened by now. Stir in the mustard and if there is a lot of liquid in the pan bring it to the boil and let it evaporate. Tip the cabbage into a serving dish.
* Serve each person one large or two small jacket potatoes, a piece of haddock with plenty of creamy peas and bacon and some cabbage.

</td></tr>
<tr><td>Afterwards</td><td>

* Put the remaining potatoes on a plate, allow to them to cool then cover them with cling film and place in the fridge.
* Break the remaining haddock pieces – you should have about 500 g – into big flakes, cover and place in the fridge ready to use in the fish pie later in the week.
* If you have any remaining pea and bacon sauce you can use it for a pasta dish (see below). Alternatively, you can strain it and keep it covered in the fridge, then use it to add flavour to the fish pie.
* Save any leftover cabbage to fry up and have with the fish pie.

</td></tr>
</table>

Added extra

Bacon, Pea and Parmesan Pasta

If you have any bacon and pea sauce left over it will make a delicious sauce for pasta with the addition of a little crème fraîche and Parmesan.

**Something
for nothing 1**

Fish Pie

There's nothing more comforting than a good home-made fish pie – except, perhaps, one where some of the work has already been done for you. This uses leftover haddock from the Big Meal from Scratch. If you have any cabbage left over from the big meal fry it in butter until it is hot and crispy and finish with a squeeze of lemon juice. If you don't have any leftover cabbage, serve the pie with greens of your choice.

3 leeks (approx. 600 g)
340 ml milk or strained sauce
   from the Big Meal from Scratch
   made up to 340 ml with milk
60 ml double cream
3 large free-range eggs
40 g butter
30 g plain flour, plus extra for
   dusting
large handful of fresh flatleaf
   parsley
300 g chilled ready-made puff
   pastry (you can buy it ready-
   rolled)

500 g cooked, flaked smoked
   haddock left over from the Big
   Meal from Scratch or 500 g
   smoked haddock covered in
   boiling water for 10 minutes,
   then flaked
juice of ½ lemon
salt and pepper

To serve
Fried cabbage left over from the
   Big Meal from Scratch (see
   above) or greens

GET AHEAD PREPARATION (optional)

The pie can be prepared a day in advance, up until the point when it goes in the oven. If you only have a little time:
* Prepare the leeks.
* Cook and peel the eggs.
* Chop the parsley.
* Roll out the pastry.

*40 minutes before
you want to eat*

* Heat the oven to 200°C/400°F/Gas Mark 6.
* Trim, slice and thoroughly wash the leeks. Bring the milk (or milk and strained sauce) and cream to the boil in a large pan, add the sliced leeks and simmer for 5 minutes.
* While the leeks are simmering, cook the eggs. Place them in boiling water for 7 minutes, then drain and leave to cool under cold running water.
* Melt the butter in a small pan, add the flour and stir to a paste. Cook for few minutes until the mixture turns to a biscuity roux.
* Strain the milk straight on to the roux and stir thoroughly to make a sauce. Use a whisk to stir out lumps as you bring the sauce to the boil. Let the sauce simmer for a few minutes to thicken. Chop the parsley and add to the sauce. Season.
* Peel and halve the eggs.
* Lightly dust a work surface with flour and roll the pastry out, or cut it if it is ready rolled, to fit over the top of a 1–1.5-litre pie dish. Let the pastry rest.
* Put a pie crown or an upside-down egg cup in the centre of the pie dish to hold up the pastry and allow steam to escape. Put the leeks in a layer on the bottom of the dish and season. Cover the leeks with the haddock and the lemon juice. Next, add the egg halves and pepper. Finally, add the sauce.
* Wet the rim of the pie dish and use trimmings from the pastry to make a 2-cm lip on the rim. Put the pastry on top of the lip and press firmly. Use a fork to press down the edges to secure them. Make a hole in the pastry for the pie crown.
* Brush the pie with milk and bake for 20 minutes until the pastry is golden.
* Serve with the left over cabbage or greens.

**Something
for nothing 2**

Stuffed Baked Potatoes

Stuffed baked potatoes may not feature on the menus of fancy dinner parties or restaurants, but they are homey and comforting and are usually wolfed down indiscriminately by young and old. The fillings need only be limited by what you have available – cooked ham, leeks in cheese sauce and anchovy butter are recommended. In this recipe we keep things simple with cheese, spinach and bacon as the flavours.

400 g frozen spinach
4 large or 8 small baked
  potatoes left over from the Big
  Meal from Scratch
2 large free-range eggs
100 g cream cheese or 100 ml
  crème fraîche
200 g rindless free-range
  smoked streaky bacon or
  cooked ham (optional)
120 g strong Cheddar or blue
  cheese (or any cheese you have
  to hand)
4 spring onions
olive oil
generous nut of butter
salt and pepper

To serve
salad leaves and chutney or
  relish

GET AHEAD PREPARATION (optional)

The potatoes can be prepared a
day in advance, up until they go
in the oven. If you only have a
little time:
* Prepare the spring onions.
* Grate the cheese.
* Defrost the spinach.
* Halve the potatoes and scoop
  out the flesh.
* Fry the bacon, if using.

*30 minutes before
you want to eat*

* Preheat the oven to 190°C/375°F/Gas Mark 5.
* Defrost the spinach according to the instructions on the packet (usually in a microwave or in boiling water).
* Cut the potatoes in half and using a teaspoon scoop out as much of the flesh as you can without tearing the skin. Place all the flesh in a large bowl and mash well with the butter, then beat in the eggs and cream cheese or crème fraîche.
* If you are using the bacon, heat a frying pan over a medium heat and use scissors to snip the bacon straight into the hot pan. When it is crisp add it to the potato mixture. If you are using ham, slice into strips and add at this point.
* Coarsely grate the Cheddar or blue cheese or crumble it into small pieces. Trim and finely chop the spring onions. Add the spring onions and three-quarters of the cheese to the potato mixture. When the spinach has defrosted drain it very thoroughly and add it to the potato mixture. Stir the potato mixture together vigorously with plenty of salt and pepper.
* Oil a dish large enough to hold all the potato shells, then fill each shell with the potato mixture and place in the dish. Sprinkle the tops with the remaining cheese and bake in the oven for 15–20 minutes until golden and crisp.
* Serve the stuffed potatoes with chutney or relish and salad leaves tossed in olive oil and lemon juice.

Seasonal supper

Goats' Cheese Bruschetta with Beetroot and Rocket Salad

The colours and flavours in this meal are vibrant and energising.

Using uncooked beetroot will require 20–25 minutes of cooking. If you don't have time for this, you can always use ready-cooked beetroot but make sure they haven't been pickled. If time is of no consequence, beetroot baked in their skins with salt and oil have an intensity that boiled beetroot lacks – roasting does, however take from 45 minutes to 2 hours, depending on the size of the beets (see below).

750 g uncooked beetroot (each beet ideally about the size of a golf ball) or 600 g cooked beetroot (not pickled in vinegar)	2 sprigs fresh rosemary
2 bay leaves	350 g soft goats' cheese, rindless
1 tsp caraway seeds (optional)	8 large slices bread (crusty, country bread would work well)
1 tbsp sherry vinegar or white wine vinegar, plus a dash for cooking the beetroot	80–100 g rocket
olive oil	5 sprigs fresh mint
80 g shelled walnuts	1 tbsp walnut oil (optional)
	2 tbsp olive oil (3 tbsp if you can't or don't want to buy walnut oil)
	salt and pepper

30 minutes before you want to eat

* If you are using raw beetroot, they will need cooking. Wash away any large clods of mud then if they are about the size of a golf ball or just over, place them directly in a pan of water. If they are larger, first cut them in half or, if they are very large, into quarters. Add the bay leaves, caraway seeds, a dash of vinegar and another of olive oil and salt and pepper. Bring to the boil, turn down the heat and simmer gently for 20–25 minutes or until tender.
* Toast the walnuts in a frying pan over a low heat for a few minutes. Strip the rosemary leaves from their stalks. Roughly chop them with the walnuts. Put the goats' cheese, rosemary, walnuts and seasoning into a bowl and mix together to a smooth paste.
* Preheat the grill to its highest setting. Drizzle the bread with olive oil and toast on both sides, then spread with the goats' cheese. Leave the grill on while you prepare the salad.
* Remove any thick stalks from the rocket, wash and dry the leaves and tip into a large salad bowl. Strip the mint leaves from their stalks, tear the leaves and add to the rocket.
* When the beetroot are tender, drain them and rinse under cold running water until they are cool enough to handle and peel. If you are using ready-cooked beetroot, peel if necessary. Cut the beets into bite-sized chunks. Mix together the vinegar and the walnut and olive oil (or just the olive oil), season and add to the beetroot.
* Put the goats' cheese toasts under the grill and let them become golden brown.
* Toss the beetroot and rocket leaves together.
* Put two bruschettas on each plate and top them with piles of salad.

To bake beetroot

Preheat the oven to 180°C/350°F/Gas Mark 4. Wash the beetroot and place them in a roasting tin with a sprinkling of coarse salt, a drizzle of olive oil, a drizzle of vinegar and a good splash of water. Cover the tin with foil and bake the beetroot until they are tender. Check them after 25 minutes and add a little more water. The beets will take about 45 minutes if they are very small and up to 2 hours if they are larger than a tennis ball. Top the water up a couple of times.

Larder feast

Spicy Sweetcorn with Sesame Seeds and Tomatoes

This spicy tortilla wrap makes a standby, crowd-pleaser supper.

Polly had a large can of sweetcorn lurking in her larder for years – it had been with her when she moved flat in her late twenties, and stayed unused at the back of the cupboard in her new home for four years. When she came to move a third time she decided the sweetcorn had to be eaten before the removal van arrived, and she turned to Madhur Jaffrey's *World Vegetarian* for inspiration. This recipe was the result.

This is a quick recipe. Don't be put off by the longish list of ingredients – most of them are spices and require no preparation.

1 medium onion, approx. 120 g
1 garlic clove
1 green chilli or ½ tsp chilli sauce (ideally green)
1 medium green pepper, approx. 150 g
2 tbsp groundnut or grapeseed oil
½ tsp brown or yellow mustard seeds
¼ tsp cumin seeds
2 tbsp sesame seeds
300 g canned new potatoes, drained weight

600 g canned sweetcorn, drained weight
½ tsp garam masala
¼ tsp turmeric
½ tsp ground cumin
½ tsp ground coriander
1 tsp paprika
1 × 400 g can chopped tomatoes or 250 ml passata
1 packet soft flour tortillas, approx. 8
handful of fresh coriander
200 g Greek yoghurt

GET AHEAD PREPARATION (optional)

The sweetcorn mixture can be prepared and cooked 2 days in advance. If you only have a little time:
* Prepare the onion and garlic.
* Deseed and chop the chilli and pepper.
* Chop the coriander.
* Combine the mustard and cumin seeds together, and the turmeric, ground cumin, ground coriander and paprika.

25 minutes before you want to eat

* Peel and finely chop the onion and garlic. Deseed and finely chop the chilli and deseed the pepper and cut it into 1-cm dice.
* Heat the oil in a large frying pan. When it is hot add the mustard and cumin seeds. When the mustard seeds start to pop, add the garlic and chilli. Stir a couple of times then add the sesame seeds. After a few seconds these will start to turn golden and pop. Stir a couple of times then add the onion and pepper. Fry for 5 minutes.
* While the onions and pepper are cooking, drain the potatoes and cut them into 2-cm pieces.
* After the onion and pepper have been frying for 5 minutes, stir in the sweetcorn, potatoes, garam masala and salt. Cook for 1 minute then add the turmeric, ground cumin, ground coriander and paprika.
* After a minute add the tomatoes or passata and bring to a simmer. Allow to simmer gently for 10–20 minutes.
* While the sweetcorn mixture is cooking down and thickening, heat the tortillas according to the instructions on the packet (either in the oven or in a little oil in a frying pan). Roughly chop the fresh coriander.
* When most of the liquid has evaporated from the sweetcorn and potato mixture place it in a warmed serving bowl, add the chopped coriander and place on the table alongside the tortillas and yoghurt.
* Take a tortilla, spoon a generous amount of the sweetcorn and potato mixture in the middle, add a dollop of yoghurt, roll up and eat.

Two for one

Rabbit (or Chicken) with Almonds, Pine Nuts and Garlic

In Spain and France rabbit is eaten as a matter of course, but it is underappreciated and less commonly eaten in Britain. Rabbits are undeniably cute and this is probably an impediment to their becoming an everyday staple. This is a shame because wild rabbits are populous, economic and delectable and are particularly suited to casseroling – they tend to have a stronger flavour and are less succulent than farmed rabbits so if you are using wild ones long slow cooking gets the best results. You should be able to get rabbits from a good butcher who will joint them for you.

If rabbit is not for you, the recipe works very well with chicken – you can either use thighs or joint a couple of chickens (see page 183).

This recipe is adapted from Penelope Casa's *The Foods and Wine of Spain*. It is incredibly easy to put together. Don't be concerned if there doesn't seem to be enough liquid; with occasional stirring and the lid on, the meat will cook. While the rabbit or chicken is cooking you could prepare some rice and green beans tossed in garlic and butter to serve with it.

2-3 rabbits, 1.8 kg total weight, jointed or 1.8 kg free-range chicken pieces (on the bone)
4 tbsp plain flour
4 tbsp olive oil
3 medium onions, approx. 360 g
4 garlic cloves
handful of fresh parsley
750 ml dry white wine
2 sprigs fresh thyme or 1 tsp dried thyme
1 bay leaf
4 tbsp pine nuts
3 tbsp slivered almonds
salt and pepper

To serve
rice and green beans (see above)

GET AHEAD PREPARATION (optional)

If you want to get well ahead, the dish can be cooked a couple of days in advance and warmed through prior to serving. If you only have a little time:
* Prepare the onions, garlic and parsley.

1½ –2 hours before you want to eat

* Dust the rabbit or chicken pieces with the flour. To do this with minimal mess and hassle, put the pieces in a plastic bag with the flour and shake well, then lift each piece out and straight into the casserole to brown.
* Heat the oil in a large casserole with a lid on a medium heat and brown the rabbit or chicken pieces. Remove them as they brown and set aside.
* Meanwhile, peel and finely slice the onions and garlic, and roughly chop the parsley. When all the meat is browned, add the onions to the pan and cook for about 7 minutes over a low heat until soft.
* Pour in the wine, scrape the bottom of the casserole with a wooden spoon then add the browned rabbit or chicken and all the remaining ingredients with the exception of half the parsley. Season with ½ teaspoon each of salt and pepper.
* Simmer over a very low heat with a lid on for up to 1 hour for chicken and more like an 1½ hours for rabbit. Stir every now and then.
* Once the casserole is cooked, taste it for seasoning then divide it into two portions, leaving one to cool for freezing later.
* Serve the remaining portion with remaining parsley sprinkled on top.

Lazy day supper – reheating instructions

Defrost the casserole completely before reheating. Tip it into a large casserole dish and warm gently through. This should take about 20–30 minutes. Serve as above with rice and garlicky green beans.

Jointing a chicken

A butcher will joint a chicken for you but it's a useful skill to have. Supermarkets sell chicken drumsticks, thighs and legs, but not breasts, on the bone. Breasts on the bone are more succulent and better for casseroles than skinned and boneless ones.

Jointing a chicken demands a very sharp knife. Here, we refer you to Hugh Fearnley Whittingstall's *The River Cottage Meat Book* as it has good instructions and clear photographs, but in case you don't have access to a copy here's a rough précis:

1 Start by removing the legs – pull them gently out from the body and slice through the skin between the body and the thigh. Pull the leg firmly out and down until the ball of the thigh bone tears free then chop firmly through the sinews. The thigh and attached drumstick should come off cleanly. If you want to divide the thigh and drumstick, bend the joint between them until the ball comes out then cut through the sinews.

2 Separate the breast from the back – turn the bird breast-side down, place the knife across the rear cavity (where the legs have been removed) and slice between the ribcage and the shoulder joints, cutting below the wings so they stay attached to the breast. You'll need to slice through the ribcage on both sides. The breast and back should now only be connected beneath the wings. Hold the breast sections down while you pull the back section firmly up, tearing it away from the shoulder bones – cut firmly through these.

3 Split the breast – put the breast section skin-side down, place your knife as close as possible to the backbone on one side and push firmly down to cut through the flat part of the bone. If you want to cut each breast in half, you could cut at an angle across the breast – so that one portion has two-thirds of the breast and the other has one-third and the wing.

April Week 4 – Overview

Pork Chops Baked in Cider with Leeks and Prunes is another Big Meal from Scratch that is easy to execute and will appeal to young and old. From start to finish it takes just over an hour to make and there are enough for leftovers to contribute to two further meals.

If being sociable is on the agenda there are two quick recipes that might be especially suitable for sharing with friends: Smoked Salmon with Potato Pancakes, one of this week's Something for Nothing dishes, and the Seasonal Supper – a Baked Omelette with Butternut Squash and Sorrel. The pancakes look and taste very special and would also make a good starter for larger numbers. The baked omelette is bright, colourful and tasty and, although it takes a little longer than is ideal for a midweek meal, there is only 20 minutes preparation time. Although sorrel is in season in April it's not always easy to find it, but as it can be replaced with spinach this doesn't pose a problem.

The other Something for Nothing recipe uses leftover broccoli to make a refreshing, zesty Greek Butter Bean and Broccoli Salad that can be on the table in just under 15 minutes. The Larder Feast this week, which takes just 20 minutes, is a Japanese Miso Noodle Soup with salmon and ginger. It not only tastes good but is also very wholesome. Miso paste and instant miso are sold in most big supermarkets. The recipe will work with either but the paste is the better of the two.

This week's Two for One, an Italian Sausage and Bean Casserole, only involves 20 minutes preparation and 40 minutes cooking.

April Week 4	Recipe	Time
Big meal from scratch	Pork chops, leeks and prunes in cider with mash and broccoli	1 hour 20 minutes
Something for nothing 1	Greek butter bean and broccoli salad	15 mins
Something for nothing 2	Smoked salmon, potato pancakes and beetroot salad	30 mins
Seasonal supper	Baked omelette with butternut squash and sorrel	40 mins
Larder feast	Japanese miso noodle soup	20 mins
2 for 1	Italian sausage and bean casserole	1 hour

All recipes serve 4 apart from the 2 for 1 recipe which makes 8 portions

SHOPPING LIST (for 4 people)

Meat and fish
4 x 200-225 g free-range pork chops (ideally loin)
200-300 g smoked salmon
4 frozen salmon fillets, approx 150-75 g each
12 good quality free-range pork sausages

Dairy
130 g butter
280 ml milk
105 ml crème fraîche
11 free-range eggs
150-200 g feta
60 g Parmesan

Fruit and vegetables
1.5 kg mashing potatoes, such as Maris Piper or baking potatoes
1 small butternut squash, approx. 600 g
2-3 heads broccoli, 800 g-1kg
400 g cooked beetroot (*not* pickled in vinegar)
3 leeks with green tops, approx. 360 g
2 little gem lettuces
60 g sorrel or 75 g baby leaf spinach and 1 lemon
salad leaves, such as baby leaf spinach
7 medium red onions, approx. 840 g
1 small onion, approx. 80 g
9-11 spring onions, approx. 1½ bunches
7 garlic cloves
4 sprigs fresh sage
6 sprigs fresh mint
1 small bunch chives
3½ lemons
200 g frozen soya beans
1 lime

Basics
135 ml olive oil
75 ml groundnut or grapeseed oil
2 slices bread (whatever you have to hand)
3 tbsp self-raising flour
2 bay leaves
1 litre chicken stock (fresh or made from a stock cube or bouillon powder)
250 ml chicken or vegetable stock (fresh or made with a stock cube or bouillon powder)
salt and pepper

Store cupboard
300 g dried udon noodles or egg noodles or ready-cooked noodles
100 g pitted prunes (preferably no-soak)
2 tbsp wheatgerm (optional)
2 x 420 g cans butter beans
3 x 410 g cans haricot beans
1 x 400 g can chopped tomatoes
1 x 220 g can sliced bamboo shoots
30 g pine nuts
30 g sunflower seeds
2 tsp sesame seeds
1-3 tbsp miso paste (according to taste) or 5 sachets instant miso soup
2 tsp creamed horseradish (optional for Smoked Salmon, Potato Pancakes and Beetroot Salad)
1 tbsp pickled ginger (optional for Japanese Miso Noodle Soup)
½ tbsp toasted sesame oil (optional for Japanese miso noodle soup)
drizzle of chilli oil (optional for Japanese Miso Noodle Soup)
2 tbsp soy sauce
generous pinch of chilli powder
500 ml cider
500 ml red wine

Serving suggestions
pitta breads (Greek Butter Bean and Broccoli Salad)
bread and green salad ingredients (Baked Omelette with Butternut Squash and Sorrel)
green vegetable, such as cabbage, or green salad ingredients, and bread or,
if want a very hearty meal, potatoes for mashing (Italian Sausage and Bean Casserole)

To download or print out this shopping list, please visit www.thekitchenrevolution.co.uk/April/Week4

**Big meal
from scratch**

Pork Chops, Leeks and Prunes in Cider, with Mash and Broccoli

Combining pork and apples, whether in the form of roast pork and apple sauce or cold pork and apple chutney, is well known and well loved. This partnership works because the sharp-sweet flavour of apple sets off the sweet flavour of pork. In this recipe the same principle is applied, but with the addition of prunes and cider.

When buying cider look out for the likes of Westons or Aspall who make traditional cider from English apples. Aim for a dry to medium cider (but certainly not sweet).

The extra broccoli in this recipe is used to make the warm Greek Butter Bean and Broccoli Salad (see page 188) later in the week and the extra mash is rehashed, literally, for Smoked Salmon, Potato Pancakes and Beetroot Salad (see page 000).

Pork chops, leeks and
prunes in cider
4 × 200-250 g free-range pork
  chops (ideally loin)
40 g butter
groundnut or grapeseed oil
3 leeks with green tops, approx.
  360 g
500 ml cider
2 garlic cloves
2 sprigs fresh sage
juice of 1 lemon
100 g pitted prunes (preferably
  no-soak)
salt and pepper

Mash
1.5 kg mashing potatoes, such as
  Maris Piper or baking potatoes;
  includes approx. 600 g extra
  for the potato pancakes
100 ml milk or 75 ml milk and
  2 tbsp double cream
50 g butter

Broccoli
2-3 heads broccoli, 800-1 kg;
  includes 500-600 g extra for
  the Greek butter bean and
  broccoli salad

GET AHEAD PREPARATION (optional)

The chops can be browned and
their accompanying sauce can be
made, ready to be popped in the
oven. If you only have a little
time:
* Prepare the potatoes and cover
  with water until required.
* Prepare the leeks, garlic and
  broccoli.

1 hour 20 minutes before you want to eat prepare the chops

* Preheat the oven to 190°C/375°F/Gas Mark 5.
* Start by browning the chops. Heat half the butter and a splash of oil in a large frying pan. Season the chops with salt and pepper and brown them over a medium to high heat for a couple of minutes on each side until they have a lovely golden colour. You will probably have to do this in two batches. While the chops are browning, slice the leeks finely, and wash very well When they are clean, drain in a colander.
* When the chops are browned, lift them out and place them, in one layer, in a roasting tin or ovenproof dish. Then pour half the cider into the frying pan and bring to the boil while stirring. Pour this liquor over the chops.
* Now make the accompaniment to the chops. Return the pan to the heat, and melt the remaining butter with another splash of oil. Add the leeks and once they have started to wilt turn the heat down, put a lid on the pan and let them cook gently for about 5-7 minutes until they begin soften.
* While the leeks are softening, peel and thinly slice the garlic and tear the sage leaves into strips. Add the sage and garlic to the leeks and cook for a few minutes more, stirring from time to time. Once the leeks are nice and soft, add the lemon juice and bring everything to the boil. Let the mixture bubble away for a couple of minutes before adding the remaining cider and the prunes. Bring back to the boil, season to taste with salt and pepper and simmer for a few minutes.
* Using a slotted spoon put a quarter of the leek and prune mixture on to each chop, and pour the cooking liquor and any stray leeks around the chops. Cover with a lid or two layers of foil and place in the oven for 30 minutes.

40 minutes before you want to eat cooks the potatoes

* Peel the potatoes, cut them into even-sized pieces and put them in a pan of salted water. Bring to the boil and simmer gently until the potatoes are just cooked – this will take 20-25 minutes, depending on the size of the pieces.
* While the potatoes are cooking, trim the broccoli and break it into even-sized florets.

10 minutes before you want to eat cook the broccoli and mash the potatoes

* The chops should be ready by now, so turn off the oven and leave them to rest at the bottom of the oven. Put some plates and serving dishes in to warm.
* Steam the broccoli for 5–7 minutes until it is just cooked and the stems retain a little bite.
* When the potatoes are cooked, drain them in a colander. Put the milk or milk and cream, and the butter into the empty potato pan over a low heat so that the butter melts and the milk heats. Place the colander containing the potatoes over the pan to dry them out and prevent a sloppy mash.
* When the milk is hot and the butter has melted, add the potatoes and mash them well with a traditional masher or, for a really smooth texture, pass them through a mouli-legumes or potato ricer.
* Taste and season as necessary, scoop just over half the mash into a serving dish and keep warm. Leave the remaining mash to cool for use later in the week.
* When the broccoli is cooked, season well, put half to one side to cool for use later in the week and the rest into a serving dish. Take the chops from the oven, lift each chop with its topping on to warm plates and ladle over lashings of pan juices. Serve with the mash and broccoli.

Afterwards

Put the mash and broccoli in separate containers, cover and place in the fridge.
You should have approx. 450 g mash and 500–600 g broccoli.

Greek Butter Bean and Broccoli Salad

Broccoli is especially delicious in a salad because the dressing seeps deeply into the florets so that each mouthful offers up an explosion of flavour. On a very hot summer day this salad is excellent cold, but as it is only April and likely to be chilly we suggest you warm the butter beans and broccoli. Served with toasted pitta bread this makes a substantial supper.

1 medium red onion, approx.
  120 g
5-7 tbsp olive oil
3 spring onions
2 garlic cloves
6 sprigs fresh mint
juice of 1 lemon
2 × 420 g cans butter beans
500–600 g broccoli left over from
  the Big Meal from Scratch or
  uncooked broccoli lightly
  steamed until just cooked
2 little gem lettuces
150–200 g feta
salt and pepper

To serve
warmed pitta breads

GET AHEAD PREPARATION (optional)

This salad is made mostly in the final assembly. If you have a little time:
* Prepare the onion, spring
  onions and garlic.

*15 minutes before
you want to eat*

* Peel and finely slice the red onion. Heat 1 tablespoon of the oil in a heavy-based pan over a medium heat. When the oil is hot, add the onion and fry until soft. This will take 7–10 minutes. Stir from time to time so that it doesn't get too brown.
* While the red onion is cooking make the dressing. Finely chop the spring onions, including any green leaves that are not too thick or tough as they add colour, texture and flavour.
* Peel and finely chop or crush the garlic, and strip the mint leaves from their stalks and roughly chop them. Put the lemon juice, spring onions, garlic and mint leaves in a small container. Mix well then add the remaining oil. Taste, season with salt and pepper and add more oil if the mixture is too acidic. Leave to one side while you finish off the salad.
* Next, drain the butter beans and rinse them under warm water. Add them to the softened red onion and warm gently.
* Make sure the broccoli is broken into just larger than bite-sized florets and add to the pan. Stir once or twice and allow to gently warm through.
* While the broccoli and beans are warming, wash and dry the little gems and tear the leaves in half. Place the leaves in a large salad bowl, then toss them with the warmed broccoli and bean mixture. Cut or crumble the feta into the salad and pour in the dressing. Mix well and serve with warmed pitta breads.

Something
for nothing 2

Smoked Salmon, Potato Pancakes and Beetroot Salad

Potato pancakes made from leftover mash have a light texture and involve minimal work. Served in this form, with smoked salmon and a horseradishy beetroot salad, humble mash is transformed to create a meal that's elegant but substantial.

Potato pancakes remind Rosie of days working for Juliet Peston, a friend and mentor – she has been the cookery brain behind some of London's best restaurants.

Smoked salmon
200–300 g smoked salmon
1 lemon, plus lemon juice for
  tossing
salad leaves, such as baby leaf
  spinach
olive oil

Potato pancakes
3 free-range eggs
2 free-range egg whites
3 tbsp crème fraîche
3 tbsp self-raising flour
450 g mashed potatoes left over
  from the Big Meal from Scratch
  or 500 g potatoes, peeled,
  cooked and mashed
groundnut or grapeseed oil

Beetroot salad
400 g cooked beetroot (not
  pickled in vinegar)
1 small bunch chives
½ lemon
4 tbsp crème fraîche
2 tsp creamed horseradish
  (optional)
salt and pepper

GET AHEAD PREPARATION (optional)

This beetroot salad and potato pancake batter can be made a couple of hours in advance. If you only have a little time:
* Chop the chives.
* Slice the beetroot

30 minutes before you want to eat

* Preheat the oven to 140°C/275°F/Gas Mark 1.
* Start by making the pancake batter. Beat the eggs, egg whites and crème fraîche together and stir the mixture and the flour into the mash until you have a smooth batter. You can easily throw it all into a food processor.
* Add a splash of oil to a large frying pan and heat until hot. When the oil is hot start making the pancakes. You should get 8 or so pancakes from the mix. Drop 2 heaped tablespoons of the mixture on either side of the pan and let them set into saucer-sized pancakes. Alternatively, you can fill the pan with half the pancake mixture then divide the mixture into two once it's cooked.
* When little bubbles start to appear, flip the pancakes over and let them get brown on the other side. Keep the warm in the oven while you cook the remaining pancakes.
* While the pancakes are cooking make the beetroot salad. Peel the beetroot if necessary and halve them. Cut them into thickish slices, place in a bowl and snip the chives over them. Season well with salt and pepper and squeeze in the juice of the half lemon. Add the crème fraîche and horseradish, mix together and turn into a serving dish.
* Place the smoked salmon on a serving plate and divide the lemon into four. Put the salad leaves in a bowl and toss with olive oil and lemon juice.
* When you have cooked all the pancakes, serve them on a plate and pass the smoked salmon, lemons, beetroot salad and the bowl of lightly dressed leaves around separately.

Seasonal supper

Baked Omelette with Butternut Squash and Sorrel

This dish is colourful, flavourful and simple to make – definitely one to share with friends. It's rather like a quiche or tart without the pastry – instead it has a crunchy topping of wheatgerm, pine nuts and sunflower seeds. Although the recipe calls for Parmesan, this is a good vehicle for using up any pieces of cheese that are knocking around.

Sorrel is a seasonal leaf that looks a little like spinach but has a sharper, more lemony flavour. It is sometimes available in supermarkets, but if you can't find it baby leaf spinach with lemon juice and zest will re-create a similar flavour and works very well in this recipe.

2 medium red onions, approx.
 240 g
20 g butter
2 tbsp olive oil
1 small butternut squash,
 approx. 600 g
60 g sorrel or 75 g baby leaf
 spinach and the juice and zest
 of
 1 lemon
2 slices bread (whatever you

have to hand)
60 g Parmesan
30 g sunflower seeds
30 g pine nuts
2 tbsp wheatgerm (optional)
6 free-range eggs
180 ml milk
salt and pepper

To serve
Warm bread and green salad

GET AHEAD PREPARATION (optional)

* Peel and slice the onions and
 butternut squash.
* Make the topping.
* Prepare the sorrel or spinach.

40 minutes before you want to eat

* Preheat oven to 190°C/375°F/Gas Mark 5.
* Peel and slice the onions. Heat half the butter and a generous splash of oil in a large heavy-based pan with a lid. When the butter has melted add the onions and cook gently until soft.
* Meanwhile, peel the squash, cut it in half and remove the seeds, then cut it into 5-mm thick slices across its length.
* By the time you have prepared the squash, the onions will be soft, so add the squash and the rest of the butter to the pan. Stir for a couple of minutes, then cover with a lid and leave the squash to soften for about 10 minutes.
* Meanwhile, wash the sorrel or spinach, remove any thick stalks and make the topping. Chop, grate or whizz the bread into breadcrumbs. Grate the Parmesan and roughly chop the sunflower seeds and pine nuts, and mix with the breadcrumbs and wheatgerm.
* When the squash has softened, add the sorrel or the spinach and lemon zest, replace the lid and allow the leaves to wilt – this will take a couple of minutes.
* When the leaves have wilted, add the lemon juice, if using spinach, and season to taste with salt and pepper. Now tip the squash mixture into an ovenproof dish and leave it while you beat the eggs and milk together and season them thoroughly.
* Pour the egg and milk over the squash mixture, sprinkle with the topping and place the dish in the oven. Bake until set – this will take about 15 minutes.
* Serve straight from the dish with warmed bread and a simple green salad.

Japanese Miso Noodle Soup

This is a quick, midweek supper that involves almost no preparation. It does rely, however, on sourcing miso – either in paste or sachet form. Japanese flavours and style of eating have taken a long time to catch on in the United Kingdom, but in the last couple of years, as noodle and sushi bars have gained in popularity, supermarkets have started to stock increasing amounts of Japanese ingredients.

Miso is as important in Japanese cooking as soy sauce – it's used as the basis for stocks and broths as well as a marinade for fish and meat. It's made from fermented soya bean curd and can range in colour from pale straw to dark brown. The paste has a texture similar to marzipan. Once the preserve of specialist shops, miso paste can now be bought from most health food shops and big supermarkets, and is a great standby supper ingredient to have in the fridge where it keeps for months without spoiling. If you cannot find miso paste it's also possible to use miso soup mixture, which comes in sachet form and has to be reconstituted with water rather like a bouillon powder.

We have suggested you top each bowl of steaming broth with a few pieces of pickled ginger which will complement the salmon very well. It is sometimes found in the 'oriental' section of supermarkets, but if you can't find it don't worry.

4 frozen salmon fillets, approx.
    150–75 g each
1 small onion, approx. 80 g
1 × 220 g can sliced bamboo
    shoots
2 tbsp groundnut or grapeseed
    oil
½ tbsp toasted sesame oil
    (optional)
300 g dried udon noodles or egg
    noodles or ready-cooked
    noodles
1 litre chicken stock (fresh or
    made from a stock cube or
    bouillon powder)

2 tbsp soy sauce
1–3 tbsp miso paste (according
    to taste) or 5 sachets instant
    miso soup
6 spring onions
juice of 1 lime
2 tsp sesame seeds
generous pinch of chilli powder
200g frozen soya beans
chilli oil, for drizzling
1 tbsp pickled ginger (optional)

GET AHEAD PREPARATION (optional)

* Prepare the onion and spring
  onions.
* Defrost the salmon.

20 minutes before you want to eat

* Place the salmon fillets in a shallow dish and cover them with boiling water.
* Peel and thinly slice the onion and drain the bamboo shoots. Heat the groundnut or grapeseed oil, and the toasted sesame oil if using, in a wok or large frying pan until very hot. Add the onion and bamboo shoots and stir-fry for 5 minutes over a high heat.
* Cook the noodles according to the pack instructions
* While the noodles are cooking, add the stock, soy sauce and miso paste or sachets to the browned and softened onion and bamboo shoots. Turn up the heat and bring to the boil, stirring so that the miso dissolves.
* Trim and finely slice the spring onions, using as much of the green parts as you can.
* The salmon fillets should now be defrosted. If not, cover with boiling water once again for a few minutes. Pat them dry, remove the skin and cut into slices the thickness of a pound coin. Place in a bowl and toss together thoroughly with the lime juice, sesame seeds and chilli powder.
* Add the salmon pieces and soya beans to the broth and let them cook through.
* Once the salmon is opaque, ladle the soup into bowls, sprinkle with the spring onions and drizzle with chilli oil, according to taste. Top each bowl with pickled ginger.

Two for one

Italian Sausage and Bean Casserole

Cooking sausages and white beans in a richly flavoured sauce creates a meal that is hearty and robust. A grown-up version of sausages and beans, this will be equally enjoyed by adults and kids. The crucial component of this meal is the sausages. Low-quality sausages have a flaccid, pulpy texture and almost no taste. This recipe calls for sausages with enough body and flavour to partner and complement garlic, sage, onions and wine.

2 tbsp groundnut or grapeseed oil
12 good quality free-range pork sausages
4 medium red onions, approx. 480 g
3 garlic cloves
500 ml red wine
250 ml chicken or vegetable stock (fresh or made from a stock cube or bouillon powder)
1 × 400 g can chopped tomatoes
2 sprigs fresh sage
1 bay leaf
3 × 410 g cans haricot beans

To serve
green vegetable, such as cabbage, or a green salad
bread for mopping up the juices or creamy mashed potatoes

GET AHEAD PREPARATION (optional)

The whole dish can be prepared 2 days in advance and and gently reheated. If you only have a little time:
* Cut the sausages and brown.
* Prepare the onions and garlic.
* Chop the sage leaves.

1 hour before you want to eat

* Heat a good splash of the oil in a large frying pan and cut the sausages into halves or thirds. When the oil is hot, add as many sausages as you can turn easily. Cook the sausages over a medium heat until they are evenly browned. When the first batch is browned, lift the sausages on to a plate and add a little more oil to the frying pan. Add more sausages and brown as before. If the pan gets very brown and crusty it's worth rinsing and drying it between batches, otherwise the sausages may catch and burn.
* While the sausages are browning, peel and slice the onions and garlic.
* Heat the remaining oil (about 1 tablespoon) in a large casserole dish. It needs to be big enough for all the sausages and beans to fit in. Soften the onions for 10 minutes over a low to medium heat. Add the garlic and stir it about for a few minutes, then splash in the wine. Bring to the boil, reduce the heat to a simmer for a couple of minutes then add the stock and tomatoes and bring back to the boil.
* Roughly chop the sage leaves. Add the sausages, sage leaves and bay leaf and stir gently while you reduce the heat to simmering point.
* Put a lid on the casserole and leave to simmer for 25 minutes.

20 minutes before you want to eat

* When the sausages have been cooking for 25 minutes add the beans. Stir them in and bring them back to a simmer. Let them heat through for another 10–15 minutes. Leave the lid off if there seems to be excess liquid so that the whole lot becomes rich and unctuous.
* Put half the casserole in a container suitable for freezing and serve the rest with warm crusty bread or dollops of creamy mash, and a salad or green vegetable.

Lazy day supper – reheating instructions

* Defrost the sausages and beans thoroughly before reheating.
* Preheat the oven to 180°C/350°F/Gas Mark 4.
* Tip the sausages and beans into a casserole with a lid and heat in the oven for about 30 minutes.

Simmering versus boiling

Understanding the difference between boiling and simmering is critical. A good rolling boil at 100°C will have the surface of the liquid bubbling away furiously. A simmer is 4 degrees or more cooler (90°–96°C), and the surface of the liquid only shows occasional tiny bubbles. The latter is crucial in cooking meat. If you boil it too quickly it will be tough and inedible – if you simmer it slowly it will be tender and melting.

Recipes usually recommend that you bring the liquid up to temperature quickly over a high heat, then reduce the heat to bring the temperature down to a simmer. But achieving a really good slow simmer can be difficult if you're cooking on gas – even the smallest ring on its lowest setting can produce too strong a flame. If you are cooking with gas you can get little mesh plates that go over the rings and help to disperse the heat, so helping you to achieve a slower simmer.

Bread Pudding

This pudding is an absolute classic and is great in cold-weather. It's also a good way to use up leftover bread, and would be ideal if you have any leftover hot cross buns. We have made this bread pudding with butter, although suet is more commonly used. If you wish, you can replace the butter with an equal amount of suet. Bread pudding is good served at room temperature as well as hot. It can also be reheated in a low oven. This recipe was given to Rosie by her friend the ice cream maker Kitty Travers.

500 g bread
125 g butter or suet, plus extra
   butter for greasing
140 g dried fruit (we favour a
   mixture of apricots, pitted
   dates, raisins and sultanas)
125 g light brown soft sugar
1 tbsp mixed spice
1 free-range egg
½ tsp ground cinnamon
2 tsp demerera or unrefined
   granulated sugar

To serve
custard or cream

1 hour before you want to eat

* Break the bread into large bite-sized pieces and put it in a bowl. Cover with water and leave to soak while you prepare everything else.
* Grease a 20 x 25 cm (approx.) tin or ovenproof dish with butter.
* Mix the light brown sugar, dried fruit and mixed spice together in a large bowl. Grate the butter into the bowl and toss it through the fruit and sugar.
* Preheat the oven to 200°C/400°F/Gas Mark 6.
* Take the bread out of the water and squeeze it to remove excess liquid. Add the bread to the bowl containing the fruit and sugar, then break in the egg and mix the whole lot together thoroughly.
* Turn the mixture into the greased tin or dish and flatten it out. Sprinkle with the cinnamon and demerara or unrefined sugar and bake for 45 minutes to 1 hour, until firm and slightly crisp and brown on top.
* Serve warm or at room temperature with custard or cream.

Koliva – Serbian Sweet Wheat Pudding

Koliva is the Greek word for the wheat taken to church to be blessed. This sweetened dish is commonly found in Greece, Russia and the Balkans. Wheat berries have a nutty, plump texture and can be located in Greek grocers and some supermarkets. The only time-consuming part of this recipe is cooking the wheat berries – they take about 45 minutes.

Polly was given this recipe by Sladja, her Serbian friend.

180 g wheat berries
150 g shelled walnuts
30 g caster sugar
2 tbsp clear honey
juice of 1 lemon
½ tsp ground nutmeg

To serve
Greek yoghurt and, if you like,
 dried fruit or slices of banana

1 hour before you want to eat

* Wash the wheat berries well, then place them in a pan and cover with water. Bring to the boil and simmer for about 45 minutes until they are soft but not mushy.
* Drain the berries well then allow them to steam-dry and cool.
* Meanwhile, put the walnuts into a food processor and pulse two or three times until they are ground – don't overprocess them as they will become greasy and compact. Alternatively chop them finely.
* Put the sugar into a small pan with the honey and lemon juice and heat gently until the sugar melts.
* Tip the wheat berries into a deep bowl and mix them with the walnuts, sugar and honey syrup and the nutmeg. Taste and add extra sugar, nutmeg and honey as desired.
* Serve with a generous dollop of Greek yoghurt and perhaps dried fruit or slices of banana.

Rhubarb and Almond Tart

This tart is very easy to make and looks fantastic. Use the best quality marzipan you can, as this will make a difference to the flavour and texture. Some ready-made marzipans contain almond essence, which gives them an overly intense, fabricated almond taste. Leftover marzipan will freeze well and can be used in a summer fruit version of this tart. Ready-made, and especially ready-rolled, puff pastry is a life saver. The ready-rolled version normally comes in a 375 g pack and is a rectangle of about 25 x 35 cm – ideal for a tart for four to six people. If you buy unrolled puff pastry you will need to roll it out to a similar size and about the thickness of a pound coin. Perhaps accompany the tart with rhubarb's great companion, custard.

500 g chilled ready-made puff
   pastry or 375 g if ready-rolled
plain flour, for dusting
400 g rhubarb, the thinner the
   better
50 g unrefined granulated sugar
250 g best quality marzipan
85 g ground almonds

To serve
custard

45 minutes before you want to eat

* Begin by rolling out the pastry if you haven't bought it ready rolled. You need a rectangle of approximately 25 x 35 cm and the pastry needs to be about the thickness of a pound coin.
* Once the pastry is rolled out, leave it somewhere cool to rest while you get everything else ready.
* Preheat the oven to 200°C/400°F/Gas Mark 6 and preheat a baking sheet.
* Next, prepare the rhubarb. Wash it well and trim off any leaves. Cut the stalks into 2.5-cm lengths. If the rhubarb is coarse and thick you may have to peel it and slice the stalks in half lengthways. Put the rhubarb in a bowl, sprinkle with the sugar and toss the two together.
* Coarsely grate the marzipan into a bowl, add half the ground almonds and mix.
* You are now ready to assemble the tart. Using a sharp knife, score lines around the pastry rectangle, 2.5 cm in from each edge (take care not to cut all the way through the pastry). Take the hot baking sheet from the oven and slide the pastry on to it.
* Next, scatter the marzipan and almond mixture over the pastry, keeping inside the lines you scored, then arrange the rhubarb on top – you can go free form or arrange the pieces in straight lines, whatever you fancy. Finally, scatter over the remaining almonds.
* Return the baking sheet to the oven and bake until the pastry is puffed up and golden, and the rhubarb is just cooked.
* Serve with lashings of custard.

April puddings

Alternative Easter Cake

Simnel cake, enjoyed throughout Britain at Easter, was originally devised as a cake for Mothering Sunday. This mid-Lent treat then somehow found its way to becoming an Easter ritual with the balls of marzipan on the top said to depict the apostles. Our Easter cake has mixed peel and spices in common with a Simnel cake, but it also contains Easter eggs. Think of this as an Easter egg hunt in a cake – a lovely, light spiced sponge studded with meltingly gooey chocolate eggs.

225 g softened butter, plus extra
   for greasing
200 g light brown soft sugar
1 tsp ground cinnamon
1 tsp ground ginger
200 g self-raising flour
4 free-range eggs
50 g chopped mixed peel
175 g dark or milk chocolate
   mini eggs or buttons
25 g cornflour
3–4 tbsp milk

To serve
mascarpone

1 hour before you want to eat

* Preheat the oven to 180°C/350°F/Gas Mark 4. Grease a 25 cm round cake tin, ideally loose-bottomed, with butter.
* Beat the butter, sugar, cinnamon and ginger together until light and fluffy.
* Sift the flour and beat the eggs.
* Beat the eggs gradually into the butter and stir in the mixed peel and three-quarters of the chocolate eggs or buttons.
* Finally, fold in the flour. Loosen the mixture with a splash of milk now and again, until you have a smooth batter that drops easily from a spoon.
* Pour the mixture into the greased cake tin and scatter the rest of the chocolate eggs or buttons over the top. Bake in the oven for 45 minutes to 1 hour, until a skewer or toothpick inserted in the cake comes out clean.
* Leave to cool on a wire rack for a while before turning out. Serve warm with mascarpone.

MAY

May brings so many good things: warmer weather, two bank holidays – and English asparagus. We love this fat, tender shoot so much that it takes centre stage in three of this month's Seasonal Suppers. May is also the month for perfumed, lace-like elderflowers, a familiar ingredient in puddings and cordials, but used here to add delicate flavour to a broth of a poached chicken served with garlic new potatoes. Though not strictly seasonal, the Peppered Steaks with Caesar Salad and Chicken Waldorf Toasts suit summery eating, so why not? Spring Vegetable Soup with Potato and Herb Dumplings and Yoghurt Chicken with Spicy Baked Lentils keep perfectly in the freezer and can be saved for hot spells. Poached Rhubarb with Hazelnut Shortbread is an ideal seasonal pudding, as is an Elderflower Cream rather like a fragrant panna cotta.

May	Week 1	Week 2	Week 3	Week 4
Big meal from scratch	Fish stew with aioli, rouille, potatoes and salad	Pot roast veal (or pork) with morel mushrooms, new potatoes and steamed watercress	Pot roast Caribbean pork, roast sweet potatoes and spring greens	Elderflower poached chicken with wine and garlic new potatoes and cabbage
Something for nothing 1	Peppered steaks with Caesar salad	Parmesan and artichoke veal (or pork) with radicchio, celery and apple salad	Pork with lime coleslaw	New potato, asparagus and egg salad
Something for nothing 2	Potato, onion and horseradish tart	Smoked mackerel salad	Sweet potato and goats' cheese flatbreads with hazelnut and chicory salad	Chicken Waldorf toasts
Seasonal supper	Baked eggs with asparagus and ham	Sea trout (or salmon) baked with asparagus and Serrano ham	Parmesan chicken goujons with roast asparagus, garlic mayonnaise and rocket salad	Spiced lamb chops with radish and orange salad
Larder feast	Smoked mussel, fennel and tomato bake	Pea and ham pasta	Tuna empanada	Mushroom stroganoff
2 for 1	Spring vegetable soup with potato and herb dumplings	Yoghurt chicken with spicy baked lentils and salad	Beef braised with celeriac and morel mushrooms	Mexican beans with a polenta topping
Puddings	Elderflower cream	Rhubarb with hazelnut shortbread	Coffee granita, pistachio cream and chocolate sauce	Dried fruit spiced flapjacks

May Week 1 – Overview

For the first May bank holiday this week's Big Meal from Scratch is a rich Fish Stew that's good enough to serve to guests but easy enough to make without needing the excuse of an occasion. As with all fresh fish, make sure you cook the fish within a day or so of purchasing, or put it straight in the freezer until required.

The Fish Stew is served with salad, simply cooked potatoes and two traditional accompaniments: a hot pepper paste called a rouille and a garlic mayonnaise called aïoli. These intensify the soup and are also used later in the week to make one of the Something for Nothing recipes – Peppered Steaks with Caesar Salad. The steaks and salad take just 20 minutes to make and it's well worth inviting friends to enjoy them.

The surplus potatoes left over from the big meal are used as part of the topping for a Potato, Onion and Horseradish Tart, this week's other Something for Nothing recipe. Using ready-made pastry means there's minimal work involved but as the onions take 20 minutes to soften and sweeten and the tart takes 20 minutes to cook, allow 40 minutes in total to make it.

The Seasonal Supper welcomes the start of the asparagus season with a recipe for Baked Eggs with Asparagus and Ham.

The Two for One recipe, a Spring Vegetable Soup, takes 1 hour. It involves a fair amount of chopping but the method is straightforward and the end result is delicious and light. The addition of cloud-like potato and herb dumplings to the soup makes a good meal excellent. As with the soup, they freeze very well.

May Week 1	Recipe	Time
Big meal from scratch	Fish stew with aïoli, rouille, potatoes and salad	1 hours
Something for nothing 1	Peppered steaks with Caesar salad	20 mins
Something for nothing 2	Potato, onion and horseradish tart	40 mins
Seasonal supper	Baked eggs with asparagus and ham	25 mins
Larder feast	Smoked mussel, fennel and tomato bake	40 mins
2 for 1	Spring vegetable soup with potato and herb dumplings	1 hour

All recipes serve 4 apart from the 2 for 1 recipe which makes 8 portions

SHOPPING LIST (for 4 people)

Meat and fish
250 g smoked haddock fillets
200 g white fish fillets, such as pollack or
   frozen coley
200 g large raw peeled prawns
4 rump or sirloin steaks, approx. 600-800 g
200-300 g good quality sliced ham

Dairy
11 free-range eggs
105 g (approx.) butter
100 ml crème fraîche
120 ml double cream
225 g (approx.) Parmesan
370 g (approx.) ricotta

Fruit and vegetables
1.5 kg waxy maincrop potatoes, such as
   Desirée
4-5 large floury potatoes, such as Maris Piper
   or baking potatoes, approx. 750 g
20 asparagus spears
2 leeks, approx. 250g
5 courgettes, approx. 500 g
9 celery sticks
7 ripe tomatoes, approx. 500 g
200 g mixed salad leaves
3 hearts of romaine or cos lettuces or 4 little
   gem lettuces
½ cucumber
2 bulbs fennel, approx. 400 g
12 small onions, approx. 1.21 kg
2 large red onions, approx. 300g
12 garlic cloves
1-4 large red chillies (depending how hot you
   like the rouille)
1 sprig fresh thyme
1 large bunch flatleaf parsley
2 small bunches chives
small handful of fresh mint
large handful of fresh basil
4 lemons
400 g frozen peas

Basics
150 ml olive oil
120 ml groundnut or grapeseed oil
4 thick slices bread (brown or white
   - whatever you have to hand)
75 g breadcrumbs or 2-3 slices bread
   suitable for crumbing
350-400 g chilled ready-made shortcrust
   pastry (you can buy it ready-rolled)
110 g plain flour
2 tsp Dijon mustard
600 ml fish stock (fresh or made from a stock
   cube or bouillon powder)
2 litres chicken or vegetable stock (fresh
   or made from a stock cube or bouillon
   powder)
100 ml beef or chicken stock (fresh or made
   with a stock cube or bouillon powder)
salt and pepper

Store cupboard
2 × 400 g cans tomatoes
200 g canned pimientoes or piquante peppers
2-3 × 85 g cans smoked mussels in oil
30 g anchovy fillets in olive oil
½ tsp saffron threads
1 tbsp creamed horseradish or horseradish
   sauce
2 tsp coarsely ground black pepper or
   crushed black peppercorns
350 ml white wine
100 ml red wine

Quick option (aïoli)
6 tbsp mayonnaise
2 garlic cloves
½ lemon
Omit 3 garlic cloves, 2 tsp Dijon mustard,
   100 ml groundnut or grapeseed oil, 50 ml
   olive oil, ½ lemon from shopping list

Serving suggestions
chips (Peppered Steak with Caesar Salad)
green salad ingredients (Potato, Onion and
   Horseradish Tart)
crusty bread and green salad ingredients
   (Baked Eggs with Asparagus and Ham)
rice, green salad ingredients or green beans
   and a few black olives (Smoked Mussel,
   Fennel and Tomato Bake)

To download or print out this shopping list,
please visit www.thekitchenrevolution.co.uk/May/
Week1

Fish Stew with Aïoli, Rouille, Potatoes and Salad

The famous Provençal fish stew, *bourride*, is served with aïoli, a garlicky mayonnaise. In this big meal recipe the aïoli is whisked into the soup to create a creamy texture and pungent taste. The fish stew is served with rouille, a fiery hot paste, made by pounding sweet red peppers, chillies, olive oil and garlic together. This stew is so rich and has so many different flavours we decided to serve it with very simple accompaniments – boiled potatoes and salad.

   To guarantee that the ingredients for this recipe are easy to source, and to make it ultimately family friendly, we've suggested using smoked haddock, a white fish such as pollack or frozen coley, and prawns – minimal fuss and minimal bones. To make llife easier the aïoli can be made using ready bought mayonnaise (see below).

   This recipe is based on a fish soup that Polly and Rosie came to love while working with Joyce Molyneux at her restaurant, The Carved Angel, in Dartmouth.

   The ingredients include extra quantities of aïoli, rouille and mash for the Peppered Steaks and the Potato, Onion and Horseradish Tart.

Fish stew
2 small onions, approx 180g
2 leeks, approx 250g
olive oil
2 bulbs fennel, approx 200g
3 celery sticks
2 garlic cloves
½ cucumber
½ tsp saffron threads
1 sprig fresh thyme
250 ml white wine
1 × 400 g can chopped tomatoes
small handful of fresh flatleaf
   parsley
600 ml fish stock (fresh or made
   from a stock cube)
½ lemon
250 g smoked haddock fillets
200 g white fish fillets, such as
   pollack or frozen coley
200 g large raw peeled prawns
salt and pepper

Aïoli
3 garlic cloves
1 free-range egg
1 free-range egg yolk
2 tsp Dijon mustard

100 ml groundnut or grapeseed
   oil
50 ml olive oil
½ lemon
or
3 garlic cloves
6 tbsp mayonnaise
½ lemon
includes 3 tbsp extra for the
   peppered steaks with Caesar
   salad

Rouille
1 garlic clove
1-4 large red chillies (depending
   how hot you like it)
200 g canned pimientoes or
   piquante peppers
2 tbsp olive oil
(half the quantity is for the
   peppered steaks with Caesar
   salad)

Potatoes
1.5 kg waxy maincrop potatoes,
   such as Desirée; includes 500-
   600 g extra for the Potato,
   Onion and Horseradish Tart

Salad
200 g mixed salad leaves of
   choice
1 small bunch chives
small handful of fresh mint
juice of ½ lemon
3 tbsp olive oil

GET AHEAD PREPARATION (optional)

The tomato base for the fish stew, the rouille and the aïoli can be made up to a day in advance. If you only have a little time:
* Prepare any of the vegetables for the stew.
* Peel the potatoes and cover with water until required.
* Prepare the salad leaves.
* Chop the parsley, chives and mint.

*1 hour before
you want to eat
prepare the fish
stew and rouille*

* Peel and slice the onions. Trim, slice and wash the leeks. Place a large pan over a medium heat, add a generous layer of oil and when it is hot throw in the onions and leeks. Allow these to soften while you prepare the other vegetables.
* Trim any brown areas or tough outer layers from the fennel and slice the bulbs finely. Wash and slice the celery and chop it into 5 mm pieces. Peel and slice the garlic and cucumber. Add all of these to the onions and leeks and cook.
* After 5 minutes add the saffron, thyme sprig, wine and tomatoes and bring to simmering point. Simmer for just over 5 minutes. Meanwhile wash, dry and finely chop the parsley.
* Add the stock, a squeeze of lemon juice and all but 1 tablespoon of the parsley. Turn the heat up and bring to the boil.
* While the broth is coming to the boil, if the smoked haddock and white fish are whole fillets cut into pieces 5-10 cm wide.
* The broth can tick away gently until you want to cook the fish – you don't want it to reduce, though, so keep a lid on.

* Now make the rouille. Peel the garlic and deseed the chillies. Put all the rouille ingredients in a food processor and whizz to an emulsified paste or blend with a hand blender. Taste and adjust the seasoning as necessary – rouille is meant to be pretty fiery. Put half of the rouille in the fridge for later in the week.

30 minutes before you want to eat cook the potatoes and make the rouille

* Peel the potatoes and cut them in half if they are larger than egg size. Fill a pan with salted water, add the potatoes and bring to the boil. Simmer gently for about 15–20 minutes until they are just cooked.
* While the potatoes are cooking, make the aïoli. To make the version with ready-made mayonnaise, peel and crush the garlic and stir it into the mayonnaise with a very good squeeze of lemon juice.
* To make the aïoli from scratch, peel and crush the garlic. Place the egg and egg yolk in a food processor with the garlic and mustard. Whizz them for 1–2 minutes and put the groundnut or grapeseed oil and the olive oil in a jug. Now very gradually, while the processor is on, start pouring the oil into the egg and mustard mixture. Do this in a very slow stream; once the mixture seems to be thickening and emulsifying it should be fine to add the oil more quickly. When all the oil is absorbed, taste the aïoli and add a squeeze of lemon juice and salt and pepper to your liking.
* Put half the aïoli in the fridge for later in the week.
* Now make the salad. Wash and trim the salad leaves and chop the chives and mint. Mix the lemon juice and oil together in a jar or other container with a lid. Place the salad in a large bowl and put a couple of serving dishes and big soup bowls in a warm oven (140°C/275°F/Gas Mark 1) to heat.

15 minutes before you want to eat add the fish

* The tomato base of the stew should still be ticking away gently. Turn the heat up and season the fish before adding it to the pan to cook very gently for 5 minutes. If you are using frozen coley give this a 5-minute head start on the smoked haddock.
* Finally add the prawns and simmer for a further couple of minutes.
* Remove the soup from the heat, lift out the thyme sprig if it hasn't disappeared completely and whisk in the aïoli – this will thicken it slightly and give it a rich, creamy texture.
* Drain the potatoes, season them with salt and pepper and toss in the remaining parsley from the stew.
* Serve the fish stew in bowls. Pass the potatoes and rouille round separately and follow with the salad.

Afterwards

Put any leftover potatoes – you should have 500–600 g – and the remaining aïoli and rouille in separate containers, cover and refrigerate for use later in the week.

Peppered Steaks with Caesar Salad

Sometimes, when you need a treat nothing but a steak will suffice. Combining this with Caesar salad is ever so slightly indulgent, but once in a while decadence should be embraced.

This recipe calls for peppered steak, but with a difference. The spicy pepper paste (rouille) from the Big Meal from Scratch is rubbed all over the meat and crushed peppercorns are pressed on top. Left to marinate, the rouille will have a tenderising effect as well as spicing up the steak. To make a rouille from scratch blend a small clove of garlic, 1–2 chillies, a handful of pimentoes or piquante peppers plus 1 tablespoon of olive oil in a blender.

Caesar salad is made from lettuce leaves tossed in a creamy, anchovy dressing with croûtons and Parmesan. Using the extra aïoli from the big meal in the dressing helps to reduce the labour. If you don't have any aïoli left over, mix ½ clove of garlic, squeeze of lemon juice, salt and pepper to 3 tablespoons of mayonnaise. Croûtons made in the oven take very little time and are a good way of using stale bread, but if you are in a real hurry you could buy some ready-made.

Peppered steaks
4 rump or sirloin steaks, approx. 600–800 g
rouille left over from the Big Meal from Scratch (or see above)
2 tsp coarsely ground black pepper or crushed black peppercorns
30 g butter
groundnut or grapeseed oil
100 ml red wine
100 ml beef or chicken stock (fresh or made from a stock cube or bouillon powder)
salt and pepper

Caesar salad
4 thick slices bread (brown or white – whatever you have to hand)
olive oil
30 g anchovy fillets in olive oil
½ lemon
3 tbsp aïoli left over from the Big Meal from Scratch (or see above)
30 g Parmesan

3 hearts of romaine or cos lettuces or 4 little gem lettuces

To serve
chips

GET AHEAD PREPARATION (optional)

* Make the croûtons and the Caesar dressing.
* Grate the Parmesan.
* Season the steak with the rouille and pepper or peppercorns.

* Preheat the oven to 180°C/350°F/Gas Mark 4.
* Prepare the steaks by trimming any excess fat. Rub the rouille thoroughly over each side and then press the pepper or peppercorns into the flesh.
* Cut the bread into 2–3 cm cubes and place them on a baking sheet. Drizzle the cubes with the oil and toss them about so that they are well coated. Place them in the oven and bake them until they are crisp for about 10 minutes. Leave to cool.
* Mash up the anchovies. Add a squeeze of lemon juice and add the aïoli. Taste the dressing and season as necessary. Grate the Parmesan and set aside. Wash and separate the lettuce leaves.
* Heat the butter and a splash of oil in a large, heavy-based frying pan over a medium to high heat. You want the fat to be very hot. Add the steaks – probably two at a time. For a rare steak, an average-sized piece of meat about 2.5 cm thick will take 3 minutes on each side; allow 4½ minutes on each side for medium and 8 minutes on each side for well done.
* Place the lettuce in a big salad bowl, breaking up any very large leaves. Add the croûtons and half the Parmesan, and season with a little salt and plenty of pepper. Drizzle most of the dressing over the leaves and toss thoroughly. Scatter the remaining Parmesan over.
* When the steaks are ready, remove them from the pan and let them rest in a warm place. Keep the pan over the heat, add the wine and let it boil for 1–2 minutes before adding the stock. Let the sauce simmer for a couple of minutes, then season to taste.
* Serve the steaks with the sauce, the salad and chips.

Something
for nothing 2

Potato, Onion and Horseradish Tart

One of the glorious qualities of onions is their capacity for turning meltingly sweet when sliced thin and cooked very slowly. Used as a topping for a tart, onions cooked like this counter and complement the richness and crumbliness of pastry. Adding horseradish and potato to a classic onion tart is delicious. This tart is very simple to make but the onions will take time to melt down to a sweet, soppy mass.

30 g butter
groundnut or grapeseed oil
4 large or 6 small onions,
    approx 600g
plain flour, for dusting
350-400 g chilled ready-made
    shortcrust pastry (it can be
    bought ready-rolled)
500-600 g potatoes left over
    from the Big Meal from Scratch
    or 600-700 g potatoes (King
    Edward or Desiree) peeled and
    boiled for 15-20 minutes
small handful of flatleaf parsley
100 ml crème fraîche
1 tbsp creamed horseradish or
    horseradish sauce
salt and pepper

To serve
green salad

GET AHEAD PREPARATION (optional)

The tart can be made up to 2
days in advance and reheated. If
you only have a little time:
* Peel, slice and cook the
onions.
* Roll out the pastry.
* Chop the parsley.

*40 minutes before
you want to eat*

* Preheat the oven to 220°C/425°F/Gas Mark 7 or its nearest setting and preheat a baking sheet. Putting the uncooked tart on to a hot baking sheet will help the bottom to become crisp.
* Melt the butter with a splash of oil in a heavy-based pan with a lid while you peel and finely slice the onions. Add the onions to the pan and stir them so that they are well coated. Add a splash of water and some salt and pepper, put on the lid and leave to cook slowly over a low heat for 20 minutes. After 10 minutes, check they aren't sticking, and stir.
* While the onions are cooking, get everything else ready for the tart. Lightly dust a work surface with flour and roll the pastry out into rough rectangle, about 25 x 30 cm, and about the thickness of a pound coin. So that the pastry can be lifted without tearing, roll it around the rolling pin and lift it on to a large piece of foil or baking paper. Leave it to rest in a cool place until you need it.
* Slice the potatoes to about the thickness of a pound coin and roughly chop the parsley. Season the crème fraîche and stir in the horseradish.
* When the onions have been cooking for 20 minutes, take the lid off the pan and simmer for about 5 minutes so that any surplus liquid evaporates. Once the liquid has gone the onions will be soft and ready to be spread on the tart. Mix the parsley with the onions and season to taste.
* Now spread the onions over the pastry in an even layer, leaving a 3-4 cm frame around the edge of the tart. Add a layer of potatoes, season the layer and cover with blobs of the crème fraîche and horseradish mixture.
* Take the hot baking sheet out of the oven and carefully slide the tart on the foil or paper on to it. Place in the oven and bake for 15-20 minutes until the pastry is crisp.
* Once cooked, cut the tart into four and serve with a green salad.

Seasonal supper

Baked Eggs with Asparagus and Ham

The English asparagus season officially starts on St George's Day and is marked in the calendar of all asparagus lovers. Although the vegetable is globally sourced and available throughout the year, English asparagus with its thick, fat stems and strong flavour is hard to beat. During its short season it's worth eating as much of it as possible. This simple dish makes the most of a classic combination: asparagus and eggs.

Knowing about baked eggs is an invaluable tool for the cook, especially one who is sometimes caught short of time, ingredients or energy. There is no limit to the combinations that can be used to make baked egg dishes – smoked haddock and bacon, goats' cheese and sorrel – even just spinach – are a few other ingredients that work especially well.

20 asparagus spears
200-300 g good quality sliced
    ham
1 small bunch chives
120 ml double cream
15 g butter
8 free-range eggs
salt and pepper

To serve
crusty bread or new potatoes
green salad

GET AHEAD PREPARATION (optional)

* Trim, wash and cook the
    asparagus.
* Finely chop the chives.

25 minutes before you want to eat

* Preheat the oven to 190°C/375°F/Gas Mark 5.
* Prepare the asparagus by bending each spear so that it snaps at the point where the base turns woody. Discard the woody parts. As asparagus can sometimes be gritty, rinse the spears under running water.
* Cook the spears in salted boiling water for 3–4 minutes until tender.
* In the meantime, cut the ham into strips about 1–2 cm thick. Finely chop the chives and stir them into the cream along with a little salt and pepper.
* When the asparagus spears are tender, lift them out of the boiling water with a slotted spoon. Keep the water for later. Run the asparagus spears under cold water to retain their vibrant colour then cut them into bite-sized lengths.
* Now melt the butter and pour it into an ovenproof dish, about 30 x 20 cm and 5 cm deep. Put the asparagus pieces into the dish, toss them in the butter and season them well. Distribute the ham pieces around the asparagus then break the eggs on top and pour over the cream.
* Place the dish in a roasting tin and pour the hot asparagus water carefully around it so that it comes about halfway up the sides of the dish.
* Bake for 15 minutes for soft runny eggs or 20 minutes for hard ones. Eat with crusty bread to mop up all the tasty juices or new potatoes and a green salad tossed in olive oil and lemon juice.

Larder feast

Smoked Mussel, Fennel and Tomato Bake

Canned seafood and fish provide the cook with a secret weapon in the face of an empty fridge and an unexpected guest. Smoked mussels are surprisingly underrated; they have an addictive flavour so it's well worth having a couple of cans in the larder at all times. They are sold either in olive oil or brine – always go for the former. If you can't find smoked mussels in oil, replace them with about 200 g canned mackerel fillets in tomato sauce.

2 large red onions, approx. 190 g
1 tbsp olive oil
2 large bulbs fennel, approx.
   400 g
2 garlic cloves
1 lemon
1 × 400 g can chopped tomatoes
2-3 × 85 g cans smoked mussels
   in oil
100 ml (approx.) white wine
handful of fresh parsley
75 g breadcrumbs or 2-3 slices
   bread suitable for crumbing
30 g (approx.) butter
salt and pepper

To serve
Rice and a green salad or cooked
   green beans tossed with olive
   oil, lemon juice and black
   olives

GET AHEAD PREPARATION (optional)

The recipe can be made a few hours in advance up to the point of going under the grill. If you only have a little time:
* Prepare the onions and garlic.
* Make the tomato and mussel mixture.
* Prepare and cook the fennel.
* Make the breadcrumbs.
* Chop the parsley.

40 minutes before you want to eat

* Peel the onions and chop them into a smallish dice.
* Heat the oil in a large heavy-based pan over a medium heat. Add the onions and cook for 7–10 minutes until soft.
* While the onions are cooking, trim the fennel bulbs of any brown or bruised outer layers then cut them into sixths.
* Put the fennel in a pan and cover with water. Add a generous pinch of salt and bring the water to the boil. Let the fennel pieces cook for about 5–10 minutes or until a sharp knife inserted into one of them meets only a little resistance.
* While the onions and fennel are cooking away, peel and slice the garlic, grate the zest from the lemon and open the cans of tomatoes and mussels.
* When the onions have softened, add a splash of oil from one of the cans of mussels. Add the garlic, stir it about for a minute or so then turn the heat up and splash in the wine. Bring the wine to the boil and reduce it for 2 minutes.
* Now add the tomatoes and lemon zest to the onions. Stir well and bring to the boil, then turn down to a vigorous simmer. Cook for 7–10 minutes.
* When the fennel pieces are cooked, drain them well and place them in an ovenproof dish.
* Next, preheat the grill to high. Roughly chop the parsley and, if necessary, chop, whizz or grate the bread into breadcrumbs. Mix half the parsley into the breadcrumbs.
* Stir the rest of the parsley into the tomato sauce along with the drained mussels. Season to taste with salt and pepper and pour the tomato and mussel mixture over the fennel. Sprinkle with the breadcrumbs and dot with the butter.
* Place under the grill for 5 minutes or until the crumbs are browned and the tomato, mussel and fennel mixture is bubbling.
* Serve with rice and a green salad or cooked green beans tossed with olive oil, lemon juice and roughly chopped olives.

Two for one

Spring Vegetable Soup with Potato and Herb Dumplings

This light soup, packed with herbs, tomatoes and vegetables, is particularly enjoyable on a late spring evening. It is based on the classic Italian minestra (a lighter version of the well-known minestrone), with the added delight of potato, herb and cheese dumplings.

    If you have the time, the dumplings are easy to make, but you could serve the soup with croûtons or fresh bread and Parmesan if you are in a particular hurry. The soup and dumplings for this Two for One have to be frozen separately.

<u>Spring vegetable soup</u>
4 small onions, approx. 300 g
olive oil
4 garlic cloves
6 celery sticks
7 ripe tomatoes, approx. 500 g
5 courgettes, approx. 500 g
400 g frozen peas
2 litres chicken or vegetable
    stock (fresh or made from a
    stock cube or bouillon powder)
grated Parmesan, for sprinkling

<u>Potato and herb dumplings</u>
4–5 large floury potatoes, such
    as Maris Piper or baking
    potatoes, approx. 750 g
175 g Parmesan
½ lemon
1 free-range egg yolk
370 g (approx.) ricotta
100 g plain flour
handful of fresh flatleaf parsley
large handful of fresh basil
salt and pepper

<u>GET AHEAD PREPARATION (optional)</u>

The soup and the dumplings can be prepared a day in advance, up until the point the dumplings are added to the soup. If you only have a little time:
* Prepare the onions and garlic.
* Prepare the potatoes and cover with water until required.
* Chop the herbs.
* Grate the lemon zest.
* Prepare the vegetables for the soup.

1 hour before you want to eat make the dumplings

* Start by making the dumplings. Peel the potatoes, chop them into quarters and bring to the boil in a large pan of salted water. Cook until soft – this will take 15–20 minutes.
* While the potatoes are cooking, grate the Parmesan and zest the lemon. Mix two-thirds of the Parmesan with the egg yolk, ricotta cheese, flour, lemon zest, 1 teaspoon salt and 1 teaspoon pepper.
* Roughly chop the parsley and half the basil and stir them into the cheese mixture.
* Drain the potatoes and mash them very well, or pass them through a potato ricer or mouli-legumes – don't be tempted to use a food processor, as you will end up with glue. Add this to the cheese and herbs. Mix together well, taste and season if necessary. Tip the mixture out on to a chopping board or work surface and flatten with the back of a spoon so that it is about 2 cm thick. Allow to cool while you make the soup.

30 minutes before you want to eat make the soup

* Peel and finely chop the onions. Heat a generous glug of oil in a large heavy-based pan. When the oil is hot, add the onions and cook for 7–10 minutes until starting to soften.
* While the onions are softening, peel and thinly slice the garlic, wash the celery sticks and chop them into small pieces. Once the onions are soft, add the celery and garlic to the onions and cook over a gentle heat for another 5 minutes.
* Meanwhile, prepare the remaining vegetables. Plunge the tomatoes in a large bowl of boiling water. After a couple of minutes, lift them out of the water, run them under the cold tap and peel them. The skins should slide off easily.
* Cut the tomatoes into quarters and then into pieces about 1 cm square.
* Slice the courgettes in half lengthways and then across into crescents a little thicker than a pound coin.
* Add the courgettes to the softened and slightly caramelised onions, garlic and celery mixture, give them a few minutes to soften then add the tomatoes, frozen peas and stock. Season, bring to a gentle simmer and cook for 15 minutes.

20 minutes before you want to eat brown the dumplings

* Cut the potato mixture into approximately 3-cm squares.
* Heat a good splash of oil in a frying pan over a medium heat. Take the potato squares in your hand one at a time, shape into rough balls and fry for 1–2 minutes until they start to brown. Turn once or twice. You can fry quite a few simultaneously. This may sound fiddly but once you have a production line going the job is quickly finished. Place half the dumplings aside for freezing.
* Pour half the soup into a bowl and allow to cool down before freezing.

* Keep the remaining soup on the heat, roughly tear the remaining basil leaves and add to the soup along with half the potato dumplings.
* Cook for 5 minutes until the dumplings are warmed through then serve in big bowls, sprinkled with a grating of Parmesan.

Lazy day supper – reheating instructions

* Defrost the soup and dumplings, and when they are completely thawed warm the soup over a gentle heat. Add another handful of roughly chopped basil leaves and the dumplings and cook for 5 minutes.
* The soup can be cooked from frozen. Turn it out of the freezer container by running the base under hot water, place in a pan, add half a cup of water and gently defrost over a medium heat, then bring up to simmering point and serve. The dumplings can't be defrosted quickly unless you have a microwave.

May Week 2 – Overview

The Big Meal from Scratch this week is Pot Roast Veal with Morel Mushrooms, New Potatoes and Steamed Watercress. The method for this is similar to making a casserole but uses a single joint of meat and slightly less liquid. As with most casseroles, once all the ingredients have been assembled everything can be left to simmer slowly. Cooking veal gently in a creamy mushroom sauce is a good way to show off the delicate flavour and texture of the meat. Veal is quite pricey so bear this in mind and, if necessary, replace the veal with a less expensive boned, rolled leg of pork. For a discussion on the best veal to buy in terms of taste and ethics see page 212. Fresh morels are in season in May, but if they are difficult to find dried morels or dried wild mushrooms will work too.

Cooking extra new potatoes for the big meal leaves you with the basis for a Warm Potato and Smoked Mackerel Salad, a Something for Nothing that takes just about 15 minutes to put together. The other Something for Nothing is a recipe for slices of veal or pork topped with a mixture of artichokes, lemon zest and Parmesan then heated under the grill. We suggest you serve this with a crisp radicchio, celery and apple salad. If there is a great deal of mushroom sauce and any steamed watercress left over at the end of the big meal these can be combined and turned into a tasty sauce for pasta.

A Seasonal Supper recipe for Sea Trout Baked with Asparagus and Serrano Ham is summery and pretty. If sea trout aren't available salmon fillets will work as a good substitute. Although the meal takes about 45 minutes from start to finish, 25 minutes of this require no involvement from the cook so this is worth bearing in mind. As with all fresh fish, make sure you cook the trout within a day or so of buying, or put it straight into the freezer until required.

The Larder Feast of Pea and Ham Pasta is sweet and salty, uncomplicated and comforting – just the sort of thing that's ideal in the middle of a wearisome week.

The Two for One recipe for Yoghurt Chicken with Spicy Baked Lentils is ready in just 40 minutes, most of which is cooking time – perfect for busy weekends.

May Week 2	Recipe	Time
Big meal from scratch	Pot roast veal (or pork) with morel mushrooms, new potatoes and steamed watercress	2½ hours
Something for nothing 1	Parmesan and artichoke veal (or pork) with raddichio, celery and apple salad	20 mins
Something for nothing 2	Smoked mackerel salad	15 mins
Seasonal supper	Sea trout (or salmon) baked with asparagus and Serrano ham	45 mins
Larder feast	Pea and ham pasta	40 mins
2 for 1	Yoghurt chicken with spicy baked lentils and salad	40 mins

All recipes serve 4 apart from the 2 for 1 recipe which makes 8 portions

SHOPPING LIST (for 4 people)

Meat and fish
1 × 1.8 kg shoulder of free-range veal, boned
  and rolled, or leg or loin of free-range
  pork, boned and rolled and fat and skin
  removed
4 smoked mackerel fillets, approx. 400 g
1 × 800 g sea trout or 2 × 400 g sea trout,
  gutted but intact, or 4 large salmon fillets.
100 g thinly sliced Serrano ham or prosciutto
200-300 g good quality ham
6 free-range chicken breasts, skinless and
  boneless

Dairy
100 g butter
2 free-range eggs
150 ml double cream
80 g Parmesan
2 heaped tbsp natural yoghurt
250 g Greek yoghurt

Fruit and vegetables
2.25 kg new potatoes
4 celery sticks
100g fresh morel mushrooms or 25-30 g dried
  morels
1 large bunch asparagus, approx. 400 g
2 heads chicory, approx. 300 g
2 heads radicchio, approx. 300 g
250 g watercress or 2-3 large bunches
80 g (approx.) salad leaves
3 leeks, approx 375g
1 medium onion, approx. 120 g
1 small onion, approx 90g
4 spring onions
6 garlic cloves
small handful fresh parsley
2 sprigs fresh basil
4 sprigs fresh thyme or ½ tsp dried thyme
1 small bunch chives
4 sprigs fresh mint (2 sprigs optional for Pea
  and Ham pasta)
handful of fresh coriander
2 little gem lettuces
2 large red chillies
8-10-cm piece of fresh root ginger
3 lemons
2 crisp dessert apples
720-920 g frozen peas

Basics
200 ml olive oil
45 ml groundnut or grapeseed oil
pinch of sugar
1 tbsp Dijon mustard
2 tbsp tomato purée
1 bay leaf
200 ml chicken stock (fresh or made from a
  stock cube or bouillon powder)
200 ml vegetable stock (made from a stock
  cube or bouillon powder)

salt and pepper
greaseproof paper or foil

Store cupboard
300 g penne or other pasta
2 x 200 g cans artichoke hearts
4 × 400 g cans brown lentils
1 x 200 g can olives stuffed with anchovies
2 tsp creamed horseradish
1 tbsp garam masala
½ teaspoon turmeric
430 ml white wine

Serving suggestions
pasta, olive oil and garlic (Parmesan and
  Artichoke Veal or Pork with Chicory, Celery
  and Apple Salad)
Parmesan (Pea and Ham Pasta)

To download or print out this shopping list,
please visit www.thekitchenrevolution.co.uk/May/
Week2

Pot Roast Veal (or Pork) with Morel Mushrooms, New Potatoes and Steamed Watercress

Veal and pork are both mild and ever so slightly sweet. In this recipe, these flavours are enhanced by pot-roasting the meat in a delicate morel sauce. Served with simple new potatoes and lightly steamed watercress, this is easy to make and feels just right for the start of summer.

Veal is not cheap so it's also fine to make this recipe with leg of free-range pork – if possible ask the butcher to bone and roll it without the fat and skin. For more information about veal production, see page 219.

This is the right time of year for fresh morels. They look nothing like conventional mushrooms – they have a pale brown upright, pitted hat, somewhat like a honeycomb and creamy stems. If fresh morels are difficult to find substitute with dried morels or, if necessary, use mixed dried mushrooms or ceps (porcini).

The recipes here include extra meat for Parmesan and Artichoke Veal (or Pork) and extra new potatoes for the Smoked Mackerel Salad.

Pot roast veal or pork
50 g butter
groundnut or grapeseed oil
1 × 1.8 kg shoulder of free-range veal, boned and rolled, or leg or loin of free-range pork, boned and rolled and fat and skin removed; includes 500-600 g extra for the Parmesan and artichoke veal (or pork)
3 leeks, approx 375g
200 ml white wine
1 bay leaf
4 sprigs fresh thyme or ½ tsp dried thyme
200 ml chicken stock (fresh or made from a stock cube or bouillon powder)

100 g fresh morel mushrooms or 25-30 g dried morels
150 ml double cream
salt and pepper

New potatoes
1.5 kg new potatoes; includes approx. 750 g extra for the smoked mackerel salad
5 tbsp olive oil
small handful of fresh parsley

Steamed watercress
250 g watercress or 2-3 large bunches watercress

GET AHEAD PREPARATION (optional)

* Prepare the leeks.
* Prepare the potatoes and cover with water until required.
* Soak the dried mushrooms.
* Chop the parsley.

2½ hours before
you want to eat
cook the meat

* Preheat the oven to 180°C/350°F/Gas Mark 4.
* Melt half the butter with a splash of oil in a large casserole over a medium heat. Season the veal or pork all over and, when the butter is foaming, add the meat to the pan and brown it thoroughly on all sides.
* Wash, trim and slice the leeks.
* Once the meat is browned, remove from the casserole and set aside in a dish. If the bottom of the casserole looks dark brown or almost burned on the bottom, wipe it out with kitchen paper and move on to the next instruction. If it doesn't look over-browned, keep the pan on the heat and deglaze by splashing in the wine and bringing it to the boil while stirring vigorously. Tip the wine over the meat and wipe the pan out with kitchen paper.
* Return the casserole to the heat, add the rest of the butter and the leeks and cook for 5 minutes.
* Put the veal or pork on top of the softened leeks and add the bay leaf, thyme, wine, stock and seasoning. Bring this to simmering point, cover with a tight-fitting lid and transfer to the oven. Leave to cook for 1¾ hours, by which time the meat will be tender. If you have a larger piece of meat, cook it for an extra 30 minutes per 500 g.
* Wash the potatoes and cut any large ones in half. Place in a pan with a lid and cover with water.
* If using dried mushrooms, cover with boiling water and leave them to soak.

*25 minutes before
you want to eat
cook the potatoes*

* Tip enough water out of the potato pan for it to come just under halfway up the potatoes. Add the oil and some salt, place the pan on a high heat and bring to the boil. Cover with a lid and leave to boil briskly for 10 minutes.

* While the potatoes are boiling, check on the meat. After about 1¾ hours in the oven, it should be tender.
* Turn the oven off and take the casserole out. Lift the meat out and set it aside to rest in a warm place while you make the sauce. Put some plates and serving dishes in the oven to warm.
* Place the casserole on a low heat and let the leeks and cooking liquor simmer.

10 minutes before you want to eat make the sauce

* If you are using dried mushrooms, lift them from their soaking liquor. Take the liquor and strain it through a fine sieve into the simmering casserole (to remove any grit). Bring to a rolling boil and let the liquid bubble away until it has reduced by a third. Then add the cream and soaked mushrooms and simmer gently until you are ready to serve.
* If you are using fresh morels, bring the cooking liquor in the casserole to the boil and reduce it by a third. Meanwhile, heat a splash of oil in a small frying pan, clean the morels and halve any large ones, then fry the morels until they are soft. Splash in a small cupful of the cooking liquor from the casserole and allow it to reduce and catch any of the mushroom flavour from the pan. When liquor has almost completely evaporated, tip the morels into the casserole. Stir them for a minute or so, add the cream and continue as with the dried mushrooms.
* After 10 minutes boiling the potatoes will be almost cooked. Take the lid off and leave them for another 5 minutes so that all the water evaporates and they are completely tender. Splash in a little more water if you think they are drying out before they are cooked.
* While the potatoes and sauce are bubbling away, bring about 2 cm water to the boil in a pan with a lid or the bottom of a steamer. Add some salt and place the watercress in the steamer or pan of water to wilt. This will take 2–3 minutes.
* Chop the parsley. If there is a lot of liquid left in the potato pan, lift the potatoes out with a slotted spoon and put them into a serving dish while you let the cooking liquid boil briskly until about 1 tablespoon remains. Pour the liquid over the potatoes in the serving dish, add the parsley and season as necessary.
* Taste the morel sauce and season.
* Place the wilted watercress in a serving dish.
* Slice the veal or pork, place on a warmed serving dish and serve with sauce, potatoes and watercress.

Afterwards

Place the remaining potatoes (600 g) and veal (enough to make 8 slices about 1-2 cm thick) in separate airtight containers or cover them with foil and keep in the fridge.

Added extra

Any leftover watercress and morel sauce can be used to go with the pasta, or to accompany a simply cooked chicken breast. It will keep in the fridge for a few days or could be frozen.

Parmesan and Artichoke Veal (or Pork) with Radicchio, Celery and Apple Salad

For this recipe, artichokes, lemon and Parmesan are mixed together then grilled on top of slices of veal or pork. This can be prepared in less than 5 minutes, and you can have it on the table to eat in 20 if you have slices of veal or pork left over from the Big Meal from Scratch. If you don't have any leftover veal or pork you can substitute with veal escalopes or free-range chicken breasts. If you are using chicken breasts, cut off the small fillets, wrap the breasts loosely in cling film and beat with a rolling pin until they are flattened to about 1–2 cm thick. Season the veal or chicken well and rub in olive oil, then grill for about 2 minutes on each side before adding the Parmesan and artichoke topping and grilling again.

Parmesan and artichoke veal (or pork)
cooked veal or pork left over from the Big Meal from Scratch, enough for 8 x 1-2 cm thick slices (see below)
2 x 200 g cans artichoke hearts
1 garlic clove
1 x 200 g can olives stuffed with anchovies (85 g drained weight)
1 lemon
80 g Parmesan
5-6 fresh basil leaves
4–5 tbsp olive oil
salt and pepper

Radicchio, celery and apple salad
2 tbsp olive oil
½ tbsp lemon juice
2 tsp Dijon mustard
pinch of sugar
2 crisp dessert apples
4 celery sticks
2 heads radicchio, approx. 300 g

To serve
pasta with olive oil and garlic (optional)

GET AHEAD PREPARATION (optional)

* Make the salad dressing.
* Wash the radicchio.
* Chop the celery.

20 minutes before you want to eat

* Remove the veal or pork from the fridge and cut into 8 x 1-2-cm thick slices. Season with salt and pepper and leave at room temperature in a single layer in an ovenproof dish.
* Preheat the grill to medium hot.
* Make the topping in a large bowl. Drain the artichokes, chop them finely and put them in the bowl. Peel and finely chop the garlic, drain and roughly chop the olives and add them both to the artichokes. Zest and juice the lemon, and add to the mixture. Grate the Parmesan into the bowl and add the shredded basil leaves. Fold the artichoke mixture together with 4 tablespoons of the oil and season well with salt and pepper. The mixture should be glistening with oil – if it isn't, add another tablespoon.
* Pile the artichoke mixture on to the veal or pork slices – 3-4 cm of topping is about right. Put the meat under the grill and cook for 5-7 minutes until the topping starts to brown.
* While the meat is under the grill, make the salad. Mix together the oil, lemon juice, mustard, sugar and salt and pepper. Peel, core and slice the apples, wash and slice the celery and break up the radicchio heads. Toss in a bowl with the dressing.
* Remove the meat from the grill and serve with the salad.

Something for nothing 2

Smoked Mackerel Salad

This is an almost instant meal and one that's full of flavour and goodness. Smoked mackerel has a distinctive, slightly peppery flavour. For something so special, it is wonderfully inexpensive.

If you have any fresh watercress left over from the Big Meal from Scratch, it can be used in this salad instead of the salad leaves. You will have to remove any large stalks first.

120 g frozen peas
600 g cooked potatoes leftover from the Big Meal from Scratch or 750 g small new potatoes, boiled
2 heaped tbsp plain yoghurt (Greek is good)
1 heaped tsp Dijon mustard
2 tsp creamed horseradish
juice of ½ lemon
4 spring onions
2 heads chicory, approx. 300 g
80 g (approx.) salad leaves
4 smoked mackerel fillets, approx. 400 g
salt and pepper

GET AHEAD PREPARATION (optional)

* Cut the potatoes.
* Prepare the spring onions.
* Prepare the chicory leaves.
* Make the dressing.

15 minutes before you want to eat

* First cook the peas and heat up the potatoes. Put some hot or boiling water into a pan and bring it to the boil. Add some salt and the peas and bring back to the boil over a medium heat. Meanwhile, chop the potatoes in half. When the peas come back to the boil, throw in the potatoes, then turn off the heat and leave them to sit for a couple of minutes to warm through.
* In the meantime, make a dressing for the salad by mixing the yoghurt, mustard, horseradish and lemon juice together. Trim and finely slice the spring onions, using as much of the green as you can. Stir them into the dressing and season to taste with salt and pepper.
* Next, prepare the rest of the salad. Separate the chicory heads into leaves and break them into bite-sized pieces. Peel the skins off the mackerel fillets and break the flesh into generous chunks.
* Drain the peas and potatoes well and place in a large bowl with a couple of generous spoonfuls of the dressing. Toss together thoroughly.
* Add the chicory, salad leaves and mackerel pieces and stir together carefully. Add more dressing, if necessary, and serve immediately.

Seasonal supper

Sea Trout (or Salmon) Baked with Asparagus and Serrano Ham

May until August is the time for sea trout and, as luck would have it, for asparagus as well. It's difficult to imagine a better matched combination than these two. Here they are cooked in a parcel – ensuring that no flavours are wasted and the fish stays moist.

It's likely that you will have to buy the sea trout (or salmon trout as they are otherwise known) from a fishmonger – they are not widely available and when they appear they are snaffled up quickly by those in the know. If you can't find sea trout, salmon fillets will work as well.

700 g new potatoes
1 large bunch asparagus, approx.
    400 g
100 g thinly sliced Serrano ham
    or prosciutto
1 small bunch chives
½ lemon
50 g butter
1 × 800 g sea trout or 2 × 400 g
    sea trout, gutted but intact, or
    4 large salmon fillets, approx.
    175 g each
2 tbsp (approx.) white wine
salt and pepper

GET AHEAD PREPARATION (optional)

* Trim the asparagus.
* Cut the ham into pieces.
* Cut the chives.
* Zest and juice the lemon.

45 minutes before you want to eat

* Preheat the oven to 190°C/375°F/Gas Mark 5.
* Scrub the potatoes clean and cut any that are larger than bite size in half. Place them in a large pan of well-salted water.
* Bend each spear of asparagus so that it snaps at the point where the base turns woody. Discard the woody parts. Rinse the spears under running water then place them in a bowl. Cut the ham into 1–2 cm pieces and cut the chives into tiny lengths. Zest and juice the half lemon. Add the lemon zest and half the lemon juice, half the ham and half the chives to the asparagus. Season well and mix together.
* To make a parcel for the fish and vegetables take a sheet of greaseproof paper at least three times the width and 1½ times the length of the fish and place on a large baking sheet. Dot the middle with some butter then pile the asparagus and ham mixture in the centre.
* Season one side of the sea trout or salmon and place this, seasoned-side down, on top of the asparagus and ham. Take the remaining ham and place it inside the sea trout's cavity with a little seasoning and another few dabs of butter. For fillets place them skin side up on top of the asparagus mixture and place the remaining ham over the skin with seasoning and butter as above.
* Pour the rest of the lemon juice and wine over the fish. Season well and dot with the remaining butter. Create an airtight, roomy parcel around the fish by bringing the sides of the paper together and folding them tightly.
* Place on a tray or in a dish in the oven and bake for 25 minutes or 15–20 minutes for fillets.
* Bring the water in the potato pan to a gentle boil and simmer for 20 minutes.

10 minutes before you want to eat

* Open the parcel. Make sure the fish is cooked by checking that the flesh is opaque and flakes easily. Return to the oven for 10 minutes if the fish isn't cooked. Otherwise, lift the fish out of the parcel and place on a large plate. Put the asparagus and ham mixture in a serving dish. Pour the fish cooking liquor into a small pan and place over a medium heat to reduce.
* Drain the potatoes. Take the sea trout fillets off the bone and place them, or the salmon fillets, on four plates. Add the remaining chives to the reduced cooking liquor and pour over the fish. Serve with the asparagus, ham and the potatoes.

Larder feast

Pea and Ham Pasta

Pea and ham is a classic combination and this reinvention of a traditional Italian dish won't disappoint. There are more peas here than pasta, and the trick is to simmer them until they are soft, sweet and ever so slightly mushy.

This recipe owes its existence to a misreading of Diane Seed's *The Top One Hundred Pasta Sauces* when Zoe first left college and was trying to fend for herself in the kitchen.

1 tbsp olive oil
1 medium onion, approx. 120 g
200–300 g good quality sliced
   ham
600–800 g frozen peas
200 ml white wine
200 ml vegetable stock (made
   from a stock cube or bouillion
   powder)
300 g penne or other pasta
handful of fresh mint (optional)
salt and pepper

To serve
grated Parmesan

GET AHEAD PREPARATION (optional)

* Chop the onion and ham.
* Chop the mint, if using.

40 minutes before you want to eat

* Heat the oil in a large heavy-based pan with a lid while you chop the onion. Add the onion and soften over a low heat for 7–10 minutes. Chop the ham into bite-sized pieces.
* When the onion is soft, add the peas and mix them together well.
  Then add the wine, turn up the heat and bring to the boil. Once it is boiling, turn the heat down slightly and reduce the liquid by half.
* When the wine has reduced, add the stock and ham, turn the heat right down, put the lid on and leave to simmer very gently for 10 minutes.
* After 10 minutes, give the peas and ham a stir, replace the lid and leave to cook gently while you start the pasta. Cook the pasta for 5 minutes less than the instructions on the packet.
* When the pasta is 5 minutes away from being cooked, drain it and add it to the pan containing the peas and ham. Replace the lid and simmer for another 5–10 minutes until the pasta is cooked and the peas are soft and slightly mushy.
* Roughly chop the mint, if using, add to the dish and season to taste with salt and pepper. Serve with a generous sprinkling of grated Parmesan.

Two for one

Yoghurt Chicken with Spicy Baked Lentils and Salad

For this recipe chicken is marinated in yoghurt and spices, fried and served with a dish of spiced lentils. Although there are lots of flavours and spices in the recipe the combination is subtle and not at all overpowering. The quantities here are for eight, on the assumption that half will be frozen for use at another time.

Yoghurt chicken
1 small onion, approx. 90 g
6 free-range chicken breasts
  approx. 200 g each, skinless
  and boneless
1 tbsp garam masala
250 g Greek yoghurt
salt

8-10 cm piece of fresh root
  ginger
handful of fresh coriander
2 free-range eggs
½ tsp turmeric
2 tbsp tomato purée
groundnut or grapeseed oil
pepper

GET AHEAD PREPARATION (optional)

The chicken can be marinated up
to 24 hours before cooking. If
you only have a little time:
* Prepare the onion, chillies,
  garlic and ginger.
* Chop the coriander.
* Wash the lettuce.

Spicy baked lentils
4 x 400 g cans brown lentils
2 large red chillies
5 garlic cloves

Salad
2 little gem lettuces
2 sprigs fresh mint
olive oil
½ lemon

40 minutes before you want to eat marinate the chicken

* Peel and finely slice the onion. Cut the chicken breasts into 2 cm wide strips.
* Mix the onion, garam masala and some salt into the yoghurt. Pour this mixture over the chicken and leave to marinate for as long as the lentils take to cook, or as long as possible. Freeze half the chicken pieces at this point.

30 minutes before you want to eat cook the lentils

* Preheat the oven to 200°C/400°F/Gas Mark 6.
* Tip the lentils into a sieve over the sink and leave to drain thoroughly.
* Meanwhile, deseed and finely chop the chillies. Peel and finely chop or crush the garlic. Peel and grate the ginger and wash and roughly chop the coriander. Place the chillies, garlic, ginger and all but a generous teaspoon of chopped coriander in a food processor and blend them with the eggs, turmeric, tomato purée and some salt and pepper. Alternatively use a hand blender.
* Tip the lentils into a bowl, stir in the spice and herb mixture and season to taste.
* Oil an ovenproof dish with groundnut or grapeseed oil and put half the lentils into the dish. Freeze the other half in a freezer bag or freezer-proof container.
* Put the lentils in the oven and bake for 20–30 minutes until they are slightly set.

10 minutes before you want to eat cook the chicken

* While the lentils are baking, finely slice the little gems, and wash and dry them. Roughly tear the mint leaves. Put the little gems and the mint in a salad bowl. Dress the salad by adding a good splash or two of olive oil, a squeeze of lemon juice, salt and pepper and mixing together.
* Heat a generous dose of oil in a frying pan, and when it is hot lift the chicken pieces and onion from the yoghurt marinade and fry them. Stir them constantly for about 5 minutes or until the chicken is lightly browned and cooked.
* When the chicken is cooked through and browned, take the lentils out of the oven – they should be slightly firm to the touch.
* Serve the chicken with a spoonful of lentils and a pile of salad for each person.

Lazy day supper – cooking instructions

* Defrost the chicken and lentils thoroughly before reheating.
* Preheat the oven to 200°C/400°F/Gas Mark 6.
* Place the lentils in a greased ovenproof dish and bake them for 20–30 minutes, until they are slightly firm to the touch.
* While the lentils are in the oven, wash and prepare the salad as above.
* When the lentils are ready, turn off the oven and leave them to sit while you heat a frying pan and quickly fry the defrosted chicken. Serve as above.

Veal

Veal has long been a controversial choice and many people, even those who may not have strong views on animal welfare, have been revolted by the cruelty inflicted on crate-raised veal calves. These animals live a confined existence, drinking a powdered-milk feed that stops their intestines developing and keeps their flesh white. According to the meat guru of our times, Hugh Fearnley Whittingstall, this practice achieves nothing of gastronomic note as the pale meat has little taste or texture. Conventionally produced veal, therefore, should be avoided, but this does not mean veal is off the menu. Eating veal that has been thoughtfully produced is no more or less ethical than eating good pork or lamb. Veal is, in fact, produced from the unwanted calves of the beef and dairy industry. Raised in a free-range system, veal calves live a decent life before they are slaughtered. These animals produce tender, sweet meat with a light pink colour. If, however, you cannot find a reliable source of veal it is probably better to use free-range or organic free-range pork.

May Week 3 – Overview

Pot Roast Caribbean Pork with Roast Sweet Potatoes and Spring Greens starts this week off with a Big Meal from Scratch that's fairly straightforward to make, attractive to look at and intensely flavoured – a good meal to share with people you like. As with most pot roasts, the pork is cooked slowly so allow 2½ hours from start to finish.

The surplus roast sweet potatoes that accompany the pork are turned into a Something for Nothing recipe for Goats' Cheese Flatbreads which are served with a Hazelnut and Chicory Salad. Meanwhile, for the other Something for Nothing meal, any extra pork is sliced thinly and served with a light, lime coleslaw guaranteed to get the mouth watering. Both take around 20 minutes to make.

Almost as quick, and just as tasty, is the Seasonal Supper of Parmesan chicken with Roast Asparagus. The Larder Feast of Tuna Empanada is something along the lines of a Spanish pasty. It involves making a rich, spicy tuna and pepper filling that is then packed into a large pastry pocket and baked for 20 minutes. In total the recipe takes around 40 minutes.

For when you have more time, there is a Two for One recipe for Beef Braised with Celeriac and Morel mushrooms. This takes 30 minutes of preparation and then cooks in the oven for 1½ to 2 hours.

May Week 3	Recipe	Time
Big meal from scratch	Pot roast Caribbean pork, roast sweet potatoes and spring greens	2½ hours
Something for nothing 1	Pork with lime coleslaw	20 mins
Something for nothing 2	Sweet potato and goats' cheese flatbreads with hazelnut and chicory salad	25 mins
Seasonal supper	Parmesan chicken goujons with roast asparagus, garlic mayonnaise and rocket salad	30 mins
Larder feast	Tuna empanada	45 mins
2 for 1	Beef braised with celeriac and morel mushrooms	1½–2½ hours

All recipes serve 4 apart from the 2 for 1 recipe which makes 8 portions

SHOPPING LIST (for 4 people)

Meat and fish
1 × 1.5-1.8 kg boned rolled skinned free-
  range pork joint (go for a lean cut such as
  leg or loin)
4 small free-range chicken breasts, skinless
  and boneless
1.2 kg brisket, stewing steak or skirt, cut
  into 1-2 cm thick slices

Dairy
140 g butter
6 free-range eggs
240 g soft goats' cheese
165 g Parmesan
4 tbsp Greek yoghurt

Fruit and vegetables
100 g fresh morel mushrooms or 25-30 g
  dried morels
8 garlic cloves
1.25 kg sweet potatoes
500 g spring greens
1 medium white cabbage, approx. 600 g
1 small bunch spring onions
3 small red onions, approx. 250 g
2 medium onions, approx. 240 g
1 large celeriac, approx. 700 g
3 heads chicory, approx. 250 g
200 g green beans
600 g asparagus
150-200 g rocket
1 small bunch fresh parsley
1 generous handful of fresh coriander
2 sprigs fresh sage†
a few sprigs fresh mint, parsley, tarragon or
  chervil, or 1 small bunch chives
1 orange
2 juicy limes
3 lemons

Basics
185 ml olive oil
80 ml groundnut or grapeseed oil
6 large soft thin flatbreads
350 g chilled ready-made shortcrust pastry
4 tbsp dried oregano
2 tsp dried thyme
1 tbsp demerara sugar
160-70 g plain flour, plus extra for dusting
1½ tbsp coarsely ground black pepper or
  1 tbsp black peppercorns
250 ml beef or chicken stock (fresh made
  from a stock cube or bouillon powder)
salt and pepper

Store cupboard
1 tbsp white wine vinegar
1 tbsp cider or white wine vinegar
a few drops of chilli sauce, such as Tabasco
6 tbsp mayonnaise
340 g pitted green olives
6 pitted dried prunes
1 × 200 g can chopped tomatoes
300 g roasted red peppers from a can or jar
  (piquillo for choice)
340-400 g canned tuna in brine
1 tsp coriander seeds
¼ tsp ground cumin
2½ tsp paprika (preferably smoked)
30 g toasted hazelnuts
400 ml (approx.) stout
500 ml white wine

Serving suggestions
potatoes for baking or pitta breads (Pork with
  Lime Coleslaw)
green salad leaves, olive oil and lemon juice
  (Tuna Empanada)
potatoes such as Maris Piper and spinach
  or greens (Beef Braised with Celeriac and
  Morel Mushrooms)

To download or print out this shopping list,
please visit www.thekitchenrevolution.co.uk/May/
Week3

Pot Roast Caribbean Pork with Roast Sweet Potatoes and Spring Greens

Prunes, orange and sugar might not be the first ingredients you'd think to partner with pork but the sweetness of these is balanced in this recipe by herbs, olives, garlic and stout. The olives and prunes are pushed deep into the pork flesh so each slice on carving is dotted with colour. This an excellent recipe for entertaining, not only because it looks so appetising but because once the pork is prepared it simmers on the stove for 2 hours leaving you a free agent.

The ingredients include extra pork for the Pork with Lime Coleslaw (see page 224) and the extra sweet potatoes make for Sweet Potato and Goats' Cheese Flatbreads with Hazelnut and Chicory Salad (see page 225).

The recipe itself is borrowed and adapted from Jeremy Round's wonderful *The Independent Cook* and, as he explains, is a 'shameless bastardisation' of a Puerto Rican recipe.

Pot roast Caribbean pork
4 garlic cloves
1 orange
1½ tbsp coarsely ground black pepper or 1 tbsp black peppercorns crushed in a pestle and mortar
2 tsp dried oregano
2 tsp salt
1 tsp dried thyme
1 tbsp olive oil
1 tbsp cider or white wine vinegar
1.5–1.8 kg boned, rolled free-range pork joint (go for a lean cut, such as leg or loin, or you will have to remove any fat); includes 600 g extra for the pork with lime coleslaw

6 pitted dried prunes
100 g pitted green olives, approx. 20 olives
400 ml (approx.) stout
1 tbsp demerara sugar

Roast sweet potatoes
2 tbsp olive oil
2 tbsp groundnut or grapeseed oil
1.25 kg sweet potatoes; includes approx. 450 g for the sweet potato and goats' cheese flatbreads
1 tsp dried thyme
salt

Spring greens
500 g spring greens
50 g butter
pepper

GET AHEAD PREPARATION (optional)

* Make the spice paste.
* Rub the pork with the paste.
* Insert the olives and prunes in the pork.
* Peel, cut and parboil the sweet potatoes.
* Prepare the greens.

2½ hours before you want to eat cook the pork

* Peel and chop or crush the garlic and put it in a bowl. Zest and juice the orange. Add the pepper, oregano, salt, thyme, orange zest, oil and cider or white wine vinegar and mix into a paste.
* Untie the pork. (If it comes in an elasticated net, keep this intact as you can use it to re-roll the joint). If the fat on the pork is more than 1 cm thick cut away the excess with a sharp knife. Place the pork on a work surface, skin side down. Rub half the spice paste on the inside of the pork, roll the joint up again and tie it securely with string or ease it back into its elasticated net .
* Halve the prunes. Cut about 20 deep slits in the meat and insert an olive or half a pitted prune into each slit.
* Rub the remaining spice paste over the outside of the joint.
* Heat a heavy casserole dish with a lid over a medium heat, add the pork and brown it all over. Turn down the heat, and add the stout, sugar and orange juice. Bring the liquid up to a gentle simmer, cover with a lid and cook gently for 2 hours.

1 hour before you want to eat cook the sweet potatoes

* After 1 hour of cooking, check on the pork to ensure there is sufficient liquid. Add a little water if it risks going dry. Turn the meat once, cover with the lid again and leave for the remaining hour.
* Preheat the oven to 200°C/400°F/Gas Mark 6. Put the olive and groundnut or grapeseed oils for the sweet potatoes in a large roasting tin and place in the oven to get hot.
* Now prepare the sweet potatoes. Peel them and cut them into chunks the size of an egg. Place in a pan of salted water and bring to the boil. Sweet potatoes take very little time to cook so they will only need 2–3 minutes simmering to be parboiled and ready to roast. Drain the potatoes in a sieve and shake them so that the edges become floury and toss in the thyme.

* Tip the sweet potatoes into the tin of hot fat, turning them over so that their sides will crisp. Return the tin to the oven and cook the potatoes for 40–50 minutes, turning them once to prevent any sticking and to ensure they are evenly roasted.

15 minutes before you want to eat cook the greens

* Wash the spring greens and cut them into 3 cm (approx.) ribbons. Place in a steamer or in a pan with a small amount of water. Bring to the boil and cook for about 5 minutes or until tender. Drain well, place in a serving bowl and season with salt and pepper. Dot with the butter and keep warm.
* Once the sweet potatoes are cooked, remove the tin from the oven, turn the oven off and put some plates and serving dishes in to warm. Put half the potatoes to one side to use later in the week and put the rest in a serving dish and keep warm while you slice the pork.
* Remove the pork from the casserole and slice thickly. Put the slices on individual plates and spoon over the gravy from the casserole. Serve with the roast sweet potatoes and spring greens.

Afterwards

Put the leftover pork and potatoes in separate containers, cover and refrigerate for use later in the week. Ideally you will have 450–550 g pork and 400 g sweet potatoes.

KITCHEN REVOLUTION EXTRA

Seasoning 'to taste'
All too often seasoning to taste is a step that is forgotten – yet it's crucial. The addition of salt and pepper can make the difference between a dish that tastes flat, and one where the flavours of the ingredients sing.

Something
for nothing 1

Pork with Lime Coleslaw

This is a meal for late spring – filling but not too heavy, and quick to prepare. If it's a nice evening you won't have to spend too long slaving in the kitchen.

Like coronation chicken and Waldorf salad, coleslaw is ruined by too much gloopy, under-seasoned and poor quality mayonnaise. In this recipe the richness of the coleslaw is cut through with zesty lime and strong spices. The pot roasted pork is sliced and placed on top. The result is lip-smackingly lovely, especially served with jacket potatoes.

If you don't have any leftover pork, replace it with 500 g pork fillet, well seasoned with herbs, salt and pepper and roasted for 30 minutes in a hot oven.

2 juicy limes
1 tsp coriander seeds
a few drops of chilli sauce, such
  as Tabasco
2 tbsp olive oil
450–550 g pork left over from the
  Big Meal from Scratch or see
  above
1 medium white cabbage, approx.
  600 g
1 small bunch spring onions
generous handful of fresh
  coriander
3 tbsp mayonnaise
2 tbsp Greek yoghurt
¼ tsp ground cumin
salt and pepper

To serve
jacket potatoes or warmed pitta
  breads

GET AHEAD PREPARATION (optional)

The coleslaw can be made a day
or two in advance – but add the
fresh coriander just before eating
so that it retains its colour. If
you only have a little time:
* Crush the coriander seeds.
* Prepare the spring onions.
* Chop the fresh coriander.

*20 minutes before
you want to eat*

* Squeeze the juice of one of the limes into a bowl. Roughly crush the coriander seeds and add half of them to the lime juice, along with a pinch each of salt and pepper, the chilli sauce and 1 tablespoon of the oil. Slice the pork thinly and cover the slices with the lime mixture.
* Shred the cabbage very finely, using a food processor if you have one. Place in a large bowl. Chop the spring onions finely and the fresh coriander roughly and add all but a tablespoon of the coriander to the cabbage.
* In a separate bowl, mix together the mayonnaise, yoghurt, the remaining oil, the remaining coriander seeds, the cumin and the juice of the remaining lime. Mix well, season generously and pour over the shredded cabbage. Toss the cabbage very well. It's important to make sure all the dressing is well incorporated.
* Pile the coleslaw on to four plates and top with the slices of pork. Tip the left over pork marinade over the top, sprinkle with the rest of the fresh coriander and serve with jacket potatoes or warmed pitta breads.

Sweet Potato and Goats' Cheese Flatbreads
with Hazelnut and Chicory Salad

For this recipe flatbreads or flour tortillas are spread with an intensely flavoured sweet potato, herb and cheese filling, rolled up and baked until hot and melting. The end result is somewhere between a pizza, a toasted cheese sandwich and a crostini – impossible to resist and very moreish. For the salad, the flavours of hazelnut and chicory, the former sweet and nutty and the latter slightly bitter and sharp, are a good match for the flatbread stuffing. You can, if you wish, replace the flatbreads with eight pitta breads. Just split them down one side and spread the filling over each half. Then place them, as they are, on an oiled baking sheet and bake them.

Sweet potato and goats' cheese flatbreads
400 g cooked sweet potatoes left over from the Big Meal from Scratch or 450 g sweet potatoes peeled and boiled
2 sprigs fresh sage
olive oil
80 g Parmesan
6 large soft thin flatbreads or tortillas, see above
240 g soft goats' cheese
salt and pepper

Hazelnut and chicory salad
200 g green beans
1 lemon
1 small red onion, approx. 180 g
3 heads chicory, approx. 250 g
30 g toasted hazelnuts
2 tbsp olive oil

GET AHEAD PREPARATION (optional)

* Crumble the goats' cheese.
* Grate the Parmesan.
* Chop the sage leaves.
* Zest and juice the lemon.
* Prepare the onion and chicory.
* Top and tail the green beans.
* Roughly chop the hazelnuts.

25 minutes before you want to eat

* First prepare the beans for the salad. Put a pan of water on to boil. Top and tail the beans and cook them in the boiling water for 3–4 minutes, depending on how crunchy you like them. When cooked, drain and run under cold water.
* Meanwhile, prepare the marinade for the onions. Grate a slightly heaped teaspoon of the zest from the lemon and put to one side for the flatbreads. Squeeze the juice of the lemon into a large bowl and stir in a pinch of salt.
* Peel and finely slice the onion, and place them in the marinade, tossing them so that they are well coated in the lemon juice (they will start to go a vibrant pink-red colour). Leave the onions to marinate.

15 minutes before you want to eat

* Preheat the oven to 200°C/400°F/Gas Mark 6.
* Put the sweet potatoes into a large bowl with the lemon zest. Roughly chop the sage leaves and add to the sweet potatoes with about 1 tablespoon olive oil. Season the sweet potatoes and mash them with a wooden spoon or large fork until you get a smoothish consistency.
* Coarsely grate the Parmesan and oil a baking sheet. Spread the potato mixture evenly over each flatbread. Now crumble the goats' cheese on top and add the Parmesan.
* Roll the flatbreads up and place them, seam sides down, on the oiled baking sheet. Bake for 10 minutes until they are crisp and the cheese has melted.
* While the flatbreads are cooking, assemble the salad. Wash, separate and dry the chicory leaves and roughly chop the hazelnuts. Put the chicory into a large bowl, along with the beans. Mix in the onions with all their juice and toss with the oil and salt and pepper.
* Once the flatbreads are cooked, cut them in half and serve with the salad.

Seasonal supper

Parmesan Chicken Goujons with Roast Asparagus, Garlic Mayonnaise and Rocket Salad

These crispy strips of Parmesan-coated chicken are an ideal partner for some simply roasted asparagus. Served with garlic mayonnaise and a rocket salad, they make a winning combination.

Parmesan chicken goujons
60 g butter
4 small free-range chicken
    breasts, skinless
2 free-range eggs
85 g Parmesan
generous pinch of paprika
120 g plain flour
salt and pepper

Roast asparagus
600 g asparagus
olive oil
zest of ½ lemon

Garlic mayonnaise
1 garlic clove
2 tbsp Greek yoghurt
3 tbsp mayonnaise
½ lemon
a few sprigs fresh mint, parsley,
    tarragon or chervil, or 1 small
    bunch chives

Rocket salad
150-200 g rocket
½ lemon
olive oil

GET AHEAD PREPARATION (optional)

The mayonnaise can be made a day in advance. If you only have a little time:
* Cut the chicken.
* Make the egg mash.
* Grate the Parmesan.
* Prepare the asparagus.
* Peel and crush the garlic.
* Strip herb leaves from their stalks and chop finely.

30 minutes before you want to eat

* Preheat the oven to 220°C/425°F/Gas Mark 7.
* Put the butter in a roasting tin and put it in the oven to melt. Cut each chicken breast lengthways into three or four strips about 2–3 cm wide.
* The coating for the chicken requires an egg wash and a dry Parmesan mixture. For the egg wash, break the eggs into a small bowl and add the melted butter. Whisk the two together with a little salt and pepper.
* For the Parmesan coating, finely grate the Parmesan into a second small bowl, and add the paprika, a good pinch of salt and the flour.
* Drop the chicken pieces into the egg mixture and then into the Parmesan and flour mixture and toss them to coat evenly. Lift the chicken out of the flour and dust off any excess, but don't be too fastidious.
* Now lay the pieces in the roasting tin and put them in the oven on the top shelf to become gold and crisp.
* While the chicken is cooking, prepare the asparagus. Bend each spear so that it snaps at the point where the base turns woody, then discard the woody parts and give the spears a rinse under cold running water. Grate the zest of the half lemon. Toss the asparagus in a bowl with a glug of oil, the lemon zest and a good dose of seasoning. Now place the spears on a baking sheet, in one layer.
* The chicken should have started to crisp and brown, so move it down to the middle shelf and put the baking sheet with the asparagus on the top shelf to roast for 10–12 minutes.
* Meanwhile, make the garlic mayonnaise. Peel and crush the garlic and mix it with the yoghurt, mayonnaise and a generous squeeze of lemon juice. If using any herbs, strip the leaves from their stalks and chop finely. If using chives, snip them into tiny lengths with scissors. Add the herb or chives to the mayonnaise mixture. Season to taste and set aside.
* Dress the rocket with a generous squeeze of lemon juice and some olive oil and divide between four plates.
* The chicken and asparagus should be ready at the same time. Take them out of the oven, put the asparagus spears on top of the rocket and drizzle with any pan juices. Divide the chicken goujons between the plates.

Larder feast

Tuna Empanada

Empanadas are small, savoury pastries served as tapas in Spain. We've taken this idea and some classic Spanish flavours to make one large empanada that can be cut into four slices. The filling in the middle includes tuna, but also peppers and tomatoes, so is intense and sharp enough to cut through the richness of the pastry. This recipe is based on one given to Rosie by her friend and excellent chef Kevin McFadden.

Filling
2 tbsp olive oil
2 small red onions, approx.
    150 g
3 garlic cloves
300 g roasted red peppers from a
    can or jar (piquillo for choice)
1 × 240 g can pitted green olives
2 tsp paprika (preferably
    smoked)
2 tsp dried oregano
1 × 200 g can chopped tomatoes
3 free-range eggs
340–400 g canned tuna in brine
½ lemon
small handful of flatleaf parsley
    (optional)
salt and pepper

Pastry
plain flour, for dusting
350 g chilled ready-made
    shortcrust pastry
olive oil
1 free-range egg
milk or water

To serve
green salad dressed with olive
    oil and lemon juice

GET AHEAD PREPARATION (optional)

The filling can be made 2 days in advance in advance and the empanada can be cooked a day in advance and reheated when required. If you only have a little time:
* Prepare the onions, garlic and peppers.
* Chop the olives.
* Boil the eggs.
* Roll out the pastry and cut it into two rectangles.

45 minutes before you want to eat make the filling

* Put a small, heavy-based pan with a lid over a gentle heat and add a generous splash of the oil. Peel and slice the onions, add them to the pan, cover and leave to soften over a low heat for 5–7 minutes.
* Peel and slice the garlic, slice the peppers and chop the olives. Add all these to the pan, with the paprika and oregano and cook for a few minutes. Add the tomatoes and bring to a simmer and cook for 10–15 minutes until thickened.
* Cook the eggs in boiling water for 8 minutes. Cool under running cold water and peel.
* Chop the parsley and open and drain tuna and mix them together in a bowl. Peel the eggs and roughly mash them into the tuna. Add a squeeze of lemon juice and season.
* Add the thickened sauce to the tuna and eggs and mix very well. Spread the mixture out on a tray to cool as quickly as possible.

25 minutes before you want to eat make up the empanadas

* Preheat the oven to 220°C/425°F/Gas Mark 7.
* Lightly dust a board with flour, and roll the pastry out to a square about 5 mm thick and approximately 40 x 40 cm. Cut the square into two equal rectangles.
* Put one rectangle on to a lightly oiled baking sheet. Beat the egg with a drop of milk or water.
* Pile the filling into the middle of the pastry on the baking sheet, leaving 2 cm round the edge. Paint this 2-cm frame with the beaten egg, then press the two rectangles together. Use a fork to press down the edges of the empanada, creating a ridge pattern and securing the edges.
* Brush the top with more beaten egg.
* Bake for 15–20 minutes until the emapanada is crisp and golden.
* Serve with a green salad dressed with olive oil and lemon juice.

Two for one

Beef Braised with Celeriac and Morel Mushrooms

This fully flavoured braise makes the most of an economic cut of beef brisket. This cut deserves to be much more popular than it is – with long, slow cooking it literally melts in the mouth. Combining it with morels and celeriac makes it well worth the wait.

If you can't get hold of brisket you could substitute stewing steak or skirt, but you may find you need to cook the meat for longer to ensure it's tender. If fresh morel mushrooms aren't available they can be replaced with dried morels or any other dried mushrooms.

Having a quantity of this braise in the freezer is a useful safety net when you really don't have the time or energy to cook from scratch.

100 g fresh morels or 25-30 g dried morels
1.2 kg brisket, stewing steak or skirt, cut into 1-2-cm thick slices
5-6 tbsp plain flour
2 tbsp groundnut or grapeseed oil
30 g butter
2 medium onions, approx. 240 g
1 large celeriac, approx. 700 g

1 tbsp white wine vinegar
500 ml white wine
250 ml beef or chicken stock (fresh or made from a stock cube or bouillon powder)
handful of fresh parsley
salt and pepper

To serve
mashed potatoes, spinach or greens

GET AHEAD PREPARATION (optional)

The entire dish can be made 3 ays in advance. If you only have a little time:
* Soak the dried mushrooms, if using, in boiling water.
* Prepare the onions.
* Prepare the celeriac.
* Season and flour the beef.

1½ –2½ hours before you want to eat

* Preheat the oven to 160–170°C/325°F/Gas Mark 3. If you are using dried mushrooms, cover them with boiling water and leave to soak.
* Toss the slices of beef in flour mixed with a good dose of salt and pepper. To do this without creating any mess put the flour, salt and pepper in a plastic bag, add the meat and shake vigorously to coat.
* Add a splash of oil and some of the butter to a large casserole and place over a medium heat. When the fat is hot, brown the beef on both sides, in batches. Add more butter and oil as and when you need to. As the beef browns, lift it from the pan and put it to one side. While the beef is browning, peel and slice the onions.
* Once the beef has browned, add the remaining butter and a splash of oil, then add the onions to the casserole and allow them to soften and brown slightly over a low to medium heat for 7–10 minutes.
* Meanwhile, peel the celeriac and chop it into 3-cm chunks. If you are using fresh morels, remove any mud with a soft, damp cloth and cut them in half.
* When the onions are soft, add the morels (if you are using dried ones, lift them out of their soaking liquor) and cook them for a few minutes until they start to soften.
* When the morels have cooked for a few minutes, add the vinegar and boil vigorously while stirring and scraping the bottom of the pan until the vinegar has evaporated. Now add the wine and bring to the boil. Simmer the wine for a couple of minutes then add the stock, celeriac and the beef. Roughly chop the parsley and add this, along with salt and pepper, to the casserole.
* Cover the casserole and place it in the oven for at least 1½ hours and up to 2 hours.
* Check the beef after about 1½ hours – it is ready if it feels tender and succulent. It may require longer so return it to the oven and check again after 30 minutes or so.
* When you want to serve, remove half the beef, mushrooms and celeriac, and half the cooking liquor, and place in a container to freeze.
* If you think there is too much liquid and want to intensify the sauce, strain into a separate pan and reduce until you have the consistency you desire. Keep the beef, celeriac and morels warm while the sauce is reducing.
* Pour the sauce over the beef slices, with the mushrooms and celeriac to the side. Serve with mashed potatoes and steamed spinach or greens.

Lazy day supper – reheating instructions

* Remove the braise from the freezer the day before you plan to serve it. Allow to defrost completely.
* Preheat the oven to 180°C/350°F/Gas Mark 4.
* Put the braise in a large casserole with a lid, cover and let it heat in the oven for 30 minutes until thoroughly hot. Serve as above.

KITCHEN REVOLUTION EXTRA

Pot roasting, braising and poaching

Many of the recipes involve cooking meat in liquid. Sometimes the dish is described as a pot roast, sometimes as a braise (or a stew or casserole) and sometimes the method is described as poaching.

Pot roasting
A whole joint is cooked very slowly with a little liquid, so that it half roasts, half steams. This is usually done in the oven, though can be done on the hob, and it works especially well for dry cuts of meat like guinea fowl, pheasant, venison, etc.

Braising
A braise, stew or casserole mostly uses meat which is cut into pieces and mixed with vegetables and different flavourings, and is then submerged in liquid to keep it moist while it cooks very gently for a long period of time. This good for cheaper cuts of meat and ones with a good marbling of fat which breaks down and baste the meat as it cooks.

Poaching
This is quicker and very simple. Poached meat or fish is generally cooked, in whole pieces, in flavoured liquid at a very slow simmer until it is just cooked.

May Week 4 – Overview

For a special meal over the bank holiday weekend, chicken poached with elderflower, served with garlic new potatoes hits the spot. This Big Meal from Scratch takes only 1 hour 20 minutes from start to finish but leaves you with the basis for two, perhaps three, meals. Any leftover chicken is used to make Chicken Waldorf Toasts and surplus garlicky new potatoes make a salad with asparagus and eggs. Both these Something for Nothing recipes take less than 20 minutes. If there is any sauce leftover from cooking the chicken it can be turned into a light and fragrant Chicken and Elderflower Soup.

Making the most of the time of year, the Seasonal Supper is a recipe for Spiced Lamb Chops with Radish and Orange Salad that takes 30 minutes. Taking inspiration from the flavours and sunny colours of the Middle East, this meal is appetising and exceptionally pretty – a good choice for supper with friends.

Digging deep into the store cupboard this week, a creamy and rich Mushroom Stroganof is a Larder Feast that will prove a challenge to any food snobs who deride canned mushrooms. Ready in 30 minutes, this is an ideal recipe when the fridge is bare and the larder beckons.

Mexican Beans with a Polenta Topping make a hearty vegetarian casserole. As with many Two for One recipes, this takes some time to prepare and cook – 1¼ hours in total – so save this for a day when you have sufficient time.

May Week 4	Recipe	Time
Big meal from scratch	Elderflower poached chicken with wine and garlic new potatoes and cabbage	1 hour 20 minutes
Something for nothing 1	New potato, asparagus and egg salad	20 mins
Something for nothing 2	Chicken Waldorf toasts	10 mins
Seasonal supper	Spiced lamb chops with radish and orange salad	30 mins
Larder feast	Mushroom stroganof	30 mins
2 for 1	Mexican beans with a polenta topping	1¼ hours

All recipes serve 4 apart from the 2 for 1 recipe which makes 8 portions

SHOPPING LIST (for 4 people)

Meat and fish
4 free-range chicken breasts (bone in, if possible) and 6 free-range chicken thighs, skin on
4-12 lamb chops (depending on the size of the chops and your appetite)

Dairy
135 ml milk
100 g butter
150-200 ml soured cream or crème fraîche
4 free-range eggs or 12 quail eggs
2 free-range eggs
40 g Parmesan
70 g Cheddar

Fruit and vegetables
900 g even-sized new potatoes (the smaller the better)
1 leek with green top, approx. 160 g
12 celery sticks
2 carrots, approx. 200 g
1 cabbage, approx 400-600g (hispy is very good at this time of year)
600 g asparagus
2 little gem lettuces or 300-500 g salad leaves
100 g rocket
2 bunches radishes (ideally the long white-tipped ones - breakfast radishes - and enough for 4 radishes per person)
3 sweet hot red peppers (the long thin ones) or normal sweet red peppers
3 medium onions, approx. 360 g
4 medium red onions, approx. 400 g
3-4 spring onions
15 garlic cloves
a few sprigs fresh thyme
6 sprigs fresh mint
2 sprigs fresh tarragon or 1 tsp dried tarragon
1 small bunch fresh coriander
small handful of fresh flatleaf parsley
2 crisp tart apples, such as Granny Smith
3 medium sweet oranges
1½ lemons
½ lime

Basics
250ml olive oil
60 ml groundnut or grapeseed oil
8 pitta breads or 4 naan breads
8 thick slices bread
2½ tbsp plain flour
1 tbsp baking powder
2 heaped tsp mustard powder
1 tsp caster sugar

1 bay leaf
300 ml chicken stock (fresh or made from a stock cube or bouillon powder)
salt and pepper

Store cupboard
185 g polenta
2 x 400 g cans chopped tomatoes
1 x 400 g can kidney beans
1 x 330 g can sweetcorn
60 g green olives (we like the ones stuffed with anchovies)
2 x 290 g cans sliced button mushrooms
4 tbsp mayonnaise
30-50 g mixed dried mushrooms
75 g walnut halves
300 g pasta, such as tagliatelle or pappardelle
1 tbsp cider or red wine vinegar
1 tbsp balsamic vinegar
½-1 tsp chilli powder (according to taste)
1 tsp ground coriander
2 tsp paprika
½ tsp ground cumin
pinch of nutmeg (ground or freshly grated)
500 ml sparkling elderflower drink or elderflower cordial diluted with water
325 ml white wine

To pick
4 heads elderflower or use a generous dash of elderflower cordial

Serving suggestions
foccacia bread (New Potato, Asparagus and Egg Salad)
avocado, cucumber, spring onions, lemon juice and olive oil (Mexican Beans with a Polenta Topping)

To download or print out this shopping list, please visit www.thekitchenrevolution.co.uk/May/Week4

Elderflower Poached Chicken with Wine and Garlic New Potatoes and Cabbage

This is the first recipe Rosie ever devised and it has become a firm favourite with us all. The chicken is moist, the sauce light and fragrant, and the potatoes are richly flavoured when cooked with wine-soaked garlic cloves.

Though the elderflower season is short, the flat white blooms are generally pretty abundant. Don't worry if you can't locate any, as you can add an additional dash of elderflower cordial. If you are going to pick elderflowers do so as near to the time of cooking as possible, preferably not from the side of a busy main road as they may have been covered in fumes. Once picked, give the heads a hearty shake to expel any bugs or dead flowers, then rinse them thoroughly in cold water and leave them to drip dry.

The recipe includes extra chicken for the Chicken Waldorf Toasts and extra potatoes for the Potato, Asparagus and Egg Salad.

Elderflower poached chicken
2 tbsp groundnut or grapeseed oil
4 free-range chicken breasts (bone in, if possible) and 6 free-range chicken thighs, skin on; includes 2 extra breasts for the chicken Waldorf toasts
1 medium onion, approx. 120 g
2 carrots, approx. 200 g
2 celery sticks
1 leek with green top, approx. 160 g
500 ml sparkling elderflower drink or elderflower cordial diluted with water
30 g butter
1 lemon
300 ml chicken stock (fresh or made from a stock cube or bouillon powder)
4 heads elderflower or a generous dash of elderflower cordial
1 bay leaf
salt and pepper

Wine and garlic new potatoes
3 tbsp olive oil
900 g even-sized new potatoes (the smaller the better); includes 600 g extra for the new potato, asparagus and egg salad
12 garlic cloves
250 ml white wine
a few sprigs fresh thyme

Cabbage
1 cabbage, approx. 400 g–600 g (hispy is very good at this time of year)
20 g butter
pinch of nutmeg (ground or freshly grated)

GET AHEAD PREPARATION (optional)

* Prepare the onion, carrots, celery and leek.
* Peel the garlic and make up the parchment envelope for the potatoes.
* Prepare the cabbage.

1 hour 20 minutes before you want to eat prepare the chicken

* Heat a good splash of oil in a large casserole and season the chicken pieces. Add the chicken to the pan and brown all over. Lift the pieces out with a slotted spoon and set aside. You may need to do this in batches.
* Peel and roughly chop the onion and carrots. Wash and chop the celery. Remove the tough green top and outer layer from the leek, then slice and wash it thoroughly.
* When all the chicken is browned, keep the casserole on the heat and add a small glassful (approx. 150 ml) of the elderflower drink or diluted cordial. Let it simmer, stirring all the time, to lift any flavours left from browning the chicken. Pour the liquor over the browned chicken pieces, wipe out the casserole with kitchen paper and return to the heat.
* Add a generous splash of oil and about half the butter, and when the pan is hot add all the vegetables and sweat them over a low heat, stirring regularly, for about 5 minutes. Zest and juice the lemon.
* Add the stock, lemon juice and remaining elderflower drink or diluted cordial to the vegetables. Season well and bring to a simmer for a few minutes.
* Next, lay the chicken thighs on the vegetables followed by the stock and elderflower. Cover with the heads of elderflower and lemon zest and the bay leaf. If you can't get elderflowers add the dash of cordial over the thighs.

* Bring to simmering point, then turn the heat right down and leave the chicken to poach gently until tender (about 50 minutes).
* While the chicken is poaching, preheat the oven to 200°C/400°F/Gas Mark 6.
* If necessary wash or scrub the potatoes.

50 minutes before you want to eat prepare the potatoes

* Heat a very generous splash of oil in a large frying pan and when it is hot add the potatoes. Brown them all over for 5–10 minutes, shaking them occasionally to make sure they colour evenly. Peel the garlic cloves and add them to the pan, so they turn a little golden too.
* When the potatoes are browned, add the wine, reduce it by half then add 150 ml water and let the potatoes cook in this liquid for about 5 minutes. By the end of 5 minutes just a few spoonfuls of liquid should remain in the pan. Add the thyme sprigs to the potatoes and season.
* Now cut a piece of foil big enough to hold the potatoes in a parcel and place it on a large baking sheet. Drizzle generously with oil and use a slotted spoon to lift the potatoes on to one half of the foil. Carefully pour the pan juices over the potatoes and create an airtight, roomy parcel by bringing the sides of the foil together and folding them tightly.
* Cook the potatoes in the oven for 30 minutes.
* Now put the chicken breasts in with the thighs to poach for 20 minutes until just cooked.

10 minutes before you want to eat cook the vegetables and sauce

* Wash and prepare the cabbage.
* Put a little water in a steamer or pan to boil. When the water boils, add the cabbage and steam for about 5 minutes. Place the cooked cabbage in a warmed serving dish with the butter, a small pinch of nutmeg and salt and pepper.
* Check that the potatoes are cooked using a knife or skewer. If they need a little more time return them to the hot oven. If they are cooked, turn the oven off and keep them warm in their parcel, while you make the sauce. Put some plates and dishes in the oven to warm.
* Check that the chicken thighs and breasts are cooked – the juices should run clear when a thigh is pierced with a skewer. Lift the meat from the sauce and place the thighs and two of the breasts in a serving dish in the still warm oven until you are ready to serve. Set aside the other breasts for later in the week.
* Put a sieve over a bowl, pour in the vegetables and their cooking liquor and strain the liquor into the bowl. Put the vegetables into a food processor. Remove the bay leaf and any elderflower stalks and purée the vegetables, gradually adding the cooking liquor until you have a smooth sauce. Taste for seasoning and add the remaining butter, give the sauce one last whizz in the food processor and pour it into a pan to reheat ready to serve.
* Pour the elderflower sauce over the chicken and scatter with the flowers from the remaining elderflower head. Serve with the cabbage and the potatoes straight from their parcel.

Afterwards

* Put the leftover potatoes – ideally there should be 600 g – and 2 chicken breasts (approx. 200–300 g) into separate containers, cover and refrigerate for use later in the week.
* Any leftover sauce can be used later in the week as the basis for a chicken and elderflower soup.

Added extra

Depending on the amount of sauce left over and the intensity of flavour, add either chicken stock, vegetable bouillon or water to make up the volume of soup you need (usually about 250 ml per person). Add a few peeled, sliced potatoes; simmer for 20 minutes till potatoes are cooked. Throw in some roughly chopped parsley and blitz with a hand blender until smooth and serve with warm crusty bread.

New Potato, Asparagus and Egg Salad

This simple salad is a quick and tasty way to enjoy the abundance of seasonal asparagus.

2 little gem lettuces or 300–500
   g salad leaves
3–4 spring onions
400g–600g cooked new potatoes
   left over from the Big Meal
   from Scratch or 600 g new
   potatoes boiled for 15 minutes
   or until just tender
600 g asparagus
4 free-range eggs or 12 quail
   eggs
4 tbsp olive oil
1 tbsp balsamic vinegar
40 g Parmesan
salt and pepper

To serve
focaccia bread (optional)

GET AHEAD PREPARATION (optional)

* Prepare the little gem lettuces.
* Trim and slice the spring
  onions.
* Halve the potatoes.
* Prepare the asparagus.

*20 minutes before
you want to eat*

* Put a kettle on to boil for the eggs and asparagus. Meanwhile, wash the little gem lettuces and tear the leaves in half. Trim and slice the spring onions, slice the potatoes in half and prepare the asparagus by bending each spear close to the base so that it snaps at the point where the base turns woody. As asparagus can sometimes be gritty, rinse under cold running water.
* Cook the asparagus in boiling, salted water for about 4 minutes. You want them to still have a bit of bite and they will carry on cooking once they are out of the water. Add the potatoes to the boiling water for the last minute to warm through. Lift out the potatoes and asparagus and set them aside until you are ready to put the salad together.
* Add the eggs to the same pan of boiling water and cook for 7 minutes (3 minutes for quail eggs). Once cooked, drain the eggs and leave them to cool under cold running water. Peel the eggs when they are completely cold. Quarter the eggs if you are using hens' eggs.
* Put the oil into a large salad bowl, add the balsamic vinegar, season and whisk the two together to make the dressing. Now throw the spring onions and lettuce into the bowl but don't toss the dressing through yet.
* Shave the Parmesan into the salad bowl – the easiest way to do this is with a vegetable peeler.
* Now add the asparagus and potatoes along with the eggs. Toss the whole lot together and season well with salt and pepper.
* This salad is fairly substantial but do serve it with warm focaccia bread if you feel so inclined.

Something
for nothing 2

Chicken Waldorf Toasts

Created at the Waldorf-Astoria hotel in New York, Waldorf salad is a much-loved classic. Like those other staples of the buffet table, Coronation Chicken and Potato salad, it is often spoiled with too much mayonnaise – here the mayonnaise is a light coating that adds rich creaminess to an otherwise crunchy combination of apples, walnuts and celery. The chicken is a good, if not classic, addition. This is quite a rich recipe so two pieces of hot, buttered toast, a generous pile of chicken Waldorf and rocket should satisfy most appetites.

4 tbsp mayonnaise
1 tbsp cider or red wine vinegar
juice of ½ lemon
1 tsp caster sugar
2 crisp, tart apples, such as
  Granny Smith
4 celery sticks
75 g walnut halves
2 poached chicken breasts
  (approx. 200–300 g) left over
  from the Big Meal from scratch
  or 2 free-range chicken breasts
  poached in stock for 15
  minutes then cooled
8 thick slices bread
butter
100 g rocket
salt and pepper

GET AHEAD PREPARATION (optional)

The chicken Waldorf can be made
up to 2 days in advance, but
remove from the fridge a good
40 minutes prior to eating. If
you only have a little time:
* Make the mayonnaise dressing.
* Chop the celery and walnuts.

*10 minutes before
you want to eat*

* Put the mayonnaise, vinegar, lemon juice and sugar into a large bowl. Mix well and taste. If the mixture is too tart add more sugar, but remember that the intensity will be diluted by the other ingredients.
* Peel and core the apples and cut them into bite-sized chunks. Add them to the mayonnaise mixture and mix well to ensure all the chunks are coated.
* Wash the celery and chop it into 5mm chunks. Roughly chop the walnuts but don't worry if there are some big pieces left. Break or shred the chicken into bite-sized pieces and add them, the celery and the walnuts to the mayonnaise and apple. Mix thoroughly, taste and season with salt and pepper.
* Toast the bread and spread generously with butter. Put a few rocket leaves on each toast then spoon a generous amount of the chicken Waldorf on top. Serve immediately.

Spiced Lamb Chops with Radish and Orange Salad

May is a good month to enjoy radishes and lamb, and this recipe makes the most of both. Combining radishes and oranges in a salad is a Middle Eastern tradition so we've suggested that you season the lamb with the spices of the region. This is a beautiful-looking supper that is surprisingly simple to get together.

1 tsp ground coriander
1 tsp paprika
½ tsp cumin
5 tbsp olive oil
4–12 lamb chops (depending on the size of the chops and your appetite)
4 medium sweet oranges
2 bunches radishes (ideally the long white-tipped ones – breakfast radishes – and enough for 4 radishes per person)
handful of fresh mint
handful of fresh flatleaf parsley
8 pitta breads or 4 naan breads
salt and pepper

GET AHEAD PREPARATION (optional)

* Season the lamb.
* Wash and slice the radishes.
* Chop the mint and parsley.

30 minutes before you want to eat

* Preheat the grill to high and the oven on to 140°C/275°F/Gas Mark 1.
* In a large shallow dish, mix together the spices, 2 tablespoons of the oil, and ½ teaspoon salt and pepper to taste. Mix well and add the lamb, rubbing the spices into the meat so that each chop is well seasoned. Set aside to marinate while you make the salad.
* To make the salad grate the zest and squeeze the juice of one of the oranges and place in a large bowl. Using a small knife, cut a small section from the top and bottom of each of the three remaining oranges so that they will stand upright on a board. Using a sharp knife, cut downwards so that you remove the skin and pith but so the orange retains its round shape. Slice the skinned oranges into 5-mm rounds and add to the zest and juice in the bowl.
* Wash the radishes, cut them into 3–4-mm slices and add to the oranges.
* Roughly chop the mint and parsley and add to the oranges. Dress with the remaining oil and season to taste. Set aside while you cook the lamb and warm the pitta breads or naan breads.
* Remove the pitta breads or naan breads from any packaging, wrap in foil and place in the oven.
* Place the lamb chops on a rack under the grill. Cook each side for 5–10 minutes, depending on whether you like your lamb rare, medium or well done.
* Serve the chops with the salad and a pile of warmed pitta breads or naan breads.

Larder feast

Mushroom Stroganof

Fried canned mushrooms are the mark of an authentic Greasy Spoon fry-up, but it's difficult to think where else they feature in our culinary landscape. They may not get the gastronomic juices flowing but they can be excellent in certain recipes. Of course, there is no denying that fresh mushrooms are ultimately superior, but when the kitchen is bare, a can of mushrooms in the cupboard and a good recipe mean you can rustle up a very passable meal at short notice and with minimal fuss. This stroganof uses canned and dried mushrooms, and as a result has plenty of texture and flavour.

30-50 g mixed dried mushrooms
2 tbsp groundnut or grapeseed
    oil
30 g butter
2 medium onions, approx. 120 g
2 × 290 g cans sliced button
    mushrooms
1 tbsp plain flour
2 heaped tsp mustard powder
1 tsp paprika

300 g pasta, such as tagliatelle
    or pappardelle
75 ml white wine
150-200 ml soured cream or
    crème fraîche
2 sprigs fresh tarragon or 1 tsp
    dried tarragon
salt and pepper

GET AHEAD PREPARATION (optional)

The stroganoff can be made 2-3 days in advance, but if there are only a few spare moments:
* Soak the dried mushrooms.
* Prepare the onions.
* Drain the mushrooms.
* Chop the tarragon, if using

30 minutes before you want to eat

* Cover the dried mushrooms with boiling water.
* Heat a generous slug of oil and the butter in a large heavy-based pan. Peel and finely slice the onions and add them to the pan. Allow them to cook gently for 7–10 minutes, until they are soft, stirring occasionally.
* While the onions are softening, drain the button mushrooms and shake off any excess water.
* After 10 minutes, turn the heat up under the onions and add the canned mushrooms. Fry the mushrooms over a medium to high heat until they are golden brown and any liquid they have released has evaporated. Add a splash more oil if they seem to be dry and sticking.
* When the mushrooms and onions are light golden, add the flour, mustard powder and paprika, turn down the heat and let them release their flavours for a couple of minutes.
* Lift the dried mushrooms from their soaking liquor and squeeze them a little (keep the liquor to add later). Add the soaked mushrooms to the onions and button mushrooms in the pan, and cook them for a couple of minutes over a medium heat.
* Bring a large pan of water to the boil. Add a generous teaspoonful of salt, add the pasta and cook according to the manufacturer's instructions.
* Turn the heat up under the mushrooms, add the wine and let it bubble for a minute or so. Then, using a sieve to catch any bits of grit, strain the mushroom liquor into the pan. Bring this to the boil and let it simmer vigorously until the liquid has reduced by half.
* Add the soured cream or crème fraîche and bring the whole lot back to the boil. Season well and leave to simmer for 5 minutes.
* If using fresh tarragon, strip the leaves from their stalks and chop finely. When the pasta is cooked, drain and return it to the pan. Add the fresh or dried tarragon and a good dose of seasoning, and toss well. Divide between four plates and serve the stroganof on top.

Two for one

Mexican Beans with a Polenta Topping

Tamales are a staple snack food in Mexico and are traditionally made by stuffing cornmeal dough and various flavourings inside corn husks or banana leaves. This recipe is Rosie's brother, Chris, and is always a hit with everyone. Instead of stuffing corn husks, polenta and cheese are used as the topping for a delicious tamale-style pie with a piquant filling made from olives, hot peppers, kidney beans, sweetcorn and coriander. You can also use any leftover vegetables you might have knocking about.

Don't be put off by the amount of time involved in preparing this dish because most of it is pie-cooking time.

The ingredients below make enough filling for eight servings, but only enough topping for four as the polenta top can't be frozen. When you take the filling out of the freezer you will need to make a fresh topping.

If really pushed for time the filling can be served with simply cooked plolenta.

4 medium red onions, approx.
   400 g
3 tbsp olive oil
3 sweet hot red peppers (ramano)
   or red peppers
6 celery sticks
3 garlic cloves
60 g green olives (we like the
   ones stuffed with anchovies)
½–1 tsp chilli powder (according
   to taste)
small handful of fresh coriander
1 x 400 g can red kidney beans
1 x 330 g can sweetcorn
2 x 400 g cans chopped tomatoes
juice of ½ lime
salt and pepper

For the topping
70 g Cheddar
185 g polenta
1½ tbsp plain flour
1 tbsp baking powder
1–2 tsp salt
2 free-range eggs
135 ml milk
1½ tbsp olive oil

To serve
Avocado, cucumber and spring
   onion salad, dressed with
   olive oil and lemon juice
   (optional)

GET AHEAD PREPARATION (optional)

The filling can be made up to 2 days in advance. If you only have a little time:
* Prepare the onions, peppers, celery and garlic.
* Chop the olives and coriander.
* Grate the cheese.

1¼ hours before you want to eat

* Preheat the oven to 200°C/400°F/Gas Mark 6.
* Peel and slice the onions, then heat a good splash of oil in a large pan over a medium heat and add the onions. Allow them to soften gently for about 5 minutes.
* Meanwhile, deseed and slice the peppers and wash, trim and slice the celery. Add these to the pan and cook for another 5–7 minutes.
* While the onions, peppers and celery are cooking away, peel and crush the garlic and roughly chop the olives and coriander.
* Now add the garlic and chilli powder to the pan and stir for a couple of minutes. Then add the olives, kidney beans, sweetcorn and tomatoes. Bring the whole lot to the boil, add the chopped coriander and lime juice and season to taste with salt and pepper. Leave to simmer gently while you make the topping.
* Grate the cheese and put it in a large bowl with the polenta, flour, baking powder and salt.
* Beat the eggs, milk and oil together. Make a well in the centre of the dry ingredients, pour in the liquid and stir until you have a well-amalgamated batter.
* Pour half the tomato filling into an ovenproof dish. Pour the polenta batter over the top and smooth out. Place in the middle of the oven and bake for about 45 minutes until the top is golden and set.
* Let the rest of the filling cool, then put it in a freezer bag and freeze.
* Serve hot with an avocado, spring onion and cucumber salad, dressed with olive oil and lemon juice, if you wish.

**Lazy day supper
– reheating
instructions**

* Remove the Mexican bean mixture from the freezer and leave at room temperature for 6–8 hours or for 24 hours in the fridge to thaw completely.
* Make the topping as above. Warm the filling in a pan on the hob then place it in an ovenproof dish and cover with the topping. Bake as before for 45 minutes.

May puddings   # Elderflower Cream

This is essentially panna cotta with a difference – instead of the milk being infused with vanilla, it is infused with elderflowers and lemon. If you can't get hold of elderflowers you can achieve the same effect by using less milk and sugar and adding elderflower cordial. This pudding would be lovely with stewed gooseberries, rhubarb or even the first of the raspberries, and crisp biscuits. It is very quick to make but takes a few hours to set.

This recipe is based on a superb panna cotta recipe that was given to Rosie by her great friend Sue Lewis.

400 ml double cream
50 g sugar or 30 g if using
  elderfower cordial (see above)
375 ml milk or 300 ml milk and
  75 ml elderflower cordial (see
  above)
4 heads elderflowers (if available)
½ lemon
4 leaves (approx. 7 g) gelatine

To serve
fresh or stewed fruit (see above)
  and biscuits

4 hours before you want to eat

* Put the cream, sugar and half the milk in a pan. If you are using cordial, reduce the amount of sugar and milk as shown in the ingredients list and add the cordial.
* If using elderflowers, shake them to remove any lurking bugs and give them a quick rinse under cold running water. Zest and juice the lemon. Drop the flowers into the milk, crushing them a little as you do, so that they release some of their perfume. Add the lemon juice and zest. Bring the milk to the boil then take it off the heat and leave it to infuse.
* While the milk is coming to the boil, soak the gelatine leaves in the rest of the milk and leave for a few minutes until soft and spongy. At this point, lift the leaves out of the milk and squeeze any excess liquid back into the milk. Stir the gelatine into the hot milk, but not over the heat. Once the gelatine has completely dissolved, add the remaining milk and leave the whole lot to become completely cold.
* When the mixture is cold, strain it into a jug and pour it into four moulds, cups or glasses and put in the fridge to set.
* Once the creams are set, dip each mould in to boiling water and invert the cream on to an individual serving plate.
* Serve with fruit and biscuits.

May puddings

Rhubarb with Hazelnut Shortbread

Rhubarb is excellent at this time of year. Lightly stewed with orange peel, sugar and perhaps a little ginger, pieces of rhubarb look like jewels suspended in syrup. Rhubarb is a treat enough on its own, so if you are short of time or energy the accompanying biscuits can be left out. That said, the flavour of the hazelnuts and the richness of shortbread complement the tart lightness of the fruit.

Rhubarb
1 kg rhubarb (as thin and as pink
  as you can find)
200 g light brown soft sugar
1-cm piece of fresh root ginger
grated zest of 1 orange

Hazelnut shortbread
125 g softened butter, plus extra
  for greasing
50 g caster sugar
100 g skinned, toasted hazelnuts
150 g plain flour
pinch of salt
caster sugar, for dusting

To serve
double or (even better) clotted
  cream (optional)

1 hour before you want to eat

* Preheat the oven to 150°C/300°F/Gas Mark 2.
* Wash the rhubarb and cut away any thick, woody ends. Cut into rhubarb into 4-cm lengths and place in an ovenproof dish with a lid. Cut the ginger in half and add to the rhubarb with the sugar and orange zest. Add two tablespoons of water.
* Stir well, then place over a medium heat and bring to the boil. Cover with the lid and place in the oven for at least 30 minutes and up to 45 minutes, until the rhubarb is completely soft.
* In the meantime, make the shortbread. Line a baking tin, approximately 26 x 16 x 2 cm, with butter. Cream the butter and sugar until fluffy and pale. You can do this with an electric whisk. Put the hazelnuts in a food processor and pulse until they are chopped into small pieces. If you don't have a food processor, put them in the middle of a clean tea towel, wrap them well and bash them with a rolling pin or the base of a pan.
* Add the hazelnuts to the butter and sugar, then fold in the flour and salt so that you have a light crumbly mixture.
* Press the shortbread dough into the baking tin, smoothing out the top as much as possible. The back of a spoon does this job well. Using a knife, score the dough without cutting all the way through so that you will be able to break fingers off once it's baked. Set aside until the rhubarb is ready.
* Once the rhubarb is soft, take it out of the oven, check for sweetness and tip it into a serving dish. Allow to cool before serving.
* Turn the oven up to 160°C/325°F/Gas Mark 3 and when it has come to temperature put the shortbread in and bake for 25–30 minutes.
* Remove the shortbread from the oven, dust it lightly with caster sugar and allow it to cool a bit before you break it up into fingers.
* Serve the rhubarb in a bowl with the shortbread on the side and an optional jug of cream.

Coffee Granita, Pistachio Cream and Chocolate Sauce

There are many classic sundae-style puddings and we based this recipe on the French café dessert *liégois*. We have pumped it up a little by adding pistachio cream and using coffee water ice (granita) instead of ice cream. If you make the granita well in advance (24 hours or more) you will be able to assemble the pudding quite easily.

Coffee granita	Pistachio cream	Chocolate sauce
2 tbsp sugar	100 g unsalted pistachios, kernels	85 g caster sugar
2 strips lemon zest	2 tbsp demerera sugar	3 tbsp rum, Cointreau or brandy (or whatever you fancy and think would go well)
5 heaped tbsp ground strong coffee	100 g mascarpone	200 g bitter dark chocolate
	100 g fromage frais	150 ml double cream

At least 4 hours in advance

* Place the sugar and lemon zest in a pan with 500 ml water and stir until the sugar is dissolved. Put the ground coffee in a bowl or jug. When the sugar has dissolved, bring the syrup to the boil, pour it over the coffee and leave it to infuse.
* After 10–15 minutes, strain the coffee-flavoured syrup through a very fine sieve or coffee filter into a large shallow dish so that it will cool down as quickly as possible.
* When the liquid is cold, pour it into a 1-litre freezer-proof container, preferably a shallow rectangular one with a lid. Freeze for 1 hour or so, by which time the liquid should have started to freeze around the sides and base of the container.
* Take a fork and mix the frozen crystals into the centre, then re-cover the container and return it to the freezer for another hour. After that, repeat with another vigorous mixing with a fork, cover again and refreeze for a further hour. At this stage give the mixture one final mix.
* The coffee granita should now be a completely frozen snow of ice crystals, which means it is ready to serve.
* It can remain at this servable stage in the freezer for a further 3–4 hours, but after that it will become too solid and it will need to be taken out and allowed to soften, then mixed with a fork again.

30 minutes before you want to eat

* Place the pistachios in a food processor with the sugar and whizz until they are finely chopped. Alternatively put them in a pestle and mortar and grind to a fine powder. Put the mascarpone and fromage frais in a bowl and beat them together, then add the pistachio and sugar mixture until you have a well amalgamated nutty cream. Put this in the fridge for later.
* Now make the chocolate sauce. Put the sugar and the rum, Cointreau or brandy in a pan and let the sugar dissolve gently over a low heat. In the meantime, break the chocolate into little pieces.
* When the sugar has dissolved, bring the syrup to the boil then simmer it for half a minute. Add the chocolate and stir thoroughly until it has melted. At this point add the cream and swirl the pan to amalgamate, then bring the sauce to the boil and simmer for a couple of minutes. Keep stirring so that the sauce doesn't stick.
* To serve this indulgence – spoon out a generous layer of granita into four dishes or glasses (for full-on glamour), then add a dollop of the pistachio cream, followed by lashings of chocolate sauce.

May puddings

Dried Fruit Spiced Flapjacks

Kitchens stocked with tins of flapjacks are the stuff of childhood nostalgia, and there aren't many people who don't enjoy them, even though they may not be associated with grown-up eating. The recipe for these ones is a little different, and perhaps a little more grown-up, but nevertheless very good. Although not normally served as a pudding, a fruity and spicy flapjack served warm from the oven with a spoonful of ice cream is an excellent end to any meal. This recipe makes enough for about 15 slices, on the understanding that it's rather nice to have spare flapjacks for snacks.

200 g butter, plus extra for
  greasing
75 g no-soak apricots
50 g no-soak prunes
50 g dried figs
50 g raisins
3 tbsp brandy (optional) or water
½ tsp ground cinnamon
½ tsp ground ginger
¼ tsp ground nutmeg
180 g demerara sugar
300 g jumbo rolled oats
pinch of salt

To serve
vanilla ice cream

45 minutes before you want to eat

* Preheat the oven to 190°C/375°F/Gas Mark 5.
* Line the base of a shallow baking tin, about 30 x 30 cm and at least 2 cm deep, with greaseproof paper and grease the unlined sides with butter.
* Cut the apricots, prunes and figs into pieces about the same size as the raisins. Put all the dried fruits in a pan with a lid, add the brandy or water and bring to the boil. Cook for a couple of minutes then take off the heat and leave to cool slightly.
* While the fruit is cooling, prepare the other ingredients. Melt the butter in a large pan and when it is foaming add the spices, sugar, oats and salt. Mix well, then remove from the heat and add the dried fruits and all their liquid.
* Tip the entire mixture into the tin, flatten with the back of a spoon and bake for 30 minutes. Cool for 10 minutes, then score the mixture into serving size squares or triangles.
* When the mixture is completely cold, cut it into individual flapjacks and lift them out of the tin. Serve with vanilla ice cream.

JUNE

June is the time for cucumbers, mackerel, salad leaves and the first gooseberries, and we use each of these at least once this month. Cucumber is a key ingredient in a Garlicky Prawn and Fennel Tzatziki Salad, and also appears in a Smoked Salmon and Cucumber sauce served with tagliatelle. With a little luck, you'll be able to eat outdoors in June, and there are recipes here that could be served cold for a picnic, or warm as part of a long and leisurely outdoor lunch: Watercress and Potato Frittata, for example, or Spiced Lentil Salad with Hummus and Lamb. The Larder Feasts have the feel of warmer climates: Chickpea Cakes with Tomato Salsa, inspired by the Middle East and Mexican-style Spicy Bean Wraps. A summer without Summer Pudding is unthinkable; ours is packed to bursting with strawberries, raspberries, blackcurrants and cherries. There is also a Gooseberry and Elderflower Sorbet – refreshing, light and very elegant.

June	Week 1	Week 2	Week 3	Week 4
Big meal from scratch	Roast haddock with crushed potatoes and spinach and Parmesan salad	Mustard baked veal (or pork) chops with roast asparagus and marjoram potatoes	Grilled poussin with lemon and olives, brown rice with herbs and pine nuts, and roast fennel and red onions	Roast leg of lamb (or kid) with new season's garlic, braised lentils and glazed baby carrots
Something for nothing 1	Haddock with French beans and green sauce	Crab and asparagus with sweet chilli and ginger	Feta lamb with rice salad	Spiced lentil salad with hummus and lamb (or kid)
Something for nothing 2	Watercress and potato frittata with tomato salad	Potatoes, eggs and ham	Prawn and fennel tzatziki salad	Braised summer vegetables with pancetta and sherry
Seasonal supper	Oatmeal herrings with warm beetroot salad	Grilled mackerel with spring onions and calcot sauce	Baked broccoli carbonara	Salmon and cucumber tagliatelle
Larder feast	Salmon with spinach and spiced rice	Spicy bean wraps with palm hearts salsa	Chickpea cakes with tomato salsa	Pearl barley and feta salad with agresto dressing
2 for 1	Giant sausage roll	Goats' cheese gnocchi with beetroot	Baked fish with summer vegetables	Rolled chicken breasts filled with asparagus and cheese, with new potatoes and salad
Puddings	Cherry and chocolate fool	Redcurrant sponge squares	Summer pudding	Gooseberry and elderflower sorbet

June Week 1 – Overview

This week's food embraces summer enthusiastically. Most of the recipes contain little or no meat but they are substantial and flavourful enough to sustain even the most committed carnivore.

The Big Meal from Scratch recipe, Roast Haddock with Crushed Potatoes and Spinach and Parmesan Salad can be made in an hour. Bear in mind the need to cook fish soon after purchasing when you're planning this week's cooking.

An Italian omelette, or frittata, uses the extra new potatoes cooked to accompany the big meal, and any leftover haddock is turned into a salad with green beans and a creamy herb sauce. Both meals are ideal for the working week as they're ready in about half an hour.

For a Seasonal Supper, herrings are coated in oatmeal, fried and served with a beetroot salad. If they are unavailable, mackerel or sardines could stand in but with all fish freshness is key so plan to cook this recipe as soon after purchasing the fish as possible.

The Larder Feast this week is a layered, spiced rice dish made with canned salmon and frozen spinach that has proved popular every time it's been served. The recipe takes 25 minutes to prepare then 20 minutes cooking, so consider making this when you have some reserves of time and energy.

The week is not completely devoid of meat with a Two for One recipe for a Giant Sausage Roll – layers of filo pastry filled with a tomato and sausage casserole. In all, the recipe involves 45 minutes preparation and 15–20 minutes cooking – best for a day when time is on your side.

June Week 1	Recipe	Time
Big meal from scratch	Roast haddock with crushed potatoes and spinach and Parmesan salad	1 hour
Something for nothing 1	Haddock with French beans and green sauce	35 mins
Something for nothing 2	Watercress and potato frittata with tomato salad	25 mins
Seasonal supper	Oatmeal herrings with warm beetroot salad	30 mins
Larder feast	Salmon with spinach and spiced rice	45 mins
2 for 1	Giant sausage roll	1 hour

All recipes serve 4 apart from the 2 for 1 recipe which makes 8 portions

SHOPPING LIST (for 4 people)

Meat and fish
1.25 kg haddock or cod loin, or skinned
  pollack fillets
4 × 350 g herrings (ask the fishmonger to
  scale them and, if you prefer, to butterfly
  them too) or other oily fish, such as
  mackerel or trout
16 good quality free-range pork sausages

Dairy
150 g butter
20 g Parmesan
7 large free-range eggs
2 tbsp milk
3 tbsp soured cream

Fruit and vegetables
1.4 kg floury potatoes, such as Maris Piper or
  baking potatoes (medium-sized if possible)
600 g new potatoes
600 g cooked beetroot (not pickled)
600 g French beans
150 g baby leaf spinach
1 small bunch watercress, approx. 100 g
6 medium ripe tomatoes, approx. 600 g
1 soft lettuce, such as a butterhead or round
  lettuce (little gem or cos will also be fine)
1 head celery
6 medium red onions, approx. 720 g
2 medium onions, approx. 240 g
4 large or banana shallots, approx. 150 g
6 spring onions
10 garlic cloves
8 sprigs fresh mint
4 sprigs fresh tarragon
1 large bunch fresh parsley
4 sprigs fresh dill or fresh chervil
5 sprigs fresh dill or 1 tsp dried dill
  (optional for Salmon with Spinach and
  Spiced Rice)
3 sprigs fresh sage
4 sprigs fresh thyme
1 small bunch chives
3½ lemons
200 g frozen spinach

Basics
330 ml olive oil
75 ml groundnut or grapeseed oil
400 g filo pastry
2½ tbsp Dijon mustard
1 tsp Worcestershire sauce
dash of Tabasco sauce
100 g plain flour
3 heaped tsp wholegrain mustard
30 g sugar (light brown soft or unrefined
  golden for preference)
2 bay leaves
salt and pepper

Store cupboard
300 g basmati rice
100 g pinhead oatmeal
2 × 400 g cans salmon
1 × 400 g can tomatoes or 4 plum tomatoes,
  peeled
100 g green olives stuffed with anchovies
1 × 50 g can anchovy fillets in olive oil
50 g toasted almonds
40 g raisins or sultanas
2 tsp capers
6 tbsp red wine vinegar
1½ tsp ground cinnamon
¾ tsp ground ginger
1½ tsp ground turmeric
½ tsp ground nutmeg
½ tsp cayenne pepper or chilli powder
poppy seeds for sprinkling (optional for Giant
  Sausage Roll)
300 ml red wine

Serving suggestions
watercress, olive oil and lemon juice
  (Oatmeal Herrings with Warm Potato Salad)
green or cucumber salad ingredients (Salmon
  with Spinach and Spiced Rice)
greens or green salad ingredients (Giant
  Sausage Roll)

To download or print out this shopping list,
please visit www.thekitchenrevolution.co.uk/June/
Week1

Roast Haddock with Crushed Potatoes and Spinach and Parmesan Salad

With fish simplicity is often the best recipe – here haddock is topped with olives and herbs and roasted in the oven for 20 minutes. This is served with mustardy potatoes and a spinach and Parmesan salad. As a nod to summer, the potatoes are served warm rather than piping hot.

If you cannot find good thick haddock loins then you could use pollack or cod fillets. The thickness of the fish will very much determine how long they need to cook. For a 2-cm thick fillet a roasting time of 10 minutes should be ample. Increase or decrease the time for thinner or thicker cuts. The fish is cooked if the flesh flakes easily and is opaque.

The recipe includes extra haddock for the Haddock with French Beans and Green Sauce and extra potatoes for the Watercress and Potato Frittata.

Roast haddock
2 garlic cloves
½ lemon
100 g green olives stuffed with
    anchovies
small handful of fresh parsley
1.25 kg haddock or cod loin, or
    skinned pollack fillet; includes
    500 g extra for Haddock with
    French Beans and Green Sauce
3 tbsp olive oil
salt and pepper

Crushed potatoes
1.4 kg floury potatoes, such as
    Mans Piper or baking potatoes
    (medium if possible); includes
    500 g extra for the watercress
    and potato frittata

3 garlic cloves
1 tbsp Dijon mustard
2 heaped tsp wholegrain mustard
3 tbsp red wine vinegar
8 tbsp olive oil
6 spring onions

Spinach and Parmesan salad
1 soft lettuce, such as butterhead
    or a round lettuce (little gems
    or cos will also be fine)
150 g baby spinach
2 large handfuls of flatleaf
    parsley
1 large or banana shallot,
    approx. 30 g
½ lemon
20 g Parmesan
3 tbsp olive oil

GET AHEAD PREPARATION (optional)

The topping for the haddock can be made a few hours in advance, as can the dressing for the crushed potatoes and the green salad. If you only have a little time:
* Chop the olives.
* Prepare the garlic and spring onions.
* Wash the potatoes.
* Prepare the lettuce leaves.
* Chop the parsley.

1 hour before you want to eat prepare the fish and the potatoes

* To make the topping for the haddock, peel and crush the garlic, grate the zest from the half lemon and finely chop the olives and parsley. Put all the ingredients into a bowl, season with salt and pepper and mix together very thoroughly.
* Pat the haddock dry and season all over. Cut the loin into six portions. Spread the olive mixture on the top side of four of the six pieces of fish. The two remaining pieces are for the haddock with French beans, and will be cooked without topping at the same time as the others. Place the haddock in the fridge until you are ready to cook.
* Wash the potatoes, if large cut in half and put them in a big pan. Cover with water and add a generous pinch of salt. Bring the potatoes to the boil and simmer for about 25 minutes until soft.

30 minutes before you want to eat cook the fish

* Preheat the oven to 200°C/400°F/Gas Mark 6 and preheat a roasting tin.
* Take the haddock out of the fridge.
* Meanwhile, make the dressing for the potatoes. Peel and crush the garlic and place it in a large bowl with the mustards and vinegar. Whisk the lot together with a pinch of salt and a good grinding of pepper. Now pour the oil in slowly and mix well. Trim and finely chop the spring onions, using as much green as you can, and add them to the dressing.
* Next, prepare the salad ingredients. Break up the lettuce and discard any damaged outer leaves. Wash and dry the lettuce leaves and the spinach. Roughly chop the parsley and place all the leaves and the parsley in a large bowl. Peel and finely slice the shallot and put it in a small bowl. Grate the Parmesan in with the shallot and add a generous squeeze of lemon juice and the oil. Mix together with salt and pepper to taste.
* The oven should be at the right temperature by now, so remove the hot roasting tin and drizzle with some oil. Lay the haddock on top and drizzle with a little more oil. Make

sure the haddock pieces without topping have a good dousing. Return the tin to the oven and cook the fish for about 10-15 minutes.

* When the potatoes are cooked, drain them and run under the cold tap for a couple of minutes until they are cool enough to handle. Pull the skin off and break crumbly, bite-sized pieces into a bowl. Add the dressing and mix thoroughly. Tip into a serving dish and set aside until you are ready to eat.

5 minutes before you want to eat

* The best way to check that the fish is cooked is to use a small-bladed knife and ease it into the thickest part. If the flesh looks opaque and lifts easily it is ready. Squeeze a little juice over the top.
* Leave the fish to rest for a couple of minutes while you dress the green salad.
* Serve the haddock with any juices from the pan drizzled over it and pass the salad and the potatoes around separately.

Afterwards

* Put the haddock and leftover potatoes in two separate containers, cover and keep in the fridge for use later in the week.
* Ideally you will have about 500 g of haddock and 500 g potatoes.

Something for nothing 1

Haddock with French Beans and Green Sauce

Other than canned tuna and the occasional appearance of poached salmon, it is relatively unusual for salads in Britain to contain fish. Mixed with a little dressing and carefully chosen leaves, flakes of fish make a salad into an excellent meal, especially when the weather is warm. If you don't have any haddock remaining from the Big Meal from Scratch, use 500 g haddock, pollack or cod, gently poached in water with a stick of celery, a carrot, parsley stalks, a couple of black peppercorns and lemon juice until tender. Allow to cool then break the flesh into large flakes.

600 g new potatoes
600 g French beans
10 anchovy fillets in olive oil
1 tbsp red wine vinegar
2 tsp Dijon mustard
1 large or banana shallot, approx. 30 g
2 tsp capers

3 tbsp olive oil
8 sprigs fresh mint
4 sprigs fresh tarragon
2 pieces of haddock, approx. 500 g, left over from the Big Meal from Scratch or see above
small handful of fresh parsley

GET AHEAD PREPARATION (optional)

* Prepare the beans.
* Roughly chop the anchovies.
* Peel and slice the shallot.
* Chop the herbs.

25 minutes before you want to eat

* Wash the potatoes and cut them in half. Put them in a pan of water, bring to the boil, then leave them to simmer until they are cooked – this will take about 15 minutes in total.
* Top, tail and wash the beans, then steam or blanch them until they are just cooked. Drain the beans and plunge them into a bowl of cold water to cool quickly and stop them cooking, so that they retain a nice bright green colour. Once cooled, leave the beans in a colander to dry.
* Next, make the dressing. Roughly chop the anchovies and place them in a bowl. Pour the vinegar over the anchovies – this should help them break up more easily. Now stir in the mustard with a wooden spoon until you have a paste. Peel and finely slice the shallot and add it to the anchovies. Add the capers (you can roughly chop the capers if you prefer them smaller) and stir in the oil. Strip the parsley, mint and tarragon leaves from their stalks. Roughly chop the leaves and add them to the bowl.
* Next, if you haven't already done so, break the fish into large flakes.
* When the potatoes are ready, drain well and place them in a large salad bowl. Add the beans and flakes of haddock and toss the lot together. Add the dressing and fold everything together gently.
* Serve immediately with a glass of good crisp white wine.

**Something
for nothing 2**

Watercress and Potato Frittata with Tomato Salad

Frittata, like its close cousin the Spanish tortilla, is a type of open omelette made with potato and other fillings and cooked until firm on the stove. Frittatas are perfect for a warm summer evening, and this one with watercress and potato left over from the Big Meal from Scratch is quick to prepare, looks good and tastes excellent.

The only slightly tricky part of this meal is where you have to invert the frittata from a frying pan on to a plate, and then slide it back into a frying pan to allow the uncooked side to brown. This requires more courage than skill. Make sure the plate is placed securely over the pan and that you have a good grip before trying to turn the pan upside down. To avoid inverting the pan the frittata can be put uunder the grill.

This frittata is served with a simple tomato salad.

Watercress and potato frittata	Tomato salad	GET AHEAD PREPARATION (optional)
6 large free-range eggs	6 medium ripe tomatoes, approx.	*Prepare the watercress and
500 g cooked crushed potatoes	600 g	tomatoes.
left over from the Big Meal	1 small bunch chives	
from Scratch or 500 g floury	1 heaped tsp Dijon mustard	
potatoes boiled, peeled and	2 tsp red wine vinegar	
roughly crushed	pinch of sugar (ideally light	
1 small bunch watercress,	brown soft)	
approx. 100 g	3 tbsp olive oil	
olive oil		
30 g butter		
Tabasco sauce		
salt and pepper		

*35 minutes before
you want to eat*

* First make the frittata. Lightly beat the eggs with a dash of Tabasco sauce, ½ teaspoon salt and ½ teaspoon black pepper in a large bowl. Add the potatoes and mix well, making sure there are no large clumps of potato.
* Wash and dry the watercress. Remove any thick stalks, coarsely chop the leaves and fold them into the potato and egg mixture.
* Now heat the oil and butter in a heavy-based frying pan (non-stick for preference) large enough to hold all the potatoes. When the butter is foaming, tip the potato, egg and watercress mixture into the pan, flatten it using the back of a spoon and cook on a low heat for about 20 minutes.
* Meanwhile, wash and slice the tomatoes. Using scissors, cut the chives over the tomatoes.
* Put the mustard into a small jug or jar and mix with the vinegar, sugar and a pinch of salt and pepper. Slowly add the oil, stirring all the while.
* When the frittata has been cooking for about 20 minutes and is starting to set, cover the pan with a large plate and, taking great care not to burn yourself, invert the pan so that the frittata ends up on the plate. Use a fish slice to lift out any bits that stick to the pan. Wipe out the pan and add splash of oil. Return the pan to the heat and slide the frittata back in so that the cooked side is facing uppermost. Fry for another 5 minutes until the frittata feels firm. (To avoid inverting the frittata, you can place it under a medium grill for 5–10 minutes. Watch carefully to make sure it doesn't burn.)
* When the frittata feels firm all over, remove it from the heat and slide it on to a plate to rest for a few minutes before slicing.
* Dress the tomatoes and slice and serve the frittata.

Seasonal supper

Oatmeal Herrings with Warm Beetroot Salad

Herrings have a good, strong, oily flavour and respond well to grilling, barbecuing, frying or baking. This old Scottish recipe involves coating them in oatmeal and dates from the nineteenth century. The method in this recipe for boning the fish while keeping it whole for cooking can be used for any small round fish such as mackerel or trout. If pinhead oatmeal proves hard to find, subsitute for matco meal or breadcrumbs.

<u>Oatmeal herrings</u>
4 x 350 g herrings or other oily
   fish such as mackerel or trout,
   scaled and gutted
100 g plain flour
1 large free-range egg
2 tbsp milk
100 g pinhead oatmeal
4 tablespoons groundnut or
   grapeseed oil
generous nut of butter
½ lemon
salt and pepper

<u>Warm beetroot salad</u>
600 g cooked beetroot (not
   pickled in vinegar)
1 tbsp red wine vinegar
2 large or banana shallots,
   approx. 60 g
6 celery sticks (inner ones,
   including the centre)
3 tbsp soured cream
1 tsp Dijon mustard
pinch of light brown soft sugar
4 sprigs fresh dill or fresh
   chervil

<u>To serve</u>
watercress and new potatoes

<u>GET AHEAD PREPARATION</u> (optional)

* Flatten and bone the herrings.
* Prepare the shallots and
   celery.
* Chop the dill or chervil.

*30 minutes before
you want to eat*

* Halve the beetroot and cover with boiling water to warm through.
* Cut along the belly of each fish with scissors and snip off the fins and the head just behind the gills. Now place the herring, flesh side down, on a flat work surface. Using a rolling pin, flatten it out so that the fish looks like a butterfly. Run your thumb firmly all along the backbone of the fish to push it out. Now turn the fish over so that the fish is now skin-side down and splayed open. Start at the head and slip a sharp knife under the backbone and gently ease the bones away. If any little bones stay behind just lift them out. Remove any blood that may still be lurking around, then give the fish a quick wash and pat dry with kitchen paper.
* Place the flour on a plate and season it thoroughly. Beat the egg with the milk. Put the beaten egg mixture, flour and oatmeal on separate plates, next to each other. Season each herring well and dip both sides into the seasoned flour, then dip the flesh side only into the beaten egg and then the oatmeal. Press the oatmeal down firmly into the flesh.
* Drain the beetroot and cut into bite-size chunks. Place in a bowl and sprinkle with the vinegar and season. Peel and then finely slice the shallots and celery and add to the beetroot.
* Mix the cream with the mustard, sugar and 1 tablespoon water. Chop the dill or chervil, add it to the dressing with seasoning and stir well. Pour the dressing over the warm beetroot and toss.
* Heat the oil and butter in a large frying pan over a high heat. Turn the heat down a little and fry the herrings, flesh side (oatmeal side) down, for 2–3 minutes. Flip them over and cook for a couple more minutes, until the skin is crisp. Drain on kitchen paper. Serve with a good squeeze of lemon juice, the beetroot salad, some dressed watercress and new potatoes.

Larder feast

Salmon with Spinach and Spiced Rice

This is a great recipe to have up your sleeve for those times when you need to entertain but have an empty fridge. The method may seem involved, but it transforms canned salmon, rice and frozen spinach into a beautifully presented layered dish.

To make this you need to prepare two separate mixtures – one with rice, spinach, almonds and raisins, the other with onions, salmon and spice. These are then layered up and cooked on the stove.

300 g basmati rice
200 g frozen spinach
2 medium onions, approx. 240 g
5 garlic cloves
olive oil
1½ tsp ground cinnamon
¾ tsp ground ginger
1½ tsp turmeric
½ tsp ground nutmeg
½ tsp cayenne pepper or chilli
   powder

30 g butter
5 sprigs fresh dill or 1 tbsp dried
   dill (optional)
2 × 400 g cans salmon
50 g toasted almonds
40 g raisins or sultanas
2 lemons
salt

To serve
Green salad or cucumber salad

GET AHEAD PREPARATION (optional)

This can be prepared up to 2 days in advance and served at room temperature. If you only have a little time:
* Peel and slice the onions and garlic.
* Juice one of the lemons.

45 minutes before you want to eat

* Put 1.5 litres boiling water into a large pan, add 1 heaped teaspoon salt and bring back to the boil. Rinse the rice in a sieve under running water. Add the rice to the boiling water, bring back to the boil and boil rapidly for 5 minutes.
* After 5 minutes, stir in the frozen spinach and bring back to the boil. Simmer until all the spinach has defrosted into the rice. Drain the part-cooked rice and spinach into a sieve and leave the mixture there so that it loses as much liquid as possible.
* Peel and finely slice the onions and garlic. Put a generous splash of oil into a pan on a medium heat. Add the onions and cook gently for 10 minutes.
* Once the onions are soft, add the garlic and spices and stir for a few minutes then add the butter. If using fresh dill, chop it finely. Add the dill to the pan and remove from the heat. Drain off any oil or liquid from the salmon and stir it into the onions.
* Tip the well-drained rice and spinach into a bowl and add the almonds, raisins, the juice of one of the lemons and a good glug of oil. Fold together taste and season.
* Pour a thin layer of oil and 80 ml water into a deep-sided (preferably non-stick) frying pan about 25 cm in diameter and set over a medium heat. Spread one third of the rice and spinach over the base of the pan, top with half the onion and salmon mixture, a squeeze of lemon juice and a generous sprinkling of seasoning. Follow with another layer of rice and spinach, one more of onion and salmon, lemon juice and seasoning and finally finish the layering with the remaining rice.
* Put a lid on the pan and turn the heat to high for 2 minutes, then turn the heat to its lowest setting for 10–15 minutes. Remove from the heat and leave to rest for 5 minutes.
* To serve, run a knife around the edge of the pan, place a large plate on top of the pan and invert it. Leave the pan on top for 1–2 minutes then give its base some robust taps. Gently lift the pan away so that the rice comes out like a cake. Serve with a green or cucumber salad.

Two for one

Giant Sausage Roll

This recipe makes two sausage-and-tomato-stuffed filo pastry rolls – sausage rolls with attitude. The combination of pastry, sausage and tomato is homely and comforting, and is bound to be popular with children and adults alike.

Filo pastry is sold ready-made in the chilled or freezer cabinets in most supermarkets. It is extremely thin and dries out easily, so while you are buttering the layers for the roll keep the rest of the pastry either covered with a moist tea towel or in its plastic wrapping.

This recipe makes two large rolls and will feed eight people in total. One roll is frozen prior to baking, so you have a ready-made meal for a night when cooking is out of the question.

Filling
6 medium red onions,
    approx. 720 g
groundnut or grapeseed oil
5 outer celery sticks
4 sprigs fresh thyme
2 bay leaves
16 free-range pork sausages
300 ml red wine
pinch of light brown soft sugar
1 × 400 g can tomatoes or 4
    plum tomatoes, peeled
1 tsp Worcestershire sauce
3 sprigs fresh sage

Pastry
400 g filo pastry
60 g butter
1 heaped tsp wholegrain mustard
poppy seeds, for sprinkling
    (optional)

To serve
steamed greens or green salad

GET AHEAD PREPARATION (optional)

The tomato and sausage filling can be made 2 days in advance. If you only have a little time:
* Prepare the onions and celery.
* Chop the sage.
* Brown the sausages.

1 hour before you want to eat

* Preheat the oven to 200°C/400°F/Gas Mark 6 and preheat a large baking sheet.
* Peel and finely slice the onions. Heat a glug of oil in a heavy-based pan with a lid, add the onions and cook them on a low heat for 10 minutes with the lid on until they become soft.
* In the meantime, cut the sausages into bite-sized lengths and place in a roasting tin or ovenproof dish in the oven for 15 minutes, until they are nicely browned. Meanwhile trim and slice the celery.
* When the onions have softened, add the celery, thyme sprigs and bay leaves, replace the lid and leave to soften for another 5 minutes.
* When the onions and celery have softened, turn up the heat and add the wine. Simmer with the lid off until the wine is completely absorbed – this will take about 5–7 minutes. Next, add the tomatoes, sugar and Worcestershire sauce and boil briskly until they have bubbled down to a dryish paste.
* After about 15 minutes in the oven the sausages will be cooked and brown, so use a slotted spoon to lift them from the tin into a large bowl. Roughly chop the sage and throw it into the bowl.
* Now prepare the filo pastry. Melt the butter (either in a small pan or in a microwave). Lay out a piece of baking parchment the size of the baking sheet in the oven, butter it and lay a sheet of filo on top. You want a sheet that is about A3 size – if it's smaller use two sheets side by side, overlapping slightly.
* Now stir the mustard into the melted butter. Brush the sheet of filo with the mustardy butter, then lay another sheet on top. Butter the second sheet and add a third, butter again and add a fourth. Reserve some of the butter and keep it warm.
* The pastry can sit like this until the tomato mixture is ready.
* Once the tomato mixture is very thick, remove the thyme stalks and stir in the sausage and sage mixture.
* Now place half the sausage and tomato mixture down the centre of the filo leaving a few centimetres at either end (make two separate rolls if you are using two smaller sheets of filo). Fold the ends into the filling and use the baking parchment to help you roll the sides of the pastry over the mixture. Use the parchment to roll the sausage roll over so that the seam ends up underneath.

* Brush the sausage roll with the reserved melted butter and sprinkle with poppy seeds, if using. Use the parchment paper to lift the sausage roll onto the hot baking sheet in the oven and cook for 15–20 minutes until the pastry is crisp and the filling hot.
* While the first sausage roll is cooking, repeat the process with the remaining filo and the filling. Wrap the roll or rolls in baking parchment and freeze.
* When the roll is cooked, slice it into four and serve with simply steamed greens or a green salad.

Lazy day supper – cooking instructions

The sausage roll can be cooked from frozen. Preheat the oven to 180°C/350°F/Gas Mark 4 and preheat a baking sheet. Unwrap the sausage roll, pop it into the oven, seam-side down, and bake for 45 minutes until crisp and heated through. Serve as above.

June Week 2 – Overview

The delicate flavour and tender texture of veal is especially suited to summer. In this week's Big Meal from Scratch recipe veal chops are coated with mustard and breadcrumbs then baked in the oven and served with roast asparagus and casseroled potatoes. The veal can be replaced with pork chops, if necessary, but for more information about buying and eating veal see page 000. From start to finish this meal will take 1½ hours but most of this is the cooking time for the potatoes.

Roasting draws out the flavour of asparagus, so it therefore makes sense to cook extra quantities so there are leftovers ready to use in another meal – in this case a quick Crab and Asparagus Stir-Fry with Sweet Chilli and Ginger. If fresh crab proves difficult to find, the recipe works well with tiger prawns. Sometimes food reminiscent of childhood is the answer to a busy week and the other Something for Nothing recipe, Potatoes, Eggs and Ham fits the bill exactly. Both this and the crab stir-fry take around half an hour to make.

Grilled or barbecued mackerel is lovely, especially in summer, so for this week's Seasonal Supper this most handsome of fish is served with spring onions and a Spanish calcot sauce.

For this week's Larder Feast, Spicy Bean Wraps are similar to Mexican burritos, and are ready in just 30 minutes. We've suggested serving these with a salsa made from canned palm hearts, but fresh avocados would work too.

Finally, the Two for One is a Roman gnocchi dish that takes 1 hour and 20 minutes to prepare – save this for when you're not in a hurry. As with all the Two for One recipes, it freezes well. It will keep for a few days in the fridge so it can be made in advance.

Remember that the crab and mackerel will need to be eaten when they are as fresh as possible so plan to cook them soon after they are purchased.

June Week 2	Recipe	Time
Big meal from scratch	Mustard baked veal (or pork) chops with roast asparagus and marjoram potatoes	1½ hours
Something for nothing 1	Crab and asparagus with sweet chilli and ginger	30 mins
Something for nothing 2	Potatoes, eggs and ham	25 mins
Seasonal supper	Grilled mackerel with spring onions and calcot sauce	45 mins
Larder feast	Spicy bean wraps with palm hearts salsa	35 mins
2 for 1	Goats' cheese gnocchi with beetroot	1 hour 20 minutes

All recipes serve 4 apart from the 2 for 1 recipe which makes 8 portions

SHOPPING LIST (for 4 people)

Meat and fish
4 x 200 g–220 g (approx.) veal loin chops or
  free-range pork chops
350 g (approx.) fresh crab meat (a mixture
  of brown and white meat but ideally with
  more white than brown) or 400 g raw peeled
  tiger prawns
250–300 g thinly sliced good quality baked
  or roast English ham
8 medium mackerel fillets (ask the
  fishmonger to prepare them)

Dairy
800 ml milk
180 g (approx.) butter
6 free-range eggs
150 ml crème fraîche
110 g Parmesan
300 g goats' cheese
100–200 ml Greek yoghurt or soured cream

Fruit and vegetables
1.5 kg baking potatoes
600 g Jersey Royals or new potatoes of your
  choice
800 g uncooked beetroot or 600 g cooked
  beetroot (not pickled in vinegar)
1 kg asparagus
200 g (approx.) sugar snap peas or mangetout
1 bunch watercress, approx. 85 g
100 g watercress
150 g rocket
2 large ripe plum tomatoes, approx. 200 g
2 large or banana shallots, approx. 60 g
7 medium red onions, approx. 760 g
2–3 bunches spring onions, approx. 18
10 garlic cloves
4-cm piece of fresh root ginger
½ bunch chives
5 sprigs fresh marjoram or thyme or 1 tsp
  dried marjoram or thyme
1 large bunch fresh flatleaf parsley
handful of fresh coriander
3 lemons
2 limes
2 juicy oranges

Basics
150 ml olive oil
60 ml groundnut or grapeseed oil
100 g breadcrumbs, or 2–3 slices bread
  suitable for crumbing
12 soft flour tortillas
2 tbsp wholegrain mustard
200 ml stock, ideally chicken (fresh or made
  from a stock cube or bouillon powder)
200 ml vegetable stock (made from a stock
  cube or bouillon powder)
salt and pepper

Store cupboard
100 g brown long grain rice or brown
  basmati rice
170 g basmati rice
400 g semolina
2 tbsp pickled ginger or 4–5 spring onions
50 g flaked almonds (toasted if possible)
30 g toasted hazelnuts
4–5 roasted red peppers from a can or jar
½ x 400g can celery hearts
1 x 400 g can pinto beans or haricot beans
1 x 200 g can reduced salt and sugar baked
  beans
1 x 410g can palm hearts
1 tbsp sherry or cider vinegar
2 tsp red wine vinegar
2½ tbsp soy sauce
2½ tbsp rice or white wine vinegar
1 tbsp sweet chilli sauce
2½ tsp ground cumin
½–1 tsp smoked paprika
pinch of paprika
½ tsp chilli powder
pinch of nutmeg (ground or freshly grated)
1 heaped tbsp sesame seeds

Serving suggestions
tomato salad ingredients (Potatoes, Eggs and
  Ham)
green salad ingredients (Mackerel with
  Spring Onions and Calcot Sauce)

To download or print out this shopping list,
please visit www.thekitchenrevolution.co.uk/June/
Week2

**Big meal
from scratch**

Mustard Baked Veal (or Pork) Chops
with Roast Asparagus and Marjoram Potatoes

Mustard sauce goes very well with the gentle flavour of veal or pork and baked
marjoram potatoes. For information about veal, see page 219.

This recipe makes a large quantity of marjoram potatoes, partly because they are
used as the basis for a bake later in the week, and also because they are so well
received. Surplus asparagus is used with some Sweet Chilli and Crab later in the week.

Mustard baked veal (or pork)
chops
4 veal loin chops or free-range
  pork chops, approx. 200-220 g
  each depending on your
  appetite
30 g (approx.) butter
groundnut or grapeseed oil
2 tbsp wholegrain mustard
small handful of flatleaf parsley
1 lemon
100 g breadcrumbs or 2-3 slices
  bread suitable for crumbing
1 bunch watercress, approx. 85 g
200 ml stock, ideally chicken
  (fresh or made from a stock
  cube or bouillon powder)
salt and pepper

Roast asparagus
1 kg asparagus; includes
  500-600 g extra for the crab
  and asparagus with sweet
  chilli and ginger
1 large or banana shallot,
  approx. 30 g
1 lemon
3 tbsp olive oil

Marjoram potatoes
Olive oil
1.5 kg baking potatoes; includes
  approx. 700 g extra for the
  potato, ham and eggs
6 spring onions
100 g butter
5 sprigs fresh marjoram or 1 tsp
  dried marjoram
3 garlic cloves

GET AHEAD PREPARATION (optional)

* Chop the parsley.
* Peel the potatoes, slice them
  as thinly as you can and cover
  with water until required.
* Prepare the garlic, shallot and
  spring onions.
* Strip and chop the marjoram
  leaves.
* Trim and rinse the asparagus.
* Make the topping for the chops.

*1½ hours before
you want to eat
cook the potatoes*

* Preheat the oven to 180°C/350°F/Gas Mark 4.
* Oil an ovenproof dish large enough to hold all the potatoes. Peel and slice the potatoes
  as thinly as possible and tip them into the dish. Trim and thinly slice the spring
  onions and add them to the potatoes.
* Melt the butter (in a small pan or a microwave). Strip the marjoram leaves from their
  stalks and chop them. Peel the garlic and crush it or grate it straight into the butter.
  Add the chopped marjoram leaves or dried marjoram.
* Pour the flavoured butter over the potatoes and spring onions, add a good dose of salt
  and pepper and mix together well – you want the potatoes to be glistening with butter
  (add a little oil if you need to). Flatten the mixture down and cover with foil so that
  it's airtight.
* Place the potatoes in the oven for about 1 hour until cooked. Once cooked, a knife will
  slip easily through them.

*40 minutes before
you want to eat
prepare the
asparagus*

* Bring a large pan of salted water to the boil. Meanwhile, prepare the asparagus by
  bending each spear so that it snaps at the point where the base turns woody. As
  asparagus can sometimes be gritty, rinse under cold running water.
* Add the asparagus to the boiling water, cover with a lid and bring to the boil again.
  Cook until the asparagus is just starting to tenderise (1–3 minutes depending on the
  thickness of the spears).
* Once cooked, drain the spears and run them under cold water so they cool quickly and
  don't lose colour. Pat dry and tip into an ovenproof dish so that the asparagus is in as
  thin a layer as possible.
* Next, finely peel and chop the shallot. Grate the zest of the whole lemon and juice half
  the lemon. Mix the shallot with the oil, lemon zest and juice, and a generous pinch
  each of salt and pepper. Pour over the asparagus and mix well. Put to one side, ready to
  be roasted just before you eat.

30 minutes before *you want to eat* *prepare the chops*	* Turn the oven up to 220°C/425°F/Gas Mark 7.
	* Season the chops very well with salt and pepper.
	* Melt the butter over a low heat in a large frying pan, Tip most of the butter out into a little bowl and set aside. Add a splash of oil to the pan and turn the heat up.
	* Now brown the chops for 3 minutes on each side, so they turn golden in colour. Once browned, sit them side by side in a roasting tin.
	* Mix the mustard with the remaining melted butter and brush it on to the uppermost sides of the chops.
	* Now make the topping. Roughly chop the parsley, juice the lemon and grate about a quarter of its zest. Mix the parsley and zest with the breadcrumbs and some seasoning and pack a quarter of the mixture on top of each chop. Press the crumbs down well so that they stick on.
20 minutes before *you want to eat* *cook the chops*	* The potatoes should be almost cooked by now. Take the foil off to let them brown.
	* Put the chops at the top of the oven for about 10–12 minutes, by which time they should be cooked and the breadcrumbs should be brown. While the chops are cooking, wash and dry the watercress and remove the thick stalks.
10 minutes before *you want to eat* *cook the asparagus* *and the sauce*	* When the chops are cooked remove them from the oven and put the asparagus in their place at the top. The asparagus will take about 10 minutes in a hot oven.
	* Move the potatoes to the very bottom of the oven until you are ready to serve. Cover them with foil if they seem to be getting too brown. Lift the chops from the roasting tin and leave them to rest in a warm place while you make a sauce in the tin.
	* Place the roasting tin over the heat, add the stock and bring it to the boil then let it reduce by a third. Add the lemon juice and season to taste.
	* To serve the meal, put a handful of watercress on each plate, drizzle with the sauce. and place a chop on top. Pass the rest of the sauce and the potatoes and asparagus round separately.
Afterwards	* Put the leftover asparagus (500 g) and potatoes (700 g) in separate containers, cover and keep in the fridge for use later in the week.
	* Keep any leftover sauce to use as the basis for a pasta sauce (see below).

Added extra

Bacon and Mustard Pasta

Fry some bacon and leeks, once they are cooked add the leftover sauce and a spoonful of crème fraiche, sour cream or double cream. Simmer for a few moments and then serve with pasta.

Crab and Asparagus with Sweet Chilli and Ginger

Crab has often been perceived as the poor cousin to lobster but there are many people, ourselves included, who would argue for the brown crab as the superior crustacean. It has a delicate, sweet flavour but can nevertheless withstand the powerful flavours of Asian food. In our favourite Singaporean restaurant, whole chunks of crab, shell and all, are served stir-fried in a wickedly hot, caramelised sweet chilli sauce.

Fresh crab, however, is not something you can always bank on finding, especially if you are limited to using a supermarket rather than a fishmonger. If this is the case, this recipe works fine with raw, peeled tiger prawns. Although tiger prawns come ready cooked, they tend to be more rubbery and have less flavour than the raw ones. Replace the crabmeat with 400 g prawns. Pat them dry and stir-fry them in a drizzle of oil over a high heat for just over 1 minute until they turn pink, then follow the instructions for using crabmeat.

170 g basmati rice
1 large or banana shallot,
    approx. 30 g
1 garlic clove
4-cm piece of fresh root ginger
2 tbsp pickled ginger or
    4-5 spring onions
2½ tbsp soy sauce
2½ tbsp rice vinegar or white
    wine vinegar
1 tbsp sweet chilli sauce
1 heaped tbsp sesame seeds
1 tbsp groundnut or grapeseed oil

200 g (approx.) sugar snap peas
    or mangetout
500 g (approx.) roast asparagus
    left over from the Big Meal
    from Scratch or 500 g
    asparagus, cooked until *al
    dente*
350 g (approx.) fresh crab meat
    (a mixture of brown and white
    but ideally with more white
    meat than brown) or raw,
    peeled tiger prawns (see
    above)

1 lime
salt and pepper

GET AHEAD PREPARATION (optional)

* Prepare the shallot, garlic and
    ginger.
* Drain the pickled ginger or
    prepare the spring onions.
* Mix the soy sauce, vinegar and
    chilli sauce in a bowl.

*30 minutes before
you want to eat*

* Wash the rice well under cold running water, tip it into a large pan and cook according to the instructions on the packet.
* Meanwhile, peel and finely slice the shallot and garlic and ginger. Peel and grate the fresh ginger. Drain the pickled ginger or finely slice the spring onions. Mix the soy sauce, vinegar and chilli sauce in a bowl.

*10 minutes before
you want to eat*

* Start by browning the sesame seeds in a large wok or large heavy-based frying pan over a medium heat. Watch them carefully as they will burn quickly. Once brown, put them to one side.
* Next, heat the oil in the wok or frying pan over a high heat and when hot add the shallot. Fry for about 1 minute, stirring all the while, until the shallot starts to brown.
* Next, add the sugar snap peas or mangetout, fry for 1 minute then add the garlic and fresh ginger and fry for a further minute.
* Cut the asparagus in half, add to the wok, and mix well. Then add half the soy sauce, vinegar and chilli mixture. Stir well while it bubbles away for a few minutes.
* Now add the crabmeat and sesame seeds. Mix well, then halve and squeeze the lime over the top. Season with salt and pepper then remove from the heat.
* Once the rice is cooked divide it between four bowls. Spoon the crab and asparagus mixture on top. Garnish with the pickled ginger or spring onions. Serve with the remaining soy, vinegar and chilli mixture on the side for extra flavour.

Something
for nothing 2

Potatoes, Eggs and Ham

The addition of chives, Parmesan and rocket to potatoes, eggs and ham turns a homely and fairly ordinary dish into something special. If there are no marjoram potatoes remaining from the Big Meal from Scratch, peel, slice and parboil 700 g large baking potatoes and toss them with melted butter, fresh or dried marjoram, and salt and pepper.

olive oil
2 medium red onions, approx.
   240 g
700 g (approx.) marjoram
   potatoes left over from the Big
   Meal from Scratch or see above
250–300 g good quality, thinly
   sliced, baked or roast English
   ham
½ bunch chives
150 ml crème fraîche
150 g rocket
50 g Parmesan
4 free-range eggs
salt and pepper

To serve
tomato salad

GET AHEAD PREPARATION (optional)

* Prepare the onions.
* Cut the ham.
* Cut the chives.
* Grate the Parmesan.

*.25 minutes before
you want to eat*

* Preheat the oven to 200°C/400°F/Gas Mark 6.
* Heat a generous splash of oil in a large heavy-based pan with a lid. While the oil is heating, peel and thinly slice the onions. Add them to the pan and let them soften for 7–10 minutes over a medium heat.
* Meanwhile, place the potatoes in a large pan. Cut the ham into approximately 2 x 5 cm strips and the chives into short lengths. Add both to the potatoes along with the crème fraîche and fold together thoroughly.
* When the onions are soft, add the rocket, put the lid on the pan and let the rocket soften and wilt for a minute.
* Once the rocket has wilted mix it into the potato and ham mixture. Let the mixture warm through over a gentle heat for about 5 minutes. While it is warming grate the Parmesan.
* When the potatoes and ham are warmed through, turn them out into a large shallow ovenproof dish. Flatten the mixture down and then make four indents in which to nestle the eggs. Break an egg into each hollow and sprinkle with the Parmesan and salt and pepper. Bake for about 5–7 minutes until the whites of the eggs are opaque and the yolks are still runny.
* This is a meal in itself but you could serve it with a tomato salad if you wish.

Seasonal supper

Grilled Mackerel with Spring Onions and Calcot Sauce

Fresh mackerel in season is meaty in texture and intense in flavour, and its succulent flesh means it can be grilled without any risk of drying. Here it is grilled on a bed of potatoes and spring onions. Calcot is the Catalan word for spring onion.

This nutty, sharp sauce goes very well with potatoes and also cuts through the oiliness of the mackerel. If you are especially tight for time, you can cook and serve the potatoes separately.

Grilled mackerel
600 g Jersey Royals or new
    potatoes of your choice
12 spring onions
olive oil
8 medium mackerel fillets (ask
    the fishmonger to prepare
    them)
1 lemon
salt and pepper

Calcot sauce
3 garlic cloves
4 tbsp olive oil
50 g flaked almonds (toasted if
    possible)
30 g chopped toasted hazelnuts
small handful of flatleaf parsley
2 large ripe plum tomatoes,
    approx. 200 g
2 tsp red wine vinegar
pinch of paprika
salt and pepper

To serve
green salad

GET AHEAD PREPARATION (optional)

The sauce can be made 2 days in advance. If you only have a little time:
* Trim the spring onions.
* Cook the potatoes.
* Peel the garlic.
* Toast the almonds.
* Chop the tomatoes.

45 minutes before you want to eat (20 minutes if the potatoes are cooked separately)

* Wash the potatoes and cut them in half lengthways. Put them in a pan of boiling water and bring them up to a simmer. Let them cook for 10–15 minutes until they are just cooked through.
* Peel the garlic cloves, put them in a small pan with 2 tablespoons water and a good slug of oil and simmer for a few minutes until the water has evaporated and the cloves are soft and golden.
* If you haven't bought toasted almonds and hazelnuts, toss them in a frying pan over a low heat for a minute or so until lightly golden.
* When the garlic is soft, place it in a food processor. Chop the parsley, add to the garlic and whizz for a minute or so, then add the nuts and repeat the process. Chop up the tomatoes and add these, along with the vinegar and paprika. Whizz to a smooth paste. Now add 2 tablespoons oil in a slow stream with the motor running. Taste and season.
* Trim the spring onions, but keep them whole.
* Preheat the grill to high. Drain the potatoes and put them on a large baking sheet in a single layer, season and drizzle with oil. Place under the grill for a few minutes (not on the very closest shelf – probably the second closest) until they start to turn golden..
* Once the potatoes are golden, remove the baking sheet from under the grill and turn the potatoes over. Scatter the spring onions over the top of the potatoes, season and drizzle with a little more oil then grill as before for a few minutes.
* When the spring onions have softened and started to colour, bring the baking sheet out again, turn the spring onions over and lay the mackerel fillets on top, skin-side up. Season, drizzle with any remaining oil and place under the grill. The fillets will take 7–9 minutes to cook and their skins should be crispy and slightly coloured.
* To serve, squeeze the lemon over the mackerel fillets and place on individual plates on top of a pile of spring onions and potatoes and with a generous dollop of sauce on the side. Serve with a green salad.

Larder feast

Spicy Bean Wraps with Hearts of Palm Salsa

These spicy bean wraps are great for family eating or informal entertaining. Avocado guacamole is the usual accompaniment for burritos and beans, but as this is a larder feast the wraps are served with a refreshing salsa made with palm hearts, lime and smoked paprika. Adding a small can of baked beans to the vegetable and pinto bean mixture is an inspired idea borrowed from cookery writer Ruth Watson.

Spicy bean wraps
100 g brown long grain rice or
   brown basmati rice
2 medium red onions, 240 g
   approx.
½ tbsp groundnut or grapeseed
   oil
3 garlic cloves
3-4 canned roasted red peppers
½ × 400 g can celery hearts
2 tsp ground cumin
½ tsp chilli powder
1 × 400g can pinto beans or
   haricot beans
1 × 200 g can reduced salt and
   sugar baked beans

12 soft flour tortillas
100-200 ml Greek yoghurt or
   soured cream
salt and pepper

Hearts of palm salsa
juice of 1 lime
1 × 410 g can palm hearts
1 canned, roasted red pepper
handful of fresh coriander
¼ tsp ground cumin
½-1 tsp smoked paprika
   (unsmoked if the smoked
   version is unavailable)

GET AHEAD PREPARATION (optional)

The beans can be made up to 2 days in advance and reheated when required. The salsa can be made a couple of hours in advance. If you only have a little time:
* Prepare the onions and garlic.
* Slice the peppers, celery hearts and palm hearts.
* Chop the coriander.

30 minutes before you want to eat

* Wash the rice under cold running water and cook according to the pack instructions.
* Peel and finely slice the onions. Put one quarter of the slices in a bowl large enough to hold all the palm hearts, squeeze the lime juice over and set aside.
* Heat the oil in a large heavy-based frying pan and when it is hot add the remaining sliced onions. Peel and finely slice the garlic, add it to the onions and stir once or twice.
* Drain the red peppers, cut them into fine slices then add these to the pan. Drain the celery hearts, chop them into a small dice and add to the pan. Fry for about 3 minutes, stirring occasionally.
* After about 3 minutes add the cumin, chilli powder and ½ tsp each of salt and pepper to the vegetable mixture. Cook for 1 minute then add the drained pinto beans and baked beans. Fill the baked bean can to just under halfway with water and it to the pan. Stir well, turn down the heat and allow the mixture to bubble away and thicken for about 10-15 minutes. Stir occasionally.
* Heat up the tortillas according to the manufacturer's instructions.
* Drain the palm hearts and slice them in half lengthways and then into small chunks no more than 1 cm thick. Add these to the onion slices.
* Drain the red pepper, chop it into small dice and add to the onions and palm hearts. Add the cumin, paprika and coriander, mix well and season.
* When the bean mixture has thickened, season then tip into a serving bowl. Place the rice, salsa, beans and warmed tortillas on the table with a bowl of yoghurt or soured cream.
* To serve, layer a spoonful of rice, then beans then salsa and a few dots of yoghurt or sour cream on top of a tortilla, roll it up and eat.

Two for one

Goats' Cheese Gnocchi with Beetroot

Gnocchi, a staple of Italy, are small dumplings made from potato, semolina or pasta dough. In this recipe a semolina dough is baked in a slab, sandwiched around a layer of goats' cheese. Accompanied by beetroot cooked with orange and walnuts, it is delicious.

Most grocers and supermarkets sell uncooked beetroot, but it is often also sold cooked in airtight plastic wraps and jars. Either is fine to use, though ready-cooked beets tend to be overcooked and have little texture which is a shame. Beetroot also comes pickled in jars – this will absolutely *not* work for this recipe. If using ready cooked beetroot it will not need to simmer for 20 minutes – just heat through for five minutes.

The gnocchi recipe takes its inspiration from the Merchant House, a restaurant owned by Shaun and Anja Hill, where Rosie was lucky enough to work.

The quantities here are for eight so that half can be frozen for eating on another day.

Goats' cheese gnocchi
groundnut or grapeseed oil
800 ml milk
pinch of nutmeg (ground or finely grated)
400 g semolina
2 free-range eggs
60 g Parmesan
300 g goats' cheese
salt and pepper

Beetroot
3 medium red onions, approx. 280 g
1 tbsp groundnut or grapeseed oil
50 g butter
800 uncooked beetroot or 600 g cooked beetroot (*not* pickled in vinegar) (see above)
1 tbsp sherry or cider vinegar
juice of 2 oranges
250 ml vegetable stock (made from a stock cube or bouillon powder)
100 g watercress

GET AHEAD PREPARATION (optional)

The beetroot mixture can be made up a day in advance, ready to be reheated, and the gnocchi can be made until the point of frying, up to 2 days in advance. But if there are only a few spare If you only have a little time:
* Prepare the onions and beetroot.
* Grate the Parmesan.

1 hour 20 minutes before you want to eat make the gnocchi

* Preheat the oven to 180°C/350°F/Gas Mark 4. Find a large ovenproof dish, approximately 30 x 15 x 5 cm, that will fit inside a roasting tin. Grease the dish with oil.
* Next, make the gnocchi. Grate the Parmesan, then put the milk in a pan with the nutmeg and a good dose of salt and pepper. Pour in the semolina and bring it to the boil over a medium heat, stirring constantly. Carry on stirring until the mixture has become almost solid then take it off the heat and beat in the eggs and Parmesan. Pour half the mixture into the prepared dish and cover it with goats' cheese – depending on the type of cheese either crumble or slice it, and distribute it evenly over the gnocchi. Add some seasoning then spread the rest of the semolina over the cheese. Cover the dish with a couple of butter papers or some lightly oiled foil and seal around the edge.
* Put the dish with the gnocchi inside a roasting tin and pour boiling water to come halfway up the sides of the dish. Place in the oven and bake the gnocchi for 25–30 minutes until it is firm to the touch. The gnocchi will become more solid as it cools.

40 minutes before you want to eat cook the beetroot

* In the meantime, start cooking the beetroot. Peel and slice the onions. Then heat the oil and butter in a large pan with a lid over a medium heat. When the fat is hot, add the onions. Stir the onions, turn the heat down, cover the pan and soften for 5–7 minutes.
* Meanwhile, peel the beetroot if necessary. Cut each beet in half and each half into 1-cm thick semicircular slices.
* When the onions are soft, add the beetroot, turn the heat up and let them get a good coating of buttery onion mixture. Splash in the vinegar and let this disappear entirely. Now add the orange juice and stock and bring to the boil. Season, cover with a lid and leave to simmer gently for 20 minutes (or 5 if using cooked beetroot).

30 minutes before you want to eat

* By now the gnocchi should be cooked, so take it out and leave to cool for at least 20 minutes or until it is completely cold. The colder and more solid it is, the easier it will be to brown. Turn the oven right down at this point.

*10–15 minutes
before you want
to eat brown the
gnocchi*

* Once the gnocchi is cold, divide it into eight pieces. Put four pieces aside to freeze and start browning the other four.
* Heat a good splash of oil in a large frying pan over a medium to high heat and add the four pieces of gnocchi. Let them cook until they are browned and crisp on the bottom then turn them over and brown them on the other side – this will take about 3 minutes on each side. If you can only fit a couple of pieces of gnocchi in the pan, keep them in the oven once browned while you cook the other two.
* Meanwhile, check on the beetroot – a sharp knife should meet no resistance when it is inserted into a beet. If there is a lot of liquid in the pan, turn the heat up and reduce until it is just coating the beetroot. Set half the beets aside to cool and then freeze.
* To serve, pile the warm beetroot on to a handful of watercress with a crispy chunk of gnocchi on the side.
* Freeze the leftover gnocchi and beetroot separately.

**Lazy day supper
– reheating
instructions**

* Thoroughly defrost the gnocchi and beetroot.
* Heat the beetroot in a pan, covered, over a low heat for a few minutes until warmed through, add a splash of water if it seems dry.
* Brown the gnocchi as above.
* Serve with watercress as suggested in the recipe.

June Week 3 – Overview

In the event of warm weather the poussin in this week's Big Meal from Scratch can be cooked on the barbecue, or under the grill. Marinated with lemons and olives and accompanied by rice roast fennel and red onion, this is a colourful meal well suited to June. Though most of the cooking can be completed in under an hour, the poussins will need to marinate for at least 1 hour before being cooked so start making the marinade about 1 hour 45 minutes before you want to eat.

By adding handfuls of herbs to the surplus rice from the big meal, Feta Lamb with Rice Salad is ready in 45 minutes. The leftover roast fennel goes to make a refreshing and light Prawn and Fennel Tzatziki which is ready in just 15 minutes.

The Seasonal Supper of Baked Broccoli Carbonara is a rich pasta that appeals to children and grown-ups alike. The Larder Feast recipe for Chickpea Cakes with Tomato Salsa is akin to falafels and equally moreish.

The Two for One recipe for Baked Fish with Summer Vegetables uses a simple method to make the most of seasonal ingredients and celebrate the delicate flavour of fish. Fresh fish will only keep for a day or two so use quickly or freeze raw immediately after purchase.

June Week 3	Recipe	Time
Big meal from scratch	Grilled poussin (or chicken) with lemon and olives, brown rice with herbs and pine nuts, and roast fennel and red onions	1¾ hours
Something for nothing 1	Feta lamb with rice salad	45 mins
Something for nothing 2	Prawn and fennel tzatziki salad	15 mins
Seasonal supper	Baked broccoli carbonara	35 mins
Larder feast	Chickpea cakes with tomato salsa	40 mins
2 for 1	Baked fish with summer vegetables	1 hour

All recipes serve 4 apart from the 2 for 1 recipe which makes 8 portions

SHOPPING LIST (for 4 people)

Meat and fish
4 × 350-450 g poussin or 1.25 kg chicken
   drumsticks or thighs
1 × 550 g neck of lamb fillet
   300 g cooked, peeled Atlantic prawns
150-200 g (approx.) free-range, rindless
   smoked back bacon (depending on taste)
1.25 kg flat fish, such as plaice, sole or brill
   cut into steaks across the fish (fillets will
   also do)

Dairy
50 g butter
6 free-range eggs
200 ml double cream
350 ml Greek yoghurt
200 ml milk
80 g Parmesan
120 g feta

Fruit and vegetables
7 bulbs fennel, approx. 1.4 kg
600 g carrots (baby ones if possible)
500 g (approx.) broccoli
600 g asparagus
6-7 ripe tomatoes, approx. 700 g
1 cucumber
7 medium red onions, approx. 840 g
3 bunches spring onions, approx. 24
24-25 garlic cloves, approx. 2 large heads
small handful of fresh flatleaf parsley
1 large bunch fresh coriander
1 large bunch fresh mint
5 sprigs fresh basil
6 sprigs fresh thyme (preferably lemon
   thyme)
6 lemons
1 lime

Basics
200 ml fish or vegetable stock (fresh or made
   with a stock cube or bouillon powder)
plain flour, for dusting
330 ml olive oil
groundnut or grapeseed oil
salt and pepper

Store cupboard
600 g brown rice (long grain or basmati)
300 g spaghetti
2 roasted red peppers from a can or jar
2 × 400 g cans chickpeas
1 tbsp jalapeno chilliess from a jar
5 no-soak apricots
3 tbsp tahini
50 g pitted black olives
50 g green olives
120 g (approx.) pine nuts (toasted if possible)
150 ml white wine

5 tbsp balsamic vinegar
2½ tsp ground cumin
1 tbsp coriander seeds
4 pinches of paprika

Serving suggestions
pitta breads and green salad ingredients
   (Prawn and Fennel Tzatziki Salad)
tomatoes and basil (Baked Broccoli
   Carbonara)
pitta breads, salad leaves and Greek yoghurt
   (Chickpea Cakes with Tomato Aalsa)
new potatoes (Fish Baked with Summer
   Vegetables)

To download or print out this shopping list,
please visit www.thekitchenrevolution.co.uk/June/
Week3

Grilled Poussin (or Chicken) with Lemon and Olives, Brown Rice with Herbs, and Pine Nuts and Roast Fennel and Red Onions

In this recipe, poussin (or chicken pieces) are marinated in lemon, thyme and olive oil then grilled until crisp. The surplus marinade is turned into a tangy gravy to serve with the finished meat, the accompanying herbed rice and roast fennel and red onions. The resulting meal is vibrant in colour and taste.

Poussin (young chickens) can be bought at most supermarkets. Here we suggest you flatten them out, otherwise known as spatchcocking. Sometimes you can buy them ready spatchcocked, but if not it's relatively simple to do it yourself. This recipe also works well with chicken thighs and drumsticks. If using chicken pieces grill for slightly less time than for poussin.

If the weather is suitable, the poussin or chicken pieces can be cooked on a barbeque. They will take 20–25 minutes and should be basted with the marinade half-way through.

The recipe includes extra brown rice for the Feta Lamb with Rice Salad and extra roast roast fennel and red onions for the Prawn and Fennel Tzatziki.

Grilled poussin with lemon and olives
4 lemons
6 sprigs fresh thyme (preferably lemon thyme)
6 garlic cloves
5 tbsp balsamic vinegar
100 ml olive oil
4 × 350–450 g poussin or 1.25 kg chicken drumsticks or thighs
50 g pitted black olives
50 g pitted green olives

Brown rice with herbs and pine nuts
600 g brown rice (long grain or basmati); includes 300 g extra for the feta lamb with rice salad

60 g pine nuts (toasted if possible)
1 tbsp olive oil
5 sprigs fresh mint
5 sprigs fresh coriander
small handful of flatleaf parsley
4 spring onions
salt and pepper

Roast fennel and red onions
7 bulbs fennel, approx. 1.4 kg
6 medium red onions, approx. 720 g
4 tbsp olive oil
(half the quantity is for the prawn and fennel tzatziki salad)

GET AHEAD PREPARATION (optional)

The poussin can marinated up to a day ahead of time – in fact the longer the better, but any of the following would be helpful:
* Wash and soak the brown rice.
* Roughly chop the thyme sprigs, coriander and parsley, and the mint leaves.
* Peel and crush the garlic.
* Toast the pine nuts, if necessary.
* Trim and cut the fennel, and cover with water until required to prevent discoloration.
* Peel and cut the onions.

1¾ hours before
you want to eat
marinate the
poussin

* Wash the rice in a sieve under cold running water. Place the rice in a large pan, cover with 1.3 litres water and soak for 1 hour.
* Now prepare the marinade. Grate the zest from one of the lemons into a small bowl. Add the juice from the zested lemon along with the juice of another 1½ lemons. Cut the remaining 1½ lemons into quarters and add to the juice and zest. Roughly chop the thyme, stalks and all, and peel and crush the garlic. Mix the thyme, garlic, vinegar and oil with the lemon zest, juice and quarters. Season well.
* Spatchcock the poussins one by one by turning them on to their breasts. Starting at the head end, cut down either side of the backbone with a pair of scissors. Cut through the ribs and along the backbone until you are able to remove the backbone from the body. The strip of meat and bone you remove will be the length of the bird and about 3 cm in width. Discard the backbone then turn the bird over and flatten it out by pressing down firmly on its breast bone.
* Place the poussin, skin-side down, in the grill tray, give the marinade a stir then pour it over the birds. Leave them to marinate for at least 1 hour.

1 hour before
you want to eat
prepare the fennel

* Preheat the oven to 190°C/375°F/Gas Mark 5. Place a roasting tin in the oven to warm up. If you have not bought toasted pine nuts place them in a single layer in the tin and cook for about 3–5 minutes in the oven until lightly golden, then put to one side.
* Put a large pan of water on to boil while you trim the bulbs of any fronds, dry ends or battered-looking layers. Cut the bulbs into half lengthways and then cut each half into

three lengthways so that each bulb is in six pieces. When the water is boiling, add 1 teaspoon salt and the fennel and leave it soften a little – this will probably take 3–5 minutes. Meanwhile, peel the onions and cut them into eight wedges through the root.

* When the fennel is ready, drain and toss it with the onion pieces and some seasoning.
* Remove the roasting tin from the oven and pour a generous splash of oil on to it. Put the fennel and onions in the tin, drizzle with more oil and return the tin to the oven. Leave the fennel and onions to roast, stirring once or twice, for 45 minutes.

35 minutes before you want to eat

* Add the oil and plenty of seasoning to the rice and bring to the boil. Once boiling, turn the heat down as low as possible, cover and cook until the rice is just soft. This will take 20–35 minutes.

30 minutes before you want to eat cook the poussin

* Preheat the grill it to its highest setting.
* Lift the poussins out of the marinade and place them on a grill rack, breast (skin-side) down, with the marinade underneath in the grill tray or roasting tin. When the grill is hot, place the birds about 5 cm away from the heat. Leave them to cook for 10–15 minutes, basting them once or twice with some of the marinade.
* After 10–15 minutes, once they are nicely browned, turn the birds over so that they are skin side up, baste them with the marinade and return them to the grill. Leave them to cook and become golden brown. This will take another 7–10 minutes.
* While the poussins are cooking, strip the mint and coriander leaves from their stalks. Roughly chop the leaves and the parsley. Trim the spring onions and chop finely.

10 minutes before you want to eat finish the rice

* Once the rice is cooked, remove it from the heat and drain if necessary. Gently fold in the herbs, spring onions and pine nuts and season to taste. Place the rice in a serving dish and leave it to rest undisturbed until just before serving.
* To check whether the poussin are ready, insert a small knife into the thickest part of the flesh and the juices should run clear. Let the birds rest in a warm place for 5 minutes.
* Leave the grill tray with the marinade under the grill and let the whole lot bubble away for a couple minutes to brown the lemon pieces, stirring occasionally. Splash in a couple of tablespoons of water and then pour the marinade into a sieve over a bowl containing the olives. Tip any remaining juices from the grill tray, then discard the contents of the sieve. Season the marinade and olives in the bowl to taste.
* Check the fennel and onions and, if they have lost heat while the poussin were cooking, pop them under the grill for a couple of minutes to warm up. Taste and season and turn into a serving dish.
* Serve the poussin with a spoonful of the marinade and olives on top, and put the rest of the marinade in a dish to serve on the side.

Afterwards

* Place the leftover fennel and onions (500 g) and the rice (700–800 g) in separate containers, cover and keep in the fridge for use later in the week.
* Any leftover marinade could be used when grilling some fish and chicken and any leftover meat would make a delicious sandwich or salad.

Something
for nothing 1

Feta Lamb with Rice Salad

Mint, feta, yoghurt and lamb are classic Greek or Cypriot ingredients and when combined are the very essence of summer eating. Adding fresh herbs, a new dressing and tomatoes to the rice left over from the Big Meal from Scratch means this recipe can be ready in less than half an hour. If starting from scratch simply cook 350 g brown rice, then mix with 1 tablespoon olive oil, a small handful of chopped mint, a small handful of chopped coriander, 3–4 chopped spring onions and salt and pepper, and increase the amount of dressing for the salad.

This recipe was very kindly donated by Bob Granleese, a great friend of Rosie's and a very accomplished cook.

1 small bunch fresh mint
1 small bunch fresh coriander
5–8 spring onions
100 ml or 3–5 tbsp Greek yoghurt
120 g feta
3½ tbsp olive oil
2 free-range egg yolks
½ tsp ground cumin
60 g (approx.) toasted pine nuts

1 × 550 g lamb neck fillet
700–800 g approx. cooked brown
   rice left over from the Big Meal
   from Scratch or see above
2–3 ripe tomatoes, approx. 250 g
juice of ½ lemon
salt and pepper

GET AHEAD PREPARATION (optional)

* Chop the herbs.
* Trim and slice the spring onions.
* Mix together the ingredients for the crust for the lamb.
* Mix together the dressing for the rice salad.

45 minutes before you want to eat

* Preheat the oven to 200°C/400°F/Gas Mark 6.
* Start by dicing the feta, roughly chopping the mint and coriander and trimming and finely slicing the spring onions.
* Next, make the topping for the lamb by mixing together the yoghurt, feta, ½ tablespoon of the oil, egg yolks, cumin, half the pine nuts, half the coriander, half the mint and half the spring onions. Put the mixture in the fridge for 5–10 minutes.
* Meanwhile, heat 1 tablespoon of the olive oil in a heavy-based frying pan over a medium to high heat. While the oil is heating, cut the lamb fillet into four and season well with salt and pepper. When the oil is hot add the lamb and brown evenly all over – this will take a couple of minutes. When browned, pat the fillets dry and leave them to cool for a few moments.
* Take the topping out of the fridge, rub it over one side of the lamb fillets and sprinkle with the remaining pine nuts. Put the fillets back in the fridge for 5 minutes so that the crust sets.
* While the lamb is in the fridge make the rice salad. Tip the rice into a large bowl. Add the remaining spring onions, coriander and mint. Chop the tomatoes into small bite-sized pieces and mix these into the rice. Mix together the lemon juice, remaining oil and a generous amount of salt and pepper and toss this through the rice. Taste for seasoning and set aside for the flavours to infuse.
* Place the lamb fillets on a baking sheet and put in the oven to bake for 15–25 minutes, depending on whether you prefer your lamb pink or well done.
* When the lamb is cooked, remove the fillets from the oven and let them rest for 5–10 minutes, then slice thickly and serve on top of generous piles of rice salad.

Prawn and Fennel Tzatziki Salad

Using the leftover roasted fennel and onion from the Big Meal from Scratch, this recipe creates a garlicky, summer salad, goodfor outdoor eating. It comprises three parts – lemon fennel, a cucumber tzatziki and seasoned prawns.

    This dish calls for the plump, pale pink coldwater prawns synonymous with a 'pint of prawns'. They are most often sold ready-peeled in supermarkets and have a sweet flavour and soft texture that works especially well in cold dishes.

For the fennel
500-600 g baked fennel and red onions from the Big Meal from Scratch or 4 large bulbs fennel, quartered and cooked in boiling salted water for 5 minutes until tender and tossed while warm with 2 finely sliced red onions, some olive oil, lemon juice and seasoning
grated zest of ½ lemon
2 tbsp olive oil
salt and pepper

For the cucumber tzatziki
1-2 garlic cloves (depending on taste)
250 ml (approx.) Greek yoghurt
1 small bunch fresh mint
1 cucumber
4 pinches of paprika

For the prawns
500 g cooked, peeled Atlantic prawns

To serve
pitta breads and a dressed green salad

GET AHEAD PREPARATION (optional)

* Peel the garlic.
* Chop the mint.
* Prepare the cucumber.

15 minutes before you want to eat

* Put the fennel and onion mixture in a bowl and mix with the lemon zest and oil. Season well with salt and pepper and set aside.
* Now make the cucumber tzatziki. Peel the garlic and crush it into a large bowl. Add the yoghurt, season and beat together. Then roughly chop the mint and add most of it to the yoghurt – leaving some for a garnish. Peel the cucumber and cut it into quarters lengthways. Remove the seeds with a teaspoon and cut the cucumber into 5-mm thick slices. Add to the yoghurt and mix well.
* Tip the prawns into a bowl. Season with a little salt and a generous amount of black pepper.
* Divide the fennel and onion mixture between four plates. Pile the cucumber tzatziki mixture on top of the fennel and the prawns on top of this. Sprinkle with the paprika and remaining chopped mint and serve with pitta breads and a dressed green salad.

Seasonal supper

Baked Broccoli Carbonara

Carbonara, that perfect mixture of eggs, Parmesan and pancetta, is a popular standby in many households. This recipe is a version of carbonara but adds broccoli and becomes a bake. The result is a simple but pleasing meal that's likely to be popular with all ages.

Broccoli, or calabrese as it is also known (after the Italian region from which it originates), has its British season in summer going into autumn. At this time of the year you should be able to get the first of the new season English crop which really is a treat. Broccoli is packed full of vitamins and antioxidants which is why it is cooked for only a couple of minutes before being baked.

This recipe is excellent served with a simple tomato and basil salad.

300 g spaghetti
500 g (approx.) broccoli
150-200 g (approx.) free-range
  rindless smoked back bacon
  (depending on taste)
80 g Parmesan
4 free-range eggs
200 ml double cream
200 ml milk
salt and pepper

To serve
tomato salad with basil

GET AHEAD PREPARATION (optional)

The whole dish can be made a day in advance ready to be baked, though it will require about 30 minutes to heat through. If you only have a little time:
* Prepare and cook the broccoli.
* Grate the Parmesan.

35 minutes before you want to eat

* Preheat the oven to 190°C/375°F/Gas Mark 5.
* Break the spaghetti in half and cook according to the instructions on the packet – usually for about 10 minutes in salted boiling water.
* While the spaghetti is cooking, break the broccoli into small bite-sized florets and rinse under a tap. A couple of minutes before the pasta is cooked drop the broccoli into the pan.
* While the broccoli cooks, heat a frying pan and when it is hot use a pair of scissors to snip the bacon into the pan. Cook until crisp.
* When the pasta and broccoli are just cooked, drain well and tip into a large ovenproof dish.
* Grate the Parmesan. Break the eggs into a bowl and whisk thoroughly with the cream, milk and Parmesan. Season very well.
* Scatter the bacon over the broccoli and spaghetti, followed by the egg mixture.
* Bake in the oven until set – this should take about 20 minutes.
* Serve with a tomato salad.

Larder feast

Chickpea Cakes with Tomato Salsa

Chickpeas are what give falafel, that wonderful snack of the Middle East, its characteristic nutty flavour and light texture. Though the cakes for this recipe are bigger than falafel, they are not dissimilar. This is a good recipe to try on people who claim meat is vital for any proper meal. The cakes are packed with flavour and are surprisingly filling. Served with pitta breads, a tangy salsa, yoghurt and green leaves this recipe is colourful, tasty and very moreish.

Chickpea cakes
2 × 400 g cans chickpeas
1 garlic clove
2 roasted red peppers from a
    can or jar
5 no-soak apricots
handful of fresh coriander
2 tsp ground cumin
1 tbsp coriander seeds
1 tbsp jalapeno chillies from a
    jar
3 tbsp tahini
3 tbsp olive oil
juice of ½ lemon
plain flour, for dusting
salt and pepper

Tomato salsa
4 ripe tomatoes, approx.
    350-400 g
handful of fresh coriander
1 medium red onion, approx.
    120 g
juice of 1 lime
2 tbsp olive oil

To serve
pitta breads, Greek yoghurt and
    salad leaves

GET AHEAD PREPARATION (optional)

The salsa can be made a few hours in advance. The chickpea cakes can be made up to the point of frying a day in advance, and kept covered in the fridge. If you only have a little time:
* Prepare the onions.
* Chop the coriander.
* Chop the red peppers and apricots.

40 minutes before you want to eat

* Preheat the oven to 150°C/300°F/Gas Mark 2.
* First make the salsa. Halve the tomatoes and, if you are so inclined, scoop out the seeds. Don't worry if some remain. Chop the tomatoes into small cubes, about 1 x 1 cm, and place in a mixing bowl. Roughly chop the coriander. Peel and finely chop the onion, and add it to the tomatoes. Add the lime juice, coriander and a generous pinch or two of salt and pepper. Pour in the oil, stir well and set aside to marinate.
* Next, make the chickpea cakes. Drain the chickpeas and tip them into a food processor. Either chop or crush the garlic and add it to the chickpeas. Roughly chop the red peppers, apricots and fresh coriander. Add the peppers, apricots, cumin, coriander seeds, jalapeno chillies and fresh coriander to the processor. Pulse a few times then add the tahini, 1 tablespoon of the oil, lemon juice and salt and pepper. Process to form a coarsely ground, well mixed and sticky mixture. If there is not enough liquid add a little water until it binds together.
* Form the mixture into eight cakes of equal size, dusting your hands with flour to prevent them sticking. Sprinkle the cakes on each side with flour and set aside.
* Heat the remaining oil in a frying pan over a medium heat and add four chickpea cakes. Fry for 5 minutes on each side until golden then place the cakes in the oven to keep warm, then cook the second batch.
* Serve the chickpea cakes with warmed pitta breads, generous spoonfuls of the salsa and Greek yoghurt and a handful of salad leaves.

Two for one

Baked Fish with Summer Vegetables

Flat fish such as plaice, sole or brill have delicate flavours and textures and are at their best in the summer months. In this recipe flat fish steaks are baked in an airtight parcel on a bed of vegetables so that the fish remains moist and is unlikely to be overcooked. Cutting a flat fish into steaks, or tronçons, is the easiest way to deal with it as it doesn't involve skinning or boning the fish.

Don't be surprised that the recipe calls for 16 garlic cloves. You might think that the subtle flavour of any flat fish would be flattened by such a quantity but, because the cloves are poached in wine and stock until soft, they lose their potency. The recipe makes an all-in-one meal but it could be accompanied by new potatoes.

The quantities here are for eight, so that half can be frozen for use later.

16 garlic cloves or 8 cloves if
    they are large
600 g carrots (baby ones if
    possible)
groundnut or grapeseed oil
50 g butter
12 spring onions
150 ml white wine
200 ml fish or vegetable stock
    (fresh or made from a stock
    cube or bouillon powder)
600 g asparagus
5 sprigs fresh basil
1.25 kg flat fish, such as plaice,
    sole or brill, cut into steaks
    across the fish (fillets will
    also do)
½ lemon
salt and pepper

To serve
new potatoes

GET AHEAD PREPARATION (optional)

The bed of vegetables can be
prepared a day in advance. If
you only have a little time:
* Prepare the carrots.
* Trim the spring onions.
* Prepare the asparagus.
* Peel and cut the garlic.

1 hour before you want to eat

* As peeling the garlic cloves is likely to take a while, start by getting this out of the way. Peel all the cloves and if you have eight large ones cut them in half.
* Scrape any baby carrots or, if the carrots are large, peel them and cut into 5 x 2 cm batons.
* Heat a very generous splash of oil and a nut of the butter (approx. 15 g) in a large frying pan and add the carrots and garlic. Let them brown a little, stirring every now and then. Meanwhile prepare the spring onions by trimming them and cutting them into 5-cm pieces.
* Add the spring onions to the carrots and toss everything about for a few minutes until golden.
* Next, add the wine and let it reduce by half. Then add the stock and let the carrots and spring onions cook in this liquid for about 5 minutes. By this time the liquid should be reduced to a small layer on the bottom of the pan.
* Preheat the oven to 180°C/350°F/Gas Mark 4.
* While the carrots, garlic and spring onions are cooking, prepare the asparagus. Bend the spears close to the base so that they snap at the point where the base turns woody, then wash them. Throw the asparagus in with the other vegetables to steam for a couple of minutes.
* Tear the basil leaves into the vegetable mixture and season to taste. Oil a large baking sheet and cover it with half the vegetables. Set the other half aside to cool for freezing.
* Dot with a little of the butter and lay half the fish on top. Season the fish well and dot with more butter. Cover with foil, make airtight and bake for 20 minutes.
* Allow the remaining vegetables to cool completely then freeze. Freeze the extra fish fillets separately.
* When the fish is cooked (if it is on the bone it will lift away easily when cooked; if the fish is in fillets the flesh will be opaque and flaky) serve on a bed of the vegetables with a squeeze of lemon juice. Serve with buttered new potatoes on the side.

Lazy day supper – cooking instructions

* The fish can be cooked from frozen, but the vegetables will need to be thoroughly defrosted before reheating.
* Preheat the oven to 180°C/350°F/Gas Mark 4 and preheat a roasting tin. When the oven and tin are hot, add the vegetables, tear a few basil leaves over the top and dot with butter. Place the frozen fish fillets on the vegetables, season them and dot them with butter. Cover with foil and bake for 25–30 minutes.

June Week 4 – Overview

By now summer should be in full swing, but that's no reason not to enjoy a roast, especially roast lamb accompanied by sweet baby carrots and summery braised lentils. As with all Big Meals from Scratch, this needs to be cooked at leisure as the lamb needs to be prepared about 2 hours before it's time to eat. The recipe calls for a 2.4 kg leg of lamb – a butcher will be able to supply a joint this size, but if the supermarkets can't oblige, a smaller one will work, though with slightly reduced cooking times. Kid, if available, could replace the lamb.

Surplus lentils and lamb from the big meal are made into a spiced salad served with hummus. This takes 30 minutes if the hummus is made from scratch, 20 minutes if it is ready-made. Leftover carrots and roasted garlic make a Summer Vegetable Braise with Pancetta that takes 30 minutes, though if using peas and broad beans in their shells add 15 minutes to this.

The Seasonal Supper of Salmon and Cucumber Tagliatelle is an original way to enjoy the season's cucumbers. The recipe works especially well with big flakes of hot-smoked salmon but regular smoked salmon will work too.

Full of strong flavours and interesting textures, the Larder Feast of Pearl Barley and Feta Salad with Agresto Dressing made from hazelnuts and parsley is a winner. This takes just over half an hour to make, most of which is the time taken to cook the pearl barley.

Rolled and flattened chicken breasts stuffed with a ricotta and asparagus filling and baked in foil are equally good served hot, warm or cold, and would be ideal for a picnic. These take an hour to make and are fiddly though not difficult – once you have a production line of flattening, stuffing and rolling it's worth batching up and making enough for the freezer, so the length of the preparation time pays off in the end.

June Week 4	Recipe	Time
Big meal from scratch	Roast leg of lamb (or kid) with new season's garlic, braised lentils and glazed baby carrots	2 hours
Something for nothing 1	Spiced lentil salad with hummus and lamb (or kid)	30 mins
Something for nothing 2	Braised summer vegetables with pancetta and sherry	35 mins
Seasonal supper	Salmon and cucumber tagliatelle	20 mins
Larder feast	Pearl barley and feta salad with agresto dressing	35 mins
2 for 1	Rolled chicken breasts filled with asparagus and cheese, with new potatoes and salad	1½ hours

All recipes serve 4 apart from the 2 for 1 recipe which makes 8 portions

SHOPPING LIST (for 4 people)

Meat and fish
1 × 2.4 kg (approx.) leg of lamb (or kid)
200 g sliced pancetta
250 g hot-smoked salmon or cold-smoked
    salmon
8 small free-range chicken breasts, skinless

Dairy
120 g butter
250 g ricotta
200 g (approx.) feta in olive oil or chilled
    feta

Fruit and vegetables
1 kg new potatoes
1 kg baby carrots
450 g shelled or frozen broad beans or 1.5 kg
    broad beans in their pods
250 g shelled or frozen peas or 800 g peas in
    their pods
2 bunches asparagus, approx. 600-800 g
1 leek, approx. 150 g
3 celery sticks
1 large cucumber
2 little gem lettuces
100 g baby spinach or any other greens you
    come across (sorrel, puntarella, rocket)
1 medium onion, approx. 120 g
5 large or banana shallots, approx. 600 g
10 spring onions, approx. 1½ bunches
6 fat heads new season's wet garlic or
    6 large heads normal garlic
4-5 garlic cloves
1 large bunch fresh parsley
1 small bunch fresh coriander
4 sprigs fresh dill
4 sprigs fresh rosemary
1 small bunch fresh mint
1 small bunch chives
5½ lemons

Basics
290 ml olive oil
½ tsp sugar
1 tsp plain flour
3½ tbsp Dijon mustard
500 ml chicken stock (fresh or made from
    a stock cube or bouillon powder)
250 ml lamb or chicken stock (fresh or made
    from a stock cube or bouillon powder)
900 ml vegetable stock (made from a stock
    cube or bouillon powder)
100 ml fish or vegetable stock (fresh or made
    from a stock cube or bouillon powder)
salt and pepper

Store cupboard
500 g tagliatelle
500 g dried brown lentils
300 g pearl barley
1 × 400 g can chickpeas
1 × 400 g can chopped tomatoes
3-4 roasted red peppers, from a can or jar
50 g (approx.) pitted green or black olives
50 g (approx.) toasted hazelnuts
100 g (approx.) shelled walnuts
2 tbsp pine nuts (toasted if possible)
2 tbsp verjuice (or ½ lemon, ½ tbsp white
    wine, ½ tbsp vinegar, 1 tsp sugar)
2 tbsp sherry vinegar
1 tbsp cider vinegar
3 tbsp tahini
1 tsp ground coriander
½ tsp ground cinnamon
150 ml white wine
150 ml dry sherry or white vermouth

Quick option
(Spiced Lentil Salad with Hummus and Lamb
    (or Kid)
300 g ready-made hummus: remove 1 × 400 g
    can chickpeas, 1-2 garlic cloves (depending
    on taste), 3 tbsp tahini, 6 tbsp olive oil
    and
    1 lemon from your shopping list.

Serving suggestions
green salad ingredients and pitta breads
    or flatbreads (Spiced Lentil Salad with
    Hummus and Lamb or Kid)
crusty bread (Braised Summer Vegetables
    with Pancetta and Sherry)

To download or print out this shopping list,
please visit www.thekitchenrevolution.co.uk/June/
Week4

**Big meal
from scratch**

Roast Leg of Lamb (or Kid) with New Season's Garlic, Braised Lentils and Glazed Baby Carrots

In this recipe lamb is roasted slowly on a bed of fresh garlic until both have become meltingly soft and sweet. If you're feeling adventurous, delicately flavoured kid rather than lamb is worth seeking out. Kid is not widely available but good butchers can source it.

Garlic fresh from the ground is known as wet garlic and has a milder flavour than when the bulb is dried. It looks very similar to ordinary garlic except the bulb tends to be bigger and the skins covering the cloves are much softer and slightly moist; they often have faintly purple tint. In this recipe the bulbs are roasted whole until soft. The cooked garlic pulp can then be squeezed out of the cloves by everyone as they eat.

The recipe includes extra lamb for the Spiced Lentil Salad and extra carrots for the Braised Summer Vegetables.

Roast leg of lamb (or kid)
6 fat heads new season's wet garlic or 6-8 large heads normal garlic; includes 2 extra heads for the braised summer vegetables
olive oil
4 sprigs fresh rosemary
1 × 2.4 kg (approx.) leg of lamb (or kid); includes 600 g extra for the spiced lentil salad
1 tsp plain flour
150 ml white wine
250 ml lamb or chicken stock (fresh or made from a stock cube or bouillon powder)
salt and pepper

Braised lentils
(includes 600 g extra for the Spiced Lentil Salad)
4 large or banana shallots
olive oil
1 medium leek – approx 150g
3 celery sticks
500 g dried brown lentils
1 tbsp cider vinegar
500 ml chicken stock (fresh or made from a stock cube or bouillon powder)
100 g baby leaf spinach (or other leaves such as sorrel or rocket
small handful of fresh mint
small handful of fresh parsley
2 tsp Dijon mustard

Glazed baby carrots
1 kg baby carrots; includes 400 g extra for the braised summer vegetables with pancetta and sherry
30 g butter
1 small bunch chives
juice of 1 lemon

GET AHEAD PREPARATION (optional)

The lentils can be cooked a day in advance up to the point of adding the spinach. If you only have a little time:
* Prepare the shallots, leek and celery.
* Wash and scrape the carrots.
* Chop the mint and parsley.

2 hours before you want to eat cook the lamb

* Preheat the oven to 220°C/425°F/Gas Mark 7.
* Place the whole, unpeeled garlic heads in a roasting tin, season and drizzle with oil. Break up the rosemary and scatter it among the garlic. Add 500 ml water to the tin. Cover the tin with foil and put the garlic in the oven for 30 minutes.
* Rub the lamb or kid with oil, salt and pepper and set aside.
* Once the garlic has been in the oven for 30 minutes, remove the foil and put the lamb or kid on top, add a bit more water and return the tin to the oven. Roast for 30 minutes until the meat is brown and crisp, then turn the temperature down to 160°C/325°F/ Gas Mark 3 and roast the meat for 1 hour 10 minutes. As a guide, we suggest that after the 30 minutes at high temperature the meat is cooked at 160°C/325°F/Gas Mark 3 for 30 minutes per kilo for pink meat and 40 minutes per kilo for well done meat.
* Baste the meat every 25 minutes or so and add a little water if the garlic looks very dry.

1 hour before you want to eat cook the lentils

* Peel and finely chop the shallots. Heat a generous splash of oil in a heavy-based casserole over a medium heat. Add the shallots, stir once or twice and allow them to soften over a low heat for 5-7 minutes. Trim, wash and finely slice the leek and celery.
* When the shallots are soft, add the leek and celery and cook with the lid on for another 10 minutes. In the meantime, tip the lentils into a sieve and rinse them well.
* Remove the lid from the vegetables and turn up the heat. Add the lentils and a generous splash of oil and stir them about for a couple of minutes. Then add the vinegar which will sizzle away in moments. Now pour in the stock and bring the lentils back to the boil. Leave them to simmer for 35-40 minutes until they are soft.
* Check on the lentils every now and then and add more water if necessary.

* Wash and scrape the carrots. Put the carrots in a large pan with a lid and add just enough water to halfway cover them. Add the butter and salt and pepper.

20 minutes before you want to eat cook the carrots and the gravy

* When the meat is cooked, take it out of the oven and leave it to rest in a warm place for 15–20 minutes.
* Turn the oven off. Remove the heads of garlic from the roasting tin and keep four of them warm on a serving dish in the cooling oven. Put a couple more serving dishes and some plates in the oven to warm.
* Put the carrots over a high heat and bring to the boil. Then put the lid on, turn the heat down and simmer for 5–7 minutes.
* If there is a lot of fat in the tin, tip some of it out. Place the roasting tin over a medium heat to make the gravy. Add the flour and let it cook while you stir for a couple of minutes. Add the wine and stir, using a whisk. Let the wine bubble for 1–2 minutes then add the stock and bring to the boil, whisking occasionally. Let the gravy simmer until it is the consistency you like
* Remove the lid from the pan of carrots and let the carrots simmer until all the water has evaporated.
* Wash and dry the spinach well, then check that the lentils are cooked. Add the spinach to the lentils and let it wilt down for a few minutes. Roughly chop the mint and parsley, then stir them into the lentils with the mustard.
* The carrots will be cooked by now, so take them off the heat. Chop the chives and add them to the carrots with the lemon juice. Taste and season and cover with the lid.
* Slice the lamb or kid and put it on a warmed serving dish with the garlic. Pour any juices that run out of the meat into the gravy and season.
* Put the lentils and carrots into warmed serving dishes and the gravy in a jug.

Afterwards

Cut the remaining lamb or kid into slices. Place the meat (600 g), 2 leftover roast garlic heads, gravy, carrots (300 g) and lentils (600 g) in separate containers, cover, and keep in the fridge for later in the week.

Something
for nothing 1

Spiced Lentil Salad with Hummus and Lamb (or Kid)

In Morocco, hummus is served topped with fried, minced lamb and caramelised onions. This turns something lovely but everyday into a luxurious and rich snack or starter. Here we use similar flavours but adapt the quantities and add a coriander and lentil salad to make a substantial supper.

Hummus is very easy and inexpensive to make and can be adapted to suit your personal taste with extra herbs and spices like coriander, cumin and paprika. That said, if you don't have the time to make the hummus you could use a ready-made tub and add any seasonings you fancy, such as paprika, ground cumin or coriander, lemon or garlic.

Spiced lentil salad
1 small bunch fresh coriander
juice of 1 lemon
4 tbsp olive oil
1 tsp ground coriander
600 g brown lentils left over
    from the Big Meal from Scratch
    or 1 x 400 g tin cooked brown
    lentils
salt and pepper

Hummus
1 x 400 g can chickpeas
1-2 garlic cloves, depending on
    taste
3 tbsp tahini
juice of 1 lemon
6 tbsp olive oil
or
300 g ready-made hummus

Lamb (or kid)
2 tbsp pine nuts (toasted, if
    possible)
1 large or banana shallot,
    approx. 30 g
½ tbsp olive oil
½ tsp ground cinnamon
8-12 slices lamb or kid left over
    from the Big Meal from Scratch
    (approx. 600 g) or 700 g neck
    fillet seasoned, browned in a
    pan with oil then roasted in a
    hot oven for about 20 minutes
    and sliced
handful of flatleaf fresh parsley

To serve
green salad and pitta breads or
    flatbreads

GET AHEAD PREPARATION (optional)

The hummus can be made up to a day in advance. If you only have a little time:
* Prepare the garlic and shallot.
* Toast the pine nuts.
* Chop the parsely and fresh coriander.

30 minutes before you want to eat

* Start by making the hummus or if using ready made check the seasoning and adjust accordingly then move onto the next instruction. Drain the chickpeas and tip them into a food processor, add about 1 tablespoon water and whizz for 1–2 seconds. Don't worry if they are not all pulverised.
* Peel the garlic, cut in half and add to the chickpeas. Add the tahini and lemon juice. Turn on the processor and pour in the oil. If the mixture seems very thick add more water. Taste and season accordingly with salt and pepper. Scoop into a bowl and set aside. If you don't have a food processor a much more textured hummus can be made by chopping the chickpeas then smashing them with a rolling pin before mixing with the other ingredients.
* If you haven't bought ready-toasted pine nuts, tip the pine nuts into a frying pan and place over a medium heat. Toast until browned then set aside.
* Peel and finely slice the shallot. Heat the oil in a frying pan, add the shallot and cook for 7–10 minutes until golden and sweet.
* Meanwhile make the lentil salad. Roughly chop the fresh coriander. Mix the lemon juice with the oil, ground coriander and salt and pepper. Place the lentils in a large bowl. Add the chopped coriander and the dressing, mix well and set aside.
* When the shallot is soft and starting to brown, add the cinnamon. Stir well, turn down the heat and then add the lamb to just warm through. Roughly chop the parsley and add half to the lamb. Stir well, season, then remove from the heat.
* To serve, place a pile of the lentil salad on each plate with slices of lamb and shallot on top. Take a generous dollop of hummus, place on the lamb and garnish with the remaining parsley and the toasted pine nuts. Serve with a green salad and some warmed pitta breads or flatbreads.

Braised Summer Vegetables with Pancetta and Sherry

This recipe creates a soupy broth with a rustic feel. The whole dish has an intense flavour, with sherry and pancetta drawing out the flavours of the vegetables. Broad beans and peas are in season for such a short time, and are so delicious, that it would be wrong not to include them as key ingredients in a few recipes in this book. Shelling 1.5 kg fresh broad beans and 800 g fresh peas however is quite a time-consuming process. For this reason, we've included quantities and instructions for using frozen and ready-shelled beans and peas. The fresh beans and peas take this from being a delicious meal into the realms of the sublime, but delicious is probably good enough for most of us midweek. Mop this up with hunks of crusty brown bread.

olive oil
200 g sliced pancetta
1 medium onion, approx. 120 g
400 g new potatoes
250 g shelled or frozen peas or
   800 g peas in their pods
450 g shelled or frozen broad
   beans or 1.5 kg broad beans in
   their pods
2 heads roast garlic left over
   from the Big Meal from Scratch
   or 6 peeled garlic cloves
   simmered in water and olive
   oil until they are soft and
   lightly browned

2 tbsp sherry vinegar
300 g baby carrots left over from
   the Big Meal from Scratch or
   300 g scraped and cleaned
   baby carrots
400 ml vegetable stock (made
   from a stock cube or bouillon
   powder) or leftover gravy made
   up to 400 ml with water
150 ml dry sherry or white
   vermouth
2 sprigs fresh mint
small handful of fresh parsley
salt and pepper

To serve
crusty brown bread

GET AHEAD PREPARATION (optional)

The recipe can be made a day in advance and reheated gently.
If you only have a little time:
* Peel and chop the onions.
* Slice the potatoes and cover them with water until required.
* Shell the peas and beans, if necessary.
* Chop the herbs.

*35 minutes before
you want to eat*

* Heat a very generous splash of oil in a heavy-based frying pan over a medium heat. Using scissors, snip the pancetta into the hot oil, cook for a few minutes until crisp, then lift it out. While the pancetta is cooking, peel and finely chop the onion.
* When the pancetta is cooked put the onion into the frying pan, lower the heat and let it soften for 7 minutes.
* Meanwhile, wash, scrub or scrape the potatoes and cut into slices the thickness of a pound coin while you wait for the onion to soften.
* Once the onion is soft, squeeze the roast garlic from its skin and add to the softened onion. Stir for a couple of minutes, adding a little more oil if necessary. Turn the heat up, splash in the sherry vinegar and let it boil away to nothing.
* Add the potatoes and carrots to the onion mixture and stir them for a couple of minutes so they start to brown. Now add the stock and bring the lot to a simmer, then season and simmer gently for 15 minutes.
* Shell the peas and beans if necessary.
* After 15 minutes add the sherry or vermouth, and the peas and beans. Cook for a further 5–7 minutes. In the meantime, strip the mint leaves from their stalks and roughly chop the leaves along with the parsley.
* Finally, add the herbs and return the pancetta to the pan. Stir everything about and serve immediately with lots of bread to mop up the juices.

Seasonal supper

Salmon and Cucumber Tagliatelle

Cucumber, salmon and dill are a classic combination. Here these well-matched ingredients are brought together in an original pasta sauce. Gently cooking the cucumber enhances its distinctive flavour and creates a light, creamy and very elegant sauce.

Smoked salmon is usually the result of long, slow cold smoking which produces its characteristic dense texture and intense flavour. Hot-smoked salmon is smoked for less time at very hot temperatures, resulting in a softer texture and a less intensely smoky flavour. Hot-smoked salmon can't be sliced thinly so it is usually sold as whole fillets. Supermarkets increasingly stock it but if you can't find it this recipe works as well with cold-smoked salmon.

6 spring onions
50 g butter
1 large cucumber
500 g tagliatelle
1 lemon
100 ml fish or vegetable stock
   (fresh or made from a stock
   cube or bouillon powder)
4 sprigs fresh dill
250 g hot-smoked salmon or
   cold-smoked salmon
salt and pepper

GET AHEAD PREPARATION (optional)

* Prepare the spring onions and
   cucumber.
* Chop the dill.
* Flake the hot-smoked salmon
   or cut the cold-smoked
   salmon.

20 minutes before you want to eat

* Trim and finely slice the spring onions, using as much green as you can.
* In a pan large enough to hold all the pasta, melt half the butter over a medium heat. Throw in the spring onions to soften for a couple of minutes. Meanwhile, peel and deseed the cucumber and slice it into 1-cm pieces.
* Add the cucumber to the spring onions, stir once or twice and allow to soften for 4–5 minutes.
* Meanwhile, cook the tagliatelle according to the instructions on the packet.
* Once the cucumber has softened slightly, squeeze the lemon and add all but 1 tablespoon of the juice to the cucumber. Let it bubble away for 1 minute, then add the stock. Turn the heat up high, bring the stock to the boil and let it reduce by a third.
* Once the stock has reduced, turn the heat down to medium and add the rest of the butter in little pieces, swirling the pan as you put in each piece so that butter emulsifies with the liquid.
* Once the tagliatelle is cooked, drain well and tip it into the pan with the cucumber.
* Roughly chop the dill and break the hot-smoked salmon into flakes or cut the cold-smoked salmon into 5-cm lengths.
* Add the dill and salmon to the tagliatelle and toss well. Season to taste – lashings of black pepper is highly advisable – add the final splash of lemon juice and serve.

Larder feast

Pearl Barley and Feta Salad with Agresto Dressing

This warm salad of pearl barley, feta, olives and peppers with a tangy dressing is substantial and packed with flavour. The nutty flavour of pearl barley goes extremely well with salsa agresto. This is an Italian sauce similar to pesto, only it is made with hazelnuts, walnuts, parsley and (if you can get it) verjuice.

Made from the juice of unripened grapes, verjuice has been used in cooking since before Roman times. It has a sharp flavour and works in much the same way as lemon or vinegar, although without their sourness. If verjuice proves impossible to find it can be replaced with a mixture of ½ tablespoon white wine, 1 teaspoon sugar, ½ tablespoon vinegar and the juice of ½ lemon.

Pearl barley and feta salad
300 g pearl barley
500 ml vegetable stock (made from a stock cube or bouillon powder
1 × 400 g can chopped tomatoes
¼ tsp sugar
200 g feta in olive oil, or chilled feta
4 spring onions
3-4 roasted red peppers from a can or jar
100 g pitted green or black olives
olive oil
salt and pepper

Agresto dressing
50 g (approx.) toasted hazelnuts
50 g (approx.) shelled walnuts
1 small bunch fresh flatleaf parsley
1 garlic clove
3 tbsp olive oil
2 tbsp verjuice or see above

To serve
green salad

GET AHEAD PREPARATION (optional)

The agresto dressing can be made up to a week in advance and stored in the fridge in an airtight container with a layer of oil over the surface. If you only have a little time:
* Cook the pearl barley.
* Prepare the garlic and spring onions.
* Cut the feta into dice.
* Prepare the red peppers.

35 minutes before you want to eat

* Rinse the pearl barley under cold running water then tip into a large pan with a lid. Cover with the stock and the tomatoes. Add the sugar and 1 teaspoon salt, stir to mix and put over a high heat. Bring to the boil then turn the heat down and allow the barley to bubble away with the lid on. Over the next 30 minutes check the level of liquid and, if necessary, add more water.
* Make the agresto dressing. Wash and rinse the parsley. Then, holding it in a bunch, chop off and discard all the stalks. Put half the parsley in a food processor, saving the rest to go with the pearl barley. Peel the garlic and crush it roughly, then add this to the parsley, along with the hazelnuts and walnuts. Pour in the oil and verjuice and process. Agresto should have similar texture to pesto. If it is too thick add more oil or verjuice, depending on taste. Season to taste. Tip the dressing into a bowl, cover with cling film and set aside.
* Cut the feta cheese into 1-2-cm dice. Trim and finely chop the spring onions using as much of the green as you can. Drain the red peppers and cut them in half lengthways, then into strips no more than 1 cm wide. Chop the remaining parsley.
* After 30 minutes the barley should be cooked. If there is surplus water either reduce it rapidly over a high heat, or drain the barley into a colander then tip back into the pan. Add the spring onions, parsley, feta and red peppers to the barley along with 2 tablespoons oil, the olives and seasoning and gently mix.
* Divide the pearl barley between four bowls, top with at least 1 tablespoon of the agresto dressing and serve with a green salad.

Two for one

Rolled Chicken Breasts Filled with Asparagus and Cheese, with New Potatoes and Salad

Chicken, asparagus and new potatoes work together well, particularly in summer. Flattening, stuffing and rolling the chicken breasts means they can be stuffed with a mixture of asparagus and cheese, which helps to prevent them drying out and fills them with flavour. Once you've discovered this way of stuffing chicken breasts you can vary the filling to suit the season and available ingredients. These ones are as good hot as they are cold and they travel well so they are especially useful for picnics. The recipe here accounts for eating four stuffed breasts immediately and freezing the remaining four. The quantities for the potatoes and salad serve four as these cannot be frozen.

Rolled chicken breasts filled with asparagus and cheese	New potatoes	GET AHEAD PREPARATION (optional)
2 bunches asparagus, approx. 600-800 g	600 g new potatoes	The asparagus can be cooked, the filling can be made and the chicken breasts can be filled and stuffed up to a day in advance.
8 small free-range chicken breasts, skinless	40 g butter	If you only have a little time:
250 g ricotta	**Salad**	* Prepare and cook the asparagus.
1 lemon	2 little gem lettuces	* Prepare the lettuce.
handful of fresh flatleaf parsley	juice of ½ lemon	* Peel and crush the garlic.
salt and pepper	1 garlic clove	* Chop the parsley.
	½ tbsp Dijon mustard	
	3 tbsp olive oil	

1½ hours before you want to eat prepare the stuffing and chicken

* Bring a large pan of salted water to the boil. Meanwhile, prepare the asparagus by bending each spear close to the base so that it snaps at the point where the base turns woody, then rinse the tips under running water.
* Add the asparagus spears to the boiling water, cover with a lid and bring back to the boil. Cook until the asparagus is just starting to tenderise – once the water starts boiling again this will take 3–4 minutes for thick spears and about 1 minute for thin spears
* Meanwhile, place four of the chicken breasts on a chopping board and cover with clingfilm. Bash with a rolling pin or the bottom of a pan until they are between 5 mm and 1 cm thick – the thinner the better as they will be easier to stuff and roll. Put the first batch aside and repeat with the remaining four breasts.
* When the asparagus is cooked, drain and rinse under cold running water to cool. Dry with kitchen paper and cut into short lengths no more than 5 mm long.
* Place the asparagus in a bowl with the ricotta and grate in the zest of the lemon. Add a small squeeze of lemon juice, ½ teaspoon salt and 1 teaspoon pepper and mix well. Chop the parsley finely and add half to the asparagus and cheese mixture.

1 hour before you want to eat make the rolls

* Preheat the oven to 190°C/375°F/Gas Mark 5.
* Lay the eight flattened breasts in two rows. Season them well and spoon 1 heaped tablespoon of the asparagus and ricotta mixture along the middle of each breast. Smooth out the mixture then roll each breast up lengthways, tucking in any stray edges, and wrap each one very tightly in foil. Twist each end of foil tightly so that the parcels are airtight and the rolled-up breast will set into a sort of sausage shape as it cooks.
* Place four of the rolls on a plate in the fridge to set for 5 minutes and put the other four in the freezer.
* While you are waiting for the oven to heat up and the rolled breasts to set, scrub the potatoes and place them in pan of well-salted water.
* Place the chicken parcels in an ovenproof dish, put them in the oven and roast them for 20–30 minutes, depending on their size.
* While the chicken breasts are roasting, bring the potatoes to the boil and simmer for 15–20 minutes until just cooked.
* Meanwhile, make the salad and dressing. Wash and dry the little gems, tear the leaves in half and put them in a salad bowl. Squeeze the lemon juice into a small bowl or jar

and peel and crush the garlic. Add the garlic and mustard to the lemon juice, mix well then stir in the oil. Season to taste with salt and pepper.

* After 20–30 minutes remove the chicken rolls from the oven. Insert a small, sharp knife into the middle of one roll and check that the tip feels hot when removed – if not return the chicken to the oven for 5 minutes. Otherwise, allow the rolls to rest for 5 minutes while you drain the potatoes and toss them in the butter, and dress the salad.

* Unwrap the chicken rolls and slice each one crossways into four pieces. Serve with the salad and potatoes.

Lazy day supper – cooking instructions

* Remove the rolled breasts from the freezer and defrost completely.
* Preheat the oven to 190°C/375°F/Gas Mark 5. Cook the rolls as above and serve with new potatoes and salad.

Cherry and Chocolate Fool

This is a wickedly lovely pudding and one that's very easy to make. The secret is to use ripe cherries and let them cook down in a sugary alcohol mixture – ideally cherry brandy or kirsch. You will need to wait for the syrup to cool before you incorporate it with the cream, then the whole lot needs to be chilled for about 1 hour. Although this recipe is simple, there is a degree of waiting between various instructions and the end result.

300 g ripe black cherries
50 g caster sugar
4 tbsp cherry brandy, kirsch or
    brandy
70 g dark plain chocolate
300 ml double cream

1½ hours before you want to eat

* Halve and stone all the cherries. Put them in a pan with a lid along with the sugar and alcohol. Bring to the boil and simmer gently for about 10 minutes or until the cherries are soft.
* Tip the cherries into a colander and catch the syrup in a bowl beneath. Put the cherries to one side to cool.
* Return the syrup to the pan, put it back on the heat and boil rapidly until reduced by about half. Allow the syrup to cool to room temperature.
* Once the syrup has cooled, grate the chocolate.
* Whip the cream to soft peaks then stir in the reduced, cooled cherry syrup. Whip the mixture so that it forms soft peaks again.
* Gently fold in all but 1 heaped tablespoon of the chocolate.
* Put the cherries in the bottom of four glasses or a large glass bowl and spoon the chocolate cherry cream over them.
* Sprinkle with remaining chocolate, cover with cling film and chill for at least 1 hour.

Redcurrant Sponge Squares

These squares are lovely as a pudding on a warm day with a glass of chilled dessert wine. This recipe is based on something Rosie's mum used to make from a fabulous New Zealand baking book called *Edmond's Sure to Rise*. The version from the book is called Loch Katrin cake and has jam instead of the redcurrant layer.

For the base
150 g plain flour, plus extra for
  dusting
1 tsp baking powder
50 g butter, chilled
3-4 tbsp milk

For the fruit layer
250 g redcurrants
200 g sugar

For the sponge
50 g butter, softened
100 g sugar
150 g plain flour
1 tsp baking powder
2 free-range eggs
4-6 tbsp milk

For the topping
20 g butter
1 lemon
100 g icing sugar

45 minutes before you want to eat

* Preheat the oven to 160°C/325°F/Gas Mark 3.
* First, make the base. Mix the flour with the baking powder in a bowl. Coarsely grate the butter into the flour and carefully rub them together until the mixture resembles coarse breadcrumbs.
* Next, add enough milk to bind the mix – you want a stiffish dough. Leave this to rest while you prepare the redcurrants and make the sponge.
* Strip the redcurrants from their stalks, give them a quick wash and toss them in the sugar.
* Cream the butter and sugar for the sponge until light and fluffy. Sift the flour and baking powder together and beat the eggs. Add half the flour and the beaten eggs to the creamed mix then stir in the remaining flour.
* Roll out the base dough on a lightly floured work surface to fit flat in a rectangular baking tin, approx. 25 x 35 cm. Scatter the redcurrants over the top and cover with the sponge mix. Bake for 30 minutes, until the sponge springs back when you touch it lightly with your finger. Leave to cool for a few moments while you make the icing.
* Melt the butter, grate the zest of the lemon and squeeze out the juice. Sift the icing sugar into a bowl and add the butter and enough lemon juice and water to make a just-runny icing. Add the lemon zest then pour this over the cake and, once set, cut the cake into squares.

Summer Pudding

Summer pudding is universally loved. The secret to a successful pudding is ensuring there's enough juice to penetrate all the bread and that the juice is given enough time to do so – a pudding where only some of the bread has mopped up the liquid is always disappointing. For this reason, we suggest dunking the bread in the fruit juice before assembling the pudding. It's important to let a summer pudding stand for a day or overnight in the fridge to give the fruits sufficient time to mascerate. The overall quantity for the fruit is important – about 1.8–2 kg fruit in total – but the mixture can be altered to suit what is to hand or any gluts there might be. Soft fruits like strawberries and raspberries give off a lot of juice so it's good to have a lion's share of these. We like cherries in our summer pudding as they add texture and splashes of either dark purple or brilliant red.

500 g ripe strawberries
300 g ripe cherries
400 g blackcurrants
200 g red and white currants
500 g raspberries
200 g caster sugar
10–12 slices day-old white bread,
  1 cm thick

To serve
clotted cream or crème fraîche

35 minutes before you want to put the pudding in the fridge for 12–24 hours

* Hull the strawberries and stone the cherries. Remove any stalks from the currants.
* Put all the fruit and the sugar in a large pan and place over a gentle heat. Stir once or twice so that the sugar mixes in, but take care not to bash the fruit too much. Bring to simmering point and cook for 4–5 minutes or until the juices start to run. When the fruit is cooked tip it into a colander and catch the juice in a bowl beneath it.
* Cut the crusts off the slices of bread then dip the slices in the fruit juice until they are completely soaked and dyed. Line the bottom and sides of a 1-litre pudding basin with the bread. You will need to cut the slices into different shapes to get them to fit with no gaps.
* Spoon the fruit into the basin adding as much liquid as will fit. Keep any juice that won't fit in the basin covered in the fridge to serve with the end product. Cover the top of the fruit with slices of bread so that there are no gaps.
* Put the basin on a saucer to catch any juice that squeezes out of the top, then cover the top of the basin with another saucer and weigh down with a bag of sugar or something of similar weight. Place in the fridge and leave overnight.
* After a couple of hours pour some of the surplus juice into the basin, then cover again and continue to chill.
* Remove the summer pudding from the fridge at least 30 minutes before you want to eat – you want it to be just under room temperature to serve.
* Use a palette knife to ease the bread away from the sides, then cover the basin with a large flat plate and invert it so that the pudding slips from the basin.
* Serve with any leftover juice, clotted cream or crème fraîche.

Gooseberry and Elderflower Sorbet

This was one of Polly's grandmother's recipes and transports Polly straight back to childhood. Elderflower and gooseberry create a perfect partnership that's difficult to imagine and hard to forget. This sorbet is the very essence of summer and it's well worth making a large batch because the gooseberry season is short. If gooseberries and elderflowers coincide all the better, but often the former are a few weeks behind the latter. If this is the case it's a shame, but you can replace the elderflowers with elderflower cordial. The quantities here will serve eight on the basis that you and anyone you live with will not mind having surplus quantities in the freezer.

2 lemons
1 kg gooseberries
300 g sugar
5 heads elderflowers or 3 tbsp
  elderflower cordial

30 minutes before you want to eat

* Peel the zest from the lemons with a peeler, then juice the lemons and cut the zest into strips. Wash the gooseberries and put them in a pan along with the sugar, lemon rind and juice and 1 litre water. Bring slowly to the boil then simmer gently for 10 minutes until the gooseberries are soft.
* Add the elderflower heads or cordial and simmer for another couple of minutes.
* Remove from the heat and press the gooseberry mixture through a fine sieve. Pour it into a flat shallow dish to help it cool as quickly as possible.
* Once the mixture is cool, tip it into a freezer container with a lid and freeze.
* After 1 hour stir the mixture with a fork, scraping into the middle any ice crystals that have formed on the edges or bottom of the container. Freeze for another hour and stir well once again, then leave the sorbet in the freezer until you are ready to eat.

JULY

At the height of summer no one wants to stand in a kitchen for hours cooking. So it's just as well that July's seasonal foods – summer fruits, aubergines, tomatoes, courgettes, herbs and peppers – make for meals that can be prepared in as little as ten or twenty minutes. July is the time to remember what a real English tomato tastes like. Regal aubergines and brilliant red and yellow peppers are abundant now, so there is a recipe for Lamb Kebabs with a Sweet-Sour Caponata Relish. A cold spicy Vietnamese Beef Salad and Hoisin Chicken Wraps are light and fresh Something for Nothings that are filled with enough flavour to make a substantial meal. Gooseberry and Almond Cake will go as well with a glass of chilled sweet wine to end a meal as it will with a cup of tea on a summer afternoon. The season for soft fruits is short so it's worth taking full advantage of it with a Greengage Clafoutis and Raspberry Water Ice.

July	Week 1	Week 2	Week 3	Week 4
Big meal from scratch	Fish and courgette parcels with potato and tomato bake and a mixed leaf salad	Red spiced poussin (or chicken) with cardamom rice and runner beans	Roast beef with a pepper crust, with garlic new potatoes and green bean and red onion salad	Duck with cherries, roast baby vegetables and spinach
Something for nothing 1	White fish salad	Baked stuffed peppers	Vietnamese beef salad	Root vegetable, caraway and feta salad with rocket salad
Something for nothing 2	Cheese and tomato stacks with rocket salad	Hoisin chicken wraps with noodle salad	Chicken and roast onion bruschetta	Duck salad with bacon and eggs
Seasonal supper	Chard risotto	Braised lettuce with ham	Soft goats' cheese salad	Chilled summer soup with prawns on toast
Larder feast	Coconut prawn noodles	Tuna Niçoise	Spiced prawn couscous	Braised lentils with herb cream cheese
2 for 1	Citrus lamb	Stilton and watercress penne	Braised chicken with celery and orange	Lamb kebabs with caponata and rice
Puddings	Raspberry water ice with prosecco	Apricot pie	Gooseberry and almond cake	Greengage clafoutis

July Week 1 – Overview

For this week's Big Meal from Scratch, fish is baked in foil with summer vegetables and crème fraîche. Baking fish this way ensures that it doesn't overcook and dry out. While the fish parcels are light and delicate, the flavours in the accompanying potato and tomato bake are intense – together they are ideal summer fare. Though the fish will cook in about 30 minutes, the bake takes 1 hour in the oven so the meal needs starting 1½ hours before serving to allow sufficient preparation time. As always, cook the fish soon after buying or place it in the freezer until required.

For a Something for Nothing when the weather is hot and cooking is unappealing, a recipe for a herby fish salad served with flatbreads is perfect. This is refreshing and light and takes no more than 10 minutes to put together. For the other Something for Nothing, the leftover potato and tomato bake from the big meal is sandwiched with tomatoes between slices of marinated halloumi cheese and then grilled.

With creamy white rice interspersed with flecks of green, the Seasonal Supper of Chard Risotto is as good to look at as it is to eat. As with all risottos, the rice needs some time to absorb the stock so this is a 45-minute recipe from start to finish. If chard proves elusive the recipe can be made with a mixture of spinach and celery instead.

The Larder Feast of Coconut Prawn Noodles is a sweet-sour noodly soup that's ready in just under half an hour.

Many meat casseroles seem too heavy for summer but the Two for One Citrus Lamb is pleasantly tart and refreshing. As with many casseroles it takes over 2 hours to cook but much of this time is when the lamb is in the oven and doesn't involve culinary labour.

July Week 1	recipe	time
Big Meal from scratch	Fish and courgette parcels with potato and tomato bake and a mixed leaf salad	1½ hours
Something for nothing 1	White fish salad	10 mins
Something for nothing 2	Cheese and tomato stacks with rocket salad	25 mins
Seasonal supper	Chard risotto	45 mins
Larder feast	Coconut prawn noodles	30 mins
2 for 1	Citrus lamb	2–3 hours

All recipes serve 4 apart from the 2 for 1 recipe which makes 8 portions

SHOPPING LIST (for 4 people)

Meat and fish
1.8 kg stewing lamb (neck fillets, scrag end
   or boned shoulder)
6 x 200 g skinless fillets of white fish, such
   as coley, pollack, haddock or cod
200–300 g frozen large raw peeled prawns

Dairy
100 ml crème fraîche
500 g (2 packets) halloumi cheese
130 g butter
60–100 g Parmesan

Fruit and vegetables
1.2 kg waxy new potatoes
4 courgettes, approx. 400 g
350 g Swiss or rainbow chard (or 50 g celery
   heart and 200 g baby leaf spinach)
4 large very ripe tomatoes, approx. 600 g
1 green pepper, approx. 150 g
1 red pepper, approx. 150 g
2 celery sticks
1 leek, approx. 150 g
200 g cherry tomatoes
200 g mixed salad leaves
100 g rocket
6 large onions, approx. 1 kg
1 small red onion, approx. 90 g
13 garlic cloves
5-cm piece of fresh root ginger
12 sprigs fresh thyme (6 lemon thyme if
   possible) or 1 tbsp dried thyme
1 large bunch fresh parsley
1 small bunch fresh coriander (optional for
   Coconut Prawn Noodles)
3 sprigs fresh basil
4½ lemons
1 orange
2 limes

Basics
275 ml olive oil
½ tbsp groundnut or grapeseed oil
60 g plain flour
pinch of sugar
salt and pepper
1.1 litres chicken stock (fresh or made from
   a stock cube or bouillon powder)
200 ml fish or chicken stock (fresh or made
   from a stock cube or bouillon powder)
400 ml lamb or chicken stock (fresh or made
   from a stock cube or bouillon powder)

Store cupboard
250–300 g (approx.) medium dried wheat or
   egg noodles
350 g risotto rice
1 x 200 g can chopped tomatoes
1 x 280 g (approx.) can button mushrooms

1 x 220 g (approx.) can water chestnuts
1 x 220 g (approx.) can sliced bamboo shoots
1 x 400 g can haricot beans
300 ml coconut milk
8 sun-dried tomatoes
180 g pitted black olives (Niçoise would be
   ideal)
20 g pine nuts (toasted if possible)
2–3 tbsp red wine vinegar
1 tbsp sweet chilli sauce
1 tsp Thai fish sauce
700 ml white wine

Serving suggestions
4 naan breads or flatbreads (White Fish
   Salad)
crusty bread (Cheese and Tomato Stacks with
   Rocket Salad)
tomato salad ingredients (Chard Risotto)
2 x 400 g cans cannellini beans, olive oil
   and rosemary, or potatoes for mashing,
   and a green vegetable or salad ingredients
   (Citrus Lamb)

To download or print out this shopping list,
please visit www.thekitchenrevolution.co.uk/July/
Week1

**Big meal
from scratch**

Fish and Courgette Parcels with Potato and Tomato Bake and a Mixed Leaf Salad

English tomatoes and courgettes start to appear around the start of July and this Big Meal from Scratch celebrates their arrival. Baking fish with courgettes and herbs in a foil parcel is a good way of protecting delicate flavours and textures. The rich tomato and potato bake is a summery accompaniment that can be enjoyed hot or at room temperature. You will need foil to make the parcels for the fish.

The quantities here include extra fish for White Fish Salad (see page 296) and extra potatoes and tomatoes for Cheese and Tomato Stacks with Rocket Salad (see page 297).

Fish and courgette parcels
4 courgettes, approx. 400 g
1 medium leek, approx. 150g
2 lemons
2 tbsp olive oil
3 sprigs fresh basil
100 ml crème fraîche
6 x 200 g skinless fillets of white fish, such as coley, pollack, haddock or cod; includes 2 extra fillets for the white fish salad

Potato and tomato bake (makes double quantities for fried potato and tomato with halloumi)
3 large onions, approx. 570 g
80 ml olive oil

4 large very ripe tomatoes, approx. 600 g
1.2 kg large waxy new potatoes
5 garlic cloves
6 sprigs fresh thyme (lemon thyme is especially good in this dish)
200 ml white wine
salt and pepper

Mixed leaf salad
200 g mixed salad leaves
20 g pitted black olives
1 tbsp lemon juice
2–3 tbsp olive oil
20 g pine nuts (toasted if possible)

GET AHEAD PREPARATION (optional)

The potato and tomato bake can be made up to a day in advance and either served at room temperature or reheated in the oven. If you only have a little time:
* Skin the tomatoes.
* Prepare the courgettes.
* Toast the pine nuts, if necessary.
* Make the salad dressing.
* Prepare the garlic and onions.
* Prepare the potatoes and cover with water until required.

1½ hours before you want to eat make the potato salad bake

* Preheat the oven to 180°C/350°F/Gas Mark 4.
* Peel and finely slice the onions. Heat a generous glug of oil in a pan, add the onions and cook gently for 7–10 minutes.
* Cover the tomatoes with boiling water and leave for a minute or so until their skins loosen. Then plunge them into cold water and pull their skins off. Slice the peeled tomatoes then peel and thinly slice the potatoes.
* Peel and crush the garlic and add it to the onions. Strip the leaves from the thyme stalks and add them to the garlic and onions. Add the wine and bring to the boil.
* Next, oil an ovenproof dish. Lay one-third of the potatoes on the bottom and season them. Spoon over half the onion and wine mixture. Lay half the tomatoes on top with a good sprinkling of salt and pepper. Now start again with another third of the potatoes, the remaining onion and wine, and the remaining tomatoes. Finish with a layer of potatoes. Season well and add the remaining oil and any wine left in the onion pan.
* Cover the dish with foil and place in the oven for 1 hour. Remove the foil after 40 minutes. This should coincide with when the fish is put in the oven to bake.

35 minutes before you want to eat prepare the fish

* Put a large baking sheet for the fish in the oven to heat.
* Prepare the vegetables for the fish. Wash the courgettes, top and tail them and cut them into batons; they should be about 1cm wide. The length is less important but 5–6cm is ideal.
* Trim the leek and remove the tough outer layers and the coarse green end. Cut the leek into similar lengths to the courgettes and then into 1-cm thick batons. Wash the leek well to remove any grit lurking between the layers of leaf.
* Grate the zest of one lemon and squeeze out its juice into a bowl. Add the courgettes and leek, all but a splash of the oil and a generous amount of salt and pepper, and mix well.
* Tear the basil leaves into small pieces and mix them into the crème fraîche along with some salt and pepper.
* Next, make the parcels. Take four squares of foil, 12 x 12 cm, and one extra-large square (big enough to hold two fillets of fish). Oil each square of foil.

* Divide the courgette and leek mixture between the four smaller squares of foil and pop a fillet on top of each portion. Season the fish, squeeze over a little juice from the remaining lemon then spread a quarter of the basil crème fraîche over each fillet. Bring the edges of the foil together, making sure there is a little space above the fish.
* Finally, place the two plain fish fillets on the last square of foil, season them, squeeze a little lemon juice over them and close up the foil parcel as before.
* Place all the foil parcels on the hot baking sheet and bake at the top of the oven until the fish is cooked. This will take 20–25 minutes.
* While the fish is cooking get the salad ready. Wash and dry the salad leaves and place in a large bowl. To make the dressing, roughly chop the olives and put them in a small jug or bowl with the lemon juice and stir in the oil and some salt and pepper.
* Remove the parcel containing the plain fish fillets from the oven after 15 minutes and set aside as the fillets will continue to cook while they cool down.

5–10 minutes before you want to eat

* When the remaining fish has been in the oven for 20 minutes check that it is cooked – it should flake easily and be opaque. If the fillets aren't ready return them to the oven for another 5–10 minutes.
* If you haven't bought them toasted, place the pine nuts on a baking sheet in the oven for a few minutes. Watch them carefully so that they don't burn.
* When the fillets are ready, let the parcels sit out of the oven while you toss the pine nuts and dressing through the salad leaves.
* Place a fish parcel on each plate and leave each diner to open their own – take care no one gets burned by escaping steam.
* Serve with the salad leaves and potato and tomato bake.

Afterwards

Put the cooled leftover fish fillets and potato and tomato bake in separate containers, cover and refrigerate for use later in the week. Ideally you will have 400 g cooked fish and 600 g potato and tomato bake.

**Something
for nothing 1**

White Fish Salad

This simple salad is quick and easy to make. It's based on a recipe for shredded salt cod salad from Sam and Samuel Clark's *Moro* cookbook. We've adapted the Clarks' delicious recipe to work with cooked white fish left over from the Big Meal from Scratch.

1 green pepper, approx. 150 g
1 red pepper, approx. 150 g
1 × 400 g can haricot beans
200 g cherry tomatoes
1 bunch fresh flatleaf parsley
1 small red onion, approx. 90 g
4 tbsp pitted black olives
    (Niçoise would be ideal)
1 garlic clove
2-3 tbsp red wine vinegar
    (depending on taste)

pinch of sugar
4 tbsp olive oil
400 g cooked fish left over from
    the Big Meal from Scratch or
    450 g white fish such as
    pollack, cod or haddock
    poached until cooked
salt and black pepper

To serve
4 naan breads or flatbreads

GET AHEAD PREPARATION (optional)

* Prepare the peppers.
* Chop the parsley.
* Slice the onion.
* Make the dressing.

*10 minutes before
you want to eat*

* Cut the peppers in half, deseed them and slice them as thinly as you can. Drain the beans. Tip the peppers into a large bowl along with the tomatoes and beans. Roughly chop the parsley and add this to the mixture. Peel, halve and finely slice the onion. Add this to the bowl along with the olives and mix well.
* Now make the dressing. Peel and chop or crush the garlic over a bowl or jam jar. Add the vinegar, sugar and a generous amount of salt and pepper. Mix well then add the oil and stir or shake until everything has amalgamated.
* Add the dressing to the salad and toss so that everything is well covered.
* Gently break the fish into large flakes. Add the flakes to the salad and fold them gently into it, trying to avoid breaking them.
* Season with salt and pepper and serve with warm naan breads or flatbreads on the side.

Something
for nothing 2

Cheese and Tomato Stacks with Rocket Salad

Some food starts out good but gets better when it's reheated a day or two after it was cooked. This is the case with the potato and tomato bake made for the Big Meal from Scratch. In this recipe it is sandwiched between two slices of halloumi cheese and cooked in the oven. It is excellent served with a rocket salad.

If you don't have any leftover potato and tomato bake you can achieve a good result using ripe fresh tomatoes and precooked potatoes. You will need 2 large tomatoes cut into 1-cm slices and 300 g (approx.) waxy new potatoes, boiled and cut into 1-cm slices. To make the filling for the stacks, put a single layer of tomato and then another of potato between the halloumi slices, seasoned with salt, pepper and thyme for added flavour.

Cheese and tomato stacks	Rocket salad	GET AHEAD PREPARATION (optional)
2 tbsp olive oil	100 g rocket	* Make the marinade for the
2 sprigs fresh thyme or 1 tsp	juice of ½ lemon	halloumi.
dried thyme	1 tbsp olive oil	* Slice the halloumi and
zest of ½ lemon		marinate.
500 g halloumi (2 packets)	To serve	* Wash the rocket.
600 g (approx.) potato and	crusty bread	
tomato bake left over from the		
Big Meal from Scratch or see		
above		
salt and pepper		

25 minutes before you want to eat

* Preheat the oven to 190°C/375°C/Gas Mark 5.
* First, make the marinade for the halloumi. Pour 1 tablespoon of the olive oil into a shallow bowl. Add the thyme, lemon zest, salt and pepper and mix well.
* Cut the halloumi lengthways into 16 slices and add them to the marinade. Taking care not to break the slices, use your hands to turn them in the oil and herb mixture so that they are all well coated.
* Place eight of the slices of halloumi on a baking sheet and carefully put a spoonful of the potato and tomato bake on top of each slice.
* Put the remaining eight slices of cheese on top of the potato and tomato mixture to make a halloumi sandwich. Drizzle the remaining oil over the top, place in the oven and bake for 15 minutes or until the filling in the middle is piping hot.
* While the cheese is baking, prepare the salad. Wash and dry the rocket leaves and tip them into a salad bowl. Squeeze about 2 teaspoons of lemon juice over the leaves and add the oil, and a generous pinch of salt. Mix well using your hands and set aside.
* Preheat the grill to high and grill the halloumi stacks for a few minutes so that the top slices of cheese start to brown.
* Remove the stacks from the grill, squeeze over a few drops of lemon juice and serve with the rocket salad and crusty bread.

Seasonal supper

Chard Risotto

Chard is a real treat at this time of year, particularly early in the season when it's young and tender. It has thick stalks and dark green, heavily veined leaves. The stalks have an earthy flavour, with a similar texture to celery, and can vary in colour from pure white to yellow or brilliant ruby red. If you can't find chard at all, however, replace the stalks with 50 g finely sliced celery heart and the leaves with 200 g bagged small-leaved spinach.

1.1 litres chicken stock (fresh or made from a stock cube or bouillon powder)
100 g butter
1 large onion, approx. 190 g
350 g Swiss or rainbow chard (or see above)
350 g risotto rice

150 ml white wine
60–100 g Parmesan
small handful of fresh flatleaf parsley
salt and pepper

To serve
tomato salad

GET AHEAD PREPARATION (optional)

* Prepare the onion and chard.
* Grate the Parmesan.
* Chop the parsley.

40 minutes before you want to eat

* If the stock is cold, put it in a pan and bring it to the boil.
* Start by softening the onion. Melt half the butter in a large heavy-based pan. Peel and finely chop the onion and add it to the butter. Stir it about to get well coated and cook it over a low heat until it is soft and translucent – about 10 minutes.
* Meanwhile, prepare the chard. Remove the stalks and put the leaves in a full sink of water. Trim the dry ends from the stalks, then wash the stalks and slice them finely.
* Add the stalks (or sliced celery) to the onion and cook gently over a low heat for about 10 minutes until they have softened. Put a lid on the pan and stir regularly to prevent them colouring.
* When you judge that the stalks are less crunchy, add the rice and turn up the heat. Stir the rice so that it's coated in the butter, onion and chard mixture.
* Now add the wine, bring it to the boil and let it evaporate entirely, stirring all the while.
* Then add 3 ladlefuls of the hot stock and turn the heat down so that the whole lot is just simmering. Stir the rice every few moments to avoid sticking and to allow the rice to absorb the liquid evenly. When the stock is all but absorbed, add another 3 ladlefuls.
* While the rice is cooking, roll up the chard or spinach leaves, a few at a time, and slice them into thin ribbons.
* When the stock needs replenishing add the leaves and another 3 ladlefuls of stock and keep stirring.
* Continue adding the stock in this way until the rice is soft to the bite and the risotto has a thick and creamy consistency. In between stirrings, grate the Parmesan.
* When the risotto is creamy, stir in the rest of the butter, all but 2 tablespoons of the Parmesan and a generous amount of salt and pepper. Cover the pan and let the risotto sit for 5 minutes before serving.
* While the risotto rests, finely chop the parsley. Stir it into the risotto just before serving. Spoon the risotto into bowls with a final sprinkling of Parmesan and serve with a tomato salad.

Larder feast

Coconut Prawn Noodles

This recipe makes a swift and easy noodle soup flavoured with lime, coconut and chilli. Frozen raw prawns have the advantage that they can be cooked from frozen, thus cutting down on labour and time.

250–300 g (approx.) dried medium wheat or egg noodles
5-cm piece of fresh root ginger
2 limes
1 x 200 g can chopped tomatoes
200 ml fish or chicken stock (fresh or made from a stock cube or bouillon powder)
3 garlic cloves
1 x 280 g (approx.) can button mushrooms
1 x 220 g (approx.) can water chestnuts

1 x 220 g (approx.) can sliced bamboo shoots
½ tbsp groundnut or grapeseed oil
200–300 g frozen large raw peeled prawns
300 ml coconut milk
1 tbsp sweet chilli sauce
1 tsp Thai fish sauce (optional)
handful of fresh coriander (optional)
salt

GET AHEAD PREPARATION (optional)

* Prepare the ginger and garlic.
* Juice one of the limes.
* Drain the mushrooms, water chestnuts and bamboo shoots.

30 minutes before you want to eat

* First cook the noodles according to the instructions on the packet. Once cooked, drain them, rinse under cold running water and leave to one side.
* While the noodles are cooking, peel and thinly slice the ginger and juice one of the limes. Put the ginger in a pan along with the tomatoes, stock and lime juice. Stir well, place over a medium heat and simmer gently for about 10 minutes while you cook the remaining ingredients.
* Now stir-fry the prawns and vegetables. Peel and finely slice the garlic. Drain the mushrooms, water chestnuts and bamboo shoots. Heat the oil over a high heat in a pan big enough to hold all the noodles and vegetables. When the oil is hot, add the garlic. Fry for 1–2 minutes then add the prawns. Stir for 3–4 minutes, until the prawns turn pink.
* Next, add the mushrooms, water chestnuts (whole or cut in half if large) and bamboo shoots and stir-fry for a minute or so.
* Once the vegetables have started to colour, add the coconut milk, chilli sauce and the fish sauce, if using. Bring to the boil then add the tomato and stock mixture. Stir well, add just under ⅓ teaspoon salt and simmer for 5 minutes. Roughly chop the coriander, if using.
* Finally, add the noodles to warm through. Taste for seasoning and add more lime juice if desired.
* Serve in large bowls with, if you wish, the coriander sprinkled over the top.

Two for one

Citrus Lamb

Lamb is more usually partnered with red wine than oranges and lemons, but these create a citrus-flavoured dish well suited to summer.

Neck fillets, scrag end or boned shoulder are ideal cuts for this slow cook. If you are shopping at a supermarket, lamb for casseroles often comes ready diced and is generically labelled as 'stewing lamb'.

As with most casseroles, this recipe is pretty straightforward but it does take some time to cook (for information about cooking casseroles, see page 301). The quantities make enough for eight, so you can freeze half for a lazy night at a later date.

For a lighter more summery alternative to mash, try white bean mash. Drain two 400 g cans cannellini beans and heat them gently in a pan with a little water, a generous slug of olive oil and a sprig of fresh rosemary. When they are hot, whizz them with a little oil in a food processor or a hand blender to get a smoothish texture. Make double this quantity if you want to freeze half with the lamb.

1.8 kg stewing lamb (see above), cut into 4-5 cm cubes
2 tbsp olive oil
30 g butter
60 g plain flour
2 large onions, approx. 380 g
2 celery sticks
½ bottle white wine
4 garlic cloves
1 lemon
1 orange
8 sun-dried tomatoes

4 sprigs fresh thyme
400 ml lamb or chicken stock (fresh or made from a stock cube or bouillon powder) or water
4 tbsp pitted black olives
salt and pepper

To serve
mashed potatoes or white bean mash (see above), and a green vegetable or salad (optional)

GET AHEAD PREPARATION (optional)

The recipe can be made 2 days in advance and then reheated. If you only have a little time:
* Prepare the onions, celery and garlic.
* Zest and juice the lemon and orange.
* Quarter the sun-dried tomatoes.
* Strip the thyme leaves from their stalks.

2–3 hours before you want to eat

* Preheat the oven to 180°C/350°F/Gas Mark 4.
* Start by browning the lamb. Put 1 tablespoon of the oil and two nuts of the butter in a large casserole and place over a medium heat. Lightly dust the lamb with the flour, season and add the meat to the casserole in batches. Allow it to brown, turning it now and then to ensure even colouring. This will take about 15 minutes in all. Remove the lamb from the casserole as it browns and put it aside on a plate.
* While the meat is browning prepare the vegetables. Peel and finely slice the onions and finely chop the celery.
* When all the lamb is browned and on a plate, add a generous splash of wine to the pan and boil it rapidly while stirring to deglaze. Tip the juices over the lamb.
* Add the rest of the oil to the casserole and return it to a medium heat. Add the onions and celery and cook slowly, making sure they don't burn.
* While the onions and celery are cooking, peel and finely slice the garlic. Add this to the pan and cook gently for a further 10 minutes.
* While the garlic is cooking, zest and juice the lemon and orange and cut the sundried tomatoes into quarters. Strip the thyme leaves from their stalks.
* When the onion mixture is soft, add the thyme leaves, tomatoes, remaining wine, stock or water and the zest and juice from the citrus fruits. Bring to the boil and simmer for 3 minutes.
* Tip the lamb into the casserole along with the olives and about ½ teaspoon each of salt and pepper. Stir once or twice, cover with a lid and place in the oven for 1½ hours and up to 2½ hours until the lamb is meltingly tender.
* Put half the lamb aside to cool and then freeze, and serve the other half with potato or white bean mash and a green vegetable or salad.

Lazy day supper – reheating instructions

Defrost the lamb thoroughly prior to reheating either on the stove over a gentle heat or for 30 minutes in the oven at 180°C/350°F/Gas Mark 4.

Casseroles and stews – basic method

Most all casseroles, stews and braises involve the same basic set of procedures. Once you are familiar with these steps and the reasons for carrying them out, making a casserole will become a logical and easy process. Knowing these basic steps means that reliance on a recipe becomes a matter of choice not necessity. The steps and the reasons behind them are:

1 Browning

The meat is seasoned then browned in fat over a high heat. This caramelises the meat and improves the overall flavour of the end dish. It's important to brown the meat sufficiently – it needs to have seared, become dark brown and have slightly crusty edges. There's no point trying to rush the process and if you continually turn and stir the meat it won't get a chance to brown. Let it sit untouched for a few minutes, then turn it so that different sides of the meat brown. Don't try to brown it in an overcrowded pan – it's more effective to brown meat in batches. Once browned, it is generally set aside or put in a large casserole. Meat is sometimes sprinkled with seasoned flour before being browned – this can help to thicken the sauce, but a sauce can also, if necessary, be thickened at the end of cooking.

2 Deglazing

The bottom of the pan in which the meat was browned will be covered with pieces of browned, caramelised meat. These are packed with flavour and should be loosened by 'deglazing' the pan with a little wine, stock or water. Splash the liquid into the pan and stir to loosen the flavours from the pan. A whisk is particularly useful for this job. This liquid is then poured over the meat.

3 Vegetables

Almost all casseroles, stews and braises contain onions, and usually garlic, leeks, celery, carrots and sometimes garlic – most often a mixture of these. Any or all of them add a depth of flavour but, again, these are best when they've been softened and browned. Generally, while the meat is browning there is time to peel and chop the vegetables. Once the meat is browned the onions can be softened and the vegetables can then be slightly browned, and the onions and vegetables are then added to the meat. The pan can be deglazed again. A casserole or braise can be prepared up to this point hours in advance meaning that the last couple of steps can be done when convenient.

4 Liquids and seasonings

Once the meat and vegetables have been browned and the pan is deglazed the herbs (usually bay and other hard herbs such as thyme and rosemary), seasonings, stock and wine are added to the casserole. The meat and vegetables should be almost completely submerged in liquid.

5 Slow cooking

Once assembled, the dish is ready to be cooked, either in a low oven or over a low heat. The key here is low. If the heat is too high and the contents of the casserole boil the meat will become tough and stringy. Low and slow is the key for a melt-in-the-mouth tender and intensely flavoured end result – this means up to an hour for chicken legs and thighs, and anywhere between 1½ to 2 hours for duck, beef, venison lamb or pork.

July Week 2 – Overview

The Big Meal from Scratch recipe this week works as well with whole chicken as with four small poussin. The birds are cooked in a fiery rich red sauce. Combined with spiced rice and runner beans this makes a very satisfying meal. The recipe will take a total of 2½ hours to come together but once the chicken is in the oven, the majority of the work has been done.

As always, the big meal leaves leftovers for two, in this case even three, further meals. Surplus chicken is turned into Hoisin Chicken Wraps, reminiscent of Peking duck and ready in 25 minutes. This Something for Nothing works especially well with small, soft pancakes sold in Asian stores but is also good with the soft flour tortilla wraps that are sold in the Mexican section of supermarkets. Extra spiced rice means making Baked Stuffed Peppers is simply a question of quick assembly then baking time in the oven – a total of 30 minutes. The big meal produces a large quantity of sauce and this can be turned into an Added Extra: tomato and aubergine curry.

There's nothing wrong with lettuce in salads but this is not the only way it can be eaten. Here it is gently braised with ham and wine to make a light vegetable casserole. The recipe takes 40 minutes but is not complex or particularly involved. Quicker and probably more familiar is a Larder Feast of Tuna Niçoise – pure summer eating in a swift 25 minutes.

Unusually, the Two for One recipe for this week – Stilton and Watercress Penne – is ready in 25 minutes. Take care to check the freshness of any watercress as it can turn from crisp and peppery to yellow and musty very quickly – ideally cook this recipe within a couple of days of buying the watercress.

July Week 2	Recipe	Time
Big meal from scratch	Red spiced poussin (or chicken) with cardamom rice and runner beans Added Extra – Tomato and aubergine curry	2½ hours
Something for nothing 1	Hoisin chicken wraps with noodle salad Baked stuffed peppers	25 mins
Something for nothing 2	Baked stuffed peppers	30 mins
Seasonal supper	Braised lettuce with ham	40 mins
Larder feast	Tuna Niçoise	25 mins
2 for 1	Stilton and watercress penne	25 mins

All recipes serve 4 apart from the 2 for 1 recipe which makes 8 portions

SHOPPING LIST (for 4 people)

Meat and fish
6 poussin or 2 × 1.2–1.5 kg (approx.) free-
  range chickens
4 thick slices roast ham, approx. 300–400 g

Dairy
150 g butter
8 free-range eggs
150 g natural yoghurt
200 ml milk
350 g Stilton

Fruit and vegetables
8 medium red onions, approx. 840 g
1 large onion, approx. 180 g
4 bunches spring onions, approx. 26
10 garlic cloves
2–3 green chillies
4 cm piece of fresh root ginger
5 large red peppers, approx. 1 kg
1 bunch radishes, approx. 200 g (the long
  breakfast variety if possible)
1 cucumber
4 ripe tomatoes, approx. 500 g
1 soft lettuce (butterhead or round are the
  best)
2 little gem lettuces
300 g watercress, approx 2 bunches
450 g runner beans
200 g green beans
200g shelled peas
1 kg small new potatoes
1 large bunch fresh parsley
1 bunch fresh mint
1 small bunch fresh coriander
1½ lemons
1 lime

Basics
120 ml olive oil
60 ml groundnut or grapeseed oil
½ tbsp Dijon mustard
1 bay leaf
1 tsp sugar
400 ml ham or chicken stock (fresh or made
  from a stock cube or bouillon powder)
250 ml chicken or vegetable stock (fresh
  or made from a stock cube or bouillon
  powder)
salt and pepper

Store cupboard
3½ × 50 g cans anchovy fillets in olive oil
2 × 200 g cans tuna in olive oil or brine
  (depending on preference)
1 × 400 g can chopped tomatoes
1 × 400 g can haricot beans
1 × 400 g can flageolet beans

12 roasted red peppers in oil, from a can or
  jar, piquante if possible
4 tbsp capers
50 g black olives, 15–20 (ideally Kalamata
  or Provençal), pitted if you prefer
400 g basmati rice
300 g clear glass noodles or egg noodles
20 wheat-flour pancakes or 8 flour tortillas
400 g penne or fusilli pasta
1 tbsp sesame seeds
½ tbsp fresh tamarind paste
4 tbsp hoisin plum sauce
2 tbsp rice vinegar (optional Hoisin Chicken
  Wraps with Noodle Salad)
1–5 tbsp white wine vinegar
splash of red wine vinegar (optional Tuna
  Niçoise)
2 tsp onion seeds
1 tsp ground cinnamon
large pinch of ground cloves
1 heaped tsp ground coriander
3 cardamom pods
½ cinnamon stick
½ tbsp clear honey
2 tsp soy sauce
1 tbsp sweet chilli sauce
60 g sultanas
250 ml white wine
300 ml cider

Serving suggestions
green salad ingredients (Baked Stuffed
  Peppers)
mustard (Braised Lettuce with Ham), optional
crusty bread (Tuna Niçoise)

To download or print out this shopping list,
please visit www.thekitchenrevolution.co.uk/July/
Week2

Red Spiced Poussin (or Chicken) with Cardamom Rice and Runner Beans

Based on Indian recipes for cooking quail or game, this meal is rich with spices but without excessive heat. Poussin are coated in a rich, Indian-spiced tomato sauce and baked, covered in foil, in the oven. The end result is succulent and flavoursome.

The recipe suggests one poussin per person. This may seem rather a lot, but there's not a huge amount of meat on poussin. If they are difficult to come by or you would prefer to cook two chickens this will work too. The birds are accompanied by a cardamom-flavoured rice.

This dish has been slightly adapted from a Josceline Dimbleby recipe.

The quantities here include extra meat for the Hoisin Wraps and extra rice for the Baked, Stuffed Peppers.

Red spiced poussin (or chicken)
40 g butter
3 red onions, approx. 240 g
1 large red pepper. approx. 200 g
4 garlic cloves
4-cm piece of fresh root ginger
2-3 green chillies
2 tsp onion seeds
1 heaped tsp ground coriander
1 tsp ground cinnamon
large pinch of ground cloves
1 tbsp white wine vinegar
1 × 400 g can chopped tomatoes
250 ml chicken or vegetable stock (fresh or made from a stock cube or bouillon powder)
½ tbsp fresh tamarind paste
6 poussin or 2 × 1.2–1.5 kg (approx.) free-range chickens; includes 2 poussin/1 chicken extra for the hoisin chicken wraps (approx 600g extra meat)
60 g sultanas
150 g plain yoghurt
salt and pepper

Cardamom rice
400 g basmati rice, includes 200 g extra for the baked stuffed peppers
60 g butter
1 tbsp groundnut or grapeseed oil
1 large onion, approx. 180 g
3 garlic cloves
3 cardamom pods
½ cinnamon stick
1 bay leaf
small handful of fresh parsley
½ lemon

Runner beans
450 g runner beans
small nut of butter

GET AHEAD PREPARATION (optional)

The tomato sauce can be made up, cooled and poured over the poussin or chickens up to a day in advance. If you only have a little time:
* Prepare the onions, red pepper, chillies and ginger.
* Peel all the garlic.
* Whizz the chillies, ginger and garlic for the paste.
* Measure out and mix the spices for the tomato sauce.
* Prepare the runner beans.
* Chop the parsley.

2½ hours before you want to eat prepare the poussin

* Preheat the oven to 180°C/350°F/Gas Mark 4.
* Melt the butter in a large heavy-based pan over a low heat, and while it melts peel and finely slice the onions. Add the onions to the pan and let them cook over a medium heat for 5 minutes.
* Deseed and finely slice the red pepper and add it to the onions. Next, peel and chop the garlic and ginger and deseed and roughly chop the chillies. Put the garlic, ginger and chillies in a food processor and whizz to a smooth paste. Tip this out into the pan with the onions and red pepper.
* When the onion mixture is soft, turn up the heat, add the onion seeds, coriander, cinnamon and cloves and stir well. After a couple of minutes, splash in the vinegar and allow it to evaporate completely before adding the tomatoes, stock and tamarind. Bring the whole lot to a simmer, stir well and leave to cook together over a low heat for 10 minutes.
* Season the poussin or chickens and place in a large roasting tin. Scatter the sultanas around the birds. Taste the sauce and season, then pour it over the birds and cover the tin with foil, tucking it in around the outside edges to make it airtight.
* Put in the oven and cook for 1–1½ hours. After an hour the legs of the poussin should come away easily and feel tender. If you are using whole chickens, after 1¼ hours pierce

a thigh and if the juices run clear they are ready. Once they are ready, they will sit in a low oven until needed.

40 minutes before you want to eat cook the rice

* Place the rice in a sieve and rinse well under cold running water. Heat the butter and oil in a large, heavy-based pan and peel and finely slice the onion. Add the onion to the hot fat, stir so that it is well coated, cover with a lid and leave to sweat over a gentle heat for 10 minutes or so.
* While the onion is softening peel and slice the garlic.
* After 10 minutes remove the lid from the onion pan, add the garlic and cook for a couple more minutes. Roughly crush the cardamom pods and cinnamon stick and throw them in with the onion; turn up the heat and let the onion brown a little. Add the washed rice and stir gently to ensure it is well coated in butter. Add enough water to come 1 cm above the level of the rice, season and add the bay leaf. Stir once and bring to the boil. Once boiling, cover the pan, turn the heat down and cook very gently for 15–20 minutes. While the rice is cooking, roughly chop the parsley.
* Wash and top and tail the beans. If they seem stringy, remove a strip from the side of each bean using a vegetable peeler. Cut the beans into 3-cm lengths.

15 minutes before you want to eat cooks the beans

* By now the poussin or chickens will be ready, so turn the oven off and leave them to rest while you finish everything else. If the sauce seems thin, lift the birds out of the roasting tin and put them in an ovenproof dish. Transfer the tin to the heat and simmer until the sauce is to your liking. When you are ready to serve, spoon the yoghurt into the sauce, but don't stir it.
* Put some plates and serving dishes in the cooling oven to warm.
* No more than 10 minutes before you want to eat, drop the beans into a pan of boiling water and let them cook for 4–5 minutes until they are tender.
* Drain them well and tip them into a warmed serving dish with seasoning and some butter.
* By now the rice should be ready. Leave to stand with its lid on for 5–7 minutes. Taste for seasoning, stir in the lemon juice and chopped parsley and turn it out into a warmed serving dish.
* To serve, put a poussin or some carved chicken on each warmed plate and pass the sauce, rice and beans round separately.

Afterwards

* Place 2 poussin or the remaining chicken meat (400 g), and rice (600 g) in the fridge, cover and keep for use later in the week.
* Any extra beans make a delicious warm salad with a simple garlic dressing. The remaining sauce can be frozen for use with more chicken or other game, or the aubergine dish below is a tasty way to use it up.

Added extra

Tomato and Aubergine Curry

Preheat the oven to 200/400/gas 6. Cut a large aubergine into bite-sized pieces and put them onto a roasting tin. Drizzle with plenty of olive oil and season with salt and pepper. Mix well, then place in the oven for 20 minutes until they are soft and golden brown. Roughly chop a handful of coriander and heat the tomato sauce. When the aubergine is ready, add it to the tomato sauce and leave to simmer for at least 10 minutes, but longer if possible. When ready to eat, throw in the conach and season the dish to taste. Serve with some naan bread and yoghurt.

Something for nothing 1

Hoisin Chicken Wraps with Noodle Salad

This recipe is inspired by Peking duck, that perfect combination of sweet and savoury, hot and cold, crunchy and soft. Here we toss shredded chicken in a plum sauce dressing then roll this mixture in wraps along with cucumber, spring onions and toasted sesame seeds.

Chicken is considerably less rich than duck so to make this a complete meal, the recipe includes a salad of noodles, coriander and mint dressed with lime juice, chilli and rice vinegar.

Hoisin chicken wraps
1 lime
4 tbsp hoisin plum sauce
½ tbsp clear honey
2 tsp soy sauce
1 tbsp sesame seeds
2 cooked poussin or 400 g
    cooked chicken meat left over
    from the Big Meal from
    Scratch, stripped from the
    bone, or 3 chicken breasts
    poached in water or stock until
    cooked
1 cucumber
12-16 spring onions
20 wheat-flour pancakes or 8
    soft flour tortillas

Noodle salad
300 g clear glass noodles or egg
    noodles
½ bunch fresh mint
½ bunch fresh coriander
1 tbsp sweet chilli sauce
1 tsp sugar
2 tbsp rice vinegar or white wine
    vinegar

GET AHEAD PREPARATION (optional)

* Prepare the spring onions and
    cucumber.
* Make the dressings for the
    chicken and the noodle salad.
* Chop the herbs.

25 minutes before you want to eat

* Cook the noodles according to the instructions on the packet and while they are cooking prepare the other ingredients.
* Then make the sauce for the chicken. Squeeze the juice from half the lime into a large bowl and reserve the remaining half lime for the noodle salad. Mix the juice with the hoisin plum sauce, honey and soy sauce. Taste and adjust according to taste – it should be lip-puckeringly sweet and sour.
* Put a frying pan over a medium heat, add the sesame seeds and toast them until browned. Add them to the plum sauce mixture and stir well.
* If you haven't done so already, shred the chicken meat and mix into the plum sauce dressing.
* Now prepare the cucumber and spring onions. Peel the cucumber, cut it into quarters lengthways and deseed. Slice the quarters into thin matchsticks about 6 cm long. Trim the spring onions and shred them into narrow strips, using as much of the green as you can. Put the cucumber and spring onions on a plate side by side, cover and keep in the fridge until you come to serve.
* Prepare the dressing for the noodle salad. Strip the mint leaves from their stalks and chop them finely. Roughly chop the coriander. Mix the chilli sauce, sugar and rice vinegar with most of the juice (any extra juice may be needed later) from the remaining half of lime.
* When the noodles are cooked, drain them thoroughly and tip them into a large bowl. Add the mint and coriander and mix well. Pour over the chilli dressing and toss so that all the different components are evenly distributed. Taste, and season with extra chilli sauce, lime juice or vinegar according to your preference.
* If you are using tortillas rather than pancakes you will have to warm them in the oven or microwave until soft – check the instructions on the packet.
* Arrange the chicken, cucumber, spring onions and pancakes so that everyone can help themselves. Take a pancake or tortilla, fill it with the chicken, cucumber and spring onions and roll it up. Serve with the noodle salad on the side.

Baked Stuffed Peppers

Stuffed peppers were an almost weekly feature of family suppers in the '70s when we were growing up – they are very easy to make if you have cooked rice to hand, the flavours can be determined by what's available and, as long as peppers are in season, they cost next to nothing. This is classic family food. Like many simple dishes, it's as easy to get stuffed peppers wrong as it is to get them right – if the filling lacks flavour or moisture, or if the peppers are raw tasting, the whole event is a disappointment. The key, therefore, is to err on the side of generosity when thinking about the filling and parboil the peppers prior to stuffing. With these two principles in place, stuffed red peppers make a tasty, simple and very satisfying meal. Serve with a dressed green salad.

4 large red peppers, approx.
 800 g
4 free-range eggs
4 spring onions
large handful of fresh parsley
2 x 50 g cans anchovy fillets in
 olive oil
4 tbsp capers
600 g cooked rice left over from
 the Big Meal from Scratch or
 200 g basmati rice cooked as
 in the big meal with onions,
 garlic and spices (see page
 305)
juice of 1 lemon
4 tbsp olive oil
salt and pepper

To serve
green salad

GET AHEAD PREPARATION (optional)

The entire dish can be made 2 days in advance up to the point of going in the oven. If you only have a little time:
* Prepare the red peppers and spring onions.
* Parboil the peppers.
* Chop the parsley.
* Chop the anchovies and capers.
* Boil the eggs.

30 minutes before you want to eat

* Preheat the oven to 200°C/400°F/Gas Mark 6.
* Cut the red peppers in half lengthways, retaining the stalks if there are any. Scoop or cut out the seeds and any thick, white, pithy ribs, but take care not to make any holes in the flesh.
* Now parboil the peppers and cook the eggs. Place the peppers in a pan of boiling water for 4–5 minutes and the eggs in a pan of boiling water for 8 minutes.
* When the peppers have softened leave them to drain. Meanwhile, continue to prepare the rest of the stuffing. Trim and slice the spring onions and chop the parsley. Place in a large bowl and add the oil from the anchovy can. Roughly chop the anchovies and capers and add them to the bowl.
* When the eggs are ready, tip them into the sink and run them under cold water for a few minutes so that they cool down quickly. If you crack the shells this helps. When the eggs are cool enough to handle, peel and chop them roughly then add them to the bowl with the spring onions, parsley, capers and anchovies.
* Now fold in the rice, lemon juice and 3 tablespoons of the oil. Mix together well and season thoroughly to taste with salt and pepper.
* Oil an ovenproof dish in which the peppers will fit snugly. Place the peppers in the dish and fill each one with the rice mixture. Drizzle a little oil over the top of each one and bake for about 15 minutes until the rice is heated through and is crisp on the top.
* Serve with a dressed green salad.

Seasonal supper

Braised Lettuce with Ham

Lettuce is at its best in midsummer and can be enjoyed in many more ways than in a salad. Here we braise little gems and a soft lettuce in white wine with ham, radishes, green beans and the new season's potatoes. As its name suggests, a butterhead lettuce will add a rich butteriness to this simple, light recipe, but most lettuce would work if it is unavailable.

Late June and early July see the start of the new crop potatoes. Of these, Jersey Royals are arguably king. They have a sweet, nutty flavour and waxy flesh.

groundnut or grapeseed oil
50 g butter
6 spring onions
600 g small new potatoes
1 bunch radishes, approx. 200 g
2 little gem lettuces
250 ml white wine
400 ml ham or vegetable stock
 (fresh or made from a stock
 cube or bouillon powder)
200 g green beans
1 soft lettuce (butterhead or
 round are best)
small handful of fresh flatleaf
 parsley
3 sprigs fresh mint
200 g shelled peas
4 thick slices roast ham, approx.
 300-400 g

To serve
mustard and bread

GET AHEAD PREPARATION (optional)

* Prepare the spring onions amd
 radishes and little gems and
 soft lettuce.
* Prepare the potatoes and cover
 with water until required.
* Top, tail and slice the beans.
* Chop the herbs.

*40 minutes before
you want to eat*

* Heat a splash of oil and the butter in a large pan or casserole. Trim the spring onions and slice them into 2–3-cm pieces using as much as possible of the green parts. Throw the spring onions into the pan and let them cook gently, while you wash the potatoes and cut them in half.
* Increase the heat under the pan or casserole and add the potatoes. Stir from time to time to stop them sticking. While the potatoes are browning, remove any radish leaves and wash the radishes well. Cut the radishes in half lengthways if they are large.
* Add the radishes to the potatoes and let them brown for 1–2 minutes, stirring to prevent them sticking. Remove any brown or bruised leaves from the little gem lettuces then cut the lettuces into sixths lengthways. Wash them well, shake off any excess water and add them to the pan.
* When the little gems have been cooking for a couple of minutes and have started to soften, splash in the wine. Let this simmer for a few minutes then add the stock. Bring to simmering point and let everything bubble away gently for 15 minutes.
* While the vegetables are cooking, top and tail the beans and cut them into 2–3-cm lengths. Discard any damaged outer leaves from the soft lettuce, wash it well and leave it to drip-dry in a colander. Strip the parsley and mint leaves from their stalks and chop them.
* When the potatoes are just cooked, add the beans and tear the soft lettuce into the pan. Leave to cook for 5–7 minutes.
* Next, add the peas, bring back to a simmer and drop in the ham slices to warm through for a few minutes.
* Once the slices of ham are warm, lift them out and set them aside on a warm plate. Add the parsley and mint to the pan and season to taste.
* Put a good pile of vegetables and some cooking liquor on each plate, with a slice of ham on top, and serve mustard on the side and bread for mopping up the juices.

Larder feast

Tuna Niçoise

Niçoise salad has to be one of the best things about summer eating. It requires very little forethought given that most of the ingredients (the most crucial ones anyway) are store-cupboard basics. Here we use canned flageolet beans but you could use fresh green beans if you prefer.

400 g small new potatoes
4 free-range eggs
1 x 400 g can haricot beans
1 x 400 g can flageolet beans
12 roasted red peppers in oil
  from a can or jar (piquante if
  possible)
1 medium red onion, approx.
  120 g
small handful of fresh parsley
  (optional)
2 x 200 g cans tuna in olive oil
  or brine (depending on
  preference)
50 g black olives, 15–20 (ideally
  Kalamata or Provençal), pitted
  if you prefer

4 ripe tomatoes, approx. 500 g
splash of red or white wine
  vinegar
1 garlic clove
juice of ½ lemon
½ tbsp Dijon mustard
4 tbsp olive oil
8–12 anchovy fillets in olive oil
  (depending on taste)
salt and black pepper

To serve
crusty bread

GET AHEAD PREPARATION (optional)

* Prepare and cook the potatoes.
* Boil the eggs.
* Drain the beans, tuna and
  anchovies.
* Prepare the red peppers and
  the onion.
* Chop the parsley.
* Halve the tomatoes.
* Peel and crush the garlic.

*25 minutes before
you want to eat*

* Wash the potatoes, cut them in half and place them in a large pan of salted water. Bring to the boil and simmer for 10–15 minutes or until the potatoes are just cooked.
* Bring another pan of water to the boil and lower the eggs in one by one. Cook for 7 minutes, or longer if you like your eggs hard-boiled.
* While the potatoes and eggs are cooking, prepare the rest of the salad. Drain and rinse the beans and tip them into a large salad bowl. Slice the red peppers into quarters and add them to the beans. Slice the onion finely and chop the parsley roughly and add these to the other ingredients, mixing well. Drain the tuna and break up any very large chunks then add it to the salad bowl and fold in gently. Add the olives to the bowl.
* Cut the tomatoes into quarters and add them to the salad bowl.
* Drain the potatoes, sprinkle them with the vinegar and toss them through the salad.
* Lift the eggs out of their pan and place under cold running water to cool. Crack their shells so they cool more efficiently.
* Meanwhile, make the dressing. Peel and crush the garlic and mix it with the lemon juice and mustard. Add the oil, stirring all the while, and season well with salt and pepper.
* Dress the salad with three-quarters of the dressing and mix very well.
* When the eggs are completely cold, peel them, cut them into quarters and place them on top of the salad. Drain the anchovies, separate them and place them on top along with lots of freshly ground pepper.
* Drizzle the remaining dressing over the eggs then serve with large chunks of crusty bread.

| Two for one | # Stilton and Watercress Penne |

The pepperiness of watercress, the sweetness of red onions and the sharpness of Stilton combine to make a rich, intense and colourful sauce. Don't be concerned about the large quantity of cheese in this recipe – you're making enough sauce for eight so that half can be frozen for a lazy night in at a later date. If you prefer, you can replace the Stilton with any cows' milk blue cheese.

The ingredients only include pasta quantities for four.

4 medium red onions, approx. 480 g
2 tbsp groundnut or grapeseed oil
2 garlic cloves
300 ml cider
400 g penne or fusilli pasta
350 g Stilton, rind removed
200 ml milk ·
300 g watercress, approx. 2–3 bunches
salt and pepper

GET AHEAD PREPARATION (optional)

The sauce can be made 2 days in advance and reheated. If you only have a little time:
* Prepare the onions and garlic.
* Prepare the watercress.

25 minutes before you want to eat

* Peel and finely chop the onions. Heat the oil in a heavy-based pan over a medium heat, add the onions and sweat them down for 5–7 minutes, stirring from time to time to prevent them sticking. Peel and crush the garlic and add it to the onions.
* After the garlic has been cooking for a couple of minutes, pour in the cider and let it bubble away.
* Meanwhile, start cooking the pasta according to the manufacturer's instructions.
* Once the cider has reduced to about 2 tablespoons, crumble the Stilton into the pan with half the milk and stir well to encourage the cheese to melt. This will take about 5 minutes. If the sauce starts to get very thick, add the rest of the milk and, if necessary, a splash or two of water. You want a thick sauce, the consistency of double cream.
* In the meantime, remove and discard any thick stems from the watercress and roughly chop what's left (there's no need to be too thorough or spend a long time doing this). Stir into the sauce.
* When the pasta is ready, drain it well, tip it into a big bowl and season it generously with salt and pepper. Mix half the sauce with the pasta and serve immediately.
* Put the remaining sauce into a freezer bag. When cool place in freezer.

Lazy day supper – reheating instructions

Remove the sauce and watercress sauce from the freezer and defrost thoroughly. When the sauce has defrosted tip it into a pan and warm gently for about 15 minutes. Stir in extra milk if the sauce is too thick. Cook 400 g pasta and drain, toss the watercress through it, then stir in the sauce.

Watercress

This attractive peppery flavoured dark green leaf with its slightly chewy stems can be served raw or cooked. It is a member of the mustard family and has a similar taste. Watercress is a good source of iron and vitamins A and C.

Watercress is sold both pre-packed in bags and loose. If possible, we prefer to buy loose watercress (look for fresh green leaves with no signs of yellowing or wilting) as it often has more flavour and is more economical. It can be found at farmers' markets and greengrocers. To prepare loose watercress trim any tough roots off and remove any damaged or yellowing leaves. Wash gently in cold water and pat dry with kitchen paper.

July Week 3 – Overview

The Big Meal from Scratch this week is Roast Beef with a Pepper Crust served with Garlic New Potatoes and a Green Bean and Red Onion Salad. Using a piece from a whole sirloin makes this meal an extra-special treat and something well worth sharing with people you love. A butcher or the meat counter at a supermarket will be able to provide whole sirloin. Though it may seem wickedly expensive, when you factor in the eight portions this recipe will serve the cost per portion seems less shocking. The recipe calls for pink and green peppercorns, which are sometimes hard to find – if so, use a dessertspoon of black peppercorns instead.

When splashing out on a cut like sirloin it seems prudent to stretch it into more than one meal. Here the surplus beef is used to make a Vietnamese-inspired salad – a Something for Nothing that takes 30 minutes to make. Extra roast onions are mixed with chicken, herbs and tomatoes to make this week's other Something for Nothing: a warm salad that's served on bruschetta and is ready from start to finish in 20 minutes.

A Soft Goats' Cheese Salad for a Seasonal Supper and a Larder Feast of Spiced Prawn Couscous will both work well however hot the weather, and each takes under 20 minutes to make.

The Two for One casserole of Braised Chicken with Celery and Orange takes about 30 minutes to assemble and then 45 minutes of gentle cooking.

July Week 3	Recipe	Time
Big meal from scratch	Roast beef with a pepper crust, with garlic new potatoes and green bean and red onion salad	1 hour 20 mins
Something for nothing 1	Vietnamese beef salad	30 mins
Something for nothing 2	Chicken and roast onion bruschetta	20 mins
Seasonal supper	Soft goats' cheese salad	15 mins
Larder feast	Spiced prawn couscous	20 mins
2 for 1	Braised chicken with celery and orange	1¼ hours

All recipes serve 4 apart from the 2 for 1 recipe which makes 8 portions

SHOPPING LIST (for 4 people)

Meat and fish
1 kg (approx.) boneless sirloin (ask the butcher to trim most of the fat from the top)
3 small free-range chicken breasts, skinless and boneless
8 free-range chicken legs (thighs and drumsticks)
400 g frozen raw peeled prawns

Dairy
2 tbsp crème fraîche
400 g soft goats' cheese (the freshest and softest you can find)

Fruit and vegetables
1.2 kg new potatoes (Pink Fir Apple if possible)
4 medium red onions, approx. 480 g
8 small red onions, approx. 720 g
6 spring onions
7 garlic cloves
2 bunches radishes, approx 400 g
1 head celery
300 g green beans
300 g mangetout
150 g beansprouts or 75 g salad leaves
100 g watercress, approx. 23 bunches
4 little gem lettuces
100 g rocket
1 cucumber
150 g cherry tomatoes
8 very ripe plum tomatoes, approx. 1 kg
1 large bunch fresh flatleaf parsley
1 large bunch fresh coriander
1 large bunch fresh mint
2 sprigs fresh rosemary
2 sprigs fresh sage
1 orange
3 lemons
2 limes

Basics
1 large ciabatta ('heat and serve' if possible)
4 poppy-seed rolls
150 ml olive oil
60 ml groundnut or grapeseed oil
1 tbsp Dijon mustard
1 tbsp sugar
300 ml orange juice
400 ml chicken stock (fresh or made from a stock cube or bouillon powder)
400 ml vegegetable stock (made from a stock cube or bouillon powder)
salt and pepper

Store cupboard
250 g basmati rice
400 g couscous
1 tbsp green peppercorns in brine and 1 tbsp pink peppercorns in brine or 2 tbsp green peppercorns in brine; or 1 tbsp dried mixed peppercorns
1 tsp crushed black peppercorns
100 g green pickled chillies
100 g green olives stuffed with pimientoes
7 heaped tbsp mayonnaise
1 tsp balsamic vinegar
4 tbsp Thai fish sauce
1 tbsp sweet chilli sauce
splash sesame oil
½ tbsp light soy sauce
2 tsp paprika
500 g passata

Serving suggestions
lime quarters (Vietnamese Beef Salad)
cucumber and avocado salad ingredients (Spiced Prawn Couscous)
potatoes for baking or couscous or polenta, and peas (Braised Chicken with Celery and Orange)

To download or print out this shopping list, please visit www.thekitchenrevolution.co.uk/July/Week3

**Big meal
from scratch**

Roast Beef with a Pepper Crust, with Garlic New Potatoes and Green Bean and Red Onion Salad

Steak *au poivre*, is a bistro classic and here we've adapted it to use a whole beef joint. Prior to cooking the meat is smothered in mustard and pink and green peppercorns. The green are fiery and sharp whereas the pink are mild and fragrant. The end result is very pretty and well balanced.

Sirloin is one of the best cuts of beef – served either as a single steak or kept as a whole joint and roasted. The recipe asks for 1 kg sirloin. In a book that claims to help a household's weekly budget this is rather extravagant and we apologise. We deliberated about whether to abandon the sirloin for less expensive ingredients but decided that for a special treat, it's acceptable to splurge. Moreover, because the beef is used for a Something for Nothing as well as a Big Meal from Scratch the overall cost per head is not too horrendous.

To serve with the beef, we suggest a salad of roasted red onions mixed with green beans. The mild, sweet flavour of this accompaniment contrasts well with the punchy bite of the steak and the garlic richness of the aïoli potatoes.

This meal can be served piping hot or at room temperature.

The recipe includes extra beef for the Vietnamese Beef Salad and extra red onions for the Chicken and Roast Onion Bruschetta.

Roast beef with a pepper crust
1 kg (approx.) boneless sirloin (ask the butcher to trim most of the fat from the top); includes 400 g extra for Vietnamese beef salad
1 tbsp groundnut or grapeseed oil
1 tbsp green peppercorns in brine and 1 tbsp pink peppercorns or 1.5 dsp green peppercorns in brine; or 1 tbsp dried mixed peppercorns
1 tsp crushed black peppercorns
1 tbsp Dijon mustard
salt and pepper

Green bean and red onion salad
8 small red onions, approx. 720 g; includes 2 extra for the chicken and roast onion bruschetta
2 tbsp olive oil
1 tsp balsamic vinegar
300 g green beans
100 g watercress, approx. 2–3 bunches

Garlic new potatoes
1.2 kg new potatoes (Pink Fir Apple if possible); includes 400 g extra for the chicken and roast onion bruschetta
7 heaped tbsp mayonnaise; includes 3 tbsp extra for the chicken and roast onion bruschetta
juice of ½ lemon
small handful of fresh flatleaf parsley
2 garlic cloves

GET AHEAD PREPARATION (optional)

The aïoli can be made 2 days in advance. If you only have a little time:
* Trim the sirloin, if necessary, and prepare the crust.
* Prepare the ingredients for the green bean salad.
* Prepare the new potatoes and cover them with water until required
* Peel the garlic.
* Chop the parsley.

*1 hour 20 minutes
before you want
to eat*

* Preheat the oven to 180°C/350°F/Gas Mark 4.
* Peel the onions and cut each one into quarters. Place in a roasting tin with a good drizzle of oil, the vinegar and some seasoning. Cover and roast in the oven for 30 minutes, stirring once or twice.
* If there is any, trim most of the fat from the top of the sirloin, leaving a thin, even coat to help the pepper crust stick. Place the beef on a baking sheet, fat side up, rub it all over with oil and leave it out of the fridge for a good 40 minutes prior to cooking.
* Now prepare the crust. Drain the green peppercorns in brine from their liquid and crush them with the pink peppercorns. Tip them into a small bowl with the crushed black peppercorns and add a dash of oil to make a paste. If you are using mixed dried peppercorns, crush them finely then mix them with oil to make a paste.
* Then cook the beans. Fill a large pan with water and bring it to the boil. Top and tail the beans and when the water is boiling add a generous dose of salt. When the water comes back to the boil, throw in the beans and cook for 3–4 minutes. Drain the beans

and plunge them into ice-cold water. Drain once more, pat dry and tip into a serving bowl with a splash of oil.

* Remove the thick stems from the watercress, wash well then dry and keep it in the fridge until you are ready to serve.
* Wash the new potatoes and cut them in half, unless they are very small. Place the potatoes in a pan of salted water.

1 hour before you want to eat

* Turn the oven to 220°C/425°F/Gas Mark 7. Remove the foil from the onions and cook at a high heat for 10 minutes.
* Give the beef a good dowsing of salt. When the oven has reached temperature remove the onions and roast the beef for 20 minutes.
* Meanwhile, put the potatoes over a high heat and bring them to the boil. Simmer until tender – about 25 minutes.
* Put the mayonnaise into a small mixing bowl and stir in 1 tablespoon of the lemon juice. Chop the parsley and crush the garlic and stir them into the mayonnaise. Put 3 tablespoons of the aïoli aside.
* When the onions have cooled slightly put aside 4 heaped tablespoons for later in the week. Tip the remaining onions and all the juices into the dish in with the beans and mix together well.

30 minutes before you want to eat

* When the sirloin has been roasting at a high temperature for 20 minutes remove it from the oven. Reduce the oven temperature to 180°C/350°F/Gas Mark 4. (After the initial 20 minutes on high, we recommend 10 minutes per 500 g for rare meat, 15 minutes for medium-rare to medium and 25 minutes for well done.)
* Spread the fatty side of the beef with the mustard. Sprinkle the crushed peppercorns over the mustard – you only want a light coating so don't be heavy handed. Press them on to the mustard and spread them on with a fish slice or palette knife. Any peppercorn crust you have left will last well in the fridge for a couple of weeks.
* Return the beef to the oven for a final 20 minutes (or longer is you prefer beef more well done – see cooking times above) for the crust to brown and set, then take it out and let it rest for 10 or more minutes.
* Drain the potatoes and put a quarter of them aside for later in the week. Tip the rest into a serving dish with the remaining aïoli. Mix well, and add a little extra salt and pepper if desired.
* Throw the watercress in with the beans and red onions, season and mix everything together well.
* Serve the sirloin in slices the thickness of a pound coin and reserve 350 g for later in the week. Spoon any juices that run out of the meat over the slices and serve with the potatoes and the salad.

Afterwards

Put the leftover sirloin (350 g), potatoes (400 g), aïoli (3 tbsp) and onions (150 g) in separate containers, cover and refrigerate for use later in the week.

**Something
for nothing 1**

Vietnamese Beef Salad

This Vietnamese Beef Salad is served on top of steaming hot rice. The combination of
hot and cold and sweet and sour flavours is very appetising. Adjust the strong flavours
such as chilli and lime to best suit your taste.

If you don't have any leftover beef, season a 400 g piece of sirloin and grill it under
a high heat for about 3 minutes each side for rare or longer for well done.

This is a version of a recipe from Vatcharin Bhumichitr's *Southeast Asian Salads.*

350 g (approx.) cooked sirloin
  left over from the Big Meal
  from Scratch or see above
250 g basmati rice
4 tbsp Thai fish sauce
2 tsp sugar (more if you prefer)
½ tbsp light soy sauce
1 tbsp sweet chilli sauce (more if
  you prefer)
juice of 1 lime (more if you
  prefer)
1 garlic clove

splash of sesame oil
300 g mangetout
generous handful fresh mint
  leaves
generous handful fresh coriander
  leaves
150 g beansprouts or 75g salad
  leaves

To serve
lime quarters

GET AHEAD PREPARATION (optional)

* Peel and crush the garlic.
* Chop the herbs.

*30 minutes before
you want to eat*

* Take the sirloin out of the fridge so that it is at room temperature by the time you
  need it.
* Wash the rice under cold running water then cook it according to the instructions on
  the packet. While the rice is cooking prepare the dressing and salad.
* Mix together the fish sauce, sugar, soy sauce and chilli sauce. Add the lime juice.
  Peel and crush the garlic and mix it with the rest of the dressing. Taste and add more
  sugar, chilli sauce or lime, according to taste. Set the dressing aside while you make
  the salad.
* Heat the sesame oil in a frying pan over a high heat and when the oil is hot add the
  mangetout and stir-fry them for about 2 minutes until they are just cooked but still
  bright green. Tip them into a large bowl.
* Roughly chop the mint and coriander and add them to the mangetout along with the
  beansprouts or salad leaves. Mix well.
* Add all but a few teaspoons of the dressing to the salad and toss thoroughly.
* Slice the sirloin as thinly as you can.
* Divide the rice between four bowls. Pile the salad on top then lay slices of sirloin over
  the salad. Drizzle the remaining dressing over the beef and serve immediately with
  lime quarters.

**Something
for nothing 2**

Chicken and Roast Onion Bruschetta

Everyone loves toast and bruschetta is basically Italian toast with excellent toppings. For this bruschetta leftover red onions, caramelised and sweet, are tossed together with rosemary-flavoured chicken, tomatoes and a creamy dressing made from aïoli.

It's important to take the potatoes and onions out of the fridge in good time so that they are at room temperature and not cold when eaten. Pop them in the oven for 5 minutes while it is warming up if there's no time for them reach the right temperature slowly.

If you have not cooked the big meal, peel and cut two medium red onions into quarters. Rub with oilve oil, then bake in a medium oven for 20 minutes until soft.

3 small free-range chicken
  breasts, skinless and boneless
2 tbsp olive oil
2 sprigs fresh rosemary
½ lemon
1 large ciabatta ('heat and serve'
  if possible)
150 g cherry tomatoes,
  approx. 20
150 g roast red onions left over
  from the Big Meal from Scratch

400 g cooked new potatoes left
  over from the Big Meal from
  Scratch, or 400 g new potatoes
  boiled until cooked
3 tbsp aïoli left over from the
  Big Meal from Scratch, or
  3 tbsp mayonnaise stirred with
  1 crushed garlic clove
2 tbsp crème fraîche
100 g rocket
salt and pepper

GET AHEAD PREPARATION (optional)

* Cook the chicken breasts.
* Halve the cherry tomatoes, if
  necessary
* Cut the potatoes.

*20 minutes before
you want to eat*

* Preheat the oven to 200°C/400°F/Gas Mark 6.
* Start by cooking the chicken. Season the chicken breasts with salt and pepper. Heat a generous splash of the oil in a heavy-based frying pan over a medium heat, and when the oil is hot add the chicken breasts. Cook for 5 minutes on each side, or until browned. While the chicken is cooking strip the leaves from the rosemary.
* Add a generous squeeze of lemon juice and the rosemary leaves to the chicken and cook for another 5 minutes.
* While the chicken is cooking, put the 'heat and serve' ciabatta in the oven for 10 minutes or according to the instructions on the packet.
* Remove the chicken breasts from the pan and set them aside to rest. Bring any juices in the pan to a rapid boil then pour over the chicken.
* Now make the topping. If the tomatoes are larger than bite sized, slice them in half. Put the tomatoes in a bowl with the onions. Cut the potatoes into bite-sized chunks and throw them in too. Add some seasoning and mix well.
* Next, make the dressing. Mix the aïoli and crème fraîche with 1 tablespoon water. Season according to taste.
* By now the chicken will have rested sufficiently. Cut the breasts widthways into slices about 5 mm thick. Add the slices to the tomato, onion and potato mixture. Pour over the aïoli dressing and fold everything together well. This salad will now sit happily until you are ready to eat.
* Take the ciabatta out of the oven when it's cooked and cut it in half. Cut each half in two lengthways so that you end up with four generous vessels for the salad. Drizzle them with a little oil and add a grinding of pepper.
* Put a ciabatta quarter on each plate and pile a handful of rocket on top, followed by the salad. Serve immediately.

Seasonal supper

Soft Goats' Cheese Salad

This salad relies on using the very best ingredients you can. The tomatoes in particular have to be ripe and sweet. If they are, this is a delightful summer meal.

8 very ripe plum tomatoes,
  approx. 1 kg
1 cucumber
2 bunches radishes, approx.
  400 g
4 little gem lettuces
small handful of fresh flatleaf
  parsley
small handful of fresh mint
  leaves
small handful of fresh coriander
  leaves
4 poppy-seed rolls
400 g soft goats' cheese (the
  freshest and softest you can
  find)
juice of 1 lemon
3 tbsp olive oil
salt and pepper

GET AHEAD PREPARATION (optional)

* Prepare the tomatoes and
  cucumber.
* Wash the radishes and little
  gems.

15 minutes before you want to eat

* Start by chopping everything up. Cut the tomatoes into chunks. Peel, deseed and slice the cucumber. Top and tail the radishes, wash them well and cut them in half. Break up, wash and dry the little gem lettuces. Roughly chop the parsley, mint and coriander.
  Throw all the salad ingredients into a bowl.
* Tear the rolls into chunks, break up the cheese and add the rolls and cheese to the salad.
* Season the salad well with salt and pepper then add the lemon juice and oil.
  Mix together thoroughly so that the cheese starts to disintegrate and becomes part of the dressing.
* Pile the salad on to plates and serve immediately.

Larder feast

Spiced Prawn Couscous

Couscous is the staple food of North Africa and has a light, fluffy texture when cooked. Most couscous purchased in Britain is made with wheat and is a delicious alternative to pasta, rice and potatoes. A simple way to cook couscous is to cover it with boiling hot stock, cover tightly with a lid and allow to steam and absorb the liquid for about 15 minutes. Once cooked, it can be fluffed up with a fork and served either with a little olive oil or butter as an accompaniment, or mixed with vegetables, meat or fish as a complete meal. In this recipe the couscous is combined with a mixture of prawns, chillies, olives and lime to create a light but very tasty meal.

450 ml vegetable stock (made
   from a stock cube or bouillon
   powder)
400 g frozen raw peeled prawns
2 tsp paprika
400 g couscous
6 spring onions
100 g green olives stuffed with
   pimientoes
100 g pickled green chillies
small handful of fresh parsley
3 tbsp olive oil
juice of 1 lime
salt and pepper

To serve
spinach

GET AHEAD PREPARATION (optional)

* Prepare the olives, chilli and
   parsley.

20 minutes before you want to eat

* Put the stock in a pan with the prawns, paprika and a pinch of salt and bring to the boil.
* When the stock is boiling pour in the couscous, take the pan from the heat and cover it either with a tight-fitting lid or cling film and leave it to puff up for 10–15 minutes. In the meantime, trim and slice the spring onions, using as much of the green parts as possible.
* Drain and roughly chop the olives and drain the chillies and cut them into thin slivers. Roughly chop the parsley.
* After 10–15 minutes run a fork through the couscous to fluff it up, then throw in the olives, chillies, spring onions and parsley.
* Stir in the oil and lime juice and season to taste with salt and pepper.
* Serve with spinach.

Two for one

Braised Chicken with Celery and Orange

The flavours of orange and lemon make this chicken braise intense but light. Chicken portions are gently braised in a piquant sauce of tomatoes, oranges, lemons and herbs until the meat is falling from the bones.

This recipe was devised by Rosie and her dad. Quantities are for eight – the intention is that half is frozen for use at a later date.

If there is masses of surplus cooking liquor the surplus can be turned into a soup. See added extra below.

3 tbsp groundnut or grapeseed oil
8 free-range chicken legs (thighs and drumsticks)
4 medium red onions, approx. 480 g
400 ml chicken stock (fresh or made from a stock cube or bouillon powder)
1 head celery
4 garlic cloves
1 orange

2 sprigs fresh sage
300 ml orange juice
500 g passata
pinch of sugar
juice of 1 lemon
4 sprigs fresh mint
salt and pepper

To serve
baked potatoes or couscous or polenta, and peas

GET AHEAD PREPARATION (optional)

The whole dish can be prepared 2 days in advance and warmed through, but if there are only a few spa. If you only have a little time:
* Prepare the onions, garlic and celery.
* Brown the chicken legs and deglaze the pan.
* Soften the vegetables.

1¼ hours before you want to eat

* First brown the chicken. Heat a good splash of oil in a large frying pan, season the chicken legs with salt and pepper and add them in batches to the hot oil. Brown the legs on both sides. While the legs are browning, peel and finely slice the onions.
* When you've finished browning the chicken legs and the onions are sliced, put the legs in a casserole. Pour the stock into the frying pan and stir until it boils, scraping the bottom of the pan. Pour the stock over the chicken legs in the casserole, return the frying pan to the heat and add the remaining oil.
* When the pan and oil are hot, add the onions, turn the heat down and let them soften for 7–10 minutes, stirring every now and then to prevent them sticking; it is fine if they pick up a bit of colour. While the onions are softening, trim, wash and finely slice the celery.
* Add the celery to the onions to soften for another 5 minutes. Add a little extra oil if necessary. While the celery is softening, peel and finely slice the garlic. Cut two slices of orange and strip the sage leaves from their stalks.
* When the celery is soft, add the garlic, orange slices and sage leaves. Stir for a couple of minutes, then add the orange juice and let it come to the boil. Simmer the juice for 5 minutes then add the passata and a pinch of sugar. Bring back to the boil and tip the mixture into to the casserole containing the chicken legs. Squeeze in the lemon juice along with the juice from the sliced orange and season with salt and pepper.
* Bring to a simmer, cover and cook very gently until the chicken is cooked and very tender – it should come away from the bone very easily. This will take 30–45 minutes.

10 minutes before you want to eat

* Preheat the oven to 120°C/250°F/Gas Mark 1.
* Lift the chicken legs out of the casserole, keep four covered in the warm oven and set four aside to cool before freezing.
* Finish the sauce by boiling it rapidly for 5 minutes. While the sauce is boiling, roughly chop the mint leaves. After 5 minutes add the mint and season to taste. If you want the sauce to have a thicker consistency one-third can be blended or liquidised. Either whizz it in food processor then return to the casserole or use a hand blender to pulse it a few times in the casserole.
* Put half the sauce to one side to cool. When it is cold pour it over the cooled chicken legs and freeze.
* Serve the chicken with baked potatoes, couscous or polenta and plenty of peas.

Lazy day supper – reheating instructions

* Defrost the braise thoroughly then preheat the oven to 180°C/350°F/Gas Mark 4.
* Put the chicken legs and sauce in an ovenproof dish, cover and let them reheat in the oven for 25 minutes.

Added extra

Tomato and Orange Soup

Put the remaining sauce in the liquidiser and blend until smooth. It is good hot or cold.

July Week 4 – Overview

Cherries are a sign of summer, and their sweet flesh and hint of sourness are especially good when combined with the juicy richness of duck. Served with roast baby vegetables and spinach, Duck Breasts with Cherries makes a memorable Big Meal from Scratch that takes just over an hour to prepare – this is definitely a meal to share with friends. Be warned, duck breasts are not cheap, but given that the recipe allows for two good meals, the expense seems less criminal. If you are cooking out of season the cherries could, at a push, be canned.

For one of this week's Something for Nothing recipes, extra roast duck breasts are utilised in a Duck Salad with Bacon and Eggs. Ready in just 25 minutes this feels rather indulgent without being difficult. The second Something for Nothing is even quicker – Root Vegetable, Caraway and Feta Salad utilises the roast vegetables from the big meal and transforms them into a salad brimming with flavour. Taking only 15 minutes to make, this is likely to be popular with cook as well as guests.

A Seasonal Supper of Chilled Summer Soup with Prawns on Toast is elegant and very refreshing, and takes 25 minutes in all to make. The recipe can be made with fresh or frozen prawns – just be sure to use fresh ones well within their sell-by date. Stewed Lentils and Tomatoes with Herb and Garlic Cream Cheese, this week's Larder Feast, makes a tomatoey lentil braise that is ready to eat in 25 minutes.

For the Two for One a sweet-sour caponata sauce is made to accompany marinated lamb kebabs. Kebabs and caponata sauce both originate in hot climates so it's no surprise that they are so suited to summer eating. If the weather permits, the kebabs work as well on the barbecue as under the grill. They benefit from being marinated so the meal will take up to 1 hour to make.

July Week 4	Recipe	Time
Big meal from scratch	Duck with cherries, roast baby vegetables and spinach	1¼ hours
Something for nothing 1	Root vegetable, caraway and feta salad with rocket salad	15 mins
Something for nothing 2	Duck salad with bacon and eggs	25 mins
Seasonal supper	Chilled summer soup with prawns on toast	25 mins
Larder feast	Braised lentils with herb cream cheese	25 mins
2 for 1	Lamb kebabs with caponata and rice	1 hour

All recipes serve 4 apart from the 2 for 1 recipe which makes 8 portions

SHOPPING LIST (for 4 people)

Meat and fish
6 free-range duck breasts
160 g free-range rindless streaky bacon
  or lardons
400 g (approx.) Atlantic coldwater cooked
  peeled Atlantic prawns (fresh or frozen)
1.5 kg neck of lamb fillet

Dairy
70 g butter
4 free-range eggs
200 g feta
200 g Boursin with garlic and herbs or cream
  cheese with herbs
300 g Greek yoghurt

Fruit and vegetables
1 kg small new potatoes
800 g baby carrots
500 g large leaf spinach
300 g baby leaf spinach
800 g small courgettes, approx. 7-8
2 large aubergines, approx. 400 g
4 medium red onions, approx. 240 g
3 garlic cloves
4-5 spring onions
100 g rocket
1 large frisée lettuce
4 celery sticks
1 large, ripe avocado
5-6 sprigs fresh thyme
1 bunch fresh mint
1 bunch fresh parsley
4-5 sprigs fresh dill
160 g black cherries (canned if you can't
  find fresh)
4 lemons

Basics
300 ml (approx.) olive oil
3 tbsp groundnut or grapeseed oil
8 slices bread suitable for croûtons and toast
6 pitta breads
1 tbsp dried oregano
2 bay leaves
5 tsp Dijon mustard
pinch of sugar (ideally brown)
1.25 litres chicken or vegetable stock (fresh
  or made from a stock cube or bouillon
  powder)
salt and pepper

Store cupboard
200 g basmati rice
2 × 400 g cans brown lentils
1 × 400 g can cherry tomatoes
2 × 400 g cans chopped tomatoes
80 g sun-dried tomatoes in oil
4 tbsp capers
4 tbsp pitted green olives
3 tbsp sherry vinegar
2 tbsp red wine vinegar
½ tsp balsamic vinegar
2 mild dried red chillies or 1 tsp chilli
  powder
2 tsp ground cinnamon
2 tsp ground cumin
1 tbsp ground coriander
1 tsp allspice
1-2 tsp caraway seeds
2-3 drops Tabasco or other chilli sauce
  (optional for Chilled Summer Soup with
  Prawns on Toast)
1 tbsp mayonnaise
150 ml white wine

Quick option (Duck Salad with Bacon and Eggs)
75-100 g ready-made croûtons; omit 4 slices
  bread from shopping list

Serving suggestions
new potatoes or crusty bread (Duck Salad
  with Bacon and Eggs)
crusty bread (Braised Lentils with Herb
  Cream Cheese)

To download or print out this shopping list,
please visit www.thekitchenrevolution.co.uk/July/
Week4

**Big meal
from scratch**

Duck with Cherries, Roast Baby Vegetables and Spinach

The duck breasts in this recipe are served with a black cherry sauce. The richness of duck meat goes especially well with fruity flavours – plum sauce with Peking duck is a well-known example.

Duck breasts are widely available and are a good alternative to the ubiquitous chicken breasts – they have more flavour and are less susceptible to becoming dry.

The recipe includes extra duck for the Duck Salad with Bacon and Eggs and extra potatoes and carrots for the Root Vegetable, Caraway and Feta Salad.

Duck with cherries
6 free-range duck breasts;
   includes 2 extra breasts
   for the duck salad with bacon
   and eggs
1 tsp ground allspice
160 g black cherries (canned if
   you can't find fresh ones)
150 ml white wine
250 ml chicken stock or
   vegetable stock (fresh or made
   from a stock cube or bouillon
   powder
salt and pepper

Roast baby vegetables
1 kg small new potatoes;
   includes 500 g extra for the
   root vegetable and caraway
   salad
800 g baby carrots; includes
   400 g extra for the root
   vegetable and caraway salad
5-6 sprigs fresh thyme
1 bay leaf
2 tbsp groundnut or grapeseed oil

Spinach
500 g large leaf spinach or 300 g
   baby leaf spinach
15 g butter
½ lemon

GET AHEAD PREPARATION (optional)

* Trim the duck breasts.
* Prepare the cherries.
* Prepare the potatoes and cover
   with water until required.
* Prepare the spinach.

*1¼ hours before
you want to eat
prepare the duck
and cook the
potatoes*

* Preheat the oven to 190°C/375°F/Gas Mark 5.
* Trim the duck breasts by removing any excess fat – the easiest way to do this is to lie each breast skin side down on a board, press it down a little and cut away any fat that protrudes from the sides of the meat. Next, if there are any hard, tube-like bits on the breast flesh, trim these off too. Often these have already been removed so don't worry if you can't find them. Turn the breast over and make three or four slashes to the skin – don't pierce the flesh. Season the breasts all over with the allspice and a couple of pinches of pepper and set them aside.
* Wash the potatoes and cut them in half lengthways if they are more than bite sized. Wash the carrots, strip the thyme leaves from their stalks and tear the bay leaf.
* Place the potatoes on a baking sheet, splash them with some of the oil, season with salt and pepper and scatter with the thyme leaves and bay leaf. Put the baking sheet in the oven so that the potatoes can get a 15-minute start on the carrots.

*45 minutes before
you want to eat*

* After the potatoes have been in the oven for 15 minutes, add the carrots and a little more oil and salt and pepper. Return to the oven for another 30 minutes or so.
* Meanwhile, prepare the cherries – pick off any stalks and wash them well or drain them if you are using canned ones.
* Then prepare the spinach by removing any large, thick stalks and plunging the leaves into a sink of cold water to remove any grit. Once washed leave it to drain in a colander.

*25 minutes before
you want to eat
cook the duck*

* Turn the oven up to 220°C/425°F/Gas Mark 7 or its nearest setting and check the potatoes and carrots. If they aren't cooked move them to the bottom of the oven, but keep checking them – the higher heat should make them brown and crisp but they must also be soft on the inside. When they are cooked, remove them from the oven – they can be warmed up in it 10 minutes before serving.
* Place a roasting tin at the top of the oven for the duck breasts.
* Heat a large heavy-based frying pan over a high heat until it is very hot. Add the duck breasts, skin-side down. Unless you have a very large pan and a very high heat, it is a good idea to cook three at a time. Leave the breasts skin-side down for 6 minutes. If a lot of fat runs out, spoon some of it into a small bowl – it will keep very well in the fridge for six weeks and is great for roasting potatoes.

* After 6 minutes turn the breasts over – the skin should be crisp and golden brown. Let them brown for a minute or so skin-side up, then set them aside while you brown the other three breasts.
* Now put all six breasts into the hot roasting tin, skin sides up. Put them in the oven and leave them to cook for 5–7 minutes, depending on size. Don't wash up the frying pan as the cherry sauce will be made in this.
* After 5–7 minutes in the oven the duck breasts should be pink. Leave them for another 5 minutes if you like them well done.
* While the duck breasts are cooking, fill the base of a steamer or large pan with a few centimetres of water and bring it up to the boil.

10 minutes before you want to eat cook the spinach and cherry sauce

* Remove the duck breasts from the oven and leave them to rest in a warm place while you make the sauce. They will benefit from 10 minutes resting. Put two breasts to one side for later in the week.
* Turn the oven right down and if you removed the roast vegetables from the oven earlier return them now to heat through for 10 minutes. You could also put in some plates and serving dishes to warm.
* Return the frying pan to a high heat and add the cherries. Shake them about for a couple of minutes then add the wine and let it reduce by two-thirds. Add the stock, bring the whole lot back to the boil and simmer gently for 5 minutes while you steam the spinach.
* Place the spinach in the steamer or in the pan of boiling water, put a lid on and let it wilt.
* Taste the cherry sauce and season as necessary.
* When the spinach is soft, lift it out of the steamer or water and drain well before tossing with the butter and and a squeeze of lemon juice. Season well and tip the spinach into a warmed serving dish.
* Take the roast vegetables out of the oven and put them into a warmed serving dish.
* You can either slice the duck breasts or serve them whole with the buttered spinach, roast vegetables and cherry sauce.

Afterwards

Cover the extra duck breasts, put the leftover roast vegetables in an airtight container and refrigerate for use later in the week. Ideally you will have 2 duck breasts and 900 g vegetables.

Something for nothing 1

Root Vegetable, Caraway and Feta Salad with Rocket Salad

The word salad doesn't really do this recipe justice – the flavours are strong and the starchy root vegetables and feta mean it's fairly substantial. Caraway seeds have a deep, nutty, anise flavour that complements the savoury flavours of feta, potato and carrot.

One thing that will make the difference between this being a good salad and a fantastic one is making sure the root vegetables are at room temperature rather than straight from the fridge. If you don't have the time to leave them out for a while before making the salad you could heat them gently in the oven or a frying pan for a few minutes.

If you use the leftover vegetables from the Big Meal from Scratch this supper can be ready in a matter of minutes. If you don't have any, scrub 500 g new potatoes and 400 g carrots and cut them into small dice. Parboil them for 5–10 minutes then drain them. Toss in olive oil, season with thyme, caraway seeds, salt and pepper and bake in a hot oven (200°C/400°F/Gas Mark 6) for 20 minutes.

We serve the salad with warmed pitta breads with a simple rocket salad, but if you're a keen barbecuer you could serve it with sausages, lamb chops or vegetables. It is also a great addition to a mezze.

Root vegetable, caraway
and feta salad
900 g cooked new potatoes and
    carrots left over from the Big
    Meal from Scratch or see above
4–5 spring onions
2 handful of fresh flatleaf
    parsley
1–2 tsp caraway seeds (according
    to taste)
1 lemon
200 g feta
4 tbsp olive oil
6 pitta breads
salt and black pepper

Rocket salad
2 tsp Dijon mustard
pinch sugar (ideally soft brown)
½ tsp balsamic vinegar
2 tbsp olive oil
100 g rocket

GET AHEAD PREPARATION (optional)

* Chop the potatoes and carrots.
* Chop the parsley and spring
  onions.
* Toast the caraway seeds.

15 minutes before you want to eat

* Start by preparing the root vegetable salad. Chop the potatoes and carrots into a fine dice and tip them into a large bowl. Slice the spring onions finely and add them to the bowl. Roughly chop the parsley and add this to the rest of the salad.
* Toast the caraway seeds – place them in a dry frying pan over a medium heat for a minute or so. Watch them like a hawk so that they don't burn.
* Next, make the dressing for the root vegetable salad. Squeeze just under 2 tablespoons juice from the lemon into a bowl or jar. Add the toasted caraway seeds and a generous pinch or two each of salt and pepper. Mix well then add the oil and shake or stir to amalgamate.
* Crumble the feta into the salad. Pour the dressing over the top and mix using a large spoon, taking care not to pulverise the feta. Season to taste.
* Next, make the dressing for the rocket. Squeeze about 1 teaspoon juice from the lemon you used for the root vegetable salad into a bowl with the mustard, sugar, vinegar and a pinch each of salt and pepper. Mix well then stir in the oil.
* Wash and dry the rocket and tip it into a bowl. Dress with the mustard dressing and toss well.
* Cut the pitta breads in half width-wise and toast.
* Put three pitta halves on each plates and pile the root vegetable and feta salad on top. Serve the rocket salad alongside.

Duck Salad with Bacon and Eggs

This is a luxurious twist on a classic French brasserie salad of bacon, eggs, croûtons and frisée lettuce. The addition of duck breast should convert even dedicated meat-eaters to the merits of a salad. Filling and packed with interesting flavours, it is simple and quick to make.

The pale green leaves of frisée have a slightly bitter taste and a crinkly texture. This means they have enough body to withstand the strong flavours and meaty textures in this salad. Making sure the duck is at room temperature will make all the difference in this salad. If it's fridge-cold it will be pretty tasteless and much tougher.

2 cooked duck breasts left over from the Big Meal from Scratch or 2 duck breasts pan-fried and then roasted as in the big meal (see page 324)
4 free-range eggs, if possible
4 slices bread (preferably a little stale) or 75–100 g ready-made croûtons
3 tbsp olive oil, plus extra for the croûtons
1 large frisée lettuce

1 tbsp Dijon mustard
2 tbsp sherry vinegar
1 tbsp groundnut, grapeseed or sunflower oil
160 g free-range streaky bacon or lardons
salt and pepper

To serve
boiled new potatoes or crusty bread

GET AHEAD PREPARATION (optional)

* Soft-boil the eggs.
* Make the croûtons.
* Trim and prepare the frisée.

25 minutes before you want to eat

* Preheat the oven to 190°C/375°F/Gas Mark 5. Remove the duck breasts from the fridge to bring them to room temperature.
* Next, cook the eggs. Boil for 7 minutes then drain and leave to cool under cold running water. When they are completely cold, peel them.
* In the meantime, make the croûtons if you haven't bought ready-made ones. Remove the crusts and then cut the bread into 3-cm cubes. Place on a baking sheet with a little olive oil and salt and pepper. Toss the cubes about to distribute the oil and seasoning and place in the oven for 10–15 minutes until the croûtons are crisp and golden brown.
* While the croûtons are in the oven, remove any tough outer leaves from the frisée, then tear the remaining leaves and wash and thoroughly dry. Thinly slice the duck breasts and set them aside. Next, make the vinaigrette in a bowl large enough to hold all the salad. Whisk together the mustard, 1 tablespoon of the vinegar, the olive and other oil and some seasoning.
* When you are ready to eat the salad, heat a frying pan until hot. Either throw in the lardons or cut the bacon into strips over the pan. Allow them to release their fat and turn crisp over a medium to high heat.
* While the lardons or bacon are cooking slice the duck. Put the frisée and croûtons in the salad bowl with the dressing. Break up two of the eggs and throw them into the salad. Season everything thoroughly.
* When the lardons or bacon are crisp, splash the remaining vinegar into the frying pan and stir to lift all the flavours from the pan. When the vinegar has all but disappeared, tip the lardons and the pan juices into the salad.
* Toss all the salad together well and divide it between four plates. Top each helping with half a soft-boiled egg and a few slices of duck, and serve immediately with boiled new potatoes or crusty bread.

Seasonal supper

Chilled Summer Soup with Prawns on Toast

Chilled soup is refreshing and flavourful, and when it is accompanied by juicy prawns dressed with lemon mayonnaise on buttered toast, it makes a filling supper.

Courgettes can be pricey when they aren't in season, but when they are, the lovely dark green, small ones can be inexpensive. Atlantic or coldwater prawns, the variety that are classically sold in pint jars at pubs or used in prawn cocktails, have a soft texture and sweet taste that works well with this recipe. They are sold frozen and fresh; if using frozen ones put them in a large bowl of water to defrost while you make the soup.

Chilled summer soup
800 g small courgettes, approx. 7–8
1 litre cold chicken or vegetable stock (fresh or made from a stock cube or bouillon powder)
1 large ripe avocado
large handful of fresh mint leaves
1 lemon
300 g Greek yoghurt
salt and pepper

Prawns on toast
400 g (approx.) cooked peeled Atlantic prawns (fresh or frozen)
4 slices bread
½ lemon
4–5 sprigs fresh fresh dill
1 tbsp mayonnaise
2–3 drops Tabasco or other chilli sauce (optional)
70 g approx. butter

GET AHEAD PREPARATION (optional)

The soup can be prepared up to a day in advance. If you only have a little time:
* Defrost the prawns, if necessary.
* Prepare the courgettes and dill.

25 minutes before you want to eat

* If using frozen prawns put them in a bowl of cold water to defrost.
* Next, make the soup. Wash the courgettes and cut them into 1–2-cm slices. Put about 500 ml of the stock into a pan with a lid over a medium heat. Add the courgettes, season well with salt and pepper, cover with the lid and cook for 7–10 minutes so that the courgettes are just soft and retain their dark green colour.
* While the courgettes are cooking zest and juice the lemon and peel and stone the avocado and cut the flesh into chunks. Put the courgettes in a food processor, along with the avocado flesh and half the mint. Add the yoghurt, most of the lemon juice and the remaining stock. Blend until smooth then tip into a large bowl. You may need to do this in two batches. You can use a hand blender if you don't have a food processor. Taste and season, then place in the fridge and chill.
* Now make the prawns on toast. Put the bread on to toast while you prepare the prawn mayonnaise. Roughly chop the dill and mix with the zest, the mayonnaise, chilli sauce, about 1 teaspoon lemon juice and plenty of salt and pepper. Squeeze any liquid from the prawns then mix them into the mayonnaise and set aside. When the toast is ready butter it liberally.
* Remove the soup from the fridge. Finely chop the remaining mint leaves and stir these into the soup. Taste for seasoning, spoon into four large bowls.
* Divide the prawns equally between the slices of toast and serve alongside the soup.

Larder feast

Braised Lentils with Herb Cream Cheese

This is a deceptively simple recipe but one that is packed with flavour – it's a meal that demands crusty bread for mopping the bowl. If you have any leftover bacon or pancetta in the fridge and want a more meaty flavour you could add this to the lentil recipe (snip it straight into the onions when they have softened).

2 tbsp olive oil
2 medium red onions, approx.
   240 g
2 × 400 g cans brown lentils
1 × 400 g can cherry tomatoes
80 g sun-dried tomatoes in oil
2 whole dried mild red chillies
   or 1 tsp chilli powder
1 bay leaf
1 tbsp sherry vinegar

250 ml vegetable stock (made
   from a stock cube or bouillon
   powder)
1 × 200 g Boursin with garlic and
   herbs or cream cheese with
   herbs
salt and pepper

To serve
crusty bread

GET AHEAD PREPARATION (optional)

The braised lentils can be made
2 days in advance. If you only
have a little time:
* Prepare the onions.
* Drain and rinse the lentils.
* Slice the sun-dried tomatoes.

*25 minutes before
you want to eat*

* Heat the oil in a large heavy-based pan over a medium heat. Peel and finely slice the onions and add them to the pan. Cover and cook gently for 7–10 minutes until the onions are beginning to soften. Meanwhile open the can of lentils and drain and rinse them. Open the can of cherry tomatoes and drain and slice the sun-dried tomatoes.
* Add the chillies and bay leaf to the onion and stir them about for a couple of minutes. Add the sun-dried tomatoes and, after a minute, turn up the heat and splash in the vinegar. When the vinegar has sizzled away, add the cherry tomatoes and when they are bubbling add the lentils and stock and bring to a simmer. Leave everything to bubble for 15 minutes.
* When you are ready to serve the lentils, lift out the chillies and season the lentils with salt and pepper to taste. Spoon the lentils into large bowls with a generous dollop of the Boursin or herby cream cheese on top – it should melt into the lentils a little.
* Serve with lots of bread to mop up all the tasty juices.

Two for one

Lamb Kebabs with Caponata and Rice

Lamb behaves wonderfully well on a barbecue or under a grill because the meat is succulent enough to take high heat without much risk of becoming dry. In the Middle East it's common for roadside stalls to sell skewers of marinated lamb cooked over hot coals – the smell fills the air and is impossible to resist.

Salads and vegetable stews often accompany the lamb, and aubergines, tomatoes, garlic and onions is a favourite combination. Versions of this unctuous dish can be found not only throughout the Middle East but all over the Mediterranean too. The version we've given is from Italy and includes the addition of capers and olives. Both these go very happily with the rich, sweetness of lamb.

There is nothing complicated about this recipe. The most time-consuming task is frying the aubergines. Do this in batches and make sure the oil is hot otherwise it will take much longer. We suggest serving this meal with rice but other grains such as couscous or cracked wheat would also work well, especially if mixed with herbs, olive oil and lemon juice. You will need 8-10 wooden or metal skewers for grilling the lamb.

There is enough here for eight, so you can freeze half for another day. The caponata freezes very well, as do the kebabs, though these should be frozen raw in their marinade.

Lamb kebabs
2 tsp ground cinnamon
2 tsp ground cumin
1 tbsp ground coriander
juice of 1 lemon
2 tbsp red wine vinegar
3 tbsp olive oil
1.5 kg neck of lamb fillet
4 lemon wedges
salt and black pepper
8-10 wooden or metl skewers

Caponata
2 large aubergines, approx.
  400 g

olive oil
2 medium red onions, approx.
  240 g
4 celery sticks
3 garlic cloves
1 tbsp dried oregano
2 x 400 g cans chopped tomatoes
4 tbsp capers
4 tbsp pitted green olives
generous handful of fresh parsley

Rice
200 g basmati rice
40 g (approx.) butter

GET AHEAD PREPARATION (optional)

The caponata can be made up to 3 days in advance, and the lamb can be cut into chunks and marinated up to 24 hours ahead of cooking. If you only have a little time:
* Prepare the onions, garlic and celery.
* Cut up and fry the aubergine.
* Chop the parsley.
* Make the marinade.

At least 1 hour before you want to eat marinate the lamb

* Start by making the marinade for the lamb. Put the cinnamon, cumin, coriander, lemon juice, 1 teaspoon each of salt and pepper into a mixing bowl or shallow dish large enough to hold all the lamb. Add the vinegar and oil and mix well.
* Cut the lamb into chunks about the size of a walnut. Add to the marinade and use your hands to rub the marinade all over the meat. Allow the meat to marinate while you make the caponata.
* Light the barbecue if you are planning to use this. If you are using wooden skewers, soak them in cold water for 30 minutes or so to stop them burning and breaking.

At least 45 minutes before you want to eat cook the caponata

* Cut the aubergines into chunks about 4 cm long and wide. Heat 4 tablespoons of the oil in large pan over a high heat. When the oil is very hot add one layer of aubergine chunks. Fry them for 2–3 minutes then turn them and continue to fry. Line a large bowl with kitchen paper and when most of the chunks are browned or starting to colour lift them with a slotted spoon into the bowl. Cook the remaining aubergine chunks in two or three batches, adding a little more oil if necessary.
* While the aubergines are cooking, peel the onions and chop finely. Heat the remaining oil in a pan large enough to hold all the aubergine. When the oil is hot add the onions and cook on a low heat for 5 minutes. Wash and slice the celery and add it to the onions. Peel the garlic cloves and crush or finely chop them.
* When the onions are soft add the aubergines, oregano and garlic and cook over a medium heat for 3–4 minutes, stirring all the while.
* Add the tomatoes, capers, olives and salt and pepper and simmer for at least 20 minutes and up to 50 minutes. The longer you cook the caponata the more intense the flavour – you want something rich and thick. Stir now and then to prevent any burning and to check there is sufficient liquid; splash in a little water if you think it's needed.

25 *minutes before*
you want to eat
cook the rice and
the lamb

* Rinse the rice under cold running water and cook according to the instructions on the packet. It will probably take 20 minutes in total.
* Preheat the grill to medium or check the heat of the barbecue. Take the kebab skewers and thread four or five pieces of lamb along each one. Set half of them aside for freezing.
* Place the remaining kebabs under the grill or on the barbecue for 3–5 minutes until the lamb is brown, then turn them and grill them for the same amount of time on the other side. When they are brown all over, leave them to rest while you get everything else ready.
* Roughly chop the parsley and throw it into the caponata, season as necessary and set half aside to freeze when cold.
* Drain the rice, return it to the pan, stir in the butter and season.
* Pile the rice on to four plates with a generous spoonful of caponata and the kebabs on top and a lemon wedge on the side.
* Freeze the kebabs and caponata separately.

Lazy day supper – reheating instructions

Defrost the kebabs and the caponata thoroughly. Then heat the caponata in a pan over a low heat for about 20 minutes, while you cook some basmati rice (as above) and grill or barbecue the kebabs as in the recipe.

Raspberry Water Ice with Prosecco

This delicate pink water ice is the perfect antidote to a hot day or a heavy meal. Prosecco is a dry, light sparkling white wine from Italy – a good, celebratory and much cheaper alternative to champagne. The recipe calls for 600 ml which means there will a small glass to enjoy while you make the pudding! Alternatively, pour any surplus prosecco over the water ice when it's served if you want to have a slightly more boozy and glamorous end to your meal. There is plenty here for seconds or to save for another day

600 ml prosecco
150 g caster sugar
350 g (approx.) ripe raspberries

1½ hours before you want to eat

* Put the prosecco and sugar into a pan and slowly bring to the boil so that all the sugar dissolves. Remove from the heat.
* Put about half the raspberries to one side. Purée the remaining raspberries using a food processor or hand blender and push the purée through a sieve into the wine mixture. Stir well and leave for about 1 hour to let the fruit macerate and until the entire mixture has cooled to room temperature.
* Once cooled, stir the mixture again and pour it into a container suitable for freezing. Add the remaining raspberries and put in the freezer.
* After 45 minutes or 1 hour give the mixture a stir with a fork, making sure you scrape any icicles from the edges of the container.
* Repeat this every 45 minutes until the raspberry water ice has frozen into slushy crystals and the fresh raspberries are evenly distributed and suspended in the mixture.
* To serve, scrape into chilled glasses.

Apricot Pie

Apricots in season are a wonderful thing. Pies are always good. This combination is excellent.

400 g approx. chilled ready-
    made puff pastry (ready rolled
    if available)
plain flour, for dusting
1 kg apricots
160 g unrefined golden caster
    sugar, plus extra for sprinkling
50 g butter
1 vanilla pod
milk, for brushing

To serve
crème fraîche or ice cream

45 minutes before you want to eat

* Roll out the pastry on a lightly floured work surface to the thickness of a pound coin and a bit bigger than a 20 x 24 cm pie dish.
* Cut the apricots in half and remove their stones.
* Put the apricots into a bowl with the sugar then melt the butter and pour this over the apricots. Split the vanilla pod and scrape the seeds into the bowl.
* Mix the apricot mixture thoroughly and tip into the pie dish. The apricots will shrink a lot when soft so pile them high.
* Preheat the oven to 200°C/400°F/Gas Mark 6.
* Dampen the edge of the pie dish with milk and cut some strips of pastry and press them on to the edge of the dish – this will to help secure the pastry top.
* Now drape the pastry top over the apricots and press it on to the pastry edges. Cut a cross in the top of the pie to let the steam escape. Use the tines of a fork to press the pastry top and pastry strips together.
* Brush the top of the pie with milk and sprinkle a little sugar over it.
* Bake the pie in the oven for 25–30 minutes until the top is golden and crisp and the apricots are soft. If the pastry seems to be getting very brown before the apricots are cooked, cover the pie with foil until the fruit is soft.
* Serve immediately with crème fraîche or ice cream

Gooseberry and Almond Cake

This cake is baked with whole gooseberries in the batter so every bite contains an explosion of sweet and sour loveliness.

125 g butter, plus extra for
  greasing
½ lemon
200 g gooseberries
240 g sugar
150 g plain flour
1 tsp baking powder
150 g whole almonds
2 free-range eggs
2 tbsp groundnut or grapeseed oil
75 ml milk
icing sugar, for dusting

To serve
whipped cream, flavoured with
  elderflower cordial (optional)

55 minutes before you want to eat

* Preheat the oven to 180°C/350°F/Gas Mark 4.
* Grease a 25 cm cake tin with butter, grate the zest from the half lemon and melt the butter. Top and tail the gooseberries, then wash them and toss them in 3 tablespoons of the sugar. Set aside while you make the batter.
* Put the lemon zest, flour, baking powder, almonds and all the remaining sugar into a food processor. Whizz the mixture until it resembles breadcrumbs.
* Whisk the eggs, butter and oil together, pour this into the food processor and pulse once or twice to just mix them through the dry ingredients.
* Finally, add the milk and whizz until the cake batter is smooth. If you don't have a food processor you can use a hand blender to make the batter.
* Pour the batter into the cake tin and scatter the gooseberries over the top. Push them into the batter a little.
* Put the tin into the middle of the oven and bake for 40 minutes until the cake is golden and springs back when you touch it with your finger.
* When the cake is cooked put it on a rack to cool. When it has cooled a little dust it with icing sugar. Serve warm with whipped cream, flavoured with elderflower cordial if you have some to hand.

Greengage Clafoutis

Clafoutis comes from the Limousin region of France and is, in its traditional form, a batter filled with cherries and baked in an earthenware dish. Other fruits work as well as cherries and greengages are no exception. You can replace them with small plums if you wish.

450 g ripe greengages
unsalted butter, for greasing
150 g plain flour
250 g sugar
4 free-range eggs
250 ml milk
2 tbsp brandy or kirsch
  (optional)
salt

45 minutes before you want to eat

* Preheat the oven to 200°C/400°F/Gas Mark 6.
* Wash the greengages, cut them in half and remove the stones.
* Butter a 25 cm pie dish and place the greengages in the dish in one layer, flesh-side down.
* Put the flour, sugar, and a pinch of salt in a bowl or food processor. Add the eggs one at a time while mixing continuously, then pour in the milk and finally the brandy or kirsch, if using. Mix until smooth then pour the batter over the greengages.
* Bake in the oven for about 30 minutes until the clafoutis is firm and puffed up. Serve immediately.

AUGUST

In August there are vegetables, fruits and salad stuffs galore – all the tastes of summer. We'll be able to make spaghetti sauce with raw, ripe tomatoes, basil leaves and olive oil, and Sea Bream with Grated Fennel and Courgettes. On especially hot days, roast chicken with Middle Eastern spices, served with a butter bean salad will taste even better cooled to room temperature. If work, commuting and the heat are taking their toll, the Tuscan Bread Salad, Chicken and Sweetcorn Tortilla Salad and Roast Tomato Tapenade Tart are quick and delicious. The pudding recipes this month continue to celebrate seasonal soft fruits and three of our four puddings use strawberries, melons, nectarines or peaches. And it would be a shame to forget chocolate just because it's hot, so there's also a recipe for an Iced Chocolate Meringue.

August	Week 1	Week 2	Week 3	Week 4
Big meal from scratch	Salmon with lemon horseradish, and wild rice salad and beetroot salad	Roast pork loin with a herb crust, and roast tomato salad and potato salad	Thyme and lemon cod with skordalia and sweet pepper potatoes and sweetcorn	Chermoula chicken, butter bean salad and mushy courgettes
Something for nothing 1	Wild rice chilli	Pork teriyaki with noodles and crunchy salad	Chicken and sweetcorn tortilla salad	Rosie's coronation chicken
Something for nothing 2	Warm salmon potato salad	Roast tomato tapenade tart	Low-rise summer soufflé with tomato salad	Butter bean and roast pepper soup
Seasonal supper	Jane's fresh tomato spaghetti	Sea bream with grated fennel and courgettes	Bagna cauda – summer vegetables with anchovy dressing	Panzanella – Tuscan bread salad
Larder feast	Spiced roast vegetables with seasoned yoghurt	Russian salad with tuna and hot buttered potatoes	Quinoa with aubergine and olive relish	Coconut mackerel with green Thai rice
2 for 1	Baked chicken with courgettes and tarragon	Gnocchi verde with puttanesca sauce	Braised pork with fennel and tomatoes	Spinach and smoked trout roulade
Puddings	Baked cheesecake with strawberries	Iced chocolate meringue	Melon, nectarine and grape salad with muscat syrup	Baked peaches

August Week 1 – Overview

Pale pink salmon, ruby-red beetroot and speckled white and brown rice mean that this week's Big Meal from Scratch is as handsome to look at as it is lovely to eat. From start to finish the meal will take 1½ hours but much of this is rice cooking time and won't involve any exertion. Beetroot can be bought uncooked or cooked, but avoid pickled beetroot. Remember to cook fresh fish soon after its been purchased or otherwise place it in the freezer and defrost as required.

The big meal leaves enough rice to make a spicy Chilli that takes 45 minutes to cook – about 30 minutes of this is when ingredients are simmering rather than involved cooking so this Something for Nothing is not too demanding. It's worth bearing in mind that cooked rice doesn't keep too well so the chilli is best cooked soon after the big meal. Extra salmon becomes the dressing for a Warm Potato Salad that is ready in 30 minutes.

The Seasonal Supper, Jane's Tomato Spaghetti, is simplicity itself and is ready in the time it takes the pasta to cook. There's no cooking involved in this recipe and the resulting dish of ripe tomatoes and basil tossed with olive oil and pasta is the essence of summer. Buy the best tomatoes you can for this. It will really pay off. A Larder Feast of Spiced Roast Vegetables with Seasoned Yoghurt takes about 40 minutes but the entire dish can be made in advance and kept in the fridge if this helps the week's order of cooking.

The Baked Chicken with Courgettes and Tarragon, the Two for One, is a light casserole well suited to hot weather. Altogether this agreeable summer supper takes about an hour so it is better cooked at leisure rather than under pressure.

August Week 1	Recipe	Time
Big meal from scratch	Salmon with lemon horseradish, and wild rice salad and beetroot salad	1½ hours
Something for nothing 1	Wild rice chilli	45 mins
Something for nothing 2	Warm salmon potato salad	30 mins
Seasonal supper	Jane's fresh tomato spaghetti	20 mins
Larder feast	Spiced roast vegetables with seasoned yoghurt	40 mins
2 for 1	Baked chicken with courgettes and tarragon	1 hour

All recipes serve 4 apart from the 2 for 1 recipe which makes 8 portions

SHOPPING LIST (for 4 people)

Meat and fish
2 × 650 g unskinned sides of salmon or 2 × 600 g skinned salmon fillets
6 free-range chicken breasts, skinless if possible

Dairy
120 g butter
300 g cottage cheese
50-75 g (approx.) Parmesan
200-300 g Greek yoghurt
600 ml sour cream
30-45 ml crème fraîche

Fruit and vegetables
1.2 kg new potatoes (Charlotte or Pink Fir Apple if possible)
400 g (approx.) uncooked beetroot or 400 g cooked beetroot (*not* pickled in vinegar)
6 medium courgettes, approx. 750 g
2 green peppers, approx. 300 g
500 g ripe tomatoes - best quality you can find
1 cucumber
80-100 g rocket
4 medium onions, approx. 480 g
1 large or banana shallot, approx. 30 g
3 large bunches spring onions
8 garlic cloves
½-1 fresh jalapeno or green chilli (depending on how hot you like it)
2 large bunches fresh parsley
10 sprigs fresh dill
3 sprigs fresh thyme
1 small bunch fresh mint
1 large bunch fresh coriander
1 small bunch fresh basil
8 sprigs fresh tarragon
4½ lemons
2 avocadoes
1 lime
700-800 g frozen grilled or chargrilled mixed vegetables, or fresh mixed peppers, courgettes and aubergines

Basics
180 ml olive oil
75 ml extra virgin olive oil
30 ml groundnut or grapeseed oil
1 tsp dried oregano
1 bay leaf
pinch of sugar
1 heaped tbsp cornflour
500ml vegetable stock (made from a stock cube or bouillon powder)
750ml chicken stock (fresh or made from a stock cube or bouillon powder)
1 bag tortilla chips
salt and pepper

Store cupboard
250 g brown long grain rice and 200 g wild rice or 400 g ready-mixed brown and wild rice
350-450 g spaghetti
1 × 400 g can kidney beans
1 × 400 g can chickpeas
2 × 400 g cans chopped tomatoes
2 tsp sesame seeds (toasted if possible)
1 tbsp balsamic vinegar
35 ml (approx.) white wine vinegar
3 tbsp grated horseradish or 4 tbsp horseradish sauce
1-2 tsp paprika
2 pinches of cayenne pepper
2-3 pinches of ground mace
generous pinch of nutmeg (ground or freshly grated)
1 tsp crushed chillies or cayenne pepper (or more depending on taste)
2 tsp ground cumin
1 tsp ground coriander
1 tsp ground cinnamon
330 ml white wine
2 tbsp sherry (optionals for Warm Salmon Potato Salad)

Serving suggestions
Couscous or flatbreads (Spiced Roast Vegetables with Seasoned Yoghurt)
Green salad ingredients, spinach or Swiss chard (Baked Chicken with Courgettes and Tarragon)

To download or print out this shopping list, please visit www.thekitchenrevolution.co.uk/August/Week1

Salmon with Lemon Horseradish, and Wild Rice Salad and Beetroot Salad

This is a great way to cook salmon; it tastes and looks fantastic, and is extremely simple to make. Two whole salmon fillets are sandwiched together with a lemon horseradish cream and baked in the oven. Baking them with wine and wrapping them in foil helps the fillets stay moist.

Rice salad, like so many other buffet table favourites, has a bad reputation. This is justified when it consists of quick-boil rice mixed with frozen peas and bottled dressing. By contrast, this rice salad recipe is made with liberal quantities of herbs and uses a mixture of brown long grain and wild rice so that it has plenty of taste and texture.

Beetroot is prolific at this time of year and its earthy flavours go well with dill and balsamic vinegar. It is fine to use red beetroot but if you come across the golden, candy striped varieties use these as they look beautiful.

The recipe includes extra wild rice salad for the Wild Rice Chilli and extra salmon for the Warm Salmon Potato Salad.

Salmon with lemon horseradish
3 tbsp grated horseradish and 3 tbsp crème fraîche or 4 tbsp horseradish sauce and 2 tbsp crème fraîche
1 generous bunch fresh parsley
4 generous sprigs fresh dill
1 lemon
2 × 650 g unskinned sides of salmon or 2 × 600 g skinned salmon fillets; includes 450g extra for the warm salmon potato salad
100 ml white wine
salt and black pepper

Wild rice salad (makes double quantities for the wild rice chilli)
200 g wild rice and 250 g brown long grain rice or 400 g ready-mixed wild and brown rice

750 ml (approx.) chicken or vegetable stock (fresh or made from a stock cube or bouillon powder)
2 bunches spring onions
1 small bunch fresh parsley
generous handful of fresh mint leaves
3 sprigs fresh dill
juice of 1 lemon
4-5 tbsp olive oil

Beetroot
400 g (approx.) uncooked beetroot or 400 g cooked beetroot (*not* pickled in vinegar)
1 tbsp olive oil
1 tbsp balsamic vinegar

GET AHEAD PREPARATION (optional)

The rice salad and beetroot salad can be made a day in advance, though hold the herbs until just before serving. If you only have a little time:
* Make the salmon filling.
* Cook the beetroot.
* Chop the parsley and dill and mix with the lemon zest.
* Chop the spring onions, parsley, mint and dill for the rice salad.

1½ hours before you want to eat cook the rice

* Start by cooking the rice as this is served at room temperature and will take a while to cook. The two types of rice will cook at different times – usually 20–35 minutes for brown rice and up to 1 hour for wild rice. Follow the instructions on the packets for both the brown and wild rice, but for the brown rice replace the water with stock.

1¼ hours before you want to eat cook the beetroot

* Preheat the oven to 180°C/350°F/Gas Mark 4.
* If you have ready-cooked beetroot continue to the next step. If you have bought raw beetroot, cook them now. Wash them thoroughly, place in a large pan of salted boiling water then leave to simmer with a lid. Ideally the beetroot should retain some bite rather than becoming completely soft but the length of time they take to cook will very much depend on how big they are. For beets the size of cricket balls reckon on simmering for about 45 minutes. Increase or decrease this approximate timing according to the size of the beets you have.

1 hour before you want to eat cook the salmon

* Once you've got the beetroot and rice on the go, start preparing the salmon. First, make the filling. Mix together the horseradish and crème fraîche in a bowl. Chop the parsley finely and roughly chop the dill – you can use scissors if this is easier. Add the herbs to the horseradish. Grate the lemon zest and add this to the creamy mixture, then squeeze in the juice of half the lemon. Season with 1 teaspoon pepper and ½ teaspoon salt, mix well and set aside.

* Now prepare the foil. Place a piece of foil well over two times the length of the salmon over the base of a roasting tin large enough to hold the salmon fillets. (If your sheets are not long enough you may have to cut the fillets in half and instead of making one long sandwich, make two shorter ones).
* Place one of the salmon fillets on the foil (skin-side down if it isn't skinned). Season the upper side with salt and pepper. Using a knife, evenly spread three-quarters of the horseradish mixture over the salmon in the roasting tin. Place the remaining fillet on top to make a sandwich (skin side up if it isn't skinned). Season the skin side with salt and pepper, any last drops of juice from the lemon and pour the wine over the top.
* Now fold the length of foil over the fish and bring the edges together by twisting them so that you have an airtight foil parcel. Place the salmon in the oven for 45 minutes.
* Cover the remaining horseradish and herb cream and place in the fridge until you come to serve.

45 minutes before you want to eat make both salads

* While the salmon is cooking, finish the rice. Check that it is cooked, drain it if necessary and place in a large serving bowl. Mix the wild and brown rice together if it isn't already mixed. Finely chop the spring onions, parsley, mint and dill and add them to the rice. Mix the lemon juice and oil and pour over the salad. Season with ½ teaspoon salt and 1 teaspoon pepper. Mix together well and set aside to allow the flavours to infuse and the rice to cool to room temperature.
* Once the beetroot are cooked, peel them under cold running water. When they are not too hot to handle, cut them into 5-mm slices and arrange them on a serving plate. Mix together the oil, vinegar and a good dose of seasoning and drizzle this over the beetroot.

5 minutes before you want to eat

* Take the salmon from the oven and let it rest for a couple of minutes before you peel back the foil. This should prevent you being burned by the steam, but do take care when you remove the foil. Peel the skin on top of the salmon away. Cut the fillets into generous slices, removing the bottom layer of skin from each helping.
* Drizzle the salmon with any juices from the bottom of the roasting tin and serve with the beetroot and rice salads, and the remaining horseradish and crème fraîche mixture.

Afterwards

Remove the skin from the leftover salmon (400 g) and break it into flakes. Put the salmon and the remaining rice (400 g) in separate containers, cover and refrigerate for use later in the week.

Wild Rice Chilli

For this chilli, kidney beans and rice are cooked with a mixture of seasonings and served with soured cream, tortillas and fresh coriander. It's unlikely that even die-hard carnivores will notice the absence of meat. The recipe takes a little longer than you'd ideally spend on a week night, but it's quick to prepare and then it just cooks gently for the best part of half an hour. Be led by your own taste buds for this recipe – add as much or as little chilli as you desire.

This recipe is inspired by Madhur Jaffrey's Tex-Mex chilli recipe.

2 tbsp groundnut or grapeseed
  oil
2 medium onions, approx. 240 g
2 green peppers, approx. 300 g
4 garlic cloves
½–1 fresh jalapeno or green
  chilli (depending on how hot
  you like it)
1–2 tsp paprika (smoked if
  possible)
3 sprigs fresh thyme
pinch of cayenne pepper
1 tsp ground cumin
1 tsp dried oregano
1 tbsp white wine vinegar

1 × 400 g can kidney beans
500 ml vegetable stock (made
  from a stock cube or bouillon
  powder)
1 × 400 g can chopped tomatoes
400 g cooked wild and brown
  rice left over from the Big Meal
  from Scratch or 150 g brown
  rice and 100 g wild rice,
  cooked
2 avocados
1 lime
large handful of fresh coriander
1 bag tortilla chips
200 ml (approx.) soured cream

GET AHEAD PREPARATION (optional)

The chilli can be prepared 2
days in advance up to the point
where you add the rice. If you
only have a little time:
* Prepare the onions, peppers,
  garlic and chilli.

*45 minutes before
you want to eat*

* Heat the oil in a large heavy-based pan over a medium heat. Peel and finely slice the onions and add them to the pan. Cook the onions gently for 7–10 minutes while you, core, deseed and finely slice the green peppers, peel and crush the garlic and deseed and finely slice the chilli.
* When the onions have softened a little, add the peppers to the pan and soften them for 3–5 minutes.
* When the peppers are soft, add the garlic and chilli and cook for a couple of minutes. Strip the thyme leaves from their stalks.
* Turn up the heat and throw in the paprika, cayenne, cumin, thyme and oregano and cook for a minute or so, stirring to prevent sticking.
* Splash in the vinegar and stir while it bubbles and evaporates. Add the kidney beans and stock, turn up the heat and bring to the boil. Add the tomatoes to the pan and boil vigorously for 15 minutes.
* After 10 minutes, stir in the rice and simmer for another 5 minutes while you prepare the accompaniments. Peel, stone and chop up the avocados, squeeze some lime juice over them and season with salt and pepper. Roughly chop the coriander.
* Put the avocados, tortilla chips, soured cream and half the coriander in separate bowls on the table. Finally taste the chilli, stir in the remaining coriander and season as necessary.
* Serve in big bowls and let people add their own toppings.

**Something
for nothing 2**

Warm Salmon Potato Salad

In this recipe salmon, new potatoes and cucumber – a classic combination – are brought together with a buttery, spiced dressing. The result is summery but substantial. If there is no salmon remaining from the Big Meal from Scratch, use 400 g fresh skinned salmon fillets. Season them with salt, pepper and a squeeze of lemon juice and bake them in foil in the oven (180°C/350°F/Gas Mark 4) for 20–30 minutes until cooked.

800 g new potatoes (each about
   the size of a small egg), such
   as Charlotte or Pink Fir Apple
1 large or banana shallot,
   approx. 30 g
2 tbsp sherry or white wine
good pinch of cayenne pepper
2-3 pinches of ground mace
generous pinch of nutmeg
100 g butter
400 g cooked salmon fillet left
   over from the Big Meal from
   Scratch or see above
2 spring onions
3 sprigs fresh dill

1 cucumber
pinch of sugar
1 tsp white wine vinegar
juice of 1 lemon
salt and pepper

GET AHEAD PREPARATION (optional)

* Prepare the potatoes and
  shallot.
* Prepare the spring onions and
  dill.
* Peel and deseed the cucumber.

*30 minutes before
you want to eat*

* First, cook the potatoes. If they are large, cut them into bite-sized pieces then put them in a pan of salted water. Bring them to the boil and simmer until cooked. This will take about about 15 minutes.
* While the potatoes are cooking, peel and slice the shallots and add them to a small pan over a high heat with the sherry or wine and the cayenne, mace and nutmeg. Boil quite briskly until the liquid has reduced so that the shallot is just glistening with moisture.
* When the liquid has reduced, add the butter to the pan. When all the butter has melted, turn the heat to its lowest setting and leave the butter and shallot mixture to cook very gently so that the flavours infuse. Check on it from time to time and stir.
* In the meantime, break the salmon into flakes.
* Trim and chop the spring onions, using as much of the green parts as you can and place them in another bowl. Chop the dill (or you may find it easier to snip it with scissors). Peel and dice the cucumber and add to the spring onions with some salt and pepper, a pinch of sugar, the vinegar and the dill
* After about 15 minutes, remove the butter and shallot mixture from the heat and leave it to cool for a minute. Stir the butter and shallot into the salmon with the lemon juice, salt and pepper to taste, and set aside.
* When the potatoes are cooked, drain them well, put them into a bowl with some seasoning and crush them gently using a fork.
* Next, add the salmon mixture and toss it with the potatoes as though with a dressing. Serve the potatoes and salmon on individual plates with piles of cucumber salad on top.

Seasonal supper

Jane's Fresh Tomato Spaghetti

Polly's mum has been serving this spaghetti dish on hot summer days for as long as Polly can remember. Other than the spaghetti, nothing is cooked for this recipe, which makes it exceedingly simple to make but deceptively easy to ruin – if the tomatoes, olive oil or Parmesan are of an indifferent quality the taste will be indifferent. If you have good quality raw materials, however, this is a summer recipe that is hard to beat.

350-450 g spaghetti (depending on how hungry you are)
500 g ripe tomatoes (the most flavourful you can find)
75 ml extra virgin olive oil, plus extra for serving
2 large handfuls of basil leaves, approx. 20-30
50-75 g Parmesan
½ lemon
300 g cottage cheese
80-100 g rocket
salt and pepper

GET AHEAD PREPARATION (optional)

The tomato mixture, minus the cheese, can be made a couple of hours in advance and allowed to marinate. If you only have a little time:
* Chop the tomatoes.
* Grate the Parmesan.

20 minutes before you want to eat

* Put the spaghetti on to cook according to the manufacturer's instructions – usually 10 minutes in boiling water.
* Meanwhile prepare the sauce. Chop the tomatoes into 1 cm chunks. Tip them into a colander sitting over a bowl as you go – this will help to remove any excess liquid or pips. It's not worth going through the onerous task of seeding all the tomatoes but get rid of any pips that can easily be discarded. When all the tomatoes are chopped, tip them into a large bowl.
* Pour in all but 1 tablespoon of the oil and all but a squeeze of the lemon juice. Roughly chop the basil leaves and add these. Add 1 teaspoon each of salt and pepper. Set aside at room temperature to infuse.
* Meanwhile grate the Parmesan and place it in a serving bowl.
* Just before the spaghetti is cooked, add the cottage cheese to the tomato mixture and stir well. Taste for seasoning then set aside.
* Drain the spaghetti thoroughly, then add the tomato and cottage cheese mixture. Toss very well and divide between four bowls. Serve with the Parmesan and extra olive oil on the side, and the rocket, tossed in the remaining oil, a squeeze of lemon, and seasoned with salt and pepper.

Larder feast

Spiced Roast Vegetables with Seasoned Yoghurt

Here, North Africa meets the Mediterranean in a mezze-style dish of roasted vegetables in a cumin and coriander flavoured dry tomato sauce. This is a dish that can be served hot or cold, and in fact improves with time – so it's a useful recipe to remember.

As this is a Larder Feast, we have suggested using the frozen chargrilled mixed vegetables that are in the freezer cabinets of most supermarkets, but this would be good using fresh peppers, courgettes and onions if available. Flatbreads or couscous work well as an accompaniment.

Spiced roast vegetables
700-800 g frozen chargrilled mixed vegetable or fresh mixed vegetables, such as peppers, courgettes and aubergines
5 tablespoons olive oil
2 medium onions, approx. 240 g
4 garlic cloves
1 tsp crushed chillies or cayenne pepper (or more depending on taste)
1 tsp ground cumin
1 tsp ground coriander
1 tsp ground cinnamon
1 tbsp white wine vinegar

1 x 400 g can chickpeas
1 x 400 g can chopped tomatoes
small handful of fresh coriander
small handful of fresh flatleaf parsley (optional)
salt and pepper

Seasoned yoghurt
200-300 g Greek yoghurt
2 tsp sesame seeds (toasted if possible)
1 tbsp olive oil
salt and pepper

To serve
couscous or warmed flatbreads

GET AHEAD PREPARATION (optional)

The spiced roast vegetables and the seasoned yoghurt can be made up to a day ahead. If you only have a little time:
* Prepare the onions and garlic.
* Toast the sesame seeds.
* Chop the herbs.
* Season and drain the yoghurt.

40 minutes before you want to eat

* Preheat the oven to 220°C/425°F/Gas Mark 7 or its nearest setting.
* Season the yoghurt with salt and pepper and tip it into a fine sieve over a bowl. This will help to thicken it. Cover the yoghurt with a plate and leave to drain.
* Put the vegetables on a large baking sheet and drizzle some of the oil over them. Season and mix them together, then spread them out into a single layer. Place in the oven for 20 minutes.
* While the vegetables are roasting, toast the sesame seeds, if necessary, on a baking sheet for 1-2 minutes until golden brown.
* Peel and finely slice the onions. Heat 2 tablespoons of the oil in a heavy-based pan over a medium heat, add the onions and cook for about 7–10 minutes, stirring every now and then, until they soften. Peel and slice the garlic.
* When the onions have softened, add the chilli or cayenne and stir for a couple more minutes, then add the cumin, coriander and cinnamon. Turn up the heat and roast the spices for a few minutes to bring out their flavour. Add the garlic and a little more oil, and cook for a minute.
* Splash in the vinegar and let it evaporate completely before adding the chickpeas. Stir the mixture well. Now add the tomatoes and bring them to the boil. Let this mixture bubble quite vigorously over a medium to high heat, with the lid off, for 10 minutes so that it becomes thick and rich.
* Stir the vegetables into the spicy tomato mixture and simmer for another 5 minutes. Chop the coriander and parsley, throw them in and season to taste. Take the vegetables off the heat to cool a little before serving.
* In the meantime, tip the yoghurt out of the sieve and stir in the oil and toasted sesame seeds.
* When you are ready to serve, put the roast vegetables in a big dish with the seasoned yoghurt on top and pass round warmed flatbreads or couscous.

Two for one

Baked Chicken with Courgettes and Tarragon

This creamy chicken dish has light, summery flavours. It is a meal in itself, but would go well with a salad, spinach or Swiss chard. Tarragon has a unique flavour that is difficult to replicate – hints of aniseed and vanilla. With tarragon, a little goes a long way, so if you have part of a packet left over you can freeze it for another time (see page 137). Most supermarkets and grocers should sell tarragon, especially in the summer, but if it's impossible to find use basil instead – the flavour will be different but good.

6 free-range chicken breasts
200 ml white wine
1 bay leaf
6 medium courgettes,
 approx. 750 g
400 g new potatoes
1 heaped tbsp cornflour
400 ml soured cream
8 spring onions
8 sprigs fresh tarragon
20 g butter
1 lemon
salt and pepper

To serve
green salad or a green vegetable
 (see above)

GET AHEAD PREPARATION (optional)

The chicken and courgette mixture can be made a day in advance, but if put in the oven cold will need a further 10 minutes cooking time. If you only have a little time:
* Poach the chicken.
* Prepare the courgettes.
* Slice and cook the potatoes.
* Prepare the spring onions.

1 hour before you want to eat

* Preheat the oven to 200°C/400°F/Gas Mark 6.
* First, poach the chicken breasts. Cut each breast into six pieces and season them well with salt and pepper. Put the pieces in a large pan with the wine, bay leaf, some salt and a generous grinding of pepper. Fill the pan with water to just cover the chicken, put over a medium heat and bring to a gentle simmer.
* While the chicken pieces are coming to a simmer, prepare the courgettes. Wash and top and tail them and, if they are thick, cut them in half lengthways and then into 1-cm thick slices.
* As soon as the courgettes are ready, add them to the chicken, put a lid on the pan and bring to a simmer. Leave to simmer for 3–5 minutes until the chicken has turned opaque and the courgettes have softened a little.
* While the chicken and courgettes are cooking, cut the potatoes into slices the thickness of a pound coin. You are going to cook them in the liquid the chicken and courgettes are poaching in.
* When the chicken and courgettes are ready, lift them out of the pan with a slotted spoon and place them in a colander to drain well. Take 4 tablespoons of the cooking liquor out of the pan and put it into a large bowl. Add the cornflour and whisk the two together.
* Now put the potatoes in the hot cooking liquor in the pan, add a pinch more salt, turn the heat up and let the potatoes come to the boil. Turn the heat down and simmer for 10 minutes or until they are just cooked.
* Add the soured cream to the cornflour mixture and stir well, then add the chicken pieces and courgettes while they are still warm. Mix well so that so that everything becomes coated in the creamy mixture.
* Trim the spring onions and chop them into 2-cm pieces using as much of the green parts as you can. Strip the tarragon leaves from their stalks. Throw the spring onions and tarragon leaves into the bowl containing the chicken and courgettes. Mix well and add a good dose of seasoning.
* Set half aside to cool and put the remaining mixture into an ovenproof dish. Make sure the chicken pieces and courgettes are evenly distributed.
* By now the potatoes should be tender, so drain and return them to the pan. Season well and add the butter. Grate the zest from half the lemon and squeeze the juice from all of it on to the potatoes and toss through.

* Put the potatoes in a layer over the chicken and courgettes, and place in the oven. Bake for 10–15 minutes until the top is crisp and golden and the underneath is bubbling and hot.
* When the reserved chicken and courgette mixture is cold freeze it.

Lazy day supper – reheating instructions

* Defrost the chicken and courgettes completely before reheating.
* Preheat the oven to 200°C/400°F/Gas Mark 6. Put the chicken and courgette mixture into an ovenproof dish and put it into the oven to warm up. Slice some potatoes and boil them until they are just cooked, then continue as above.

August Week 2 – Overview

If friends or family are visiting over the bank holiday weekend, Roast Pork Loin with a Herb Crust, Roast Tomato Salad and Potato Salad might prove popular. The recipe calls for pork loin but this could, at a push, be replaced with a leg. Either way, the pork benefits from marinating at least 40 minutes so this needs to be taken into account.

To make a Roast Tomato and Tapenade Tart, one of this week's Something for Nothings surplus roast tomatoes from the big meal are used. It's an easy and tasty recipe that you'll be happy to serve to friends and family. Leftover pork, meanwhile, is a key ingredient in the recipe for Pork Teriyaki with Noodles. Teriyaki sauce is quick to make, and the ingredients are available in most supermarkets.

For entertaining, a meal that's less substantial than the big meal, but which is elegant and attractive, is the Sea Bream with Grated Fennel and Courgettes. With a food processor to help with grating it can be on the table in 25 minutes. Without a processor, factor in some arm-aching grating. It isn't absolutely necessary to find sea bream as grey mullet or sea bass can be used instead. Be sure to cook this recipe soon after purchasing the fish or otherwise place the fish in a freezer until you are ready to cook it.

An up-to-date interpretation of an old classic is the Larder Feast of Russian Salad with Tuna. Making this recipe will only take as long as new potatoes take to cook – 25 minutes or thereabouts.

This week the Two for One of Gnocchi Verde with Puttanesca Sauce can be cooked according to mood and time. If you're feeling relaxed and enthused about being in the kitchen there's a recipe for making the gnocchi as well as an intense puttanesca sauce. If the kitchen is not where you want to be, your labours can be halved by making the sauce but buying the gnocchi ready-made. The sauce takes half an hour to assemble but has to cook slowly for 1 hour for the flavours to marry and intensify. While the sauce is cooking there's time to make the gnocchi, if you are so inclined.

August Week 2	Recipe	Time
Big meal from scratch	Roast pork loin with a herb crust, and roast tomato salad and potato salad	2 hours 50 mins
Something for nothing 1	Roast tomato tapenade tart	35 mins
Something for nothing 2	Pork teriyaki with noodles and crunchy salad	30 mins
Seasonal supper	Sea bream with grated fennel and courgettes	25 mins
Larder feast	Russian salad with tuna and hot buttered potatoes	25 mins
2 for 1	Gnocchi verde with puttanesca sauce	1½ hours

All recipes serve 4 apart from the 2 for 1 recipe which makes 8 portions

SHOPPING LIST (for 4 people)

Meat and fish
8-bone free-range loin of pork or rack (ask
the butcher to chine and skin it) or 1 x 1.3
kg skinned, boned and rolled loin of pork
200 g thinly sliced pancetta or free-range
rindless smoked back bacon
4 x 200 g approx. sea bream fillets

Dairy
85 g butter
200 ml natural yoghurt
150 g Parmesan
2 large free-range eggs

Fruit and vegetables
1 kg new potatoes
1.4 kg mashing potatoes, such as Maris Piper
or baking potatoes
2-3 carrots, approx. 250 g
3 courgettes, approx. 300 g
100 g beansprouts
1 small mooli (white radish), approx. 300 g,
or 150 g salad radishes
12 large ripe tomatoes, approx. 1.2 kg (plum
tomatoes it possible)
250 g rocket
6 celery sticks
2 bulbs fennel, approx. 400 g
2 heads chicory (red if possible)
6 medium onions, approx. 720 g
6 small red onions, approx. 420 g
2 large or banana shallots, approx. 60 g
1 bunch spring onions
9 garlic cloves
2 red chillies
1 small bunch chives
10-12 sprigs fresh thyme
1 large bunch fresh flatleaf parsley
1 large bunch fresh basil
2 sprigs fresh sage
2½ lemons
1 lime
150 g frozen peas

Basics
180 ml olive oil
100 g breadcrumbs or 2-3 slices bread
suitable for crumbing
1 tsp Dijon mustard
2 tbsp tomato purée
2 bay leaves
2½ tbsp sugar
260 g plain flour
500 ml chicken stock (fresh or made from a
stock cube or bouillon powder)
salt and pepper

Store cupboard
4 tbsp mirin
300 g dried soba, buckwheat or egg noodles
250 g chilled filo pastry
1 x 400 g can artichoke hearts
1 x 185 g can tuna (ideally in olive oil, but
in brine if you prefer)
4 x 400 g cans chopped tomatoes
1 x 400 g can celery hearts
200 g pickled beetroot (approx. 3-4)
150 g capers
150 g pitted black olives
2 tbsp sesame seeds
1 tbsp toasted sesame oil
2 tsp balsamic vinegar
5 tbsp white wine vinegar
6 tbsp mayonnaise
4 tbsp soy sauce
3 tbsp tapenade
300 ml white wine
4 tbsp sake
1-2 pinches chilli powder

Quick options
6-8 tbsp ready-made teriyaki sauce (Pork
Teriyaki with Noodles and Crunchy Salad);
omit 4tbsp sake and 4 tbsp mirin from
shopping list
400 g ready-made dried gnocchi or 800
g fresh gnocchi (Gnocchi Verde with
Puttanesca Sauce); omit 1.4 kg mashing
potatoes and 2 free-range eggs from
shopping list

Serving suggestions
green salad ingredients (Roast Tomato
Tapenade Tart and Gnocchi Verde with
Puttanesca Sauce)
bulghar wheat or couscous (Sea Bream with
Grated Fennel and Courgettes)

To download or print out this shopping list,
please visit www.thekitchenrevolution.co.uk/August/
Week2

**Big meal
from scratch**

Roast Pork Loin with a Herb Crust, and Roast Tomato Salad and Potato Salad

This recipe is for a roast joint of pork with a herb and lemon breadcrumb crust that is delicious either hot or cold. It is served with a salad of roast tomatoes with rocket and balsamic vinegar, and a light fresh potato salad.

The recipe works best with a joint that is relatively lean but has enough fat for the herb and breadcrumb crust to stick. The 'best end' is ideal for this. The 'best end' is usually divided into separate loin chops but here is roasted as a whole piece. It has knuckle-like bones running through it and eight knuckles, or eight chops will be sufficient for this recipe and for leftovers. If it proves difficult to find, a boned leg a rolled shoulder will work too. Try to buy it skinless or you will have to remove the skin yourself

This is based on an Elizabeth David recipe in *French Provincial Cooking*.

The recipe includes extra pork for Pork Teriyaki with Noodles and tomatoes for the Roast Tomato Tapanade.

Roast pork loin
8-bone loin of pork or rack (ask the butcher to chine and skin it) or 1.3 kg skinned boned loin (see note above); includes 500 g extra for the Pork Teriyaki
2 garlic cloves
300 ml white wine
2 medium onions, approx. 240 g
1 bay leaf
2 sprigs fresh thyme
500 ml chicken stock (fresh or made from a stock cube or bouillon powder)
100 g breadcrumbs or 2-3 slices bread suitable for crumbing
8 fresh sage leaves
small handful of fresh flatleaf parsley
1 lemon
salt and pepper

Roast tomato salad
12 large ripe tomatoes, approx. 1.2 kg (plum if possible); includes 6 extra for the roast tomato tapenade tart
3-4 sprigs fresh thyme
2 tbsp olive oil, plus extra for drizzling
2 tsp balsamic vinegar
250 g rocket

Potato salad
600 g new potatoes
150 ml natural yoghurt
3 tbsp mayonnaise
1 small bunch chives
6 celery sticks
2 large or banana shallots, approx. 60 g
1 tbsp white wine or cider vinegar
2 heads chicory (red if possible)
small handful of fresh flatleaf parsley

GET AHEAD PREPARATION (optional)

The tomatoes can be roasted and the potato salad can be made up to 2 days in advance, but take it out of the fridge a good 40 minutes before you want to eat. The pork can be marinated several hours in advance. If you only have a little time:
* Roast the tomatoes.
* Prepare the crust for the pork.
* Prepare the garlic and onions.
* Prepare all the vegetables for the potato salad.

3 hours before you want to eat roast the tomatoes and marinate the pork

* Preheat the oven to 170°C/325°F/Gas Mark 3.
* Wash and halve the tomatoes. Strip the leaves from one of the thyme sprigs. Place the tomatoes on a baking sheet and add a drizzle of oil. Scatter the thyme leaves over them and season. Roast the tomatoes for 45 minutes.
* If the pork joint still has its rind remove this with a sharp knife. Peel and thinly slice the garlic. Grind pepper all over the meat and season with salt, then make small incisions with a knife around the bones. Slip the slivers of garlic into the incisions. Place the pork in a roasting tin, fat side up, and pour the wine over the top. Peel and roughly chop the onions and scatter them around the pork with the bay leaf and remaining thyme sprig. Leave to marinate for at least 30 minutes and up to 3 hours, basting from time to time.

2 hours 20 minutes before you want to eat cook the pork

* Turn the oven up to 220°C/425°F/Gas Mark 7. Keep the tomatoes in the oven as it heats up. When the oven reaches temperature, remove the tomatoes and leave them to cool.
* Cover the pork with foil and roast for 20 minutes.
* Then turn the oven down to 180°C/350°F Gas Mark 4, add all but about 2 tbsp of the stock to the pork and cook for a further hour.

1 hour 20 minutes
before you want
to eat prepare the
potato salad

* While the pork is cooking, wash the potatoes and cut them into bite sized pieces. Place the potatoes in a large pan of salted water. Bring them to the boil then simmer for 15–20 minutes or until they are just cooked.
* Beat together the yoghurt and mayonnaise until smooth and season to taste. Use scissors to snip the chives into the mixture. Trim, wash and slice the celery, add to the dressing, stir well and set aside.
* Peel and finely slice the shallots and set aside in a large bowl.
* When the potatoes are cooked, drain them well, place them in a bowl with the sliced shallots and toss with the vinegar and seasoning.

1 hour before you
want to eat add the
pork crust and
finish the salads

* Chop, whizz or grate the bread into breadcrumbs. Chop the sage and parsley, grate the zest of the lemon, add all three to the breadcrumbs and whizz briefly or mix with a fork to amalgamate them.
* When the pork has been cooking at 180°C/350°F/Gas Mark 4 for 1 hour take it out of the oven. Remove the foil. Press the herbed breadcrumb mixture all over the layer of fat on the pork using a palette knife.
* Return the pork to the oven and cook for a further 30 minutes, uncovered, until the crumbs have formed a golden herby crust.
* When the potatoes have cooled to room temperature, wash the chicory, slice it into rounds and add it to the potatoes. Fold in enough dressing to coat all the ingredients generously. Chop the parsley and fold this into the potato salad. Season to taste and keep at room temperature until you are ready to serve.
* Put half the roast tomatoes and all the pan juices into a salad bowl. Set the rest of the tomatoes aside for later in the week. Add the vinegar and oil to the tomatoes in the bowl. Then wash and dry the rocket and remove any thick stalks.

20 minutes before
you want to eat

* By now the pork should have a golden crust, so take it out of the oven (turn the oven off) and leave it to rest in a warm place while you make the gravy. Put a serving dish for the pork in the oven to warm up.
* Skim any fat from the cooking juices in the roasting tin. If there is a lot of juice, simmer to reduce for a few minutes. If there is not much gravy add the few remaining tablespoons of stock and warm through.
* Add the rocket to the roasted tomatoes and toss well. Serve alongside the potato salad.
* Cut the pork into slices and serve with the gravy.

Afterwards

Cut the leftover pork into 12-16 5-mm thick slices. Put the meat and 12 reserved tomato halves in separate containers, cool and refrigerate for use later in the week

**Something
for nothing 1**

Roast Tomato Tapenade Tart

This tart is simple to make and very moreish – a good meal to rustle together for impromptu summer meals. The base of the tart is made from layers of filo pastry sandwiched together with olive tapenade. This makes a rich, salty and crispy base that is a good contrast to the sweetness of the roast tomatoes and red onions.

Tapenade is a paste made from olives, anchovies and garlic that is easy to make (see page 000) or can be found at any supermarket or delicatessen.

Filo pastry can be found in the chiller cabinet of most supermarkets. It tends to come in 400 g packets. This recipe uses just over half a packet, but the remainder could be frozen to use at a later date. If you don't have any leftover tomatoes, use 12 tomato halves drizzled with olive oil, sprinkled with thyme leaves and roasted in a warm oven (170°C/325°F/Gas Mark 3) for 45 minutes.

4 small red onions, approx.
   280 g
2 tbsp olive oil
2 garlic cloves
60 g butter
250 g filo pastry
3 tbsp tapenade
4 sprigs fresh basil
12 roasted tomato halves leftover
   from the Big Meal from Scratch
   or see above
salt and pepper

To serve
green salad

GET AHEAD PREPARATION (optional)

If there are a few spare moments any of the following would be helpful:
* Prepare the onions and garlic and cook until soft.

*35 minutes before
you want to eat*

* Preheat the oven to 220°C/425°F/Gas Mark 7.
* First, cook the onions. Peel and finely slice the onions. Heat a glug of oil in a pan over a medium heat and when it is hot add the onions. Turn down the heat and cook gently for about 7–10 minutes. Meanwhile peel and crush the garlic.
* While the onions are cooking prepare the tart base. Brush a baking sheet, about 30 x 40 cm, with melted butter. Lay a sheet of filo on the baking sheet. The tart base should be about 30 x 35 cms so it may be necessary to lay two filo sheets side by side, slightly overlapping to create the right size.
* Butter the base layer and put another sheet on top of this. Butter the second layer and then spread it with half the tapenade. Lay a third layer of filo, brush melted butter over the top and add a fourth layer of filo. Butter this fourth layer and spread it with the remaining tapenade. Then add two more layers of filo with butter in between each sheet. Butter the top sheet and set aside.
* Now add the garlic to the onions and stir the mixture for a couple of minutes. Tear up the basil and stir it into the onions with a good dose of salt and pepper.
* Spread the onion mixture over the filo base. Distribute the tomatoes evenly and drizzle with oil.
* Put in the oven to cook for 15–20 minutes until the pastry is crisp.
* Cut the tart into four slices and serve with a green salad.

Pork Teryaki with Noodles and Crunchy Salad

In this recipe pork left over from the Big Meal from Scratch is given a completely new lease of life when grilled with a teriyaki sauce and served with noodles and a salad of crunchy vegetables. The sweet flavour of pork goes very well with the sour sweetness of teriyaki.

For the noodles, the nutty flavour of soba is ideal but rice or even egg noodles will be fine too. Mooli is a form of Japanese radish and looks like a huge white carrot. Most supermarkets and Asian stores stock it but but if you can't find it you can replace it with ordinary radishes – 150 g will be sufficient.

If you have no pork left over from the Big Meal from Scratch buy 500 g fillet, rub with teriyaki marinade, season with salt and pan fry until brown, then cook in the oven at 180°C/350°F/Gas Mark 5 for about 20 minutes.

Pork teriyaki
400 g (approx.) cold roast pork,
    12-16 slices, left over from the
    Big Meal from Scratch or see
    above
olive oil, for greasing
4 tbsp soy sauce
4 tbsp sake
4 tbsp mirin
1½ tbsp sugar
or
6-8 tbsp ready-made
    teriyaki sauce

Crunchy salad
1 small red onion, approx. 70 g
juice of 1 lime
2-3 carrots, approx. 250 g
1 small mooli, approx. 300 g, or
    150 g salad radishes
100 g beansprouts
1 garlic clove
1 small red chilli
2 tsp sugar
2 tbsp hot water
1 tbsp white wine vinegar

Noodles
300 g dried soba, rice or egg
    noodles
1 tbsp toasted sesame oil
2 tbsp (approx.) sesame seeds

GET AHEAD PREPARATION (optional)

The teriyaki sauce can be made in advance as it will keep for weeks in the fridge. The dressing can be made up to 1 day in advance. If you only have a little time:
* Toast the sesame seeds.
* Prepare the onion, carrots, mooli and garlic.
* Deseed and chop the chilli.

30 minutes before you want to eat

* Preheat the grill to its highest setting.
* Cook the noodles according to the pack instructions.
* Next make the sauce. Put the soy sauce, sake, mirin and sugar in a pan, bring to the boil reduce the heat and simmer gently for about 10 minutes or until the mixture has reduced by about one-third. Remove the sauce from the heat and set it aside.
* While the teriyaki sauce is cooking prepare the other ingredients. Drain and refresh the noodles with cold water, tip them into a large bowl and dress with the sesame oil.
* Toast the sesame seeds in a hot pan until they start to brown. Tip half the sesame seeds in with the noodles and reserve the remainder.
* Next prepare the crunchy salad. Peel and thinly slice the onion. Place in a bowl with the lime juice and set aside. Peel the carrots and mooli. Slice as finely as possible into matchsticks and place in a serving bowl. Add the beansprouts and mix well.
* Make the dressing. Peel the garlic and crush it into a bowl. Deseed and finely chop the chilli and add it to the garlic. Add the sugar to the hot water and stir to dissolve. Mix this and the vinegar with the garlic and chilli. Mix well, then add the onion and lime mixture. Pour the dressing over the salad and mix thoroughly.
* Finally cook the pork. Grease a piece of foil with oil and lay it on a grill pan. Place the pork slices on the foil and brush generously with the teriyaki sauce. Grill for about 2 minutes or until the sauce is bubbling.
* Divide the noodles between four bowls. Put a pile of salad on top then lay the pork slices on top and sprinkle them with the remaining sesame seeds.

Seasonal supper

Sea Bream with Grated Fennel and Courgettes

Serving sea bream on a salad of grated fennel and courgettes draws out the delicate flavours of all the ingredients. August is when courgettes and fennel appear in the shops - firm, gleaming and considerably less expensive than at other times of the year. Sea bream is a large rounded fish with sweet-flavoured flesh. This recipe also works well with grey mullet or sea bass. Be led by whatever looks freshest or by the recommendation of the fishmonger.

If you're extra hungry serve the sea bream with bulghar wheat or couscous dressed with olive oil and any herbs you have.

1 small red onion, approx. 70 g
1 lemon
2 bulbs fennel, approx. 400 g
3 courgettes, approx. 300 g
3 tbsp olive oil
4 × 200 g (approx.) sea bream fillets
small handful of fresh flatleaf parsley
4 sprigs fresh basil
salt and pepper

To serve
bulghar wheat or couscous

GET AHEAD PREPARATION (optional)

* Prepare and marinate the onion.
* Grate the courgettes and fennel.
* Chop the parsley.

25 minutes before you want to eat

* First, marinate the onion. Peel and finely slice the onion and place it in a large bowl. Add the zest of half the lemon and all the juice. Mix together, along with a pinch or two of salt.
* Next, prepare the vegetables. Trim any brown outer layers from the fennel and wash the bulbs well. Top and tail the courgettes, and wash thoroughly. If you have a food processor use the coarse grater to grate the fennel and courgettes. If you don't have a processor grate by hand. Add the grated courgettes and fennel to the onion and mix together well with 2 tablespoons of the oil, then set aside.
* Now cook the sea bream. Heat a large frying pan and add a generous glug of oil. Season the fish, making sure to salt the skin well to help it crisp. Place the fillets in the pan, skin sides down, and leave to cook for 3–4 minutes. Turn the heat down a little after the first minute to stop the skin burning. Turn the fillets over when you can see the edges of the flesh becoming opaque. Let them cook, flesh-side down, for 3–5 minutes. Check the fillets are cooked by peeling a bit of skin back to the thickest part; if the skin comes away easily and the flesh is opaque all the way through the fish is ready. Squeeze a spot of lemon juice over the fillets and set them aside.
* Roughly chop the parsley and tear up the basil then stir them through the fennel and courgettes.
* Serve each fillet on a pile of the salad with a little of the dressing over the top.

Larder feast

Russian Salad with Tuna and Hot Buttered Potatoes

Canned artichokes and celery should not be compared with their fresh counterparts but should be taken as a different kind of thing altogether. Yes, the earthy fleshiness of fresh artichoke and the crunch and bite of raw celery are deserving of much praise, but their canned cousins should not be discounted as necessarily inferior. For some purposes the luxury of being able to eat an artichoke heart without any labour, and the soft intensity of canned celery, should be applauded.

In the recipe that follows we do just that, combining both with peas and beetroot to make a salad that is dressed with a light, creamy dressing that goes well with tuna. Hot buttered potatoes are served alongside.

150 g frozen peas
1 × 400 g can artichoke hearts
½ × 400 g can celery hearts
3-4 pickled beetroot, approx. 200 g
1 tbsp capers
1 bunch spring onions
1 × 185 g can tuna (ideally in olive oil, but brine if you prefer)

For the dressing
3 tbsp mayonnaise
juice of ½ lemon
2 tbsp natural yoghurt or crème fraîche
1 tsp Dijon mustard
salt and pepper

Hot buttered potatoes
400 g new potatoes
25 g (approx.) butter

GET AHEAD PREPARATION (optional)

The Russian salad can be made up to a day in advance, but remove from the fridge 30 minutes before serving. If you only have a little time:
* Prepare potatoes and cover with water until required.
* Drain the artichoke and celery hearts, beetroot and tuna.
* Prepare the spring onions.

25 minutes before you want to eat

* Start by cooking the potatoes. Wash them well and cut them into bite-sized pieces. Place them in a large pan of salted water and bring to the boil. Turn down the heat and simmer for 15 minutes or until just cooked.
* While the potatoes are cooking, prepare the salad dressing. Put the mayonnaise, lemon juice, yoghurt or crème fraîche and the mustard in a bowl and whisk together well. Season to taste with salt and pepper and set aside.
* Next, prepare the salad. Put the peas in a pan, cover with water and bring to the boil. Drain the artichokes, celery and beetroot and cut into small pieces about 1 cm square. Place in a bowl with the capers and the cooked, drained peas. Dress with just over half the dressing, stir well and season to taste.
* Next, prepare the tuna. Trim and thinly slice the spring onions. Put half of them in a bowl to mix with the tuna and set the other half aside to mix with the potatoes. Drain the tuna, flake it into bowl containing the spring onions and add the remaining dressing. Mix well and season to taste.
* When the potatoes are cooked, drain them and return to the pan. Add the butter along with the remaining spring onions, a pinch of salt and a few grinds of pepper. Put the lid back on the pan, hold it down and give the potatoes a good shake so that the butter and onions are evenly distributed.
* Divide the potatoes between four plates and top with a spoonful of the Russian salad and then a spoonful of the tuna.

Two for one

Gnocchi Verde with Puttanesca Sauce

Potato gnocchi are easy to make but the process does involve a number of different stages – cooking and mashing the potatoes, making a dough by adding flour and eggs, forming this into balls, poaching the balls and then baking them with a cheese or other sauce. If you are spending time making gnocchi it seems sensible to double the quantity and save a batch for another day. Gnocchi are also a good way to involve kids in cooking, as they usually enjoy shaping the dough into little balls. If you are short of time then use ready-made gnocchi instead.

The puttanesca sauce that accompanies the gnocchi is unctuous, sweet, sour and ever so slightly chilli-hot. Puttanesca is Italian for prostitute so this sauce, as the name suggests, is not supposed to be subtle – big, brassy flavours are what's required. It only takes 15 minutes to prepare, but it must be left to cook for at least 50 minutes so that the flavours develop. Once the sauce is made it is poured over the gnocchi and the dish is baked for 20 minutes.

Puttanesca sauce
200 g pancetta or free-range
  rindles smoked back bacon
4 medium onions, approx. 480 g
4 tbsp olive oil
4 garlic cloves
½ red chilli
5-6 sprigs fresh thyme or 1 tsp
  dried thyme
3 tbsp white wine or sherry
  vinegar
4 × 400 g cans chopped tomatoes
2 tbsp tomato purée
1 bay leaf
150 g pitted black olives
100 g capers
150 g Parmesan
pinch of sugar (optional)
1-2 pinches of chilli powder
  (optional)
butter, for greasing
salt and pepper

Gnocchi verde
1.4 kg mashing potatoes, such as
  Maris Piper or baking potatoes
2 large free-range eggs
6 (approx) sprigs fresh basil
1 handful of flatleaf parsley
250 g plain flour, plus extra for
  dusting
olive oil, for tossing
or
400 g dried ready-made gnocchi
  or 800 g fresh ready-made
  gnocchi, green if you can get it

To serve
green salad

GET AHEAD PREPARATION (optional)

The gnocchi can be made a day in advance; be careful to store them so that they are not touching otherwise they will stick together. The tomato sauce can be made up to 4 days ahead of time. If you only have a little time:
* Prepare the onions and garlic.
* Deseed and chop the chilli.
* Prepare and cook the potatoes.

*1½ hours before
you want to eat
make the sauce*

* Start with the puttanesca sauce because the longer it can cook the more delicious it will be. Using a pair of scissors, snip the pancetta or bacon into 2-cm lengths, straight into a large heavy-based pan. Fry over a medium heat until it starts to brown and lets off some of its fat. While it is cooking, peel and finely slice the onions. Once browned, lift the pancetta or bacon out with a slotted spoon and put it to one side.
* Add a splash of the oil to the pan and cook the onions on a gentle heat for about 10 minutes until they are very soft and starting to brown. Meanwhile, peel and slice the garlic. Deseed and finely chop the chilli.
* When the onion has been cooking for 10 minutes, add the garlic, fry it for a couple of minutes then add the chilli. Turn the heat up, stir the mixture for another couple of minutes, then splash in the vinegar. Use a wooden spoon to scrape the bottom of the pan and cook until the vinegar has all but disappeared.
* Then add the tomatoes, along with the pancetta or bacon, tomato purée, thyme leaves or dried thyme, bay leaf, olives and capers, and some seasoning. Stir well, bring to the boil then allow to simmer over a low heat, uncovered, for at least 50 minutes or until the liquid has reduced to a thick sauce. While the sauce is simmering away grate the Parmesan, and – if you wish – make the gnocchi.

*1 hour before
you want to eat
make the gnocchi*

* If using ready made gnocchi skip to the next section.
* To make the gnocchi peel the potatoes and cut them into 2–3-cm pieces. Put them in a large pan of salted water, bring them to the boil and then simmer for 10–15 minutes until they are soft.
* Once the potatoes are cooking, beat the eggs and season them with 1 teaspoon salt and 1 teaspoon pepper. Roughly chop the basil and finely chop the parsley and add these to the eggs.
* Once the potatoes are cooked, drain them thoroughly and mash them very well. Put the mashed potato in a large bowl and make a hollow in the centre.
* Pour the eggs into the hollow and sprinkle with some of the flour. Mix together well adding more flour as you go until the dough reaches a consistency that is easy to form into balls with floured hands.
* Put a large pan of water on to boil. Flour your hands and a work surface, break off a quarter of the dough and roll it out into a rope, about 1–2 cm in diameter. Cut the rope into 4-cm lengths and put the finished gnocchi on a floured tray while you shape the rest of the dough.
* When the water is boiling add 1 teaspoon salt and carefully drop in a quarter of the gnocchi; poach them for 5 minutes until they rise to the surface. Tip them gently into a colander and allow them to drain. Continue paching the gnocchi until they are all cooked.
* Tip half the gnocchi into a buttered ovenproof dish and continue as above.
* Toss the remaining gnocchi in a little oil and lay them on a tray to cook.
* Once the gnocchi and sauce are cool, freeze the gnocchi in a plastic box with paper between the layers and the sauce in a freezer bag or freezer-proof container.

*25 minutes before
you want to eat
bake the gnocchi*

* Preheat the oven to 200°C/400°F/Gas Mark 6.
* If using ready made gnocchi bring a large pan of salted water to the boil, and cook according to the instructions on the packet.
* Once the sauce has thickened taste it for seasoning. If it's not sweet enough add a pinch sugar and if it's not sufficiently hot add a pinch or two of chilli powder. Put half aside to cool, ready for freezing.
* Grease a large ovenproof dish with butter. Place half the gnocchi (or all of it if you are using the ready-made version) in the dish in no more than a double layer. Pour the remaining half of the sauce over the top and sprinkle the Parmesan evenly over.
* Bake in the oven for 20 minutes or until the cheese is bubbling and brown.
* Serve immediately with a green salad.

**Lazy day supper
– reheating
instructions**

* Defrost the puttanesca sauce thoroughly. The gnocchi can be cooked from frozen.
* Preheat the oven to 200°C/400°F/Gas Mark 6. Warm the sauce in a pan. Meanwhile bring a large pan of salted water to the boil and add the gnocchi. When they start to float, drain them well then place in a buttered dish and pour the sauce over the top. Sprinkle with 50 g Parmesan. Bake in the oven for 20 minutes, or until the cheese is bubbling and brown.

August Week 3 – Overview

There are four components to the Big Meal from Scratch this week: Thyme and Lemon Cod, Skordalia, an accompanying Greek Garlic Sauce, Sweet Peppers and Potatoes and Fresh Sweetcorn. To become suitably sweet and soft, the pepper and potato dish benefits from long, slow cooking. The skordalia and the fish marinade have to be started 1 hour 40 minutes before eating. In other words, this is not a meal that can be rushed.

For midweek meals, the two Something for Nothings use surplus cod to delicately flavour a summer soufflé and extra sweetcorn is turned into a Chicken and Sweetcorn Tortilla Salad. Cooking a soufflé may sound daunting midweek but this is a cheat's version that only involves 20 minutes preparation and 25 minutes cooking. The salad is quicker and takes just 20 minutes to make.

Summer Vegetables with Anchovy Sauce, this week's Seasonal Supper, requires relatively little cooking – 30 minutes should be sufficient to chop all the vegetables and make the sauce.

For the Larder Feast, sourcing the ingredients for Quinoa with Aubergine and Olive relish might be rather challenging. A super-healthy but rather unknown grain, quinoa is stocked by most supermarkets but it can be swapped for bulghar wheat if necessary. Jars of aubergines in oil may also prove tricky to track down; if so, use peppers in oil (not oil and vinegar) instead. The recipe takes 30 minutes.

The meat in the Braised Pork with Fennel and Tomatoes, this week's Two for One, has to cook long and slow to soften to the point of falling apart. Half an hour of assembly followed by about 1½ hours of gentle casserole cooking will do it, but the longer the better. The end result combines a light and delicate braise with meltingly soft meat.

August Week 3	Recipe	Time
Big meal from scratch	Thyme and lemon cod with skordalia and sweet pepper potatoes and sweetcorn	1 hour 40 mins
Something for nothing 1	Chicken and sweetcorn tortilla salad	20 mins
Something for nothing 2	Low-rise summer soufflé with tomato salad	45 mins
Seasonal supper	Bagna cauda – summer vegetables with anchovy dressing	30 mins
Larder feast	Quinoa with aubergine and olive relish	30 mins
2 for 1	Braised pork with fennel and tomatoes	2 hours 10 mins

All recipes serve 4 apart from the 2 for 1 recipe which makes 8 portions

SHOPPING LIST (for 4 people)

Meat and fish
1.6 kg free-range boneless pork belly, skin scored and trimmed
2 free-range chicken breasts, skinned
6-8 x 150-200 g cod steaks or pieces of cod loin

Dairy
140 g butter
12 large free-range eggs
60 ml crème fraîche
140 ml (approx.) double cream
150 g Cheddar

Fruit and vegetables
1.3 kg large waxy new potatoes
200 g small new potatoes
1 small head broccoli
8 corn on the cob
4 red peppers
1 green pepper
1 bunch radishes
5 large bulbs fennel, approx. 750 g
2 kg large ripe tomatoes, approx. 16
120 g cherry tomatoes
200 g baby leaf spinach
3 little gem lettuces
1 head chicory
1 cucumber
2 medium onions, approx. 240 g
12-15 spring onions (approx. 2 bunches)
40 garlic cloves (approx. 4 large heads)
8 sprigs fresh thyme
1 small bunch fresh parsley
3-4 sprigs fresh tarragon or 1 generous handful of parsley
1-2 sprigs fresh rosemary
1 small bunch fresh coriander
handful of chives
4½ lemons
2 limes
200 g frozen spinach

Basics
1½ slices white bread
300 ml olive oil
2 tbsp groundnut or grapeseed oil
2 bay leaves
½ tsp dried thyme
3 tbsp tomato purée
salt and pepper

Store cupboard
200 g quinoa
4-8 soft flour tortillas
2 x 50 g cans anchovy fillets in olive oil
1 x 400 g can chopped tomatoes
200 g (approx.) aubergines in oil (drained weight approx. 150 g) or roasted red peppers in oil
150 g (drained weight) pitted olives (a mixure of black and green and as flavoursome as possible)
½ tbsp mayonnaise
2 tsp paprika (ideally smoked)
½ tsp ground cumin
1-2 generous pinches of cayenne pepper
1 tbsp fennel seeds
1 tbsp Pernod (optional for Braised Pork with Fennel and Tomatoes)
100 ml white wine

Serving suggestions
crusty bread (Low-Rise Summer Soufflé; Bagna Cauda - Summer Vegetables with Anchovy Dressing)
courgettes and rocket or other salad leaves of choice (Braised Pork with Fennel and Tomatoes)

To download or print out this shopping list, please visit www.thekitchenrevolution.co.uk/August/Week3

**Big meal
from scratch**

Thyme and Lemon Cod with Skordalia, Sweet Pepper Potatoes and Sweetcorn

It's difficult to imagine a meal more suited to summer than this – marinated cod served with sweet pepper potatoes, corn on the cob and a garlic bread sauce. The sweet pepper potatoes involve cooking peppers, potatoes and tomatoes slowly so that all their flavours infuse. Baking the cobs of corn means they can be served ready seasoned and smeared with butter.

Traditionally, skordalia is a potent Greek sauce made using raw garlic. Here we've adapted the recipe so that the garlic is roasted in olive oil before being blended to a paste with bread and olive oil.

The recipe will also work well with pollack, haddock or halibut.

The recipe includes extra fish for the Low-Rise Summer Soufflé and extra sweetcorn for the Chicken and Sweetcorn Tortilla Salad.

Thyme and lemon cod
4 tbsp olive oil
juice of ½ lemon
4–5 sprigs fresh thyme or ½ tsp
   dried thyme
1 garlic clove
handful of fresh parsley
6–8 × 150–200 g cod steaks or
   pieces of cod loin; includes
   2 steaks or 400 g extra for the
   low-rise summer soufflé
20 g butter
salt and pepper

Skordalia
6–7 large garlic cloves
120 ml olive oil
1½ slices crustless white bread
2–3 tbsp hot water
½ lemon

Sweet pepper potatoes
3 red peppers
500 g large waxy new potatoes
1 medium onion; approx. 120 g
1 green pepper
2 tbsp olive oil
1–2 sprigs fresh rosemary
4 ripe tomatoes, approx. 600 g

Sweetcorn
8 corn on the cob; includes
   4 extra for the chicken and
   sweetcorn tortilla salad
50 g (approx.) butter

GET AHEAD PREPARATION (optional)

The skordalia can be made up to a day before eating. The sweet pepper potatoes can be made a day before eating and gently reheated. The cod can be marinated up to 2 hours before eating. If you only have a little time:
* Peel and roast the garlic for the skordalia.
* Prepare the marinade.
* Prepare the onion and peppers for the sweet pepper potatoes.

*1 hour 40 minutes
before you want
to eat*

* Preheat the oven to 200°C/400°F/Gas Mark 6.
* Peel the garlic cloves for the skordalia and put them in the centre of a piece of foil. Add 1 tablespoon of the oil then bring the foil together to make an airtight parcel and place in the oven for 20 minutes.
* Place the red peppers in a roasting tin and roast in the oven until their skins peel easily –25–35 minutes.
* Prepare the marinade. Mix together 2 tablespoons of the oil, the lemon juice and the thyme sprigs or dried thyme. Crush the garlic and chop the parsley and add them to the marinade. Season and mix well.
* Place the cod in a single layer in a large dish. Pour the marinade over the top and set aside. After about 15 minutes turn the fish so that both sides have been in contact with the marinade.
* Now prepare the corn. Strip away the outer leaves from the sweetcorn and cut off any dry or tough ends or stalks. Cover a large baking sheet with a piece of foil big enough to wrap up all eight corn cobs. Dot each cob with the butter, season well then cover the cobs with another piece of foil to make an airtight parcel.
* Remove the garlic from the oven and check that it is completely soft. If not, return it to the oven for 10 minutes.

*1 hour before
you want to eat*

* Put the corn in the oven and bake for about 1 hour until tender.
* Scrub the potatoes thoroughly and cut them into large, chip-shaped chunks. Peel and thinly slice the onion. Halve and deseed the green pepper and slice it into pieces about the same size as the potatoes.

* Heat the oil in a large heavy-based pan with a lid, over a medium heat. When the oil is hot add the onion, green pepper and potatoes. Strip the rosemary leaves from their stalks and add them to the pan. Season, stir well, cover and cook gently.
* When the red peppers are cooked, remove them from the oven. Put them in a plastic bag and set them aside to cool. Steaming while they cool means the skins will lift off more easily.
* When the red peppers are cold, peel and deseed them, then rinse to remove any excess pieces of skin or seeds. Slice into pieces similar-size to the green pepper then add them to the pan containing the onion, potatoes and green pepper.
* Cut the tomatoes in half and scoop out the seeds. Chop the tomatoes into 1 cm dice. Add these to the potato mixture and cook gently for about 45 minutes. If the mixture looks very dry add a few tablespoons of water.
* Make the skordalia. Put the bread, hot water and the roast garlic into a food processor. Add the lemon juice and ½ teaspoon salt. Pulverise to a paste and while the blade is running slowly pour in the remaining oil. Taste for seasoning, then tip the skordalia into a serving bowl and set aside.

10 minutes before you want to eat cook the fish

* When the corn is cooked, turn off the oven and leave the corn inside, wrapped up in foil to keep warm. Put some plates and serving dishes in to warm at the same time.
* Taste the sweet pepper potatoes for seasoning and check that they are completely cooked. If not, remove the lid and increase the heat for a few more minutes. Otherwise keep warm on a very low heat.
* Heat the remaining oil and the butter in a frying pan. When the butter is foaming add as many steaks as will fit in a single layer. Fry steaks about 3 cm thick for 3 minutes on each side – fry for less or more time, depending on the thickness. When the steaks are cooked, place on the warmed serving dish and cover loosely with foil.
* Remove the corn cobs from the oven, cut four of them in half and put in them a serving dish. Pour any buttery juices over the top. Put the remaining four cobs aside to cool, for use later in the week. Remove two of the cod steaks from the serving dish and set them aside to cool for use later in the week.
* Serve the cod with a spoonful of skordalia on top with the potatoes and corn separately.

Afterwards

Skin and bone the reserved cod steaks and shuck the corn from the cobs by standing the cobs vertically on a board and using a sharp knife to cut downwards between the corn husk and kernels. Put the fish (300 g) and corn (200 g) in separate containers, cover and refrigerate for use later in the week.

**Something
for nothing 1**

Chicken and Sweetcorn Tortilla Salad

This is very quick and one of our favourite supper dishes – grilled tortillas with cheese feels like indulgent snack food but in this recipe they are piled high with a spicy salad, sweetcorn and grilled chicken so the guilt is kept to a minimum.

    Although roast corn is more intense and less soggy than the canned version, you can use 300 g canned sweetcorn if necessary.

½ tsp ground cumin
2 tsp paprika (ideally smoked)
generous 1-2 pinches of cayenne
  pepper
2 free-range chicken breasts,
  skinned
2 tbsp olive oil
juice of 2 limes
1 tbsp crème fraîche or Greek
  yoghurt
½ tbsp mayonnaise
3 ripe tomatoes, approx. 360 g
1 little gem lettuce

large handful of fresh coriander
kernels from 4 roasted corn
  cobs, approx. 200g, left over
  from the Big Meal from Scratch
  or see above
salt and pepper

For the base
4-8 soft flour tortillas
150 g Cheddar
4 spring onions

GET AHEAD PREPARATION (optional)

* Grate the Cheddar.
* Trim and finely slice the
  spring onions.
* Prepare the vegetables for the
  salad.
* Make the salad dressing.

*20 minutes before
you want to eat*

* Preheat the grill to its highest setting.
* Start by preparing the chicken. Mix half the cumin, paprika and cayenne with salt and pepper. Cut the chicken breasts into 1-cm strips and toss them in the spice mixture. Place the strips in a single layer on a well-oiled baking tray, drizzle oil over the strips and cook under the grill for about 3–4 minutes or until the chicken is starting to colour. Turn the strips over and cook them for another couple of minutes. Remove the strips from the grill and set aside. Turn the grill to medium.
* Meanwhile, make the dressing for the salad. In a bowl or jar mix together the remaining cumin, paprika and cayenne. Add the lime juice, crème fraîche or yoghurt and the mayonnaise and mix well. While stirring, add the oil to create a pouring consistency. The dressing should be tangy and intense – check for seasoning and set aside.
* Next, assemble the base. Place 4 tortillas on a baking sheet. Grate the Cheddar and finely slice the spring onions. Mix these together and sprinkle them over the tortillas. Place under the medium-hot grill and allow the cheese to melt and bubble. If you are cooking 8 tortillas keep the first batch warm while you melt the cheese on the second batch.
* While the cheese is melting make the salad. Roughly chop the tomatoes. Wash and dry the little gem leaves and the coriander. Rip the lettuce leaves into bite-sized pieces, roughly chop the coriander and place in a bowl with the tomatoes. Add the corn kernels to the salad along with the chicken strips.
* Pour the dressing over the salad and mix well.
* Put the cheese tortillas on four plates and pile the chicken strips and sweetcorn salad on top.

Something
for nothing 2

Low-Rise Summer Soufflé with Tomato Salad

This recipe is for a cheat's low-rise soufflé and the method is a good one to have up your sleeve. Unlike a proper soufflé, you don't have to make a roux with flour, butter and egg yolks. Instead you combine the yolks with a few strong-flavoured ingredients, then fold this mixture into beaten egg whites. The result will be something between a risen soufflé and a quiche filling.

Tarragon has a unique flavour, one that is impossible to replicate. If you can't find fresh tarragon we also give an option to use parsley mixed with lemon rind – this won't be the same as the taste of tarragon but will equally complement the cod and spinach.

Low-rise summer soufflé
butter or oil, for greasing
200 g baby leaf spinach
3 tbsp crème fraîche
3–4 sprigs fresh tarragon or
  1 generous handful of fresh
  parsley
1 lemon
2–3 spring onions
8 large free-range eggs
300g (approx.) cooked, flaked
  cod, left over from the Big
  Meal from Scratch or
  2 cooked, skinned and boned
  pieces cod, haddock or pollack
salt and pepper

Tomato salad
5 large ripe tomatoes, approx.
  600 g
handful of chives
2 tbsp olive oil

To serve
warmed crusty bread

GET AHEAD PREPARATION (optional)

Everything can be prepared ahead of time other than beating the egg whites, which has to be done at the last moment. If you only have a little time:
* Wash the spinach and cook until wilted.
* Trim and finely chop the spring onions.

45 minutes before you want to eat

* Preheat the oven to 220°C/425°F/Gas Mark 7 and grease an ovenproof dish about 30 cm square or 25 cm in diameter and 7 cm deep with butter or oil.
* Wash the spinach and without bothering to dry the leaves put it in a large pan. Cover and place over a high heat. Cook until the spinach has wilted then tip into a colander. Use the back of a spoon to press any excess liquid from the spinach, then set aside until cool.
* Put the crème fraîche in a large bowl. Roughly tear the tarragon leaves (if you are using parsley, chop it) and add to the bowl. Add the juice of half the lemon and if you are not using tarragon, grate the zest of the lemon and add this to the crème fraîche. Trim the spring onions, chop them and add them to the bowl.
* Separate the eggs. Put the whites in a large clean bowl and add the yolks to the crème fraîche mixture. Add the fish flakes and seasoning to the yolk mixture and mix well.
* Squeeze any remaining liquid from the spinach and roughly chop the leaves. Fold this into the crème fraîche mixture.
* Beat the egg whites with a pinch of salt until they form soft peaks. Take a spoon of the egg whites and gently fold it into the crème fraîche mixture. Tip the remaining egg whites into the bowl and gently fold together.
* Pour this mixture into the prepared dish, place in the middle of the oven and bake for 20–25 minutes.
* Slice the tomatoes thickly and lay them on a plate. Using scissors, cut the chives finely over the tomatoes. Squeeze about 1 teaspoon lemon juice over the top, drizzle with the oil and season.
* Remove the soufflé from the oven, put a knife through the middle and if it comes out clean the soufflé is ready. If not cook it for another 5 minutes.
* When the soufflé is cooked serve immediately with the salad and crusty bread.

Seasonal supper

Bagna Cauda - Summer Vegetables with Anchovy Dressing

This supper of boiled eggs, fresh seasonal vegetables and crusty bread dipped into a rich anchovy sauce is especially good for a summer evening.

In Italy bagna cauda literally translated means 'warm bath', referring to the intense anchovy sauce. This is a speciality of Piedmont in northern Italy and on high days and holidays they grate white truffle into the sauce.

Any seasonal vegetables are suitable for this meal. The amounts and varieties below are just a rough guide.

Summer vegetables	Bagna cauda	GET AHEAD PREPARATION (optional)
200 g new potatoes	12 garlic cloves	The bagna cauda and vegetables can be prepared in advance. If you only have a little time:
1 small head broccoli	140 ml (approx.) double cream	
4 free-range eggs	2 × 50 g cans anchovy fillets in	
6-8 spring onions	olive oil	* Peel the garlic and soften it down in the cream.
1 cucumber	60 g butter	
1 red pepper	½ lemon	
2 little gem lettuces	salt and pepper	
1 large bulb fennel		
1 head chicory	To serve	
1 bunch radishes	crusty bread	
120 g cherry tomatoes		
salt		

30 minutes before you want to eat

* First, make the bagna cauda. Peel the garlic and, leaving the cloves whole, put them in a small pan and cover with the cream. Bring the cream to the boil and simmer very gently until the garlic is soft – this will take about 15 minutes. Stir from time to time to prevent the cream sticking and burning. When stirring the pan check on how the garlic cloves are cooking by pressing to test their softness.
* Next, cook the potatoes. Wash and cut them in half (unless they are much bigger than bite-sized, in which case cut them into quarters). Place in a pan of water with a generous pinch of salt. Bring to the boil then simmer for about 15 minutes until the potatoes are cooked.
* Next, blanch the broccoli. Break it into florets and place them in boiling water for a couple of minutes until they are just cooked. Lift from the pan, refresh under cold water and leave to drain.
* Boil the eggs – use the water you cooked the broccoli in. Cook the eggs for 8 minutes then drain and leave them to cool under cold running water for a few minutes. When they are completely cold, peel and leave them whole.
* Now wash, trim and chop the other vegetables. Cut the spring onions, cucumber and red peppers into chunky dipping batons. Cut the little gems and fennel lengthways into quarters or eighths. Separate the chicory leaves and keep the radishes and cherry tomatoes whole.
* Now finish the bagna cauda. When the garlic is soft use a fork to crush it into the cream. Chop the anchovies and stir them and their oil into the garlic cream over a gentle heat. Crush the anchovies with the spoon until you have a brownish sauce. Cut the butter into little cubes and add a few cubes at a time, whisking as they melt, so that the sauce emulsifies. Add a couple of squeezes of lemon juice to the bagna cauda and season to taste.
* To serve, divide the potatoes and vegetables between four plates, halve the eggs and put two halves on each plate. Put the sauce into four small dishes or bowls and place one dish on each plate. Serve with small pieces of crusty bread for dipping and mopping.

Larder feast

Quinoa with Aubergine and Olive Relish

Quinoa is a grain that grows in the Andes. It is highly nutritious, but, most importantly, it is very tasty and easy to cook. Most health food stores and supermarkets stock quinoa but if you can't find it you can substitute it for the same quantity of bulghar wheat.

For this recipe you cook the quinoa with canned tomatoes and spinach and serve it with stewed aubergines cooked with olives and lots of garlic.

Greek and Turkish grocers sell aubergines marinated in olive oil. These are sleek, slippery and voluptuous and, with the addition of some garlic and seasoning, they complement the subdued flavours of the quinoa, tomato and spinach. If you cannot find aubergines in oil, replace them with about 200 g peppers marinated in olive oil – the flavours will be different but equally good.

Quinoa
200 g quinoa
1 medium onion, approx. 120 g
1 tbsp olive oil
200 g frozen spinach
1 × 400 g can chopped tomatoes
2 tbsp tomato purée
½ tsp dried thyme
salt and pepper

Aubergine and olive relish
1 tbsp olive oil
4 garlic cloves
150 g pitted olives (a mixture of black and green), drained weight
200 g aubergines in oil (drained weight approx. 150 g)
1 tbsp tomato purée

GET AHEAD PREPARATION (optional)

The relish can be made up to 2 days in advance. If you only have a little time:
* Rinse the quinoa and cover with boiling water.
* Prepare the onion and garlic.
* Defrost the spinach.
* Chop the olives and slice the aubergines.

30 minutes before you want to eat

* Rinse the quinoa under cold running water then tip it into a large bowl. Cover with boiling water, stir once and set aside.
* Peel and finely slice the onion. Heat the oil in a large heavy-based pan and add the onion. Cook over a medium heat for 7–10 minutes until the onion is soft.
* Defrost the spinach according to the pack instructions. Tip it into a colander and press with the back of a wooden spoon to get rid of excess water.
* When the onion is soft, stir in the tomatoes and tomato purée. Add the thyme, ½ teaspoon salt and some black pepper. Mix well, then simmer over a low heat for a couple of minutes with the lid off.
* Next, roughly chop the spinach and add it to the tomato sauce. If there is a lot of liquid in the quinoa tip it into a sieve and press it with the back of a wooden spoon before adding it to the tomato sauce. Stir once or twice, cover with a lid and steam over a very gentle heat.
* Now make the aubergine and olive relish. Heat the oil in a frying pan over a gentle heat. Peel and finely slice the garlic and add it to the oil. Cook for about 3–4 minutes without letting the garlic burn.
* Drain and roughly chop the olives. Drain the aubergines and slice them into 2–3-cm wide slivers.
* Add the aubergines, olives and tomato purée to the garlic and cook gently for 5 minutes. Taste the relish and adjust the seasoning if necessary.
* Using a fork, fluff up the quinoa, taste it for seasoning, and divide between four large bowls. Spoon the aubergine and olive relish on top of the quinoa and serve immediately.

Two for one

Braised Pork with Fennel and Tomatoes

This dish is a light summer braise, where pork is cooked on a bed of citrus-flavoured tomatoes, fennel and potatoes. This method of cooking ensures that no flavours or moisture are wasted.

Pork belly is one of the least expensive cuts of pork and is very succulent. With pork it's always worth buying meat that's either free-range, organic or from a reputable source. Intensively reared pork tends to be insipid rather than sweet, flabby rather than rich. The potatoes in this recipe could, if you prefer, be replaced with large butter beans.

This meal is not particularly labour intensive, but it's not quick either. Once the pork is in the oven the braise cooks slowly for 1½ hours so the recipe doesn't tie the cook to the kitchen. Even so, this probably isn't one to embark on at the end of a long day when there are hungry people to feed. The meal reheats well, though, so it is something that can be made well ahead of time and, of course, the quantities are for eight so half the braise can be frozen for a labour-free meal in the future.

1.6 kg free-range boneless pork belly, skin scored and trimmed
2 tbsp groundnut or grapeseed oil
16 garlic cloves
4 large bulbs fennel, approx. 600 g
4 very ripe tomatoes, approx. 500 g
2 lemons
1 tbsp Pernod (optional)
100 ml white wine

1 tbsp fennel seeds
2 bay leaves
4 sprigs fresh thyme
800 g large waxy new potatoes, such as Charlotte
small handful parsley
salt and pepper

To serve
courgettes or rocket or other salad leaves of choice

GET AHEAD PREPARATION (optional)

The entire meal can be made up to 3 days in advance and reheated. If you only have a little time:
* Prepare the garlic and fennel.
* Mix the lemon juice with the Pernod, wine and fennel seeds.

2 hours 10 minutes before you want to eat

* Preheat the oven to 220°C/425°F/Gas Mark 7.
* Pat the pork belly dry with kitchen paper and rub the skin very well with salt and oil. Season the whole piece of pork with salt and pepper and place it at the top of the oven in a large roasting tin.
* Roast on high for 30 minutes until the pork is brown all over. Don't worry if the rind is still soft – it can be crisped under the grill at the end.
* While the pork is browning, prepare the vegetables. Peel and slice the garlic, then trim the fennel and cut each bulb lengthways into eighths. Peel the tomatoes by placing them in a bowl and covering them with boiling water for a couple of minutes. Plunge them into cold water and pull the skins off. Peel a couple of strips of zest from the lemons and squeeze their juice into a jug. Mix the lemon juice with the Pernod, if using, wine and fennel seeds.

1¾ hours before you want to eat

* After 20 minutes turn the oven down to 160–170°C/325°F/Gas Mark 3 and take out the pork. Lift it out of the roasting tin and pour off any excess fat (this can be kept for roasting potatoes and frying chops). Place the tin over a medium heat and pour the lemon juice and fennel seed mixture into it; use a whisk to lift the extra flavours that will be stuck to the bottom. Put the fennel, garlic and tomatoes into the tin with the cooking liquor, season with salt and pepper and scatter in the bay leaves, thyme and lemon zest. Place the pork on top. Cover the tin with foil so that it is airtight and return it to the oven for 1½–2 hours until the meat is absolutely tender. The length of time here isn't crucial; a 2.5 kg pork belly will cook in the about the same time, and, as the meat is being cooked in an almost steamy atmosphere, a smaller piece won't dry out.
* While the pork is cooking, peel the potatoes, cut them into 4-cm chunks and boil them for about 8–10 minutes, until they are almost cooked.

40 minutes before you want to eat

* When the pork has been cooking for 1 hour add the potatoes to the roasting tin and let them finish cooking.

15 minutes before you want to eat

* When the pork has been cooking at a low temperature for 1½–2 hours, check that it is meltingly tender and, if it is, remove the roasting tin from the oven. Turn the oven off and put some plates and serving dishes in to warm.
* Lift the pork from the tin, cut it in half and set one of the halves aside for freezing. Spoon half the fennel, tomato and potato mixture into a container suitable for freezing and set it aside to cool alongside the pork. Put the rest of the mixture back in the oven to keep warm.
* If you are keen to have crisp skin on the pork you will be serving, preheat the grill to its highest setting and set the pork under it so that the skin crisps. Once the skin is crisp let the pork rest while you get everything else ready.
* Roughly chop the parsley and add it to the vegetables in the roasting tin.
* Cut the pork you will be serving into 2–3-cm slices and serve it with the warm fennel, tomatoes and potatoes.
* To freeze, put the cooled vegetables in a freezer bag or plastic container and wrap the pork tightly in foil.

Lazy day supper – reheating instructions

* Defrost the pork and the fennel, tomato and potato mixture thoroughly.
* Preheat the oven to 180°C/350°F/Gas Mark 4. Place the pork on top of the vegetables, cover with foil and warm through. This will take about 25 minutes. If you are keen to have crisp skin, preheat the grill and when the pork is hot place it under the grill for a few minutes before serving as above.

August Week 4 – Overview

This week's Big Meal from Scratch is a Middle Eastern-flavoured roast of Chermoula Chicken, served with a Butter Bean Salad and Mushy Courgettes. Every component of the meal will work served piping hot or at room temperature, taking pressure off the cook in terms of timing and allowing the weather to dictate how the food will be best enjoyed. In total this big meal takes around 2¼ hours, depending on the size of the chicken, but much of this is cooking time rather than preparation.

Leftover chicken is used to make Rosie's Coronation Chicken with optional rice and green salads – this Something for Nothing is a great interpretation of a classic recipe that takes 25 minutes without the rice salad and 45 minutes with it. Extra butter beans from the big meal are used to make a smooth Butter Bean and Roast Pepper Soup that can be on the table in 25 minutes.

For a Seasonal Supper that makes the most of the summer's tomatoes, Panzanella Salad is the perfect vehicle. It only takes about 5 minutes to assemble but it benefits from sitting and marinating for at least 30 minutes at room temperature before eating. A Larder Feast of Coconut Mackerel with Green Thai Rice Cakes its inspiration from South-East Asia and doesn't pull any punches. It takes about 30 minutes of busying in the kitchen.

Smoked trout is a good partner for spinach and in this week's Two for One they come together in a cold roulade that is particularly suited to outdoor eating. From beginning to end the recipe takes 1 hour to make but as it makes two roulades, one for the freezer, this time is well spent.

August Week 4	Recipe	Time
Big meal from scratch	Chermoula chicken, butter bean salad and mushy courgettes	2¼ hours
Something for nothing 1	Butter bean and roast pepper soup	20 mins
Something for nothing 2	Rosie's coronation chicken	45 mins (or 25 mins)
Seasonal supper	Panzanella – Tuscan bread salad	35 mins
Larder feast	Coconut mackerel with green Thai rice	30 mins
2 for 1	Spinach and smoked trout roulade	1 hour

All recipes serve 4 apart from the 2 for 1 recipe which makes 8 portions

SHOPPING LIST (for 4 people)

Meat and fish
2 × 1.2-1.5 kg free-range chickens
450 g smoked trout fillets (or hot-smoked
  salmon or 300 g cold-smoked salmon)

Dairy
110 g (approx.) butter
200 ml milk
2 tbsp natural yoghurt or crème fraîche
200 g cream cheese
6 free-range eggs

Fruit and vegetables
800 g large leaf spinach or 600 g baby
  leaf spinach
750 g medium courgettes
4 red peppers
2 little gem lettuces
4 celery sticks
10 very ripe tomatoes, approx. 1 kg
1½ cucumbers
3 medium onions, approx. 360 g
1 medium red onion, approx. 120 g
2 bunches spring onions, approx. 16
23 garlic cloves
6-cm piece of fresh root ginger
1-2 green chillies (depending on taste)
1 fresh lemon grass stick or 2 tbsp lemon
  grass paste
1½ large bunches fresh coriander
4 sprigs fresh dill
1 sprig fresh rosemary
handful of fresh parsley
5 sprigs fresh mint
1 bunch fresh basil
1 small bunch chives
7-10 sprigs fresh thyme or 1 tsp dried thyme
4 lemons
2 limes
300 g frozen spinach

Basics
500 g coarse-textured rustic white bread
2 tbsp tomato purée
350 ml olive oil
50 ml groundnut or grapeseed oil
1 bay leaf
700 ml chicken stock (fresh or made from a
  stock cube or bouillon powder)
salt and pepper

Store cupboard
250 g Thai jasmine rice
100 g long grain rice
4 × 400 g cans butter beans
1½ × 290 g jars roased red peppers in oil
  or 3 large red peppers for peeling and
  roasting

4 × 125 g cans mackerel fillets in lightly
  salted water
2 tbsp tamarind paste
8 tbsp dessicated coconut (if you can get
  dried ribbon coconut even better)
60 g no-soak dried apricots
50 g toasted flaked almonds
2 tsp capers
5 tbsp mayonnaise
1 tbsp horseradish cream
40 ml red wine vinegar
25 ml white wine vinegar
4 tsp Thai fish sauce
4 tbsp clear honey
1 tsp ground cumin
2 tsp ground coriander
1 tbsp garam masala
1 tsp paprika (smoked if possible)
1 tsp cayenne pepper
pinch of nutmeg (ground or freshly grated)
350 ml white wine

Serving suggestions
crusty bread, butter (Butter Bean and Roast
  Pepper Doup)
soft white cheese or Parma ham (Panzanella
  - Tuscan Bean Dalad)
new potatoes and tomato salad ingredients
  (Spinach and Smoked Trout Roulade)

To download or print out this shopping list,
please visit www.thekitchenrevolution.co.uk/August/
Week4

**Big meal
from scratch**

Chermoula Chicken, Butter Bean Salad and Mushy Courgettes

This Moroccan roast chicken is flavoured with chermoula – a North African sauce or marinade made from fresh coriander, cumin, garlic, lemon juice and olive oil. It is rubbed over chicken prior to cooking, so that the flavours infuse into the meat.

Recipes for chermoula vary considerably, and much is down to personal taste. In this recipe tomato purée binds all the ingredients so the chermoula can be smeared over and inside the chicken.

We have written this recipe for whole birds but if you prefer it would work very well on the barbeque (see page 183 for jointing a chicken). Simply rub the chermoula all over the chicken pieces, leave to marinade for an hour or so, then barbeque.

The recipe includes extra chicken for Rosie's Coronation Chicken and extra butter bean salad and pepper for Butter Bean and Roast Pepper Soup.

Chermoula chicken
1 large bunch fresh coriander
3 large garlic cloves
1 tsp ground cumin
2 tsp ground coriander
½ tsp (approx.) cayenne pepper
1½ lemons
2-3 tbsp olive oil
2 tbsp tomato purée
2 × 1.2-1.5 kg free-range chickens; includes 1 chicken or 600 g extra meat for Rosie's coronation chicken
1 tbsp white wine vinegar
250 ml white wine
salt and black pepper

Mushy courgettes
750 g courgettes
3 garlic cloves
50 g (approx.) butter

2 tbsp olive oil
3-4 sprigs fresh thyme or ½ tsp dried thyme

Butter bean salad (makes double quantities for the bean and pepper soup)
4 red peppers
1 medium onion, approx. 120 g
3 tbsp olive oil
1 tbsp red wine vinegar
4 × 400 g cans butter beans (approx. 900 g drained weight)
handful of fresh parsley
2 ripe tomatoes, approx. 200 g
juice of ½ lemon
4-6 sprigs fresh thyme or ½ tsp dried thyme
1 tsp paprika (smoked if possible)

GET AHEAD PREPARATION (optional)

The chermoula and salad can be made up to a day in advance. The chicken can be prepared up until the point it goes in the oven or on the barbecue. If you only have a little time:
* Prepare the parsley and fresh coriander.
* Prepare the garlic for the chermoula.
* Prepare the remaining garlic and the onion.
* Prepare the courgettes.
* Chop the tomatoes.
* Roast and peel the red peppers.

2¼ hours before you want to eat make the chermoula

* Preheat the oven to 190°C/375°F/Gas Mark 5.
* Wash the fresh coriander and remove any long, thick stalks. Put the stalks to one side and put the leaves in the food processor. Peel the garlic, crush it a little and add it to the processor with the cumin, ground coriander, cayenne, salt, pepper and the juice of 1 lemon (don't throw away the squeezed lemon halves). Pulse the processor to create a rough paste. Finally stir in the oil and tomato purée or add them to the processor and pulse a couple more times to amalgamate. If you don't have a processor chop the coriander leaves, crush the garlic and mix together in a bowl with other ingredients.

2 hours before you want to eat cook the chicken

* Place the chickens side by side in one large roasting tin if possible, or in two separate tins. Stuff the chicken cavities with the squeezed lemon halves and the coriander stalks. Now rub all but 1 tablespoon of the chermoula over the birds. Carefully prise the skin from the chicken breasts near the head cavities and fill with the chermoula paste and push as far under the skin as it will go.
* Cover the chickens with foil and place them in the oven. Roast for 1 hour under the foil. Then remove the foil, baste and return to the oven, uncovered, for a further 30 minutes.
* Place the whole peppers on a baking sheet and put them in the oven until they are soft and skins peel easily - about 45 minutes.

1¼ hours before you want to eat cook the courgettes

* Wash and top and tail the courgettes. Cut them in half lengthways and then slice across the halves to create half-moons about 2 cm thick.
* Peel and thinly slice the garlic.

* Melt the butter and oil over a medium heat in a pan large enough to hold the courgettes. When the butter is foaming, add the courgettes and garlic. Season with salt and pepper, mix well and cover. Turn the heat to its lowest setting – you want the courgettes to collapse – this may take up to 1 hour.

1 hour before you want to eat make the butter bean salad

* Remove the RED peppers from the oven, put them in a sealed plastic bag to steam in their own heat and set them aside to cool.
* Peel and finely slice the onion. Heat 1 tablespoon of the oil in a pan over a medium heat and soften the onion for 7–10 minutes. For the last minute or so add the vinegar and allow it to evaporate almost completely.
* Drain and rinse the butter beans and place in a large serving bowl. Chop the parsley and add to the beans. Halve the tomatoes and scoop out the seeds with a teaspoon. Roughly chop the tomatoes into 1-cm squares, then mix these with the beans, the remaining oil and the juice of the half lemon.
* Strip the thyme leaves from their stalks. When the onion is soft, add the thyme leaves or dried thyme and paprika and fry for a minute. Add the onion mixture to the butter beans and stir well.
* When the peppers are cool enough to handle remove the softened skins, under a running tap if you find it easier. Remove the seeds from the peppers. Put the equivalent of one of the peppers aside for use later in the week, then cut the other three into strips about 1 cm wide and add these to the salad.
* Mix well, taste and season as necessary. Place in a serving dish.
* The chickens will have been cooking for about 1 hour by now – so remove the foil, baste them and return them to the oven, uncovered, for 30 minutes.

15 minutes before you want to eat make the gravy

* After 1½ hours take the chickens from the oven and place them on a carving board to rest.
* Tip or spoon away any fat from the roasting tin and place it over a medium heat. Using a wooden spoon, scrape any juices from the bottom of the tin. Add the vinegar and boil vigorously, stirring, until it has all but disappeared. Add the wine and bring to the boil. Reduce by half then add the remaining chermoula and about 150 ml water. Bring to the boil, stir well, then turn the heat down to low to reduce and intensify the gravy while you carve the chickens.
* To finish the courgettes, strip the leaves from the thyme stalks and add these or the dried thyme to the purée. Stir well, season and place in a serving dish.
* Serve the carved chicken with the courgette purée, salad and gravy.

Afterwards

Strip any remaining flesh (600 g) from the chickens. Put this and the leftover peppers (4–6 pieces) and butter bean salad (600 g) in separate containers, cover and refrigerate for later in the week.

Something
for nothing 1

Butter Bean and Roast Pepper Soup

Using the butter bean salad left over from the Big Meal from Scratch provides the basis for this rich, colourful soup served with a crispy garlic and red pepper paste. If you don't have any butter bean salad, replace it with 2 cans drained and rinsed butter beans mixed with 2 tomatoes, roughly chopped, 1 tablespoon olive oil, and salt and pepper. If there are no remaining pieces of pepper, char 1–2 red peppers under the grill or in the oven and peel them.

Butter bean soup
1 medium onion, approx. 120 g
2 tbsp olive oil
1 garlic clove
600 g (approx.) butter bean salad
    left over from the Big Meal
    from Scratch or see above
200 ml milk
700 ml chicken stock (fresh or
    made from a stock cube or
    bouillon powder
1 sprig fresh rosemary

Pepper paste and crispy garlic
6 garlic cloves
1 roasted and skinned red
    pepper, left over from Big Meal
    from Scratch or see above
3 tbsp olive oil
2 pinches of cayenne pepper
salt and pepper

To serve
crusty bread and butter

GET AHEAD PREPARATION (optional)

Everything can be made 1–2 days in advance and reheated. If you only have a little time:
* Prepare and soften the onion.
* Peel the garlic.

20 minutes before you want to eat

* If you are using the butter bean salad from the Big Meal from Scratch as the basis for this soup, fish out the slices of pepper and put them with the other pieces of pepper. It's not necessary to fish out every last piece.
* Peel and finely slice the bit. Heat 2 tablespoons of the oil in a large heavy-based pan over a medium heat. When the oil is hot add the onion and soften for 7–10 minutes.
* Meanwhile, peel the garlic. Slice one of the cloves thinly and add it to the onion. Keep the remaining six for the pepper paste and crispy garlic.
* When the onion is soft, add the butter bean salad, milk and stock to the pan. Add the rosemary sprig and cayenne pepper, season and simmer for 10 minutes.
* Now make the pepper and garlic paste. Slice the remaining six garlic cloves into slivers about 2 mm thick. Cut the peppers into rough slices. Heat 1 tablespoon of the oil in a frying pan over a medium heat. Add half the garlic (keep the other half for the crispy garlic) and soften gently for 3 minutes, stirring all the while to ensure it doesn't burn. When the garlic is softened, add the peppers and a pinch of cayenne and cook for another couple of minutes. Tip this mixture into a food processor or use a hand blender to blend it into a paste. If you don't have a processor or blender chop the mixture finely. Set the pepper paste aside.
* Now make the crispy garlic. Heat the remaining oil in the frying pan over a high heat. When the oil is very hot, add the rest of the garlic slices and fry until they are crisp and brown. Tip them on to kitchen paper and set aside while you finish the soup.
* Take the soup off the heat. Remove the rosemary sprig, pour the soup into a food processor, or use a hand blender, and blend until smooth.
* Season to taste, ladle the soup into four bowls and put a spoonful of the pepper paste in the middle of each. Scatter with the crispy garlic and serve with crusty bread and butter.

Something
for nothing 2

Rosie's Coronation Chicken

This is Rosie's version of a classic recipe. It bears little resemblance to the gloopy and overly sweet coronation chicken that appears on buffet tables across the land. We suggest you serve the chicken with a rice salad and a green salad.

If you have no chicken left over from the Big Meal poach 2–3 skinned chicken breasts in stock for about 20 minutes until cooked.

Coronation chicken
1 medium onion, approx. 120 g
1 tbsp groundnut or grapeseed oil
1-2 garlic cloves
2-cm piece of fresh root ginger
1 tbsp garam masala
100 ml white wine
4 tbsp clear honey
½ lemon
1 bay leaf
5 tbsp mayonnaise
2 tbsp natural yoghurt or crème fraîche
600 g (approx.) cooked chicken left over from the Big Meal from Scratch or see above
60 g no-soak dried apricots
1 small bunch chives
salt and pepper

Rice salad (optional)
100 g long grain rice
2 tsp white wine or cider vinegar
1½ tbsp olive oil
4 spring onions
50 g flaked almonds (toasted if possible)

Green salad (optional)
4 celery sticks
½ cucumber
2 little gem lettuces
5 sprigs fresh mint
juice of ½ lemon
olive oil, for drizzling

GET AHEAD PREPARATION (optional)

The rice salad and coronation chicken can be made 2 days in advance and kept in the fridge (remove 40 minutes before serving). If you only have a little time:
* Prepare the onion, ginger and garlic.
* Prepare the ingredients for the green salad.
* Cook the rice.

45 minutes before you want to eat

* Cook the rice according to the pack instructions.
* Then cook the sauce. Peel and roughly slice the onion. Heat the oil in a small pan over a medium heat, add the onion and cook gently for 5 minutes. Peel and chop the garlic and ginger. After 5 minutes add the ginger and garlic to the pan and cook over a low heat for another 3 minutes. Increase the heat, add the garam masala and a pinch of salt. Let this cook for 2 minutes then add the wine and honey. Cut the half lemon into slices and add the pieces to the mixture with the bay leaf. Simmer for 10 minutes.
* While the sauce is cooking, drain the rice. To cool it down quickly, spread it over a flat dish.
* Next prepare the salad. Trim and wash the celery, then chop it finely and place in a salad bowl. Peel the cucumber and halve it lengthways. Slice the cucumber and add it to the celery. Remove any outer leaves from the little gems, wash them well then dry. Shred the leaves and add them to the celery and cucumber. Strip the mint leaves from their stalks, tear and add to leaves.
* When the sauce has simmered for 10 minutes tip the contents of the pan into a sieve over a bowl and press the lemon pieces with the back of a spoon to extract all the liquid. Leave the liquid in the bowl to cool.
* Once the rice is cool, tip it into a bowl, stir through the vinegar and oil and season. Trim the spring onions and slice them finely. Toast the almonds, if necessary, in a frying pan over a low heat for a couple of minutes, then stir the almonds and spring onions into the rice.
* Season the green salad, add the lemon juice and a drizzle of oil and toss together.
* Stir the mayonnaise and yoghurt into the cooled sauce, taste and season. Shred the chicken into a bowl. Spoon the sauce over the chicken and stir well. Use scissors to snip the apricots and nearly all the chives into the chicken.
* Put a spoonful of rice salad, green salad and coronation chicken on the plates. Snip the remaining chives over the top.

Panzanella – Tuscan Bread Salad

Sometimes the simplest things are really the best. This is based on a delicious Tuscan bread salad called panzanella. It was originally a solution to the problem of left over bread too tough to chew. This recipe is especially refreshing on hot summer days, and makes excellent picnic food.

If you don't have any suitably stale bread, slice your bread as described in the recipe and dry it out in a low oven (160°C/325°F/Gas Mark 3) for 15–20 minutes until it is no longer doughy. If it doesn't completely dry out, don't worry – it will still soak up the delicious juices.

500 g white bread, several days old (coarse-textured rustic bread works best); see above if you only have fresh bread
2 garlic cloves
8 very ripe large tomatoes, approx. 800 g
1 medium red onion, approx. 120 g
1½ × 290 g jars roasted red peppers in oil or 3 large red peppers, roasted and peeled (see page 360–61)

2 tsp capers
4 tbsp olive oil
1½ tbsp red wine vinegar
2 handfuls of fresh basil leaves
1 cucumber
salt and pepper

To serve
soft white cheese or Parma ham

GET AHEAD PREPARATION (optional)

* Dry the bread in the oven, if necessary.
* Peel and slice the onion.
* Peel the tomatoes.
* Slice the peppers.

35 minutes before you want to eat (50 minutes if you are roasting the peppers)

* First, prepare the bread. Slice into 3–4-cm thick slices, then cut the garlic cloves in half. Rub both sides of each slice of bread thoroughly with the raw garlic. Rip the bread slices into generous bite-sized pieces.
* Next, peel the tomatoes. Make a small incision in the top of each tomato and cover with boiling water. After 30 seconds, run them under the cold tap and peel off skin. Cut the tomatoes into quarters and then each quarter in half again, so that you have nice bite-sized chunks.
* Peel and finely slice the onion and cut the red peppers into thick slices.
* Now place the chopped tomatoes, onion, peppers and capers in a bowl, season them with salt and pepper and dress them with the oil and vinegar.
* Add the bread pieces to the tomatoes and peppers. Tear the basil leaves in half, add these to the bread, tomato and peppers and leave to infuse for 20–30 minutes (up to 2 hours if you are ahead of time) at room temperature. Taste the salad and season as necessary.
* To serve, peel, deseed and cube the cucumber and add it to the salad. Spoon the salad on to individual plates and scatter a few torn basil leaves on top. A little soft white cheese or Parma ham is delicious served alongside.

Larder feast

Coconut Mackerel with Green Thai Rice

This is one of those recipes which at first glance seems rather bold. In fact, it's worth the risk as it produces a very moreish meal with relatively little effort. The powerful, contrasting flavours are typical of South-East Asian cooking.

Canned mackerel fillets are marinated in a sour dressing, coated in coconut and then fried until brown. It is served with a fragrant coriander, ginger and chilli rice. The recipe takes its inspiration from New Zealand chef Peter Gordon.

Coconut mackerel
2 garlic cloves
juice of 1½ limes
4 tsp Thai fish sauce
2 tbsp tamarind paste
2 tbsp lemon grass paste or
  1 stick fresh lemon grass
4 × 125 g cans mackerel fillets
  in lightly salted water
8 tbsp dessicated coconut (if you
  can get dried ribbon coconut
  even better)
groundnut or grapeseed oil

Green Thai rice
4 garlic cloves
4-cm cube of fresh root ginger
1-2 green chillies (depending on
  taste)
small handful fresh coriander
500 ml boiling water
300 g frozen spinach
250 g Thai jasmine rice
1 bunch spring onions, approx.
  8 10
juice of ½ lime
salt and pepper

GET AHEAD PREPARATION (optional)

* Marinate the mackerel.
* Prepare the flavouring for the rice.
* Trim and chop the spring onions.

30 minutes before you want to eat

* Preheat the oven to 160°C/325°F/Gas Mark 3.
* Make the marinade. Peel and crush the garlic and mix it in a bowl with the lime juice, fish sauce, tamarind and lemon grass. If you are using fresh lemon grass, slice this finely first.
* Drain the mackerel fillets and cover them with the marinade, keeping the pieces of fish as large as you can. Cover and set aside.
* Next prepare the flavours for the rice. Peel and chop the garlic and ginger. Deseed and chop the chillies. Put the garlic, chopped ginger or ginger paste and the chillies in a food processor, add the coriander and whizz it to a paste. Then tip the paste into a large pan with a lid. Add the boiling water, ½ teaspoon salt and the spinach. Place on a medium heat to let the spinach defrost.
* Now add the rice to the fragrant spinach water and bring to the boil over a medium heat. Stir once, then cover, and leave the rice to cook over a very low heat until the liquid is absorbed and the rice is soft – about 10 minutes. Do not disturb the rice once the lid is on the pan. After 10 minutes remove the rice pan from the heat and leave it to sit for another 10 minutes with the lid on.
* Lift the pieces of mackerel from their marinade (scrape away any pieces of lemon grass that stick) and toss them in about 7 tablespoons of the coconut.
* Heat a generous splash of oil in a frying pan. When it is hot add the coconut-coated fish. Fry on both sides until the coconut is brown and the fish hot.
* Set the fish aside in the preheated oven while you finish everything else. Pour the marinade into a jug – if you used fresh lemon grass, strain the marinade first.
* To finish the rice, trim and chop the spring onions. Stir them into the rice with the lime juice and season to taste.
* Place the mackerel pieces on a bed of rice and scatter the rest of the coconut over them. Serve the remaining marinade on the side.

Two for one

Spinach and Smoked Trout Roulade

A roulade looks kitschly sophisticated, but is surprisingly easy to make. It can be made in advance, and freezes well, so is a useful recipe for summer entertaining.

There are two stages to this recipe. Chopped fresh spinach is cooked and mixed with eggs and seasoning so that it can spread flat on a baking sheet and baked. This is then covered with a mixture of smoked trout and horseradish cream, and rolled into a roulade. If you can't find smoked trout use 300 g smoked salmon, finely chopped, or, if possible, 450 g hot-smoked salmon, flaked like trout. You will need baking parchment or greaseproof paper to line the baking sheet.

This recipe makes enough for eight so that half can be frozen.

Roulade
800 g large leaf spinach or
    600 g baby leaf spinach
groundnut or grapeseed oil
2 free-range egg yolks
pinch of nutmeg (ground or
    freshly grated)
6 free-range egg whites
salt and pepper

Filling
450 g smoked trout fillets
1 lemon
4 sprigs fresh dill
4 spring onions
60 g butter
1 tbsp horseradish cream
200 g cream cheese

To serve
new potatoes and tomato salad

GET AHEAD PREPARATION (optional)

The roulade can be made up to 2 days in advance and kept in the fridge. If you only have a little time:
* Prepare and cook the spinach, drain it well and whizz with the egg yolks and nutmeg.
* Flake the smoked trout and make the filling.

1 hour before you want to eat

* Preheat the oven to 180°C/350°F/Gas Mark 4.
* Line a baking tray (approx. 30 x 40 cm) with parchment or greaseproof paper.
* Next cook the spinach for the roulade mixture. Wash it thoroughly and, if using large leaf spinach with thick stalks, remove these. Heat a splash of oil in a large pan and cook the spinach for 4–5 minutes until limp. Then tip the spinach into a colander, run it under the cold tap to cool, and squeeze very thoroughly to remove excess liquid.
* To make the roulade mixture, put the spinach in a food processor with the egg yolks and nutmeg, season with salt and pepper and whizz to a purée. If you don't have a processor you can use a hand blender.
* Next, whisk the egg whites until they form stiff peaks when the whisk is removed. Fold the egg whites into the spinach mixture.
* Pour the roulade mixture on to the baking tray, flatten to an even thickness covering the base and bake in the oven for 10 minutes.
* While the roulade is cooking, make the filling. Flake the trout into a mixing bowl (removing any skin or bones). Grate the zest from half the lemon and squeeze out all the juice. Add the zest and juice to the trout. Roughly chop the dill, trim and finely slice the spring onions and add both to the bowl. Finally, melt the butter and add this, along with the horseradish cream and cream cheese. Beat everything together until blended – this will work in a processor or with a hand blender but try not to overwork the mixture as it's best when it retains some texture. Season to taste with salt and pepper.
* Once the roulade is cooked, turn it out on to a clean damp tea towel and remove the paper backing. Leave it to cool for 10-15 minutes. Keep the tea towel underneath, as this will be used to roll up the roulade.
* Carefully spread the trout filling over the roulade when it is cool, then roll the roulade up, along the longest side, using the tea towel to help you pull it into a log shape. Twist the tea towel at either end of the log. Place the roulade in the fridge to set for at least 10 minutes. It could sit like this for up to 2 days before serving.
* After 10 minutes, or when you want to serve, unwrap the roulade and cut it in half (use a serrated knife). Wrap one of the halves in foil and place in the freezer.
* Slice the other half into even slices and serve with hot new potatoes and a tomato salad.

Lazy day supper   Take the roulade out of the freezer and let it defrost completely. Cut it into four slices and serve as above.

Spinach

In terms of flavour and texture the best spinach for cooking is all but completely unavailable at supermarkets since bags of baby spinach for salad are the norm. Spinach with larger leaves and stalks has been grown for longer and has more flavour and texture but, admittedly, it involves more labour than the bags of baby spinach – it has to be well washed and the thick stalks have to be removed. If you are able to buy spinach from a grocer and have been used to buying supermarket spinach you'll be surprised not only at the improved taste but also at the price – bagged baby spinach while delicious raw for salads is more expensive than it's scruffier, dirtier but more substantial older brother. Where recipes in the book ask for spinach the weights specified refer to the amount required for cooking. In other words, if a recipe calls for 200 g spinach this could either come from a 200 g bag of ready-prepared leaves, or from 250–300 g large-leaved loose spinach once the stalks have been discarded.

Baked Cheesecake with Strawberries

This baked cheesecake has a layer of strawberries and strawberry purée running through the middle. It is rich and very wicked. The recipe for the cheese filling is adapted from Jill Norman's definitive *The New Penguin Cookery Book*.

Filling
300 g strawberries
100 g caster sugar
3 free-range eggs
500 g mascarpone
100 g cream cheese
100 ml double cream

Base
60 g butter
120 g digestive biscuits
3 tbsP demerara sugar

1½ hours before you want to eat

* Preheat the oven to 180°C/350°F/Gas Mark 4.
* Grease a 20-cm cake tin with butter and line the base with greaseproof paper.
* Hull the strawberries and put half of them in a pan with half the caster sugar. Add 1 tablespoon water and bring slowly to the boil. Simmer for about 5 minutes or until the fruit softens. While these strawberries are cooking cut the others in half and set them aside.
* When the strawberries are cooked pass them through a sieve. Mix the halved strawberries in to the purée and leave to one side to cool.
* Melt the butter in a pan or in the microwave. Put the biscuits and sugar into a food processor, whizz to form crumbs and add the melted butter. If you don't have a processor put the biscuits and demerara sugar in a plastic bag and bash them to crumbs with a rolling pin or the back of a pan, then tip the crumbs into a bowl and stir in the butter.
* Put the biscuit mixture on the bottom of the prepared tin, pressing it down so that it forms an even layer.
* Beat the eggs until they are thick then add the remaining sugar. Beat until the mixture is light and fluffy then beat in the mascarpone and cream cheese. Whip the cream until it is just starting to thicken then fold it gently into the cheese mixture.
* Cover the biscuit base with half the cheese mixture then tip the strawberry mixture on top. Cover the strawberries with the remaining cheese and egg mixture.
* Bake in the oven for about 1¼ hours but check after 45 minutes to make sure the top is not browning too much. If it is, cover it with foil for the remaining cooking time.
* Take the cheesecake out of the oven and allow it to cool completely before removing it from the cake tin and serving.

Melon, Nectarine and Grape Salad with Muscat Syrup

This pudding has the look and taste of summer. It can be made well ahead of time and left to chill in the fridge.

½ lemon
100 g caster sugar
200 ml muscat wine
1 sprig fresh mint
4 ripe nectarines
1 ripe melon, approx. 800 g
  (preferably charentais)
300 g seedless small sweet white
  grapes (preferably muscat)

To serve
Ice cream, sorbet or cream

50 minutes before you want to eat

* Start by making the muscat syrup. Put the sugar, wine, mint and lemon peel in a pan. Bring slowly to the boil and simmer for about 5 minutes. Remove from the heat, pour into a serving dish and leave to cool.
* While the syrup is cooling prepare the fruit. Put a large pan of water on to boil. When the water is boiling immerse the nectarines for about 30 seconds then drain and peel them. The skins should come away easily. Cut the nectarines in half, remove the stones then slice the flesh into bite-sized slithers.
* Cut the melon into quarters and scoop out the seeds. Slice the flesh away from the skin then chop it into cubes.
* Separate the grapes from their stalks and if they are large cut them in half.
* Remove the mint sprig and lemon peel from the syrup then when it is completely cold, add the prepared fruit. Stir to mix, chill for 30 minutes or so, then serve.

August puddings   # Iced Chocolate Meringue

This recipe can be made using shop-bought meringues but if you have egg whites to use up, or have the time, they are easy to make. They do take a while to cook in the oven, though, so if you make the meringues factor in starting at least 2¼ hours before you want to freeze the pudding (it needs to be frozen for 3–4 hours). Meringues keep very well for days in an airtight container so you could make them well ahead of time. This pudding is good with strawberries and raspberries.

groundnut or grapeseed oil for
   greasing
2 free-range egg whites
110 g sugar
or
8 ready-made meringues

125 g dark chocolate, broken into
   smallish pieces
2 tbsp brandy
200 ml double cream

To serve
soft fruit

2½ hours before you want to freeze the pudding

* First, make the meringues. Preheat the oven to 140°C/275°F/Gas Mark 1 and grease a baking sheet with oil.
* Whisk the egg whites until they are stiff but not dry and add half the sugar. Whisk again until the mixture becomes shiny then add the remaining sugar and whisk again.
* Spoon the meringue mixture on to the prepared baking sheet, and bake for up to 1¼ hours until the meringues are dried out but not brown.

25 minutes before freezing

* Line a 900 g loaf tin with parchment paper then start to make the chocolate mixture.
* Put the chocolate and brandy in a pan with 2 tablespoons water and stir constantly over a gentle heat until the chocolate has melted. Put to one side to cool.
* Crush the meringues. Lightly whip the cream, fold in three-quarters of the chocolate mixture and add the meringues. Make sure everything is well incorporated, then swirl the rest of the chocolate through the mix. Pour into the prepared loaf tin and freeze for 3–4 hours, until firm to the touch.
* Transfer the pudding to the fridge 10 minutes before serving with the fruit.

August puddings   # Baked Peaches

These are so simple but so good.

50 g butter
juice of 1 lemon
80 g light brown soft sugar
generous pinch of nutmeg
   (ground or freshly grated)
4 ripe peaches

To serve
cream or pistachio ice cream

45 minutes before
you want to eat
* Preheat the oven to 190°C/375°F/Gas Mark 5.
* Melt the butter and mix it with the lemon juice, sugar and nutmeg.
* Halve the peaches, remove their stones and place them snugly in an ovenproof dish.
* Scatter the sugar and butter mixture over the peaches. Put the dish in the oven and bake for 30 minutes until the peaches are soft and golden brown. Check them halfway through and spoon the syrupy liquid from the bottom of the dish over them.
* Serve with cream or pistachio ice cream.

SEPTEMBER

In late summer, it should still be possible to eat outdoors. Butterflied lamb with baba ganoush could be cooked on the barbecue if the weather permits, and our rich shellfish stew with saffron potatoes takes its inspiration from the Mediterranean. As autumn arrives and the weather grows brisker, we have duck legs roasted with quinces or pears and a traditional Roast Rib of Beef with Yorkshire Puddings. September is the month for making chutneys and jams. Plums, grapes, figs, quinces and blackberries come into their own, and tomatoes, aubergines and red peppers can still be had. Baking figs with balsamic vinegar and orange juice intensifies their plump loveliness and chicken cooked with grapes develops a gently perfumed flavour. There are puddings for all weathers this month: an Iced Blackberry Fool for warmer days, a Plum Crumble for when the temperature drops and a Chocolate and Fig Cake suitable for rain or shine.

September	Week 1	Week 2	Week 3	Week 4
Big meal from scratch	Sweet charred lamb with baba ganoush, green and runner beans and potatoes	Rich shellfish stew, saffron potatoes and lemon fennel	Roast rib of beef with Yorkshire puddings, roast potatoes and parsnips and steamed squash and marrow	Duck with quinces (or pears) in red wine with roast potatoes and lemon courgettes
Something for nothing 1	Spiced lamb with pearl barley pilaff	Fideua – shellfish spaghetti	Bread and butter squash and marrow	Duck and lentil salad
Something for nothing 2	Green beans on toast	Fennel Niçoise	Yoghurt baked fish with chilli parsnips and chutney	Courgette and ricotta lasagne
Seasonal supper	Plaice, potato and spinach bake	Baked figs and green bean, potato and walnut salad with smoked duck or bacon	Sausages with peperonata	Chicken with grapes
Larder feast	Bean burgers	Lentil and chorizo stew	Quick kedgeree	Cauliflower, chickpea and preserved lemon salad
2 for 1	Salmon parcels with watercress and lemon butter	Chicken with sun-dried tomatoes	Imam bayaldi – rich aubergine stew	Fish and red pepper stew
Puddings	Iced blackberry fool	Apple butterscotch meringue	Chocolate and fig cake	Plum crumble

September Week 1 – Overview

If there's an Indian summer and barbecuing is still a possibility, consider cooking much of this week's Big Meal from Scratch outside. The lamb and the aubergines for the baba will benefit from being cooked over hot coals. That said, the meal will not be lacking if only the grill and oven are in operation. In terms of timing, the lamb requires marinating and the aubergine needs to be cooked for at least 2 hours before you want to eat, so this is probably a recipe for the weekend. Aside from the extra ingredients for the Something for Nothing recipes, there should be enough baba ganoush remaining at the end of this meal to enjoy during the week with pitta breads, cold lamb and pickles.

For one of the Something for Nothings, surplus lamb from the big meal is dipped in a spicy marinade and served with a Pearl Barley Pilaff that takes 30 minutes to make. For the other, extra green and runner beans are stewed down with wine and anchovies and served on toast with soft-boiled eggs.

The Seasonal Supper, a Plaice, Potato and Spinach Bake, is simple and tasty but takes 20–25 minutes to prepare and 20 minutes to cook, so bear this in mind when planning the week's cooking. The fish should be cooked soon after purchase or, if not, be placed in the freezer until required. For a Larder Feast that will be loved by children and adults alike, try the Bean Burgers served in white rolls with salad and a relish.

The Two for One, Salmon Parcels with Watercress and Lemon Butter, is a meal that can be prepared ahead of eating, looks impressive and tastes delicious so it is a good choice if you've invited friends over. The recipe takes around 20 minutes to prepare, 20–30 minutes to cook and freezes very well.

September Week 1	Recipe	Time
Big meal from scratch	Sweet charred lamb with baba ganoush, green and runner beans and potatoes Added Extra Lamb pittas with baba ganoush	2 hours
Something for nothing 1	Green beans on toast	30 mins
Something for nothing 2	Spiced lamb with pearl barley pilaff	30 mins
Seasonal supper	Plaice, potato and spinach bake	50 mins
Larder feast	Bean burgers	35 mins
2 for 1	Salmon parcels with watercress and lemon butter	45 mins

All recipes serve 4 apart from the 2 for 1 recipe which makes 8 portions

SHOPPING LIST (for 4 people)

Meat and fish
1.6–1.8 kg butterflied leg of lamb (buy 1 ×
  2.5kg leg of lamb and ask the butcher to
  butterfly it)
2 large plaice, filleted and skinned, divided
  into 4 fillets per fish
1.2–1.6 kg skinned side of salmon or 2 ×
  600–800 g skinned salmon fillets

Dairy
340 g butter
5 free-range eggs
150 ml milk
275 ml double cream
100 ml soured cream
60 g Parmesan

Fruit and vegetables
750 g potatoes (ideally King Edward)
600 g new potatoes
600 g green (or fine) beans
600 g runner beans
2–3 aubergines, approx. 800
2 small bunches watercress or 85g bagged
  watercress
500 g large leaf spinach or 300 g baby leaf
  spinach
3 large carrots, approx. 400 g
2 large leeks, approx. 350g
2 celery sticks
5 medium red onions, approx. 600 g
2 large or banana shallots, approx. 60 g
15 garlic cloves
5 sprigs fresh coriander
1 small bunch mint
9 sprigs fresh thyme or 1½ tsp dried thyme
1 large bunch fresh parsley
1 small bunch chives
2 lemons

Basics
625 g chilled ready-made shortcrust pastry
4 slices thick crusty white bread
100 ml olive oil
80 ml groundnut or grapeseed oil
450 ml vegetable stock (made from a stock
  cube or bouillon powder)
50 g (approx.) plain flour
2 tsp mustard powder
salt and pepper

Store cupboard
300 g pearl barley
150 g matzo meal or dried breadcrumbs
2 × 400–420 g cans red kidney beans
1 × 50 g can anchovy fillets in olive oil
3 tbsp tahini
4 tbsp mayonnaise
2 tbsp clear honey

2 tbsp tomato ketchup
1 tbsp ground cinnamon
2 tsp ground cumin
2 tsp ground coriander
pinch of nutmeg
pinch of cayenne pepper
good shake of Tabasco sauce
1 tsp paprika
300 ml sherry (preferably oloroso or fino)
250 ml white wine

Serving suggestions
radish and lettuce salad ingredients (Spiced
  Lamb with Pearl Barley Pilaff)
toMatoes, salad ingredients, Soft rolls and
  relish of choice (Bean Burgers)
frozen peas (Salmon Parcels with Watercress
  and Lemon Butter)

To download or print out this shopping list,
please visit www.thekitchenrevolution.co.uk/
September/Week1

**Big meal
from scratch**

Sweet Charred Lamb with Baba Ganoush, Green and Runner Beans and Potatoes

The sweet flavour of lamb goes well with baba ganoush, a smoky, rich Middle Eastern dip made from aubergines, tahini, lemon juice and garlic. A butterflied leg of lamb is one that's been boned, kept in one piece, split lengthways and splayed out – or butterflied. This cut can be successfully cooked on a barbecue (or in a very hot oven) so that the outside is well seared and the inside remains pink. With the meat laid flat, any marinade permeates deep into the flesh, so it is well worth factoring some marinating time into your planning.

Ideally the aubergines can be roasted on a barbecue until their skins are charred and the flesh is completely soft. This gives the dip an intensely smoky flavour. If you're not lighting the barbecue they can be cooked until very soft in a hot oven with adequate results.

The recipe includes extra lamb for the Spiced Lamb with Pearl Barley Pilaff and extra green beans for Green Beans on Toast.

Sweet charred lamb
2 garlic cloves
2 tbsp clear honey
300 ml sherry
6 sprigs fresh thyme
handful of fresh parsley
1 tsp paprika
1.6–1.8 kg butterflied leg of lamb (buy 1 × 2.5kg leg of lamb and ask the butcher to butterfly it; includes 700 g extra for the spiced lamb with pearl barley pilaff)
salt and black pepper

Baba ganoush
2–3 aubergines, approx. 800 g total weight)
2 garlic cloves
3 tbsp tahini
juice of 1 lemon
3 tbsp olive oil

Green and runner beans and potatoes
600 g green (or fine) beans; includes 300 g extra for the green beans on toast
600 g runner beans; includes 300 g extra for the green beans on toast
600 g new potatoes
50 g butter

GET AHEAD PREPARATION (optional)

The marinade can be made, and the lamb can be marinated, up to 24 hours in advance. The baba ganoush can be made a day or two in advance. If you only have a little time:
* Chargrill the aubergines.
* Prepare the beans.
* Peel the garlic.

At least 2 hours (and up to 24 hours) before you want to eat marinate the lamb

* To make the marinade, peel and crush the garlic and place it in a dish large enough to hold the lamb. Add the honey and sherry and mix until the honey has dissolved. Strip the thyme leaves from their stalks, roughly chop the parsley and add the herbs to the sherry mixture. Stir in 2 teaspoons salt, 1 teaspoon pepper and the paprika and mix well. Place the lamb, flesh-side down, in the marinade. Using a spoon, baste the top of the lamb with the marinade, then set aside in a cool place or, if you aren't planning to eat within 4 hours, in the fridge. Baste the lamb at least twice prior to cooking.

At least 1½ hours before you want to eat make the baba ganoush

* Preheat the oven to 200°C/400°F/Gas Mark 6 and preheat the grill to high, or light the barbecue.
* If you are using a barbecue, place the aubergines on a griddle over the heat and cook until their skins are completely charred. You will need to turn them once or twice. When the skins are completely black and the aubergines are soft to the touch, remove them from the heat and set aside until they are cool enough to handle. If you're cooking them using a stove place them under the hot grill for 5 minutes until one side is blackened. Turn them and repeat once more, then turn off the grill and place the aubergines on a high shelf in the oven and cook for about 20–30 minutes or until they are soft and floppy.
* Peel and crush the garlic and place it in a large mixing bowl. Add the tahini and mix well.
* When the aubergines are cool enough to handle, hold them over the bowl containing the garlic tahini by their stalk ends and scrape out the flesh with a metal spoon. Don't worry if some charred skin ends up in the bowl as this will add flavour. Using a fork, mix and mash the aubergines into the tahini mixture. Add about 1 tablespoon lemon

juice and season. Using a whisk, mix the mixture very well while adding the oil. Taste for seasoning and add additional lemon juice, salt or pepper if necessary. Cover and set aside in a cool place.

* Next, top and tail the green beans. Remove any tough strings from the runner beans and cut into lengthways slices, as thin as possible.

45 minutes before you want to eat cook the lamb

* Turn the oven to 220°C/425°/Gas Mark 7 or make sure the barbecue is smoulderingly hot.
* Remove the lamb from the marinade and either place it, skin side up, on a rack in a roasting tin and put it in the middle of the hot oven, or place the rack over the hot barbecue. Baste with the marinade and cook for 15 minutes.
* After 15 minutes, baste the meat with liberal amounts of marinade and, if cooking on the barbecue, turn the meat. Cook for a further 20–30 minutes, depending on whether you like your lamb pink or well done

25 minutes before you want to eat cook the potatoes

* While the meat is cooking wash and scrub the potatoes and, if they not very small cut them in half, then bring them to the boil in a large pan of salted water. When the water boils turn the temperature down and allow to simmer for 10–15 minutes.

15 minutes before you want to eat cook the beans

* After a total of 30–40 minutes cooking time (longer if you like your meat well done), remove from the lamb from the oven or barbecue, and leave it in a warm place to rest for 15 minutes. Turn the oven off and put some plates and serving dishes in it to warm.
* Next cook the beans in salted boiling water for 4–5 minutes until just cooked.
* When the beans and potatoes are cooked, drain them well. Tip half the beans into a serving dish, add half the butter and season, cover until ready to serve. Set the rest of the beans aside for use later in the week. Tip the potatoes into a serving dish, dot with the remaining butter, season and cover until ready to serve.
* Cut one-third of the meat from the lamb and set aside for later in the week.
* Slice the remaining lamb and serve it with a generous spoon of baba ganoush on the side and the beans and potatoes.

Afterwards

Put the remaining lamb (400-600 g) and beans (600 g) in separate containers, cover and refrigerate for use later in the week. There may be additional lamb and baba ganoush spare, in which case they make excellent pitta brad sandwiches.

Added extra

Lamb Pittas with Baba Ganoush

Stuff warm pitta brads with thin slices of the cold lamb, baba ganoush, cucumber and little gem lettuce. Dress with lemon, pickled cucumbers and chilli sauce. Eat immediately.

Green Beans on Toast

This is an excellent way of transforming leftover green and runner beans into a new meal – it's extremely simple and very good. The inspiration for this recipe came to Rosie from her friend and colleague Andy Tyrell, who is a great chef and champion of seasonal food.

2 large or banana shallots,
    approx. 60 g
1 × 50 g can anchovy fillets in
    olive oil
50 g butter
2 garlic cloves
600 g cooked green and runner
    beans from the Big Meal from
    Scratch or 600 g green and
    runner beans cooked in salted
    water for 7–10 minutes
4 free-range eggs
4 slices thick crusty white bread
100 ml white wine
salt and black pepper

GET AHEAD PREPARATION (optional)

* Peel and slice the shallots.
* Peel and crush the garlic.

30 minutes before you want to eat

* Start by cooking the shallots in the anchovy oil. Peel and finely slice the shallots, then splash a generous amount of oil from the anchovy can into a heavy-based pan with a lid, large enough to hold all the ingredients. Heat gently with a large nut of butter. When the oil is hot, add the shallots to the pan and let them cook over a low heat for 5 minutes, stirring from time to time. While the shallots are softening, peel and crush the garlic.
* When the shallots are soft, add the garlic and cook gently for 1–2 minutes. Then add the anchovies and let them melt into the shallots for 5 minutes.
* When everything has amalgamated, add another generous nut of butter and the beans to the pan. Make sure everything is mixed together well and let the flavours converge for a couple of minutes.
* After a few minutes add 75 ml water and bring up to a simmer. Put the lid on the pan and leave the beans to tick over very gently for 15 minutes. Preheat the oven to 140°C/275°F/Gas Mark 1.
* Now soft-boil the eggs. Lower them into a pan of boiling water. Do this carefully, without cracking any of them. Put a timer on for 7 minutes. When the timer goes off, drain off the hot water and leave them to cool under cold running water for 5 minutes or so. Give them a shake around and their shells will crack a little allowing the cooling process to work more efficiently. When they are completely cold, peel them and leave whole.
* While the eggs are cooking, toast the bread, butter it liberally and keep warm in the oven.
* After 15 minutes take the lid off the beans, increase the heat and add the wine and the remaining butter. Season to taste with salt and pepper and simmer for a few minutes while you peel and halve the eggs.
* To serve, place a slice of toast on each plate and use a slotted spoon to pile the beans on top. Finish each serving with two egg halves and a little ground black pepper.

Something for nothing 2

Spiced Lamb with Pearl Barley Pilaff

Pilaff refers to a dish where a grain such as rice, cracked wheat or pearl barley is fried then cooked with different vegetables and flavours. It can be a very simple mixture of rice cooked with onions or an elaborate dish served as part of a banquet with meats, vegetables, herbs, spices, fruits and nuts. The pilaff recipe for this meal uses pearl barley, which has a plump, fat texture and a distinctive nutty taste. The leftover lamb from the Big Meal from Scratch is marinated in Middle Eastern spices and lemon juice and this mixture doubles as a dressing for the pearl barley when you come to serve. If you have no lamb left over, marinate 500 g lamb neck fillet in a little olive oil, lemon juice and seasoning, brown in a pan then roast in a hot oven for about 15–25 minutes.

Spiced lamb
1½ tbsp olive oil
½ tbsp lemon juice
good shake of Tabasco sauce
1 tsp ground cinnamon
2 tsp ground cumin
2 tsp ground coriander
5 sprigs fresh coriander
400–600 g cold lamb left over
    from the Big Meal from Scratch
    or see above
salt and pepper

Pearl barley pilaff
300 g pearl barley
450 ml vegetable stock (made
    from a stock cube or bouillon
    powder)
30 g butter
1 medium red onion, 120 g
2 tbsp olive oil
2 celery sticks
2 garlic cloves
150 ml white wine
3 large carrots
½ tbsp lemon juice
small handful mint leaves
small handful parsley

To serve
radish and lettuce salad

GET AHEAD PREPARATION (optional)

The pilaff can be made a day in advance, minus the herbs. If you only have a little time:
* Prepare any of the vegetables.
* Chop the coriander and parsley.
* Slice the lamb.

30 minutes before you want to eat cook the pilaff

* Rinse the pearl barley in a sieve and put it into a pan with the stock and butter. Bring to the boil then turn the heat down and leave to simmer.
* Meanwhile, peel and finely slice the onion. Heat a generous splash of oil in a heavy-based pan. Add the onion and cook gently while you trim, wash and slice the celery. Add the celery and leave to soften for 5–10 minutes. Meanwhile, peel and crush the garlic. Once the onion and celery are soft, add the garlic and cook for a couple of minutes. Then add the wine and simmer for 3 minutes, stirring all the time.
* Once the wine has reduced to two thirds, tip the onions and celery into the pan containing the pearl barley and mix them in thoroughly. Now leave the whole lot to simmer while you prepare the lamb.

15 minutes before you want to eat prepare the lamb

* In a large bowl whisk together the oil, lemon juice, Tabasco, cinnamon, cumin and ground coriander. Wash and chop the fresh coriander and add it to the bowl, taste the dressing and season. Slice the lamb, throw it into the bowl and toss it about thoroughly.

5 minutes before you want to eat

* When the pearl barley is soft all the liquid should be absorbed. Turn the heat off and put the lid on. If there is still liquid in the pan, continue to simmer for another 5 minutes or so.
* Peel and coarsely grate the carrots, season them and toss them in the oil and lemon juice. Stir the carrots through the pilaff when it is ready, then tear up the mint leaves and stir them through.
* Put the lamb slices with their dressing on a serving plate and the pilaff in a serving dish.
* Serve with a radish and lettuce salad.

Seasonal supper

Plaice, Potato and Spinach Bake

This recipe is for flat fish layered with spinach and potatoes in a creamy sauce. The plaice can be replaced with lemon sole or dab – but we think fresh plaice is a real treat even though it's not the most expensive of the flat fish. Fresh is the key here though; these delicate white fish lose their flavour and have an unpleasant taint if they are left hanging about too long.

750 g potatoes, ideally King
   Edward
1 tbsp groundnut or grapeseed oil
60 g butter
2 large leeks, approx. 350 g
500 g large leaf spinach or 300 g
   baby leaf spinach
3 garlic cloves
pinch of nutmeg (ground or
   freshly grated)
150 ml milk
275 ml double cream
60 g Parmesan
2 large plaice, filleted and
   skinned, divided into 4 fillets
   per fish

juice of ½ lemon
salt and pepper

GET AHEAD PREPARATION (optional)

* Prepare the potatoes and cover
   with water.
* Prepare the leeks and spinach.
* Peel and slice the garlic.
* Grate the Parmesan.

50 minutes before you want to eat

* Preheat the oven to 200°C/400°F/Gas Mark 6.
* Peel and thinly slice the potatoes and place them in a pan of salted boiling water. Bring them back to the boil then simmer until they are just soft – about 7–10 minutes.
* Gently heat the oil and all but a generous nut of the butter in a large heavy-based pan. Trim, slice and thoroughly wash the leeks.
* Add the leeks to the pan and cook them over a high heat until they start to soften – stirring occasionally. When they have started to soften, season, turn the heat down, put the lid on and leave the leeks to cook for 5 minutes.
* Destalk the spinach if necessary and wash it thoroughly in plenty of cold water – you may find you need to change the water a couple of times. Leave it to drain in a colander.
* When the leeks are soft, turn the heat up, add the spinach to the pan and stir for a couple of minutes before lowering the heat and replacing the lid. Leave the spinach to wilt for a couple of minutes while you peel and slice the garlic. After 2 minutes, shake the pan a few times to ensure the heat is evenly distributed. Leave for another 2 minutes.
* When the spinach is soft, add the nutmeg and a touch of seasoning then tip the contents of the pan into a colander.
* Use the same pan to make the creamy sauce. Don't worry about washing it – just add the milk, cream and garlic and bring them to the boil. Turn down the heat and simmer gently for a few minutes.
* Drain the potatoes and tip them into the milk and cream mixture in the pan. Take the pan off the heat. Grate the Parmesan.
* Use some of the remaining butter to grease a large ovenproof dish.
* Now start layering up the bake. Using a slotted spoon, lift one-third of the potatoes from their liquid and arrange on the base of the dish. It is important to season each layer as you go. Add half the fish fillets and give them a squeeze of lemon juice. Cover them with half the leek and spinach mixture and a light dusting of cheese. Repeat the layering one more time ending with potatoes. Pour over the cooking liquor. Dot the potatoes with the remaining butter and cheese.
* Bake for 20 minutes. Serve right away.

Larder feast

Bean Burgers

The description 'bean burger' may seem an oxymoron to a hardened meat lover, but believe us, these end up being popular with the most carnivorous eaters. This recipe is an excellent store-cupboard standby so long as you have a few onions and some garlic knocking about. Serve with soft rolls, plenty of relish, a few slices of tomato and a good salad.

4 medium red onions, approx. 480 g
groundnut or grapeseed oil
4 garlic cloves
2 × 400-420 g cans red kidney beans
3 sprigs fresh thyme or 1 tsp dried thyme
150 g matzo meal or dried breadcrumbs

2 tsp mustard powder
2 tbsp tomato ketchup
4 tbsp mayonnaise
2-3 tbsp plain flour
pinch of cayenne pepper
salt and pepper

To serve
soft rolls, salad leaves, tomato slices and relish of choice

GET AHEAD PREPARATION (optional)

The bean burgers can be made up 1-2 days in advance if kept in the fridge - just coat them in flour before frying. If you only have a little time:
* Prepare the onions and garlic.
* Soften the onions.
* Mash and season the beans.

35 minutes before you want to eat

* Peel and finely dice the onions, then heat a splash of the oil in a heavy-based pan over a medium heat. When the oil is hot, stir in the onions, turn down the heat and cook gently for 7–10 minutes until soft.
* In the meantime, peel and crush the garlic and prepare the beans. Drain the beans, and roughly mash them, using either a masher or food processor, so that the mixture is two-thirds mashed and one-third whole or almost whole beans. Strip the thyme leaves from their stalks if using fresh thyme. Add the matzo meal or breadcrumbs, fresh or dried thyme, mustard, tomato ketchup and mayonnaise to the beans. Season with salt and pepper and mix together well.
* Add the garlic to the onions when they have softened. Cook for a couple more minutes then tip the onions and garlic into the bean mixture and mix together.
* Preheat the oven to 140°C/275°F/Gas Mark 1.
* Season the flour with salt and a pinch of cayenne and place it on a plate. Then, with wet hands to stop the mixture sticking, shape the bean mixture into eight patties and coat them in the flour.
* When all the burgers are shaped, heat 1-cm of oil in a large frying pan over a medium-high heat. When the oil is sizzling hot, add two or three burgers at a time, and fry them for about 3 minutes on each side. Keep the cooked burgers warm in the oven while you cook the rest.
* Serve the bean burgers with sliced tomatoes, salad, soft rolls and relish

Two for one

Salmon Parcels with Watercress and Lemon Butter

These salmon pastry parcels are appetising to look at and excellent to eat. Salmon in pastry is a dinner-party classic – delicious, but very rich and perhaps a bit old-fashioned. In this recipe watercress, herbs and plenty of lemon ensure that the end result is light and fresh. Good to serve to friends and a treat to serve to family.

The recipe includes the quantities to make eight parcels so that four can be frozen for a later date. The parcels can be cooked from frozen.

150 g butter
1.2–1.6 kg skinned side of
   salmon or 2 × 600–800 g
   skinned salmon fillets
625 g chilled ready-made
   shortcrust pastry
plain flour, for dusting
2 small bunches watercress or
   85g watercress

small handful of fresh parsley
2 lemons
1 free-range egg
1 small bunch chives
100 ml soured cream
salt and pepper

To serve
peas

GET AHEAD PREPARATION (optional)

The salmon parcels can be made and kept in the fridge for up 12 hours, then cooked as per the instructions. If you only have a little time:
* Make the watercress butter.

45 minutes before you want to eat

* Put the butter in a warm place to soften or soften it in the microwave (do not allow to melt completely).
* Cut the side of salmon into four equal pieces, or cut each fillet in half. The recipe makes two large salmon parcels. Each parcel contains two pieces of salmon with a watercress butter filling.
* Cut the pastry into four pieces, place on a lightly floured work surface and roll into four rectangles, two of them just a little bigger than the fillets and two about 5 cm wider and longer so that they wrap round the fish. Rest the pastry in the fridge while you get on with making the watercress butter.
* Pick the watercress leaves from any particularly thick stalks, then discard the stalks and chop the leaves. Roughly chop the parsley. Grate the zest of one lemon and squeeze out the juice of both. Mix watercress, the grated lemon zest, half the lemon juice and the parsley into the softened butter and season with salt and pepper. This job can be done in a food processor or with a hand blender if you prefer.
* Spread half the watercress butter over two f the fillets. Place the other two fillets on top, skinned-side up and spread the remaining watercress butter on top of these
* Preheat the oven to 200°C/400°F/Gas Mark 6 and preheat a baking sheet in the oven.
* Place the two smaller rectangles of pastry on the work surface and put one of the salmon and watercress-butter sandwiches on top. Break the egg into a small bowl and beat. Paint the edge of the pastry with the egg and place the larger rectangles of pastry on top of the salmon. Pull the pastry over the fish, press the pastry edges together and paint the tops of the parcels with the egg. Make a couple of slashes in the top of each parcel.
* One of the parcels is now ready to be frozen. Wrap it in greaseproof paper or cling film, put it in a freezer bag and freeze.
* To cook the remaining salmon parcel, place it on the hot baking sheet – and cook in the oven for 20–30 minutes until the pastry is golden and crisp.
* While the salmon is cooking, make the sauce. Chop the chives and mix them with the soured cream and remaining lemon juice, then season to taste.
* After 25 minutes check the salmon is cooked by inserting a thin knife into the centre of the parcel. If it feels hot to the touch and the pastry is crisp remove from the oven. If not return to the oven for a further 5 minutes. Cut the salmon parcel into four slices and serve with the soured cream sauce and a pile of peas.

Lazy day supper – cooking instructions

* The salmon parcel is best cooked from frozen.
* Preheat the oven to 180°C/350°F/Gas Mark 4 and preheat a baking sheet. Place the salmon parcel on the baking sheet and cook in the oven for 45 minutes. Cover it with foil if the pastry starts browning before the fish is hot. You can turn the oven up to 200°C/400°F/Gas Mark 6 for the last 5 minutes if the top isn't becoming golden.
* While the salmon is cooking, make the soured cream sauce as above.

KITCHEN REVOLUTION EXTRA

Buying salmon

Salmon presents a rather complicated conundrum for the cook. On the one hand, salmon farming has made it widely available and it can be inexpensive, particularly in the summer. On the other hand, badly managed intensive salmon farming is held to be responsible for contaminating the environment and for causing a decline in the number of wild salmon. However, buying British wild salmon is not the solution to this set of problems – it would only exacerbate the problem of stock decline and wild salmon is fiercely expensive.

As a basic standard, Scottish farmed salmon tends to be farmed more widely than Norwegian salmon and with more stringently regulated feeds and chemical inputs, and is therefore less damaging to the environment and raises fewer questions about stocking densities. In recent years organic salmon farming has taken off and this may be the solution to some of the concerns raised by intensive salmon production. Wherever you buy salmon, look for products that have Marine Stewardship Council approval.

When buying fresh salmon it's worth remembering that a farmed salmon spends less time exercising than its wild counterpart, and as a consequence it can be fatty and flabby. For the sake of taste and texture, however your salmon has been produced, try to buy one without large thick strips of fat between the pink flesh.

Canned salmon comes from Alaskan and Pacific wild salmon. This is MSC certified and therefore, at present, safe to buy.

September Week 2 – Overview

The Big Meal from Scratch of Rich Shellfish Stew, Saffron Potatoes and Lemon Fennel is definitely a feast that deserves to be shared. As an added bonus there's very little preparation and cooking involved so the whole meal can be on the table in about 1¼ hours. It's imperative that everything for this stew is as fresh as possible, so it will need to be cooked the day, or day after, all the shellfish and fish are purchased.

No recipe this week takes longer than half an hour, and though each is simple to execute none of them disappoint on flavour. For one of the Something for Nothings, Fiduea – Shellfish Spaghetti makes use of any surplus stew from the big meal. The other Something for Nothing uses the leftover baked lemon fennel and transforms this into a light and lovely warm Fennel Niçoise.

A Seasonal Supper of Baked Figs and Green Bean, Potato and Walnut Salad with Smoked Duck or Bacon is more substantial than it sounds. The duck breasts have a luxurious smoky flavour but if they are not available the salad works just as well with smoked bacon or even Parma ham, both of which have an intense flavour.

A Lentil and Chorizo Stew is a Larder Feast that can rescue a cook from an empty fridge at the drop of a hat. The recipe takes 30 minutes using canned lentils, but if there is an hour or more to spare it's worth replacing these with dried ones as these are better able to soak up all the wonderful flavours of the chorizo and seasonings.

The Two for One of Chicken with Sun-Dried Tomatoes is a relatively short recipe – it takes 40 minutes.

September Week 2	Recipe	Time
Big meal from scratch	Rich shellfish stew, saffron potatoes and lemon fennel	1¼ hours
Something for nothing 1	Fideua – shellfish spaghetti	30 mins
Something for nothing 2	Fennel Niçoise	30 mins
Seasonal supper	Baked figs and green bean, potato and walnut salad with smoked duck or bacon	25 mins
Larder feast	Lentil and chorizo stew	35 mins
2 for 1	Chicken with sun-dried tomatoes	40 mins

All recipes serve 4 apart from the 2 for 1 recipe which makes 8 portions

SHOPPING LIST (for 4 people)

Meat and fish
400 g monkfish fillet
350 g mussel meat, approx. 900 g fresh
   mussels in their shells
300 g scallops, out of their shells
400 g cooked peeled Atlantic prawns (fresh
   or frozen)
3 smoked duck breasts or 150 g free-range
   rindless smoked streaky bacon or 8 slices
   Parma ham
75 g piece of unsliced pancetta or free-range
   smoked streaky bacon
3-4 chorizo sausages, each approx. 20 cm
   long (hot or mild depending on taste)
6-8 free-range chicken breasts, skinless

Dairy
140 g approx. butter
75 ml milk
300 ml, approx. double cream
150-200 g Gruyère or other strong cheese

Fruit and vegetables
1.2 kg waxy potatoes, such as Desirée or
   Charlotte
7 bulbs fennel, approx. 1.5 kg
400 g green beans
100 g baby leaf spinach
60-70 g rocket
3 medium onions, approx. 360 g
2 medium red onions, approx. 240 g
4 large or banana shallots, approx. 120 g
14 garlic cloves
1 small bunch chives
1 large bunch fresh parsley
generous pinch of herbes de Provence or
   leaves from 3-4 sprigs fresh thyme and
   a handful of chopped fresh parsley or a
   generous pinch of dried herbes de Provence
4 sprigs fresh tarragon or 1 tsp dried
   tarragon
5½ lemons
1 orange
12 fresh figs

Basics
150 ml olive oil
2 tbsp groundnut or grapeseed oil
3-4 thick slices crusty bread, such as pain
   de campagne
2 tbsp plain flour
½ tsp sugar
700 ml vegetable stock (made from a stock
   cube or bouillon powder)
275 ml fish stock (fresh or made from a stock
   cube or bouillon powder)
salt and pepper

Store cupboard
300 g green tagliatelle
400 g spaghetti
3 × 400 g cans brown lentils or 350 g dry
   lentils
2 × 400 g cans chopped tomatoes
250 g passata
4-5 canned Piquillo peppers or any other red
   peppers in oil from a can or jar
14-20 sun-dried tomatoes, the best part of a
   280 g jar (ideally preserved in oil)
150 g (approx.) pitted black olives
100 g new season's walnuts in their shells or
   50 g shelled walnut halves
1 tbsp balsamic vinegar
1 tbsp sherry vinegar
2 tbsp white wine vinegar
2 tsp cayenne pepper
1 tsp approx. red chilli powder
1 tbsp paprika
small pinch saffron threads
300 ml white wine
400 ml red wine

Serving suggestions
crusty bread, green salad ingredients (Fiduea
   - Shellfish Spaghetti)
new potatoes, spinach, olive oil and lemon
   juice (Fennel Niçoise)
crusty bread (Lentil and Chorizo Stew)

To download or print out this shopping list,
please visit www.thekitchenrevolution.co.uk/
September/Week2

Rich Shellfish Stew, Saffron Potatoes and Lemon Fennel

Though the method for this recipe is very simple, the resulting rich stew with its intense flavours is excellent. It's worth bearing in mind that the large quantity of seafood in this meal makes it fairly costly. We considered removing it but then decided that there are always occasions when it's worth pushing the boat out.

The recipe includes extra stew for the Fiduea and extra fennel for the Fennel Niçoise.

Rich shellfish stew (includes one third extra for the fiduea)
350 g mussel meat, approx. 900 g mussels in their shells
400 g monkfish fillet
2 tbsp plain flour
2 tsp cayenne pepper
30 g butter
2 tbsp groundnut or grapeseed oil
200 ml white wine
4 large or banana shallots, approx. 120 g
3 garlic cloves
300 g scallops, out of their shells
400 g cooked peeled Atlantic prawns
100 g baby leaf spinach
2 tbsp white wine vinegar
75 ml milk
275 ml fish stock (fresh or made from a stock cube or bouillon powder)
salt and pepper

Saffron potatoes
800 g waxy new potatoes, such as Desirée or Charlotte
700 ml vegetable stock
small pinch saffron threads
40 g butter
1 small bunch chives

Lemon fennel
7 bulbs fennel, approx. 1.5 kg; includes 2 extra for the fennel Niçoise
small handful of fresh flatleaf parsley
2 lemons
3 tbsp olive oil

GET AHEAD PREPARATION (optional)

The sauce for the shellfish stew can be made up to 2 days in advance. Keep it refrigerated until required then warm it through gently before adding the fish and shellfish. If you only have a little time:
* Clean the mussels, if using.
* Prepare the fennel and dress in the lemon and oil mixture.
* Prepare the shallots and garlic.
* Chop the parsley.
* Prepare the potatoes and cover with water until required.

1¼ hours before you want to eat prepare the fennel

* Preheat the oven to 180°C/350°F/Gas Mark 4.
* Bring a large pan of salted water to the boil. Trim any tough outer layers from the fennel bulbs and cut them into quarters or sixths lengthways, depending on the size of each bulb. Add the fennel to the water and leave to simmer until the fennel is just soft – about 5 minutes. Drain the fennel.
* While the fennel is cooking, make the dressing in a small bowl. Roughly chop the parsley. Grate the zest from one of the lemons and add the juice from both. Mix with the oil and the parsley.
* Oil a large, deep ovenproof dish. Arrange some of the fennel in a single layer in the dish, season and pour over some of the lemon and oil mixture. Arrange another layer of fennel and pour over more lemon and oil. Repeat the process until all the fennel is in seasoned layers. After the final layer, add any remaining lemon and oil mixture. Cover with an airtight layer of foil and leave to steam gently in the oven for 40 minutes until the fennel is meltingly tender.

1 hour before you want to eat prepare the shellfish and sauce

* If using mussels in their shells, clean them and remove their beards – scrub off any mud, take hold of the small hairy beard protruding from the shell and pull hard to remove it. Once cleaned, put the mussels in a bowl and leave them to sit under a barely running cold tap until you need them. Discard any mussels that don't close when you give them a sharp tap.
* Trim off any membranes from the monkfish and cut the fish into 2-cm thick medallions. Cut the medallions a little thicker towards the tail end. Put the flour and cayenne on a plate, season well and mix together. Toss the monkfish pieces in the flour. Heat half the butter and half the oil in a large flameproof casserole dish, and when the butter is foaming pat any excess flour from the fish and add a few pieces of fish at a time to the dish, over a medium heat. Keep the leftover flour as it's used later. Brown each piece of monkfish evenly then lift it out into another dish.

* When you have browned all the monkfish, deglaze the casserole dish by adding the wine. Bring to a simmer, stirring constantly. When the wine has been simmering for a minute, pour it over the fish, wipe the dish dry and return it to the heat.
* Heat the remaining butter and oil in the casserole dish over a low heat and peel and thinly slice the shallots. Throw the shallots into the casserole and let them soften gently for 5 minutes while you peel and thinly slice the garlic.
* Add the garlic to the pan and let it soften for a few more minutes.
* Mix the scallops, prawns and mussel meat together, season well and place in the fridge. If you are using mussels in their shells don't mix them with the scallops and prawns. Wash and drain the spinach.
* When the shallots and garlic are soft and sweet, add any reserved flour. Stir once or twice and cook for 1–2 minutes.
* Turn the heat up, splash in the vinegar and cook until it's completely evaporated. When the vinegar has evaporated, stir in the milk and stock and bring to a simmer. Simmer for 5 minutes over a low heat so that the sauce thickens a little.
* Season the sauce and set it aside until a few minutes before serving when the fish and spinach are finally added.

35 minutes before you want to eat cook the prawns

* Peel the potatoes and cut them into large even-sized chunks.
* Place the potatoes in a pan, add the stock and top it up with water so that they are just covered. Add the saffron, butter and a good dose of seasoning.
* Put the potatoes over a medium heat and bring them to the boil, then simmer until they are cooked – about 20 minutes.

20 minutes before you want to eat make the stew

* Return the sauce for the fish stew to a medium heat and bring it to a simmer.
* The fennel should be very soft by now so turn the heat down to a warming temperature and put some plates and serving dishes in the oven.
* When the fish sauce is simmering, take the scallops, prawns and mussels out of the fridge. Add the cleaned mussels in their shells. Cover the casserole dish with a lid and steam the mussels until they open. This will take 4–5 minutes. Discard any mussels that don't open.
* When the mussels are starting to open, add the monkfish and let it cook gently in the sauce for 3–4 minutes.
* Add the spinach, prawns and scallops (and mussel meat if using). Heat through gently, for 4–5 minutes with the lid on.
* By now the potatoes should be ready. Drain them from their cooking liquid and snip the chives over the top, then toss them and put them into a warmed serving dish.
* Season to taste and serve with the saffron potatoes to mop up all the tasty juices and the lemon fennel.

Afterwards

Drain the remaining seafood from its sauce. Put the seafood (approx 300 g), sauce (approx 250 ml) and leftover fennel (approx 400 g) in separate containers, cover and refrigerate for use later in the week.

Something
for nothing 1

Fiduea – Shellfish Spaghetti

In this recipe spaghetti is broken into small pieces and cooked in a shellfish and tomato stock until the liquid is completely absorbed and the pasta is cooked. At this point seafood is stirred into the pasta with herbs and a little lemon juice. This dish is goes well with crusty bread and a green salad.

If you have no leftover seafood or sauce, poach about 100 g of white fish, 100 g peeled prawns, 50 g clams and 50 g scallops in stock. Make the stock by frying a chopped onion and a celery stick in butter until soft, then adding ½ glass wine and a pinch of pepper and 200 ml water. Bring the liquid to a boil then simmer for a minute or two before adding the seafood and cooking for a few minutes. Use the stock to make or add up to the sauce used to cook the pasta.

1 medium onion, approx. 120 g
1 tbsp olive oil
2 garlic cloves
½ lemon
400 g spaghetti
250 ml sauce left over from the
    Big Meal from Scratch or see
    above
250 g passata
handful of fresh flatleaf parsley
300 g cooked seafood left over
    from the Big Meal from Scratch
    or see above
salt and black pepper

To serve
crusty bread and a green salad.

GET AHEAD PREPARATION (optional)

* Prepare the onion and garlic.
* Zest the lemon.
* Chop the parsley.

30 minutes before
you want to eat

* Peel and finely slice the onion. Heat the oil in a large, heavy-based pan over a medium heat. Add the onion and cook gently for 7–10 minutes until quite soft. While the onion is cooking, peel and finely slice the garlic, and grate the zest of the half lemon.
* When the onion has softened, break the spaghetti into 3–5-cm long pieces and add them to the onion. Stir once or twice then add the garlic and lemon zest.
* Add the sauce and passata, season to taste with salt and pepper and leave to simmer without a lid for 15–20 minutes or until all the liquid is absorbed and the spaghetti is cooked. If the liquid evaporates before the spaghetti is cooked, add more liquid.
* While the spaghetti is cooking roughly chop the parsley.
* When the spaghetti is just cooked, add the seafood and parsley, and allow to warm through for 1–2 minutes. Season to taste.
* Squeeze the lemon half over the top, add more pepper, stir well and serve immediately with crusty bread and a green salad.

**Something
for nothing 2**

Fennel Niçoise

This is a very simple dish to prepare and a good kitchen standby – easy to make and easy to eat. Niçoise usually refers to tomatoes and black olives, and for this recipe, ready-cooked fennel and black olives are topped with a rich tomato sauce, bread and grated cheese, then baked in the oven until bubbling and hot. This is a meal in itself, but it would also go very well with lightly grilled white fish, such as cod or pollack. The basis of this recipe comes from Jane Grigson, but we have added the garlic bread to make it more substantial.

If you don't have any leftover fennel, quarter 3½ bulbs fennel, cook in boiling water for 5–7 minutes until they are soft, then drain and season them with salt, pepper and the juice of half a lemon.

2 medium red onions, approx. 240 g
2 tbsp olive oil
2 garlic cloves
1 tbsp red wine vinegar
1 x 400 g can chopped tomatoes
generous pinch of herbes de Provence or leaves from 3–4 sprigs fresh thyme and a handful of chopped fresh parsley
400 g (approx.) cooked lemon fennel left over from the Big Meal from Scratch or see above

150 g (approx.) pitted black olives
150–200 g Gruyère or other strong cheese
handful of fresh parsley
3–4 thick slices crusty bread
100 ml white wine
½ tsp sugar
salt and pepper

To serve
boiled new potatoes and sautéed spinach dressed with olive oil and lemon juice

GET AHEAD PREPARATION (optional)

The entire dish can be assembled a few hours in advance then baked when required. If you only have a little time:
* Prepare the onions and garlic.
* Make the tomato sauce.
* Chop the bread.
* Grate the cheese.

30 minutes before you want to eat

* Preheat the oven to 220°C/425°F/Gas Mark 7.
* Peel and thinly slice the onions. Put the oil in a heavy-based pan over a medium heat. Add the onions and fry for 5 minutes while you peel and finely slice the garlic. After 5 minutes, turn the heat up under the pan and add the garlic. Stir for 2–3 minutes so that the onions and garlic start to brown, then add the vinegar and let it bubble away. Turn the heat down to medium, add the tomatoes and herbs and leave to bubble for 10 minutes.
* Meanwhile, lay the fennel on the bottom of an ovenproof dish. Drain the olives and distribute them evenly around the fennel. Grate the cheese, roughly chop the parsley and cut the bread into small cubes, then mix together and set aside.
* When the tomato sauce has been cooking for 10 minutes add the wine, sugar and salt and pepper and allow to bubble vigorously for 5 minutes.
* Taste the tomato sauce and season if necessary, then pour it over the fennel. Sprinkle the cheese and bread over the top and place at the top of the oven for 10 minutes so that the cheese melts and the middle is bubbling hot.
* Serve with boiled new potatoes and sautéed spinach dressed with olive oil and lemon juice.

Seasonal supper

Baked Figs and Green Bean, Potato and Walnut Salad with Smoked Duck or Bacon

Both figs and walnuts come into season in September, and this recipe makes the most of both. The figs are baked with orange, balsamic vinegar and red wine and the juice from this is used for a dressing for a salad of green beans, potatoes and walnuts.

For a real luxury, serve this with slices of smoked duck which can be found at good butchers and some large supermarkets. Alternatively serve the figs and salad with rashers of good quality smoked bacon or 8 slices of Parma ham.

The new season's walnuts usually come in their shells, and have a moister, sweeter flavour than their older relatives. If you can't get new season walnuts in the shell buy walnuts halves instead.

Baked figs
12 fresh figs
1 orange
150 ml red wine
1 tbsp balsamic vinegar
olive oil
salt and pepper

Green bean, potato and walnut salad with smoked duck or bacon
3 large waxy new potatoes, such as Charlotte, approx. 360 g
1 tbsp sherry vinegar

400 g green beans
2 garlic cloves
olive oil
3 smoked duck breasts or 150 g free-range smoked, streaky bacon or 8 slices Parma ham
100 g new season's walnuts in their shells or 50 g shelled walnut halves
60–70 g rocket
salt and pepper

GET AHEAD PREPARATION (optional)

* Make the dressing for the figs.
* Dice the potatoes and cover them with water until required.
* Top and tail and cook the green beans.
* Peel and slice the garlic.
* Fry the bacon, if using.

25 minutes before you want to eat

* Preheat the oven to 200°C/400°F/Gas Mark 6.
* Wash the potatoes and cut them into a 2-cm dice. Put the potatoes in a pan of salted water over a high heat, bring them to the boil then simmer for 10 minutes or until soft. When the potatoes are cooked, drain them well, sprinkle them with some of the sherry vinegar and set aside.
* Meanwhile bake the figs. Take the stalk off each fig and then cut a cross in the top of each one. Put the figs in an ovenproof dish. Grate the zest from half the orange and squeeze all its juice into a small bowl. Mix the orange zest and juice with the wine, balsamic vinegar, a good splash of oil and plenty of salt and pepper. Pour the dressing over the figs then put them in the oven for 10–15 minutes.
* Cook the beans in well-salted boiling water for 3–4 minutes until they are just tender.
* When the beans are cooked, drain them and plunge them into very cold water to cool, then dry them well and put them in a large bowl. Add a splash of oil and the remaining sherry vinegar, and toss the slivers of garlic through them with seasoning to taste.
* Peel and finely slice the garlic. If using duck breasts, cut them into 5-mm slices. If using bacon, fry the rashers until crisp in a hot frying pan. Crack the walnuts and break up the kernels.
* When the figs have been cooking for about 10–15 minutes, remove them from the oven. Tip the potatoes into the bowl containing the beans and add the rocket. Spoon over a few tablespoons of the juice from the figs and toss the salad together. Taste and add more seasoning if necessary.
* Put some salad on each plate and place slices of duck, Parma ham, or bacon on top. Arrange three figs around the salad and sprinkle the walnuts over. Pour any left over juice over the figs and serve immediately.

Larder feast

Lentil and Chorizo Stew

Packed with flavour but requiring minimum effort, this is a wonderful recipe for the exhausted, uninspired or just plain lazy cook. Having a couple of chorizo to hand in the fridge is the culinary equivalent of a secret weapon. The sausages impart a wonderful deep flavour to even the most lacklustre dish. In this recipe the lentils do a good job of soaking up and intensifying the rich chorizo flavour, and this is set off by the fiery kick of the piquillo peppers. Piquillo means 'little beak' and these peppers are a regular feature of food in northern Spain. They are traditionally handpicked and roasted over a beech wood open fire, then packed in jars or cans. The roasting gives them a rich, spicy flavour. Added to stews and salads piquillo peppers impart a smoky, sweet loveliness. Spanish food shops and some large supermarkets sell them, but if they are not easy to find they can be easily replaced by the ordinary roasted sweet red peppers in oil that are available in cans and jars.

If you have the time, dried lentils will enhance the flavour of the resulting dish, but using them will add about half an hour to the total cooking time. You will need to wash them well, then follow the recipe as below – but add enough water to cover the lentils with 2 cm of liquid and cook the dish for a minimum of 30 minutes.

2 medium onions, approx. 240 g
1 tbsp olive oil
3–4 chorizo sausages, each
   approx. 10 cm (hot or mild,
   depending on taste)
75 g piece of pancetta or free-
   range smoked streaky bacon
3 garlic cloves
4–5 piquillo peppers or any red
   peppers in oil from a can or
   jar
1 × 400 g can chopped tomatoes
250 ml red wine
3 × 400 g cans brown lentils or
   350 g dry lentils (see above)
¼–½ tsp red chilli powder
handful of fresh flatleaf parsley
salt and pepper

To serve
crusty bread

GET AHEAD PREPARATION (optional)

The entire dish can be made up
to days in advance and reheated
slowly when required. If you only
have a little time:
* Prepare the onions and garlic.
* Slice the chorizo and pancetta.
* Slice the peppers.
* Chop the parsley.

35 minutes before you want to eat

* Peel and thinly slice the onions. Heat the oil in a heavy-based pan over a medium heat. Add the onions and cook for 7–10 minutes until soft. While the onions are cooking, slice the chorizo and pancetta into 1-cm thick pieces, peel and slice the garlic and slice the peppers into 1-cm thick strips.
* When the onions are soft, add the chorizo and pancetta and cook for 3–4 minutes they are until starting to brown. Then add the tomatoes, garlic and wine, stir well and cook gently for 3 minutes.
* Next, stir in the peppers, lentils and chilli powder to taste (according to how hot you like your food). Season well with salt and pepper and add sufficient water to just cover the lentils. Simmer gently for at least 20 minutes, longer if you have time.
* When you are ready to serve, season to taste. Roughly chop the parsley and add it to the stew. Serve in big bowls with crusty bread and red wine.

Two for one

Chicken with Sun-dried Tomatoes

In this recipe the intense flavours of sun-dried tomatoes and paprika combine to make a flavoursome sauce for chicken.

When sun-dried tomatoes hit the supermarkets shelves in the early 1990s they became an essential ingredient for any aspiring domestic cook. Polly's mum took to making them herself, though in London, without the necessary amount of sun, they had to be dried in the oven before being put in jars with olive oil. In the mid–1990s the much-loved and respected cookery writer Josceline Dimbleby brought out a book called *The Almost Vegetarian Cookbook* and this, almost more than any book Polly can remember, epitomised the food her family ate through that decade. This particular recipe, adapted from Josceline Dimbleby's original, was a family favourite seeming, as it did back then, to be both perfectly comforting and rather exotic.

Aside from the tagliatelle, the quantities of the ingredients in this recipe make enough for eight people with half intended for the freezer.

6-8 free-range chicken breasts, skinless
juice of 3 lemons, approx. 150 ml
1 tbsp paprika
2 large garlic cloves
14-20 sun-dried tomatoes, the best part of a 280 g jar (ideally preserved in oil)
4 sprigs fresh tarragon or 1 tsp dried tarragon

70 g (approx.) butter
300 ml (approx.) double cream
1-2 pinches chilli powder
300 g dried green tagliatelle

GET AHEAD PREPARATION (optional)

The chicken can be cooked 2 days in advance and warmed through while the pasta is cooking. If you only have a little time:
* Prepare the marinade.
* Cut the chicken and marinate for up to an hour.
* Slice the tomatoes.

40 minutes before you want to eat

* Start by marinating the chicken. Cut the chicken breasts crossways into slices about 1–2 cm thick and place in a large bowl. Add the lemon juice to the chicken along with the paprika. Peel and crush the garlic and mix it in with the chicken. Set aside to marinate for at least 20 minutes.
* Meanwhile, slice the tomatoes into thirds or quarters, and strip the leaves from the fresh tarragon, if using.
* When the chicken has been marinating for 20 minutes or more, heat the butter in a large heavy-based frying pan over a medium heat. Add the chicken slices with their marinade and cook gently, stirring every now and then, for 5–10 minutes or until cooked through.
* Once the chicken is cooked, remove it from the pan with a slotted spoon and keep to one side.
* Cook the tagliatelle in boiling water according to instructions on the packet.
* Increase the heat under the pan and boil any remaining marinade rapidly for about 2 minutes.
* Remove the pan from the heat and stir in the cream. Return the pan to the heat, add the tomatoes, tarragon and chilli powder and bring the sauce to the boil for 5 minutes or until it has started to thicken. Add the chicken to the sauce, turn down the heat and allow to simmer while the tagliatelle cooks.
* When the pasta is cooked, drain it well and distribute it between four bowls. Spoon half the chicken evenly over the tagliatelle and serve.
* Let the remaining chicken cool then place it in an airtight container suitable for the freezer and freeze until required.

Lazy day supper – reheating instructions

Allow the chicken and sauce to defrost completely. Warm through in a pan with a lid over a gentle heat for about 20 minutes, stirring a couple of times, while you cook the green tagliatelle as above.

Paprika

The flavour and colour of paprika imparts a lovely warmth and depth to food. It is made from mild, sweet red pepper and is a classic seasoning in Hungarian goulash. We especially love smoked paprika, which adds a deep, smoky intensity whenever it is used. This can be found in the 'specialty' sections of big supermarkets or in delicatessans.

Chilli powder

Chilli powder is often described as though there is one generic type – in fact there are masses of varieties of chilli and as many versions of powder. Different types of chilli will have varying heat levels and flavours – if you are a fan of hot food it's worth experimenting to find a favourite. Indian and Asian grocery stores are usually well stocked with different types of chilli and their prices usually beat the supermarkets hands down. Sometimes chilli powders are a blend of herbs, spices and chilli, which can give a different, though not necessarily bad, flavour – check the packet before buying.

September Week 3 – Overview

The Big Meal from Scratch this week is a roast to beat all roasts – Roast Rib of Beef with Yorkshire Puddings, Roast Potatoes and Parsnips and Steamed Squash and Marrow. When roasting beef, it's generally agreed that rib is the best cut. Rib of beef should have a good marbling of fat through the meat and a thick layer of fat over the top. As with all roasts, the trick is in preparation and timings, but the methods themselves are not complicated or fiddly. The whole meal, from start to finish, will take around 2 hours but for much of this time the cook has little or nothing to do. It hardly needs saying that any surplus beef from the roast rib will make magnificent beef sandwiches.

The surplus steamed squash and marrow from the Big Meal is used to make a savoury tomato version of bread and butter pudding and leftover roast parsnips become Yoghurt Baked Fish with Chilli Parsnips. If possible, cook the fish within a day of purchase or place it in the freezer until required.

Red peppers and tomatoes are in season until the end of September and in this week's Seasonal Supper they combine to make a sweet peperonata, or thick pepper and tomato stew, as an accompaniment to sausages.

Kedgeree is mostly made with just rice these days but for this week's Larder Feast the recipe harks back to the Indian origins of the dish and uses lentils as well as lightly spiced rice. Served with eggs, coriander and canned kippers this is ready in just 30 minutes.

The Two for One is an intense and deeply flavoured Middle Eastern aubergine stew called Imam Bayaldi. To create a suitably rich and slippery texture the aubergines have to be fried and this does take a while – as a compromise it's possible to roast half of them in the oven, but it's important that at least half feel the heat and oil of a frying pan. Altogether this will take 1½ hours.

September Week 3	Recipe	Time
Big meal from scratch	Roast rib of beef with Yorkshire puddings, roast potatoes and parsnips and steamed squash and marrow	2 hours
Something for nothing 1	Bread and butter squash and marrow	45 mins
Something for nothing 2	Yoghurt baked fish with chilli parsnips and chutney	35 mins
Seasonal supper	Sausages with peperonata	35 mins
Larder feast	Quick kedgeree	30 mins
2 for 1	Imam bayaldi – rich aubergine stew	1½ hours

All recipes serve 4 apart from the 2 for 1 recipe which makes 8 portions

SHOPPING LIST (for 4 people)

Meat and fish
1 x 2 kg rib of beef, 2-3 ribs
goose or duck fat (optional for Roast Rib
  of Beef with Yorkshire Puddings, Roast
  Potatoes and Parsnips and Steamed Squash
  and Marrow)
4 x 125-150 g skinned pieces firm white fish
  or salmon
8 good quality large sausages

Dairy
130 g butter
300 ml milk
8 free-range eggs or organic eggs if possible
125 g natural yoghurt
90 g Parmesan

Fruit and vegetables
800 g roasting potatoes, such as Maris Piper
  or King Edward
1.25 kg parsnips
2 small butternut squash, approx. 1.2 kg
750 g marrow
4 large red peppers, approx. 800 g (a mixture
  of red and yellow will also be fine)
6 large tomatoes, approx. 800 g
7 medium red onions, approx. 720 g
3 large onions, approx. 1 kg
1 small onion, approx. 90 g
16 garlic cloves
2 celery sticks
5 large aubergines, approx. 2 kg
1 small mild green chilli
3-cm piece of fresh root ginger
a few sprigs fresh basil
3 sprigs fresh sage
2 bunches fresh coriander (including 1 large
  bunch)
1 small bunch fresh parsley
6 sprigs fresh thyme
1 small bunch fresh mint
2½ lemons
2 limes

Basics
250-350 ml olive oil
100 ml groundnut or grapeseed oil
½ small loaf of bread (approx. 200 g),
  8 slices (white, wholemeal or granary)
300 g plain flour
2 tbsp tomato purée
pinch of sugar
pinch of soft brown sugar
200 ml beef, chicken or vegetable stock
  (fresh or made with a stock cube or
  vegetable bouillon powder)
200 ml chicken stock (fresh or made with a
  stock cube)

800 ml vegetable stock (fresh or made from a
  stock cube or bouillon powder)
salt and pepper

Store cupboard
150 g dried red split lentils
300 g basmati rice
4 x 400 cans chopped tomatoes
1 x 190 g can kippers in oil
1 tbsp harissa paste
3 tbsp mild curry paste (optional Quick
  Kedgeree)
1 tsp ground cinnamon or 1 x 5 cm cinnamon
  stick
1 tsp ground allspice
3½ tsp ground coriander
1 tbsp ground cumin
4 tsp coriander seeds
½ tsp cayenne pepper
½ tsp paprika
1 tsp ground cardamom
1 tsp turmeric
100 ml white wine

Quick option
Add 1 tbsp tomato purée, ½ tsp chilli powder,
  2 pinches paprika and 2 pinches ground
  cumin to shopping list. Delete 1 tbsp
  harissa paste (Yoghurt Baked Fish with
  Chilli Parsnips and Chutney)

Serving suggestions
horseradish sauce or strong mustard (Roast
  Rib of Beef with Yorkshire Puddings, Roast
  Potatoes and Parsnips and Steamed Squash
  and Marrow)
spinach, olive oil and lemon juice (Bread
  and Butter Squash and Marrow)
naan breads, green vegetable or salad leaves
  (Yoghurt Baked Fish with Chilli Parsnips)
potatoes, olive oil and thyme (Sausages with
  Peperonata)
green or cucumber salad ingredients (quick
  kedgeree)
rice, Greek yoghurt and garlic (Imam Bayaldi
  – Rich Aubergine Stew)

To download or print out this shopping list,
please visit www.thekitchenrevolution.co.uk/
September/Week3

**Big meal
from scratch**

Roast Rib of Beef with Yorkshire Puddings, Roast Potatoes and Parsnips and Steamed Squash and Marrow

Roast beef 'with all the trimmings' would probably be the chosen desert island meal for a great many people. Cooking roast beef with roast potatoes, Yorkshire puds and a couple of vegetables is not complicated –sucess depends on co-ordinating the timing and order of cooking the various component parts. Hopefully the recipe below will guide you through clearly. For the Yorkshire pudding we have borrowed a recipe from Jane Grigson.

One thing is for certain: the better the beef, the better the end result. Best of all is a well-hung rib of beef with well-marbled flesh and a good thick layer of fat over the top. The fat provides flavour and succulence and the bones add to the flavour, too. Wherever you buy your beef, look for fat and for meat that isn't brilliant red – if it is, it probably hasn't been hung long enough for the flavour to develop.

For this recipe we've given the roasting time for a 2 kg rib of beef cooked until medium rare. If you prefer meat well done or very rare, or have a different sized piece of meat see below.

The recipe includes extra parsnips for the Yoghurt Baked Fish with Chilli Parsnips and Chutney and extra squash and marrow for the Bread and Butter Squash and Marrow.

Guidelines for roasting beef:
* Take the beef out of the fridge at least 40 minutes before you want to cook it. After an initial 30 minutes in a very hot oven (220°C/425°F/Gas Mark 7) cook the beef at 170°C/325°F/Gas Mark 3.
* For rare beef: 10 minutes per 500 g
* For medium rare beef: 15 minutes per 500 g
* For well-done beef: 20 minutes per 500 g

Roast rib of beef
1 × 2 kg rib of beef
1-2 tbsp groundnut or grapeseed oil or beef dripping
salt and pepper

For the gravy
100 ml white wine
1 tbsp plain flour
200 ml beef, chicken or vegetable stock (fresh or made from a stock cube or bouillon powder)

Roast potatoes and parsnips
800 g roasting potatoes, such as Maris Piper or King Edward
1 tbsp plain flour
1.25 kg parsnips; includes 750 g extra for the chilli parsnips

goose or duck fat (optional) and/or groundnut or grapeseed oil

Steamed squash and marrow
2 small butternut squash, approx. 1.2 kg; includes 600g extra for the bread and butter squash and marrow
750 g marrow; includes 350g extra for the bread and butter squash and marrow
1 tbsp olive oil
2-3 sprigs fresh sage

Yorkshire puddings
4 free-range eggs
300 ml milk
½ tsp salt
250 g plain flour
1-2 tbsp groundnut or

grapeseed oil

To serve
horseradish sauce or strong mustard

GET AHEAD PREPARATION (optional)

The potatoes could be part boiled and the squash and marrow steamed in advance. If you only have a little time:
* Prepare the squash, marrow, potatoes and parsnips and cover the potatoes and parsnips with water for up to 2 hours before cooking them.
* Make the pudding batter.

*2 hours before
you want to eat
cook the beef*

* Preheat the oven to 220°C/425°F/Gas Mark 7.
* Rub the beef generously with the oil or dripping, season well and place in a large roasting tin. Roast the beef for 30 minutes at a high temperature.
* After 30 minutes, turn the oven down to 170°C/325°F/Gas Mark 3. Cook the beef at this lower temperature (see above for guidelines). For a 2 kg medium rare rib of beef this means 1 hour of cooking time after the initial 30 minutes at a high temperature.

*1½ hours before
you want to eat
prepare the
vegetables*

* Peel the potatoes and cut them into egg-sized pieces. Place the potatoes in a large pan, cover with salted water, bring to the boil and simmer for 8 minutes. Drain the potatoes in a sieve then shake them so that they rough up. Return to the pan and add the flour, replace the lid and shake vigorously.

* Peel the parsnips, halve them and cut into halves or thirds again. Remove any woody cores.
* Put the goose or duck fat and/or the oil in a roasting tin large enough to hold the potatoes and parsnips. The oil and/or melted fat needs to cover the base of the tin to a depth of about 5 mm. Place the tin in the oven.
* Peel the squash and cut them in half lengthways. Scoop out and discard the seeds then cut the halves into 2–3 cm squares. Put the chopped squash into a steamer or pan with 2–3 cm salted water. Cut the marrow into 2-3 cm chunks and place on top of the squash.

1 hour before you want to eat

* Remove the roasting tin from the oven and tip the parsnips and potatoes in. Shake them so they are evenly distributed, and return to the oven.
* Mix the eggs, milk and salt together using an electric whisk. Allow to stand for 15 minutes then whisk in the flour until the batter is smooth.

30 minutes before you want to eat cook the Yorkshire puddings, squash and gravy

* Remove the beef from the oven, place it on a carving board and leave to rest for 20–30 minutes.
* Turn the oven up to 220°C/425°F/Gas Mark 7.
* Divide the oil evenly between the six or eight wells in a Yorkshire pudding or muffin tin or put in an ovenproof dish about 30 x 20 x 7 cm and preheat in the oven.
* Put the squash and marrow over a high heat and steam the vegetables for 10–15 minutes.
* When the oil is hot pour the Yorkshire pudding batter into the wells in the hot tin, or into the dish, and cook at the top of the oven for 15–20 minutes for individual Yorkshires and 25–30 minutes for a large one until puffed up and golden. Give the potatoes and parsnips a quick shake while the oven is open. Once the pudding is cooking they can sit for a short while in a low oven –not too long or they'll dry out. When the oven is turned low put some plates and dishes in to warm.
* After 10–15 minutes check whether the squash and marrow are cooked. When a knife can pass easily through the squash and marrow flesh, remove the pan from the heat and drain well, reserving the cooking water for the gravy. Set half the mixture aside.
* Splash the oil into a large frying pan over a medium heat. When the oil is hot tear the sage leaves in half and add them to the pan. When the sage starts to crisp, add the remaining squash and marrow to the pan and toss for 1–2 minutes. Season well and keep warm.
* To make the gravy pour off most of the fat from the roasting tin then place over a low to medium heat. Add the flour, stir for a minute or two, then add the wine. Allow the wine to bubble furiously, stirring all the while. Add the stock and about 200 ml of the cooking liquid from the drained squash and marrow. Bring the mixture back to the boil, reduce the heat and simmer, stirring regularly to dissolve any lumps. Tip any bloody juices from the carving board into the gravy.
Allow the gravy to simmer gently.
* Put half the parsnips to one side, then tip the roast potatoes and the remaining parsnips into a serving dish.
* Check on the Yorkshire puddings (or pudding) and remove them from the oven if they are golden and puffed.
* Taste the gravy for seasoning.
* Carve the roast beef and serve it with the Yorkshire puddings, vegetables and gravy.

Afterwards

Put the remaining squash and marrow (400-500 g) and the parsnips (500-700 g) in separate containers, cover and refrigerate for use later in the week.

Added extra

The Best Beef Sandwich

If you have any leftover beef, butter a thick slice of bread with butter and another with either horseradish or mustard. Add slices of beef, tomatoes and lettuce. Season then eat.

**Something
for nothing 1**

Bread and Butter Squash and Marrow

This savoury bread and butter pudding with butternut squash and marrow makes a warm and comforting supper. A simple tomato sauce is made with garlic and herbs. This is poured over bread and the squash and marrow left over from the Big Meal from Scratch, and the dish is then baked to create a substantial hearty meal. If you have no remaining squash and marrow, peel 600 g squash and 400 g marrow, chop them into bite-sized chunks and steam them until they are just cooked, then season with salt and pepper.

good splash of groundnut or
   grapeseed oil
2 medium red onions, approx.
   240 g
4 garlic cloves
1 × 400 g can chopped tomatoes
6 sprigs fresh thyme or ½ tsp
   dried thyme
60 g Parmesan
2 sprigs fresh sage
300 ml vegetable stock (made
   from a stock cube or bouillon
   powder)

pinch of light brown soft sugar
½ small loaf of bread (approx.
   200 g), white, wholemeal or
   granary
50 g butter
400–500 g cooked squash and
   marrow left over from the Big
   Meal from Scratch or see above

To serve
sautéed spinach

GET AHEAD PREPARATION (optional)

The whole dish can be made up
to a day in advance ready to go
in the oven. If you only have a
little time:
* Prepare the onions and garlic.
* Make the tomato sauce.
* Grate the Parmesan.
* Chop the sage.
* Prepare the bread.

*45 minutes before
you want to eat*

* Heat the oil in a heavy-based pan. Peel and finely slice the onions, add them to the oil and cook them over a medium heat while you peel and crush the garlic. Add the garlic and cook for a further couple of minutes.
* Let the onions and garlic brown a little, then add the tomatoes and thyme and bring to the boil. Bubble vigorously for 5 minutes. While the tomatoes are bubbling, grate the Parmesan, and roughly chop the sage.
* Now add the stock, sugar and a good dose of salt and pepper to the tomato sauce and let it simmer gently for about 10 minutes.
* Preheat the oven to 200°C/400°F/Gas Mark 6.
* While the tomato sauce is simmering away, cut the bread into eight 1-cm thick slices. Butter the slices, sprinkle them with a little sage and Parmesan and cut each slice in two diagonally so that you have triangles of bread. Keep some butter back for greasing an ovenproof dish.
* Toss the squash and marrow with any remaining sage, all but 2 heaped tablespoons of the Parmesan and some seasoning.
* Rub the remaining butter around an ovenproof dish and put half of the bread on the bottom of the dish. The triangles may have to overlap but that's fine. Cover the bread with the squash and marrow, then put another layer of bread on top.
* By now the tomato sauce will have been simmering for long enough. Pour it over the bread, lift out the thyme sprigs and scatter over the last of the Parmesan.
* Bake in the oven for 20 minutes or until the bread and the squash and marrow have absorbed the tomato sauce.
* Remove from the oven and serve with sautéed spinach.

Yoghurt Baked Fish with Chilli Parsnips and Chutney

Harissa is a Tunisian and Moroccan spicy paste made from chillies and other seasonings. In the Middle East it is used to season food and as a marinade for meat and fish. In this recipe it is mixed with yoghurt to make a coating for fish which is then baked in the oven. If you can't find harissa, replace it with a mixture of 1 tbsp tomato purée, ½ tsp chilli powder, 2 pinches of paprika and 2 pinches of ground cumin. The spicy fish and parsnips are accompanied by a refreshing and zingy chutney.

If you don't have any leftover roast parsnips parboil 600 g peeled and sliced parsnips for 3 minutes. Follow the recipe below but bake the parsnips for 15 minutes instead of 5.

Yoghurt baked fish
1 tbsp harissa paste or see above
125 g natural yoghurt
4 × 125–150 g skinned pieces
  firm white fish or salmon
salt and pepper

Chilli parsnips
2 garlic cloves
3-cm piece of fresh root ginger
1 lemon
1 tsp coriander seeds
1 tsp ground cumin
½ tsp paprika
1 tbsp groundnut or grapeseed
  oil, plus extra for greasing
500–700 g roasted parsnips left
  over from the Big Meal from
  Scratch

Chutney
1 small onion, approx. 90 g
pinch of sugar
1 small mild green chilli
large handful of fresh coriander
½ lemon

To serve
naan breads and a green
  vegetable or salad leaves

GET AHEAD PREPARATION (optional)

The fish can be marinated up to
2 hours in advance. If you only
have a little time:
* Make the spice mixture for
  seasoning the parsnips.
* Make the chutney.

*35 minutes before
you want to eat*

* Preheat the oven to 200°C/400°F/Gas Mark 6.
* First, coat the fish. Mix the harissa and yoghurt together and season with a little salt (add more harissa if you like spicy food). Place the fish fillets in a row in an ovenproof dish, season them with salt and pepper and pour over the harissa and yoghurt mixture. Leave the fish to soak up the flavours at room temperature while you start the parsnips off.
* Make the spice mixture for the parsnips. Peel and finely grate the garlic and ginger, then grate the zest from half the lemon. Roughly crush the coriander seeds, either in a pestle and mortar or place them under a tea towel and bash them with the base of a pan or a rolling pin. Mix these ingredients with the cumin, paprika and oil.
* Oil a roasting tin and add the parsnips and spice paste. Mix the paste thoroughly through the parsnips and put them in the top of the oven to roast for 5 minutes.
* After 5 minutes, move the parsnips down a shelf and put the fish on the top shelf. Bake the fish for 10–15 minutes, until a sharp knife meets no resistance when inserted into one of them.
* While the fish and parsnips are baking, make the chutney. Peel the onion and either grate it or put in a food processor and pulse it a few times. Put the onion into a bowl with some salt and the sugar. Deseed and finely chop the chilli and add it to the onion. Wash, dry and finely chop the coriander then add to the onion with a squeeze of lemon juice and more salt to taste.
* When the fish and parsnips are ready remove them from the oven. Squeeze some lemon juice over the fillets and serve them next to a pile of parsnips. Pass the chutney and warm naan breads around separately and serve with a green vegetable or salad leaves.

Seasonal supper

Sausages with Peperonata

As summer comes to an end, peperonata is a handy way to use up the last of the peppers and tomatoes. This recipe turns them into a sweet stew that goes very well with sausages. For a tasty accompaniment, bake wedges of skin-on potatoes coated in olive oil and thyme alongside the sausages.

olive oil
8 good quality large sausages
30 g butter
3 medium red onions, approx.
   360 g
4 large red peppers, 800 g (a
   mixture of red and yellow will
   also be fine)
6 large beef tomatoes, approx.
   800 g
2 garlic cloves
a few sprigs fresh basil
salt and pepper

To serve
potato wedges (see above)

GET AHEAD PREPARATION (optional)

The peperonata can be made up to 2 days in advance and warmed through when required. If you only have a little time:
* Prepare the onions and garlic.
* Cut the peppers into strips.
* Peel the tomatoes.

35 minutes before you want to eat

* Preheat the oven to 200°C/400°F/Gas Mark 6.
* Lightly grease a roasting tin with oil, add the sausages and put them in the oven for 25 minutes until they are brown and cooked through.
* Heat the butter and some oil in a heavy-based pan with a lid. Peel and finely slice the onions and add them to the pan. Put on the lid and leave them to soften for 7–10 minutes.
* While the onions are cooking, cut the peppers in half lengthways, deseed them and cut them into 2–3-cm wide strips. Add them to the pan, put the lid back on and let them cook quite vigorously while you prepare the tomatoes. Stir them from time to time as you don't want them to colour.
* Peel the tomatoes by plunging them into boiling water for 2–3 minutes, then running them under cold water until you can slip off their skins. Once they are peeled, chop the tomatoes into bite-sized chunks, then peel and slice the garlic.
* Add the tomatoes and garlic and a good dose of salt and pepper to the onions and peppers. Now cook the onions, tomatoes and peppers for 7–10 minutes with the lid on and for 5 minutes without the lid.
* The peperonata should be fairly dry. Tear in some basil leaves and serve it with the sausages, and potato wedges if you wish.

Larder feast

Quick Kedgeree

This quick kedgeree reunites the favourite English country-house breakfast of rice, fish and eggs with its roots. Kedgeree is derived from an Indian dish called 'khichri' that consists of rice and lentils. In this recipe rice and lentils are cooked with a curry paste and then served with a topping of hard-boiled eggs, kippers and chopped coriander.

Red lentils need no presoaking and are used regularly in Indian food. The recipe gives you options for using ready-made curry paste or making your own if you have time.

50 g butter
splash of groundnut or grapeseed oil
2 medium red onions, approx. 240 g
2 cloves garlic
5 cm pice of ginger
1-2 green chillies (depending on taste)
1 tsp turmeric
1 tsp ground cardamom
1½ tsp ground coriander
1 tsp cumin

300 g basmati rice
150 g dried split red lentils
4 free-range eggs
500 ml approx. vegetable stock (made from a stock cube or bouillon powder)
1 x 190 g can kippers in oil
small handful of fresh coriander
2 limes
salt and pepper

To serve
green or cucumber salad

GET AHEAD PREPARATION (optional)

* Prepare the onion, garlic and ginger.
* Deseed and chop the chilli.
* Hard-boil the eggs.

30 minutes before you want to eat

* Heat one-third of the butter and the oil in a large heavy-based pan with a lid over a medium heat. Peel and finely slice the onions and add them to the pan.
* Leave the onions to cook over a low heat for 10 minutes. (To make your own spice mix peel and crush the garlic and ginger, deseed and finely chop the chilli, then mix together with the spices.)
* While the onions are cooking, wash the rice and lentils then boil the eggs. Lower the eggs into a pan of boiling water, cook for 8 minutes then leave them under cold running water for a few minutes to cool.
* Once the onions have softened, add the curry paste. Turn the heat up and let the paste cook, stirring continuously for a minute or so.
* Turn the heat down to medium and add another third of the butter. When it has melted, add the lentils and rice and let them become coated in the spicy buttery mixture. Then add enough stock to just cover the rice and lentils by a cm or so and bring them to the boil. Reduce the heat, cover the pan and cook over a very low heat for 15–20 minutes, stirring occasionally (add more stock if the rice is beginning to look dry or is sticking; but be cautious, you don't want to end up with sloppy rice).
* Meanwhile make the topping. Once the eggs are cold, peel and roughly chop them and put them in a bowl. Open and drain the can of kippers and break them into the bowl with the eggs. Chop the coriander. Grate the zest from one of the limes and mix this with the coriander. Combine with the eggs and kippers.
* Squeeze the juice from both the limes into a small bowl and when the rice and lentils are cooked, stir in the lime juice and season. Let the rice and lentils sit for 5 minutes before serving with a generous sprinkle of the egg and kipper mixture on top, and a simple green or cucumber salad.

Two for one

Imam Bayaldi – Rich Aubergine Stew

A deep purple and gleaming aubergine is a beautiful thing that demands to be handled. Once cooked, its flesh absorbs liquids and flavours and changes from being spongy into a mass of wonderful, slippery voluptuousness.

Imam bayaldi, a Middle Eastern recipe, calls for aubergines to be fried then cooked slowly in an unctuous, spicy tomato sauce. The recipe is fairly simple but it does take some time as you have to fry the aubergine and make a thick tomato sauce. To help curtail the cooking time we've given instructions for half the aubergines to be cooked in the oven. Even so, this is not a recipe to embark on when time is short and your temper is frayed. Moreover, as you're making double quantities (to freeze half for later) you know that time spent now is saved later.

Imam bayaldi is delicious on its own, but is also wonderful with garlicky Greek yoghurt and hunks of crusty bread. It freezes well and as frying the aubergines and cooking the tomatoes takes a while it's worth bulking up quantities.

150-250 ml olive oil
3 large onions, approx. 1 kg
4 celery sticks
8 garlic cloves
5 large aubergines, approx. 2 kg
1 tsp ground cinnamon or 5-cm
    piece of cinnamon stick
1 tsp ground allspice
2 tsp ground coriander
1 tbsp coriander seeds
1 tsp ground cumin
½ tsp cayenne pepper
zest ½ lemon
3 × 400 g cans chopped tomatoes
2 tbsp tomato purée
1 bunch fresh coriander
1 small bunch fresh mint
salt and pepper

To serve
rice, Greek yoghurt mixed with
    salt, pepper and crushed
    garlic

GET AHEAD PREPARATION (optional)

The enitre mean can be cooked 3
days in advance. If you only
have a little time:
* Prepare the onions, garlic and
    celery.
* Cut the aubergines into chunks.

1½ hours before you want to eat

* Preheat the oven to 200°C/400°F/Gas Mark 6. Put 3 tablespoons of the oil in a large roasting tin and place in the oven to heat up.
* Start by getting the tomato sauce ready. Peel and thinly slice the onions. Put your largest, heavy-based pan over a medium heat and add about 2 tablespoons of the oil. When the oil is hot add the onions and fry gently over a low heat while you prepare the other ingredients. Chop the celery into thin slices and add them to the onions. Peel and thinly slice the garlic. Add half the garlic to the onion and celery mixture and leave the rest to one side. The vegetables will need to sweat for about 20 minutes.
* While the vegetables are sweating, cut the aubergines into about 5 x 5-cm chunks ready for frying. Remove the roasting tin from the oven and add about half the aubergines to the hot oil. Mix and turn well so they are well coated in oil, then place in the oven to bake for about 20 minutes until the aubergines are soft. Put the remaining aubergines in a large bowl to one side of the stove. Put another large bowl or a large baking sheet on the other side of the stove. Line the bottom with a layer or two of kitchen paper towels to absorb excess oil from the fried aubergines.
* Before you fry the aubergines, add the remaining ingredients to the softened onion, celery and garlic mixture. First, turn the heat up a little and stir in the spices and lemon zest. Cook for 1–2 minutes, stirring all the while. Then add the tomatoes, tomato purée and 1 teaspoon each of salt and pepper. Stir well, bring to the boil then simmer gently.
* Now fry the aubergines. Pour enough oil into a large frying pan to generously cover its base – it should be about 4 mm deep. Place over a high heat until the oil is very hot, but not quite smoking. If the oil isn't hot enough, frying the aubergines will take ages and they will absorb too much oil. Add the aubergine chunks to the pan so that they

form a roomy single layer and fry them, turning them every now and then so that they are well browned. Once browned, spoon them on to the prepared kitchen paper. Continue this process, adding more oil to the pan when necessary, until all the aubergines are browned. Check on the aubergines in the oven once or twice and give them a stir.

* Taste the tomato sauce and season it accordingly, then add all the baked and fried aubergines. Stir well once or twice, then roughly chop the coriander, strip the mint leaves from their stalks and chop them roughly. Add the coriander, mint and the remaining garlic to the pan. Allow to simmer for at least 15 minutes, and up to 30 minutes, until you have a rich, sweet and very flavourful dish.
* Put half aside for freezing and serve what's left with rice and garlic yoghurt

**Lazy day supper
– reheating
instructions**

Defrost the stew thoroughly, then tip it into a pan and slowly reheat it. This will take about 20 minutes. Serve as above.

September Week 4 – Overview

This week starts with a Big Meal from Scratch of Duck with Quinces (or Pears) in Red Wine with Roast Potatoes and Lemon Courgettes. Served with refreshing lemon courgettes this meal seems appropriate for the start of autumn – not too heavy but with some bold flavours. To ensure the duck legs absorb the flavours of the fruit and brandy marinade, they need to start soaking about 3½ hours before you want to eat. That said, once the legs are marinating there is nothing more to do until just over an hour before eating.

Cooking extra duck legs for the big meal leaves you with leftovers to make a Duck and Lentil Salad – a Something for Nothing that is ready in 30 minutes. Almost as quick is a light and refreshing recipe for Courgette and Ricotta Lasagne that uses the surplus lemon courgettes.

September is the month when grapes are at their sweetest and for a Seasonal Supper they are used as part of a chicken casserole that's bursting with flavour. As long as this is cooked in a generous sized casserole so the heat distributes evenly and easily it can be ready in about 40 minutes.

Cauliflower, Chickpea and Preserved Lemon Salad, served with Spiced Pitta Breads, creates a Larder Feast that's rich with flavour and texture and that works as well in hot as in cold weather. If preserved lemons prove hard to find they can be replaced with marinated sweet peppers and canned palm hearts for a different but good end result.

Fish and Red Pepper Stew is the sort of meal that's particularly suited to weekend cooking and eating – relaxed and not showy, but really very satisfying. This Two for One recipe takes 1 hour to cook, makes sufficient quantities for eight and freezes well. Always cook fresh fish within a day or two of purchase or place in the freezer until required.

September Week 4	Recipe	Time
Big meal from scratch	Duck with quinces (or pears) in red wine with roast potatoes and lemon courgettes	3½ hours
Something for nothing 1	Duck and lentil salad	25 mins
Something for nothing 2	Courgette and ricotta lasagne	40 mins
Seasonal supper	Chicken with grapes	50 mins
Larder feast	Cauliflower, chickpea and preserved lemon salad	30 mins
2 for 1	Fish and red pepper stew	1 hour

All recipes serve 4 apart from the 2 for 1 recipe which makes 8 portions

SHOPPING LIST (for 4 people)

Meat and fish
7 free-range duck legs
200 g free-range rindless smoked
 streaky bacon
8 free-range chicken thighs, skin on
1.2-1.6 kg firm white fish, skinned and boned

Dairy
90 g butter
250 g (approx.) ricotta
80-100 g Parmesan
100-125 g (approx.) mozzarella

Fruit and vegetables
2 kg roasting potatoes, such as Maris Piper
 or King Edward
2 medium aubergines, approx. 400 g
1 kg courgettes
1 small cauliflower, approx. 400 g
200 g baby leaf spinach, rocket or watercress
 or a mixture of these leaves
4 large ripe beef tomatoes or 6 ripe plum
 tomatoes, 500 g
4 celery sticks
2 carrots, approx. 200 g
3 red peppers, approx. 450 g
5 medium red onions, approx. 600 g
12 large or banana shallots, approx. 360 g
10 garlic cloves
4-5 sprigs fresh thyme or ½ tsp dried thyme
1 small bunch fresh parsley
4 sprigs fresh mint
handful of fresh coriander
4 sprigs fresh oregano or marjoram or 1 tbsp
 dried oregano or marjoram
1 small bunch chives
2 large or 4 small quinces or firm English
 pears, approx. 400 g
2½ lemons
1 orange
700 g green seedless grapes

Basics
270 ml (approx.) olive oil
50 ml (approx.) groundnut or grapeseed oil
6 pitta breads
5 tbsp plain flour
1 tbsp Dijon mustard
2 bay leaves
300 ml duck, chicken or vegetable stock
 (fresh or made from a stock cube or
 bouillon powder)
salt and pepper

Store cupboard
2-3 cans brown lentils, total weight approx.
 800-900 g
300-400 g fresh egg lasagne
200 g couscous
2 × 400 g cans chickpeas
2 × 400 g cans chopped tomatoes
1 tbsp redcurrant jelly
120 g (approx.) pitted black olives
2 tbsp pesto
2-3 preserved lemons (or 2-3 marinated
 roasted red peppers and 400g can palm
 hearts)
2½ tbsp sherry or cider vinegar
2-3 blades of mace
1 tsp ground cumin
1½ tsp ground coriander
2 tsp sesame seeds
2 tsp dried thyme
1 tsp paprika
500 ml red wine
200 ml white wine
120 ml brandy

Serving suggestions
crusty bread (dDuck Salad with Lentils)
rocket leaves or leaves of choice
 (Courgette and Ricotta Lasagne)
potatoes for mashing, green vegetable
 (Chicken with Grapes)
crusty bread, green salad or vegetable
 (Fish and Red Pepper Stew)

To download or print out this shopping list,
please visit www.thekitchenrevolution.co.uk/
September/Week4

Duck with Quinces (or Pears) in Red Wine with Roast Potatoes and Lemon Courgettes

Fruity and flavoursome, this recipe is one of our favourites. Quinces have a yellow, slightly dusky skin and look like a cross between a pear and an apple. When they are ripe, quinces have a perfumed aroma that will flavour sauces, pies or, in this case, a roast. The quince season is fairly short – the end of September through to the end of October. If you can't get hold of quinces, this recipe works well with pears that are ever so slightly firm.

This recipe is borrowed from *The Carved Angel Cookery Book* by Joyce Molyneux. Joyce is an inspirational chef who used to run and own the Carved Angel restaurant in Dartmouth. She is unquestionably one of our heroes – her approach to cooking, with its emphasis on seasonal, top quality ingredients and unfussy but original recipes has influenced generations of chefs.

The recipe includes extra duck for the Duck and Lentil Salad and extra courgettes for the Courgette and Ricotta Lasagne.

Duck with quinces (or pears) in red wine
7 free-range duck legs; includes 3 extra legs for the duck and lentil salad
120 ml brandy
2 large or 4 small quinces or firm English pears, approx. 400 g
90 g butter
groundnut or grapeseed oil
500 ml red wine
300 ml duck or chicken stock (fresh or made from a stock cube or bouillon powder)
1 tbsp redcurrant jelly
1 orange
1 heaped tbsp plain flour
salt and black pepper

Roast potatoes
1.2 kg roasting potatoes, such as Maris Piper or King Edward
1 heaped tbsp plain flour
2-3 tbsp groundnut or grapeseed oil

Lemon courgettes
1 lemon
1 tbsp olive oil
1 kg courgettes; includes 500 g extra for the courgette and ricotta lasagne

GET AHEAD PREPARATION (optional)
* Marinate the duck.
* Prepare the potatoes and cover with water until required.
* Prepare the courgettes.

3½ hours before you want to eat (and up to 7 hours beforehand) marinate the duck

* Cut any excess fat from the duck legs and place them in a large flat dish or roasting tin, along with the brandy and mix well.
* Peel, quarter and core the quinces or pears, keeping the trimmings to one side to make a juice to go into the sauce. Cut the fruit into slices about 5 mm thick, and add them, along with about 200 ml red wine to the duck legs. Mix well and marinate for 2–5 hours.
* Place the fruit trimmings in a pan with 300 ml water, bring to the boil, simmer for 15 minutes then leave to cool completely. Strain and set the strained liquid aside.

1½ hours before you want to eat

* Preheat the oven to 220°C/425°F/Gas Mark 7.
* First prepare the potatoes. Peel the potatoes, cut into chunks and cook in boiling water for 5–10 minutes. Drain the potatoes in a sieve and shake them vigorously. Put the potatoes back in the pan, sprinkle the flour over the top and shake the pan.
* Add about half the butter to a large frying pan over a medium heat. Lift the duck legs from the marinade and season. Fry the legs in the butter, turning them now and then, until they are evenly browned. You will have to do this in two batches.
* Then prepare the duck. As you finish browning each batch, pour off all the excess fat into a roasting tin. You will need about 1 cm fat on the bottom of the roasting tin so add extra oil if necessary. Put the roasting tin in the oven to heat the fat. Put each batch of browned legs into a large casserole with a lid.
* Strain the duck marinade through a sieve into the frying pan, setting the fruit aside. Deglaze the pan over a medium heat. Bring to the boil, scraping the bottom of the pan then tip the juice on to the duck legs.

* Add the reserved fruit liquid, wine and stock to the frying pan. Turn up the heat, bring the mixture to the boil then add it to the casserole containing the duck legs. Add the redcurrant jelly, a strip of orange zest about 3 cm wide and 4 cm long and the juice of the orange. Stir once to make sure everything is well incorporated, then cover the casserole with a lid and allow the duck to simmer gently over a very low heat for 1 hour. It's important to simmer very gently or the meat will become tough. Set the frying pan aside for use later.

45 minutes before you want to eat

* Carefully add the potatoes to the roasting tin. Using a spoon, turn the potatoes in the oil so that they are well coated, then return the tin to the oven to roast the potatoes for about 35–45 minutes.

20 minutes before you want to eat prepare the courgettes, fruit and sauce

* Check the potatoes and shake the roasting tin a few times.
* Grate the lemon zest into a large bowl with about 1 tsp of juice. Add about 1 teaspoon pepper and ½ teaspoon salt and mix well with the oil. Wash the courgettes and cut them diagonally into chunky 2–3-cm slices. Put the courgettes in the bowl with the lemon and oil mixture and mix together very well.
* Next cook the quinces or pears. Heat all but a walnut of remaining butter in a frying pan over a high heat until foaming, then add the reserved fruit from the marinade and cook for 5–10 minutes or until the fruit is tender and starting to caramelise. Once the fruit is caramelised, lift it out and set it to one side.
* Now make the sauce. Add the remaining butter to the pan and add the flour. Whisk to a smooth paste over a medium heat for 1–2 minutes then add about 200 ml of liquid from the duck legs. Whisk so that it forms a smooth sauce then set it aside to thicken the sauce once the duck legs are ready.

10 minutes before you want to eat cook the courgettes

* Place the courgettes in the top of a steamer or in a pan with about 2 cm water over a medium heat and cook for just over 5 minutes.
* Now check the potatoes. They should be crisp, golden, soft inside. If they are turn, the oven off and lift them into a serving dish. Return the potatoes to the cooling oven to keep warm.
* Lift the duck legs out of the casserole and put three to one side. Arrange the remaining legs on a warmed serving dish along with the fruit and keep warm in the oven.
* Place the casserole over a high heat, add the flour-thickened sauce from the frying pan and bring to a simmer. Taste the sauce and season. Strain some of the sauce from the casserole over the duck legs and fruit and put the rest in a jug.
* Once the courgettes are cooked, set half of them aside for use later in the week and put the rest into a warmed serving dish.
* Serve the duck legs with the sauce and vegetables.

Afterwards

Put the duck legs (3) and the extra courgettes (500 g) in separate containers, cover and refrigerate for later in the week.

Duck and Lentil Salad

Shredded duck meat is succulent and rich and this works well with the earthy flavours of lentils. Removing the duck skin and roasting it in a very high oven produces delicious pieces of crispy duck crackling – an ideal topping for a salad. If there are no duck legs left over from the Big Meal from Scratch, replace them with 3 duck legs, seasoned, browned in a frying pan and then roasted in a medium oven (190°C/375°F/ Gas Mark 5) for 25 minutes until cooked.

We suggest that the lentils are mixed through the salad leaves, but if preferred they can be served on the side.

This recipe takes it inspiration from one that Margot Henderson cooks at the Rochelle Canteen.

3 cooked duck legs left over from
  the Big Meal from Scratch or
  see above
4 tbsp olive oil
2 large or banana shallots,
  approx. 60 g
2 garlic cloves
4 celery sticks
2–3 cans brown lentils, total
  weight approx. 800–900 g
2½ tbsp sherry or cider vinegar

200 g baby leaf spinach, rocket
  or watercress or a mixture of
  these leaves
small handful of fresh parsley
4 sprigs fresh mint
1 tbsp Dijon mustard
salt and pepper

To serve
crusty bread

GET AHEAD PREPARATION (optional)

* Prepare the shallots, garlic
  and celery.
* Cook the lentils and reheat
  them when required.
* Crisp the duck skins in the
  oven.
* Chop the parsley.

*25 minutes before
you want to eat*

* Preheat the oven to 220°C/425°F/Gas Mark 7.
* First, crisp the duck skins. Remove the skins from the duck legs – they don't have to come away in one piece. Place them on a baking sheet in the oven to crisp. You may need to pour off fat from time to time. Keep an eye on them as they burn quite easily.
* Next, start on the lentils. Put a generous splash of oil in a heavy-based pan over a medium heat. Peel and slice the shallots, add them to the pan and cook them gently for 5 minutes. Meanwhile, peel and finely slice the garlic and wash, trim and slice the celery.
* Once the shallots are soft, add the celery to the pan and let it soften for another 5 minutes. While it is softening, shred the meat from the duck legs, discarding any chewy or sinewy pieces. Drain the lentils from their cans and rinse them well.
* When both the shallots and the celery are soft, add the garlic and let it cook for 2–3 minutes. Then increase the heat and splash in 1 tablespoon of the vinegar. Let it evaporate completely before stirring in the lentils. Turn the heat down to medium and leave the lentils to warm through, stirring from time to time. Add a little liquid if they are very dry.
* Now make the salad. Wash and dry the salad leaves and place them and the duck in a large mixing bowl, with a little seasoning and a splash of the vinegar. Roughly chop the parsley and strip the mint leaves from their stalks and tear them.
* When the lentils are warm, stir in the remaining vinegar, the remaining oil and the mustard. Season to taste and add the parsley and mint leaves.
* Now add the lentils to the duck and salad leaves and mix the lot together.
* By now the duck skins should be crisp. Remove them from the oven and let them cool a little before breaking them into bite-sized pieces – use scissors if it is easier.
* Pile the salad on to plates and sprinkle the crispy skins over the top. Serve with crusty bread.

Courgette and Ricotta Lasagne

Though conventional lasagne is undoubtedly delicious it is also a fiddle to prepare and filling to eat. By contrast, this lasagne is made with ricotta, lemon zest and courgettes, and is easy to make and light and creamy to eat. If you have the lemon courgettes from the Big Meal from Scratch this is primarily an assembly rather than a cooking job. If there are no leftover courgettes, replacing them will only add another 15 minutes or so to the total cooking time. Simply cut 500 g courgettes into 1-cm diagonals, mix them with the grated zest of ½ lemon and 2 tablespoons olive oil, season them with salt and black pepper and steam them for 5–7 minutes until they are tender.

250 g (approx.) ricotta
2 tbsp pesto
½ lemon
½ small bunch chives
80–100 g Parmesan
4 large ripe beef tomatoes or 6
   ripe plum tomatoes, 500 g
olive oil
10 sheets lasagne, approx. 300 g
   (either fresh or no-need-to
   precook)
500 g cooked lemon courgettes
   left over from the Big Meal
   from Scratch or see above
100–125 g mozzarella
salt and pepper

To serve
Rocket leaves or leaves of choice

GET AHEAD PREPARATION (optional)

The lasagne can be assembled
up to 2 days in advance and
heated in a hot oven when
required. If you only have a
little time:
* Mix together the ricotta, pesto,
   lemon zest, half the chives
   and half the Parmesan.
* Cook the sheets of lasagne.
* Cut the courgettes.
* Peel the tomatoes.

40 minutes before you want to eat

* Preheat the oven to 220°C/425°F/Gas Mark 7.
* Put a large pan of hot water on to boil while you prepare the sauce. Spoon the ricotta and pesto into a large bowl, grate the zest from the lemon and add it to the bowl. Using scissors, cut the chives into tiny pieces into the bowl. Grate half the Parmesan into the bowl, add a good dose of salt and pepper and mix together very well.
* Once water is boiling, and before you cook the lasagne, make a small incision in the base of each tomato, then drop all the tomatoes into the water and leave them for 1–2 minutes, then lift them out and plunge them into cold water. Leave them to cool while you put the lasagne sheets on to cook.
* Add salt and a glug of oil to the pan of boiling water and drop in the lasagne sheets. When they have started to soften, stir them about so that they don't stick together. If they do they can be pulled apart later. Cook according to the instructions on the packet, then drain and set aside.
* While the lasagne is cooking, prepare the other ingredients. Cut the lemon courgettes into 1–2-cm cubes.
* Next, peel the now-cold tomatoes; their skins should slip off easily. Cut the tomatoes into slices about 5–10 mm thick. Slice the mozzarella to the same thickness.
* Now build the lasagne. Take a large, ovenproof dish and line the bottom with half the courgettes. Place half the tomatoes on top and season well. Add a layer of lasagne sheets and spread this with half the ricotta and pesto mixture. Repeat this layering once again, then finish by laying the mozzarella across the top of the ricotta and sprinkling it with the remaining Parmesan.
* Place the dish in the centre of the oven and bake the lasagne for 20 minutes or until it is piping hot and golden on top.
* Serve with a salad.

Seasonal supper

Chicken with Grapes

This delightful dish is an ideal herald to autumn when grapes are at their most juicy and perfumed. It is based on an Elizabeth David recipe.

½ tbsp groundnut or grapeseed oil
200 g free-range rindless smoked streaky bacon
10 large or banana shallots, approx. 300 g
4 garlic cloves
2 carrots, approx. 200 g
700 g green seedless grapes
8 free-range chicken thighs, skin on
2-3 blades of mace
4-5 sprigs fresh thyme or ½ tsp dried thyme
1 bay leaf
salt and pepper

To serve
mashed potatoes and a green vegetable

GET AHEAD PREPARATION (optional)

The dish can be made up to 1 day in advance and reheated gently when required. If you only have a little time:
* Prepare the shallots, garlic and carrots.
* Prepare the grapes.

50 minutes before you want to eat

* Heat a splash of oil in a large casserole with a lid over a medium heat. Use a pair of scissors to cut 2-cm lengths of the bacon into the pan. Let the bacon cook for 5 minutes while you start to prepare the other vegetables. Peel and finely slice the shallots and garlic. Peel the carrots and slice them into 5-mm rounds. Separate the grapes from their stalks.
* Once the bacon is cooked, remove it from the casserole. Season the chicken thighs and add them to the casserole to brown over a medium-high heat. This will take 5-10 minutes. While the chicken is browning, continue preparing the vegetables. Once the chicken thighs are browned, remove them from the casserole and put to one side.
* Add the shallots and carrots to the casserole and let them soften for a few minutes over a medium heat. Then add the garlic and bacon and three-quarters of the grapes. Squash the grapes with a wooden spoon until they start to release some juice. At this point, return the chicken thighs to the casserole, add a good dose of salt and pepper, the mace blades and the thyme sprigs or dried thyme and the bay leaf. Mix well, bring to simmering point then cover with a lid. If there isn't much liquid add some water or stock. The thighs should be ⅔ immersed. Turn down the heat and cook gently for 20-30 minutes. Stir once during this cooking time.
* While the chicken is cooking, cut the remaining grapes in half.
* When the chicken thighs are tender and completely cooked. Lift them out and keep them warm. Press the sauce through a sieve and return it to the casserole. Simmer for a few minutes if it seems thin then taste and season as necessary. Serve sprinkled with the halved grapes, a generous pile of mash and a green vegetable.

Larder feast

Cauliflower, Chickpea and Preserved Lemon Salad

This salad is substantial enough to count as a main meal, particularly when served with spiced pitta breads. The lip-puckering loveliness of preserved lemons is particularly good if you are fed up with the cold or feeling under the weather. Preserved in salt, these lemons are a staple over much of the Middle East where they are used to add a distinctive flavour and texture to stews and salads. Unlike fresh lemons, their skin is edible and the inside pulp tends to be discarded. Preserved lemons are available in Mediterranean, Arabic and Indian stores, and some supermarkets stock them in their 'speciality' food sections.

200 g couscous
1 medium red onion, approx.
    120 g
8 tbsp olive oil
1 small cauliflower, approx.
    400 g
handful of fresh flatleaf parsley
handful of fresh coriander
2–3 preserved lemons or 2–3
    marinated red peppers and 1 x
    400 g can palm hearts
1 tsp ground cumin
1½ tsp ground coriander
2 x 400 g cans chickpeas
1 lemon
salt

Spiced pitta breads
6 pitta breads
2 tsp sesame seeds
2 tsp dried thyme
1 tsp paprika
salt and pepper

GET AHEAD PREPARATION (optional)

The salad can be assembled, minus any fresh herbs, 2 days in advance, but remove from the fridge at least 40 minutes before serving. If you only have a little time:
* Cook the couscous.
* Peel and slice the onion.
* Cook the cauliflower.
* Toast the sesame seeds.
* Make the pitta topping.
* Chop the parsley and coriander.

30 minutes before you want to eat

* Place the couscous in a large bowl and just cover it with boiling water (you will need approx. 240 ml). Cover with cling film and leave until the grains have soaked up all the water – about 15 minutes.
* Next, peel and slice the onion, heat 1 tablespoon of the oil in a frying pan over a medium heat and add the onion, cook gently for 7–10 minutes.
* Remove any leaves from the cauliflower and break it into bite-sized florets. Place the florets in a steamer and cook until just tender.
* Chop the parsley and fresh coriander. Then cut the preserved lemons in half, scrape out and discard any flesh and chop the skins into a smallish (1–2-cm) dice. If replacing with pepper and palm hearts, drain them well and chop into 1–2 cm slies then continue with the recipe.
* When the onion is soft, add the cumin and the ground coriander and stir over the heat for a minute. Then tip the spiced onion into a large salad bowl.
* Drain the chickpeas and add them to the bowl along with the preserved lemons, parsley, fresh coriander and cauliflower.
* Check the couscous is ready, then use a fork to separate the grains. If the couscous is very wet, tip it into a sieve and press it with the back of a wooden spoon to get rid of any excess water.
* Add the couscous to the chickpea, cauliflower and preserved lemon mixture along with the juice from the lemon, ½ teaspoon salt and all but about 1 tablespoon of the remaining oil. Fold together gently, season and, then set aside.
* Preheat the oven to 190°C/375°F/Gas Mark 5. Halve the pitta breads lengthways and warm in the oven.
* Wipe the pan used to cook the onion with kitchen paper then place it over a medium heat. Add the sesame seeds and toast them until they are brown.
* Mix together the thyme, paprika and toasted sesame seeds. Grate the zest of half the lemon, and add it to the herb and spice mixture, season and stir well.
* Remove the pitta breads from the oven, brush them with the remaining oil and sprinkle over the herb and spice mixture. Return the breads to the oven for 2–3 minutes.
* Serve the salad with the spiced pitta breads.

Two for one

Fish and Red Pepper Stew

This is a simple Mediterranean-flavoured fish stew – a mixture of tomatoes and aubergines, red peppers and olives. It's easy to make but requires about 45 minutes cooking on the hob. However, any time you spend now will be saved later as the quantities are for eight servings, half of which are to be frozen for a 'no effort' meal at a later date.

3 red peppers, approx. 450 g
4 tbsp olive oil
4 medium red onions, approx. 480 g
2 medium aubergines, approx. 300 g
1.2–1.6 kg firm white fish, skinned and boned
4 sprigs fresh oregano or marjoram or 1 tbsp dried oregano or marjoram
2 tbsp plain flour
200 ml white wine
4–5 large potatoes, such as Maris Piper or King Edward, approx. 800 g
4 garlic cloves
2 × 400 g cans chopped tomatoes
1 bay leaf
120 g (approx.) pitted black olives
salt and pepper

To serve
Green salad or vegetable, crusty bread

GET AHEAD PREPARATION (optional)

The vegetables can be cooked up to a day in advance and the cooked fish added to them just prior to eating. If you only have a little time:
* Bake then peel the peppers.
* Prepare the onions, garlic and aubergines.
* Prepare the potatoes and cover with water until required.
* Chop the herbs, if using.
* Cut the fish.

1 hour before you want to eat

* Preheat the oven to 220°C/425°F/Gas Mark 7.
* Place the peppers on a baking sheet, toss them with some of the oil and salt and pepper, and bake them in the oven until they are soft and their skins peel easily – this will take 20–25 minutes.
* Next, start to prepare the remaining vegetables. Peel and slice the onions. Cut the aubergines into 2–3-cm cubes and put them in an ovenproof dish. Toss in a generous splash of oil and some seasoning and place in the oven for about 20 minutes until the cubes are soft and browned. Leave the remaining vegetables to one side while you prepare the fish.
* Now prepare the fish. First cut the fillets into 3–4-cm chunks, then strip the leaves of fresh oregano or marjoram, if using, from their stalks. Chop the leaves and throw half of them, or half the dried herbs, and the fish into a bowl along with the flour and plenty of seasoning. Mix well so that the fish is evenly coated.
* Heat 2 tablespoons of the oil in a large heavy-based pan with a lid. When the oil is hot, add the chunks of fish and fry them over a medium heat, turning now and then, until they are golden. Remove the fish with a spoon, and put to one side.
* Splash half the wine into the pan, bring it to the boil, and stir well. Pour the wine into a cup or jug. Now wipe out the pan with kitchen paper before starting on the vegetables.
* Heat 1 tablespoon oil to the pan and when it is hot add the onions. Cook them over a medium heat, stirring from time to time, for about 7 minutes until they have softened a little.
* While the onions are cooking, peel the potatoes and cut them into 2–3-cm cubes. When the potatoes are ready, add them to the onions and turn the heat up so that they brown all over. You will need to stir them regularly.
* While the potatoes brown, peel and roughly chop the garlic. The potatoes will take about 7–10 minutes. When they have, add the garlic and stir it through the potatoes and onions for a couple of minutes, being careful not to let it get too much colour. By now the aubergines should be ready, so take them out of the oven and tip them into the pan.

* Next, add the tomatoes, remaining wine, bay leaf, remaining oregano or marjoram, and salt and pepper, and simmer for a further 35 minutes with the lid on, stirring now and again. If the stew seems very liquid, remove the lid for the last 15 minutes.
* When the red peppers have softened, remove them from the oven and put them in a plastic bag or in a bowl covered with cling film. Allow the peppers to cool then peel off the skins – they should slip off easily. Cut the peppers in half, remove the seeds and slice or tear the flesh into 1-cm strips.
* When the vegetables in the pan are tender, add the olives and peppers and cook with the lid off for a couple of minutes to heat through.
* Put half the vegetables into a container suitable for freezing and put half the fish into a freezer bag. Set them aside to cool before placing them in the freezer.
* Add the rest of the fish to the remaining vegetables on the stove and simmer for 5 minutes until the fish is firm.
* Serve with a robust red wine, a green salad or vegetable and crusty bread.

Lazy day supper – reheating instructions
* Defrost the fish and the vegetables thoroughly.
* Place the vegetables in a large pan and heat them over a gentle heat with the lid on until they are piping hot, then add the fish and cook for 5 minutes more.

KITCHEN REVOLUTION EXTRA

Roasting peppers
Polly and Rosie both have different ways of roasting peppers, which give slightly different results. Most of the recipes use Rosie's method, because it's less likely to cause burnt fingers, but Polly's method is far quicker. Here are both methods, so you can choose which works best for you:

Polly's method is to cut the peppers into halves or quarters and lie them, skin-side down, on the direct flame or heat of a stove ring so that the skins blacken. Turn them from time to time to make sure they blacken evenly – take great care not to burn your fingers. Once the peppers are blistered and blackened, remove them from the heat and hold them under cold running water to remove the charred skin.

Rosie's method is to place the whole peppers in a roasting tin with some oil and seasoning in a hot oven. Once they are soft and their skins have coloured, tip them into a bowl and cover with cling film so that they steam as they cool and their skins lift off more easily. Once the peppers are cool, peel and deseed them, catching any juices that escape. Finally run them under the tap to get rid of any bits of skin or seeds.

Iced Blackberry Fool

This is somewhere between a fool and a sorbet – wonderfully refreshing but also rich enough to feel slightly wicked. There are two parts to the recipe: making a fruit syrup and freezing it, then folding this semi-frozen fruit ice into Greek yoghurt and crème fraîche. You don't need an ice-cream maker for this recipe – in fact it's better made without one, because you want the frozen syrup to have quite large crystals rather than a smooth sorbet consistency.

The same method can be used for any soft fruit – strawberries, raspberries and peaches – but fruits like blackberries and gooseberries which have an edge of tartness work especially well. The excuse to pick blackberries from the hedgerows when they are in season is an added bonus of this recipe. If you are lucky enough to collect a bumper crop of berries the fruit syrup recipe can be doubled or even tripled for use later in the year.

The time it takes for the mixture to freeze will depend on the volume of the liquid – the shallower and wider the container the sooner the syrup will freeze. If the mixture has been in a freezer longer than a few hours you will need to take it out and leave it at room temperature for about 10 minutes, then use a fork to break it up. You can make the frozen fruit syrup up to 2 months before using it, but you can also make it on the day you want to eat as long as there's time for it to freeze. The quantities for sugar are approximate – be led by your senses as much as by the recipe, and add more or less sugar as required.

800 g (approx.) blackberries
200–300 g (approx.) caster sugar
½ lemon
100 ml crème fraîche
100 ml Greek yoghurt
handful of blackberries, to
   garnish (optional)
icing sugar, for dusting (optional)

To serve
biscuits

* Wash the blackberries in a bowl of water, drain them and put them into a large pan. Add the sugar and 2 tablespoons water. Peel a couple of lengths of zest from the half lemon, add this to the pan and squeeze in the juice. Place the pan over a medium heat, stir for a couple of minutes until the sugar has all but dissolved then leave to simmer for 10 minutes or until the berries have turned into a mush. Taste for sugar and add more if necessary.
* Strain the blackberry syrup through a sieve and into a plastic box with a lid. Put to one side and allow to cool to room temperature. If you are in a rush divide the mixture between two boxes so that it cools down more quickly. When the mixture is at room temperature put the lid on the boxes and place in the freezer.
* Set a timer for 45 minutes, then use a fork to stir the mixture so that the mixture freezes into soft crystals rather than a hard block. Return the mixture to the freezer and repeat this process again at least once until the mixture is nearly completely frozen.
* Mix together the crème fraîche and yoghurt.
* Divide the blackberry freeze between four bowls then use a fork to mix in the crème fraîche and yoghurt mixture.
* If you have the inclination, sprinkle some blackberries over each bowl and dust with a little icing sugar before serving.

Apple Butterscotch Meringue

This has three undisputably delicious things in one pudding.

Base
300 ml milk
55 g cornflour
125 g dark brown soft sugar
500 g eating apples – Russets
  would be good, approx 4 apples
55 g butter
2 free-range egg yolks

Meringue topping
3 free-range egg whites
85 g caster sugar

*45 minutes before
you want to eat*

* Preheat the oven to 200°C/400°F/Gas Mark 6.
* First, prepare the base. Pour the milk into a saucepan, add the cornflour and sugar. Heat slowly to dissolve the sugar and bring up to the boil – as the cornflour heats it will start to thicken. Whisk the mixture to disperse any lumps. Once boiling, let it cook for about a minute until very thick and smooth. Remove from the heat and leave to cool for a few minutes in the pan while you peel, quarter and core the apples.
* Next beat the butter into the warm mixture in the pan, a few pieces at a time. Once smooth and shiny, stir in the egg yolks. Now add the apple and combine the mixture well. Spoon the apple mixture into an ovenproof dish and make the meringue.
* Whisk the egg whites until you have soft peaks, then gradually whisk in half the caster sugar. Fold in the rest of the sugar and carefully spoon the meringue on top of the butterscotch mixture, and bake until golden and firm to the touch, about 20 minutes.
* Serve with crème fraîche to cut through richness.

Chocolate and Fig Cake

For this pudding a light chocolate mousse cake is baked in the oven until it is just setting. At this point pieces of ripe fig are plunged into the cake batter to cook for another 15 minutes.

250 g plain chocolate
125 g butter, plus extra for
  greasing
1 tbsp brandy, Cointreau or Tia
  Maria
5 free-range eggs
125 g caster sugar
pinch of salt
4 ripe fresh figs

To serve
crème fraîche

*45 minutes before
you want to eat*

* Preheat the oven to 180°C/350°F/Gas Mark 4.
* Break the chocolate into smallish pieces and place them in a bowl. Cut the butter into pieces and add to the chocolate along with the alcohol. Cover the bowl with cling film and place it over a pan of simmering water, making sure the base of the bowl doesn't touch the water. Leave the chocolate to melt.
* Line the base of a 20-cm cake tin with greaseproof paper, then grease the paper and sides with butter. Separate the eggs. Whisk the egg yolks with the sugar until very thick. Wash the whisk, make sure it is dry and whisk the whites with the salt until they form soft peaks. By now, the chocolate should be melted, so give it a stir and carefully amalgamate it with the yolk mixture. Add a good spoonful of whites to the chocolate mixture, stir thoroughly then fold in the remaining whites.
* Pour the cake mixture carefully into the prepared cake tin and bake for 15 minutes until it is just beginning to set.
* While the cake is cooking, quarter the figs lengthways. When the cake is just set, push the fig quarters into the top of the cake and return it to the oven.
* Bake for another 15 minutes until the cake is just firm and cracking a little on the top.
* Leave to cool on a rack before taking the cake out of the tin.
* Serve with crème fraîche.

Plum Crumble

Plums are at their best in September and October and when the crop is particularly good they hang dripping from trees. The oats in the topping make a well-textured crumble. The 1 kg of plums in the recipe can be replaced with 500 g plums and 500 g damsons.

175 g plain flour
75 g light brown soft sugar
125 g butter
50 g oats
1 kg plums (Victoria plums are
  really good)
160 g caster sugar

To serve
vanilla ice cream or thick cream

55 minutes before you want to eat

* Preheat the oven to 180°C/350°F/Gas mark 4.
* Start by making the crumble. If you have a food processor, sift the flour into the processor bowl, add the brown sugar and the butter cut into small pieces and whizz the mixture until it resembles breadcrumbs. At this point add the oats and whizz very quickly to disperse them. The crumble can also be made by hand. Sifting the flour into a large bowl, grate in the butter and gently rub it into the flour gently until the mixture resembles breadcrumbs. At this point add the sugar and oats and mix together thoroughly.
* Now wash the plums, cut them in half, stone them and then cut them in half again. Toss the plum quarters in the 160 g sugar then pile into a pie dish that they fill very well. Cover them with the crumble mixture, spreading it evenly all over the fruit.
* Put the crumble in the oven and bake it for 40 minutes until the plums are soft and the top is golden.
* Serve with vanilla ice cream or thick cream.

OCTOBER

As the days grow darker and colder, there are compensations to be had in October's seasonal produce. Mushrooms, apples and pears appear in dizzying variety, but most of them won't find their way into supermarkets so it's well worth seeking out a good greengrocer or the nearest farmers' market. There are fewer salads on the menu now, and more casseroles and curries. That said, October eating doesn't need to be stodgy – there is still plenty of fruit around, and lots of good herbs and vegetables. Ham with Parsley Sauce and New Potatoes somehow feels perfectly seasonal. Though its ingredients aren't particular to October, this meal is a good way to ease into wintry eating. Halloween means pumpkins – there's a pumpkin curry with coconut, and a Spanish Pumpkin Casserole. As for wonderful English pears, we caramelise them in a Ginger Pear Pudding with a light sponge on top.

October	Week 1	Week 2	Week 3	Week 4
Big meal from scratch	Poussin (or chicken) in paper with shallots, mushrooms and potatoes, and spinach	Ham and parsley sauce with carrots and new potatoes	Pot roast venison (or beef) with root vegetable mash, and curly kale	Baked fish with caper, parsley and garlic topping, boiled potatoes and steamed chard
Something for nothing 1	Glazed chicken with orange and date couscous	Croque monsieur with quick pickled onions	Crispy venison (or beef) with stir-fried vegetables and noodles	Potato crush fish cakes with herb sauce
Something for nothing 2	Steak, chips and creamed spinach	Goats' cheese and rosemary tortilla with tomato salad	Sausages with root vegetable colcannon cakes and onion gravy	Chard and mushroom rice
Seasonal supper	Mussel (or fish) and potato stew	Curried coconut pumpkin	Midweek mushroom curry	Spanish pumpkin casserole
Larder feast	Artichoke, gnocchi and Parmesan bake with garlic bread	Cod with tartare sauce and mushy peas	Fish and chorizo cassoulet	Smoked mussel spaghetti
2 for 1	Butter bean and bacon casserole with garlic bread	Chilli con carne with corn muffins	Lemon butternut lasagne	Lamb and pearl barley stew
Puddings	Hazelnut and chocolate torte	Apple charlotte	Pear and ginger Eve's pudding	Baked figs with yoghurt

October Week 1 – Overview

Wrapping poussin (or chicken), shallots, mushrooms and potatoes in paper and baking them in the oven is a wonderful way to retain moisture and flavour. It's well worth considering this Big Meal from Scratch if you're inviting friends or family over for something to eat. The recipe works fine with either six poussin or two medium-sized chickens. Altogether the recipe will take about 2 hours, but once the birds and vegetables are in the parcels and baking only the spinach has to be prepared.

For a Something for Nothing, spare poussin or chicken from the big meal makes a Glazed Chicken with Orange and Date Couscous that, again, could proudly be shared with friends. Most people get a craving for steak once in a while, so the second Something for Nothing which uses leftover spinach and potatoes to make Steak and Chips with Creamed Spinach is likely to be well received. From start to finish, this will take about half an hour.

Allow a little more time for this week's Seasonal Supper of Mussel (or Fish) and Potato Stew. Most places sell mussels ready cleaned, in which case the recipe will take 40 minutes, but if you have to scrub and debeard the mussels yourself allow another 20 minutes. Fresh mussels should be cooked within a day or so of buying them but if that isn't feasible the recipe will work with skinless, firm white fish like monkfish or pollack.

Canned artichokes are a luxurious convenience – nothing like their fresh cousins, but very nice nonetheless. In our Larder Feast they are used for an Artichoke, Gnocchi and Parmesan Bake. As this is a midweek recipe using ready-made gnocchi means the meal can be cooked and on the table in half and hour.

The Two for One Butter Bean and Bacon Casserole is an ideal antidote to a cold and wet day. This recipe also has the advantage of being very quick to cook so in just 30 minutes you can make a meal and stock the freezer.

October Week 1	Recipe	Time
Big meal from scratch	Poussin (or chicken) in paper with shallots, mushrooms and potatoes, and spinach	2 hours
Something for nothing 1	Glazed chicken with orange and date couscous	35 mins
Something for nothing 2	Steak, chips and creamed spinach	30 mins
Seasonal supper	Mussel (or fish) and potato stew	40 mins
Larder feast	Artichoke, gnocchi and Parmesan bake with garlic bread	30 mins
2 for 1	Butter bean and bacon casserole with garlic bread	30 mins

All recipes serve 4 apart from the 2 for 1 recipe which makes 8 portions

SHOPPING LIST (for 4 people)

Meat and fish
6 poussin or 2 × 1.5 kg (approx.) free-range chickens
4 × 200 g (approx.) rump or sirloin steaks, 3-4 cm thick
1 kg fresh mussels or 600 g monkfish or other skinless firm white fish
600 g free-range rindless streaky bacon (smoked or unsmoked)

Dairy
275 g (approx.) butter
100-150 ml double cream
200 g crème fraîche
150 g Parmesan
300 g garlic and herb soft cheese

Fruit and vegetables
2 kg new potatoes
3 large potatoes, approx. 850 g (ideally King Edward or Maris Piper)
800 g baby leaf spinach or 1 kg large leaf spinach
300-400 g kale or other dark greens
200 g wild or domestic mushrooms (chestnut are good)
4 large leeks, approx. 600 g
1 medium red onion, approx. 120 g
11 large or banana shallots, approx. 330 g
1 small bunch spring onions, approx. 6
10 garlic cloves
1 large head celery
1 bulb fennel, approx. 150 g
6 cm piece fresh root ginger
3 small red chillies
4 sprigs fresh thyme
1 large bunch fresh parsley
1 small bunch fresh coriander
1 large orange
2 lemons

Basics
90 ml olive oil
120 ml groundnut or grapeseed oil
2 baguettes
50 g bread (brown or white, stale or fresh; leftover crust will do)
1 tbsp wholegrain mustard
3 tbsp clear honey
5 bay leaves
1 litre vegetable stock (fresh or made from a stock cube or bouillon powder)
400 ml ham or vegetable stock (fresh or made with a stock cube or vegetable bouillon powder)
salt and pepper
baking parchment or greaseproof paper

Store cupboard
500 g ready-made fresh gnocchi
400 g couscous
2 × 400 g cans artichoke hearts
800 g butter beans from cans or jars
30 g dried ceps (porcini) or other dried wild mushrooms
75 g soft dried dates or 150 g fresh dates
20 g shelled, unsalted pistachio nuts
1 tsp paprika
½ tsp ground cinnamon
1 tsp ground cumin
1 tsp ground coriander
small pinch saffron threads
1 tsp nutmeg (ground or freshly grated)
925 ml approx. white wine
200 ml orange juice
400 ml cider

Quick option (Butter Bean and Bacon Casserole with Garlic Bread)
ready-made garlic bread: omit 2 baguettes and 300 g garlic and herb soft cheese

Serving suggestions
English or Dijon mustard (steak, chips and creamed spinach)
crusty bread, radicchio, carrot salad ingredients (Mussel (or Fish) and Potato Stew)
frozen peas or broad beans (Artichokes, Gnocchi and Parmesan Bake)

To download or print out this shopping list, please visit www.thekitchenrevolution.co.uk/October/Week1

Poussin (or Chicken) in Paper with Shallots, Mushrooms and Potatoes, and Spinach

In this recipe poussin (small chickens) are wrapped in a parcel of parchment paper and baked with potatoes and mushrooms. Roasting the birds this way ensures that they remain moist. Although this isn't a complicated or fiddly dinner the end result is pretty impressive, so it's a good one to share with friends or for a special occasion.

If you can't find poussin, the recipe works equally well using two medium-sized chickens – the cooking times will be different, and rather than serving each person an individual parcel the chicken has to be carved and the potatoes, mushrooms and juices served separately.

These delicious parcels need nothing more than simply cooked spinach to make the meal complete.

The ingredients for this recipe include two extra poussin (or one extra chicken), extra spinach and extra potatoes for dishes later in the week. The potatoes and spinach are used for Steak and Chips with Creamed Spinach (see page 435) and the leftover poussin or chicken is dressed in an orange glaze for Glazed Chicken with Orange and Date Couscous (see page 434). You will need baking parchment or greaseproof paper to make the parcels for the birds

Poussin (or chicken) in paper
with shallots, mushrooms and
potatoes
30 g dried ceps (porcini) or other
　dried wild mushrooms
6 poussin or 2 × 1.5 kg (approx.)
　free-range chickens; includes
　2 extra poussin or 1 extra
　chicken for the glazed chicken
1 tbsp groundnut or grapeseed oil
8 large or banana shallots,
　approx. 240 g
200 g wild or domestic
　mushrooms (chestnuts are
　good)
250 ml white wine
100 g butter

4 sprigs fresh thyme
2 kg new potatoes; includes 1 kg
　extra for the chips
3 bay leaves
salt and pepper

Spinach
800 g baby leaf spinach or
　1 kg large-leaved spinach;
　includes 400-500g extra for
　the creamed spinach
1 tbsp olive oil
30 g butter
pinch of nutmeg (ground or
　freshly grated)

GET AHEAD PREPARATION (optional)

The parcels can be made a few hours in advance and kept in the fridge; be sure to take them out 40 minutes before you want to cook them. If you only have a little time:
* Soak the dried ceps (porcini) or other mushrooms.
* Season and brown the poussin.
* Prepare the shallots.
* Slice the fresh mushrooms.
* Prepare the spinach.

*2 hours before
you want to eat
prepare and cook
the parcels*

* Preheat the oven to 180°C/350°F/Gas Mark 4.
* Cover the dried ceps or mushrooms with boiling water and leave to soak.
* Next, brown the birds. Season the poussin (or chickens) inside and out. Heat a splash of oil in a large frying pan and brown them all over in batches. As they brown, place them in a large dish. While the birds are browning, peel and quarter the shallots and slice the fresh mushrooms.
* When you've finished browning the birds, lift them out and put them in a dish. Then splash half the wine into the frying pan and stir once or twice, scraping the bottom of the pan. Pour the wine over the birds, then dry the pan with kitchen paper.
* Next, cook the shallots and mushrooms in the frying pan. Add a splash of oil and a generous nut of butter to the pan. When the butter is foaming, add the shallots to brown for a couple of minutes. Then add the fresh mushrooms and let them cook for a couple of minutes until they soften. When the fresh mushrooms are soft, lift the ceps or other mushrooms out of their soaking liquor and add them to the fresh mushrooms to cook down for a couple of minutes – don't discard the soaking liquor.
* Once the shallots and mushrooms are soft, turn up the heat, add the remaining wine and strain in the dried mushroom liquor. Let it boil away until it has reduced by two-thirds. Strip the thyme leaves from their stalks, add them to the frying pan and season to taste with salt and pepper.
* While the liquid is reducing, wash the new potatoes and, if they are large, cut them in half lengthways. If they are very large, cut them in half again.

* Now make the parcels. You will need six rectangles of baking parchment or greaseproof paper large enough to wrap the poussin (or two large reactangles if you are using two chickens). Place a layer of potatoes on each rectangle and season well. Spoon the mushroom mixture over the potatoes on four of the rectangles (one rectangle if you are cooking two chickens). Place a bird on top of the vegetables on each rectangle. Dot them with the rest of the butter, tear the bay leaves in half and pop half a leaf into the cavity of each bird, then season well. Bring the paper up to envelop the birds and fold the edges down to secure the parcels.
* Place the parcels on a baking sheet and bake in the oven for 45 minutes to 1 hour, or 1¼ hours if you are cooking two chickens.
* While the birds are cooking, wash and destalk the spinach if necessary.

15 minutes before you want to eat cook the spinach

* Open one of the parcels to see whether the birds are cooked. If a leg pulls away with little resistance the birds are ready.
* Remove them from the oven and leave to rest for 10 minutes. Turn the oven off and put plates and serving dishes in to warm. Set aside the two poussins or one chicken without mushrooms and allow to cool completely.
* Now cook the spinach. Heat a glug of oil and half the butter in large heavy-based pan. Add as much spinach as will fit, allow it to wilt, then add any remaining spinach. Once the spinach is evenly cooked, toss it with salt and pepper and the nutmeg, then drop it into a colander to remove any liquid. Let the spinach drain for 1–2 minutes, then put half into a serving dish with the remaining butter. Let the other half cool.
* Serve a poussin parcel to each person and pass the spinach around in a warmed serving dish. If you have cooked a chicken, carve as you would a roast chicken and divide the potato and mushroom mixture between four plates.

Afterwards

* Remove the breasts and legs from the leftover birds, keeping them as whole as possible. Place the meat and the leftover spinach and potatoes in separate containers, cover and refrigerate for use later in the week. Ideally you will have 800 g or more new potatoes, between 350 and 450 g spinach and four poussin breasts and legs or two chicken breasts and legs.
* The stripped poussin or chicken carcasses will make good stock (see page 495).

Glazed Chicken with Orange and Date Couscous

This is as far from a 'leftover' meal as it's possible to imagine and it's worth inviting friends over (again) for this. There are more ingredients than you'd usually use for a midweek supper, but the end result justifies the means. Essentially the recipe is very simple – it involves making a glaze with garlic, ginger, wine and honey, pouring this over the chicken and grilling it. While the glaze is bubbling away in the pan, the couscous is cooked in orange juice, stock and spices.

If you don't have any poussin or chicken left over from the Big Meal, season 8 chicken thighs and rub with oil. Turn the oven to 200°C/400°F/Gas Mark 6 and bake the thighs for 15–20 minutes until just cooked, then continue with the recipe.

Glazed chicken
3 garlic cloves
6 cm piece fresh root ginger
2 small red chillies
1 tbsp olive oil
175 ml white wine
3 tbsp clear honey
4 cooked poussin breasts and 4 poussin legs or 2 chicken breasts and 2 chicken legs left over from the Big Meal from Scratch or see above
20 g shelled, unsalted pistachio nuts
salt and pepper

Orange and date couscous
250 ml vegetable stock (made from a stock cube or bouillon powder)
200 ml orange juice
1 tsp paprika
½ tsp ground cinnamon
1 tsp ground cumin
1 tsp ground coriander
3 tbsp olive oil
400 g couscous
6 spring onions
75 g soft dried dates or 150 g fresh dates
1 large orange
handful fresh parsley
handful fresh coriander
juice of 1 lemon

GET AHEAD PREPARATION (optional)

The glaze and the couscous can be cooked up to 2 days in advance. If you only have a little time:
* Prepare the garlic and ginger.
* Deseed and chop the chillies.
* Prepare the stock and orange juice for cooking the couscous.
* Prepare the orange.
* Chop the herbs.
* Chop the pistachios.

35 minutes before you want to eat make the glaze

* Peel and grate the garlic and ginger, and deseed and finely chop the chillies.
* Heat the oil in a pan over a medium heat, add the garlic, ginger and chillies and cook for 3–5 minutes, stirring regularly. Then add the wine, turn up the heat and boil until the wine has reduced by half.
* Stir in the honey and simmer until the sauce starts to thicken.

25 minutes before you want to eat make the couscous

* Place the stock and orange juice in a large pan with a generous pinch of salt, the spices and a slug of oil, and bring to the boil. When the stock and orange juice are boiling, pour over the couscous, cover with cling film and leave for 10–15 minutes.
* Check the glaze; if it coats the back of a metal spoon it is ready, so set it aside until required.
* Trim and slice the spring onions. Stone and dice the dates. Peel and segment the orange, and roughly chop the segments. Chop the parsley and fresh coriander.
* After 10–15 minutes fluff the couscous up with a fork. Stir in the oil and lemon juice, dates, orange pieces, spring onions, coriander and parsley. Mix well and season to taste.

10 minutes before you want to eat grill the chicken

* Bring the pan of glaze back to the boil and preheat the grill to its highest setting.
* Place the breasts and legs in a roasting tin, skin sides up, season and pour the hot glaze over them, then put the tin under the grill. The skins will start to caramelise as the birds heat through – this will take 5–7 minutes.
* Roughly chop the pistachios.
* To serve, divide the couscous between four plates and place a poussin breast and leg on top. Pour over a little extra glaze and sprinkle with the pistachios.

Something
for nothing 2

Steak and Chips with Creamed Spinach

About two or three times a year we get a hankering for steak. Others feel the need more often, but there are very few people who don't ever experience those moments when a juicy and plump steak is all their heart desires.

A steak should have a decent amount of fat either around the outside or running through the flesh. Fat is not bad – it holds flavour and keeps meat from being dry and chewy.

Creamed spinach is a lovely way of utilising leftover spinach, and the texture and flavour complement the steak and chips. This creamed spinach recipe owes its existence to a chef friend of Rosie's, Tim Dillon.

If you have no potatoes left over from the Big Meal ffrom Scratch, parboil 800 g peeled, diced new potatoes for about 5 minutes then continue with the recipe as below.

Steak
groundnut or grapeseed oil, for
    drizzling
4 × 200 g (approx.) rump or
    sirloin steaks, cut into slices
    2.5-3.5 cm thick
20 g (approx.) butter
salt and pepper

Chips
3-4 tbsp groundnut or
    grapeseed oil
800 g cooked potatoes left over
    from the Big Meal from Scratch
    (or see above)

Creamed spinach
350-450 g cooked spinach left
    over from the Big Meal from
    Scratch or 800 g uncooked
    spinach, trimmed, washed,
    cooked and drained
40 g (approx.) butter
2-3 pinches of nutmeg (ground or
    freshly grated)
100-150 ml double cream

To serve
English or Dijon mustard

GET AHEAD PREPARATION (optional)

The creamed spinach can be
made a few hours in advance and
gently heated when required.

30 minutes before
you want to eat

* Preheat the oven to 220°C/425°F/Gas Mark 7.
* Pour the oil for the chips into a roasting tin large enough to hold all the potatoes in one layer and put it in the oven. Remove the steaks from the fridge. Make sure the potatoes are dry.
* Squeeze any excess liquid from the spinach. Melt the butter in a pan until it is foaming and add the spinach. Stir well and heat gently. Season with the nutmeg, salt and pepper and stir in one-third of the cream. Bring to simmering point and when the cream has been absorbed, add another third of the cream. Repeat this process until all the cream is absorbed. Keep the spinach simmering very, very gently until you are ready to serve.
* Remove the roasting tin from the oven and add the potatoes to the hot oil. Toss them in the oil and roast for 20 minutes.
* When the potatoes have 10 minutes left in the oven, cook the steaks. Heat a small drizzle of oil in a frying pan and place over a medium heat, until the oil is hot but not smoking. Pat the steaks dry and season them well. Add two to the pan at a time. Cook the steaks for about 45-50 seconds on one side without moving them at all, then shake the pan a few times to prevent them sticking. Add half the butter to the pan and once the steak is brown turn it over. Fry a 2.5 cm thick steak for about 2 minutes on each side if you want it rare. For a medium rare steak fry for 3 minutes on each side. For medium fry for 4 minutes on each side and for well done fry for 5-6 minutes on each side. For thicker or thinner steaks adjust the cooking time accordingly.
* Cook the steaks according to taste then place in a warm place to rest. Cook the two remaining steaks then rest for 5-10 minutes.
* Line a colander with kitchen paper. Use a slotted spoon to lift the potatoes on to the paper so that any excess fat is absorbed. Season well and season the creamed spinach.
* Serve the steaks with chips and creamed spinach.

Mussel (or Fish) and Potato Stew

Mussels should be plump and sweet at this time of year so this recipe is a fine seasonal treat. Mussels require very little cooking and, when in season, are surprisingly inexpensive – in other words, it is well worth getting hold of them when they are about. Mussels will not stay fresh for more than a day or two, so when shopping and planning the week's food bear this in mind. If you can't find or don't like mussels this recipe works well with any skinless firm white fish.

2 tbsp groundnut or grapeseed
  oil
30 g butter
3 large or banana shallots,
  approx. 90 g
1 small red chilli
4 large celery sticks
1 bulb fennel, approx. 150 g
3 garlic cloves
3 large potatoes, approx. 850 g
  (ideally King Edward or Maris
  Piper)
small pinch saffron threads
750 ml vegetable stock (made
  from a stock cube or bouillon

powder)
½ lemon
1 bay leaf
1 kg fresh mussels or 600 g
  monkfish or other skinless firm
  white fish
250 ml white wine
small handful of fresh parsley
salt and pepper

To serve
crusty bread and radicchio and
  carrot salad

GET AHEAD PREPARATION (optional)

The soup can be made a day in advance up to the point of adding the mussels and reheated gently when required. If you only have a little time:
* Prepare the shallots, chilli, celery and garlic.
* Prepare the potatoes and cover with water until required.
* Clean and debeard the mussels.

40 minutes before you want to eat

* Heat 1 tablespoon of oil and the butter in a large pan over a gentle heat. Peel and slice the shallots, add to the pan and cook over a low heat for 5–7 minutes.
* Meanwhile deseed and finely chop the chilli, and trim and slice the celery. Trim the fennel, remove the outer layer then finely slice and wash.
* Add the chilli, fennel and celery to the shallots and cook for 7 minutes. Meanwhile peel and crush the garlic. Peel the potatoes and chop them into 2-cm cubes.
* When the fennel and celery are soft, add the garlic, saffron and potatoes. Increase the heat and stir for a couple of minutes.
* Add the stock and bring to a simmer. Peel a strip of zest about 6 cm long from the lemon. When the mixture starts to simmer, add the bay leaf and lemon zest. Season and simmer until the potatoes are just soft – about 10 minutes.
* While the potatoes are cooking, clean the mussels under cold running water and remove their beards (see page 396). If you find a mussel that is open, give it a sharp tap. If it doesn't close it must be discarded. Throw away any mussels that have broken shells or feel heavier than the others. If you are using fish, cut it into bite-sized chunks.
* When the potatoes are soft, put a hand blender in the pan and whizz it a couple of times. If you don't have a hand blender lift about 4 tablespoons of potato out and push through a sieve back into the stew. The stew will sit over a very low heat until you want to add the mussels.
* Heat the remaining oil in a large pan and add the mussels. Shake them about for a minute then add the wine. Cover the pan and let the mussels steam open – about 5 minutes. If you are using fish instead of mussels, brown it in a pan, add the wine and simmer for a couple of minutes, then add the fish and liquid to the stew.
* When the mussels are open, remove with a slotted spoon and place in the stew. Discard any that have not opened. Sieve the mussel cooking liquor into the stew. Chop the parsley, add it to the stew, season as necessary. Stir thoroughly.
* Serve with bread and carrot and radicchio with lemon juice and olive oil.

Larder feast

Artichoke, Gnocchi and Parmesan Bake

Baked gratin dishes are understandably popular – the combination of a crispy, cheesy top with a creamy filling is wickedly moreish. Once all the ingredients for this recipe are assembled all the work is done. Making gnocchi, small dumplings made from potato or flour, is not difficult but when time is short the ready-made version is a useful standby. You can, if you wish, replace the gnocchi with 500 g cooked pasta, such as macaroni or farfalle. This is delicious served with broad beans or peas.

1 medium red onion, approx.
  120 g
25 g (approx.) butter, plus extra
  for greasing
½ lemon
150 g Parmesan
50 g bread (brown or white, stale
  or fresh; leftover crusts will
  do)
handful of fresh parsley
250 ml (approx.) white wine
2 × 400 g cans artichoke hearts
500 g ready-made fresh gnocchi
200 g crème fraîche
salt and pepper

To serve:
frozen peas or broad beans

GET AHEAD PREPARATION (optional)

The entire dish can be prepared a day in advance, prior to going into the oven. If you only have a little time:
* Prepare the onion.
* Grate the lemon zest and Parmesan.
* Make the breadcrumbs
* Chop the parsley

30 minutes before you want to eat

* Preheat oven to 200°C/400°F/Gas Mark 6.
* Peel and slice the onion. Melt the butter in a heavy-based pan and fry the onion for about 7 minutes until soft.
* While the onion is cooking, grate the zest of the half lemon and squeeze out its juice. Chop, grate or whizz the bread into breadcrumbs. Roughly chop the parsley and grate the Parmesan.
* Add the wine to the onion, turn up the heat and reduce the wine to about half.
* Meanwhile, drain the artichokes and cut them in half. Add them to the onion along with the gnocchi, crème fraîche, lemon zest and juice, parsley, half the Parmesan and salt and pepper. Stir well, allow the mixture to warm through for a couple of minutes then remove from the heat.
* Grease an ovenproof dish big enough to hold all the ingredients.
* Tip the gnocchi and artichoke mixture into the dish and top with the breadcrumbs and the remaining Parmesan. Bake for 15–20 minutes or until golden brown and bubbling.
* Serve with peas or broad beans.

Two for one

Butter Bean and Bacon Casserole with Garlic Bread

This recipe makes a filling but not heavy casserole that is ideal for a cold night, casual supper party or family meal. If you can get Spanish judion butter beans all the better – they are fatter, juicier and sweeter than their more ordinary cousins. They are available from Spanish and Italian stores and some good delicatessens. For a real treat, there is a recipe for home-made garlic bread to accompany the casserole.

This quantity will feed eight – half for eating now, and half for freezing.

Butter bean and bacon casserole
1 tbsp groundnut or grapeseed oil
30 g butter
600 g free-range rindless streaky
    bacon
4 large leeks, approx. 600 g
6 celery sticks from the centre of
    a head of celery
4 garlic cloves
800 g butter beans from cans or
    jars
1 tbsp wholegrain mustard
400 ml cider
400 ml ham or vegetable stock
    (fresh or made from a stock
    cube or bouillon powder)

1 bay leaf
300–400 g kale or other dark
    greens
small handful of fresh parsley
salt and pepper

Garlic bread
2 baguettes
300 g garlic and herb soft cheese
olive oil, for drizzling
black pepper
or
ready-made garlic bread

GET AHEAD PREPARATION (optional)

The casserole can be made up to 2 days in advance and kept in the fridge then heated when required. The garlic bread can be made up to 1 day in advance, to the point of going in the oven, if it is wrapped in foil and refrigerated. If you only have a little time:
* Prepare the leeks, celery and garlic.

30 minutes before you want to eat

* Heat the oil and butter in a large casserole pan with a lid over a medium heat. When the butter is foaming, use scissors to cut the bacon straight into the pan in 2-cm pieces. Let the bacon sizzle away gently while you trim and wash the leeks and cut them into 1 cm thick slices. Then wash the celery sticks and cut them into similar size slices.
* When the bacon has been cooking for about 5 minutes, add the leeks and celery to the casserole. After another few minutes, cover the casserole with a lid and let the vegetables soften further while you peel and crush the garlic and drain and rinse the beans.
* Preheat the oven to 200°C/400°F/Gas Mark 6.
* When the leeks and celery are soft, add the garlic and stir for a couple of minutes.
* Next, add the mustard and cider and bring to the boil. Boil vigorously for a minute or so then add the drained and rinsed beans, stock and bay leaf and bring back to the boil. Turn the heat down and leave to simmer gently while you prepare the garlic bread and greens.
* Cut the baguettes in half, then split each half open and spread the cheese all over one side. Drizzle the cheese with oil and season it with lots of pepper, then sandwich the slices together. Wrap them very well in foil and put one of the baguettes in the oven for 15 minutes. Set the other one aside to freeze.
* Now wash, trim and shred the greens. Ten minutes before you want to eat, put the shredded greens into the casserole and cover with a lid. The greens will need stuffing into the pan but will wilt down quickly. Let them steam for 7–8 minutes.
* When the greens have wilted down and the garlic bread is crisp, roughly chop the parsley and add it to the casserole.
* Season the butter beans to taste and put half of them aside to freeze when they are cold.
* Serve the remaining beans in big bowls with the creamy garlic bread on the side.

Lazy day supper – reheating instructions

* Defrost the butter beans and garlic bread thoroughly.
* Preheat the oven to 200°C/400°F/Gas Mark 6. Heat the butter beans very gently in a pan until they are piping hot. Put the garlic bread in the oven for 15 minutes until it is crisp.

Leeks

Like onions and garlic, leeks often provide the basis for flavouring stews and sauces. Larger leeks can be tough, but they're perfect for long, slow casserole cooking. Smaller leeks are good for sauces and as a vegetable in their own right. The layers of a leek often contain mud and grit, so thorough washing is essential. Either cut off the roots, slice and wash, or cut of the roots, slice in half lengthways and rinse under cold running water until all the mud and grit have gone.

Garlic

It is difficult to imagine now, but within recent memory garlic was regarded with suspicion and disgust by many British people. Thankfully times have changed. The garlic most widely sold has been picked fresh then dried in the sun. Green or fresh garlic is also sometimes available through spring and summer – this has a more delicate flavour than dried garlic. If a recipe calls for lots of garlic, soaking the cloves in boiling hot water for a few minutes will help soften the skins and make peeling easier.

October Week 2 – Overview

Ham and Parsley Sauce with Carrots and New Potatoes is British cooking at its most simple and sublime. Gammon is widely available and once cooked is wonderfully versatile. The total cooking time for this Big Meal from Scratch is 3 hours but as there's nothing tricky involved this shouldn't cause much anxiety.

Surplus ham from the big meal is used to make a 30-minute Something for Nothing, Croque Monsieur with Quick Pickled Onions, and the remaining potatoes are turned into a Goats' Cheese and Rosemary Tortilla. The tortilla takes around 40 minutes to make but minimal involvement is required from the cook.

A warming Seasonal Supper of Curried Coconut Pumpkin is just right for chilly October and takes 35 minutes to cook. A variation on a British classic, Cod with Tartare Sauce and Mushy Peas is a satisfying and familiar Larder Feast. Given that it only takes half an hour to make and that it's made almost entirely with ingredients from the larder (or freezer) it's also an extremely convenient recipe to have up your sleeve.

The Two for One recipe, Chilli Con Carne, can be made with mince in 1 hour and with braising steak in 2½ hours. Both versions taste delicious but the braising steak adds a body and texture that takes the chilli to another dimension. A recipe for corn muffins is included and if you're in the mood these are well worth making.

October Week 2	Recipe	Time
Big meal from scratch	Ham and parsley sauce with carrots and new potatoes	3 hours
Something for nothing 1	Goats' cheese and rosemary tortilla with tomato salad	40 mins
Something for nothing 2	Croque monsieur with quick pickled onions	30 mins
Seasonal supper	Curried coconut pumpkin	35 mins
Larder feast	Cod with tartare sauce and mushy peas	30 mins
2 for 1	Chilli con carne with corn muffins	1 hour or 2½ hours

All recipes serve 4 apart from the 2 for 1 recipe which makes 8 portions

SHOPPING LIST (for 4 people)

Meat and fish
1 × 1.4 kg free-range boned gammon/ham joint (smoked if you like a strong flavour)
900 g braising steak or good quality beef mince
4 frozen cod or haddock fillets, approx. 600 g

Dairy
225 g (approx.) butter
450 ml milk
450 ml buttermilk or 300 ml plain yoghurt and 150 ml milk
300 ml (approx.) crème fraîche
10 free-range eggs
100-150 g soft goats' cheese
320 g hard cheese (ideally Gruyère or Comté)

Fruit and vegetables
1.4 kg new potatoes
1.3 kg (approx.) pumpkin (ideally the green- and white-skinned variety)
8 carrots, approx. 800 g
2 red peppers
8 celery sticks
80-100 g rocket
4-8 plum or beef tomatoes
3 large onions, approx. 760 g
6 medium red onions, approx. 720 g
4 spring onions
17 garlic cloves
4 cm piece of fresh root ginger
5 red chillies (small or large depending on taste)
1 fresh lemon grass stick
1 small bunch fresh flatleaf parsley
1 large bunch fresh curly parsley
2 sprigs fresh rosemary
handful of fresh basil leaves
1 bunch fresh coriander
1½ lemons
1-2 limes
800 g (approx.) frozen petit pois peas

Basics
135 ml olive oil
45 ml groundnut or grapeseed oil
8 slices white toasting bread, approx. 1 cm thick
115 g plain flour
1 tsp sugar
2 bay leaves
5 black peppercorns
salt and pepper

Store cupboard
300 g basmati rice
275 g polenta
1 × 330 g can sweetcorn
1 × 400 ml can unsweetened coconut milk
1 × 400 g can chopped tomatoes
1 × 400 g can kidney beans
1 × 400 g can black-eye beans
3 tbsp mayonnaise
1 tbsp Dijon mustard (optional for Croque Monsieur with Quick Pickled Onions)
1 tbsp capers
4-5 cornichons
200 ml red wine vinegar
1 tsp bicarbonate of soda
6 cloves
1 tbsp ground cumin
5 tsp ground coriander
1 tsp medium chilli powder
800 ml dry cider
200 ml red wine

Quick option (Cod with Tartare Sauce and Mushy Peas)
6-8 tbsp ready-made tartare sauce; omit 200 ml crème fraîche, 3 tbsp mayonnaise and 4-5 cornichons from shopping list

Serving suggestions
sweet chilli sauce, mango and lime pickles (Curried Coconut Pumpkin)
potatoes for chips (Cod with Tartare Sauce and Mushy Peas)
yoghurt or crème fraîche (Chilli Con Carne with Corn Muffins)

To download or print out this shopping list, please visit www.thekitchenrevolution.co.uk/October/Week2

**Big meal
from scratch**

Ham and Parsley Sauce with Carrots and New Potatoes

This meal is very simple and very excellent. On a blustery, rainy day the smell of ham simmering slowly and the taste of parsley sauce and buttered new potatoes are heavenly

The terms gammon and ham are interchangeable, so don't be daunted if you find one and not the other as they are essentially the same. The jury is out about whether you need to soak a ham prior to cooking. It really depends on how it has been cured – but that's not much use if you don't have this information. To be safe, it is best to bring the ham joint to the boil in a large pan of water, then discard the water then either bake or boil the joint to cook it properly. The first boiling removes most of the salt, but when serving ham always be careful about the amount of salt you add to any accompanying vegetables or other dishes. For this recipe carrots cook with the meat for the last 15 minutes so they soak up the ham flavour.

The ingredients includes extra ham for Croque Monsieur with Quick Pickled Onions (see page 445) and extra potatoes for Goats' Cheese and Rosemary Tortilla with Tomato Salad (see page 444) later in the week.

Ham
1 × 1.4 kg free-range boned ham joint (smoked if you like a strong flavour); includes 400 g extra for the croque monsieur
1 large onion, approx. 190 g
6 cloves
4 celery sticks
800 ml dry cider
5 black peppercorns
1 bay leaf
8 carrots, approx. 800 g

Parsley sauce
450 ml milk
50 g butter
50 g plain flour
1 large bunch curly parsley
salt and pepper

Potatoes
1.4 kg new potatoes; includes 600 g extra for the goats' cheese and rosemary tortilla butter

GET AHEAD PREPARATION (optional)

* Make the parsley sauce. Cover with buttered greaseproof paper until required, then warm gently on the stove.
* Boil and drain the gammon.
* Prepare the onion, celery and carrots.
* Scrub the potatoes and cover with water until required.

2¼ hours before you want to eat cook the ham

* Put the ham joint in a very large pan with a lid and cover with cold water. Place over a medium heat and bring to the boil. While the ham is coming to the boil prepare the ingredients for flavouring. Peel the onion, cut it into quarters and stick the cloves into it. Wash the celery and chop the sticks in half.
* When the ham comes to the boil drain well. We only bring it to the boil once to remove the salt, but if you are very sensitive to salty food repeat the process.
* Put the ham back in the pan and add the cider, onion, celery, peppercorns and bay leaf. Pour in enough water to completely cover the joint. Slowly bring the ham to the boil and skim away any residue. Turn the heat down very low and simmer gently for 1¼ hours. As a guide, allow 25 minutes per 500 g.

40 minutes before you want to eat cook the vegetables and parsley sauce

* Scrub the potatoes and place them in a large pan of salted water over a medium heat. Bring the water to the boil then simmer for 20 minutes or until the potatoes are cooked.
* Peel the carrots and cut off the root ends, but leave the carrots whole. Add them to the simmering ham. If you don't have room for all of them in the pan, simply cook separately in a little of the stock from the ham pan and some boiling water for 20–30 minutes until tender.
* Next, make the parsley sauce. Put the milk in a small pan and heat it very gently without boiling. Melt the butter in a heavy-based pan over a gentle heat and when it is foaming add the flour. Stir for about 2–3 minutes then whisk in the milk and about 50 ml liquid from the poaching ham. Heat the sauce, whisking constantly as it thickens. When the sauce coats the back of a wooden spoon set it aside while you chop the parsley. Remove any thick stalks from the parsley and either tip the sauce into a food processor and whizz it with the parsley, or chop the parsley very finely and stir it into the sauce. Season as necessary with salt and pepper then pour the sauce into a warmed serving jug to keep warm.

❋ Drain the potatoes and place just under half aside for later in the week. Put the remaining potatoes in a warmed serving dish and dot with butter. Remove the ham and carrots from the pan (keep the cooking liquor for later in the week). Place the carrots in a warmed serving dish, cut the ham into thickish slices and serve with lots of parsley sauce.

Afterwards

Strain the cooking liquor and put the leftover ham, potatoes and liquor in separate containers, cover and refrigerate for use later in the week. Ideally you will have 400 g ham and 12 potatoes (approx. 600 g). The ham stock will be useful to keep in the freezer – to be used as when required.

Something
for nothing 1

Goats' Cheese and Rosemary Tortilla with Tomato Salad

Tortilla is a thick Spanish omelette made with egg and potatoes and cooked until firm. It is delicious served hot or at room temperature. A basic but by no means inferior tortilla is made using just potatoes, sliced onions and eggs, but you can add any number of ingredients to create variety or to use up ones like bacon, chorizo, cheese or peppers. In this recipe we suggest a soft goats' cheese and rosemary.

Traditionally a tortilla is cooked on the stove in a frying pan and turned halfway through (see intructions on page 251). Easier than turning the tortilla is to finish it off in the oven, but because many frying pans have plastic handles the recipe here suggests gently grilling the tortilla to set the top and middle.

Though simple, a good tomato salad is entirely dependent on finding decent tomatoes. Depending on how the weather has been, early October will see the last of the English grown tomatoes. Although supermarkets sell a range of varieties and even ones grown 'for flavour', a flavourful tomato is still a rare thing. When a tomato is ripe the skin and flesh will yield slightly to a gentle squeeze.

Goats' cheese and rosemary
tortilla
1 large onion, approx. 190 g
3 tbsp olive oil
8 free-range eggs
100-150 g soft goats' cheese
12-16 cooked potatoes (approx.
  600 g) left over from the Big
  Meal from Scratch or 600 g
  new potatoes, cooked
2 sprigs fresh rosemary
salt and pepper

Tomato salad
4-8 plum or beef tomatoes
handful of fresh basil leaves
2 tbsp olive oil

GET AHEAD PREPARATION (optional)

* Peel and slice the onion.
* Cut up the cheese and potatoes
  and cover the potatoes with
  water until required.
* Slice the tomatoes.
* Beat the eggs.
* Make the salad dressing.

*40 minutes before
you want to eat*

* Peel and thinly slice the onion then heat 2 tablespoons of the oil in a large heavy-based frying pan over a medium heat. Add the onion and cook gently for 5–7 minutes until it has started to soften.
* Beat the eggs in a large bowl and season. Cut the cheese into 1-cm chunks, and the potatoes into halves or quarters so that they are no more than 3 cm long at any point. Fold the potatoes and cheese into the eggs.
* Remove the rosemary leaves from their stalks, chop them and add to the onion for the last minute of cooking.
* Once the onion is soft, tip it into the beaten eggs, potatoes and cheese, season and mix well.
* Wipe the frying pan out with kitchen paper and put it over a gentle heat. Add the remaining oil, swirl it around the pan while it heats, then pour in the egg mixture. Using a wooden spoon, pat down any pieces of potato or cheese that poke up.
* Cook gently for 15–20 minutes, until the eggs in the middle of the pan appear to be setting. While the tortilla is cooking run a knife around the edge to gently loosen it.
* Slice the tomatoes and place them in a shallow dish. Tear up the basil leaves and sprinkle them over the tomatoes along with the oil and seasoning. Leave to marinate while the tortilla finishes cooking.
* Preheat the grill to medium. Brown the top of the tortilla by placing the entire pan under the grill for a couple of minutes. If the handle of the frying pan is wood or plastic keep it away from direct heat.
* Remove the tortilla from the grill, turn it onto a plate or board, cut into slices and serve with the tomato salad.

Something for nothing 2

Croque Monsieur with Quick Pickled Onions

What better way to use up leftover ham than to make the classic French brasserie sandwich of ham and cheese? We have added quick pickled onions to the sandwich and suggest you eat it with a salad of hot peppery rocket.

The recipe for quick pickled onions is based on one that was given to Rosie by a chef she knows called Scott. We have suggested you make a jar of them because they are extremely moreish.

Croque monsieur
30 g butter
8 slices white bread, approx.
    1 cm thick
1 tbsp Dijon mustard (optional)
320 g hard cheese (ideally
    Gruyère or comté)
400 g cooked sliced ham leftover
    from the Big Meal from Scratch
    or 400g thickly sliced baked
    ham
80–100 g rocket
1 tbsp olive oil
juice of ½ lemon

Quick pickled onions
½ tsp salt
1 tsp sugar
200 ml red wine vinegar
100 ml hot water
1 bay leaf
2 medium red onions, approx.
    240 g
black pepper

GET AHEAD PREPARATION (optional)

The quick pickled onions can be made a week or more in advance and the sandwiches can be made up to the point where they are cooked a day ahead. If you only have a little time:
* Melt the butter.
* Slice or grate the cheese.

30 minutes before you want to eat

* Start by making the quick pickled onions. Put the salt, sugar, vinegar, hot water, bay leaf and a good grinding of pepper in a small pan and bring them to a rapid boil. Bubble vigorously for 3–4 minutes until the liquid becomes syrupy.
* Meanwhile, peel the onions, slice them as finely as you can and put them into a bowl.
* When the pickling liquid has thickened a bit, pour it over the onions and leave them to soften for 5 minutes or so.
* Now make the sandwiches. Melt the butter and brush on one side of each slice of bread.
* Preheat the oven to 200°C/400°F/Gas Mark 6.
* Slice or grate the cheese and start assembling the sandwiches. Lay four slices of the bread buttered-side down and spread with a little mustard (if using), divide the ham between them. Scatter with the cheese and a spoonful of the pickled onions. Press the other slices of bread, butter-side up, on top.
* Heat a frying pan, (preferably non-stick) and when it is hot brown each sandwich on both sides. Once the sandwiches are browned, put them on a baking sheet and place them in the oven for 10 minutes while you dress the rocket with the oil and lemon juice.
* When the sandwiches are hot through, remove them from the oven and cut each one into four.
* Pile the salad on to four plates and serve a sandwich on top with a few more pickled onions.
* Put any left over pickled onions into a clean jar and keep in the fridge for use with sandwiches, pork pies, cold meats, etc.

Curried Coconut Pumpkin

Most grocers and supermarkets sell pumpkin cut into largish chunks so you can buy a piece that is the size to suit your needs. There are many different varieties and the ubiquitous orange type does not necessarily have the best flavour. If you can find pumpkin with green and white skin use this. You could also replace the pumpkin with butternut squash. This recipe is inspired by the chef Peter Gordon.

1.3 kg (approx.) pumpkin (ideally the green-and white-skinned variety)
1 large onion, approx. 190 g
3 tbsp groundnut or grapeseed oil
3 garlic cloves
4 cm piece of fresh root ginger
2 red chillies
1 fresh lemon grass stick
2 tsp ground coriander
1 x 400 ml can unsweetened coconut milk
1-2 limes
300 g basmati rice
handful of fresh coriander
salt and pepper

To serve
sweet chilli sauce
mango and lime pickles

GET AHEAD PREPARATION (optional)

The curry can be cooked 2 days advance and warmed through. If you only have a little time:
* Peel and deseed the pumpkin.
* Prepare the onion, garlic and ginger.
* Deseed and chop the chillies.
* Chop the fresh coriander.

35 minutes before you want to eat

* The biggest task for this meal is dealing with the pumpkin. The skin needs removing, and although some peelers are up to the job a sharp knife is probably better for getting rid of the tough skin. You may find it easier to cut it into manageable pieces before trying to peel it. Remove the seeds from the middle and cut the pumpkin into 3-4-cm chunks.
* Next, peel and finely slice the onion. Heat the oil in a pan large enough to hold all ingredients over a medium heat, add the onion and cook for 7–10 minutes so that it softens and starts to brown.
* While the onion is cooking, peel and slice the garlic, peel and finely grate the ginger and deseed and finely chop the chillies. Smash the lemon grass stick with a rolling pin or the base of a pan so that it splits and looks bashed and bruised (this unleashes the flavours).
* When the onion is softened and browned, add the garlic, ginger, chillies, ground coriander and lemon grass and cook, stirring constantly, for 1 minute.
* Add the pumpkin, coconut milk, the juice of one of the limes and ½ teaspoon salt. If the pumpkin is not covered with liquid add some water. Bear in mind that pumpkin contains a lot of moisutre which it will release whilst cooking, so be sparing with the water you add. Bring slowly to the boil and simmer uncovered for 20 minutes, stirring once or twice.
* Meanwhile, wash the rice under running water until the water runs clear then cook according to the instructions on the packet.
* When the pumpkin has been cooking for 20 minutes and is just tender, roughly chop the coriander and add half to the curry. Taste for seasoning and add more lime juice or salt if necessary.
* Divide the rice between four bowls and spoon a generous helping of the pumpkin curry on top. Garnish with the remaining coriander and serve with sweet chilli sauce and mango and lime pickles.

Larder feast

Cod with Tartare Sauce and Mushy Peas

Fish served with mushy peas is an old favourite – especially when it is served with tartare sauce and chips. As this recipe is a Larder Feast you can have the ingredients in the cupboard or freezer just waiting for when you have the urge. Serve with chips, of course. This recipe for mushy peas is made with roasted garlic – but you could leave this out or replace with a small handful of chopped fresh mint.

Cod with tartare sauce
4 frozen cod or haddock fillets
    (approx. 600 g)
50 g butter
1 lemon
salt and pepper

For the tartare sauce
1 tbsp capers
4-5 cornichons
3 tbsp mayonnaise
2 tbsp crème fraîche
small handful of fresh flatleaf
    parsley
1 lemon
black pepper

Mushy peas
1 head garlic, approx. 10 cloves
1 tbsp olive oil
800 g frozen petit pois peas
25 g butter
4 tbsp crème fraîche

To serve
chips, tartare sauce, lemon

GET AHEAD PREPARATION (optional)

The mushy peas and tartare sauce can be made a day in advance. If you only have a little time:
* Roast the garlic.
* Prepare the capers and cornichons.
* Chop the parsley.
* Cut the lemon.

30 minutes before you want to eat

* Preheat the oven to 190°C/375°F/Gas Mark 5.
* Separate the garlic cloves but don't peel them. Place them in the middle of a 20 cm square of foil. Drizzle with the oil then bring the edges of the foil together to form an airtight parcel. Roast for 20 minutes.
* Put the peas in a pan of salted water and bring them to the boil for 3–4 minutes. Once cooked, turn off the heat and leave the peas sitting in hot water.
* Now make the tartare sauce. Rinse the capers under running water, drain well then chop them and tip them into a mixing bowl. Drain and slice the cornichons. Add these to the capers along with the mayonnaise and crème fraîche. Chop the parsley and add it to the sauce. Cut the lemon into five wedges. Squeeze one wedge over the sauce. Season with pepper and mix well.
* Place the frozen fillets in one layer in a large dish. Cover them with boiling water and leave for 10 minutes.
* Drain the cooked peas, retaining about 2 tablespoons of the cooking water, and tip the peas and water into a food processor. Add a generous nut of butter, the remaining crème fraîche and season. Blend until smooth, adding more pea water if necessary – you want the peas to slide very slowly from a vertical spoon. If you don;t have a processor you can mash the peas but the texture will be coarser.
* Remove the garlic from the oven and open the foil parcel. Leave until the cloves are cool enough to handle, then squeeze the garlic from its skin into the mushy peas.
* Pulse a couple of times in the food processor to incorporate the garlic. Scrape the peas back into the pan they were cooked in, cover, and place on a gentle heat to warm through.
* Carefully remove the fish fillets from the water. Place them on a plate and pat them dry with kitchen paper. Melt the butter in a frying pan over a medium-high heat. Season the uppermost sides of the fillets. When the butter is foaming add the fillets, seasoned-side down. Cook for 3 minutes, then season the uppermost sides and flip the fillets over. Cook for 3 minutes. When the fillets are cooked and the edges are starting to caramelise remove them from the heat.
* To serve, place a large spoonful of mushy peas in the middle of each plate. Put the fish on top. Serve with tartare sauce, lemon wedges and chips.

Two for one

Chilli Con Carne with Corn Muffins

When cooked slowly with ground cumin, coriander and pepper, chilli con carne has a deep, mellow and rich flavour. For a real treat it can be made with braising steak, but if you are making an everyday chilli you can use good quality mince and it will cook in just 30 minutes.

The chillies you choose to use will influence the flavour and heat level significantly. Scotch bonnet and bird's eye chillies are fiercely hot and probably should be avoided for this recipe. Mexican dried chillies include ancho, pasilla and chipotle, the last of which has a smoky, mellow taste. Some supermarkets sell these preserved in oil in jars, or dried, in their Mexican sections. The ones sold in jars are delicious, particularly when added to guacamole or chicken fajitas or made into a dip with soured cream. You could also use fresh red or green chillies, the sort most widely available in supermarkets, but make sure to remove the seeds as they are ferociously hot. Adding fresh coriander at the end is important as it helps to unite all the flavours and brings the dish alive.

The corn muffins we've suggested as an accompaniment to the chilli are simple to make and will freeze well, but they are in no way essential. If you prefer, just serve the chilli with rice or flour tortillas and soured cream. The muffins are very simple, however, so if you have the time don't be daunted. If you don't have muffin tins, use a loaf tin. The recipe was given to Rosie by her sister Annabel – the muffins are very popular with her daughters.

The quantities here will serve eight, with the intention that half the chilli is frozen. That said, chilli is an excellent meal for a crowd so it may not get as far as the freezer!

Chilli con carne
900 g braising steak or good
    quality beef mince
2 tbsp olive oil
4 medium red onions, approx.
    480 g
4 garlic cloves
4 celery sticks
2 red peppers
3 red chillies
1 tbsp ground cumin
1 tbsp ground coriander
1 tsp medium chilli powder
200 ml red wine
1 x 400 g can chopped tomatoes
1 x 400 g can kidney beans
1 x 400 g can black-eye beans
small handful of fresh coriander
salt and pepper

Corn muffins
50 g butter, plus extra for
    greasing
4 spring onions
2 free-range eggs
450 ml buttermilk or 300 ml
    natural yoghurt mixed with
    150 ml milk
65 g plain flour
1 tsp bicarbonate of soda
1 tsp salt
1 x 330 g can sweetcorn
275 g polenta

To serve
yoghurt, crème fraîche or
    leftover buttermilk

GET AHEAD PREPARATION (optional)

The whole dish can be made 2–3 days in advance and reheated. The muffins can be made a day or so in advance. To reheat, wrap in foil and place in a cool oven (140°C/275°F/Gas Mark 1). If you only have a little time:
* Prepare the onions, garlic, celery and red peppers.

1 hour before you want to eat, if using mince – 2½ hours if using braising steak

* First brown the meat. If using braising steak, cut it into 2–3-cm cubes. Heat a generous glug of oil in a large frying pan, season the meat and brown it all over. All the mince should fit in the pan but if you are using chunks of steak it may be necessary to brown them in batches. Once browned, set the meat aside.
* In the meantime, peel and finely slice the onions, and as soon as they are sliced heat a generous splash of oil in a casserole big enough to take all the ingredients. Add the onion stir them about, then cover the pan and leave them to soften for 10 minutes over a medium-low heat. Meanwhile, peel and crush the garlic, wash and finely slice the celery, and deseed and finely chop the red peppers and chillies.
* When the onions have softened, add the peppers, celery and chillies, and cook over a medium to high heat, stirring regularly, for a further 5 minutes. Finally, stir in the garlic and the ground cumin, ground coriander and chilli powder.
* A minute after adding the garlic and spices, tip the meat into the casserole. Add the wine to the casserole and, shortly afterwards, the tomatoes.

* Bring to the boil, add all the beans, season, cover and turn the heat right down. If you are using mince simmer it for 30–45 minutes. If you are using steak simmer it very gently for 1½–2 hours. From time to time check that there is sufficient liquid. If the chilli seems to have a lot of liquid simmer it with the lid off.
* If you want to make corn muffins, make these now – they will take about 40 minutes.
* To serve, chop the fresh coriander and add it to the chilli. Serve half the chilli with yoghurt, crème fraîche, or buttermilk with warm muffins or rice or tortillas.
* Freeze the remaining chilli and corn muffins or loaf separately.

To make the corn muffins

* Preheat the oven to 200°C/400°F/Gas Mark 6.
* Melt the butter over a gentle heat.
* Grease patty tins, muffin tins or a 500 g loaf tin with butter, or alternatively use paper cupcake cases. Trim and finely slice the spring onions.
* Whisk the eggs until frothy, then add the buttermilk and melted butter. Sift in the flour, bicarbonate of soda and salt. Stir in the sweetcorn and onions and fold in the polenta.
* Spoon dollops of the mixture into the tins or paper cases, so that they are three-quarters full or into the loaf tin.
* Bake for 25–30 minutes until the muffins are firm and an inserted skewer comes out clean. It may take 5 minutes longer if you used a loaf tin.
* Allow the muffins or loaf to cool for a minute before turning them out.

Lazy day supper – reheating instructions

* Defrost the chilli con carne completely before reheating. Place in a casserole with a couple of tablespoons of water and bring gently to simmering point over a medium heat. Simmer for 15 minutes to ensure the meat is warmed through then serve as above.
* The corn muffins or loaf can be reheated from frozen. Preheat the oven to 160°C/325°F/Gas Mark 3. Wrap the muffins/loaf in foil and heat in the oven for 20–30 minutes, until piping hot. Test with a skewer.

October Week 3 – Overview

This week's Big Meal from Scratch – Pot Roast Venison (or Beef) with Root Vegetable Mash and Curly Kale – is proper food for winter. Venison, or the cheaper but nevertheless very good, brisket of beef, both respond well to pot roasting as it prevents the meat drying out. Half an hour is spent preparing the vegetables and meat and then everything bar the kale is left to cook slowly for 2 hours.

In contrast to the big meal, the first Something for Nothing of Crispy Venison (or Beef) with Stir-fried Vegetables and Noodles is Asian in inspiration and flavour. With leftover venison or beef this will take about 30 minutes. Leftover mash and greens are transformed into colcannon cakes to serve with sausages. The cakes are rather like bubble and squeak, only shaped into cakes. The recipe includes roast onion gravy and takes 40 minutes, but without the gravy the meal will take as long as it takes to cook sausages.

Mushrooms are at their best in October so to make the most of these the week's Seasonal Supper is a spinach and mushroom curry that's spicy and filling. The recipe requires making a masala paste and while this involves nothing complicated it will take 50 minutes altogether – don't cook this if time is of the essence.

The Larder Feast, an intensely flavoured Fish and Chorizo Cassoulet, is another recipe that is useful to have up your sleeve in the event of unexpected guests and an empty fridge. Although cod, pollack or haddock can be used, the recipe specifies the much overlooked coley. Its flavour is noticeably stronger than more commonly eaten white fish but this works well in a recipe with so many punchy ingredients. Coley is sold frozen by most supermarkets and fishmongers, is relatively inexpensive and, as an added bonus, comes from sustainable stocks.

The Two for One recipe this week is for a Lemon Butternut Lasagne. This has the comfort-food quality of classic lasagne without being quite so heavy. The recipe takes 1 hour in total and makes enough for two generous lasagnes.

October Week 3	Recipe	Time
Big meal from scratch	Pot roast venison (or beef) with root vegetable mash,and curly kale	2½ hours
Something for nothing 1	Crispy venison (or beef) with stir-fried vegetables and noodles	25 mins
Something for nothing 2	Sausages with root vegetable colcannon cakes and onion gravy	40 mins
Seasonal supper	Midweek mushroom curry	50 mins
Larder feast	Fish and chorizo cassoulet	40 mins
2 for 1	Lemon butternut lasagne	1 hour

All recipes serve 4 apart from the 2 for 1 recipe which makes 8 portions

Fish and meat
1 × 1.8 kg haunch of venison or 1 × 2 kg
  brisket of beef
8 good quality free-range sausages
150 g piece pancetta or free-range rindless
  smoked streaky bacon
2 small cooking chorizo sausages, approx.
  250 g
300-400 g frozen coley, pollack, haddock or
  cod fillets

Dairy
130 g butter
60 ml Greek yoghurt
3 tbsp double cream
2 free-range eggs
200 g mozzarella
170 g Parmesan
500 g ricotta
250 g mascarpone or crème fraîche
4 tbsp crème fraîche
a little milk

Fruit and vegetables
2 large floury potatoes, approx. 300 g
  (ideally Maris Piper or baking potatoes)
2 medium butternut squash, approx. 1.2 kg
4 parsnips, approx. 500 g
2 large outer sticks celery
1 small celeriac, approx. 500 g
8 leeks, approx. 1.2 kg
5 medium carrots, approx. 400 g
1 small swede, approx. 400 g
600 g curly kale or other greens
200 g Chinese cabbage or other cabbage
150-200 g baby leaf spinach
600 g chestnut mushrooms
6 medium onions, approx. 720 g
2 large or banana shallots, approx. 60 g
6 spring onions
8 garlic cloves
5-6-cm piece of fresh root ginger
2 mild red chillies (1 optional)
7 sprigs fresh thyme (approx.)
large bunch fresh coriander
small bunch fresh parsley
3 sprigs fresh sage
1 lemon

Basics
30 ml olive oil
270 ml groundnut or grapeseed oil
6 tbsp plain flour
2 tbsp cornflour
3 tbsp tomato purée
1 tbsp wholegrain mustard
2 bay leaves

600 ml beef or strong chicken stock (fresh
  or made from a stock cube or bouillon
  powder)
200-300 ml fish, chicken or vegetable
  stock (fresh or made from a stock cube or
  bouillon powder)
1 tsp vegetable bouillon powder
salt and pepper

Store cupboard
200 g basmati rice
10 sheets lasagne (fresh or no-need-to-
  pre-cook)
250 g dried rice or egg noodles
3 × 400 g cans haricot beans
1 × 400 g can chopped tomatoes
1 tbsp redcurrant jelly
1 tsp sesame seeds
2 tbsp ground almonds
75 g pine nuts (you can buy them toasted)
3 tbsp cashew nuts
1 tbsp toasted sesame oil
1 tbsp balsamic vinegar
1 tbsp dark soy sauce
1 tsp paprika
1 tsp five-spice powder
½ tsp ground turmeric
½ tsp cumin seeds
1 tsp garam masala
3 pinches of nutmeg (ground or freshly
  grated)
425 ml red wine
3 tbsp dry sherry or white wine

Serving suggestions
mango chutney and lime pickle (Midweek
  Mushroom Curry)
crusty bread (Fish and Chorizo Cassoulet)
spinach (Lemon Butternut Lasagne)

To download or print out this shopping list,
please visit www.thekitchenrevolution.co.uk/
October/Week3

Pot Roast Venison (or Beef) with Root Vegetable Mash and Curly Kale

A pot roast is a simple way of cooking meat, particularly leaner cuts which respond well to long, slow cooking. The end result is tender meat and richly flavoured vegetables.

Venison used to be the preserve of butchers and game dealers but it is now widely available in supermarkets. Leaner than beef, pork or lamb, it has dark red flesh which has a rich and slightly gamy flavour. Venison does well when it is marinated or cooked slowly to ensure succulence. If you feel slightly daunted by the prospect of venison, or you are unable to find any, you could replace it with brisket of beef. Brisket is economical and works especially well as a pot roast. If you can't find curly kale use other greens of choice.

Leftover venison or beef is used later in the week in Crispy Venison (or Beef) with Stir-fried Vegetables and Noodles (see page 454) and there is extra vegetable mash and gravy for Sausages with Root Vegetable Colcannon Cakes with Onion Gravy (see page 455).

Pot roast venison (or beef)
1.8 kg haunch of venison or 2 kg
  brisket of beef; includes 500 g
  extra for the crispy vension (or
  beef)
40 g butter
1 tbsp groundnut or grapeseed oil
250 ml red wine
500 ml beef or strong chicken
  stock, plus extra for the
  vegetables, if necessary
  (includes 200 ml extra for
  onion gravy)
1 tbsp redcurrant jelly

Root vegetable mash (makes
double quantities for the
colcannon cakes)
1 medium onion, approx. 120 g
4 carrots, approx. 350 g

4 parsnips, approx. 350 g
2 large outer celery sticks
2 large potatoes, approx. 300 g,
  such as Maris Piper or baking
  potatoes
1 small swede, approx. 400 g
1 small celeriac, approx. 500 g
1 bay leaf
5 sprigs fresh thyme
30 g butter
4 tbsp crème fraîche
2 pinches of nutmeg (ground or
  freshly grated)
salt and pepper

Curly kale
600 g curly kale or other greens;
  includes 200 g extra for the
  colcannon cakes
20 g butter

GET AHEAD PREPARATION (optional)

If there are a few spare moments
any of the following would be
helpful:
* Remove any tough membranes
  from the venison or beef.
* Prepare the onion, carrots,
  parsnips and celery.
* Prepare the potatoes and cover
  with water until required.
* Prepare the kale.

* Preheat the oven to 170°C/325°F/Gas Mark 3.
* Start by preparing the vegetables for the root vegetable mash. Peel the onion, cut it in half and slice it finely. Peel the carrots and parsnips and slice them into 3–4-cm rounds. Wash and slice the celery. Peel the potatoes, swede and celeriac and chop them into even-sized pieces that correspond to the size of the carrots.
* Trim any tough membranes and sinews from the venison or beef, and season the meat thoroughly all over. Heat half the butter and oil in a very large casserole or roasting tin and brown the meat well on all sides. Lift the meat out and place it in a large shallow dish. Add half the wine to the casserole. Allow the wine to bubble furiously while stirring, then pour the wine over the meat.
* Wipe the casserole dry with kitchen paper, add the remaining butter and oil and when the fat is hot fry the vegetables for 5–10 minutes until they are starting to brown. Add the remaining wine and scrape the bottom of the casserole to lift any delicious flavours stuck to the bottom. After a minute or so remove the casserole from the heat and add the bay leaf, thyme leaves and a good dose of salt and pepper.
* Lay the venison on top of the vegetables and add all the stock. Bring to simmering point, cover with foil and a tight-fitting lid – if not, two layers of foil. Put in the oven for up to 2 hours, (we advise 30 minutes per 500 g). If the vegetables and meat don't fit in the casserole cook as many vegetables as necessary in a pan with a lid. Add just enough stock to come halfway up the vegetables and simmer with the lid on until very soft.

* While the meat is cooking, wash the kale, remove any hard stalks and cut it into 2–3-cm thick ribbons. Place in a steamer or a pan with a lid and add about 2 cm water. Leave until the meat has been taken out of the oven.

1 hour before you want to eat

* After the meat has been cooking for a good hour, check there's sufficient liquid in the casserole.

20 minutes before you want to eat cook the greens, and make the gravy and mash

* When the meat has been cooking for about 2 hours, remove it from the casserole and leave it somewhere warm, loosely covered with foil, while you finish the vegetables.
* Put the pan of kale over a medium heat and steam for 7–10 minutes or until soft.
* Meanwhile make the gravy. Strain the liquor from the vegetables into a pan; if you don't seem to have much liquid add more stock – you will need about 400 ml. Add the redcurrant jelly, place on a gentle heat, stir and bring to the boil then leave to simmer while you finish the vegetables.
* Add the butter and crème fraîche to the vegetables and season with the nutmeg and salt and pepper. For a completely smooth and puréed mash use a hand blender but otherwise use a potato masher to mash the vegetables. Taste for seasoning then tip them into a serving dish and keep them warm while you finish the gravy and greens.
* When the greens are tender, drain them well, tip them into a serving dish, add the butter and season with salt and pepper.
* Taste the gravy, season as necessary then pour it into a jug.
* To serve, slice the venison or beef and serve with the root vegetable mash, curly kale and gravy.

Afterwards

Slice the venison or beef into thin strips. Put the meat, vegetable mash, curly kale and gravy in separate containers, cover and refrigerate for use later in the week. Ideally you will have 500 g venison or beef, 500 g mash, 200 g curly kale and 200 ml gravy.

Something
for nothing 1

Crispy Venison (or Beef) with Stir-fried Vegetables and Noodles

Like many stir-fried Asian dishes, this has what looks like rather a daunting number of ingredients. Once assembled, however, everything is cooked hot and fast so you have a meal completed in a jiffy. By coating the venison or beef with flour, then egg, then flour again you ensure a crisp outer bite. The Chinese cabbage we've specified is white-leafed and stays crunchy when cooked, but if you can't find it use another type of cabbage.

Crispy venison or beef
1 free-range egg
1 tbsp toasted sesame oil
3 tbsp plain flour
2 tbsp cornflour
1 tsp five-spice powder
1 tsp sesame seeds
500 g (approx.) strips of cooked venison or beef left over from the Big Meal from Scratch or 500 g raw sirloin or rump steak, cut into strips
8 tbsp (approx.) groundnut or grapeseed oil
salt

Stir-fried vegetables and noodles
250 g rice or egg noodles
2 garlic cloves
4-cm piece of fresh root ginger
1 red chilli (optional)
6 spring onions
1 medium carrot, approx. 100 g
200 g Chinese cabbage
3 tbsp groundnut or grapeseed oil
1 tbsp soy sauce
3 tbsp dry sherry or white wine
small handful of fresh coriander

GET AHEAD PREPARATION (optional)

* Mix the egg and sesame oil and make the flour coating.
* Prepare the garlic, ginger, spring onions, carrot and Chinese cabbage.
* Deseed and chop the chilli, if using.
* Cook the noodles.

25 minutes before you want to eat

* Whisk the egg with the sesame oil and 1 tablespoon water and season with salt.
* Mix the flour, cornflour, five-spice powder and sesame seeds together in a plastic bag. Add the meat and toss it in the bag until it is well coated with the mixture.
* Take out the coated meat, shake off excess flour and drop it into the egg mixture. Put the meat back in the bag and shake it well to ensure it is well coated. Take the meat out of the bag, shaking off excess coating as you do, and put it on a tray in one layer.
* Cook the noodles according to the packet instructions, drain and cool under running water. Peel and finely grate the garlic and ginger. Deseed and finely chop the chilli, if using. Trim and finely slice the spring onions. Peel the carrot and cut it in half lengthways, then slice each half as thinly as you can. Wash and shred the Chinese cabbage.
* Preheat the oven to 140°C/275°F/Gas Mark 1 and put some bowls in to warm.
* Heat a wok or frying pan over a high heat. Add 2 tablespoons of the oil, when it is smoking add the meat. Stir fry the meat for 3–4 minutes, it should be crisp. If you are using raw meat, stir fry it for a couple more minutes. Put some kitchen paper on a plate and, using a slotted spoon, lift the meat out and put it on the plate. Put it in the warm oven.
* Heat the remaining oil in the wok or frying pan and add the ginger. Stir the ginger for 30 seconds, then add the garlic, carrot, chilli, spring onions and cabbage and toss these for 3–5 minutes, over a high heat, stirring all the time.
* Add the soy sauce, sherry or wine and 100 ml water. Chop the coriander. Let the liquid come to the boil, add the noodles and coriander and stir-fry for a couple of minutes.
* Pile the vegetables and noodles into the bowls and serve the meat on top.

Something
for nothing 2

Sausages with Root Vegetable Colcannon Cakes and Onion Gravy

Sausages always go well with potatoes but here we've borrowed the Irish classic colcannon and added root vegetables to make a mash with a difference. Colcannon is traditionally a mixture of mashed potatoes with cooked shredded cabbage but using root vegetable mash adds a sweetness that goes very well with sausages. Gravy is an obvious partner for sausages and mash, and the recipe below is quick to knock up.

With sausages you really get what you pay for. Better quality sausages are better value – they are much more filling and are packed with flavour.

If you have no root vegetable mash left over peel 200 g parsnips and 300 g potatoes, cook until soft, then drain and mash well.

Sausages
8 good quality free-range
  sausages
groundnut or grapeseed oil

Root vegetable colcannon cakes
1 free-range egg
500 g root vegetable mash from
  the Big Meal from Scratch or
  see above
200 g curly kale from the Big
  Meal from Scratch or 200 g
  curley kale, cooked
plain flour for dusting
20 g (approx.) butter
1 tbsp groundnut or grapeseed oil

Onion gravy
2 medium onions, approx. 240 g
1 tbsp groundnut or grapeseed oil
1 tbsp balsamic vinegar
1 bay leaf
200 ml gravy left over from the
  Big Meal from Scratch or 200
  ml beef or strong chicken stock
100ml beef or strong chicken
  stock (fresh or made from a
  stock cube or bouillon powder)
1 tbsp wholegrain mustard
salt and pepper

GET AHEAD PREPARATION (optional)
The gravy can be made up to 2
days ahead of time and reheated
as required. The colcannon can
be mixed, shaped and left to rest
on a well-floured board. If you
only have a little time:
* Prepare the onions and toss in
  oil, vinegar and the broken-up
  bay leaf.
* Chop the greens.

40 minutes before
you want to eat

* Preheat the oven to 200°C/400°F/Gas Mark 6.
* Peel and slice the onions, then throw them into a roasting tin with a generous glug of oil and the vinegar. Break up the bay leaf and mix this with the onions, then tightly cover the tin with foil. Put the onions in the oven for 15–20 minutes.
* Place the sausages in a lightly oiled roasting tin and put them in the oven for 25 minutes.
* Beat the egg in a mixing bowl and add the mash. Squeeze any excess liquid from the curly kale or greens and chop. Add the kale or greens to the mash and mix well.
* Lightly flour a board. Divide the mixture into four pieces, roll them into balls and flatten them into cakes on the board. Rest for 5–10 minutes.
* To finish the gravy, check that the onions are softly roasted. If they require longer, remove the foil and roast them for a further 5 minutes. Put the gravy and stock in a pan with the mustard and bring to the boil over a medium heat. When the gravy is boiling, tip in the onions (keep the roasting tin for the colcannon cakes) and stir well. Let the gravy simmer gently.
* Heat the oil and butter in your largest frying pan. Roll each cake thoroughly in the flour on the board. Pat off any excess flour then fry the cakes, two at a time. Brown the cakes on both sides.
* Put the cakes into the onion roasting tin and put in the oven for 5–10 minutes.
* When the sausages are done, remove them and the cakes from the oven. Season the gravy to taste then place a couple of sausages and a colcannon cake on each plate. Serve with the gravy.

Seasonal supper

Midweek Mushroom Curry

The richness of mushrooms in a creamy curry sauce gives a luxurious feel to this deceptively uncomplicated supper. You start this recipe by making a masala paste, which forms the basis for the curry's texture and flavour. The paste is cooked until it loses its raw flavour and then the mushrooms are added. Mushrooms are plentiful and inexpensive in October so it's worth using them for recipes that demand large quantities. You can use ordinary white mushrooms here but the brown chestnut ones are best if you can get them.

2 large or banana shallots, approx. 60 g
1 mild red chilli
3 tbsp groundnut or grapeseed oil
200 g basmati rice
600 g chestnut mushrooms
150 g–200 g baby leaf spinach
3 tbsp double cream
1 bunch fresh coriander
salt

For the masala paste
2 medium onions, approx. 240 g
4 garlic cloves
1–2-cm piece of fresh root ginger
2 tbsp ground almonds
3 tbsp cashew nuts
½ tsp ground turmeric
1 tsp garam masala
4 tbsp Greek yoghurt
½ tsp cumin seeds

To serve
mango chutney and lime pickle

GET AHEAD PREPARATION (optional)

The curry can be made 1–2 days ahead of time and reheated. If there are only a few spare moments:
* Prepare the onions and shallots.
* Deseed and chop the chilli.
* Rinse the rice.
* Wash and drain the spinach.
* Chop the coriander.

50 minutes before you want to eat

* Start by peeling the shallots and chopping them finely. Halve the chilli, then deseed and chop half or all of it, depending on how much heat you like.
* Heat 2 tablespoons of the oil in a large, heavy-based pan over a medium heat. Add the shallots and chilli and cook for 5 minutes.
* Meanwhile, make the masala paste. Peel and roughly chop the onions and place them in a food processor. Peel the garlic and ginger and add these to the onions, along with the ground almonds and cashew nuts, turmeric, garam masala, yoghurt and cumin seeds. Blend to a thick paste.
* Once the shallots are soft, reduce the heat and add the masala paste. Stir slowly for about 5 minutes.
* Turn the heat to low, cover the pan with a lid and cook, stirring every now and then, until the oil begins to separate out from the paste – around 5 minutes.
* Cook the rice according to the packet instructions.
* Once the oil has separated from the masala paste, add about 300 ml water and ½ teaspoon salt to the paste and shallots and simmer gently for 15 minutes.
* Cut the mushrooms into quarters and wash and drain the spinach. Heat the remaining oil in a frying pan over a high heat, then add the mushrooms and brown them rapidly – this will take about 5 minutes.
* Add the mushrooms, spinach and cream to the masala and cook for 5 minutes.
* Check that the rice is cooked and chop the coriander. Stir the coriander into the mushrooms and spinach and taste for seasoning.
* Serve the curry on top of the rice, accompanied by mango chutney and lime pickle.

Larder feast

Fish and Chorizo Cassoulet

In its commonest form cassoulet is made from cuts of meat cooked with haricot beans and some kind of pork and sausage. Though the traditional cassoulet is a celebration of meat and beans, there are some old recipes for cassoulet made with beans and salt cod. In this version, chorizo, pancetta and haricot beans combine with white fish to form an intensely rich casserole that is wonderfully warming. Served with a hunk of crusty bread and a glass of red wine this is difficult to beat.

Coley is a firm-fleshed white fish that is easy to cook and, because it's underrated, inexpensive. It has a stronger flavour than cod or haddock, but this means it can stand up well to the robust flavours in this recipe. It's widely available in the frozen food sections of supermarkets. Much frozen fish is frozen at sea the moment it's caught so is likely to be some of the freshest available.

1 medium onion, approx. 120 g
2 tbsp olive oil
150 g pancetta or free-range smoked streaky bacon
2 cooking chorizo sausages, approx. 250 g
2 garlic cloves
1 tsp paprika
175 ml red wine
3 × 400 g cans haricot beans
1 × 400 g can chopped tomatoes
3 tbsp tomato purée
200–300 ml fish, chicken or vegetable stock (fresh or made from a stock cube or bouillon powder)
handful of fresh flatleaf parsley
300–400 g frozen coley, pollack, haddock or cod fillet
salt and pepper

To serve
crusty bread

GET AHEAD PREPARATION (optional)

The recipe can be made a day in advance up to the point of defrosting the fish. The bean and chorizo mixture should be kept in the fridge and warmed through gently when required. If you only have a little time:
* Prepare the onion and garlic.
* Dice the pancetta or bacon.
* Cut up the chorizo.
* Chop the parsley.

At least 40 minutes before you want to eat

* Peel and slice the onion. Heat the oil in a large heavy-based pan over a medium heat. Add the onion and fry it for about 7 minutes.
* While the onion is cooking, slice the pancetta or bacon into 1–2-cm dice, cut the chorizo into 1-cm thick slices, and peel and chop the garlic. Add these, along with the paprika, to the softened onion and fry for about 3 minutes over a high heat.
* Add the wine and reduce it by about half.
* Drain and rinse the beans and when the wine is reduced add them to the pan with the tomatoes and purée. Stir well then add the stock, ensuring the beans are well covered – add more water if necessary. Roughly chop the parsley. Season and add half the parsley to the pan.
* Heat the beans, chorizo and tomatoes to simmering point and cook for 15–45 minutes – the longer the cassoulet cooks the more the flavours will come together. Check the liquid level occasionally and add more water if necessary.
* Take the fish out of the freezer and place it in a shallow container. Cover it with boiling water and leave for about 10 minutes.
* Five minutes before you want to eat, break the fish into large chunks and add it to the pan. Stir very gently to avoid breaking the fish and simmer for about 5 minutes.
* Taste for seasoning and serve in big bowls with the remaining parsley on the top and crusty bread on the side.

Lemon Butternut Lasagne

As autumn starts to bite, a lasagne can bring some homely comfort. This colourful variation is lighter and easier to make than traditional lasagne. The recipe here involves cooking squash and leeks and layering these with ricotta and mascarpone, sheets of lasagne and generous amounts of pine nuts. This recipe is good served with pan-fried spinach dressed with a squeeze of lemon and a little butter.

The quantities are enough for two lasagnes, each feeding four people. One can be frozen and eaten at a later date.

2 medium butternut squash,
    approx. 1.2 kg
8 leeks, approx. 1.2 kg
1 lemon
2 sprigs fresh thyme
3 sprigs fresh sage
300 g mozzarella
170 g Parmesan
75 g pine nuts (you can buy them
    ready toasted)
2 tbsp olive oil
20 g (approx.) butter
500 g ricotta
250 g mascarpone or crème
    fraîche
a little milk
pinch of nutmeg (ground or
    freshly grated)
10 sheets lasagne, approx. 300 g
    (either fresh or no-need-to-
    precook)
salt and pepper

To serve
pan-fried spinach

GET AHEAD PREPARATION (optional)

The entire dish can be prepared
2 days in advance up to the point
where it goes into the oven. If
you only have a little time:
* Prepare the leeks.
* Grate the cheeses.
* Zest the lemon.
* Prepare the herbs.
* Toast the pine nuts, if
    necessary.

1 hour before you want to eat

* First, cook the squash and leek mixture. Peel, deseed and cut the squash into 1 cm thick slices. Cook in boiling salted water for 3 minutes. Meanwhile wash and slice the leeks.
* After 3 minutes add the leeks to the squash and cook together for another 6–8 minutes, until the leeks are soft and the squash is collapsing.
* Preheat the oven to 200°C/400°F/Gas Mark 6.
* Cook the sheets of lasagne in boiling salted water according to the packet instructions.
* While the leeks are cooking, zest and juice half the lemon. Strip the thyme and sage leaves from their stalks and roughly chop the sage. Coarsely grate the mozzarella and finely grate the Parmesan. If the pine nuts aren't already toasted, place them on a baking sheet in the oven as it heats up. Watch them like a hawk so that they don't burn.
* When the leeks and the squash are ready, drain them very well. Once drained, toss both the leeks and the squash with the oil, butter and herbs. Add the lemon juice and zest and season well with salt and pepper. Now add the mozzarella and one-third of the Parmesan.
* Next, make the ricotta mixture. Mix together the ricotta and mascarpone or crème fraîche and loosen them with some milk so that you have a dropping consistency. Stir in another third of the Parmesan and season with the nutmeg and salt and pepper.
* Now the lasagne can be assembled. These quantities make enough for two – one lasagne for now and one to freeze – so choose suitable dishes. Place half of the squash mixture in the bottom of each dish, sprinkle over about half the pine nuts and then cover with a layer of lasagne sheets. The sheets can overlap a little and can be cut to shape to fit all the corners. Add a layer of half the ricotta mixture over the lasagne. Repeat the process once more, finishing with the ricotta mixture on top. Finally, sprinkle with the remaining Parmesan.
* Set one lasagne aside to cool, ready for freezing, and place the other in the oven for 30 minutes until the top is golden and a knife inserted in the centre meets no resistance. Serve with pan-fried spinach or a green vegetable.

Lazy day supper – cooking instructions

For the best results, defrost the lasagne thoroughly and cook it as above.

October Week 4 – Overview

To start the week of recipes, Baked Fish with Caper, Parsley and Garlic Topping, Boiled Potatoes and Steamed Chard is a well-balanced meal with some intense flavours. Unusually for a Big Meal from Scratch, there is relatively little preparation involved so it shouldn't overly tax the cook. When using fresh fish be sure to cook it within a day or two of purchase or put it in the freezer until required.

Using leftover potatoes and fish from the big meal from scratch means that a midweek Something for Nothing of Potato Crush Fish Cakes with Herb Sauce is ready in just 20 minutes. Slightly longer is a 35-minute recipe for Chard and Mushroom Rice. It takes 20 minutes to assemble the ingredients and 15–20 minutes to cook on the stove.

October is the month for pumpkins so a Seasonal Supper of Spanish Pumpkin Casserole seems fitting. The recipe takes 40 minutes in all so save it for when you're not too pressed for time.

Canned smoked mussels are often overlooked when making a beeline for tuna, anchovies or sardines. Once discovered, their concentrated smoky flavour and juicy texture can be put to many culinary uses. For a Larder Feast that takes just 25 minutes, smoked mussels are mixed with peas to make a sauce for pasta. It's imperative to buy smoked mussels in oil rather than brine, and if these are not available use canned mackerel in tomato or provençal sauce instead.

In this week's Two for One recipe for Lamb and Pearl Barley Stew, the added grains soak up the flavours of the meat and add bulk and texture. After 30–40 minutes of assembly the stew cooks gently for about 1½ hours until the grains are plump and soft and the meat is meltingly tender. A butcher will sell boned and cubed shoulder but this recipe will also work with neck of lamb or other stewing cuts.

October Week 4	Recipe	Time
Big meal from scratch	Baked fish with caper, parsley and garlic topping, boiled potatoes and steamed chard	1 hour
Something for nothing 1	Potato crush fish cakes with herb sauce	20 mins
Something for nothing 2	Chard and mushroom rice	35 mins
Seasonal supper	Spanish pumpkin casserole	40 mins
Larder feast	Smoked mussel spaghetti	25 mins
2 for 1	Lamb and pearl barley stew	2¼ hours

All recipes serve 4 apart from the 2 for 1 recipe which makes 8 portions

SHOPPING LIST (for 4 people)

Meat and fish
6 portion-sized pieces unskinned pollack, cod or haddock fillets, approx. 1.2-1.5 kg
1.8-2 kg stewing lamb (we would favour boned shoulder, trimmed of all its fat and diced or neck fillets)

Dairy
130 g (approx.) butter
4 tbsp crème fraîche
100 g Parmesan

Fruit and vegetables
1.5 kg potatoes suitable for boiling, such as Charlotte or Desirée
350 g new potatoes (optional for Lamb and Pearl Barley Stew)
800 g chard
400 g pumpkin or butternut squash
3 medium carrots, approx. 300 g
4 celery sticks
250 g green beans
150 g field mushrooms
9 small onions, approx. 810 g
2 medium red onions, approx. 240 g
4 spring onions
11 garlic cloves
2 large bunches fresh flatleaf parsley
1 small bunch curly parsley
1 small bunch fresh coriander
1 small bunch chives
4 sprigs fresh dill
4 sprigs fresh rosemary
4 sprigs fresh thyme
4 sprigs fresh mint
4 firm pears
3 lemons
200 g frozen peas

Basics
75 ml groundnut or grapeseed oil
145 ml olive oil
100 g breadcrumbs or 3-4 slices bread suitable for crumbing
3 slices bread
5 tbsp plain flour
1 bay leaf
250 ml chicken or lamb stock (fresh or made from a stock cube or bouillon powder)
4 tsp vegetable bouillon powder
salt and pepper

Store cupboard
300 g spaghetti
200 g basmati rice
2 tbsp pearly barley
1 x 400 g can chopped tomatoes
1 x 400 g can chickpeas

3 x 65 g cans smoked mussels, in oil, not brine, or 2 x 125 g cans mackerel in provençal/tomato sauce
50 g (approx.) raisins
50 g (approx.) sultanas
2 tbsp ground almonds
25 g toasted pine nuts
50 g shelled walnut halves
2½ tbsp capers
2 tbsp sherry vinegar
½ tsp ground cinnamon
½ tsp ground cumin
1 tsp ground coriander
2 tsp paprika or 1 heaped tsp smoked paprika
850 ml white wine

Serving suggestions
frozen peas (Potato Crush Fish Cakes with Herb Sauce)
green salad ingredients (Chard and Mushroom Rice)
flatbreads (Spanish Pumpkin Casserole)
Spinach (Smoked Mussel Spaghetti)
cabbage or sprout tops (Lamb and Pearl Barley Stew)

To download or print out this shopping list, please visit www.thekitchenrevolution.co.uk/October/Week4

Big meal
from scratch

Baked Fish with Caper, Parsley and Garlic Topping, Boiled Potatoes and Steamed Chard

The flavours in this recipe are sharp and fresh and the combination makes a balanced, satisfying meal. The method is also straightforward – fish fillets, smothered with a mixture of capers, parsley, garlic and breadcrumbs are baked in the oven and served with boiled potatoes and steamed chard.

Chard has a taste akin to spinach but with a slightly more mineral quality. Its leaves are dark green and not unlike large spinach leaves, but the stalks can vary from being a creamy ivory colour (as in Swiss chard) or red, yellow and pink. Either type of chard will work well in this recipe. Chard, particularly Swiss chard, is usually available at greengrocers and supermarkets in October but if it is difficult to locate this recipe will work with spinach. You will need 1 kg loose large leaf spinach or 800 g baby leaf spinach.

Pollack is the lesser-known cousin of cod. If you cannot find pollack you could use haddock or cod just as well.

The extra fish and potatoes in this recipe are used for Potato Crush Fish Cakes with Herb Sauce later in the week and the extra chard for Chard and Mushroom Rice.

Baked fish with caper, parsley and garlic topping
2 small onions, approx. 180 g
3 garlic cloves
40 g (approx.) butter
2 tbsp capers
½ bunch fresh flatleaf parsley
1 lemon
100 g breadcrumbs (brown or white), approx. or 3-4 slices bread suitable for crumbing
1.2-1.5 kg pollack, cod or haddock fillets; includes 400 g extra for the Potato Crush Fish Cakes
salt and black pepper

Boiled potatoes and steamed chard
1.5 kg potatoes suitable for boiling, such as Charlotte or Desirée; includes 750 g extra for the potato crush fish
800 g chard; includes 400 g extra for the chard and mushroom rice
40 g (approx.) butter

GET AHEAD PREPARATION (optional)

The topping mixture for the fish can be made up to a day in advance. If you only have a little time:
* Prepare the onions and garlic.
* Chop the capers and parsley.
* Zest and juice the lemon.
* Make the breadcrumbs.
* Prepare the potatoes and cover with water until required.
* Prepare the chard.

1 hour before you want to eat cook the potatoes and fish

* Preheat the oven to 180°C/350°F/Gas Mark 4.
* Start by preparing the potatoes. Peel and cut the potatoes into even-sized chunks, then place them in a large pan with a lid and cover with water.
* Next, make the topping for the fish. Peel and finely chop the onion and garlic. Melt about half the butter in a small pan over a medium heat and add the onions and garlic. Cover and cook over a low heat for 10 minutes, stirring from time to time. Meanwhile, roughly chop the capers and parsley and put both in a large bowl. Grate the zest from the lemon and squeeze out its juice. Chop, whizz or grate the slices of bread into breadcrumbs if necessary. Add the lemon zest and juice and the breadcrumbs to the parsley and capers. When the onions and garlic are soft and golden add them to the breadcrumb mixture and season with a generous few pinches of salt and lots of pepper.
* Before you start to top the fish with the breadcrumb mixture put the pan of potatoes over a medium heat, bring it to the boil then turn down the heat and simmer gently until the potatoes are cooked. This will take 20–25 minutes.
* Grease an ovenproof dish large enough to hold the fish fillets in a single layer with the remaining butter. Lay the fillets skin-side down, season them well, then spread the breadcrumb topping evenly over each fillet. Bake near the top of the oven for 20 minutes, basting once with the buttery juice.

20 minutes before you want to eat cook the chard

* While the potatoes and fish are cooking, prepare the chard. Wash it very well in a basin of water then drain it. Cut off and discard the dry edges at the ends of the stalks, then cut the stalks off. Slice the leaves into 1-cm wide shreds and cut the stalks into 2-cm

lengths. Keep the stalks and leaves separate – as the stalks take slightly longer to cook. Put the stalks in a steamer or a large pan containing about 2 cm of salted water. Steam the stalks for 3–4 minutes then throw in the leaves, cover with a lid and cook for another 5–6 minutes until the chard is soft. Once the chard is cooked, drain it well, season with salt and pepper, dot with a nut of butter and put it into a serving dish. Cover and keep warm until ready to serve.

* Check that the potatoes are cooked, then drain them well and put them in a serving dish with a nut of butter, salt and pepper.
* Check that the fish fillets are cooked – you can tell because the flesh will look very white and will flake easily. Put one third of the fillets aside for use later in the week, but keep the topping to serve with the fish for this meal.
* Serve the remaining fillets with the extra topping, pan juices, boiled potatoes and steamed chard.

Afterwards

Remove the skin from the remaining fillets and flake the flesh. Put the fish and the remaining chard and potatoes in separate containers, cover and refrigerate for use later in the week. Ideally you will have 600 g potatoes, about 400 g fish and 300 g chard.

Potato Crush Fish Cakes with Herb Sauce

Fish cakes are a well-loved crowd-pleaser – and if you have a bowl of leftover mashed or boiled potatoes and some fish to hand, they can be ready in 15–20 minutes. In this recipe we suggest you crush rather than mash the boiled potatoes, leaving chunks that add texture and body.

Potato crush fish cakes
500 g cooked potatoes left over
    from the Big Meal from Scratch
    or 600 g new potatoes, such as
    Charlotte or Desirée, boiled for
    about 20 minutes until soft
4 spring onions
handful of fresh parsley
handful of fresh coriander
1 tbsp crème fraîche
½ lemon
400 g cooked fish left over from
    the Big Meal from Scratch or
    400 g pollack, cod or haddock
    simmered in water for about 5
    minutes until just cooked
2 tbsp plain flour
50 g butter
1 tbsp groundnut or grapeseed oil
salt and pepper

Herb sauce
1 tsp capers
1 small bunch chives
handful of fresh coriander
handful of fresh flatleaf parsley
4 sprigs fresh dill
3 tbsp crème fraîche
½ lemon

To serve
peas

The fish cakes can be assembled a day in advance, then dipped in flour at the last minute and then fried. The herb sauce can be made a day in advance. If you only have a little time:
* Prepare the spring onions.
* Chop the parsley, coriander, capers, chives and dill.
* Mix the fish cake ingredients.

20 minutes before you want to eat

* Turn the oven to its lowest setting.
* First, make the fish cakes. Place the potatoes in a large bowl and use a masher or the back of a fork to crush them into roughly mashed chunks. Trim and thinly slice the spring onions, roughly chop the parsley and coriander and add to the potatoes. Add the crème fraîche and a squeeze of lemon juice and mix well. Finally, flake the fish and add it to the potato mixture. Using a fork or knife mix well, taking care not to mush the fish too much. You want the mixture to come together but you also want some big flakes of fish and chunks of potato to remain. Taste and season accordingly with salt and pepper.
* Put the flour on to a plate and season it well. Mould the fish cake mixture into eight cakes and dip both sides of each cake into the flour.
* Now cook the fish cakes. Heat half the butter and half the oil in a large (preferably non-stick) frying pan over a medium heat. When the fat is hot, add four of the fish cakes. Allow them to cook for 3–4 minutes, resisting the urge to move them about, then turn them over and let the other sides brown. When the first four fish cakes are finished, put them on a baking sheet in the oven to keep warm. Heat the remaining butter and oil and cook the rest of the fish cakes.
* While the last four fish cakes are cooking, make the herb sauce. Roughly chop the capers, chives, coriander, parsley and dill and mix them all into the crème fraîche. Grate in the zest of the half lemon, mix thoroughly and season to taste.
* When all the fish cakes are cooked serve with a generous spoonful of herb sauce and a pile of peas.

**Something
for nothing 2**

Chard and Mushroom Rice

This Persian inspired rice recipe is flavoured with spices, nuts, dried fruit, mushrooms and chard. If you are using up leftover chard from the Big Meal from Scratch the entire meal can be cooked in one pan on the stove which means there is minimal washing-up. This is a really good standby supper – interesting enough to serve to friends, simple enough to make midweek. If you don't have any chard from the big meal use 400 g chard or spinach chopped and steamed or 300 g frozen spinach.

3 small onions, approx. 270 g
2 tbsp olive oil
4 garlic cloves
150 g flat mushrooms
200 g basmati rice
½ tsp ground cinnamon
½ tsp ground cumin
1 tsp ground coriander
1 lemon
50 g (approx.) sultanas
50 g (approx.) raisins
250 ml white wine

600 ml chicken or vegetable
    stock (fresh or made from a
    stock cube or bouillon powder)
300 g cooked chard left over
    from the Big Meal from Scratch
    or see above
2 handfuls of fresh flatleaf
    parsley
25 g toasted pine nuts
50 g walnut halves
salt and black pepper

To serve
green salad

GET AHEAD PREPARATION (optional)

The dish can be made a day in advance, up to the point of adding the parsley, lemon and nuts, and then reheated slowly on the stove until warm. If you only have a little time:
* Prepare the onions, garlic and mushrooms
* Rinse the rice.

*35 minutes before
you want to eat*

* Peel and slice the onions. Heat the oil in a heavy-based pan over a medium heat. When the oil is hot, add the onions and cook for about 5–7minutes until soft. While the onions are cooking peel and thinly slice the garlic and clean the mushrooms (you can peel them if you have the time or inclination). Then cut them into 1-cm thick slices.
* When the onions are soft, add the garlic and stir once or twice, then cook gently for another few minutes. While the garlic and onions are cooking wash the rice under cold running water. Drain and set to one side.
* When the onions and garlic are both soft, add the cinnamon, cumin and coriander and stir for 1–2 minutes.
* Turn the heat up under the onion mixture and add the mushrooms. Stir and turn the mushrooms until they start to brown – this will take a few minutes. Grate the zest of half the lemon.
* When the mushrooms have started to brown, add the rice, sultanas and raisins to the pan and the zest of half the lemon. Throw in the wine and stir once or twice. Bring to the boil then add the stock and 1 teaspoon salt. Allow to boil, then reduce the heat and simmer, uncovered, for about 15–20 minutes.
* When the rice has been cooking for about 10 minutes stir in the chard.
* Allow to cook for another 10 minutes or until the rice is just cooked. Then roughly chop the parsley and stir it into the rice along with the juice of the lemon, the pine nuts and walnut halves and a generous amount of pepper. Taste and season as necessary.
* Serve with a green salad

Spanish Pumpkin Casserole

This Spanish dish is full of flavour and chunky in texture. Adding pears is unusual, but they provide pockets of sweetness that contrast beautifully with the nutty, savoury whole. The meal is cooked in two parts then brought together at the end. The pumpkin is cooked until soft and disintegrating with the chickpeas and pears. While this is cooking onions are softened with garlic and paprika, then cubes of bread followed by ground almonds and tomatoes are added. In the last few moments green beans are cooked in the pumpkin mixture and the separate elements are then combined to form a rich and wonderful whole. This is excellent served with flatbreads, rice or simply as it is. If you wish, you can replace the pumpkin with butternut squash.

400 g pumpkin or butternut
 squash
400 ml vegetable stock
1 x 400 g can chickpeas
4 firm pears
100 ml olive oil
2 medium red onions, approx.
 240 g
2 garlic cloves
2 tsp paprika or 1 heaped tsp
 smoked paprika
3 slices bread
2 tbsp ground almonds
2 tbsp sherry vinegar
1 x 400 g can chopped tomatoes
250 g green beans
small handful of fresh flatleaf
 parsley
salt and pepper

To serve
Flatbreads

GET AHEAD PREPARATION (optional)

* Prepare the pumpkin.
* Drain and rinse the chickpeas.
* Top and tail the green beans.
* Prepare the onions and garlic.
* Cut the bread into small
 cubes.

40 minutes before you want to eat

* Peel, deseed and dice the pumpkin and cut it into 3-cm cubes.
* Put the pumpkin in a pan large enough to hold all the ingredients. Add the stock and enough water to just cover the cubes. Add some salt and a splash of olive oil, bring to the boil, then simmer for 5 minutes.
* Drain and rinse the chickpeas, add them to the pan and bring back to the boil. Simmer the pumpkin and chickpeas for 10 minutes until the pumpkin is beginning to soften.
* Peel, core and quarter the pears and set them to one side.
* Heat a generous glug of oil in a large frying pan over a medium heat. While the oil is heating peel and finely slice the onions. Add the onions to the oil and fry them until they are starting to soften and turn golden – this will take 5–7 minutes.
* Peel and crush the garlic and add it to the softened onions along with the paprika.
* Cut the bread into small cubes and add them to the onions, garlic and paprika with another generous glug of oil. Brown the bread a little then add the almonds. Let the almonds toast for 1–2 minutes then splash in the vinegar. Let the vinegar evaporate then add the tomatoes. Bring the mixture to the boil and simmer with the lid off until it starts to thicken.
* When the pumpkin and chickpea mixture has been simmering for 10 minutes add the pear slices and simmer for 5 minutes.
* Top and tail the beans and chop the parsley.
* Add the beans to the pumpkin, pears and chickpeas and simmer until they are tender – about 4–5 minutes.
* Once the beans are tender, stir in the tomato mixture and let it simmer and thicken up for a couple of minutes.
* Stir in the parsley and a good splash more of olive oil, season and serve with warmed flatbreads.

Larder feast

Smoked Mussel Spaghetti

Given how popular fresh mussels are, it seems surprising that their smoked and canned cousins aren't more widely used in everyday cooking. Having a couple of cans lurking in the larder is a good plan because they can add a touch of luxury and a rich flavour to rice, pasta or potato dishes. Here they are combined with peas in a light winey sauce for spaghetti. This is as simple and straightforward as supper gets – but it's nevertheless completely satisfying.

It is important to use smoked mussels stored in oil rather than brined mussels. The former are juicy and full of flavour. The latter are chewy and salty. Big supermarkets and good delicatessens should sell smoked mussels but if they prove difficult to find replace them with flaked mackerel in tomato or provençal sauce which has a different but equally potent flavour; you will need two 125 g cans.

1 small onion, approx. 90 g
1 tbsp olive oil
2 garlic cloves
300 g spaghetti
200 g frozen peas
100 ml white wine
3 x 65 g cans smoked mussels,
    or 2 x 125 g cans mackerel in
    tomato/provençal sauce
handful of fresh flatleaf parsley
100 g Parmesan
salt and pepper

To serve
steamed spinach

GET AHEAD PREPARATION (optional)

If there are a few spare moments any of the following would be helpful:
* Prepare the onion and garlic.
* Defrost the peas.
* Chop the parsley.
* Grate the Parmesan.

25 minutes before you want to eat

* Peel and finely slice the onion. Heat the oil in a heavy-based pan or frying pan over a medium heat and add the onion. Cook gently for about 10 minutes until soft. Meanwhile, peel and finely slice the garlic.
* After the onion has been cooking for about 7 minutes, add the garlic and cook for another 3 minutes.
* Cook the spaghetti according to the instructions on the packet – usually 8–10 minutes in salted boiling water.
* Add the peas to the onions and garlic. Stir once or twice then add the wine, bring to the boil then reduce to about half.
* While the wine is reducing, drain the mussels and roughly chop the parsley.
* Add the mussels and parsley to the pan, season with salt and pepper and cook over a low heat to warm through for about 5 minutes.
* Grate the Parmesan and set aside.
* Drain the spaghetti then toss it in the pea and mussel mixture. Season well and add half the Parmesan.
* Serve in big bowls with the remaining Parmesan on the side and steamed spinach.

Two for one

Lamb and Pearl Barley Stew

Lamb is wonderfully versatile and makes a fine stew whatever the season. British lamb is especially good from late summer through to the autumn when the animals have had plenty of time to feed on spring and summer grasses. Lamb can be cooked as a dark and rich stew in the cold, winter months and a light and citrussy casserole in the hotter summer months. The pearl barley and potatoes in this recipe suit the autumnal weather. This recipe is simple to assemble but benefits from long, slow cooking.

1.8-2 kg lamb for stewing (we would favour boned shoulder, trimmed of all its fat and diced, or neck fillet)
3 tbsp plain flour
4 tbsp groundnut or grapeseed oil
3 small onions, approx. 270 g
3 medium carrots, approx. 300 g
4 celery sticks
500 ml white wine
250 ml chicken or lamb stock (fresh or made from a stock cube or bouillon powder)
handful of fresh curly parsley
2 sprigs fresh mint
4 sprigs fresh rosemary
4 sprigs fresh thyme
1 bay leaf
350 g new potatoes (optional)
2 tbsp pearl barley
salt and black pepper

To serve
cabbage or sprout tops

GET AHEAD PREPARATION (optional)

The entire dish can be made 2 days in advance and warmed through when required. If you only have a little time:
* Brown the meat .
* Prepare the onions, carrots and celery.
* Prepare the potatoes, if using, and cover with water until required.

2¼ hours before you want to eat

* Preheat the oven to 180°C/350°F/Gas Mark 4.
* If the meat isn't already diced, cut it into 2–3-cm chunks then put it into a bowl or plastic bag with the flour and a little salt and pepper and mix well.
* Heat 1 tablespoon of the oil in a large, heavy-based casserole with a lid over a medium heat. When the oil is hot, lift the meat out of the flour and brown it in the casserole. This will have to be done in a couple of batches. Once browned, transfer the meat to a bowl and set it aside.
* While the meat is browning, prepare the vegetables. Peel and chop the onions and carrots and wash and slice the celery.
* When the meat is browned, lift it out of the casserole and add a generous splash of the wine to deglaze. Scrape all the meat flavours from the bottom of the casserole, then pour the wine over the resting meat.
* Add another tablespoon of the oil to the casserole, and when it is hot add the chopped vegetables. Brown these for about 5 minutes over a medium heat.
* When the vegetables are browned, add the remaining wine and the stock and scrape the flavours from the bottom of the casserole again. Return the meat to the casserole, scatter over a couple of sprigs of parsley, one sprig of the mint, all the rosemary and thyme sprigs and the bay leaf.
* Cover the casserole with a lid or two layers of foil and place in the oven for 1½ hours.

45 minutes before you want to eat

* Wash the potatoes, if using, and if they are larger than bite-size cut them into halves. Add these to the casserole, sprinkle in the pearl barley, stir well, and return the stew to oven.

5 minutes before you want to eat

* When the stew has been in the oven for 1½ hours, check that the meat is completely tender and the potatoes are cooked. If not, return the casserole to the oven and check again after another 20 minutes.

* When the meat is tender, spoon off any excess fat that rises to the surface. Taste the cooking liquor and season it to your taste. Remove the rosemary and thyme sprigs and the bay leaf. If you would like the liquor to be thicker you can strain it into a pan and boil it down for a few minutes. This is really a matter of taste.
* When the meat is cooked, remove the stew from the oven and place half in a container to freeze when cold.
* Chop the remaining mint and parsley and add them to stew. Serve with cabbage or sprout tops.

Lazy day supper – reheating instructions

Allow the stew to defrost thoroughly. Then tip it into a casserole and either warm it through slowly in the oven at 150°C/300°F/Gas Mark 1 or on the hob until piping hot. Add chopped mint and parsley to the stew before serving as above.

Hazelnut and Chocolate Torte

When nuts start appearing in the shops autumn really feels like it has started. Hazelnuts and chocolate, a perfect partnership, are the main ingredients in this moist torte or cake. Two hazelnut cakes sandwich layers of chocolate and whipped cream. The cakes can be made ahead of time – if anything they improve in flavour if left in a tin or wrapped in foil for a night. Do not attempt to sandwich the cakes together if the chocolate is still warm as it will melt the cream.

Hazelnut cakes
110 g shelled hazelnuts, skin-on if
   possible
butter, for greasing
4 free-range eggs
140 g caster sugar
cocoa powder, for dusting

Chocolate and cream fillings
100 g dark chocolate
200 ml double cream
½ tsp vanilla extract
20 g butter

At least 2 hours and up to 2 days before you want to eat

* Preheat the oven to 180°C/350°F/Gas Mark 4.
* Grind the hazelnuts in a food processor until finely chopped. But don't whizz them for too long or the oil from the nuts will seep out and you'll have an oily, unusable mess.
* If you don't have a food processor, chop the nuts as finely as you can.
* Grease two 15 cm round cake tins with butter.
* Separate the eggs. Whisk the egg yolks with 110 g of the sugar until they are light and fluffy.
* Thoroughly clean the whisk then whisk the egg whites, starting slowly and gradually speeding up. You want the mixture to form stiff peaks. As soon as the egg whites begin to stiffen, add the remaining sugar. Carry on whisking until the whites are shiny and firm.
* Fold the ground hazelnuts and egg whites alternately into the egg yolks and sugar until they are completely amalgamated.
* Divide the mixture between the two prepared tins and bake for 30 minutes. The cakes are ready when you leave no impression if you press them with your finger. Remove the cakes from the oven and leave them to cool for a few minutes before turning them out of their tins.
* If you've made the cakes ahead of time allow them to cool completely and store them in an airtight container until you are ready to add the fillings.
* Next, make the two fillings starting with the chocolate one. Chop the chocolate into small pieces. Put 100 ml of the cream and the vanilla extract, butter and chocolate into a non-stick pan. Warm gently and bring to the boil so that the chocolate is completely melted. Remove from the heat and whisk until the mixture is smooth and thickened. Spoon it thickly over the middle of one of the hazelnut cakes and place the cake on a serving plate.
* Put the remaining double cream in a bowl and whisk until it is thick enough to be spread on the torte and hold its shape. When the chocolate icing is completely cool spread a layer of cream on the underside of the remaining cake and sandwich the cakes together.
* Dust the top of the torte with cocoa powder and serve.

October puddings

Apple Charlotte

Charlottes are made by lining a pudding mould with bread and filling it with fruit. The bread is often buttered and sometimes fried. Apple charlotte is probably the most famous version and is especially good when apples are at their autumnal best.

900 g sweet apples, such as Cox, Russet or Discovery
½ lemon
80 g (approx.) butter
½–1 tbsp light brown soft sugar (depending on how sweet the apples are)
pinch of nutmeg (ground or freshly grated)
1 tsp ground cinnamon
8 thin slices bread (brown or white)

To serve
thick double cream or vanilla ice cream.

1 hour before you want to eat

* Preheat the oven to 190°C/375°F/Gas Mark 5.
* Peel and core the apples and cut them into eighths.
* Melt about one-third of the butter in a pan and add the apples. Fry for 3–5 minutes then add the juice of the half lemon, a couple of strips of its zest, the sugar, nutmeg and a pinch of cinnamon. Stir well, then cook over a gentle heat until the apples start to soften. This will take about 10 minutes. You want the apples to be soft but not puréed.
* While the apples are cooking remove the crusts from the bread. Butter both sides of the slices and sprinkle one side of them with the remaining cinnamon.
* Use six of the slices to line the base and sides of a deep cake tin or pudding mould approximately 20 cm in diameter. Cut the bread into shapes as necessary and try not to leave any gaps. Put the cinnamon side facing inwards.
* When the apples are softened tip them into the bread-lined tin or mould. Cover with the remaining slices of bread and bake in the oven for 30 minutes or until the top is starting to brown.
* Remove the charlotte from the oven, leave to stand for 5 minutes before inverting on to a serving dish.
* Serve with thick double cream or vanilla ice cream.

Pear and Ginger Eve's Pudding

This recipe comes from one of our favourite recipe books, *Roast Chicken and Other Stories, Second Helpings* by Simon Hopkinson. The recipes can seldom be improved on, and this one is no exception. The traditional version of this pudding is made with apples rather than pears – either is delicious but the pear and ginger combination is a real winner. Although not conventional, we suggest turning the cooked pudding out so that the pears end up on top for serving.

90 g butter
90 g sugar
2 tbsp syrup from a jar of preserved ginger
500 g pears (Conference or Comice)
1 lemon

Sponge
125 g butter
125 g caster sugar
2 large free-range eggs
3 tbsp syrup from a jar of preserved ginger
100 g self-raising flour
1 tsp baking powder
30 g ground almonds
4-5 pieces of preserved ginger

To serve
crème fraîche or double cream

1 hour before you want to eat

* Preheat the oven to 190°C/375°F/Gas Mark 5.
* Grease the inside of a 23–25-cm cake tin or ovenproof dish with a little of the butter.
* Next, prepare the caramel and pears. Melt the remaining butter in a heavy-based pan or frying-pan. When it has melted, add the sugar and ginger syrup and heat until they are bubbling and starting to turn golden brown. Remove from the heat and tip the syrupy caramel into the tin or ovenproof dish.
* Peel, core and quarter the pears and place them in a bowl. Grate the zest of half the lemon and add it to the pears along with the juice of the whole lemon so that they don't brown. Place the pears as neatly as possible in the caramel on the bottom of the tin or dish.
* Next, make the sponge, using a food processor if you have one. Tip all the ingredients apart from the preserved ginger into a food processor and blend until smooth. If you don't have a processor, cream the butter and sugar they are until pale and fluffy, then beat in the eggs and the ginger syrup followed by the dry ingredients. Chop the pieces of preserved ginger and fold them into the sponge batter, then pour the batter over the pears.
* Bake in the oven for 45 minutes. The pudding is ready when the sponge starts to come away from the sides of the tin or dish. If the edges start to burn before the pudding is finished, cover with foil.
* Remove the pudding from the oven and leave it to cool for 10–15 minutes, then run a knife round the edge, place a large plate over the top and turn the pudding out so that the pears end up on the top.
* Serve hot with double cream or crème fraîche.

October puddings **Baked Figs with Yoghurt**

Italian purple-skinned figs with their luscious red centres start appearing in markets and greengrocers in October. It is hard to improve on the simple treat of a ripe fig in season but the addition of butter, orange and honey creates a sticky, sweet syrup that emphasises the figs' flavour. Buy figs that are ripe, almost bursting.

12 ripe to bursting fresh figs
25 g butter
4 tsp clear honey
juice 1 orange
300 ml Greek yoghurt

To serve
biscotti or other hard sweet
  biscuits

30 minutes before you want to eat

* Preheat the oven to 180°C/350°F/Gas Mark 4.
* Stand the figs in ovenproof dish. Cut a cross on the top of each fig and squeeze the fig open.
* Put a small dab of the butter and 1 teaspoon of the honey on each cross.
* Pour the orange juice over the figs.
* Add 2 tablespoons water to the dish and bake the figs in the oven for 20 minutes.
* Spoon a generous dollop of yoghurt onto the warm figs and serve immediately with biscotti or other hard sweet biscuits if you have them to hand.

NOVEMBER

Winter is here, and with it root vegetables, cabbages, cauliflowers, onions and game. Now is the time for Pheasant and Chestnut Soup, and Braised Rabbit with Mushrooms. Winter is not only for carnivores, though. We have five fish recipes for November, including Brill with Prawn Bisque and Citrus Onions, and Smoked Haddock with Bacon and Mustard Sauce. For vegetarians there is Root Vegetable and White Bean Minestrone, Squash and Feta Pasta and Romanesque (or Cauliflower) Cheese. For afters, there is a Spiced Pumpkin Cake, a rice pudding made with incredibly sticky dates that appear at this time of year and also a Queen of Puddings made with quince paste.

November	Week 1	Week 2	Week 3	Week 4
Big meal from scratch	Boiled beef and carrots, with horseradish mash, cabbage and saffron broth	Roast pheasant (or chicken) with roast squash, mash and greens	Brill with prawn bisque, citrus onions and new potatoes	Lamb en croûte with roast root vegetables and broccoli
Something for nothing 1	Cottage pie	Pheasant (or chicken) and chestnut soup	Linguine with tomato prawn sauce	Baked salmon with watercress dauphinoise
Something for nothing 2	Smoked haddock, with onion skirlie with cabbage and bacon	Squash and feta pasta	Cheese and onion bread pudding	Root vegetable and white bean minestrone
Seasonal supper	Red coleslaw with baked potatoes	Smoked haddock with bacon and mustard sauce and spinach	Mushrooms on toast with rocket salad	Romanesque (or cauliflower) cheese
Larder feast	Catalan style beans and chorizo	Sardines with tomato bulghar and walnut pesto	Spinach and chickpea soup	Prawn and corn fritters with chilli-fried broccoli
2 for 1	Pistachio chicken curry	Chinese braised lamb	South American beef hotpot	Braised rabbit (or chicken) with mushrooms
Puddings	Spiced pumpkin cake with maple syrup and pecans	Queen of puddings	Rice pudding with dates	Bramley apple cream

November Week 1 – Overview

Boiled beef served with carrots and mash or dumplings is quintessentially British. A more accurate description would be 'long, slow simmered beef' but that doesn't sound as catchy. Gentle cooking like this is particularly suited to inexpensive cuts such as silverside or brisket so this meal shouldn't break the budget. Horseradish mash is ideal for soaking up the tasty cooking liquor. The beef starts cooking just over 3 hours before it's ready to serve but once it is gently poaching there's nothing more to do until 45 minutes before you're ready to eat.

Leftover beef, potato and onions are all utilised in this week's Something for Nothings. For a housekeeping classic, mash and beef are turned into Cottage Pie. With most of the work already done, the pie takes 20 minutes to assemble and is 20 minutes in the oven. The second Something for Nothing of Skirlie with smoked haddock is a version of an old Scottish recipe and uses oatmeal cooked with leftover onions, celery and cabbage to accompany grilled smoked haddock.

For an understated but scrumptious Seasonal Supper there is Red Coleslaw with Baked Potatoes. This takes as long as potatoes take to bake – about 40 minutes – and the quantities for the coleslaw are generous on the basis that having leftover coleslaw in the fridge is never a bad thing. A Larder Feast of Catalan Style Beans and Chorizo makes a thick, soupy bean casserole that takes just half an hour to make and is another good recipe for when the fridge is bare or when energy levels are low.

The Two for One Pistachio Chicken Curry is delicately flavoured with spices. The given quantities will serve eight so either freeze half or perhaps invite people over for a bonfire night supper. Other good bonfire night recipes this week are the Cottage Pie and the Red Coleslaw with Baked Potatoes.

November Week 1	Recipe	Time
Big meal from scratch	Boiled beef and carrots, with horseradish mash, cabbage and saffron broth	3¼ hours
Something for nothing 1	Cottage pie	40 mins
Something for nothing 2	Smoked haddock, with onion skirlie with cabbage and bacon	30 mins
Seasonal supper	Red coleslaw with baked potatoes	40 mins
Larder feast	Catalan style beans and chorizo	30 mins
2 for 1	Pistachio chicken curry	1 hour

All recipes serve 4 apart from the 2 for 1 recipe which makes 8 portions

SHOPPING LIST (for 4 people)

Meat and fish
1.8 kg piece of silverside or brisket of beef
   (salted if you like),
200 g small chorizos
225 g free-range rindless smoked streaky
   bacon
2 kg bone-in free-range chicken thighs, or
   1.5 kg skinless boneless thighs
4 200 g (approx.) pieces of smoked haddock
60 g duck fat or dripping (or butter)

Dairy
190-210 g butter
150 ml milk or 100 ml milk and 4 tbsp
   double cream
200 ml natural yoghurt
150 g Cheddar cheese
280 ml single cream

Fruit and vegetables
2.8 kg floury potatoes, such as Maris Piper
   or baking potatoes (4 of a suitable size for
   baking)
10-11 medium carrots, approx. 1.1 kg
1 medium Savoy cabbage
450 g (approx.) red cabbage
2 celery sticks
9 medium onions, approx. 960 g
2 medium red onions, approx. 140 g
3 garlic cloves
7 green chillies
3-5 cm piece of fresh root ginger
2 sprigs fresh thyme
4-5 sprigs fresh mint
1 large bunch fresh parsley
handful of fresh coriander
1½ lemons
1 medium crunchy apple
1 orange
400 g frozen broad beans

Basics
20 ml olive oil
75 ml groundnut or grapeseed oil
250 ml ham, chicken or vegetable stock
   (fresh or made from a stock cube or
   bouillon powder)
2 tbsp tomato ketchup
2 tsp Worcestershire sauce
3 bay leaves
12 black peppercorns
pinch of sugar
salt and pepper

Store cupboard
200 g medium oatmeal
1 × 400 g can whole green beans (haricot
   verts if possible)
1 × 200 g can butter beans

3 tbsp horseradish cream
150 g shelled pistachio nuts (unsalted)
1 tbsp pumpkin seeds
1 tbsp sunflower seeds
3 tbsp mayonnaise
2 tsp ground coriander
½ tsp ground cumin
pinch of ground cinnamon
½ tsp turmeric
1½ tsp fennel seeds
6 cardamon pods
2 blades of mace
5 saffron threads
pinch of nutmeg (ground or freshly grated)
150 ml white wine
100 ml (approx.) red wine
100 ml sherry or white vermouth

Serving suggestions
English mustard (Boiled Beef and Carrots
   with Horseradish Mash, Cabbage and
   Saffron Broth)
peas or green beans (Cottage Pie)
crusty bread or garlic bread (Catalan Style
   Beans and Chorizo)
basmati rice, fresh or frozen spinach
   (Pistachio Chicken Curry)

To download or print out this shopping list,
please visit www.thekitchenrevolution.co.uk/
November/Week1

**Big meal
from scratch**

Boiled Beef and Carrots with Horseradish Mash, Cabbage and Saffron Broth

This traditional, simple meal is full of flavour and somehow very comforting. It is ideal for a cold, wet winter day. To accompany the beef there is a sauce inspired by a 300-year-old English recipe that uses saffron, orange juice and sherry.

    The best cuts for this dish are silverside or brisket. They are perfectly suited to slow poaching and also have the advantage of being inexpensive. You need a 2 kg piece of beef for this recipe as the leftovers are used to make a quick Cottage Pie (see page 481). This may mean there isn't room in the pan to hold all the carrots. If this is the case, we suggest you cook them separately in some beef cooking liquor. The onions and celery cooked with the beef are used withe the leftover cabbage to make a Scottish Skirlie.

Boiled beef and carrots
1.8 kg piece silverside or brisket of beef (salted if you like); includes 600 g extra for the cottage pie
2 celery sticks for the skirlie
3 medium onions, approx. 360 g for the skirlie
12 black peppercorns
2 bay leaves
2 sprigs fresh thyme
2 blades of mace
1 orange
8 medium carrots, approx. 800 g; includes 2-3 extra for the cottage pie
salt

Horseradish mash
1.8 kg floury potatoes, such as Maris Piper or baking potatoes; includes 900 g extra for the cottage pie
150 ml milk or 100 ml milk and 4 tbsp double cream
80 g butter
3 tbsp (approx.) horseradish cream
pepper

Cabbage
1 medium Savoy cabbage; includes 300 g extra for the onion skirlie with cabbage and bacon
50 g butter
generous pinch of nutmeg (ground or freshly grated)

Saffron broth
5 saffron threads
100 ml sherry, white vermouth or white wine
pinch of sugar
To serve
English mustard

GET AHEAD PREPARATION (optional)

* Prepare the celery, onions and carrots.
* Prepare the potatoes and cover with water until required.

3¼ hours before you want to eat cook the beef

* Place the brisket in your largest heavy-based pan and completely cover it with water. and bring it to the boil. If it is salted beef lift it out of this water and start again with fresh water.
* While the beef is coming to the boil, trim, wash and roughly chop the celery, and peel and quarter the onions.
* If the beef isn't salted, you will not need to change the water, so once it has come to the boil skim off any scum and turn the heat to its lowest.
* Add the celery, onions, peppercorns, bay leaf, thyme, mace, orange zest and a generous pinch of salt. Cover the pan almost completely and leave the beef to simmer away as gently as possible for 2½ hours.
* Periodically skim off any scum and top up the water levels if they have dropped. Make sure it is only just simmering – anything more rigorous will make the beef tough.

45 minutes before you want to eat cook the potatoes and carrots

* Peel the potatoes, cut them into even, egg-sized chunks and put them in a pan of salted water. Bring to the boil and simmer gently until the potatoes are just cooked – this will take 20–25 minutes depending on the size of the chunks.
* Peel and trim the carrots, leaving them whole. About half an hour before the beef is cooked fit them into the pan with the beef. If this seems like an impossibility, ladle about 750 ml of the cooking liquor into a medium pan and add all the carrots. Add more water if they're not covered by the liquor and bring them to the boil, then simmer them very gently until they are just soft. This will take about 20 minutes.

25 minutes before you want to eat cook the cabbage

* Preheat the oven to 120°C/250°F/Gas Mark ½.
* Prepare the cabbage by cutting it in half lengthways, then removing the core and shredding it finely. Place it in a pan with enough water to come halfway up the cabbage. Add half the butter and generous amounts of salt and pepper, then cover with

a lid and place over a medium heat. Bring to the boil and stir the cabbage so that it softens evenly. Cook for 10–15 minutes until the cabbage is meltingly soft.

10 minutes before you want to eat make the mash and sauce

* Lift the beef from its liquor and put it on a serving plate with the carrots arranged around it. Cover with foil and place in the oven to keep warm. Put some plates and other serving dishes in the oven at the same time.
* When the potatoes are cooked, pour them into a colander. Put the milk, or milk and cream, and the butter into the empty potato pan over a low heat so that the butter melts and the milk heats. While this is happening, place the colander containing the potatoes over the pan. This helps ensure the potatoes are very dry and prevents the mash being sloppy.
* When the milk is hot and the butter has melted, add the potatoes and mash them well with a traditional masher or, for a really smooth texture, pass them through a mouli-legumes or potato ricer.
* Stir the horseradish cream into the mash, taste and season as necessary; add more horseradish cream according to taste. Put just over half into a serving dish and keep warm. Leave the remaining mash to cool for use later in the week.
* Drain the cabbage very thoroughly and put it in a serving dish. Add the rest of the butter and the nutmeg and toss well. Leave in the warm oven while you make the sauce.
* Strain 450 ml of the beef cooking liquor into a small pan with the saffron and the sherry, vermouth or wine and bring it to a rolling boil (see page 485 for more on thickening sauces). Boil for 2 minutes, season to taste and add a pinch of sugar. Squeeze in the juice of the whole orange. Strain the sauce into a jug.
* To serve, slice the beef and serve it on a dish with the carrots. Pass the mash, cabbage and broth around separately with English mustard.

Afterwards

Strain the beef cooking liquor. Put the leftover onions (2-3) and celery (several pieces), beef (500 g), carrots (2-3), horseradish mash (800 g) and 300 ml of the beef liquor in separate containers, cover and refrigerate for use later. You can freeze the rest of the beef liquor for use as stock, but it would be worth reducing it down.

Smoked Haddock with Onion Skirlie with Cabbage and Bacon

Skirlie is an old-fashioned Scottish dish, originally eaten as a complete meal and now more often served as a side dish with game or used as a stuffing for poultry. Here we suggest serving it as an accompaniment to smoked haddock with cabbage and bacon.

Smoked haddock
4 × 200 g, approx. pieces of
  smoked haddock
30 g butter
1 lemon
salt and pepper

Onion skirlie with cabbage
and bacon
1 tbsp groundnut or grapeseed oil
100 g free-range rindless smoked
  streaky bacon
2-3 cooked onions and some
  pieces of celery left over from
  the Big Meal from Scratch or
  2-3 onions, quartered and
  2 roughly chopped celery
  sticks simmered in boiling
  stock until soft

300 g cooked Savoy cabbage left
  over from the Big Meal from
  Scratch or 400 g Savoy
  cabbage, finely sliced and
  steamed until soft
50 g dripping or duck fat or 50 g
  butter
200 g medium oatmeal
150 ml beef liquor leftover from
  the Big Meal from Scratch or
  150 ml beef stock (fresh or
  made from a stock cube or
  bouillon powder)
small handful of fresh parsley

GET AHEAD PREPARATION (optional)

* Roughly chop the cooked
  cabbage and make sure it is
  very dry.
* Prepare the onions and celery.
* Chop the parsley.

30 minutes before you want to eat

* Preheat the grill to its highest setting.
* Heat the oil in a large frying pan over a medium heat. Using scissors, cut the bacon into the pan and let it brown.
* While the bacon is cooking, slice the onions, chop the celery and roughly chop the cabbage. Pat the cabbage dry.
* Add the onions, celery and cabbage to the bacon and fry over a high heat until golden brown.
* When the vegetables are golden brown add the dripping, duck fat or butter and when the butter has melted add the oatmeal and mix it in well. Turn the heat down and cook for about 3 minutes, stirring frequently. The oatmeal will start to crisp a little.
* Add the beef cooking liquor and leave to simmer until all the liquid is absorbed.
* In the meantime, cook the smoked haddock. Rub with the butter and sprinkle with a good dose of salt and pepper. Place the pieces of fish under the grill, skin sides up, and leave to cook thoroughly until the skins are golden and crisp, then turn the haddock over and cook until the flesh is firm to the touch. Leave the fish to rest for a couple of minutes.
* Check on the skirlie. When all the liquid is absorbed it should be soft with a little bite. If too chewy, add a little more liquid and cook for another couple of minutes. When it is ready, remove from the heat. Roughly chop the parsley and quarter the lemon. Add the parsley to the skirlie along with seasoning to taste. Divide the skirlie between four plates and serve the smoked haddock on top, with a quarter of lemon.

Something
for nothing 2

Cottage Pie

Cottage pie (made with leftover beef) and its close relative shepherd's pie (made with leftover lamb) are classic examples of old-fashioned kitchen housekeeping. They may epitomise kitchen economy but they are, when carefully made, some of the best meals imaginable – rich, satisfying and filling. Using the beef from the Big Meal from Scratch, this has to be one of the best cottage pies Zoe has ever eaten.

It's worth noting that if you use leftover beef or lamb from a roast to make a cottage or shepherd's pie the meat initially toughens on being heated, so it requires at least 1 hour of further cooking to make sure it's tender. If you use meat left over from a braise or pot roast it can be reheated for a shorter time.

If you have no left overs from the Big Meal you can make this cottage pie using beef mince –the end result willl have less texture and intensity but it will be tasty nonetheless. If this is the case, fry 400–500 g beef mince in a little butter and oil until brown then follow the recipe as normal. Replace the beef liquor with the same quantity of chicken or beef stock. Make mash in the normal way but add 1 tbsp horseradish cream at the end (see page 479).

2 medium onions, approx. 240 g
1 tbsp groundnut or grapeseed oil
500 g boiled beef left over from the Big Meal from Scratch
2-3 carrots left over from the Big Meal from Scratch
1 garlic clove
150 ml beef liquor from the Big Meal from Scratch or see above
100 ml (approx.) red wine
2 tbsp tomato ketchup
2 tsp Worcestershire sauce
800 g horseradish mash left over from the Big Meal from Scratch or see above
30 g butter
salt and pepper

To serve
buttered peas or green beans

GET AHEAD PREPARATION (optional)

The whole pie (or just the meat part) can be assembled up to 2 days in advance and heated when required. If you only have a little time:
* Prepare the onions, carrots and garlic.
* Chop the beef into chickpea-sized pieces.

40 minutes before you want to eat

* Preheat the oven to 220°C/425°F/Gas Mark 7.
* Peel and slice the onions. Heat the oil in a casserole dish over a medium heat then add the onions and sweat them for about 7 minutes until they are soft.
* Meanwhile, chop the beef into small pieces. You can use a food processor to do this but be careful not to pulverise the beef to a paste.
* Cut the carrots into half lengthways, and then into 5-mm chunks. Peel and slice the garlic and add it and the carrots to the onions. Cook for 2–3 minutes, stirring all the while.
* When the carrots have warmed through, add the beef. Turn up the heat and cook until it is starting to brown.
* Once the beef has started to brown, add the beef liquor or stock, wine, ketchup and Worcestershire sauce. When the mixture starts to boil, turn the heat down, season with salt and pepper and simmer gently for 10 minutes. Add more stock or water if it looks very dry.
* Before assembling the pie, taste the beef mixture – add more ketchup, Worcestershire sauce or seasoning if necessary. Tip the meat into a pie dish, but if you want to save on washing up, and presentation is not a priority, make the pie in the casserole dish.
* Spread the horseradish mash evenly over the top of the meat. If the mash is very cold it will be hard to spread. If this is the case, warm it through in a pan or microwave with a tablespoon of milk and stir it well before attempting to spread it. Dot the mash with the butter and place the cottage pie in the oven for 10–20 minutes or until the mash has browned and the filling is bubbling.
* Serve with buttered peas or beans.

Seasonal supper

Red Coleslaw with Baked Potatoes

This coleslaw is refreshing, light and zingy – a world away from the soggy gloop found in supermarkets. The recipe below probably makes more than is required for four servings but as it keeps very well in the fridge for a couple of days, we decided to err on the generous side. With a food processor it's incredibly simple to make.

Red coleslaw
450 g (approx.) red cabbage
1 medium red onion, approx. 120 g
2-3 medium carrots, approx. 300 g
1 medium crunchy apple
juice of ½ lemon
1 tbsp pumpkin seeds
1 tbsp sunflower seeds
3 tbsp mayonnaise
3 tbsp natural yoghurt
4-5 sprigs fresh mint
small handful of fresh parsley
salt and pepper

Baked potatoes
8 small baking potatoes, such as Maris Piper, approx. 1 kg
olive oil
150 g Cheddar

GET AHEAD PREPARATION (optional)

The coleslaw can be made up to 2 days in advance. If you only have a little time:
* Prepare the carrots and onion.
* Slice the red cabbage.
* Salt the cabbage, then rinse and dry thoroughly.
* Toast the pumpkin and sunflower seeds.
* Make the dressing.

40 minutes before you want to eat

* Preheat the oven to 190°C/375°F/Gas Mark 5.
* Prick the potatoes with a fork, rub with oil and salt and bake in the oven for 40 minutes.
* Next, start chopping the vegetables. De-core the cabbage and slice very finely, either in a food processor or by hand. Put the sliced cabbage into a colander and sprinkle with 2 teaspoons salt. Mix well and leave the cabbage in a colander while you prepare the rest of the ingredients.
* Peel the onion and slice it very finely. Peel and grate the carrot, either in a food processor or by hand. Peel and quarter the apple and remove the core. Grate the apple into a large bowl, then squeeze over some of the lemon juice to prevent it turning brown. Toss well, then add the carrots and onion.
* Put the pumpkin and sunflower seeds in a small pan over a medium heat so that they toast and start to brown. Make sure they don't burn. As soon as they start to brown remove them from the heat and set aside.
* Next, make the dressing. Mix together the mayonnaise and yoghurt. Add most, but not all, of the remaining lemon juice. Strip the mint and parsley leaves from their stalks and chop them well. Add these to the mayonnaise mixture along with 3–4 pinches of salt and a generous amount of pepper. Mix well and set aside.
* When the cabbage has been salted for about 10 minutes and up to 30 minutes, rinse it quickly under cold water and pat it dry.
* Add cabbage to the onion, carrots and apple. Add the toasted seeds and pour the dressing over the top. Toss very well, season to taste and add the remaining lemon juice if required.
* Grate the cheese.
* Check that the potatoes are cooked all the way through then remove them from the oven. Cut a line down the middle of each one and, using a tea towel to protect your hands, squeeze the potato open. Fluff up the middle using fork. Add a spoonful of the cheese, then a spoonful of coleslaw then another of cheese. Serve the potatoes with extra coleslaw on the side.

Larder feast

Catalan Style Beans and Chorizo

Having a few chorizo knocking about in the fridge is every cook's lifeline – they add a unique paprika and garlic flavour to any dish. Chorizo works especially well with broad beans – there's something about the earthiness of the beans and the piquant kick of the chorizo that is a heavenly combination. This is one of those recipes where a little more or less of any particular ingredient is not crucial, so let the recipe expand or contract as suits your larder. The dish can be ready in around 30 minutes but it can just as easily simmer away gently for up to 45 minutes.

1 tbsp (approx.) olive oil
125 g free-range rindless smoked
 streaky bacon
200 g chorizo
1 medium onion, approx. 120 g
2 garlic cloves
1 × 400 g can whole green beans
 (haricot verts if possible) or
 400g frozen green beans
1 × 200 g can butter beans
400 g frozen broad beans
150 ml white wine

250 ml ham, chicken or
 vegetable stock (fresh or made
 from a stock cube or bouillon
 powder)
1 bay leaf
handful of fresh parsley
 (optional)
salt and pepper

To serve
crusty bread or garlic bread

GET AHEAD PREPARATION (optional)

* Slice the chorizo.
* Prepare the shallots and
 garlic.
* Drain and rinse the canned
 beans.
* Cut the green beans.
* Chop the parsley.

30 minutes before you want to eat

* Heat the oil in a heavy-based pan over a medium heat. Using a pair of scissors cut the bacon into bite-sized pieces straight into the pan. Cook for a couple of minutes while you slice the chorizo.
* Add the chorizo to the pan and cook for 5 minutes until it is slightly browned. While the bacon and chorizo are cooking, peel and slice the onion and peel and crush the garlic.
* Lift the bacon and chorizo from the pan with a slotted spoon and set them aside.
* Put the onions and a little more oil, if necessary, in the pan and cook over a low heat for 7 minutes until soft. Add the garlic and cook for a couple more minutes, stirring from time to time.
* While the onions are cooking, drain and rinse the canned beans. Bundle the green beans and cut them into 1–2 cm pieces.
* When the garlic has cooked for a couple of minutes, add all the beans along with the wine. Bring the wine to the boil and let it bubble away to almost nothing.
* Then add the stock and bay leaf, return the chorizo and bacon to the pan and leave the whole lot to simmer for 15–20 minutes with the lid off. Add more liquid if it seems to be drying up – to serve the beans should be just covered with liquid.
* Meanwhile, roughly chop the parsley, if using.
* After 15 minutes or so add the parsley to the beans and chorizo and season to taste with salt and pepper. Serve with crusty bread or garlic bread.

Two for one

Pistachio Chicken Curry

Pistachio nuts, with their pale green colour and mild distinctive flavour, were first cultivated in Persia – so it makes sense that they work well with the Persian flavours of this delicate chicken recipe. The curry would be good served with basmati rice and, perhaps, a simple dish of wilted spinach.

   The quantities below make enough for eight, so half can be frozen for a later date.

3 medium onions, approx. 360 g
2 tbsp groundnut or grapeseed oil
3–5-cm piece of fresh root ginger
7 green chillies
1½ tsp fennel seeds
6 cardamom pods
2 kg free-range bone-in chicken thighs or 1.5 kg skinless boneless thighs
2 tsp ground coriander
½ tsp ground cumin

pinch of ground cinnamon
½ tsp turmeric
280 ml single cream
150 g shelled pistachio nuts (unsalted)
150 ml natural yoghurt
handful of fresh coriander
salt and pepper

To serve
basmati rice
wilted spinach

GET AHEAD PREPARATION (optional)

The pistachio sauce can be made a day in advance and the chicken prepared and browned a few hours beforehand. They can then be put together to be cooked for 30 minutes. If you only have a little time:
* Prepare the onions, ginger and chillies.
* Remove the skin from the chicken thighs.

1 hour before you want to eat

* Peel and thinly slice the onions. Heat some of the oil in a heavy-based casserole dish over a medium heat and cook the onions until they are soft and starting to brown. This will take about 7–10 minutes.
* Meanwhile, peel and roughly chop the ginger and place it in the bowl of a food processor or liquidiser. Halve, deseed and roughly chop the chillies and add them to the ginger. Use the back of a spoon or a rolling pin to slightly crush the fennel seeds. Open the cardomom pods and remove the seeds.
* Now prepare the chicken. Use a clean tea towel or dry cloth to pull the skin off the chicken thighs. Season the thighs and leave them to one side.
* When the onion has softened, add the fennel and cardomom seeds, ground coriander, cumin, cinnamon and turmeric, and cook over a medium heat for 1–2 minutes. Add the cream and some salt and bring to the boil.
* Once the mixture is boiling, add the spicy onion mixture to the ginger and chillies in the food processor. Add the pistachio nuts and yoghurt and blend to a paste. Add water so that the sauce has the pouring quality of single cream. You can use a hand blender to mix these ingredients if you don't have a food processor (you may need to roughly chop the pistachios first).
* Now brown the chicken thighs. Wipe out the casserole with kitchen paper and add a little oil. Place over a high heat and cook the chicken thighs until they are golden brown. Once they are browned, pour the pistachio and sauce over them. If necessary, add more liquid to cover the chicken, then leave to simmer gently for about 25 minutes, without a lid. While the chicken is gently ticking away, roughly chop the fresh coriander.
* When the thighs are cooked through and tender put half of them in a freezerproof container with half the sauce and set aside to cool and then freeze.
* To serve, stir in the fresh coriander and serve with rice and fresh or frozen spinach wilted in butter and lemon juice.

Lazy day supper – reheating instructions

Remove the curry from the freezer and defrost thoroughly. Then tip it into a casserole and warm slowly over a gentle heat with a lid on. This will take about 25 minutes. If there is a lot of liquid simmer the curry with the lid off for the last 10 minutes of reheating.

Thickening sauces
The two most usual ways of thickening a sauce are by boiling off some of the liquid (reducing) or by thickening the liquid with the addition of flour (making a roux):

Reducing
Reducing the liquid in a recipe means evaporating the excess liquid and intensifying the flavours. Sometimes you're asked to do this on a high heat with a rapid boil, and sometimes on a low heat with a long slow simmer. A low simmer is mainly used if there's meat in the pan – if you boil it rapidly it will become tough. If the sauce is too thin at the end of cooking a casserole or stew, you can always remove the meat, bring the sauce up to a rapid boil and reduce the liquid to the desired consistency, then return the meat to the sauce to warm through.

Making a roux
A roux is a sauce made with flour and it's a technique that comes up time and time again, whether you are cooking cauliflower cheese, fish pie or a soufflé. Making a white sauce or a thickened stock-based sauce is one of the basics of cooking. The technique for making a roux involves melting butter over a medium heat until it is foaming, blending in the flour over a low heat for 2–3 minutes until a smooth paste is formed and finally whisking in milk or stock (ideally warmed and infused with flavours), stirring all the time until the sauce boils and thickens. If the sauce turns lumpy it can be put through a sieve or blended.

November Week 2 – Overview

This is the season for game so a Big Meal from Scratch of Roast Pheasant, Roast Squash, Mash and Greens is just right. Pheasant has lean flesh with a slightly gamey flavour and can be roasted just like a chicken. A pheasant will generally feed two or three people, so to make sure there's ample meat for this meal and a Something for Nothing, the recipe specifies cooking three. If pheasant is difficult to find, or if you prefer, you can use chicken, but the resulting dish will be quite different. Altogether the meal takes 1 hour 40 minutes or 2 hours if you are roasting a chicken.

For a heartening Something for Nothing that's perfect for cold weather, extra meat from the big meal is used for a Pheasant (or Chicken) and Chestnut Soup. Most delicatessens stock packets or cans of cooked chestnuts and supermarkets generally have them in their frozen food sections or with their dry goods. For a super-quick and tasty Something for Nothing, the leftover squash is mixed with feta cheese and turned into a sauce for pasta that takes just 15 minutes to make. The Seasonal Supper of Smoked Haddock with Bacon is warming, straightforward and ready in half an hour. When buying fish, remember to use it within a day or two or place it in the freezer until required. The Larder Feast is an intense and satisfying Tomato Bulghar with sardines and walnut pesto that takes just 20 minutes.

The Two for One this week is a Chinese Braised Lamb – an unusually flavoured casserole but with atypical flavours. Altogether this will take 1½ hours, so plan to cook it when you have plenty of time.

November Week 2	Recipe	Time
Big meal from scratch	Roast pheasant (or chicken) with roast squash, mash and greens	1 hour 40 mins (2 hours)
Something for nothing 1	Squash and feta pasta	15 mins
Something for nothing 2	Nick's Pheasant (or chicken) and chestnut soup	40 mins
Seasonal supper	Smoked haddock with bacon and mustard sauce and spinach	30 mins
Larder feast	Sardines with tomato bulghar and walnut pesto	20 mins
2 for 1	Chinese braised lamb	1½ hours

All recipes serve 4 apart from the 2 for 1 recipe which makes 8 portions

SHOPPING LIST (for 4 people)

Meat and fish
3 pheasants or 1 × 1.8–2 kg free-range
  chicken
12 rashers free-range rindless smoked
  streaky bacon (10 rashers if you are cooking
  a chicken)
500 g (approx.) smoked haddock fillet
1 × 1.4 kg shoulder of lamb or any other good
  cut for slow cooking (ask the butcher to
  bone and cube it)

Dairy
235 g butter
50–60 g Parmesan
200 g feta
100 ml milk and/or cream
250 ml double cream

Fruit and vegetables
1 kg mashing potatoes, such as Maris Piper
  or baking potatoes
2 butternut squash, approx. 600 g each
200 g pumpkin flesh (ideally from a variety
  with green-and-white skin)
4 celery sticks
2 carrots, approx. 200 g
500–600 g (approx.) winter greens, 200–300 g
  if presliced
800 g large leaf spinach or 500 g baby leaf
  spinach
2 green peppers, approx. 300 g
200 g pak choi or other oriental greens
1 large or banana shallot, approx. 60 g
3 medium onions, approx. 420 g
2 medium red onion, approx. 300 g
4 spring onions
8 garlic cloves
4-cm piece of fresh root ginger
small bunch fresh flatleaf parsley
small handful of fresh curly parsley
3–4 sprigs fresh fresh thyme
2 sprigs fresh sage
2½ lemons
handful fresh basil leaves

Basics
60 ml groundnut or grapeseed oil
135 ml olive oil
1 tbsp tomato purée
200 ml chicken or ham stock (fresh or made
  from a stock cube or bouillon powder)
1.45 litres chicken or vegetable stock (fresh
  or made from a stock cube or bouillon
  powder)
2 tsp Dijon mustard
1 tbsp plain flour
2 bay leaves
60 g light brown soft sugar
salt and pepper

Store cupboard
400 g penne or fusilli pasta
300 g bulghar wheat (ideally coarse grain)
50 g pearl barley
100 g cooked peeled chestnuts
1 × 400 g can chopped tomatoes
2 × 120 g cans sardines in oil
1 tbsp capers
100 g shelled walnut halves
2 tbsp smooth peanut butter
1 tbsp hoisin plum sauce
2 tbsp sherry or white wine vinegar
3 tbsp light soy sauce
½ cinnamon stick
2 star anise
1 tsp ground allspice
250 ml red wine or Calvados
100 ml sherry or white wine
300 ml white wine

Quick option (for Sardines with Tomato
  Bulghar)
2 tbsp pesto; remove walnuts, 2 garlic
  cloves, ½ lemon, basil leaves, capers from
  the shopping list

Serving suggestions
green salad ingredients (Squash and Feta
  Pasta)
crusty bread, watercress, rocket or other
  peppery or bitter leaves, olive oil, lemon
  juice (Pheasant/Chicken and Chestnut Soup)
potatoes for baking or boiling (Smoked
  Haddock with Bacon, Mustard Sauce and
  Spinach)
dried egg noodles (Chinese Braised Lamb)

To download or print out this shopping list,
please visit www.thekitchenrevolution.co.uk/
November/Week2

Big meal from scratch

Roast Pheasant (or Chicken) and Roast Squash with Mash and Greens

Pheasant in season is cheap and bountiful, and is usually available in bigger supermarkets. It does have a reputation, for being dry but when a good bird is properly cooked, the slightly gamey lean meat is delicious. If, however, pheasant doesn't appeal, this recipe works just as well with chicken.

To ensure full flavour and tenderness pheasant needs to be well hung, just on the edge of turning 'high', and must be cooked quickly in a hot oven. There is enough meat on a pheasant to feed two people.

The vegetables accompanying the pheasant are plentiful in November. The squash roast underneath the birds so they will soak up any juices and add flavour to the gravy.

After you have finished, it is really worth using the left over pheasant (or chicken) carcasses to make a stock. This can be used as the basis for the Something for Nothing soup and will create a superb flavour. See page 495 for making stock.

Roast pheasant or chicken
3 pheasants or 1 x 1.8-2 kg free-range chicken; includes
  1 pheasant or 250 g extra chicken meat for the pheasant (or chicken) and chestnut soup
100 g butter
6 rashers free-range rindles smoked streaky bacon or 4 rashers if you are cooking chicken
250 ml red wine or Calvados
salt and pepper

Roast squash
1.2 kg butternut squash, includes 600 g extra for the squash and feta pasta
200 g pumpkin flesh (ideally from a variety with green-and-

white skin)
1 medium red onion, approx. 120 g
2 tbsp olive oil
3-4 sprigs fresh thyme

Mash
1 kg mashing potatoes, such as Maris Piper or baking potatoes
100 ml milk/and or cream
60 g (approx.) butter

Greens
500-600 g (approx.) winter greens, 200-300 g if presliced; includes double quantities for the pheasant and chestnut soup

GET AHEAD PREPARATION (optional)

* Prepare the pheasants or chicken for the oven.
* Prepare the squash and greens.
* Prepare the potatoes and cover with water until required.

1 hour 20 minutes before you want to eat prepare the squash and pheasant (1 hour 40 minutes if cooking chicken)

* Preheat the oven to 220°C/425°F/Gas Mark 7.
* Peel and deseed the squash and pumpkin. Chop them into 2-3-cm chunks (you'll need a sharp knife for this job) and put on the bottom of a roasting tin large enough to hold them and the birds. If necessary, divide the mixture between two tins. Peel the onion, cut it into eighths and add it to the squash. Add the oil, salt and pepper and thyme and mix well.
* Now place the pheasants or chicken on top of the squash and pumpkin. Rub them with some of the butter – it's messy but it will improve their flavour and texture so is well worth doing. Put a good blob of butter in the cavity of each bird and season with salt and pepper. Put two of the rashers of bacon over the breast of each pheasant or four rashers over the chicken breast.

1 hour before you want to eat (1 hour 20 minutes if cooking chicken)

* Roast the birds in the oven for 20 minutes. After 20 minutes remove the bacon rashers, turn the oven down to 180°C/350°F/Gas Mark 4 and cook for another 20 minutes for pheasants (or 1 hour for chicken). If you are roasting the pheasants in two different tins and at two heights in the oven, swap them round at this point. Keep the bacon rashers to serve later.

40 minutes before you want to eat cook the potatoes

* Peel the potatoes and cut them into pieces the size of a small egg. Place them in a large pan, cover with water and add a good dose of salt. Put over a medium heat and bring to the boil. Simmer the potatoes for 15-20 minutes or until they are just cooked.
* Wash the greens, remove any thick stalks and shred the leaves. Place the greens in about 2 cm of water in a steamer with a lid.

20 minutes before you want to eat cook the greens, make the mash and the gravy

* The birds should be cooked by now so remove them from the oven. If you are cooking a chicken check whether it is done by inserting a skewer or sharp knife into its thigh. If the juices run clear it is cooked – if not, return it to the oven for another 20 minutes. This is less crucial for the pheasants, which are best served slightly pink.
* Put one of the pheasants to one side for use later in the week.
* Place the remaining pheasants or the chicken on a carving board and set aside to rest in a warm place for 20 minutes. Turn the oven to very low, or switch it off, and put half the roast squash and pumpkin into a serving dish, cover and return it to the oven to keep warm. Set the rest of the squash and pumpkin aside to cool. Put some plates and serving dishes in the oven to warm.
* Meanwhile, add some salt to the greens, place them over a high heat and cook them for 7–10 minutes.
* When the potatoes are cooked, drain them into a colander. Put the milk and/or cream and the butter into the empty potato pan and place over a low heat so that the butter melts and the milk heats. While this is happening, put the potatoes in the colander over the pan – this helps dry the potatoes and prevents the mash being sloppy.
* When the milk and/or cream is hot and the butter has melted, add the potatoes and mash them well with a traditional masher or, for a really smooth texture, pass the potatoes through a mouli-legumes or potato ricer.
* Taste and season as necessary, then turn the mash into a serving dish, cover it with a butter paper or some greaseproof paper and keep it warm while you make the gravy.
* Next make the gravy. Place the roasting tin over a medium heat. Add the wine or Calvados and stir well, scraping the bottom of the pan – a whisk does this very effectively. Let the gravy bubble for a couple of minutes.
* The greens will be ready by now, so drain well, saving a cupful of their cooking liquor to put in the gravy. Season with salt and pepper and turn them into a warmed serving dish. Add the reserved water from the greens to the gravy, stir once or twice and season to taste. Leave to simmer while the pheasants or chicken are carved.
* If you cooked a chicken set about one-third of the meat aside – brown meat is best.
* Pour the gravy into a jug and put the potatoes into a warmed serving dish. Put everything on the table and let people help themselves.

Afterwards

Strip the meat (250-350 g) from the pheasant or the remaining chicken. Put the meat, squash (500 g), greens (100-200 g) and gravy in separate containers, cover and refrigerate for use later. The carcasses will make excellent stock (see page 495).

Something for nothing 1

Squash and Feta Pasta

This recipe is simple to prepare and full of flavour. Adding feta and sage to the squash left over from the Big Meal from Scratch creates a creamy rich sauce to accompany pasta. If you don't have any remaining squash replace it with 600 g butternut squash peeled, deseeded and chopped into 2–3-cm pieces, then steamed for 10–15 minutes.

400 g penne or fusilli pasta
1 medium red onion, approx. 120 g
2 tbsp olive oil
2 garlic cloves
2 sprigs fresh sage
200 g feta
small handful of fresh parsley
500 g (approx.) roasted squash left over from the Big Meal from Scratch or see above
juice of ½ lemon
50–60 g Parmesan
salt and pepper

To serve
green salad

GET AHEAD PREPARATION (optional)

* Prepare the onion and garlic.
* Crumble or cut the feta.
* Chop the parsley.
* Grate the Parmesan.

15 minutes before you want to eat

* Put the penne or fusilli on to cook according to the instructions on the packet (usually 8–10 minutes).
* Meanwhile, soften the onion. Heat the oil in a heavy-based pan over a medium-low heat. Peel and slice the onion, add it to the pan and stir for about 1–2 minutes then cover the pan and leave the onion to soften for 7–10 minutes, stirring from time to time.
* While the onion is cooking, peel and slice the garlic and roughly tear the sage leaves in half. Crumble the feta or cut it into smallish (1–2-cm) chunks, and roughly chop the parsley.
* When the onion begins to soften, add the garlic and cook for a further couple of minutes, stirring regularly to prevent burning.
* Add the sage leaves and cook for a minute, then add the squash and stir a couple of times to ensure the heat distributes evenly. Season with salt and pepper and the lemon juice.
* Grate the Parmesan. Drain the pasta and add the squash, feta and the parsley. Mix well and serve with the grated Parmesan.

Nick's Pheasant (or Chicken) and Chestnut Soup

Pheasant or chicken soup is just what's called for when the evenings start to turn chilly.

Soup is often best when it's made from leftovers. For a hearty soup like this use the recipe below as a general guide but be led by your instinct, taste buds and the contents of your fridge.

The soup is given extra body by the addition of pearl barley. The chestnuts add a nutty sweetness that works particularly well with the gamey flavours of pheasant. Cooked and peeled chestnuts are sold by most supermarkets but if they are impossible to find, the soup will work fine without them.

This recipe was devised and perfected by Nick Lawson.

If you haven't cooked the Big Meal from Scratch roast 3 or 4 chicken legs in the oven for 20 minutes, then strip them of meat.

50 g pearl barley
25 g butter
1 tbsp groundnut or grapeseed oil
1 medium onion
4 celery sticks
2 carrots
2 garlic cloves
1 lemon
1 tsp ground allspice
any gravy left over from the Big Meal from Scratch, made up to 800 ml with pheasant or chicken stock from the Big Meal or 800 ml chicken stock (made from a stock cube or bouillon powder)
1 bay leaf

100 ml sherry or white wine
100 ml double cream
100 g whole cooked peeled chestnuts
250–350 g (approx.) cooked pheasant or chicken meat left over from the Big Meal from Scratch or see above
small handful of fresh flatleaf parsley
200 g (approx.) cooked greens left over from the Big Meal from Scratch or 300 g greens sliced finely and cooked
salt and pepper

To serve
crusty bread and watercress dressed with olive oil and lemon juice

GET AHEAD PREPARATION (optional)

The soup can be made 2 days in advance and reheated gently when required. If you only have a little time:
* Cook the pearl barley.
* Prepare the onion, carrots and celery.
* Shred the meat.
* Chop the parsley.

40 minutes before you want to eat

* Place the pearl barley in a large pan with a lid. Pour in boiling water to just cover the barley, add a little salt and bring back to the boil. Cover and leave to simmer for 30 minutes.
* Heat the butter and oil in a large heavy-based pan over a medium heat. Peel and finely chop the onion, add it to the pan and let it soften for 5 minutes. Trim, wash and slice the celery, and peel and finely chop the carrots.
* When the onion is soft, add the carrots and celery to the pan and cook for another 5 minutes. Peel and crush the garlic.
* Once the celery and carrots have softened a little, add the garlic and allspice to the pan and cook for a few minutes. Add 700 ml of the stock and bring to a simmer. Add a small length of zest from the lemon and the bay leaf, cook gently for 15 minutes.
* Place the remaining stock in a small pan and add the sherry or wine and cream and crumble in the chestnuts. Cover and simmer gently for 10 minutes.
* Shred the meat and chop the parsley. Squeeze the juice from the lemon and shred the greens.
* Once the cream and chestnuts have been simmering for 10 minutes, add the meat, parsley and lemon juice. Whizz this mixture to a smooth purée in a food processor.
* Add the purée to the soup and season to taste.
* Drain the cooked barley and add it to the soup with the greens. Heat through really gently for 5–7 minutes. If necessary thin it with a little hot water or stock.
* Serve the soup with dressed watercress and crusty bread.

Seasonal supper

Smoked Haddock with Bacon and Mustard Sauce and Spinach

Smoked haddock with a bacon and mustard sauce is a classic combination. The haddock in this recipe is cooked very simply by covering it with water, bringing it to the boil then immediately removing it from the heat so that the fish poaches very, very gently in the hot liquid. This ensures that it cooks but doesn't overcook.

Whether you buy dyed (yellow) or undyed haddock makes no difference to the taste, but as the colour adds no flavour it seems rather superfluous.

Smoked haddock
500 g (approx.) smoked haddock
   fillet
salt

Bacon and mustard sauce
1 large or banana shallot, approx
   60g
6 rashers free-range rindless
   dry-cure streaky bacon
   (smoked or unsmoked)
25 g butter
2 tbsp sherry vinegar or 3 tbsp
   white wine vinegar
300 ml (approx.) white wine

200 ml ham or chicken stock
   (fresh or made from a stock
   cube or bouillon powder)
150 ml double cream
2 tsp Dijon mustard

Savoy cabbage
800 g large leaf sinach or 500 g
   baby leaf spinach
25 g butter
pepper

To serve
jacket or boiled potatoes

GET AHEAD PREPARATION (optional)

The sauce can be made a day in advance and kept in the fridge, then heated very gently when required. If you only have a little time:
* Prepare the shallot.
* Cut the bacon.
* Shred the cabbage.

30 minutes before you want to eat

* Start by making the sauce. Peel and finely slice the shallot and cut the bacon into 2–3-cm pieces. Melt the butter in a heavy-based frying pan over a medium heat, add the shallot and bacon and fry for 5–7 minutes. Stir from time to time to prevent them sticking.
* When the bacon is cooked and the shallots are soft, increase the heat and add the vinegar. Reduce it until there is almost no liquid remaining. Then add the wine and reduce until about one-third remains.
* Once the wine in the sauce has reduced, add the stock, turn up the heat and reduce to half once more.
* Meanwhile, cook the haddock. Cut the haddock into four fillets and place in a pan with a lid. Cover with cold water, add a pinch of salt and bring to the boil. The minute the water is boiling, remove the pan from the heat and set aside for 5 minutes while you finish the sauce.
* When the stock has reduced, turn down the heat, add the cream to the pan and beat in the mustard. Cook over a medium heat for 2–3 minutes then season to taste with salt and pepper. Either serve the sauce as it is or, if you would like a smooth sauce, whizz it in a food processor or with a hand blender for a minute.
* Meanwhile, cook the spinach. Place in a pan with a little water, the butter and a generous pinch of salt, then cover and cook until wilted over a gentle heat.
* To serve, carefully life the haddock fillets out of the cooking liquor, taking care to keep them whole. Put them on individual plates with the spinach and pour the sauce generously over both. Serve with jacket or boiled potatoes.

Larder feast

Sardines with Tomato Bulghar and Walnut Pesto

In this recipe canned sardines are quickly fried and served on rich, warm bulghar wheat with a lemon and walnut pesto as a dressing.

Bulghar wheat is most commonly eaten as tabbouleh, but it works well when cooked in a tomato stock and accompanied by the powerful flavours of garlic, lemon, caper and walnut. Bulghar wheat comes in a variety of different size grains. The coarse grain retains a bite and is less likely to turn into a sloppy mush, so use it if you can find it.

This is especially nice if you have the ingredients and time to make the walnut pesto from scratch, but if you don't you can replace it with 2 heaped tablespoons of ready-made basil and pine nut pesto.

Tomato bulgar	Pesto	Sardines
1 litre chicken or vegetable stock (made from a stock cube or bouillon powder)	100 g shelled walnut halves	2 × 120 g cans sardines in oil
	2 garlic cloves	1 tbsp plain flour
	juice of ½ lemon	salt and pepper
1 × 400 g can chopped tomatoes	5 tbsp olive oil	
1 tbsp tomato purée	handful basil leaves	
1 bay leaf	1 tbsp capers	GET AHEAD PREPARATION (optional)
½ tsp light brown soft sugar	or	* Prepare the pesto.
300 g bulghar wheat (ideally coarse grain)	2 tbsp ready-made pesto	

20 minutes before you want to eat

* Place the stock, tomatoes, tomato purée, bay leaf, sugar and 1 teaspoon salt in a pan with a lid and bring to the boil over a high heat. Stir well so that the tomatoes break up and are incorporated into the liquid.
* Rinse the bulghar under cold running water and tip into the pan with the boiling tomato stock. Stir once or twice, remove the pan from the heat, cover with a lid and leave for about 15–20 minutes or until all the liquid is absorbed by the wheat.
* While the bulghar is cooking prepare the walnut pesto. Chop or bash the walnuts into small pieces – the easiest way to do this is to wrap the walnuts in a clean tea towel and give them a good bashing with a rolling pin or the bottom of a heavy pan. Tip the walnuts into a bowl. Peel the garlic and crush into the bowl containing the nuts. Add the lemon juice and half the oil and stir well. Roughly tear the basil leaves and add them to the nut mixture. Roughly chop the capers and mix them, along with a pinch of salt and a few grinds of pepper, to the nuts.
* When the bulghar has absorbed all the liquid, remove the lid from the pan and stir the bulghar to separate the grains. It should be moist but not soggy. If there is surplus liquid, tip it out, place the pan over a medium heat and allow any remaining liquid to evaporate. Stir constantly while doing this to prevent the bulghar sticking and burning. Cover the bulghar with a lid to keep warm while you cook the sardines.
* Drain the sardines and pat them dry with kitchen paper. Season the flour well with salt and pepper and toss the sardines in it. Heat about 1 tablespoon of the oil in a frying pan over a medium heat and when it is hot add the sardines. Fry them for about 2 minutes on each side until warmed through and slightly crispy.
* To serve, add the remaining oil to the bulghar, taste for seasoning, stir well and divide between four large bowls. Place two sardine pieces on top of each serving with a generous helping of the walnut pesto.

Two for one

Chinese Braised Lamb

This dish is essentially a lamb stew with Chinese seasonings and flavours. It takes a while to prepare but once everything is in the pot it's just a case of leaving it to its own devices. We suggest eating it with egg noodles and pak choi, but any Chinese greens would be fine.

The recipe is adapted from a book that was very popular in Rosie's household when she was growing up – *Sainsbury's Book of Casseroles* by Norma McMillan. It makes enough for eight, so that half can be frozen for a later date.

Chinese braised lamb
groundnut or grapeseed oil
1.4 kg shoulder of lamb or other
  good cut for slow cooking (ask
  the butcher to bone and cube it)
2 medium onions, approx. 240 g
4 garlic cloves
2 green peppers, approx. 300 g
4-cm piece of fresh root ginger
450 ml chicken stock (fresh or
  made from a stock cube or
  bouillon powder)
50 g light brown soft sugar

3 tbsp light soy sauce
½ cinnamon stick
2 star anise
2 tbsp smooth peanut butter
1 tbsp hoisin plum sauce
4 spring onions

Serve with
noodles, pak choi

GET AHEAD PREPARATION (optional)

The entire dish can be made 2 days in advance and warmed through. If you only have a little time:
* Prepare the onions, garlic and green peppers.
* Cut the ginger into rounds.
* Trim the pak choi.

1½ hours before you want to eat

* First brown the lamb. Heat the oil in a large heavy-based casserole with a lid. Season the lamb with salt and pepper and fry it very quickly, stirring most of the time, until it is browned. While the lamb is browning, peel and finely slice the onions and garlic, and deseed and slice the green peppers. Cut the ginger into rounds.
* Lift out the browned lamb and add the onions. Turn the heat up and let them brown for a couple of minutes, then add the peppers, garlic and ginger and stir-fry for 5 minutes. Return the lamb to the pan and mix well.
* Now add the stock, sugar, soy sauce, cinnamon, star anise, peanut butter and hoisin sauce. Bring everything to the boil. Cover and leave to simmer over the lowest possible heat for about 1 hour until the lamb is tender. Check the lamb after 45 minutes and remove the lid if there seems to be a lot of liquid.
* In the meantime, trim and slice the spring onions and trim the pak choi.

* When the lamb is tender, season it to taste, remove it from the heat and leave it with a lid on to keep warm while you cook the accompaniments.
* Spoon half the lamb out of the casserole and set it aside to cool for freezing. Add the spring onions to the remaining lamb.
* Put a pile of noodles on each plate, place the lamb on top of and serve with the pak choi tossed in a little soy sauce and a squeeze of lemon.
* Freeze the rest of the lamb once it is cold.

Lazy day supper – reheating instructions

Defrost the braised lamb thoroughly. Place the lamb in a pan and reheat over a low heat for 25–30 minutes. Cook noodles and pak choi and serve as above.

Stock

A good stock, rich with flavour, brings depth and roundness to a recipe – but this is rarely achieved with the average overprocessed stock cube. If you can, we would strongly recommend using leftover bones to make your own stock (see below); it involves little or no preparation and the stock can be left to cook on the hob. Life, however, has a habit of getting in the way of good intentions. Luckily, there are a range of alternatives for those who haven't been organised enough to make their own. Fresh stock is readily available in supermarkets. Some supermarkets also do a range of vacuum-packed stocks, with a longer shelf life. Stock cubes tend to have a very distinctive, basic flavour, but there are some varieties that have a bit more to offer. Kallo do a range of organic stock cubes that are pretty good, but the best alternative we've found to fresh stock is a vegetable bouillon powder – Marigold is a good brand.

Making stock
This recipe can be expanded or contracted to suit what is to hand. (It is not, however, a final resting place for everything that has been lurking in the fridge or larder for weeks).

1 chicken or other poultry carcass (skin or fatty bits will not enhance the stock)
2 large onions, peeled and quartered
1 leek, roughly chopped and thoroughly washed
1 medium carrot, peeled and roughly chopped
2 celery sticks, washed and roughly chopped
large glass of white wine
4 garlic cloves, roughly crushed (no need to remove the skin)
a few sprigs of fresh thyme and rosemary
a few fresh parsley stalks
2 bay leaves

Place all the ingredients in a large pan and cover with water. Bring to the boil, then turn the heat down to the barest simmer, skim off any scum and leave to bubble gently for about an hour. Check the stock at regular intervals, to skim or to add a cupful of water if it is getting dry. Skimming helps to keep the stock clear and clean tasting. Leave it uncovered or it will become murky. An hour and half later, strain the stock through a fine sieve into a container. It will keep in the fridge for 3–4 days and freezes well.

If you don't have a chicken carcass, you can use about 1 kg chicken wings.

For a darker stock, use beef, veal or lamb bones, and brown them and all the vegetables in a hot oven. Then simmer them, as above, with red wine and 1 tablespoon tomato purée or a couple of ripe tomatoes for 2–3 hours.

November Week 3 – Overview

Countering any wintry tendencies towards eating too much meat, this week's Big Meal from Scratch recipe is for Brill with Prawn Bisque, Citrus Onions and New Potatoes. Brill is not always available but can easily be replaced by another flat, white fish such as plaice. As with all fish and shellfish, make sure to use the brill and prawns within a day or two of purchase or store them in the freezer until required.

For a Something for Nothing, the brill and prawn bisque is good enough to utilise again, this time in a simple Linguine with Tomato Prawn Sauce which takes about 20 minutes to make. The leftover citrus onions from the big meal are made into a Cheese and Onion Bread Pudding that's just what's required at the end of a long and weary day. Altogether this takes 40 minutes to make – 20 minutes assembly and 20 minutes in the oven.

Sometimes familiar food is the best and it's difficult to better Mushrooms on Toast, particularly when they incorporate pine nuts, garlic and lots of butter. This simple Seasonal Supper can be ready in 25 minutes. For a healthy but satisfying supper look to the Spinach and Chickpea Soup. Made almost entirely from larder ingredients this takes 35 minutes and is very straightforward and very good.

For a meaty end to the week the Two for One is South American Beef Hotpot. From start to finish this will take 2 hours to cook, including half an hour of preparation so it is definitely one to save for when there's plenty of time available.

November Week 3	Recipe	Time
Big meal from scratch	Brill with prawn bisque, citrus onions and new potatoes	1¼ hours
Something for nothing 1	Cheese and onion bread pudding	40 mins
Something for nothing 2	Linguine with tomato prawn sauce	20 mins
Seasonal supper	Mushrooms on toast with rocket salad	25 mins
Larder feast	Spinach and chickpea soup	35 mins
2 for 1	South American beef hotpot	2 hours

All recipes serve 4 apart from the 2 for 1 recipe which makes 8 portions

SHOPPING LIST (for 4 people)

Meat and fish
4 x 175-200 g thick pieces of brill or other
flat fish fillets
600 g large raw shell-on Atlantic prawns
1.25 kg stewing steak, cut into small even-
sized pieces
500 g piece of chorizo

Dairy
160 g butter
142 ml soured cream
275-300 ml double cream
170 g (approx.) blue cheese (Roquefort would
be good)
30 g Parmesan

Fruit and vegetables
800 g new potatoes
1 small bulb fennel, approx. 150 g
5 carrots, approx. 500 g
4 large lettuce leaves (ideally cos or Webb)
600 g mushrooms (a mixture of button,
chestnut, oyster -whatever is around)
1 medium onion, approx. 120 g
16 medium red onions, approx. 2 kg
4 large or banana shallots, approx. 240g
16 garlic cloves
100 g rocket
1 large bunch chives
4 sprigs fresh dill
1 large bunch fresh parsley
4 sprigs fresh rosemary
1½ lemons (½ optional)
400 g frozen spinach

Basics
30 ml groundnut or grapeseed oil
225 ml olive oil
10 slices rustic bread, approx. 200 g (such as
pain de campagne or pane rustica)
4 large or 8 small thick slices white toasting
bread
1 tsp light brown soft sugar
1 bay leaf
200 ml fish stock (fresh or made from a stock
cube or bouillon powder)
400 ml chicken or vegetable stock (fresh or
can be made with a stock cube)
salt and pepper

Store cupboard
350-400 g linguine
2 x 400 g cans chopped tomatoes
1 x 400 g can cherry tomatoes
4 x 400 g cans chickpeas
1 x 330-340 g can sweetcorn
1 tbsp cider or sherry vinegar
30 g pine nuts (you can buy them ready
toasted)

20 g pumpkin seeds
20 g sunflower seeds
2-3 blades of mace
1 tbsp paprika
1 tbsp ground cumin
1 tsp crushed dried chillies
pinch of saffron threads
550 ml white wine
650 ml red wine

Serving suggestions
watercress or beetroot salad ingredients
(Cheese and Onion Bread Pudding)
butternut squash, tortillas or other
flatbreads, green salad ingredients,
avocado, ½ lime (South American Beef
Hotpot)

To download or print out this shopping list,
please visit www.thekitchenrevolution.co.uk/
November/Week3

**Big meal
from scratch**

Brill with Prawn Bisque, Citrus Onions and New Potatoes

For this recipe the delicate flavour and texture of a flat fish like brill is protected by being wrapped in a softened lettuce leaf, then gently poached in butter and wine in the oven. The fish parcel is served with a bisque or sauce made from fresh prawns, fennel, shallots and herbs. This recipe works well with the hardier lettuce leaves that are still around at this time of year. Chard or spinach leaves would also work well. Accompanying this is a simple dish of baked red onions and new potatoes. Make sure you buy skinned fish fillets unless you are very adept with a knife. If brill is unavailable, replace it with another flat white fish such as plaice.

The extra citrus onions are used for Cheese and Onion Bread Pudding later in the week, and the prawn bisque is used for Linguine with Tomato Prawn Sauce.

Brill
4 large lettuce leaves (ideally cos or Webb)
4 x 175-200 g thick pieces of brill or other flat fish fillets,
4 sprigs fresh dill
small handful of fresh flatleaf parsley
30 g approx. butter
150 ml white wine
salt and pepper

Prawn bisque (includes double quantities for the linguine with tomato prawn sauce)
600 g large raw shell-on prawns
groundnut or grapeseed oil
2 large or banana shallots, approx. 120 g
1 small bulb fennel, approx. 150 g
1 medium carrot, approx. 100 g

400 ml white wine
200 ml fish stock (fresh or made from a stock cube or bouillon powder)
1 bay leaf
2-3 blades of mace
275-300 ml double cream

Citrus onions
12 medium red onions, approx. 1.5 kg; includes 5 extra (600 g) for the cheese and onion bread pudding
3 tbsp olive oil
juice of 1 lemon
generous handful parsley

New potatoes
800 g new potatoes
1 small bunch chives
20 g approx. butter

GET AHEAD PREPARATION (optional)

The prawn stock for the bisque can be made a day in advance and reheated when required. If you only have a little time:
* Prepre the onions, shallots, carrot and fennel.
* Peel the prawns and keep the shells and shelled prawns in the fridge until required.
* Prepare the potatoes and cover with water until required.

1¼ hours before you want to eat roast the onions

* Preheat the oven to 200°C/400°F/Gas Mark 6.
* Peel the onions and cut them into 1-cm thick slices. Oil a large roasting tin with some of the oil, add the onions, season them with salt and pepper and drizzle more oil over the top.
* Place the onions in the oven for 10–15 minutes until they start to brown, then turn the oven down to 160°C/325°F/Gas Mark 3 and continue cooking the onions for 40–50 minutes until they are meltingly soft.

45 minutes before you want to eat prepare the bisque and the fish

* Peel the prawns and keep their shells. Put the peeled prawns back in the fridge.
* Splash a little oil into a large pan over a medium heat, and while it heats up peel and roughly chop the shallots. Add the shallots to the pan, turn down the heat and cook gently. Meanwhile, trim and roughly chop the fennel, and peel and chop the carrot; don't worry too much about size, as the vegetables will be strained out later.
* Add the fennel and carrot to the pan and stir for 1–2 minutes. Next, add the prawn shells to the pan and stir until they start to turn pink.
* At this point, turn up the heat, pour in 250 ml of the wine and bring to the boil. Turn the heat down low and simmer for 2 minutes, then add the stock, bay leaf and mace. Let the shell and vegetable stock simmer for 25 minutes.
* Meanwhile, prepare the fish. Take the largest four lettuce leaves available and trim off any thick stalks. Place the trimmed leaves in a deep-sided flat dish, and pour boiling water over them so that they soften. When the leaves have been sitting in hot water for a couple of minutes run them under cold water. Lay the leaves out flat on a tray and pat dry.

* Lay a fish fillet on each lettuce leaf. Remove any thick stalks from the dill and parsley. Add the stalks to the shell and vegetable stock, roughly chop the dill and parsley leaves and scatter them over the brill with a good dose of seasoning. Wrap the brill in the lettuce leaves to make four parcels, tucking the ends underneath.

25 minutes before you want to eat

* Wash the potatoes and if any are larger than bite-sized cut them in half. Place the potatoes in a pan of salted water and bring to the boil over a high heat, then turn the heat down and simmer gently for 10–15 minutes until the potatoes are cooked.

20 minutes before you want to eat cook the brill and finish the bisque

* Melt the butter in a large ovenproof casserole with a lid over a medium heat. When the butter is foaming add the brill parcels, seam-side down. After a minute add the remaining wine and season with salt and pepper. Put the lid on and place the casserole in the oven for 15–20 minutes.
* Take the onions out of the oven – by now they will be soft and a slightly browned. Place the softened onions in a flat dish and dress them with the lemon juice, remaining oil and the parsley. Leave them to sit at room temperature while the remaining dishes are completed.
* To finish the prawn bisque, strain the stock through a fine sieve into a bowl. Press the solid contents in the sieve to extract all their flavour. Rinse the stock pan, dry it with kitchen paper and tip the strained stock back into it. Place over a gentle heat, add the cream and simmer until the sauce has a consistency to your liking.
* Check the brill by inserting a knife into the middle of one of the parcels. If the knife meets no resistance the fish is ready. Turn the oven off, lift the parcels on to a serving dish and return them to the oven to keep warm. Pour any liquid from the casserole into the simmering sauce.
* Add the prawns to the sauce so that they cook through. Take care not to overcook them as they will turn rubbery.
* By now the potatoes should be ready. Chop the chives, then drain the potatoes well and return them to the pan. Add the butter and chives, season and turn into a serving dish.
* Taste the prawn bisque and season as necessary. Set half the bisque aside.
* To serve, spoon the remaining prawn bisque over the fish parcels and let everyone help themselves to the citrus onions and new potatoes.

Afterwards

Strain the remaining prawn bisque and put the prawns, liquor and citrus onions in separate containers, cover and refrigerate for use later in the week. Ideally you will have 250–300 ml bisque, several prawns and 300 g citrus onions.

Something for nothing 1

Cheese and Onion Bread Pudding

Savoury bread puddings are easy to make and usually very popular. This one, based on a French panade, has a cheese and onion flavour and is robust and warming – just right for a cold night. If you don't have any citrus onions from the Big Meal from Scratch replace them with 5 medium red onions, peeled, sliced and gently fried in 1 tablespoon olive oil until they are soft.

50 g butter
300 g (approx.) citrus onions left over from the Big Meal from Scratch or see above
2 garlic cloves
2 sprigs fresh rosemary
150 ml red wine
250 ml chicken or vegetable stock (fresh or made from a stock cube or bouillon powder)
8 x ½–1-cm slices rustic bread, approx. 200 g (such as pain de campagne or pane rustica)
olive oil
170 g (approx.) blue cheese (Roquefort would be good)
salt and pepper

To serve
watercress or beetroot salad with poppy seeds

GET AHEAD PREPARATION (optional)

The entire dish can be prepared a day in advance. If you only have a little time:
* Peel and crush the garlic.
* Strip and chop the rosemary leaves.

40 minutes before you want to eat

* Preheat the oven to 180°C/350°F/Gas Mark 4.
* Heat the butter in a heavy-based pan and add the onions. Warm them over a medium to high heat for a few minutes. Meanwhile, peel and crush the garlic, strip the rosemary leaves from their stalks and chop them roughly.
* Add the garlic to the onions and let it cook for 2 minutes. Then add the rosemary leaves and give them a good stir before pouring in the wine. Bring the wine to the boil and let it simmer for 2 minutes. Lift half the contents of the pan out into a small bowl. Add the stock to the pan and bring it to the boil, then leave it to simmer while you prepare the bread.
* Oil a large baking sheet, place the slices of bread on top and crisp them in the oven for 5 minutes.
* Now build the bread pudding. When the bread is crisp, break each slice into 4-cm squares. Use one-third of the bread to line the bottom of an ovenproof dish about 25 cm square or in diameter and 10 cm deep. Spoon over half of the onions you set aside in the bowl, season well and crumble over one-third the cheese. Follow with another layer of one-third of the bread, the remaining onions you set aside, more seasoning and another third of the cheese. Finally cover with the remaining bread. Pour over the onion and stock mixture until the bread is just visible. Season well and crumble over the remaining cheese.
* Place in the oven for 20–25 minutes until the top is browned and the liquid has been absorbed.
* Serve in bowls with peppery watercress or a simple beetroot salad scattered with a few poppy seeds.

Linguine with Tomato Prawn Sauce

Sometimes the simplest and quickest pasta dishes are the best. This one combines the prawn bisque made for the Big Meal from Scratch with tomatoes and white wine. If you don't have any leftover bisque it will take you an extra 20 minutes to make the sauce – just halve the quantities for the prawn bisque in the big meal and make it according to the recipe. Either way, this will be very quick to assemble with absolutely minimal cooking. As with most of our recipes the quantities here are approximate, so feel free to add or subtract as necessary and to your taste.

1 tbsp olive oil
1 large or banana shallot,
  approx. 30 g
2 garlic cloves
1 x 400 g can cherry tomatoes
140 ml (approx.) white wine
350–400 g linguine
250–300 g prawn bisque left over
  from the Big Meal from Scratch
  or see above
prawns from the Big Meal or see
  above
1 small bunch chives
½ lemon (optional)
salt and black pepper

GET AHEAD PREPARATION (optional)

The sauce can be cooked in a day
in advance and gently warmed
through when required. If you
only have a little time:
* Prepare the shallots and
  garlic.
* Peel the tomatoes.
* Chop the chives.

*20 minutes before
you want to eat*

* First prepare the sauce. Put the oil in a heavy-based pan over a medium heat, and while it's heating peel and finely slice the shallot. Add the shallot to the pan, turn down the heat and let it soften for a few minutes.
* Meanwhile, peel and finely chop or crush the garlic. Drain the tomatoes and roughly chop.
* When the shallot is soft, add the garlic and stir for 1–2 minutes so that the garlic starts to soften. Don't let it turn brown or burn as this will add a bitter flavour.
* Next, add wine to the pan, season with a generous pinch of salt and a good grinding of pepper and boil fairly rapidly until the wine has reduced by about half. This will take about 5 minutes.
* Cook the linguine in salted boiling water, stir once and cook according to the instructions on the packet until al dente.
* When the wine in the pan has reduced, add the tomatoes and cook them for a few minutes, then add the prawn bisque. Bring this to a simmer, turn the heat down and leave to gently bubble while the remainder of the meal is assembled.
* Roughly chop the chives. Add half to the sauce along with the prawns.
* Drain the linguine well and return to the pan. Taste the sauce, season it as you see fit and tip it over the linguine. Toss well so that the linguine is evenly coated with tomato sauce.
* Serve in large bowls with the remaining chives sprinkled over the top. Add a squeeze of lemon juice if you like.

Seasonal supper

Mushrooms on Toast with Rocket Salad

There's nothing more simple, or simply excellent, than mushrooms on toast. It's almost impossible to make them badly but there are a couple of things that can make an otherwise decent dish sublime. The first is that the toast has to be thick – a thin piece of bread turns into a soggy mess. Second, the mushrooms should be cooked over a high heat in very hot fat so that they crisp and cook rather than releasing all their moisture and steam-cooking into a soft mush. Oh, and plenty of seasoning is pretty crucial too.

30 g pine nuts (you can buy them
   ready toasted)
600 g mushrooms (a mixture of
   button, chestnut, oyster –
   whatever is around)
2 garlic cloves
60 g butter
2 tbsp fresh flatleaf parsley
2 tbsp olive oil
4 large or 8 small thick slices
   white bread
salt and pepper

Rocket salad
100 g rocket
1 large or banana shallot,
   approx. 30 g
3 tbsp olive oil
1 tbsp cider or sherry vinegar
30 g Parmesan

GET AHEAD PREPARATION (optional)

* Prepare the mushrooms.
* Make the garlic and parsley
   butter.
* Toast the pine nuts.
* Make the salad dressing.

*35 minutes before
you want to eat*

* Preheat the grill to medium.
* If you haven't bought the pine nuts ready toasted, put them on a baking sheet and toast them under the grill while it warms up – keep an eye on them as they catch very easily.
* In the meantime, clean and slice the mushrooms then make the garlic and parsley butter. Soften the butter, then peel and crush the garlic and roughly chop the parsley. Stir all the garlic and half the parsley into the softened butter with 1 tablespoon of the olive oil and a little pepper until they are thoroughly amalgamated.
* Now cook the mushrooms. Heat a splash of oil in a pan and when the oil is hot add the mushrooms and sauté them over a medium to high heat until they are soft and starting to brown. Add a good tablespoon of the garlic and parsley butter and carry on cooking until the mushrooms have reabsorbed any liquid they might have exuded.
* At this point, toast the bread under the grill and spread the slices with any remaining garlic and parsley butter.
* Prepare the salad. Wash and dry the rocket, place in a bowl and set aside while you peel and finely slice the shallot. Combine the shallot with the oil and vinegar and some seasoning in a salad bowl. Shave the Parmesan, using a potato peeler or coarsely grate it.
* Finally, taste and season the mushrooms, throw in the pine nuts and add the remaining parsley.
* Toss the rocket through the dressing, divide it between the toasts and pile the mushrooms on top.

Larder feast

Spinach and Chickpea Soup

This is an invaluable recipe when your kitchen is apparently bare. With a tin of chickpeas and some frozen spinach you can create a very passable soup. We've written this as a vegetarian recipe, but it is also excellent with the addition of chopped cured ham or salt cod. If you want to add these, do so when you add the garlic bread purée and follow the recipe as normal. If using salt cod, make sure you've soaked it in at least three changes of cold water for 24 hours prior to use.

We have adapted this recipe from Penelope Casas's definitive *The Foods and Wine of Spain.*

pinch of saffron threads
1 medium onion, approx. 120 g
3 tbsp olive oil
6 garlic cloves
400 g frozen spinach
2 slices rustic bread, approx.
   50 g (*pain de campagne* or
   pane rustica)
2 × 400 g cans chickpeas
handful of fresh parsley
400 ml chicken or vegetable
   stock (fresh or made from a
   stock cube or bouillon powder)
salt and pepper

To serve
rustic bread

GET AHEAD PREPARATION (optional)

The whole dish can be cooked 2 days in advance and heated when required. If you only have a little time:
* Prepare the onion and garlic.
* Defrost the spinach.
* Chop the parsley.

35 minutes before you want to eat

* First, put the saffron in about 1 tablespoon boiling water and set it aside to soften and soak. Next, peel and finely chop the onion.
* Heat 2 tablespoons of the oil in a large heavy-based pan and when the oil is hot add the onion. Cook for 7 minutes or until the onion is soft.
* While the onion is softening, peel the garlic cloves and cut all but one in half. Then defrost the spinach according to the instructions on the packet – either in a microwave or on the hob. When the spinach is completely defrosted, tip it into a sieve or colander and put it to one side, ideally weighted with a plate or tin so that the surplus liquid drains away.
* When the onion is soft, add the halved garlic cloves to the pan and cook gently for about 5 minutes or until they are starting to soften.
* In a separate frying pan, heat the remaining oil and when it is hot add the whole garlic clove and the bread and fry until golden brown.
* When the bread is golden brown, tip the bread and garlic into a food processor, add the saffron and about 4 tablespoons of the liquid from the canned chickpeas and blend to a smooth paste. You can use a hand blender if you don't have a food processor.
* Roughly chop the parsley. Once the onion and garlic are soft, add all the other ingredients to the pan – the spinach, chickpeas, stock, parsley and the bread and garlic purée. Stir well and bring to a simmer, then cover and cook for about 10 minutes.
* Season to taste with salt and pepper and serve with hunks of rustic bread.

Two for one

South American Beef Hotpot

In this recipe warming flavours – chorizo, paprika, cumin and chilli – combine to create a punchy casserole. Once the casserole is cooked, soured cream, crushed pumpkin and sunflower seeds and fresh rosemary are stirred in. The end result is powerfully flavoured and very welcome in the winter. As with casseroles in general, this is not difficult to cook but does require a long time simmering on the stove. Not a recipe to start on when you're in a rush.

This casserole goes very well with roast butternut squash. Deseed the squash (no need to peel it) and cut it into chunks, toss it in some olive oil, lemon zest, sage and seasoning and bake in a moderate oven (180°C/350°F/Gas Mark 4) for 45 minutes to 1 hour until the squash is meltingly soft. Salad dressed with a chopped-up avocado and lime juice goes very well alongside as well.

The quantities here allow for eight helpings, with half the hotpot intended for the freezer.

3 tbsp olive oil
1.25 kg stewing steak, cut into
    even-sized pieces
500 ml red wine
500 g piece of chorizo
4 medium red onions, approx.
    480 g
4 carrots, approx. 400 g
4 garlic cloves
1 tbsp paprika
1 tbsp ground cumin
1 tsp crushed dried chillies
2 × 400 g cans chickpeas
1 × 330–340 g can sweetcorn
2 × 400 g cans chopped tomatoes
1 tsp light brown soft sugar
2 sprigs fresh rosemary
20 g pumpkin seeds
20 g sunflower seeds
142 ml soured cream
salt and pepper

To serve
roast butternut squash (see
    above), tortillas or other
    flatbreads, green salad,
    avocado, ½ lime, olive oil

GET AHEAD PREPARATION (optional)

The entire dish can be cooked
3 days in advance and reheated.
If you only have a little time:
* Prepare the onions, carrots and
    garlic.
* Brown the meat and deglaze
    the pan.
* Soften the vegetables.
* Chop the rosemary leaves and
    the pumpkin and sunflower
    seeds and mix together.

2 hours before you want to eat

* First, brown the beef. Heat half the oil in a large heavy-based casserole over a medium heat. Season the beef with a little salt, increase the heat and brown the meat in batches. While the beef is browning, slice the chorizo into 2-cm chunks and peel and finely slice the onions.
* If the base of the pan isn't burnt once all the meat has been browned, splash in half the wine and stir it to lift off the flavours from base. Once the wine comes to the boil, pour it over the beef. If the base of the pan is burnt, wash it out thoroughly before cooking the chorizo.
* Once you have deglazed the pan with the wine, wipe it dry with kitchen paper, add a glug of oil and return the pan to a medium heat. When the oil is hot add the chorizo and let it cook until it starts letting some oil out.
* When the chorizo has let out some oil and started to soften, use a slotted spoon to lift it out of the pan and set it aside with the beef.
* Now add the onions to the pan and soften them for 5 minutes while you peel the carrots and slice them into rounds about 5 mm thick. Add the carrots to the pan and let them cook for a few minutes while you peel and crush the garlic.
* Once the carrots have been cooking for about 5 minutes, add the garlic and stir it about for a minute. Add the paprika, cumin and chilli and stir them so that they start to toast. After 1–2 minutes add the rest of the wine and bring it up to a simmer.

* After a couple of minutes add the chickpeas, sweetcorn, tomatoes and sugar. Return the beef and chorizo to the pan and bring to a simmer. Cover the pan and leave the hotpot to simmer over the very lowest heat until the beef is tender. This will take 1½–2 hours.
* While the beef is cooking, strip the rosemary leaves from their stalks. Grind or roughly chop the pumpkin and sunflower seeds with the rosemary. Mix half into the soured cream and put the other half in a small bag to freeze.
* When the beef is tender, season the hotpot to taste, then remove half from the pan and set it aside to cool, ready to freeze.
* Add the soured cream to the remaining beef and stir well. Serve the beef straight away with warmed tortillas or other flatbreads, roast butternut squash and green leaves tossed with roughly chopped avocado and dressed with lime and olive oil.
* When the rest of the hotpot is cold put it in a freezer bag or box and freeze.

Lazy day supper – reheating instructions

Defrost the hotpot and seed mixture thoroughly. Tip it into a casserole and heat gently until it is warmed through. While it is heating up, stir the seeds you put in the freezer into 142 ml soured cream. When the beef is hot, stir in the soured cream, taste and season as necessary, and serve as above.

November Week 4 – Overview

For a Big Meal from Scratch that's easy enough to make for family but special enough to share with guests the Lamb en Croûte with Roast Root Vegetables is one to try. The lamb is stuffed with a watercress purée then wrapped in pastry and baked. Altogether the meal takes 1½ hours and this includes the 30 minutes it will take to make the watercress purée and wrap the lamb in pastry. Once the lamb is assembled, however, the rest of the meal is straightforward.

For a Something for Nothing, extra watercress purée is used to make a light and vibrant version of Dauphinoise potatoes which are served with salmon. This will take 20 minutes of preparation and 20 minutes baking in the oven, but the results are more than worth the cooking time. The other Something for Nothing – Root Vegetable and White Bean Minestrone – uses up surplus roast root vegetables from the big meal to make a chunky, thick soup in just 30 minutes.

Similarly warming and comforting is a seasonal recipe for Romanesque (or Cauliflower) Cheese which takes around 25 minutes from start to finish. The Larder Feast of Prawn and Corn Fritters takes longer – 40 minutes – and is more labour intensive but the fritters are very satisfying to make and excellent to eat, so provided you're not in a huge hurry it shouldn't cause too much grief.

Ideal for a cold winter night is a Braised Rabbit with Mushrooms recipe. This can also be made with chicken but rabbit does add to the flavour. Like most slow casseroles and braises it takes a while to cook – around 1½ hours. This is a Two for One, though, so the quantities specified will feed eight and the recipe freezes well.

November Week 4	Recipe	Time
Big meal from scratch	Lamb en croute with roast root vegetables and broccoli	1½ hours
Something for nothing 1	Baked salmon with watercress Dauphinoise	40 mins
Something for nothing 2	Root vegetable and white bean minestrone	30 mins
Seasonal supper	Romanesque (or cauliflower) cheese	25 mins
Larder feast	Prawn and corn fritters with chilli fried broccoli	40 mins
2 for 1	Braised rabbit (or chicken) with mushrooms	1½ hours

All recipes serve 4 apart from the 2 for 1 recipe which makes 8 portions

SHOPPING LIST (for 4 people)

Meat and fish
2 x 300-400 g pieces of loin fillet of lamb
4 x 150-200 g pieces salmon fillet
300-400 g frozen cooked peeled Atlantic
  prawns
2 x 1 kg (approx.) rabbits, jointed or 2 kg
  free-range chicken thighs and drumsticks
the livers of the rabbits or 150 g chicken
  livers

Dairy
230 g approx. butter
2 free-range eggs
280 ml double cream
775-925 ml milk
275 ml natural yoghurt
100 g Parmesan
150 g mature Cheddar or 100 g Parmesan

Fruit and vegetables
900 g (approx.) waxy potatoes, such as
  Desirée or Charlotte
1 medium swede, approx. 400 g
1 medium celeriac, approx. 500 g
1 small butternut squash, approx. 600 g
4 carrots, approx. 400 g
4 parsnips, approx. 500 g
1 small leek, approx. 100 g
2 bunches watercress, approx. 200 g
400 g chestnut or field mushrooms (or any
  mushroom of your choice)
700 g (approx.) Romanesque or cauliflower
1 kg broccoli (frozen if you wish)
4 medium red onions, approx. 480 g
4 medium onions, approx. 480 g
1 large or banana shallot, approx. 40 g
6 spring onions
18 garlic cloves
5 sprigs fresh rosemary
7 sprigs fresh sage
3 large sprigs fresh thyme
1½ lemons

Basics
120 ml approx. olive oil
105 ml groundnut or grapeseed oil
75 g breadcrumbs or 3 slices bread suitable
  for crumbing
60 g plain flour
300 g self-raising flour
3½ tbsp Dijon mustard
1 bay leaf
850 ml chicken or vegetable stock (fresh
  or made from a stock cube or bouillon
  powder)
600 ml chicken stock (fresh or made from a
  stock cube or bouillon powder)
salt and pepper

Store cupboard
450 g chilled ready-made shortcrust pastry
200 g macaroni
100 g polenta
1 x 330 g can sweetcorn
1 x 300 g can cannellini beans
1 x 200 g can chopped tomatoes
pinch of nutmeg (ground or freshly grated),
  (optional for Romanesque/Cauliflower
  Cheese)
½ tsp crushed dried chillies (or more
  depending on taste)
2 tbsp white vermouth or white wine
500 ml white wine

Serving suggestions
little gem lettuces, cucumber, dill, lemons,
  olive oil (Baked Salmon with Watercress
  Dauphinoise)
baby vine tomatoes, olive oil (Romanesque/
  Cauliflower Cheese)
potatoes for mashing, peas or beans (Braised
  Rabbit/Chicken with Mushrooms)

To download or print out this shopping list,
please visit www.thekitchenrevolution.co.uk/
November/Week4

**Big meal
from scratch**

Lamb en Croûte with Roast Root Vegetables and Broccoli

For this meal, lamb loin fillet is filled with watercress and wrapped in pastry. Fillet is one of the sweetest parts of lamb and it goes especially well with the peppery flavour of watercress. If you are using ready-made pastry this meal is very simple to execute but the end result looks and tastes impressive.

The root vegetables here are roasted together until they are caramelised and starting to turn sticky – some vegetables will melt beyond recognition, others will retain their shape and some bite.

This recipe includes extra watercress purée for Baked Salmon with Watercress Dauphinoise (see page 510) and extra root vegetables for Root Vegetable and White Bean Minestrone (see page 511) later in the week.

Lamb en croûte
1-2 tbsp groundnut or grapeseed
   oil
50 g butter
1 large or banana shallot,
   approx. 30 g
2 bunches watercress, approx.
   200 g; includes 100 g extra for
   the watercress dauphinoise
2 tbsp white vermouth or white
   wine
2 x 300-400 g loin fillet of lamb
plain flour, for dusting
450 g chilled ready-made
   shortcrust pastry
1 free-range egg, for glazing
salt and pepper

Roast root vegetables (double
quantities for the root vegetable
and white bean minestrone)
1 medium swede, approx. 400 g
1 medium celeriac, approx.
   500 g
1 small butternut squash,
   approx. 600 g
4 carrots, approx. 400 g
4 parsnips, approx. 500 g
4 medium red onions, approx.
   480 g
5 sprigs fresh rosemary
3-4 tbsp olive oil

Broccoli
600 g broccoli

GET AHEAD PREPARATION (optional)

The lamb parcels can be
prepared a day in advance. Keep
them in the fridge and remove
40 minutes before you plan to
put them in the oven. If you only
have a little time:
* Prepare all the vegetables for
   the roast root vegetables and
   cover with water.
* Make the watercress purée.

*1½ hours before
you want to eat
roast the vegetables*

* Preheat the oven to 180°C/350°F/Gas Mark 4.
* Peel the swede and celeriac, cut them into 2-3 cm chunks. Peel and deseed the squash and cut it into similar size pieces. Peel the carrots and parsnips and cut them into lengths about 4 cm long. Peel the onions and cut them into quarters and strip the rosemary leaves from their stalks. Put all the root vegetables and the rosemary in a large roasting tin, season well with salt and pepper and drizzle with the oil. Mix everything with your hands and place in the oven for at least 1 hour and up to 1½ hours.

*1 hour before
you want to eat
prepare the lamb*

* Heat a splash of the oil and a nut of the butter in a pan with a lid over a medium heat while you peel and slice the shallot. Add the shallot to the pan and leave to sweat gently for 7-10 minutes.
* When the shallot is soft, roughly chop the watercress and add it to the pan with the rest of the butter and the vermouth or wine. Put the lid on and let the watercress wilt and become completely soft – this will take about 5 minutes.
* Once the watercress has wilted, blend to a purée using a food processor or hand blender. Leave to cool then put half the purée aside for later in the week.
* Take the lamb out of the fridge and cut it into four even-sized pieces.
* Now brown the lamb. Heat a generous splash of the oil in a frying pan over a high heat, season the meat thoroughly and quickly brown it all over. Remove the browned lamb from the pan and leave it to cool.
* Lightly dust a work surface with flour. Cut the pastry into four pieces and roll each one into a rectangle big enough to wrap around each piece of lamb. Ideally the pastry should be about 5 mm thick. Leave the rectangles to rest in a cool place.
* Now make three deep slashes diagonally across each piece of lamb and put a good-sized spoonful of the watercress purée in each one. Cover the outside of the meat with a thin layer of the remaining purée. Leave to set for 20 minutes or there abouts in the fridge.

* While the lamb is resting, check on the root vegetables and give them a stir.
* After 20 minutes or so, place each piece of lamb, slashes facing downwards, in the centre of each pastry rectangle. Brush the edges of each rectangle with a little beaten egg, then fold the long sides of the pastry over the lamb so that they join. Make sure the join is secure, then press the pastry on the short sides together, as though you were wrapping a present. If there seems to be excess pastry on these short sides trim it off, then make sure they are well sealed by pressing them with the tines of a fork.
* Place the lamb parcels, seam-side down, on a baking sheet and brush the beaten egg all over the top. Leave the parcels to rest until it is time to cook them.

30 minutes before you want to eat cook the lamb and the broccoli

* Turn the oven up to 220°C/425°F/Gas Mark 7. Give the roasting vegetables a stir in their tin and move them to the bottom of the oven.
* Place the lamb parcels in the oven and leave them to roast for 20–25 minutes until the pastry is golden and crisp. (If you want the meat to be well done leave the parcels for closer to 30 minutes.)
* While the lamb is cooking, trim the broccoli and break it into florets. Put the florets into the top of a steamer or in a pan with 2 cm of water, cover with a lid and bring to the boil. Let the broccoli steam for 4–5 minutes until it is tender.
* After 20–25 minutes take the parcels out of the oven and leave them to rest for 5 minutes while you check on the vegetables.
* By now the roast vegetables should be ready to eat. Check they are soft and season them to taste. Set a generous one-third aside for later in the week and place the rest in a warmed serving dish.
* When the broccoli is cooked, drain it well and place it in a warmed serving dish.
* Serve the lamb parcels on four warmed plates and pass the roast vegetables and broccoli around separately.

Afterwards

Put the leftover watercress purée and roast vegetables in separate containers, cover and refrigerate for use later in the week. Ideally you will have 80–100 g watercress purée and 600 g vegetables. If you have any leftover broccoli you could use it with the root vegetables.

Something for nothing 1

Baked Salmon with Watercress Dauphinoise

Instead of making the more usual gratin dauphinoise of potatoes layered with cream and garlic, the recipe here uses leftover watercress purée from the Big Meal from Scratch to make watercress dauphinoise. Salmon and watercress are classic partners and, as with many classics, simplicity is a good thing. Here the salmon is quickly baked in the oven with butter and lemon. This dish would be lovely served with a simple cucumber salad dressed with a little lemon juice, olive oil, salt and pepper and dill.

To make watercress purée from scratch soften 1 chopped shalot in butter, add 100 g chopped watercress and allow to soften. Add a splash of wine, reduce a little, then purée.

Baked salmon
25 g butter
juice of ½ lemon
4 × 150–200 g pieces salmon
   fillet
salt and pepper

Watercress dauphinoise
900 g (approx.) waxy new
   potatoes, such as Charlotte or
   Desirée

1 small leek, approx. 100 g
25 g (approx.) butter
100 g (approx.) watercress purée
   left over from the Big Meal
   from Scratch or see above
280 ml double cream
150 ml milk (optional)

To serve
lemon quarters and a little gem,
   cucumber and dill salad

GET AHEAD PREPARATION (optional)

The watercress dauphinoise can
be assembled up to 2 hours
before cooking. If you only have
a little time:
* Prepare and parboil the
   potatoes.
* Slice and wash the leek.

40 minutes before you want to eat

* Preheat the oven to 220°C/425°F/Gas Mark 7.
* First, prepare the potatoes. Peel and slice the potatoes (just under 1 cm thick) and parboil for 3–5 minutes in salted boiling water or until they are al dente. Don't let them overcook or the watercress dauphinoise will turn into a mash. When cooked drain immediately.
* While the potatoes are cooking, start making the watercress and leek sauce. Slice the leek finely and wash it thoroughly. Melt the butter in a pan over a medium heat and when it's foaming add the leek. Cook slowly for 5–10 minutes until the leek is soft.
* When the leek is soft, add the watercress purée and cream and stir well. Season to taste with salt and pepper, simmer for 1–2 minutes then remove from the heat.
* Next, build the watercress dauphinoise. If you haven't already done so drain the potatoes then place a single layer on the bottom of a wide, shallow ovenproof dish. Pour the watercress and leek sauce over the top until the potatoes are just about covered. Season with salt and pepper then continue adding layers of potato followed by sauce until the dish is full. If the liquid runs out you can add more cream or the milk. Place in the bottom of the oven and cook for 20–25 minutes or until the top is browned and the liquid is bubbling.
* While the potatoes are cooking, bake the salmon. Put the butter in a small roasting tin and melt it over a low heat. Add the lemon juice, remove the tin from the heat and add a generous pinch or two of salt and pepper. Put the salmon fillets in the tin and roll them in the buttery mixture, then place them at the top of the oven for 10 minutes.
* After 10 minutes check to make sure the salmon is just cooked, then remove.
* Serve the salmon with the watercress dauphinoise and a squeeze of lemon.

**Something
for nothing 2**

Root Vegetable and White Bean Minestrone

Minestrone is substantial a soup which, when served with a handful of grated
Parmesan and perhaps some bread, becomes a meal in itself. Using roast vegetables
from the Big Meal from Scratch means this recipe is especially easy to cook and helps
to intensify the flavour. If there are no leftover vegetables, peel 100 g carrots, 1
medium onion, 1 parsnip and 200 g swede and chop them into bite-sized chunks, then
roast them in olive oil at 200°C/400°F/Gas Mark 6 until they are soft and starting to
caramelize at the edges.

olive oil
1 medium onion, approx. 120 g
6 garlic cloves
600 g roast root vegetables left
   over from the Big Meal from
   Scratch or see above
200 ml white wine
1 x 300 g can cannellini beans
850 ml chicken or vegetable
   stock (fresh or made from a
   stock cube or bouillon powder)
1 x 200 g can chopped tomatoes
200 g macaroni
4 sprigs fresh sage
100 g Parmesan
juice of ½ lemon

GET AHEAD PREPARATION (optional)

The entire recipe can be made a
day in advance, up to the final
additions of the sage, Parmesan
and lemon juice, and reheated
when required. If you only have
a little time:
* Prepare the onion and garlic.
* Grate the Parmesan.

*30 minutes before
you want to eat*

* Heat a large glug of oil in a large heavy-based pan and while it is heating up peel and
   finely slice the onion. Add the onion to the pan and sweat it gently over a medium heat
   for 7–10 minutes until softened while you peel and finely slice the garlic.
* When the onion is soft, add the garlic and cook for a couple of minutes, stirring every
   now and then. If the root vegetables are larger than bite sized, cut them into smaller
   pieces. Next, add the root vegetables to the pan and warm them through.
* When the vegetables are warm, turn the heat up and splash in the wine. Reduce the
   wine to almost nothing. While the wine is simmering away, drain and rinse the
   cannellini beans.
* When the wine has reduced, add the beans to the pan and stir them for a minute or so,
   then stir in the stock and tomatoes and bring everything up to a simmer.
* Once the soup is simmering add the macaroni and bring the soup back to the boil.
   Reduce the heat and simmer for 10 minutes until the macaroni is just cooked.
* While the macaroni is cooking in the soup, strip the sage leaves from their stalks and
   finely grate the Parmesan.
* When the macaroni is cooked, add the sage and half the Parmesan and simmer for a
   minute more, stirring to amalgamate everything. Add the lemon juice and season to
   taste with salt and pepper.
* Serve the soup in big bowls, sprinkled with the remaining Parmesan.

Romanesque (or Cauliflower) Cheese

With its brilliant green, spiralling florets and delicate flavour, Romanesque broccoli provides a pretty alternative to the popular but rather everyday cauliflower cheese.

Romanesque comes into season towards late October and should be available from most supermarkets or grocers. Unlike Calabrese broccoli (the dark green variety), the thick stem on a Romanesque has little flavour and should be removed before cooking. Of course, if you can't find Romanesque broccoli you could always use cauliflower but you will need to adjust the steaming time.

This recipe relies on making a roux-based cheese sauce – for more on this see page 485.

700 g (approx.) Romanesque or
   cauliflower
50 g butter
50 g plain flour
1 tsp Dijon mustard
500 ml milk
150 g mature Cheddar or 100 g
   Parmesan
pinch of nutmeg (ground or
   freshly grated), optional
salt and pepper

GET AHEAD PREPARATION (optional)

The dish can be made up to 2
days in advance and warmed
through at 180°C/350°F/Gas Mark
4 until piping hot. If you only
have a little time:
* Grate the cheese.

25 minutes before you want to eat

* Cut the central stalk from the Romanesque or cauliflower and break the florets into generous, bite-sized pieces. Steam the florets in a steamer or over about 2 cm water in a pan with a lid for about 3 minutes (nearer 4 for cauliflower). Be careful not to overcook them because the Romanesque and cauliflower will quickly turn into a pulp. Remove the florets from the heat and place them in a deep ovenproof dish. Cover and put aside to keep warm. Keep the cooking water to use in the white sauce if you like.
* Meanwhile, preheat the grill to medium and make the cheese sauce. Melt the butter in a heavy-based pan over a gentle heat. When the butter is foaming add the flour and stir for a couple of minutes. Add the mustard, stir to incorporate it and then add the milk, whisking well to remove any large lumps. Bring the sauce to a gentle simmer, stirring with a whisk constantly. If the mixture gets too thick to pour or flow easily, add some of the water you cooked the florets in, or a little more milk.
* Grate the cheese. When the sauce coats the back of a wooden spoon add all but a handful of the cheese and stir until the cheese is melted.
* Then pour the sauce over the Romanesque or cauliflower. Sprinkle the remaining cheese over the top and place the dish under grill for about 5 minutes or until the top is browning and crisp.

Larder feast

Prawn and Corn Fritters with Chilli-Fried Broccoli

These crispy, crunchy fritters are a great hit with kids and incredibly moreish. The quantities below make a generous amount of the fritter mixture – far more than you might think possible to eat, but we're always amazed at how many are wolfed down. There's something about the way they puff up when they're cooked that's very satisfying.

We suggest you serve the fritters with chilli-fried broccoli. As the idea behind a larder feast is to not rely on fresh ingredients, you could use frozen broccoli.

<u>Prawn and corn fritters</u>
300-400 g frozen cooked peeled
   Atlantic prawns
1 x 330 g can sweetcorn
6 spring onions
300 g (approx.) self-raising flour
100 g polenta
275 ml milk
275 ml natural yoghurt
1 free-range egg
2 tbsp groundnut or grapeseed
   oil
salt and pepper

<u>Chilli-fried broccoli</u>
400 g broccoli (fresh or frozen)
1 tbsp olive oil
½ tsp crushed dried chillies
juice of ½ lemon

<u>GET AHEAD PREPARATION (optional)</u>

The prawn batter can be made a day in advance and kept covered in the fridge. If you only have a little time:
* Prepare the spring onions.
* Boil the broccoli.

40 minutes before you want to eat

* Defrost the prawns in a large bowl of cold water (changing the water two or three times will speed the process up). While the prawns are defrosting, drain the sweetcorn, and trim and slice the spring onions.
* Mix the flour and polenta together in a large bowl. Make a well in the centre and pour in the milk and yoghurt, then break in the egg. Beat until the mixture is smooth.
* When the prawns are defrosted drain them well and dry them thoroughly with kitchen paper. Stir the sweetcorn, prawns and spring onions into the batter and season to taste. Let the batter sit in a cool place while you prepare the broccoli.
* Cook the broccoli in salted boiling water for 3–5 minutes. Drain and set aside. (If using frozen broccoli, defrost according to manufacturer's instructions.)
* Preheat the oven to 140°C/275°F/Gas Mark 1. Check the consistency of the batter – it should drop slowly from a wooden spoon held vertically over the bowl; add a little more flour if necessary.
* Heat a generous splash of oil in a large frying pan (non-stick if possible) over a medium-high heat. When the oil is hot, drop 3–4 generous tablespoons into the pan to make four fritters – the batter will spread out in the heat but stop once it has reached its natural size. Cook the fritters for a couple of minutes then flip them over when they are solid and light brown on the bottom. Cook them through and brown on the other side, then transfer them to the oven while you cook the remaining batter. You may need to put a little more oil in the pan between batches.
* When all the fritters are cooked, fry the broccoli. Wipe out the frying pan with kitchen paper and heat the oil over a high heat. Add the broccoli and toss it about for a couple minutes. Add the chilli and some salt and carry on cooking until the broccoli is just starting to brown at the edges, tossing it all the time.
* After a minute or so, squeeze the lemon juice over the broccoli and serve straight away with the prawn and corn fritters.

Two for one

Braised Rabbit (or Chicken) with Mushrooms

This meaty, gamey casserole is ideal for a cold night. To thicken the sauce, rabbit (or chicken) livers are puréed with thyme, breadcrumbs and mustard, then stirred into the sauce. This does not produce a sauce with a discernible taste of liver but rather adds a depth of flavour and body. Zoe served this dish to liver-averse friends and they raved about it.

Although excellent and very inexpensive, rabbit isn't always available and doesn't appeal to all tastes. If this is the case, chicken pieces can be used instead.

Like most casseroles and stews, this is very good served with mash and sprout tops or something similar. The quantities here are for eight so half gets stored in the freezer for a later date.

3 medium onions, approx. 360 g
3 sprigs fresh sage
80 g butter
3 tbsp groundnut or grapeseed oil
2 x 1 kg (approx.) rabbits, jointed, or 2 kg free-range chicken thighs and drumsticks
300 ml white wine
12 garlic cloves
600 ml chicken stock (fresh or made from a stock cube or bouillon powder)
400 g chestnut or field mushrooms (or any mushroom of your choice)

1 bay leaf
3 large sprigs fresh thyme
the rabbit livers or 150 g chicken livers
3 tbsp Dijon mustard
75 g breadcrumbs or 3 slices of bread suitable for crumbing
salt and pepper

To serve
mashed potatoes, peas or beans

GET AHEAD PREPARATION (optional)

The entire dish can be made 2 days in advance and reheated gently when required. If you only have a little time:
* Prepare the onions and garlic.
* Cut the mushrooms.
* Chop the sage leaves.

1½ hours before you want to eat

* Peel and finely slice the onions and chop the sage leaves. Heat a large nut of the butter and a glug of oil over a medium heat in a large heavy-based casserole with a lid. Add the onions and stir them around until they are coated in the fat, then add the sage leaves. Turn the heat down very low and put the lid on the casserole. Leave the onions cooking slowly while the meat is browned.

* Add a splash of oil in a large frying pan, season the rabbit or chicken pieces with salt and pepper and brown them in batches. Wipe the pan dry with kitchen paper and heat a splash more oil before browning each batch of meat. As each batch is finished, put the meat in with the onions. Give the onions a stir each time you do this, just to stop them sticking or browning too much – it's fine if they get a little bit of colour. Replace the lid each time.

* Between each batch, deglaze the frying pan by splashing in a small glass of the wine, stirring it once or twice to remove any flavours from the bottom of the pan and then tipping the liquor on to the meat and onions.

* While the meat is browning, peel the garlic and cut any large cloves in half. When all the rabbit or chicken is cooked, heat another large nut of butter and a splash of oil in the frying pan and cook the garlic cloves until they are just beginning to turn golden. Using a slotted spoon, lift out the cloves and add them to the meat and onions.

* Next, tip the stock into the casserole, stir well and leave it to come to a simmer while you cut the mushrooms in half.

* Cook the mushrooms in the frying pan with the oil and butter from cooking the garlic (add a spot more butter if there isn't much in the pan). When the mushrooms have browned, tip them in with the meat. Pour any remaining wine into the frying pan and bring it to the boil, then pour it into the casserole. Add the bay leaf and a little seasoning.

* Now bring everything up to a simmer. When the casserole is simmering, turn the heat down low and cover with a lid. Most of the meat will take about 30–40 minutes to cook. The rabbit saddles, however, will only take 15 minutes so lift these out. Keep one of them warm and set the other aside to cool for freezing. Just as it's name implies, the saddle refers to the rabbit's back and ribcage.

* Preheat the oven to its lowest setting, to warm plates and keep the casserole warm.
* In the meantime, make the liver purée to thicken the stew. Strip the thyme leaves from their stalks. Trim any sinewy or green bits from the livers. Place them in a food processor or, if you are using a hand blender, place them in a bowl. Add the mustard, breadcrumbs and thyme leaves and whizz to a smooth purée.
* When the meat is tender lift it out of the casserole. Keep half warm and set the other half aside for freezing.
* Once the meat has been lifted from the casserole, stir in the liver purée and bring the sauce up to a simmer. Cook for a few minutes until the sauce is thick, then taste and season as necessary. Remove half the sauce and cool for freezing.
* Serve the rabbit or chicken with mashed potatoes and peas or beans.
* Freeze the meat and sauce separately.

Lazy day supper – reheating instructions

* Defrost the rabbit or chicken and its sauce thoroughly.
* Place the sauce in a casserole and heat it gently until it is piping hot, then add the rabbit or chicken pieces and let them heat through very gently in the sauce for about 15–20 minutes with a lid on. Serve as above.

Spiced Pumpkin Cake with Maple Syrup and Pecans

Pumpkin, maple syrup and pecans are ingredients that Americans know taste wonderful together but they are much underused by the British. In this pudding the pumpkin in the cake keeps the texture rich and moist and the maple syrup mixed with cream cheese and sprinkled with pecans makes a simple but lovely icing.

Cake
125 g butter
100 g dark brown soft sugar
100 g caster sugar
2 free-range eggs
280 g self-raising flour
1 tsp salt
2 tsp baking powder
1 tsp bicarbonate of soda
2½ tsp ground cinnamon
250 g canned pumpkin or 500 g
  pumpkin, peeled, deseeded and
  steamed until soft
140 ml soured cream
80 ml milk

Icing
200 g cream cheese
4 tbsp maple syrup
60 g pecan nuts

*1¼ hours before
you want to eat*

* Preheat the oven to 180°C/350°F/Gas Mark 4 and grease a deep 20 cm cake tin with butter.
* Cream the butter and sugars, then add the eggs, one at a time, with a spoonful of flour between each one.
* Sift the rest of the flour with the salt, baking powder, bicarbonate of soda and cinnamon. Mix the pumpkin, soured cream and milk together.
* Add the sifted flour and the pumpkin mixture alternately to the butter, sugar and egg mixture.
* Pour the cake mix into the buttered tin and bake for 35 minutes. The cake is cooked when an inserted skewer comes out clean.
* Turn the cake out on to a rack and while it is cooling make the topping.
* Put the cream cheese in a bowl and gradually stir in the maple syrup.
* When the cake is completely cold, use a hot knife to smooth the cream cheese topping over the cake. Roughly chop the pecans or cover them with a tea towel and crush them with a rolling pin or the bottom of a heavy pan. Scatter them over the topping and the cake is ready to eat.

Rice Pudding with Dates

Rice pudding is one of those things you either love or loathe. There's no convincing someone who claims to dislike it, so you only have to feel sorry for them because they are missing out on one of life's great pleasures. Finding good quality dates at this time of year is pretty easy as delis, grocers and supermarkets are starting to stock up for Christmas. Cooked with rice they break down and release their intense sweetness and flavour. Save for weighing a few ingredients, almost no preparation is required to make a rice pudding, but traditionally it's cooked for a couple of hours at a low heat in the oven so it can't be thrown together at the last minute. Here we suggest you start the pudding off on the hob and then finish it off in the oven. This knocks about 1 hour off the cooking time.

50 g butter
1.2 litres (approx.) milk
150 g pitted sticky fresh dates
50 g caster sugar
1-2 strips of lemon zest
1 tsp vanilla extract
140 g pudding rice
1 tbsp light brown soft sugar

To serve
thick double cream

1½ hours before you want to eat

* Melt the butter in a large heavy-based pan over a medium heat. When the butter has melted, pour about half into a pudding dish approximately 8 cm deep and 25 cm square. Brush the butter all over the dish and set aside.
* Add the milk to the pan and bring it to the boil.
* While the milk is coming to the boil cut the dates into quarters.
* When the milk starts to boil add half the dates and the caster sugar, lemon zest, vanilla and rice, then stir well once or twice.
* Bring the rice mixture to a boil then turn down the heat and allow it to simmer very gently for about 40 minutes. Stir every now and then and check the level of liquid. It should be creamy, not dry. If the rice is drying out add a little more milk.
* Meanwhile preheat the oven to 180°C/350°F/Gas Mark 4.
* When the rice has been cooking on the hob for 35–40 minutes tip it into the pudding dish. Stir in the remaining dates, sprinkle with the light brown sugar and bake for 20 minutes until the top is browned and bubbling.
* Serve with thick double cream.

Bramley Apple Cream

In Britain October and November are synonymous with apples. The number of different varieties, each with a distinct flavour, texture and appearance, is impressive. In this recipe eating and cooking apples are combined to provide tart and sweet flavours. Bramley apples are particularly suitable here because they dissolve easily and can be whipped into a purée. If you find the end result too tart, add a little sugar but remember that the brown sugar on top will add to the overall sweetness.

200 g Bramley apples
300 g sweet apples, such as Cox,
　Russet or Discovery
1 strip of lemon zest
3 cloves
2 tbsp caster sugar
200 ml double cream
200 ml natural yoghurt
4 tbsp light brown soft sugar

*1½ hours before
you want to eat*

* Peel and core the apples, then cut them into small pieces so that they will cook down quickly. Stud the strip of lemon zest with the cloves.
* Put the apples in a pan with the caster sugar, the strip of lemon studded with cloves and a splash of water.
* Put a lid on the pan and place it over a low heat so that the apples soften and fluff up.
* Once the apples have softened, put them in a large flat dish so that they cool down as quickly as possible.
* When the apples are cool, pile them into one big dish or into four individual dishes.
* Now whip the cream until it is quite firm, then fold in the yoghurt. Spoon the cream and yoghurt mixture over the apples, smooth it down and sprinkle it with the brown sugar.
* Place in the fridge for at least 40 minutes, if not overnight, until the brown sugar has dissolved to make a lovely caramel top.

Queen of Puddings

This is a classic pudding which is normally made with raspberry or strawberry jam, but we thought that as quince paste (membrillo) is now readily available it would make an interesting change. Of course, if you can't get membrillo, substitute your favourite jam – but do go for a good quality one if you want this pudding to shine. You could otherwise use poached quinces (see below).

500 ml milk
½ vanilla pod or a few drops of
    vanilla extract
1 lemon
50 g butter
4 large free-range eggs
125 g plus 1 tbsp caster sugar

150 g fresh white breadcrumbs
80 g quince paste

To serve
cream or crème fraîche

45 minutes before you want to eat

* Preheat the oven to 180°C/350°F/Gas Mark 4.
* Put the milk in a pan. Split the vanilla pod, scrape out the seeds and add them and the pod to the milk. Peel a couple of strips of zest from the lemon and add these to the milk. Bring the milk to boiling point, then take it off the heat, add the butter and cover it so that it infuses while you prepare the rest of the pudding.
* Separate the eggs. Whisk the yolks with the tablespoon of sugar until they are light and fluffy. Fold in the breadcrumbs and pour on the milk, stirring until amalgamated.
* Pour the mixture into an ovenproof dish and bake it in the oven for 15 minutes until it is starting to set.
* Now squeeze the juice of the lemon into a small pan. Add the quince paste and melt it over a low heat, stirring regularly, until it is a loose, spreadable consistency.
* Whisk the egg whites in a clean dry bowl until they are firm. Add half the sugar and carry on whisking until the whites begin to look shiny and firm. Now carefully fold in the rest of the sugar little by little, making sure it is very well incorporated.
* By now the breadcrumb base should be firm enough to hold the weight of the quince paste and meringue.
* Pour, or brush, the quince paste on to the base and pile the meringue on top.
* Bake for another 20–25 minutes until the meringue is firm and brown. If it browns too quickly, turn the oven down.
* Serve immediately with a little cream or crème fraîche.

Poached Quinces

Poached quinces are a good standby pudding and very tasty on top of cereal for breakfast, so it is probably worth doing double the recipe if you have time.

500 ml water
200 ml orange juice or 5 oranges
    for juicing

300 g golden granulated sugar
1 vanilla pod
1 star anise

4–6 quinces depending on their
    size approx 800 g

* First make make the poaching syrup by putting the water, orange juice, sugar, vanilla pod and star anise into a large heavy-based pan and bring it gently up to simmer so that all the sugar has dissolved by the time it has reached a rolling boil. Let it boil for 5–7 minutes so that it becomes syrupy.
* Peel, core and cut the quinces into eighths. Add them to the poaching syrup and put some baking paper on top. Poach them over a gentle heat until they are tender – this will take 15–20 minutes. They will be ready when an inserted knife meets no resistance. Watch them carefully as they will become mushy if overcooked.

DECEMBER

Nuts, dates, satsumas, cranberries, mince pies, goose, turkey, bread sauce and Brussel sprouts: December is the month for festive foods and traditional dishes. Yet we decided against a recipe for a Christmas roast – there are excellent versions in so many cookery books, and anyway most people have their own way of tackling the Christmas Day cooking. Instead, there is a recipe for Honey-Baked Ham with Mustard Leeks. This works wonderfully alongside a Christmas roast when hoards need to be fed, but also makes a terrific meal in its own right. Other dishes will lift the spirits in bitter weather – Coq au Vin and Venison with Pickled Walnuts and Vegetable Curry – but some are designed for larger numbers or for easy entertaining. Koulibiac, for example, is a salmon, rice and herb pie that looks stunning and is ideal for feeding a crowd, while after a long walk Pea and Ham Soup is just the thing. Finally, December is the time for trifles and chestnuts so here are two suitable puddings: one for Citrus Trifle with toasted sugared almonds and the other for a mad and wonderful Mont Blanc Mess with chestnuts.

December	Week 1	Week 2	Week 3	Week 4
Big meal from scratch	Venison (or beef) with pickled walnuts, hasselback potatoes, and cabbage with bacon	Baked salmon with saffron rice and creamed leeks	Roast pork with red cabbage and chestnuts, carrot and swede mash and apple and cranberry sauce	Honey-baked ham with mustard leeks
Something for nothing 1	Venison (or beef) tagliatelle	Koulibiac – Russian fish pie	Stir-fried pork with cashew nuts	Baked field mushrooms with ham and leeks
Something for nothing 2	Sausages with fried potatoes and apples	Lamb chops with creamy white bean mash	Swede and Lancashire cheese soufflé	The London particular – pea and ham soup – with potato bread
Seasonal supper	Leek and chicory gratin	Vegetable curry	Venison (or lamb) with polenta and cranberry sauce	Stilton and celery strudel
Larder feast	Warm haddock and chickpea salad	Ham and macaroni bake	Spinach and mushroom pasta	Smoked haddock, spinach and macaroni bake
2 for 1	Coq au vin	Beef goulash	Dhal with coriander and onion rotis	Nut bake
Puddings	Stuffed apples baked with cinnamon custard	Mont Blanc mess	Citrus trifle	Mulled pears with ginger cream

December Week 1 – Overview

December's recipes have been written with a view to cooking for large numbers. This week's Big Meal from Scratch recipe, for example, is Venison with Pickled Walnuts, Hasselback Potatoes and Cabbage with Bacon, and is ideal for a special Sunday lunch or Saturday night with friends. Most good butchers will supply venison and, if your budget will stretch, it's well worth seeking out. If your budget is tight or it's not convenient to visit a butcher, an economical cut that can replace the venison is beef brisket. Pickled walnuts are stocked by most supermarkets and delicatessens – they are excellent with cheese, cold meats or pâtés, but also add a wonderful sweet-sour note to casseroles and stews. Hasselback potatoes are a cross between roast and baked potatoes and look rather impressive. If you are cooking for more than four, increase the quantities as necessary or forfeit the Something for Nothing recipes later in the week. The venison has to cook long and slow so altogether this meal will take 3 hours.

For the Something for Nothings, leftover venison (or beef) from the big meal is turned into a quick, rich tomato sauce for pasta and surplus hasselback potatoes are fried until crisp and then served with sausages and apples.

Leek and Chicory Gratin is a rich and creamy Seasonal Supper that is ready in 35 minutes and will be very welcome on a cold, blustery night. And the Larder Feast uses haddock from the freezer to make a warm salad that is nutritious and delicious.

The Two for One is Coq au Vin, is another recipe that's worth inviting friends to share. Towards the start of making it the cook is kept busy browning chicken and shallots, but once everything is browned and assembled the casserole sits simmering gently for up to 1¼ hours.

December Week 1	Recipe	Time
Big meal from scratch	Venison (or beef) with pickled walnuts, hasselback potatoes and cabbage with bacon	3 hours
Something for nothing 1	Venison (or beef) tagliatelle	35 mins
Something for nothing 2	Sausages with fried potatoes and apples	25 mins
Seasonal supper	Leek and chicory gratin	35 mins
Larder feast	Warm haddock and chickpea salad	30 mins
2 for 1	Coq au vin	1¾ hours

All recipes serve 4 apart from the 2 for 1 recipe which makes 8 portions

SHOPPING LIST (for 4 people)

Meat and fish
1 × 1.5 kg saddle or haunch of venison or
   brisket of beef
2 × 1.5 kg free-range chickens, jointed
   (ask your butcher to do this for you) or 12
   free-range chicken joints: 4 thighs and 4
   drumsticks (bone in, skin on) and 4 breasts
   (skin on)
480-500 g free-range rindless smoked
   streaky bacon
8 good quality free-range sausages
   (Lincolnshire or herb sausages would be
   particularly good)
400-500 g frozen haddock fillets

Dairy
300 g approx. butter
650 ml milk
120 g hard cheese, such as Cheddar

Fruit and vegetables
8-10 large potatoes, such as Desirée or King
   Edward (approx. 2 kg)
3 leeks, approx. 500 g
4 heads chicory, approx.. 400 g
2 medium carrots, approx. 200 g
1 large Savoy cabbage, approx. 700 g
400 g button mushrooms
4 medium onions, approx. 480 g
12 large or banana shallots, approx. 360 g
19 garlic cloves
9-10 sprigs fresh thyme
4 fresh sage leaves
1 bunch fresh parsley
1 small bunch fresh coriander
2 sweet firm eating apples, such as Cox's
   or Braeburn
1 lemon

Basics
75 ml olive oil
150 ml groundnut or grapeseed oil
2-3 black peppercorns
5 bay leaves
550 g plain flour
pinch of caster sugar
300 ml beef or chicken stock (fresh or made
   from a stock cube or bouillon powder)
250 ml chicken stock (fresh or can be made
   from a stock cube or bouillon powder)
300 ml vegetable stock (made from a stock
   cube or bouillon powder)
salt and pepper

Store cupboard
400 g egg tagliatelle
2 × 400 g cans chickpeas
200 g roasted red peppers from a can or jar
250 ml passata

1-2 tbsp capers (depending on taste)
50 g pickled walnuts
1 tbsp redcurrant, bramble, damson or quince
   jelly
2 tbsp cider vinegar
1 tsp sherry vinegar
4 juniper berries (optional for Venison/Beef
   with Pickled Walnuts, Hasselback Potatoes
   and Cabbage with Bacon)
1-2 tsp paprika (preferably smoked)
1.1 litres (approx.) red wine

Serving suggestions
green salad ingredients (Venison/Beef
   Tagliatelle; Leek and Chicory Gratin; Warm
   Haddock and Chickpea Salad)
chard or spinach (Sausages with Fried
   Potatoes and Apples)
rice or baking potatoes, green vegetable
   (Coq au Vin)
green salad ingredients and Parmesan
   (Venison/Beef Tagliatelle)

To download or print out this shopping list,
please visit www.thekitchenrevolution.co.uk/
December/Week1

**Big meal
from scratch**

Venison (or Beef) with Pickled Walnuts, Hasselback Potatoes, and Cabbage with Bacon

As Christmas approaches this recipe for venison is appropriately festive. The venison is roasted in a flour-and-water dough (huff paste) parcel. At the end of cooking the paste is cracked open to reveal a perfectly cooked and succulent piece of meat. This is served with hasselback potatoes – a Scandinavian recipe that takes a little preparation but results in crisp golden, fanned-out potatoes. For a vegetable, cabbage is cooked very slowly with bacon, onions and stock until meltingly soft. The rich flavour of venison is excellent for this recipe but if you'd prefer or your budget will not stretch then use brisket of beef.

The gravy is made using pickled walnuts. These are fresh walnuts that have been salted and pickled until they turn soft and black. They are stocked by most supermarkets and grocery stores, and once you've bought a jar you won't look back. If they prove difficult to find the gravy can be made without the walnuts.

This recipe includes extra quantities of meat and gravy for Venison (or Beef) Tagliatelle (see page 526) later in the week, and extra potatoes for Sausages with Fried Potatoes and Apples (see page 527).

Venison (or beef)
500 g plain flour, plus extra for dusting
60 g butter
1 × 1.5 kg saddle or haunch of venison or brisket of beef; includes 500 g extra for the venison or beef tagliatelle
salt and pepper

For the gravy
300 ml beef or chicken stock (fresh or made from a stock cube or bouillon powder)
50 g pickled walnuts
200 ml red wine
1 tbsp redcurrant, bramble, damson or quince jelly
3 sprigs fresh thyme

Hasselback potatoes
8-10 large potatoes, such as Desirée or King Edward, approx. 2 kg; includes 1 kg extra for the fried potatoes
85 g butter
3 bay leaves
2 tbsp groundnut or grapeseed oil

Cabbage with bacon
40 g butter
groundnut or grapeseed oil
200 g free-range rindless smoked streaky bacon
2 medium onions, approx. 240 g
2 medium carrots approx. 200 g
1 large Savoy cabbage, approx. 700 g .
4 juniper berries (optional)

2 tbsp cider vinegar
300 ml vegetable stock (fresh or made from a stock cube or bouillon powder)
salt and pepper

GET AHEAD PREPARATION (optional)

You can make the huff paste and wrap it around the meat 12 hours in advance – keep it refrigerated until required. Remove from the fridge at least 40 minutes before cooking. If you only have a little time:
* Prepare the potatoes and cover with cold water until required.
* Prepare the onions, carrots and cabbage.

*3 hours before
you want to eat
prepare the meat*

* First, make the 'huff' paste. Put the flour in a large bowl with 2 teaspoons salt. Make a well in the centre, gradually add 300 ml water and mix to a stiff paste – you need a consitency you can roll out. Once you have a paste, knead it until it is smooth and elasticated.
* Rub the venison or beef thoroughly with the butter so that it is very well coated and season it well with salt and pepper.
* Roll out the paste until it is large enough to wrap around the meat – huff paste is very elastic, so you might find it easier to stretch as well as roll it into shape. Place the meat in the middle and wet the edges with some water, then pull them together and seal thoroughly. Leave to stand.
* Preheat the oven to 220°C/425°F/Gas Mark 7 and preheat a large roasting tin.

*1¾ hours before
you want to eat
cook the meat*

* Put the meat parcel on to the preheated tray and cook in the oven for 20 minutes, then turn the oven down to 180°C/350°F/Gas Mark 4 and carry on cooking the meat. After the initial hot blast cook the meat for about 1 hour. As a guide allow 10 minutes per 500 g for very rare meat, 20 minutes per 500 g for pink meat and more like 30 minutes per 500 g if you like your meat well done.

1½ hours before you want to eat cook the potatoes	* Peel the potatoes and cut them in half lengthways.

* Now comes the tricky bit. You need to stand each potato flat-side down on a chopping board and make cuts at 5-mm intervals along the potato that go nearly all the way, but not through to the base. One way to do this is to insert a metal or wooden skewer about 5 mm from along the potato base and use this to block the knife from cutting all the way through. Once you have sliced the potatoes put them in a bowl of very cold water for 10 minutes. In the meantime, rub a baking sheet with some of the butter and tear each bay leaf into quarters.
* Place the potatoes on the baking sheet and insert a sliver of bay leaf in the centre of each one. Dot them very generously with the butter, drizzle with the oil and season thoroughly with salt and pepper.
* Cook the potatoes at the top of the oven for 1 hour.

1 hour before you want to eat cook the cabbage and the gravy

* Heat 30 g of the butter in a large pan with a lid over a medium heat. Using scissors, chop the bacon straight into the pan and let it sizzle away and release some of its fat.
* While the bacon is cooking peel and finely slice the onions then add them to the pan. Let the onions sweat for 5–7 minutes while you peel the carrots, cut them in half lengthways and then slice them. Cut the cabbage in half, remove the tough core and shred the leaves into 1-cm thick ribbons.
* When the onions are soft, add the carrots and let them soften for 5 minutes. Then stir in the cabbage so that it's well mixed with the buttery bacon, onions and carrots and cook until it starts to soften. If you are using juniper berries, roughly crush them and add them to the pan.
* Once the cabbage has started to soften, turn the heat up and splash in the vinegar. Add the stock, season with salt and pepper and bring to a simmer. Once simmering, turn the heat down as low as possible and cover the cabbage with a couple of butter papers or greaseproof paper and then the lid. Leave the cabbage to cook very slowly for 35–45 minutes.
* Check on the potatoes and baste them.
* Now make the gravy. Put the stock into a pan, cut the walnuts into 1-cm thick slices and add them to the stock, along with the wine, jelly and thyme. Bring to a simmer and leave to cook slowly on a very gently heat.

25 minutes before you want to eat

* Take the meat out of the oven and, if the potatoes need crisping, turn the temperature back up to 220°C/425°F Gas Mark 7 and give them a 10 minute blast.
* Crack open the hard huff paste shell and carefully remove and discard the shell. Leave the venison or beef to rest in a warm place for 15–20 minutes. Strain the cooking liquor from the meat into the pickled walnut gravy.
* Check on the cabbage – it should be very soft by now. If there is a lot of liquid in the pan take off the lid and simmer for a few minutes to reduce, then season to taste.
* Check on the potatoes – if they are golden, crisp and soft in the middle they are ready. Turn the oven down and keep the potatoes warm until you are ready to serve. Put some plates and serving dishes in the oven to warm.
* Check the gravy for seasoning and remove the thyme sprigs.
* To serve, slice the venison or beef thinly and serve on a warmed plate, with the potatoes and cabbage alongside and the gravy in a jug, with a ladle to fish out the pickled walnuts.

Afterwards

Roughly dice the remaining venison or beef and strain the gravy and discard the walnuts. Cut the remaining potatoes into quarters. Put the meat, gravy and potatoes in separate containers, cover and refrigerate for use later in the week. Ideally you will have 300 g meat, 100 ml gravy and 800 g potatoes.

Venison (or Beef) Tagliatelle

Adding diced venison or beef to a rich tomato sauce makes an excellent and slightly luxurious ragu for tagliatelle. The tomato sauce takes about 10 minutes to prepare and then 20 minutes to cook – once it's all assembled and bubbling away there is little else to do. Because the meat is already cooked, you simply add it to the tomato sauce at the very end for a few minutes to warm through. Be warned, if you do any more than warm the meat through, it will toughen and require another 1–2 hours to tenderise again. If there is no meat leaft over from the Big Meal fry 300 g beef mince until brown and continue with the recipe as below. The mince will need cooking in the tomato sauce for at least 40 minutes and ideally longer.

1 medium onion, approx. 120 g
1 tbsp olive oil
2 garlic cloves
4 rashers free-range rindless
  smoked streaky bacon
125 ml red wine
3-4 sprigs fresh thyme or ½ tsp
  dried thyme
250 ml passata
100 ml gravy leftover from the
  Big Meal from Scratch or beef
  stock (fresh or made from a
  stock cube or bouillon powder)
400 g egg tagliatelle
300 g cooked venison or beef left
  over from the Big Meal from
  Scratch or 300 g minced beef
  (see above)
salt and pepper

To serve
green salad, Parmesan

GET AHEAD PREPARATION (optional)

The sauce can be cooked 2 days
in advance and gently heated. If
you only have a little time:
* Prepare the onion and garlic.

* Peel and finely slice the onion. Heat the oil in a large heavy-based pan over a medium heat. When the oil is hot add the onion and let it sweat over a low heat for 10 minutes. While the onion is cooking peel and finely slice the garlic.
* When the onion has been cooking for just over 5 minutes, add the garlic and use scissors to cut 2–3-cm lengths of the bacon straight into the pan. Stir once or twice and cook for 5 minutes. Altogether, the onion should cook for about 10 minutes and the garlic and bacon for about 5 minutes.
* Turn up the heat, add the wine and bring it to the boil, then add the thyme, passata and gravy or stock. Season with a generous pinch each of salt and pepper and simmer, fairly rapidly for about 20 minutes. The aim is to intensify the sauce flavour by evaporating as much liquidd as possible.
* While the sauce is cooking, put the tagliatelle on to cook according to the instructions on the packet. Meanwhile finely chop the venison or beef into very small pieces. You can use a processor but be careful not to pulversie the meat.
* A few minutes before you want to eat, turn down the heat under the tomato sauce, add the meat and stir once or twice. Let the meat warm through gently for about 5 minutes but don't allow it to boil. Taste the sauce and adjust the seasoning as necessary.
* Once the tagliatelle is cooked, drain it well and divide it between four serving bowls. Spoon the meat ragu on the top and serve with parmesan and a green salad.

Sausages with Fried Potatoes and Apples

Sausages go extremely well with fruity flavours – think of tomato sauce or HP sauce – so they are very good with these slightly softened pieces of apple. Served with crisp, fried potatoes this is a meal for a cold night or are feeling in need of comforting, homely food. If there are no potatoes remaining from the Big Meal from Scratch replace them with 1 kg potatoes, peeled, cut into dice-sized cubes and boiled in salted water until they are just cooked.

This would be nice with wilted spinach or chard tossed in butter and lemon juice.

8 good quality free-range
   sausages (Lincolnshire or herb
   would be particularly good)
groundnut or grapeseed oil
800 g (approx.) hasselback
   potatoes left over from the Big
   Meal from Scratch or see above
2 sweet firm eating apples, such
   as Cox's or Discovery
25 g (approx.) butter
4 fresh sage leaves
salt and pepper

To serve
spinach or chard

GET AHEAD PREPARATION (optional)

* Prepare the apples and keep
   covered in water to which a
   few drops of lemon juice have
   been added until required.

*25 minutes before
you want to eat*

* Preheat the oven to 200°C/400°F/Gas Mark 6 and take the sausages out of the fridge to come to room temperature.
* Next, start cooking the potatoes. Heat a splash of oil in a frying pan (non-stick if possible) over a high heat. Cut the potatoes into bite-sized chunks and, when the oil is hot, add them to the pan. The potatoes should crisp as much as possible, so only turn them when they are becoming crunchy and golden on the bottom – this will take about 15 minutes in all.
* While the potatoes are frying, put the sausages in the oven to cook for 15–20 minutes.
* While the sausages and potatoes are cooking, peel and core the apples. Cut them into quarters and then halve the quarters so that you have bite-sized chunks.
* After about 15 minutes the potatoes should be crispy. Remove them from the pan and place them in a warmed dish, under the grill pan to keep warm.
* Next, heat the butter in the frying pan over a medium heat and when it is foaming add the apples and a good dose of salt and pepper. Tear the sage leaves in half. Let the apples cook for 4–5 minutes, then add the sage leaves for the final couple of minutes.
* When the sausages are cooked, serve them on top of the fried potatoes with the sage and apples on the side, accompanied with wilted spinach or chard.

Seasonal supper

Leek and Chicory Gratin

This gratin is warm and rich and takes full advantage of leeks and chicory – two seasonal treats. It makes a good supper on its own, perhaps with a green salad, or if you like you could bake some fish or chicken alongside it in the oven.

60 g butter
80–100 g free-range rindless
    smoked streaky bacon
3 leeks, approx. 500 g
4 heads chicory, approx. 400 g
50 g plain flour
650 ml milk
120 g hard cheese, such as
    Cheddar
salt and pepper

To serve
green salad

GET AHEAD PREPARATION (optional)

The white sauce, or the entire dish (up until it goes into the oven), can be made a day in advance. If you only have a little time:
* Prepare the leeks and chicory.
* Grate the cheese.

35 minutes before you want to eat

* Preheat the oven to 220°C/425°F/Gas Mark 7.
* Heat half the butter in a heavy-based pan and, using scissors, snip the bacon into the pan. Let it cook away gently for a few minutes while you trim, slice and wash the leeks.
* Add the leeks to the pan and stir them for 1–2 minutes, then put a lid on and leave them to soften for 5 minutes over a medium heat.
* In the meantime, fill a pan with water and while it comes to the boil cut the chicory into quarters lengthways and trim any brown from their bases. When the water is boiling add some salt, drop in the chicory quarters and let them cook for 3–4 minutes until just soft.
* By now the leeks will be soft. Take the lid off the pan and boil the leeks rapidly to evaporate most of the liquid.
* Now add the rest of the butter to the leeks and when it has melted add the flour and stir to amalgamate. Cook the flour for a couple of minutes then add the milk.
* Bring the lot to the boil then reduce the heat and simmer, stirring, until the sauce is smooth and thick – about the consistency of whipped cream.
* At this point, leave the leeks over a very low heat and coarsely grate the cheese. Stir three-quarters of the cheese into the leek mixture and season to taste with salt and pepper.
* Now put half the leeks in a deep ovenproof dish and cover them with all the chicory and finish with the rest of the leeks. Scatter with the remaining cheese and bake in the oven for 15 minutes until the gratin is golden and bubbling. Serve with a green salad and baked fish or chicken.

Larder feast

Warm Haddock and Chickpea Salad

This is a warm, wintry salad – quick and easy to make with powerful flavours and interesting textures. The recipe uses frozen haddock, so has the advantage of being ready to go as long as you have some haddock fillets in the freezer. You could use pollack or coley instead of haddock – though coley has a stronger flavour, so bear this in mind. You can use any red peppers that have been preserved in a can or jar. If they are marinated in olive oil they will not need rinsing, but if they are in a vinegar and oil solution you need to wash them well under running water.

1 medium onion
1 garlic clove
4 tbsp olive oil
400–500 g frozen haddock fillets
2–3 black peppercorns
1 bay leaf
2 × 400 g cans chickpeas
1–2 tbsp capers
200 g crushed red peppers from a can or jar, approx. 5
1–2 tsp paprika (preferably smoked)
½ lemon
1 tsp sherry vinegar
handful of fresh coriander
handful of fresh parsley
salt and pepper

To serve
green salad

GET AHEAD PREPARATION (optional)

* Prepare the onion, garlic an red peppers.
* Cook and flake the haddock.
* Drain and rinse the chickpeas and capers.
* Make the dressing.
* Chop the herbs.

30 minutes before you want to eat

* Peel and finely slice the onion and garlic. Heat a generous splash of oil in a frying pan on a medium heat. When the oil is hot, add the onion and soften for about 10 minutes.
* Place the frozen haddock in a pan with a lid and add about 2 cm water. Add the peppercorns, bay leaf and a pinch of salt and place over a gentle heat with the lid on. Bring to the boil then remove the pan from the heat without removing the lid.
* Next, prepare the red peppers and chickpeas. Drain both well. If the peppers are marinated in olive oil use some of the oil to make the dressing. Rinse the chickpeas and capers under running water and if the peppers were marinated in a sharp vinegar and oil solution rinse these well. Cut the peppers into 2 cm strips and set aside.
* When the onion is soft, add the paprika and about ½ teaspoon salt and ½ teaspoon pepper. Mix well, then stir in the chickpeas, peppers and capers. Warm through gently while you finish the haddock and make the dressing.
* Check the haddock is cooked – the flesh should flake very easily and be opaque throughout. If it isn't cooked, bring it to the boil once more then drain immediately. Put the fillets into a sieve or colander to drain while you make the dressing.
* Pour the remaining oil into a small jar or jug. Squeeze in about 1 teaspoon lemon juice and add the vinegar. Chop the coriander and parsley and mix them into the oil and vinegar.
* Tip the chickpea mixture into a bowl. Break the haddock into bite-sized flakes and add them to the chickpeas. Pour the dressing over the top and very gently fold everything together, taking care not to smash the haddock flakes to pieces.
* Taste for seasoning and serve in bowls with a green salad on the side.

Two for one

Coq au Vin

Coq au vin is probably the French dish that people cook more than any other. It is a casserole where chicken pieces are browned and then cooked very slowly with red wine, bacon, mushrooms and lots of herbs until they are tender. During the 1970s and 1980s coq au vin was served with such regularity it was almost an epidemic. Its popularity seems to have waned in recent years, but whenever it appears at the table everyone is happy.

Traditionally, the bird used for this slow-cooking dish would be a cockerel at the end of its life. Cockerels have darker, leaner meat than standard roasting birds and benefit from gentle, long cooking. They are difficult to locate and coq au vin will work fine with a standard free-range chicken. Although chicken legs and thighs can be cooked for a long time without toughening, breasts will dry out so these are only added towards the last 15 minutes of cooking.

2 × 1.5 kg free-range chickens, jointed or 12 free-range chicken joints: 4 thighs and 4 drumsticks (bone in, skin on) and 4 breasts (skin on)
groundnut or grapeseed oil
12 large or banana shallots, approx. 360 g
16 garlic cloves
750 ml red wine
pinch of caster sugar
30 g butter
a few sprigs fresh thyme

250 ml chicken stock (fresh or made from a stock cube or bouillon powder)
2 bay leaves
100 g free-range rindless smoked streaky bacon
400 g button mushrooms
small handful of fresh parsley
salt and pepper

To serve
rice or baked potatoes and a green vegetable

GET AHEAD PREPARATION (optional)

The entire dish can be cooked in advance and reheated prior to eating. If you only have little time:
* Joint the chicken, if necessary.
* Prepare the garlic and shallots.
* Clean and cut the mushrooms.
* Chop the parsley.

1½ hours before you want to eat

* Joint the chicken, if necessary (see page 183).
* Heat a generous glug of oil in a casserole over a medium-high heat, season the chicken joints thoroughly on both sides and brown them, in batches, in the hot oil until they are deep golden in colour. Once browned, put the chicken in a large bowl and set aside.
* While the chicken is browning, put the shallots and garlic in a bowl, cover with boiling water and leave them for a couple of minutes before draining them – this should make them easier to peel.
* Once all the chicken joints are browned, tip any excess fat out of the casserole dish and set it to one side to use for frying the shallots and garlic later.
* Return the casserole to the heat, add a large glass (approx. 250 ml) of the wine and allow it to bubble for 1–2 minutes. Stir well to lift all the lovely flavours from the bottom of the casserole. Pour this cooking liquor over to the chicken.
* Wipe the casserole dry with kitchen paper and return it to the heat with the fat you set aside earlier – if there is not very much, add another glug of oil.
* Peel and halve the shallots, add them to the casserole and cook them over a medium heat for 5 minutes while you peel the garlic cloves. Once all the cloves are peeled, add them to the casserole.
* After a couple of minutes, cover the shallots and garlic with water and add the sugar, butter and thyme. Bring this lot to the boil and let simmer away until the liquid has completely evaporated, then stir the shallots and allow them to caramelise slightly.
* Preheat the oven to 180°C/350°F/Gas Mark 4.
* When the shallots have browned add the remaining wine and bring it to the boil, then reduce the heat to a simmer. After a few minutes add the stock and bay leaves, season with salt and pepper and bring to the boil. Add all the chicken joints except the breasts to the casserole.
* Cover the casserole and put the chicken joints into the oven to cook very gently for 45–55 minutes, until they are very tender.
* While the chicken is cooking, heat a little oil in a frying pan and, using scissors, snip the bacon straight into the pan. Let this fry for a couple of minutes while you clean the mushrooms. Cut them into halves or quarters if they are larger than bite-sized.

* Add the mushrooms to the frying pan and cook them until they are soft, then turn off the heat and leave them until later.
* After about 45 minutes, check on the chicken joints – they should be very tender. Add the bacon and mushrooms to the casserole and stir to mix them in. Set the chicken breasts on top. Return the casserole to the oven for 10–15 minutes until the breasts are just cooked but not dry.
* Once the breasts are ready, take the casserole out of the oven. Remove two legs, two thighs, two breasts and half the sauce, and set aside to cool for freezing.
* Roughly chop the parsley. Check the remaining coq au vin for seasoning and add the parsley. If you feel the sauce is too thin, you can lift all the chicken out and keep it warm while you simmer the sauce until it is the consistency you like.
* Return the chicken to the sauce and serve immediately with rice or baked potatoes and a green vegetable.

Lazy day supper – reheating instructions

Defrost the coq au vin completely. Put it in a large casserole and reheat it gently for about 00 minutes with the lid on. Serve as above.

December Week 2 – Overview

The Big Meal from Scratch this week can feed four or be adapted to feed eight with no particular difficulty. Either way, Baked Salmon with Saffron Rice and Creamed Leeks is a meal that is easy to produce, striking to look at and good to eat. For numbers larger than four seek out a whole salmon, but if numbers are small it's sensible to cook two fillets of about 600 g each. There will still be plenty left over for later in the week. Altogether the meal will take 1½ hours to make.

The extra salmon and rice from the big meal are mixed with herbs and seasoning to become the filling in a Koulibiac, a beautiful pastry-wrapped Russian fish pie. This is another meal that is well worth sharing. Given that cooked rice doesn't last well, it's best to make this Something for Nothing within a day or two of the big meal. The Koulibiac takes around 45 minutes to assemble and cook, and once completed is great served hot or cold. The soft, sweet leftover leeks from the Big Meal become part of a recipe for Lamb Chops with Creamy White Bean Mash which takes just 25 minutes to get on the table.

The Seasonal Supper uses winter root vegetables to make a simple Vegetable Curry. It takes 45 minutes to make, but 30 minutes of that is cooking time. The Larder Feast is a quick, comforting and warming Ham and Macaroni Bake, ready in just half an hour.

In the depths of winter the sweet flavours of paprika and beef seem particularly appealing so the Two for One recipe for Beef Goulash is likely to please. As with many casseroles, the goulash takes 2 hours though much of this time involves no exertion by the cook.

December Week 2	Recipe	Time
Big meal from scratch	Baked salmon with saffron rice and creamed leeks	1½ hours
Something for nothing 1	Koulibiac – Russian fish pie	45 mins
Something for nothing 2	Lamb chops with creamy white bean mash	25 mins
Seasonal supper	Vegetable curry	45 mins
Larder feast	Ham and macaroni bake	30 mins
2 for 1	Beef goulash	2 hours

All recipes serve 4 apart from the 2 for 1 recipe which makes 8 portions

SHOPPING LIST (for 4 people)

Meat and fish
4 lamb chops (loin or chump)
1.2-1.5 kg stewing steak, cut into even-sized
    pieces
200-300 g sliced cooked ham
1 × 1.5 kg salmon or 2 × 600 g unskinned
    salmon fillets

Dairy
265 g (approx.) butter
2 free-range eggs
140 ml double cream
650 ml (approx.) milk
100 g strong cheese, such as mature Cheddar
60 g lard (optional for Beef Goulash)

Fruit and vegetables
1.1 kg potatoes, such as King Edwards
9 carrots, approx. 900 g
9 large leeks, approx. 1.4 kg
5 celery sticks
2 small green peppers, approx. 250 g
100 g mushrooms, such as chestnut or button
1 medium onion, approx. 120 g
3 large onions approx. 600 g
3-4 large or banana shallots, approx. 120 g
5 garlic cloves
3-cm piece of fresh root ginger
1 bunch chives
13-15 sprigs fresh dill
1-2 sprigs fresh rosemary
2 sprigs fresh thyme
generous handful of fresh parsley
2 lemons
150 g frozen peas

Basics
small splash of olive oil
100 ml groundnut or grapeseed oi
2-3 slices bread
2 tsp mustard powder
1 tbsp wholegrain mustard
2 tbsp tomato purée
1 bay leaf
40 g plain flour
600 ml chicken stock (fresh or made from a
    stock cube or bouillon powder)
salt and pepper

Store cupboard
300 g basmati rice
350 g macaroni
packet 12 cocktail blinis (optional for
    Koulibiac - Russian Fish Pie)
450 g chilled ready-made puff pastry
2 × 400 g cans cannellini or haricot beans
1 × 400 g can chopped tomatoes
1 × 200 g can chopped tomatoes

75 g (approx.) slivered almonds (you can buy
    them ready toasted)
1 tbsp red wine vinegar
1½ tbsp paprika
½ tsp cayenne pepper
2-3 tsp garam masala
½ tsp turmeric
1½ tsp caraway seeds
1½ dried red chillies (preferably Hungarian
    paprika type)
2 generous pinches of saffron threads
200 ml white wine

Serving suggestions
watercress, lemon juice, olive oil and soured
    cream; fish roe if you wish (Koulibiac
    - Russian Fish Pie)
greens (Lamb Chops with Creamy White Bean
    Mash)
naan breads or rice, Indian pickles
    (Vegetable Curry)
green salad (Ham and Macaroni Bake)
crème fraîche, noodles, frozen peas (Beef
    Goulash)

To download or print out this shopping list,
please visit www.thekitchenrevolution.co.uk/
December/Week2

**Big meal
from scratch**

Baked Salmon with Saffron Rice and Creamed Leeks

Cooking a whole salmon is great for a special occasion – this meal looks impressive and it's easy to execute, so it's ideal if you want to entertain or treat yourself around Christmas or New Year. The salmon is baked in foil with shallots, lemon, herbs and white wine. If you prefer, two 600 g fillets of salmon will work just as well. The rice is cooked in stock with onions and dill, and the leeks are cooked in butter and cream. Each dish is distinctive but the flavours also work well together.

   The recipe includes extra salmon and rice for the Koulibiac and extra leeks for the Lamb Chops with Creamy White Bean Mash later in the week.

Baked salmon
3-4 large or banana shallots
5-6 sprigs fresh dill
1 lemon
½ bunch chives
1 × 1.25 kg salmon or 2 × 600 g unskinned salmon fillets; includes 500 g extra for the koulibiac
50 g butter
200 ml white wine
salt and pepper

Saffron rice
75 g slivered almonds
1½ tbsp groundnut or grapeseed oil

1 large onion, approx. 200 g
300 g basmati rice; includes 30 g extra for the Koulibiac.
2 generous pinches of saffron threads
3-4 sprigs fresh dill
600 ml chicken stock (fresh or made from a stock cube or bouillon powder)
20 g butter

Creamed leeks
7 large leeks, approx. 1.4 kg; includes 400 g extra for the creamy white bean mash
65 g butter
140 ml double cream

GET AHEAD PREPARATION (optional)

The salmon can be prepared and wrapped in foil, then refrigerated, up to 5 hours before cooking. If you only have a little time:
* Prepare the shallots, onion and leeks.
* Prepare the roasting tin and foil.
* Toast the almonds.

1½ hours before you want to eat prepare the salmon

* Lay a sheet of foil over the base of a tin, large enough to hold the salmon. You need enough foil to enable you to wrap the salmon and create a roomy, airtight parcel if you are using a whole samlon.
* Peel and thinly slice the shallots and place them in a line along the middle of the foil. Remove any thick stalks from the dill then roughly chop the fronds and sprinkle them over the shallots. Cut half the lemon into about four slices (keep the other half to squeeze over the salmon) and add the slices to the shallots and dill. Using scissors, cut half the chives into 5-mm lengths and add them to the tin.
* Next, place the salmon on top of the shallot mixture. Stuff the cavity of the whole salmon with the dill stalks and some of the remaining chives. Squeeze the juice of the remaining half lemon over the salmon, then cut the lemon into four rounds and stuff these into the salmon cavity. Season the salmon with about ½ tsp salt and 1 tsp pepper. If using salmon fillets, place one of the fillets skin-side down on the bed of shallots, scatter with the dill stalks and lemon rounds season and then place the other fillet on top skin-side up.
* Dot the fish with butter and pour in the wine. Bring the edges of the foil over the salmon and fold them together to make an airtight but roomy parcel.
* Place the prepared salmon in a cool place.

50 minutes before you want to eat cook the rice

* Preheat the oven to 150°C/300°F/Gas Mark 2.
* Toast the almonds on a baking sheet in the oven while it heats.
* Prepare the rice. Heat the oil in a pan and place over a medium heat. Peel and finely slice the onion. When the oil is hot add the onion and cook for about 10 minutes.
* Wash the rice under cold running water until the water runs clear, then drain it. Put the saffron in a cup and add about 2 tablespoon warm water so it softens. Strip the dill fronds from any thick stalks and chop them,
* When the onion is soft add half the dill and stir well. Add the rice, saffron, stock and about ¼ teaspoon each of salt and pepper. Stir well once or twice, bring to the boil over a medium heat, then reduce the heat, cover the pan with a lid and simmer very gently for about 20 minutes.

35 minutes before you want to eat cook the leeks and the salmon	* Trim, finely slice and wash the leeks. Melt the butter in a large pan with a lid over a medium heat and when it is foaming add the leeks and some salt. Stir once, then cover with a lid, turn the heat down to its lowest setting and cook the leeks for about 15 minutes with the lid on and 10 minutes with the lid off. If they look as if they are drying out, add a little more butter. * Next put the salmon in the oven. Cook a 1.25 kg salmon in the oven for 25–30 minutes or as a guide cook at 150°C/300°F/Gas Mark 2 for 10–12 minutes per 500 g. Two 600 g salmon fillets will take 20 minutes. * Prepare the butter and almonds. Melt the butter in a pan and add the almonds then tip into a small container and set aside.
5 minutes before you want to eat	* When the leeks are completely soft, stir in the cream and some pepper. Stir once or twice, and leave simmering very gently. * Remove the salmon from the oven. Unwrap the foil and check that the fish is cooked by pulling out a fin. If it comes away easily and flesh flakes it is ready. * Let the fish cool a little then peel back the skin on the uppermost side, lift from the parcel and place it on a large serving dish. * Turn the oven off and put some plates and serving dishes in it to warm. * Strain any juices from the foil in the roasting tin into a small pan. Place over a medium heat and bring the juices to simmering point. Whisk in the remaining butter and use scissors to cut small lengths of the remaining chives into the pan. Stir well, season and pour into a jug. * Remove the lid from the pan of rice and check the rice is cooked, then stir in the remaining dill. Tip the rice into a serving dish and top with the toasted almonds. * Slice the salmon and serve it with rice, leeks and juices. When the skinned side has been served, remove the bones, turn the fillet below over, remove the skin and continue serving.
Afterwards	Put the leftover salmon (500–600 g), rice (90 g) and leeks (300 g) in separate containers, cover and refrigerate for use later. The rice will only keep for 24 hours, so try to make the koulibiac the following day.

**Something
for nothing 1**

Koulibiac

Koulibiac is a Russian fish pie where fish is mixed with herbs and rice and wrapped in a yeast dough. The end result is a far cry from our standard potato-topped fish pie. Koulibiac looks impressive and is good for entertaining – particularly as it doesn't have to be cooked or served at the last minute. For this recipe puff pastry rather than the yeast dough is used.

To make the koulibiac a pastry base is rolled out, then piled with salmon and rice, covered in more pastry and baked. In the traditional version the fish is wrapped in buckwheat pancakes before it is wrapped in dough. In an attempt to make this recipe a little less complicated we suggest you use a layer of ready-made blinis. They are, however optional.

450 g chilled ready-made puff
  pastry
plain flour, for dusting
100 g mushrooms, such as button
  or chestnut
30 g butter
2 free-range eggs
90 g cooked rice left over from
  the Big Meal from Scratch or
  30 g basmati rice, cooked
½ bunch chives
5 sprigs fresh dill

1 lemon
400 g cooked salmon left over
  from the Big Meal from Scratch
  or 950 g raw salmon, cooked
12 cocktail blinis (optional)
milk, for brushing
salt and pepper

To serve
watercress dressed with lemon
  juice and olive oil, soured
  cream; fish roe (optional)

GET AHEAD PREPARATION (optional)

The koulibiac can be made up to
1 day in advance and served cold
or at room temperature. If you
only have a little time:
* Cut and roll out the pastry.
* Slice and cook the mushrooms.
* Make the filling.
* Chop the herbs.

*45 minutes before
you want to eat*

* Cut the pastry in half and lightly dust a work surface with flour. Roll the pastry halves into two rectangles about 5 mm thick, one about A4 size and the other 28 x 40 cm. Put the pastry aside to rest in the fridge.
* Finely slice the mushrooms and heat the butter in a pan. When the butter is foaming, add the mushrooms and cook them until they are soft. When they are soft, turn the heat up and evaporate any liquid.
* Break the eggs into a large mixing bowl and add the rice. Roughly chop the chives and dill, grate the zest of half the lemon, and add the herbs and zest to the rice along with the juice of the lemon. Flake in the salmon, mix well and season.
* Preheat the oven to 220°C/425°F/Gas Mark 7 and preheat a baking sheet.
* Put the smaller pastry rectangle on a piece of baking parchment. If using, put eight of the blinis on to the pastry base and cover them with the rice filling. Shape the rice into a neat block either over the blinis or directly on the middle of the pastry. Cover the top of the rice with the remaining blinis. Brush the edge of the pastry base with milk and lay the larger pastry rectangle over the filling. Press the pastry edges together. If there is excess pastry around the edge trim it off. Press the edges of the pastry together with a fork and cut a cross in the top of the pie.
* Brush the pastry all over with milk, take the hot baking sheet out of the oven and lift the koulibiac on to it using the baking paper. Put the koulibiac in the oven to cook for 20–25 minutes until the pastry is golden and crisp and the filling is piping hot.
* Serve immediately with watercress dressed with lemon juice and olive oil, a dollop of soured cream and, if you like, a spoonful of fish roe.

Lamb Chops with Creamy White Bean Mash

White beans make a tasty alternative to the more usual mashed potato and here they are cooked with a little garlic, rosemary and milk then mashed or processed into a coarse or smooth purée. Creamed leeks from the Big Meal from Scratch are stirred into the mash and this is served with simply grilled lamb chops. This is good served with buttered greens. If you don't have any leftover leeks, trim, wash and slice 400 g leeks. Cook them very slowly with about 40 g butter until they are soft, then season them and mix them with 1 tablespoon of cream.

4 lamb chops (loin or chump)
300 g (approx.) creamed leeks
   left over from the Big Meal
   from Scratch or see above
small splash of olive oil
2–3 garlic cloves
2 × 400 g cans cannellini or
   haricot beans
200 ml milk
1–2 sprigs fresh rosemary
salt and pepper

To serve
greens

GET AHEAD PREPARATION (optional)

The white bean mash can be made 1–2 days in advance and gently reheated when required. If you only have a little time:
* Season the lamb chops.
* Prepare the garlic.

25 minutes before you want to eat

* Preheat the grill to its highest setting. Take the leeks and lamb chops from the fridge so they come to room temperature.
* Next, cook the beans. Heat the oil in a pan with a lid over a medium heat and peel and slice the garlic. When the oil is hot, add the garlic to the pan and cook slowly for 2–3 minutes until it is starting to soften. While the garlic is cooking, drain and rinse the beans. When the garlic is soft, add the beans, milk and rosemary sprigs to the pan and season with salt and pepper. Add 80 ml water and bring to a simmer over a medium heat, then cover the pan with a lid, turn down the heat and leave for 5–7 minutes to infuse.
* Meanwhile, season the lamb chops and place under the grill. Cook them for 3–5 minutes, then turn them over and cook the other sides. Cook the chops for a few minutes longer for well-done meat.
* When the beans have been simmering for about 7 minutes, drain the liquid from the beans (keep a little to add to the mash, if necessary), remove the rosemary sprigs and either mash the beans with a traditional potato masher for a coarse texture, or whizz them with a hand blender or in food processor for a smooth purée. Add the cooking liquid saved from draining the beans if the texture is too solid, but remember the leeks will add some liquid too so don't go overboard.
* When the chops are cooked, leave them to rest for about 5 minutes while you finish the beans.
* Return the bean mash to the heat and stir in the leeks. Season to taste and let the leeks warm through for a few minutes, stirring from time to time.
* Serve the chops on a pile of mash, with the juices from the grill pan and a pile of buttery greens.

Seasonal supper   ## Vegetable Curry

According to Madhur Jaffrey, the doyenne of Indian cookery, this is a typical lunch for Punjab villagers – a simple curry of carrots, peas and potatoes. At this time of the year carrots should be very sweet and crisp. Easy and quick to cook, this makes a good filling supper, especially when served with naan breads.

Indian food in Britain is so ubiquitous and popular that Indian pickles and spices are widely available. Masses of companies sell Indian pickles and chutneys but if you are lucky enough to live close to a food shop that specialises in Indian food, especially in an area with a large Indian or Pakistani community, you can find some excellent locally made versions. These are often well worth hunting out.

2 tbsp groundnut or grapeseed
  oil
1 medium onion, approx. 120 g
3-cm piece of fresh root ginger
½ tsp cayenne pepper
2-3 tsp garam masala
½ tsp turmeric
1 × 200 g can chopped tomatoes
2 tbsp tomato purée
5 carrots, approx. 500 g
400 g potatoes (King Edward
  would be good)
150 g frozen peas
salt and pepper

To serve
naan breads or rice, Indian
  pickles (lime is especially
  good with this curry)

GET AHEAD PREPARATION (optional)

The curry can be made 2 days in advance and gently reheated. If you only have a little time:
* Prepare the onion, ginger and carrots.
* Prepare the potatoes and cover with water until required.

45 minutes before you want to eat

* Heat the oil in a wide, heavy-based pan over a medium heat. Peel and finely slice the onion. Add the onion to the oil and fry it for 4–5 minutes until it begins to soften and brown. Meanwhile, peel and grate the ginger.
* When the onion is soft, add the ginger and cook for a minute, stirring constantly to prevent any burning.
* Next, add the cayenne, garam masala and turmeric and stir for a minute. Then add the tomatoes, tomato purée and 1 teaspoon salt. Half fill the empty tomato can with water. Pour the water into the pan, stir once or twice, then cook over a high heat for about 5 minutes, letting the tomato mixture thicken a little.
* Meanwhile, peel and thickly slice the carrots and peel the potatoes and cut them into 1-2-cm chunks.
* Once the tomato mixture has thickened, add the carrots and potatoes and enough water to just cover the vegetables. Stir and bring to simmering point, then cook for about 30 minutes until the potatoes are tender.
* Once the potatoes are cooked, add the peas and simmer the vegetables, uncovered, for another 4–5 minutes.
* Season to taste and serve with naan breads or rice, with pickles on the side.

Larder feast

Ham and Macaroni Bake

Macaroni is synonymous with homely suppers and here this good old store-cupboard staple is mixed with leeks, ham and a mustardy cheese sauce and baked until the top is crisp and golden.

When buying ham we encourage you to aim as high as your budget will allow – there is a world of difference between slimy squares of processed ham and the drier texture and full flavour of good quality ham. Although it costs more, the flavour of decent ham means a little goes a long way.

350 g macaroni
2 leeks, approx. 300 g
100 g strong cheese, such as
   mature Cheddar
40 g butter
30 g plain flour
2 tsp mustard powder
400 ml (approx.) milk
1 tbsp wholegrain mustard
200-300 g sliced cooked ham
2-3 slices bread
2 sprigs fresh thyme
salt and pepper

To serve
green salad

GET AHEAD PREPARATION (optional)

The whole dish can be prepared 2
days in advance and baked when
required. If you only have a
little time:
* Prepare the leeks.
* Grate the cheese.
* Make the breadcrumbs.

30 minutes before you want to eat

* Preheat the oven to 190°C/375°F/Gas Mark 5.
* First, cook the macaroni in a large pan of boiling water for 6–8 minutes or according to the instructions on the packet.
* While the macaroni is cooking, trim, slice and wash the leeks. Three minutes before the macaroni is ready, throw in the sliced leeks and cook until the macaroni is cooked.
* While the macaroni and leeks are cooking, make the cheese sauce. Melt the butter in a small pan over a gentle heat. When it is foaming add the flour and mustard powder and stir well until the mixture smells biscuity – probably about 3 minutes.
* At this point gradually add the milk, whisking continuously to avoid lumps – you don't need to be too fastidious, though. By now the macaroni and leeks should be ready. You will need about 200 ml of the cooking water for the sauce so when you drain the macaroni be sure to retain some. Add the retained water to the sauce and give it a good whisk to remove any large lumps.
* Bring the sauce to a gentle simmer, stirring constantly. If it gets too thick to pour or flow easily, add another couple of tablespoons of milk. Grate the cheese and when the sauce coats the back of a wooden spoon add two-thirds and the wholegrain mustard. Stir until the cheese is melted.
* Shake the macaroni and leeks very well to get rid of any excess moisture and tip them into an ovenproof dish. Use scissors to cut the ham into strips and add to the macaroni and leeks. Mix together well and season to taste, then pour in the cheese sauce. Shake the dish a couple of times so that everything distributes evenly.
* Chop, grate or whizz the bread into breadcrumbs. Strip the thyme leaves from their stalks. Mix the breadcrumbs with the remaining cheese and the thyme leaves and season. Sprinkle the mixture over the macaroni bake.
* Place in the oven and bake until the top is crisp and golden – this will take about 10 minutes.
* Serve with a simply dressed green salad.

Two for one

Beef Goulash

For a meal on a cold day this is hard to beat. There's little preparation involved and once all the ingredients are assembled you just leave everything simmering away gently on the hob for an hour or so.

Goulash supposedly originated in Hungary. According to *The Oxford Companion to Food*, however, the dish that has become synonymous with the name is not something that it would be easy to find there. One thing is certain, though – paprika is always in a goulash and this is what creates its characteristic flavour and appearance.

With this goulash, as with casseroles in general, it is important to keep it at a very low simmer. It will boil if the heat is just a fraction of a degree too high, and the meat will take longer to soften.

3 tbsp groundnut or grapeseed
  oil
60 g lard or butter
1.2–1.5 kg stewing beef, cut into
  even-sized pieces
2 large onions, approx. 400 g
4 carrots, approx. 400 g
5 celery sticks
2 small green peppers, approx.
  250 g
3 garlic cloves
1½ tbsp paprika
1½ tsp caraway seeds
generous handful of fresh parsley
1 tbsp red wine vinegar
1 × 400 g can chopped tomatoes
1 bay leaf
1½ dried red chillies (preferably
  Hungarian paprika type)
4 potatoes, such as King
  Edwards, approx. 700 g
salt and pepper

To serve
crème fraîche, noodles and peas

GET AHEAD PREPARATION (optional)

The whole dish can be prepared
2–3 days in advance and heated
when required. If you only have
a little time:
* Prepare the onions, carrots,
  celery, green peppers and
  garlic.
* Chop the parsley.

2 hours before you want to eat

* Heat a generous splash of the oil and one-third of the lard or butter in a large casserole dish over a high heat. Season the beef with salt and pepper and brown it all over. You may need to do this in two batches.
* Tip the beef and any cooking juices into a bowl, deglaze the pan with a little water and add this to the meat in the bowl.
* Peel and thinly slice the onions. Now add the remaining oil and butter and the onions to the casserole dish and soften the onions over a medium heat for about 5 minutes. While the onions are cooking, peel and thinly slice the carrots and trim, wash and finely slice the celery. Add the carrots and celery to the casserole, turn the heat up and lightly brown them while you deseed and slice the green peppers and peel and crush the garlic. Add these to the pan along with the paprika and caraway seeds. Stir the whole lot from time to time while you roughly chop the parsley.
* Next, splash in the vinegar and let it evaporate. When it has evaporated, return the beef to the pan with all the juices and the tomatoes, bay leaf, the chillies and nearly all the parsley. Add a little water to just cover.
* Bring the goulash back to the boil, add a good dose of salt and pepper, then turn the heat right down. Cover with a lid and leave to simmer very, very gently for about 1 hour until the beef is meltingly tender.
* Taste the goulash a few times while it is cooking – if you think it is too fiery and hot you can always fish the chilli out.
* While the goulash is cooking, peel the potatoes and cut them into 1-cm dice.

20 minutes before you want to eat

* Once the beef is tender, add the potatoes and simmer very gently for about 10–15 minutes or until they are soft.
* At this point, lift half the goulash out of the casserole and set it to one side to cool for freezing.
* Scatter the remaining goulash with the rest of the parsley and serve. Buttery noodles, crème fraîche and peas would be good accompaniments.

Lazy day supper – reheating instructions

Defrost the goulash thoroughly. Reheat it in a casserole with a lid over a low heat – don't allow it to boil. Once the goulash has heated through – this will probably take 20–30 minutes – serve as above.

December Week 3 – Overview

Straightforward, comforting and very appetising best describes this week's Big Meal from Scratch of Roast Pork with Red Cabbage and Chestnuts, and Carrot and Swede Mash. The recipe specifies belly of pork which has a number of advantages – it produces abundant crackling, is meltingly tender and flavourful when roasted and is pretty cheap. Belly can usually be found as rolled joints in supermarkets or unrolled in butchers' shops. Either will work, but unrolled is preferable. To accompany the pork there is an apple and cranberry sauce made with fresh or frozen cranberries. The cabbage is cooked with chestnuts – in the run-up to Christmas cranberries and chestnuts should both be readily available. For the pork to be sufficiently tender and melting it is best cooked long and slow, so factor in this meal taking 2¾ hours from beginning to end.

For a Something for Nothing later in the week any pork left over from the big meal is used to make Stir-Fried Pork with Cashew Nuts. The surplus swede and carrot mash is transformed into a cheat's Swede and Lancashire Cheese Soufflé which takes 40 minutes –15 minutes assembly and 25 minutes baking.

A Seasonal Supper of Venison with Polenta and Cranberry Sauce is somewhat luxurious, even though it's not hugely complicated to put together and can be made in 40 minutes. At this time of the year most supermarkets and butchers stock venison medallions, but if these cost more than you intended to spend, lamb steaks are a good substitution. For a 40-minute Larder Feast Spinach and Mushroom Pasta turns often ignored canned mushrooms into a great sauce.

To end the week there is a Two for One recipe for Dhal with Coriander and Onion Roti. The dhal recipe is plain and simple, but the addition of fresh coriander, garlic, mustard and poppy seeds at the end transforms it into something very special. The recipe for coriander and onion rotis is optional, but if you have the time and inclination they are well worth making. Altogether this recipe takes 1 hour though if you omit the rotis you will reduce the time and effort required.

December Week 3	Recipe	Time
Big meal from scratch	Roast pork with red cabbage and chestnuts, carrot and swede mash and apple and cranberry sauce	2¾ hours
Something for nothing 1	Stir-fried pork with cashew nuts	25 mins
Something for nothing 2	Swede and Lancashire cheese soufflé	40 mins
Seasonal supper	Venison (or lamb) with polenta and cranberry sauce	40 mins
Larder feast	Spinach and mushroom pasta	35 mins
2 for 1	Dhal with coriander and onion rotis	1 hour

All recipes serve 4 apart from the 2 for 1 recipe which makes 8 portions

SHOPPING LIST (for 4 people)

Meat and fish
1 × 1.5 kg unrolled belly of pork (ask the butcher to score the rind)
4 × 150-200 g venison medallions or lamb steaks

Dairy
280 g butter
100 ml milk
250 ml crème fraîche
200 g Lancashire cheese
50 g Parmesan
8 large free-range eggs

Fruit and vegetables
1 small sweet potato approx. 100 g
1 small-medium swede, approx. 700 g
7 carrots, approx. 700 g
1 small red cabbage, approx. 500 g
1 small bunch spring onions, approx. 6
200 g pak choi or other Chinese greens
4 medium onions, approx. 480 g
1 large onion, approx. 200 g
3 small red onions, approx. 240 g
9 garlic cloves
2-cm piece of fresh root ginger
2 green chillies
a few sprigs fresh thyme
2 sprigs fresh sage
2 large bunches fresh coriander
2 medium Bramley apples, approx. 300 g
2 eating apples, such as Cox's Orange Pippins
230 g cranberries (fresh or frozen)
1½ lemons
1 lime
1 large orange
300 g frozen spinach

Basics
210 ml groundnut or grapeseed oil
260 g wholewheat flour
2 tsp mustard powder
1 bay leaf
2 tbsp light brown soft sugar
1 tbsp caster sugar
pinch dark brown soft or molasses sugar
200 ml chicken stock (fresh or made from a stock cube or bouillon powder)
salt and pepper

Store cupboard
200 g basmati rice
500 g dried split red lentils
250 g polenta or 500 g ready-made polenta
250 g pasta shapes, such as fusilli
2 × 290 g cans button mushrooms
200 g cooked peeled chestnuts
30-50 g dried wild mushrooms

150 g cashew nuts
2 tsp mustard seeds
2 tsp poppy seeds
3 tbsp white wine or cider vinegar
3 tbsp cranberry sauce or redcurrant, bramble or damson jelly
2 tsp soy sauce
2 tbsp Thai fish sauce
1 tbsp red curry paste
2 pinches of nutmeg (ground or freshly grated)
2 cloves
1 small cinnamon stick
1 tbsp crushed dried chillies
1 tsp cumin seeds
2 tsp turmeric
2 tsp paprika
1 tsp chilli powder
125 ml white wine
250 ml cider
60 ml port or red wine

Quick option
(Dhal with Coriander and Onion Rotis)
chapattis or naan breads; omit 250g wholewheat flour, 2 tbsp groundnut or grapeseed oil, 1 small or ½ medium onion, 2 handfuls fresh coriander, 1 tsp coriander seeds and 2 green chillies from shopping list.

Serving suggestions
green salad ingredients, new potatoes (Swede and Lancashire Cheese Soufflé)
Savoy cabbage, butter (Venison/Lamb with Polenta and Cranberry Sauce)
green salad ingredients (Spinach and Mushroom Pasta)
yoghurt, pickles such as lime, mango, etc (Dhal with Coriander and Onion Rotis)

To download or print out this shopping list, please visit www.thekitchenrevolution.co.uk/December/Week3

**Big meal
from scratch**

Roast Pork with Red Cabbage and Chestnuts, Carrot and Swede Mash and Apple and Cranberry Sauce

Apples, cabbage and pork complement each other so well that they appear together in various guises. In this recipe roast belly of pork is served with apple and cranberry sauce, cabbage cooked slowly with chestnuts and a sweet mash of carrots and swede. This is warming winter food, and good for treating yourself or friends.

Pork belly is succulent, sweet and flavoursome with a good amount of crackling. It is also inexpensive. Supermarkets tend to sell it rolled and boneless, whereas butchers sell it unrolled with the bones still in. For this recipe unrolled is what's required, so if necessary cut any string holding the meat together and then score the rind well – this will encourage crackling to form. Use a very sharp knife and make a series of parallel lines, cutting through the rind to the depth of the flesh but not into it.

The recipe includes extra pork for the Stir-Fried Pork with Cashew Nuts and extra carrot and swede mash for the Lancashire Cheese Soufflé.

Roast pork
1 × 1.5 kg unrolled belly of pork, includes 600 g extra for the stir-fried pork with cashew nuts
groundnut or grapeseed oil
4 medium onions, approx. 480 g
1 bay leaf
a few sprigs fresh thyme
75 ml white wine
200 ml chicken stock (fresh or made from a stock cube of bouillon powder
salt and pepper

Red cabbage and chestnuts
1 tbsp groundnut or grapeseed oil
60 g butter
3 small red onions, approx. 240 g
2 eating apples, such as Cox's Orange Pippins
1 small red cabbage, approx. 500 g
1 small cinnamon stick
2 tbsp light brown soft sugar
3 tbsp white wine or cider vinegar
250 ml cider
200 g cooked peeled chestnuts

Carrot and swede mash
1 swede, approx. 700 g; includes 250 g extra for the swede and Lancashire cheese soufflé
7 carrots, approx. 700 g; includes 250 g extra for the swede and Lancashire cheese soufflé
60 g butter
generous pinch of nutmeg (ground or freshly grated)

Apple and cranberry sauce
50 ml white wine
2 medium Bramley apples, approx. 250 g
½ lemon
2 cloves
1 tbsp caster sugar
15 g butter
2 sprigs fresh sage
80 g cranberries (fresh or frozen)

GET AHEAD PREPARATION (optional)

* Prepare the onions.
* Shred and cook the cabbage.
* Prepare the apples and make the apple and cranberry sauce.
* Prepare the swede and carrots.

2¼ hours before you want to eat cook the pork

* Preheat the oven to 220°C/425°F/Gas Mark 7.
* Make sure the rind of the pork is very dry then rub with oil and season thoroughly.
* Peel the onions, slice them into 3-cm thick circles and place them in a roasting tin. Tear the bay leaf, scatter the thyme and bay leaf over the onions, season and pour in the wine.
* Season the underside of the pork and place the meat on a rack over the onions. Place high in the oven and cook for 30 minutes.
* Turn the oven down to 170°C/325°F/Gas Mark 3 and cook for 1½ hours. As a guide after the initial 30 minutes at a higher temperature cook at a lower temperature for 30 minutes per 500 g.

2 hours before you want to eat cook the cabbage	* Heat the oil and half the butter in a heavy-based casserole with a lid, over a medium heat. Peel and slice the onions, add them to the hot fat and cook for 10 minutes. * Peel, core and finely slice the apples. Discard the tough outer leaves from the cabbage, cut into quarters and remove the central, hard stalk. Finely shred the leaves. * Add the cabbage to the onions and stir until it starts to soften. Add the apples, cinnamon and sugar and stir well. * Increase the heat and add the vinegar. Allow the vinegar to evaporate then add the cider and season. * Stir for a final time and add the remaining butter. Cover and cook in the oven at 170°C/325°F/Gas Mark 3 for 45 minutes to 1 hour, stirring occasionally.
1 hour before you want to eat cook the apple sauce and the root vegetables	* Pour the wine into a pan and bring it to a simmer. Peel, core and dice the apples. Peel a 5-cm strip of zest from the half lemon and stud it with the cloves. Add the apples and lemon zest to the wine. Cover, stir and cook gently for 15 minutes. * Peel the swede and carrots and cut them into even-sized chunks, then put them in a large pan of salted water. * Stir the apples every few minutes to make sure they don't stick. Once they have transformed into a fluffy mass, about 15 minutes, add the sugar and stir until it is absorbed. Add the cranberries to the apples, return the pan to a medium heat and bring the sauce to a simmer, stirring constantly. Cover, turn the heat to low and cook for about 10 minutes or until the cranberries collapse, stirring occasionally. Strip the sage leaves from their stalks and chop them. Beat the butter, sage and seasoning into the apple and cranberry mixture.
25 minutes before you want to eat make the mash and the gravy	* Bring the carrots and swede to the boil and simmer for 20–30 minutes until cooked. * The pork belly is done when the thin straight rib bones on the underside of the meat pull away easily. Remove these bones for carving but keep them to one side for making the gravy later. To tell if a piece of pork without bones is cooked, insert a knife into the meat. If it meets very little resistance the pork is ready. If the crackling isn't very crisp, preheat the grill to high and, leaving about 7 cm clearance between the crackling and heat source, place the pork under it for a couple of minutes to crisp it up. * Leave the pork to rest for about 20 minutes in a warm place. Strain all the pan juices into a bowl and set aside to cool as quickly as possible. * Pour the stock into the roasting tin and, if you have them, add the bones. Stir over a medium heat until the stock is boiling, then turn down the heat and leave to simmer very gently. * Stir the chestnuts into the cabbage and if there is a lot of liquid leave the lid off and cook over a medium heat until it has evaporated. Taste the cabbage and season. * Drain the cooked carrots and swede, return them to their pan and let them dry over a low heat for a few minutes. Add the butter and nutmeg and mash thoroughly. Taste and season if necessary, and turn the mash into a warmed serving dish. * At this point the fat and pan juices in the bowl will have separated and the fat can be skimmed off to reveal the juices. Pour these into the gravy, bring the gravy back to a simmer, then taste and season before straining into a warmed jug. * Carve the pork into slices and pass the cabbage and mashed sweded and carrot around in separate warmed serving dishes, along with the apple and cranberry sauce and the gravy.
Afterwards	* Put the remaining pork (300-400 g), leftover carrot and swede mash (450 g) in separate containers, cover and refrigerate for use later. * If you have any leftover apple and cranberry sauce you could add more cranberries and sugar to make a speedy cranberry sauce to accompany Chritmas turkey or goose.

Stir-fried Pork with Cashew Nuts

A stir-fry, packed with crunchy textures and full flavours is always popular. Belly of pork is a good cut to use in one as its high fat content prevents it drying out. As with all stir-fries, the way to keep it simple and quick is to prepare all the ingredients before cooking starts. That way it's just a matter of throwing the ingredients into the frying pan or wok in the correct order.

200 g basmati rice
1 small sweet potato, approx. 100 g
3 garlic cloves
1 small bunch spring onions, approx. 6
200 g pak choi or other Chinese greens
300–400 g cooked pork belly left over from the Big Meal from Scratch or 350 g pork tenderloin, thinly sliced

2 tbsp groundnut or grapeseed oil
1 tbsp crushed dried chillies
150 g cashew nuts
1 tbsp Thai red curry paste
2 tsp soy sauce
2 tbsp Thai fish sauce
pinch of dark brown sugar or molasses
small handful of fresh coriander
juice of 1 lime

GET AHEAD PREPARATION (optional)

All the vegetables other than the sweet potato can be prepared a day in advance and kept covered in the fridge.

25 minutes before you want to eat

* Wash the rice well under cold running water and cook according to the instructions on the packet. If it cooks before the stir-fry is completed cover with a lid to keep it warm.
* Next, prepare the vegetables and pork for the stir-fry. Peel the sweet potato, cut it into matchsticks. Peel and roughly chop the garlic. Trim and slice the spring onions. Trim and shred the pak choi or other Chinese greens. Cut the pork into 3-cm cubes. Once all these ingredients are prepared, start to stir-fry.
* Heat the oil in a large frying pan or, for preference, a wok, over a high heat. Add the garlic and chilli flakes to the hot oil and cook until the chilli flakes are dark and the garlic is golden.
* Pass the oil through a metal sieve,and discard the chilli and garlic. Return the garlic and chilli oil to the pan, add the cashew nuts and toss them from time to time over a medium heat until they are golden. Once they are golden, lift the nuts out with a slotted spoon and dry on kitchen paper.
* Now add the pork to the pan and fry it for a couple of minutes until it starts to brown and let out some of its fat, and is getting crispy.
* Next, add the sweet potato and stir-fry for 3–5 minutes until it starts to soften.
* When the sweet potato has lost its crunchiness and is starting to soften down, add the spring onions. After a couple more minutes add the curry paste and let it cook for 1–2 minutes.
* Next, add the soy sauce, fish sauce, sugar and 5 tbsp water and bring to the boil, then simmer for 4–5 minutes.
* After 4 or 5 minutes add the pak choi or Chinese greens to the wok and allow to soften for 2–3 minutes, stirring every now and then.
* While the greens are cooking roughly chop the coriander. Return the cashew nuts to the pan, add the lime and coriander and toss them through. Serve immediately with the rice.

Something
for nothing 2

Swede and Lancashire Cheese Soufflé

To save time for a midweek supper this recipe is for a cheat's soufflé made without a roux. This means it won't rise quite as high as a classic soufflé but the flavours will still be excellent and the texture light and fluffy. The pronounced flavours of swede and Lancashire cheese ensure the soufflé isn't bland. If you don't have Lancashire cheese use a strong Cheddar instead. If you don't have any carrot and swede mash from the Big Meal from Scratch, replace it with 450 g swede, peeled and cut into chunks, then simmered until tender – this will take 25 minutes or so. Drain the swede then mash the swede with a pinch of nutmeg and a little milk.

The recipe calls for a 1-litre soufflé dish, but you could use any high-sided ovenproof dish of about 20 cm in diameter. You could also make the soufflé in individual (approx. 250 ml) ramekins in which case they will need about 5 minutes less cooking.

butter, for greasing
200 g Lancashire cheese
8 large free-range eggs
450 g carrot and swede mash left
    over from the Big Meal from
    Scratch or see above
1 tsp mustard powder
½ lemon
salt and pepper

To serve
green salad
new potatoes

GET AHEAD PREPARATION (optional)

The soufflé can be made a few hours in advance up to the point of whisking the egg whites. If you only have a little time:
* Grease the soufflé dish with butter.
* Grate the cheese.

40 minutes before you want to eat

* Preheat the oven to 200°C/400°F/Gas Mark 6 and preheat a baking sheet. Thoroughly grease a large soufflé dish (about 1 litre) with butter, especially at the rim.
* Grate the cheese and set it aside. Separate the eggs, putting the whites in a very clean large bowl.
* Use a fork to break up the mash, then use a wooden spoon to stir in the cheese, egg yolks, mustard powder and plenty of salt and pepper.
* Now whisk the egg whites with a pinch of salt using an electric or hand whisk. As the whites start to become firm, add a squeeze of lemon juice – this will strengthen the protein and make the soufflé less likely to collapse.
* When the egg whites stand in soft peaks, stir one-third of them into the mash to loosen it. Now gently fold in the rest of the whites and the cheese – don't stir too hard or you will knock all the air out of the whites.
* Carefully spoon the mixture into the prepared soufflé dish. Bake the soufflé for about 20–25 minutes until it is set but still wobbles slightly in the centre.
* When the soufflé is ready, serve it immediately with new potatoes and a green salad.

Seasonal supper

Venison (or Lamb) with Polenta and Cranberry Sauce

This is a real midweek treat. Venison medallions are available in most big supermarkets, but they are expensive – if your budget doesn't stretch to these, you can substitute with lamb steaks.

The cranberry sauce that accompanies the venison is refreshingly fruity and slightly tart at the same time. If you have trouble finding quick-cook polenta, you can use the ready-made version. This is sold by most supermarkets as plastic-wrapped slabs that have to be grilled, baked or poached before serving. If you are using ready-made polenta, follow the poaching instructions on the packet – it usually takes 15–20 minutes in a pan of water, then add the butter, milk and nutmeg as in the recipe below.

Venison (or lamb)
2 tbsp groundnut or grapeseed oil
4 × 150–200 g venison medallions or lamb steaks
salt and pepper

Polenta
250 g polenta or 500 g ready-made polenta (see above)
60 g butter
100 ml milk
pinch of nutmeg (ground or freshly grated)
salt

Cranberry sauce
3 tbsp cranberry sauce or redcurrant, bramble or damson jelly
150 g fresh cranberries
1 tsp mustard powder
2-cm piece of fresh root ginger
1 large orange
½ lemon
4 tbsp port or red wine

To serve
buttered Savoy cabbage

GET AHEAD PREPARATION (optional)

If there are a few spare moments the following would be helpful:
*Make the cranberry sauce.

40 minutes before you want to eat

* Turn the oven to its lowest setting.
* First, make the sauce. Put the cranberry sauce, fresh cranberries and mustard in a pan. Peel and grate the ginger, zest and juice the orange and lemon and add to the pan. Place the pan over a medium heat and bring everything to the boil, whisking all the while. As the cranberries heat they will pop and disintegrate into the sauce. When the mixture starts to boil remove it from the heat and stir in the port or wine. Set aside.
* Now make the polenta. Boil the kettle and pour 1.2 litres boiling water into a large pan with 1 teaspoon salt. Let the water come back to the boil then pour the polenta into it in a slow stream. Whisk well as the mixture thickens.
* When the polenta has thickened, add the butter, milk and nutmeg. Beat these ingredients into the polenta – the polenta is ready when it drops softly from the spoon. Tip the polenta into a serving dish, cover and put it in the oven to keep warm.
* Now cook the venison or lamb. Heat the oil in a frying pan. Pat the venison or lamb dry with kitchen paper, then season both sides well before frying them in the hot oil. Fry a medallion about 4 cm thick for 2 minutes on each side for rare, 3 minutes for medium rare and 4–5 minutes for well done. Adjust the cooking time for thinner medallions or lamb steaks.
* Remove the venison or lamb from the frying pan and set aside to rest for 5–10 minutes.
* Add the sauce to the pan in which the meat was cooked and bring to a gentle simmer for a few minutes.
* Serve the venison or lamb with a good dollop of polenta and a generous helping of the sauce. Buttered Savoy cabbage would make a good accompaniment.

Larder feast

Spinach and Mushroom Pasta

Creamy, colourful and full of flavours, no one will believe this is made with canned mushrooms. The recipe was originally intended to be for cannelloni but as life (particularly midweek) is too short to stuff cannelloni, here is the same sauce with a simple baked pasta. If cannelloni is your thing, however, simply follow the recipe below but stuff the spinach and mushroom mixture inside the cannelloni and put them in a dish, then pour the creamy sauce over them and bake them for 20–30 minutes.

30–50 g dried wild mushrooms
300 g frozen spinach
2 × 290 g cans button
   mushrooms
70 g butter
2 garlic cloves
250 g pasta shapes, such as
   fusilli
50 g Parmesan
250 ml crème fraîche
salt and pepper

To serve
green salad

GET AHEAD PREPARATION (optional)

* Soak the dried mushrooms.
* Defrost the spinach.
* Peel and crush the garlic.

35 minutes before you want to eat

* Preheat the oven to 200°C/400°F/Gas Mark 6.
* Pour enough boiling water over the dried mushrooms to just cover and leave them to rehydrate.
* Defrost the spinach according to the instructions on the packet (usually in boiling water or in a microwave).
* Next, cook the canned mushrooms. Melt half the butter in a heavy-based pan and peel and crush the garlic. When the butter is melted add the garlic and leave it to soften gently over a very low heat while you drain the canned mushrooms. Add them to the garlic in the pan, turn the heat up and brown them for a couple of minutes.
* Now purée the garlicky canned mushrooms – either in a food processor or with a hand blender. The purée will be added to the spinach and wild mushrooms.
* Next, cook the dried mushrooms and the spinach. Return the pan to the heat and add the rest of the butter. Lift the dried mushrooms from their soaking liquor with a slotted spoon (reserve the liquid to use in the sauce) and cook them in the butter over a medium heat for about 5 minutes. Stir in the spinach, turn up the heat a little and mix the mushrooms and spinach together, letting any excess liquid evaporate as you do so.
* Now return the mushroom purée to the pan. Amalgamate everything thoroughly and season to taste with salt and pepper. Take the mixture off the heat while you make the sauce.
* Put the pasta on to cook according to the instructions on the packet (usually in boiling water for about 10 minutes).
* To make the sauce, pass the dried mushroom soaking liquor through a fine sieve into a small pan and bring it to the boil. Reduce it by one-third while you grate the Parmesan. Then add the crème fraîche and all but 1 heaped tablespoon of the Parmesan to the liquid, blend thoroughly and season very well.
* Preheat the grill to its highest setting.
* When the pasta is cooked, drain and stir it into the mushroom and spinach mixture. Season to taste.
* Tip the pasta mixture into a large ovenproof dish and pour the sauce over it and sprinkle it with the rest of the Parmesan.
* Put the pasta under the grill until it is bubbling and browned on top.
* Serve immediately with a green salad

Two for one

Dhal with Coriander and Onion Rotis

Recipes for dhal, almost the staple food of India, vary enormously and can be either very simple or rich in texture and intense in flavour. In this one garlic, spices and fresh coriander are stirred in at the end for a dhal that packs a punch but is very easy to make.

Dried, hulled and split red lentils (masoor dal) are found in supermarkets and all Indian grocery stores. It is well worth locating your nearest Indian store – even if it is a drive away – to stock up on spices, dried beans and lentils, canned coconut milk, chutneys and pickles. You will find a much bigger range of products than at standard supermarkets and the prices, especially for spices, are much lower.

Dhal is filling and nutritious – a meal in itself and perfectly satisfying when accompanied by pickles or chutneys. But for added interest home-made onion and coriander rotis add an extra-special dimension. These are optional and could be replaced by ready-made chapattis or naan breads.

Popular recipes journey across generations and lands, and this one is no exception. It was given to Polly by her sister-in-law Kate who inherited it from a friend.

This recipe makes enough for eight servings – half to eat right away and the rest to be frozen for when you don't feel like cooking.

Dhal
1 large onion, approx. 200 g
5 tbsp groundnut or grapeseed
 oil
500 g dried split red lentils
2 tsp turmeric
2 tsp paprika
1 tsp chilli powder
4 garlic cloves
2 generous handfuls coriander
 leaves
2 tsp mustard seeds
2 tsp poppy seeds
salt

Onion and coriander rotis
1 small onion, approx. 60 g
2 handfuls of fresh coriander
 leaves
2 green chillies
2 tbsp groundnut or grapeseed
 oil, plus extra for greasing
250 g wholewheat flour, plus
 extra for dusting
1 tsp cumin seeds
salt
or
ready-made chapattis or naan
 breads

To serve
yoghurt and Indian pickles
 (lime, mango)

GET AHEAD PREPARATION (optional)

The entire dish can be made
2 days in advance and reheated
when required. If you only have
a little time:
* Prepare the roti dough, if
 making.
* Prepare the onion and garlic.
* Wash the lentils.
* Chop the coriander.

1 hour before you want to eat make the rotis

* To make rotis, peel and very finely chop the onion, finely chop the coriander and deseed and finely chop the chillies. Otherwise skip the next instructions and head on to make the dhal.
* Put half the oil in a pan or microwave and warm gently. Put the flour and 1 teaspoon salt into a bowl then stir in the warm oil. Add all the remaining ingredients (minus the rest of the oil) and use your hands to bring the mixture together and knead. Add cold water, a little at a time, to make a firm dough.
* Lightly dust a work surface with flour, then turn the dough out and knead it for about 5 minutes so that the onion, coriander, cumin and chillies are well mixed into it. Add more flour if the mixture is very sticky. You could mix and knead the roti dough in a food processor.
* Lightly oil a clean bowl, put the dough in it, cover with cling film and leave to rest for 30 minutes. While the dough is resting start the dhal.

35 minutes before you ant to eat make the dahl

* To make the dhal first peel and finely slice the onion. Heat approximately 2 tablespoons of the oil in a heavy-based pan with a lid over a medium heat. Add the onion and fry it for 10 minutes until it is soft and just turning brown.
* While the onion is cooking, wash the lentils under cold running water to remove any dust or dirt and set aside.
* When the onion is soft and starting to brown add the lentils, turmeric, paprika, chilli powder and 1½ teaspoons salt. Turn up the heat, add 1 litre of water, stir well and bring to the boil. When the water is boiling scrape off any froth from the top, turn down the

heat, cover the pan with a lid and allow the lentils to simmer gently for about 25 minutes. Check now and then to ensure they are not boiling dry or sticking – if they are drying out add a little more water.

* Peel and thinly slice the garlic and roughly chop the coriander.
* Heat the remaining oil in a frying pan. When it is hot add the garlic and nearly all the coriander, and the mustard seeds and poppy seeds. Cook until the coriander starts to go smoky brown just before burning and the pan is very smoky – up to 5 minutes.
* Remove the pan from the heat and leave it to one side while you fry the rotis.

10 minutes before you ant to eat

* Wipe out the frying pan with kitchen paper and place it over a medium-high heat. Line a bowl or pan with a lid with a clean tea towel or kitchen paper.
* While the pan is heating up, divide the dough into eight balls. Using the palm of your hand, flatten them out into circles no more than 5 mm thick.
* Add a drizzle of the remaining oil to the pan and fry the rotis one at a time. They should take about 30 seconds per side to cook. Put the fried rotis in the bowl or pan and cover to keep them warm while you fry the others. the final four can be put aside for freezing later. Freeze in layers between foil or greaseproof paper.
* When the rotis are ready, divide the dhal mixture into two. Put half aside to cool and freeze then add the coriander, garlic and spice mixture to the remaining dhal and mix well.
* Garnish the dhal with the rest of the coriander and serve with yoghurt and Indian pickles.

Lazy day supper – reheating instructions

* Defrost the dhal thoroughly. Put it in a casserole with a lid and leave it over a low heat to warm through very gently. This will take 20–40 minutes. The rotis can be reheated from frozen. Wrap them in foil in a pile. preheat the oven to 200°C/400°F/Gas mark 6 and leave them to warm through for about 15–20 minutes. If you want to crisp them up remove from the foil when warm and place on a hot oven tray in a single layer for about 5–10 minutes.
* Serve the dhal with fresh coriander fried with a garlic and spice mixture as above, yoghurt, pickles and rotis.

December Week 4 – Overview

Rather than reproducing a traditional recipe for Christmas turkey or goose, the Big Meal from Scratch this week is Honey-Baked Ham with Mustard Leeks. This can stand alone as a meal in itself but is also a fantastic accompaniment to roast turkey or goose on Christmas Day if you are catering for large numbers. If you will be eating it on its own but are serving more than four, increase the ingredients accordingly and adjust the cooking time, as suggested in the recipe. When buying ham it may also be called gammon – don't be confused by this they are pretty much interchangeable terms.

The Something for Nothing recipes this week make the most of the leftover ham and ham stock. The London particular (pea and ham soup) is warming and very welcome on a cold day and Baked Field Mushrooms with Ham and Leeks are filling but not too heavy.

If you have a glut of turkey when Christmas is over, the following recipes could provide good ways of using it up:

* Cheat's Cassoulet (see page 50)
* Upside-Down Chicken Pie (see page 31)
* Guinea Fowl (or Chicken) Pie (see page 77)
* Pheasant (or Chicken) and Chestnut Soup (see page 491)

For the Seasonal Supper there's a chance to use up leftover Stilton and utilise the season's crisp and crunchy celery in a strudel. A Smoked Haddock, Spinach and Macaroni Bake made from larder ingredients is especially good if you've run out of fresh ingredients, can't face shopping and feel like something other than meat.

The Two for One recipe for a Nut Bake is one to consider if vegetarians are visiting or when the season's excessive meat consumption starts to pall. Light and full of flavour, the bake is wonderfully moreish and will go as well with a salad as with steamed spinach or greens.

If you're planning a feast for New Year's Eve, Venison (or Beef) with Pickled Walnuts, Hasselback Potatoes and Cabbage with Bacon from December week 1 (see page 524) or Baked Salmon with Saffron Rice and Creamed Leeks from week 2 (see page 534) might be suitable.

December Week 4	Recipe	Time
Big meal from scratch	Honey-baked ham with mustard leeks	2 hours
Something for nothing 1	Baked field mushrooms with ham and leeks	35 mins
Something for nothing 2	The London particular – pea and ham soup – with potato bread	40 mins (55 mins)
Seasonal supper	Stilton and celery strudel	50 mins
Larder feast	Smoked haddock, spinach and macaroni bake	40 mins
2 for 1	Nut bake	50 mins

All recipes serve 4 apart from the 2 for 1 recipe which makes 8 portions

SHOPPING LIST (for 4 people)

Meat and fish
1 × 2-2.2 kg free-range ham or gammon joint
300 g (approx.) frozen haddock fillets
   (smoked or unsmoked)

Dairy
335 g butter
200 ml crème fraîche (100 ml optional for
   Smoked Haddock, Spinach and Macaroni
   Bake)
150 ml (approx.) milk
60 g Parmesan
170 g Stilton
6 large free-range eggs (includes 1 optional
   egg for Potato Bread)

Fruit and vegetables
1 medium potato, approx. 175 g (optional for
   potato bread)
2 carrots, approx. 200 g
10 large field mushrooms
1 large head celery (ideally English white
   celery)
1 bunch watercress, approx. 85 g
10 leeks, approx. 1 kg
5 medium onions, approx. 600 g
6 garlic cloves
1 large bunch fresh parsley
2-3 sprigs fresh mint
4-6 sprigs fresh thyme (includes a few
   optional sprigs for Potato Bread)
4-5 sprigs fresh sage (includes 2-3 optional
   sprigs for Potato Bread)
3 lemons
1 orange

Basics
60 ml groundnut or grapeseed oil
250 ml vegetable stock (made from a stock
   cube or bouillon powder)
275 g soft white breadcrumbs, 10-12 slices
   bread
250 g soft brown breadcrumbs, or 8-10 slices
   bread suitable for crumbing
½ tbsp plain flour
180 g self-raising flour (optional for potato
   bread)
3 tbsp Dijon mustard
1 tsp mustard powder (optional for potato
   bread)
½ tbsp wholegrain mustard
2 bay leaves
salt and pepper

Store cupboard
1 x 400 g can creamed spinach, canned
   spinach or frozen leaf spinach
350 g dried green or yellow split peas (no-
   soak)
250 g macaroni
150 g (approx.) filo pastry
450 g mixed shelled nuts (pine nuts, cashew
   nuts, brazil nuts, hazelnuts or almonds)
30 g shelled walnuts
4-5 tbsp clear honey
½ tsp ground allspice
10 cloves
2 tbsp ground almonds
500 ml dry cider
400 ml white wine

Serving suggestions
bread or potatoes for baking, salad
   ingredients or green vegetable (Baked Field
   Mushrooms with Ham and Leeks)
mixed salad leaves, lemon juice, olive oil
   (Stilton and celery Strudel)
green salad ingredients or green vegetable
   (Smoked Haddock, Spinach and Macaroni
   Bake)
green vegetable, cranberry or Cumberland
   sauce (Nut Bake)

To download or print out this shopping list,
please visit www.thekitchenrevolution.co.uk/
December/Week4

Honey-Baked Ham with Mustard Leeks

Serving a ham at Christmas, either as an accompaniment to turkey or on it's own, is a wonderful tradition. It's especially suited to entertaining as it can be served hot with mash and vegetables, or cold with pickles, mustard or mayonnaise.

Honey and cider are perfect partners for ham, drawing out its sweetness and countering any saltiness. As ham is a salted pork joint it has to be brought to the boil in a pan of water to remove excess salt. Once this is completed, the ham is baked in the oven on a low heat for just over 1 hour, then coated with a sticky mixture of honey and spice and roasted at a high heat for 15–20 minutes.

Accompanying the ham are leeks grilled with crème fraîche and mustard. As this is Christmas you may already be having a lot of vegetable dishes. If not, some mash would go well with the ham and leeks.

The recipe includes extra ham and leeks for the Baked Field Mushrooms and extra ham and stock for the London Particular.

Honey-baked ham
1 × 2–2.2 kg free-range ham (or gammon) joint; includes 400 g extra for the baked field mushrooms with ham and leeks and the London particular – pea and ham soup
1 lemon
1 orange
4–5 tbsp clear honey
½ tsp ground allspice
2 tbsp Dijon mustard
½ tsp freshly ground black pepper
10 cloves
350 ml (approx.) dry cider
2 bay leaves

For the gravy
½ tbsp plain flour
150 ml dry cider
salt and pepper

Mustard leeks
10 leeks, approx. 1 kg; includes 400 g extra for the baked field mushrooms with ham and leeks
3 tbsp crème fraîche
1 tbsp Dijon mustard

To serve
mashed potatoes

GET AHEAD PREPARATION (optional)

* Bring the ham to the boil and drain.
* Make the honey and cider mixture for the gammon.
* Mix the mustard and crème fraîche for the leeks.
* Zest the lemon and orange.
* Prepare the leeks.

2¼ hours before you want to eat cook the ham

* Preheat the oven to 160°C/325°F/Gas Mark 3.
* Put the ham in a large pan and cover with cold water. Place over a medium heat and bring to the boil, then drain. We only do this once but if you are very sensitive to salty food, repeat the process. Once boiled, leave the ham until it is cool enough to handle.
* While the ham is coming to the boil, grate the zest of lemon and orange, mix them together and set aside. Don't throw away the lemon and orange as you will be using the juice later. Mix together the honey, allspice, mustard and pepper and set aside.
* When the ham is cool enough to handle, use a sharp knife to make incisions in the flesh and rind and fill them with the cloves. Take half the orange and lemon zest mixture and rub it over the ham rind. Mix the remianing zest with the honey mixture.
* Place the ham on a rack in a roasting tin. Pour in the cider and squeeze in the juice of the orange and throw in the bay leaves. Cover the joint with an airtight tent of foil so that it will steam while it's in the oven. Bake in the oven for 1½ hours. (If you have a bigger or smaller joint calculate the cooking time at 20 minutes per 500 g, plus 15–20 minutes for glazing.)

1 hour before you want to eat prepare the leeks

* While the ham is baking prepare the leeks.
* Trim the leeks and if they are less than 2 cm in diameter leave them whole. If not, slice them in half lengthways (or quarter them if they are very fat). Wash very well and make sure there is no grit remaining remove the roots.
* Place the leeks in a large pan with a lid. Steam in about 2 cm of water over a high heat for about 10 minutes until they are soft. While the leeks are cooking, mix the crème fraîche and mustard together with a good dose of salt and pepper. Once the leeks are softened, drain them well. Keep the cooking liquor to use in the gravy. Tip the leeks into a gratin dish that will fit under your grill or into a grill pan. Dollop the crème

fraîche and mustard mixture over the top of the leeks, using a spoon to spread it thinly. Squeeze the juice of one lemon over the leeks.

40 minutes before you want to eat glaze the ham

* When the ham has been cooking for 1½ hours take it out of the oven. Remove the foil, taking care not to get burned by escaping steam. Reserve the cooking liquor for use later in the week.
* Turn the oven up to 220°C/425°F/Gas Mark 7.
* Use a sharp knife to remove any rind or fat from the gammon. Spoon the honey and mustard mixture over the ham and use the back of a spoon to spread it evenly over the entire joint. Put the ham back into the oven to bake for 15–20 minutes.
* Next, remove the ham from the oven and turn the oven off. Place the ham on a carving board and leave it to rest for 10–15 minutes. Put some plates and serving dishes and a jug in the bottom of the cooling oven to warm.

15 minutes before you want to eat cook the leeks and the gravy

* Preheat the grill to high. When it is hot, put the leeks underneath the grill and cook for 5–10 minutes or until they start to brown.
* While the leeks are grilling, make a simple gravy from the juices in the roasting tin. Spoon as much fat as possible out of the tin and place over a medium heat. Sprinkle in the flour, stir it well and let it cook for a minute, then add the cider. Bring to the boil, scraping the tin all the while to lift off all the tasty flavours. When the cider has reduced by half, add 100 ml of the leek cooking liquor (or stock or water). Whisk or stir well then allow the gravy to bubble away while you finish the leeks and carve the ham.
* Remove the leeks from the grill, put one-third to one side for use later in the week and keep the rest in a warm while you finish the ham.
* Season the gravy then strain it into the warmed jug.
* Slice the ham and pass the leeks and gravy around separately.

Afterwards

Put the remaining ham (500 g), leeks (300 g) and the cooking liquor (500 ml) from the ham in separate containers, cover and refrigerate for use later.

Baked Field Mushrooms with Ham and Leeks

These flavourful stuffed mushrooms are especially suited to a Boxing Day supper after the excess of Christmas.

Large field mushrooms provide a very good platform for 'stuffing' – or what is more accurately described as 'topping' – with different tasty ingredients. In this case we use leeks, ham and cheese. If there are no leeks remaining from the Big Meal from Scratch, slice and thoroughly wash 400 g leeks. Sweat them in butter until they are soft, then mix them with a little mustard and crème fraîche.

10 large field mushrooms
100 g butter
1 tbsp groundnut or grapeseed oil
2 garlic cloves
300 g (approx.) leeks left over
   from the Big Meal from Scratch
   or see above
small handful of fresh parsley
300 g cooked ham left over from
   the Big Meal from Scratch or
   300 g slices roast ham
60 g Parmesan
salt and pepper

To serve
bread or baked potatoes, and a
   green salad or green vegetable

GET AHEAD PREPARATION (optional)

This dish can be prepared a day in advance up to the point of going in the oven. If you only have a little time:
* Clean the mushrooms.
* Chop the mushroom stalks and two of the mushrooms.
* Prepare the garlic, leeks and parsley.
* Cut the ham into dice.

* Preheat the oven to 200°C/400°F/Gas Mark 6.
* First, make the topping mixture. Wipe or peel the mushrooms to remove any dirt and remove their stalks. Cut the tough ends from the stalks and finely chop the rest along with two of the mushrooms. Melt a generous nut of the butter with the oil in a pan over a medium heat. When the fat is hot add the chopped mushrooms. Cook for about 5–7 minutes until the mushrooms are soft.
* While the mushrooms are cooking, put the remaining butter in a roasting tin or ovenproof dish big enough to hold all the whole mushrooms snugly. Place in the oven for a few minutes so that the butter melts. Meanwhile, peel and crush the garlic and add it to the cooking mushrooms.
* Roughly chop the leeks and parsley, cut the ham into 1-cm dice and mix all three together.
* When the mushrooms have softened, stir in the leek, parsley and ham mixture and season to taste with salt and pepper.
* Take the roasting tin out of the oven and brush the remaining eight mushrooms, inside and out, with the melted butter. Tip any excess butter out of the tin and into the topping mixture.
* Place the mushrooms in the tin and spread the topping over them. Grate the Parmesan over the top, cover with foil and bake them in the oven for 15 minutes until they are soft and cooked through. At the end remove the foil and let them brown for 5 minutes.
* Pour any pan juices over the mushrooms and serve immediately with bread or baked potatoes and a green salad or vegetable.

The London Particular – Pea and Ham Soup – with Potato Bread

The combination of sweet peas and salty ham in this soup is incredibly moreish. The name originated in nineteenth-century London when thick fogs were referred to as 'pea soupers'. The recipe for potato bread is excellent but optional. If you leave it out the soup takes 40 minutes, otherwise add on another 15 minutes.

The London Particular – pea and ham soup
350 g dried green or yellow split peas (no-soak)
30 g butter
1 tbsp groundnut or grapeseed oil
200 g cooked ham left over from the Big Meal from Scratch or 200 g good quality baked ham
2 medium onions
2 carrots
2 large celery sticks
500 ml ham cooking liquor left over from the Big Meal from Scratch, made up to 1.5 litres with vegetable stock or 1.5 litres vegetable stock (made from a stock cube or bouillon powder)
handful of fresh parsley
few sprigs fresh mint
salt and pepper

Potato bread (optional)
175 g self-raising flour, plus extra for dusting
1 tsp mustard powder
1 medium potato, approx. 175 g
few sprigs fresh thyme
few sprigs fresh sage
1 large free-range egg
2 tbsp milk
butter, for greasing

GET AHEAD PREPARATION (optional)

The soup and the bread can be made a day in advance. If you only have a little time
* Prepare the onions, carrots and celery.

55 minutes before you want to eat make the potato bread

* Preheat the oven to 190°C/375°F/Gas Mark 5
* Sift the flour, mustard and 1 teaspoon salt into a bowl. Grate the potato into the flour. Strip the thyme and sage leaves from their stalks, chop them well and add them to the flour mix. Combine everything together with your hands.
* Mix the egg and milk, then make a well in the centre of the dry ingredients and pour in the liquid – combine to form a soft, rough dough.
* Grease a baking sheet and lift the dough onto it. Shape the dough into a 5 cm high round and dust with flour. Bake the bread for 25–30 minutes.
* When the bread is golden and light to lift, let it cool on a rack.

40 minutes before you want to eat make the soup

* Put the split peas in a large bowl, cover them with boiling water.
* Heat the butter and oil in a pan. Shred the ham and add three-quarters to the pan, reserve the remainder for garnish. Cook for a couple of minutes.
* Peel and slice the onions and add them to the pan, stirring once or twice. Peel the carrots, cut them in half lengthways and slice them into 1-cm thick pieces, then add them to the pan. Wash and finely slice the celery and add it to the pan. Cook over a medium heat for about 10 minutes until the vegetables are softened and golden.
* Once the vegetables are starting to soften, drain the split peas, add them to the pan and stir.
* Add the ham liquor and bring to simmering point. Chop the parsley and tear the mint leaves. Add half the herbs to the vegetables and split peas, put the lid on and simmer very gently for at least 25 minutes, until the peas are soft and have broken down.
* To make the garnish, fry the remaining ham in a frying pan without any fat in it, until it is crisp. Transfer it to a plate using a slotted spoon.
* While the soup is cooking make the bread.
* When the peas are soft, the soup is ready. If you want a smooth texture liquidise at this point and season to taste.
* Toss the remaining herbs with the crispy ham, if using. Ladle the soup into bowls and sprinkle some of the ham mixture or herbs, into each bowl. Serve with the bread.

Seasonal supper

Stilton and Celery Strudel

Leftover Stilton is common after Christmas and this recipe is a good way to use it up and create a lovely meal. English celery with white sticks is more likely to be in the shops at this time of the year. It has a more pronounced flavour than the standard green version sold year round and is the perfect foil for Stilton. If you can't find white celery, green celery is fine too.

8 large celery sticks
60 g butter, plus extra for
  greasing
200 ml white wine
250 ml vegetable stock (made
  from a stock cube or bouillon
  powder)
30 g shelled walnuts
1 free-range egg
170 g Stilton
small handful of fresh parsley
juice of ½ lemon
2 tbsp ground almonds
150 g filo pastry
salt and pepper

To serve
mixed salad leaves

GET AHEAD PREPARATION (optional)

The strudel can be assembled up
to 2 hours in advance, up until
the point it goes into the oven.
If you only have a little time:
* Prepare and cook the celery.
* Toast the walnuts.
* Crumble the Stilton and mix
  with the egg, lemon juice,
  parsley and seasoning.

50 minutes before you want to eat make the filling

* Wash, trim and cut the celery into 2-cm thick slices. Plunge the celery into cold water and wash thoroughly.
* Heat half the butter in a large pan with a lid and add the celery. Let it cook over a high heat for 5 minutes so that it starts to soften and brown.
* Once the celery has started to brown, splash in the wine and let it reduce by half. Add the stock and bring it up to a simmer. Then put the lid on and let the celery cook down over a medium heat for 10 minutes while you prepare the rest of the filling.
* Preheat the oven 200°C/400°F/Gas Mark 6.
* Put the walnuts on a baking sheet in the oven and toast them while the oven heats up.
* Beat the egg in a bowl and crumble in the Stilton. Roughly chop the parsley and add the parsley and lemon juice to the bowl. Season and mix the whole lot together.
* Melt the remaining butter and set it aside. Roughly chop the walnuts and mix them with the almonds.
* Once the celery has been cooking for 10 minutes, take the lid off, bring the celery to a vigorous boil and boil away all the liquid.
* When all the liquid has evaporated, tip the celery on to a large plate so that it cools down quickly.

30 minutes before you want to eat make the strudel

* Grease a baking sheet with butter and lay a sheet of filo pastry on the tray. If the filo is small (just under A4 size) lie two sheets side by side so that they overlap by about 2 cm.
* Brush the filo with some of the melted butter and sprinkle a quarter of the nuts over it. Now repeat this three times – a layer of filo, butter then nuts.
* Now mix the celery with the Stilton mixture. Pile this mixture into the middle of the pastry leaving a 5-cm gap at each end.
* Fold the edges onto the filling then roll the pastry around. Brush the outside of the strudel with any remaining butter and make sure the seam is on the bottom.
* Bake the strudel for 20 minutes until the outside is crisp and golden.
* Serve with mixed leaves dressed with lemon juice and olive oil.

Larder feast

Smoked Haddock, Spinach and Macaroni Bake

Baked macaroni is always welcome on a cold day and adding smoked haddock and creamed spinach makes a bake that is above the ordinary (even though all the ingredients come from the larder). Canned creamed spinach seems incredibly old-fashioned, a remnant of the 1950s or 1960s, but it is actually rather nice and comforting. It works well mixed with smoked haddock, macaroni and a little crème fraîche. If you can't find it use 350 g canned leaf spinach in brine, or 350 g defrosted frozen spinach, drained and mixed with 100 ml crème fraîche.

The quantities below will feed four, but they could easily be increased to cater for more.

250 g macaroni
300 g (approx.) frozen smoked
   haddock fillets
1 tbsp groundnut or grapeseed oil
1 medium onion, approx. 120 g
200 ml white wine
1 × 400 g can creamed spinach,
   canned leaf spinach or see
   above
½ tbsp wholegrain mustard
3–4 tbsp crème fraîche
½ lemon
75 g white breadcrumbs
salt and pepper

To serve
green salad or a green vegetable

GET AHEAD PREPARATION (optional)

* Peel and slice the onion.
* Defrost, drain and flake the
   haddock.

40 minutes before you want to eat

* Preheat the oven to 200°C/400°F/Gas Mark 6.
* Cook the macaroni according to the instructions on the packet (usually for 10 minutes in boiling, salted water).
* Next, defrost the smoked haddock. Place the fillets in a pan with a lid and cover with water. Place over a medium heat and bring to the boil. Cover with the lid, turn off the heat and set aside. You will use the water later so do not throw it away.
* While the haddock is coming to the boil, start cooking the onion and spinach mixture. Put the oil in a heavy-based pan over a medium heat while you peel and thinly slice the onion. When the oil is hot, add the onion and cook for about 7 minutes until it softens and starts to brown.
* When the macaroni is cooked, drain well and set aside.
* When the onion is softened and starting to brown, add the wine and bring it to the boil over a medium heat. Allow the wine to boil for about 2 minutes, then add 200 ml of the water used to cook the haddock. If using tinned leaf spinach drain well. Bring the liquid to a simmer then add the spinach and stir in the mustard and crème fraîche. Grate the zest of the half lemon, squeeze out its juice and add these. Mix well, season boldly and warm through gently.
* Meanwhile, drain any remaining water from the haddock, break it into large flakes and add it to the spinach. Add the macaroni and fold together gently. Season to taste, with salt and pepper.
* Tip into a shallow ovenproof dish and cover with the breadcrumbs or matzo meal.
* Place in the oven and bake for 15 minutes until browned and bubbling.
* Serve with a simple green salad.

Two for one

Nut Bake

After the excesses of Christmas, here is something festive, meat-free and unbelievably good for you. If you have vegetarian guests over Christmas or New Year, this is a great dish to offer them. Nut bake has received a bad press over the years because the mass-produced versions served in canteens are usually dry, solid and completely devoid of flavour. The nut bake recipe here includes a layer of herby breadcrumbs and is light, well seasoned and moist. It is delicious in its own right but also goes well with cranberry sauce. It is based on a recipe that Polly and Rosie cooked while they were at the Carved Angel.

The quantites below are enough to make two loaves, feeding eight people in total. One loaf is intended for the freezer.

60 g butter
1 tbsp groundnut or grapeseed oil
2 medium onions, approx. 240 g
4 garlic cloves
450 g mixed shelled nuts (pine nuts, cashew nuts, brazil nuts, hazelnuts or almonds)
4 large free-range eggs
200 g white breadcrumbs, or 6-8 slices bread suitable for crumbing
8 tbsp milk, approx. 120 ml
salt and pepper

For the breadcrumb filling
1 lemon
250 g brown breadcrumbs, or 8-10 slices bread suitable for crumbing
2 sprigs fresh sage
4 sprigs fresh thyme
small handful of fresh parsley
1 bunch watercress, approx. 85 g
85 g butter

To serve
green vegetable, cranberry or Cumberland sauce

GET AHEAD PREPARATION (optional)

The nut bake can be prepared 1-2 days in advance, up to the point of going in the oven. If you only have a little time:
* Prepare the onions and garlic.
* Chop the nuts.
* Chop the sage, thyme, parsley and watercress.

50 minutes before you want to eat

* Preheat the oven to 200°C/400°F/Gas Mark 6.
* Start by making the nut layers. Heat the butter and oil in a small pan over a low heat. Peel and finely chop the onions and add them to the pan. Leave the onions to soften for 10 minutes.
* Peel and crush the garlic and when the onions have softened add the garlic to the pan and cook for a couple more minutes.
* While the onions are cooking, roughly chop the whole mixed nuts – either pulse them a few times in a food processor or cover them with a clean tea towel and bash them with a rolling pin. Place the nuts in a large mixing bowl and add the white breadcrumbs, milk, beaten eggs and a good dose of salt and pepper. When the onions and garlic are cooked add these too.
* Now make the breadcrumb filling. Grate the zest of the lemon. Place the breadcrumbs in a second bowl and add the zest. Chop the sage and thyme leaves with the parsley and watercress. Add the chopped herbs and watercress to the breadcrumbs along with the melted butter. Mix together well and season to taste.
* You are now ready to build the loaf. Thoroughly grease two cake or loaf tins with butter. Put a qurter of the nut mixture in the bottom of each tin. Smooth out to form an even layer then cover each with half the bvreadcrumb mixture. Cover the breadcrumbs with the remaining nut mixture.
* Cover the tins with foil and place one of the nut bakes in the oven to bake for 30 minutes. Leave the other one to cool for freezing.
* Once the nut bake in the oven is firm to the touch, remove from the heat and let it sit for about 5 minutes before turning it out. Serve with a green vegetable and leftover cranberry or Cumberland sauce.

Lazy day supper – cooking instructions

Defrost the nut bake thoroughly then preheat the oven to 200°C/400°F/Gas Mark 6 and bake it as above.

Different types of nuts

Nuts come in various shapes, sizes and colours, each with their unique flavour. If possible, and time permits for shelling, buy nuts in their shells as shelled nuts go rancid quite quickly. Choose clean, unbroken shells, the nuts should feel heavy for their size – if they are light the nuts inside may be old and shrivelled. If you buy shelled nuts choose those that are plump and firm and uniform in colour and size.

Almonds The seeds of a Mediterranean tree which is related to the peach family, almonds are believed to have originated in the Near East and are one of the most popular and versatile nuts. For the best flavour, buy almonds unblanched and skin and roast or toast them just before using.

Brazil nuts Large dark brown skinned nuts with a creamy white interior and a sweet, milky flavour. The majority of nuts are harvested from wild trees rather than from plantations. The fruit from the Brazil tree are similar in shape and appearance to a coconut, and each one contains up to 20 nuts.

Cashew nuts The cashew is a distant relative of the pistachio and mango and is grown mainly in Brazil and India. They are plump nuts with a subtle sweet flavour – add them at the end of cooking to preserve this.

Hazelnuts These crunchy round, brown-skinned nuts, which are also known as cobnuts or filberts, have a distinctive bitter flavour. If they are roasted the bitter flavour becomes less apparent.

Pine nuts Tiny cream-coloured nuts with a subtle flavour and a high oil content. They are the seeds of many different species of pine – the majority of which are exported from Italy and Spain.

Stuffed Apples Baked with Cinnamon Custard

Oven baked custard is a great treat and when served with stuffed apples is terrific.

Stuffed baked apples	Cinnamon custard
butter, for greasing	4 free-range eggs
½ lemon	100 g caster sugar
4 heaped tbsp mincemeat	1½ tsp ground cinnamon
1 tbsp brandy or rum	pinch of salt
4 large cooking apples, such as	275 ml milk
Bramleys	60 ml double cream

*1¼ hours before
you want to eat*

* Preheat the oven to 180°C/350°F/Gas Mark 4.
* Start by greasing a shallow ovenproof dish large enough to comfortably fit the four apples with butter.
* Grate the zest of the lemon. Mix together the mincemeat, brandy or rum and lemon zest.
* Using a sharp knife, scoop out the cores of the apples so that you have a generous pocket you can fill with the mincemeat mixture. Run the knife all the way around each apple to score the skin a little and prevent it from popping.
* Use a spoon to fill the apples with the mincemeat, then place them in the dish with a splash of water. Cover with foil and bake in the oven for 30 minutes.
* Meanwhile, make the cinnamon custard.
* Beat the eggs and sugar together with the cinnamon and salt. Pour in the milk and cream and stir everything together until you a have a thoroughly amalgamated mixture.
* When the apples have been cooking for 30 minutes, turn the oven down to 160°C/325°F/Gas Mark 3. Stir any liquid that might have come out of the apples into the custard.
* Pour the custard into the bottom of the dish and return to the dish to the oven to bake for a further 30–40 minutes or until the custard has just set.
* Once the custard is cooked, remove the dish from the oven and serve.

**December
puddings**

Mont Blanc Mess

A 'mess' dessert is usually associated with the summer months and strawberries; this version takes another classic pudding called Mont Blanc that includes meringue with chestnut purée and cream.

It will take a while if you make all the elements yourself (meringues take about 3 hours to cook). If you don't have the time or inclination to make meringues you can replace them with eight ready-made ones – do buy the best quality you can as some are full of all sorts of additives. Rather than make you own you could use ready made sweetened chestnut purée. This is readily available at most supermarkets and is an utterly delicious store-cupboard treat – just stir some into yoghurt for a quick midweek pudding. If you decide to use it, you will need a 500 g can (ideally French crème de marrons).

2 tbsp rum or brandy (optional)
100 g caster sugar
a few seeds from a vanilla pod
   or a drop of vanilla extract
500 g cooked peeled chestnuts
   (fresh or frozen)
300 ml double cream
4 marrons glacé or 40 g dark
   chocolate

For the meringue
2 large free-range egg whites, at
   room temperature
100 g caster sugar

2–3 hours before you want to eat

* Whisk the egg whites in a clean dry bowl until they are firm.
* Add half the sugar and carry on whisking until the whites begin to look shiny and firm. Now carefully fold in the rest of the sugar bit by bit, making sure it is very well incorporated.
* Preheat the oven to 140°C/275°F/Gas Mark 1.
* Line a baking sheet with very lightly oiled baking parchment or foil. Tip the egg white mixture on to the sheet and spread it out to form an even layer about 2.5 cm deep.
* Put the mixture in the oven and after about 45 minutes turn the oven down to 120°C/250°F/Gas Mark ½ and leave the meringue to dry out for a further 1¼–2¼ hours.
* The meringue is ready when it feels light and sounds hollow when gently tapped on the bottom.
* If using ready made chestnut puree stir a tablespoon of rum into 500 g and assemble the pudding according to the instructions below.

45 minutes before you want to eat

* To make the chestnut purée, put the rum or brandy, sugar and vanilla in a pan with 200 ml water. Heat gently until the sugar has dissolved, then bring the liquid up to a brisk boil and simmer for a few minutes until it is syrupy.
* Place the chestnuts in a bowl and cover with boiling water and leave them to soften for a few minutes – longer if using frozen chestnuts.
* Drain the chestnuts then put them in a food processor and whizz them to a purée. They will be very dry, so add the syrup in a slow stream through the spout while you are whizzing them. Stop adding the syrup when you have a smooth but firm purée.
* Take the purée out of the food processor and spread it out on a tray to cool quickly.

10 minutes before you want to eat

* While the purée is cooling, roughly chop the *marrons glacé*, or grate the chocolate.
* When the purée is cool and the meringue is cool, whip the cream to soft peaks in a large bowl.
* Smash the meringues into 5-cm chunks and fold them and the chestnut purée gently through the cream.
* Pile the 'mess' into individual serving bowls or glasses, top with the *marron glacé* or grated chocolate.

Citrus Trifle

Trifle is a classic Christmas treat, as are clementines – so we decided that a lighter sharper take on the old family favourite, using a clementine and orange jelly, would be cheerful addition to the Christmas repertoire.

For the sponge
1 lemon
175 g soft butter
175 g caster sugar
175 g self-raising flour
3 eggs

For the jelly
75 g caster sugar
500 ml clementine juice (10–15 clementines)
3 leaves (approx. 5 g) gelatine or 1 packet powdered gelatine
2 tbsp gin (optional)
2 navel oranges

For the lemon curd cream
200 ml double cream
150 ml fromage frais
100 g lemon curd

To top it off
60 g almonds
sherry or brandy, for sprinkling
icing sugar

2 hours before you want to eat

* Preheat the oven to 170°C/325°F/Gas Mark 3.
* Oil a 20–25-cm round spring-form tin or a 30 x 20-cm Swiss roll tin.
* Grate the zest from the lemon and squeeze out its juice. Sift the flour into a bowl.
* Cream the butter and sugar with the lemon zest until pale and creamy – using an electric whisk will make this easier. Mix in the eggs one by one adding a large spoonful of flour between each one,
* Gently fold in the remaining flour and add the lemon juice and a little milk so it has a dropping consistency.
* Put the mixture into the cake tin.
* Bake for 30–35 minutes or until it springs back when you touch it.
* Leave the sponge to cool on a wire rack.

1½ hours before you want to eat

* Cut the sponge into slices. Line the bottom of a glass bowl with them and sprinkle with the lemon juice.
* Make the jelly. Put the sugar in a small pan with 100 ml water. Keep the heat low while you dissolve the sugar then increase the heat and boil the liquid for a few minutes until it is syrupy.
* Pour the syrup into a jug, then measure out 80 ml and pour it into another pan. Add the clementine juice and bring to the boil.
* If you are using leaf gelatine, put it into water for a few minutes.
* Once the clementine juice has boiled, take it off the heat and add the powdered gelatine or squeeze out the leaf gelatine and stir it into the hot liquid.
* Add the gin, if using, and stir until the gelatine has dissolved. Pour the jelly over the sponge in the bowl.
* Leave the jelly to set in the fridge.
* Peel the oranges and cut them into segments, removing all the pith. Add the segments to the jelly while it is still slightly liquid so that they slowly sink.
* Toast the almonds.
* Preheat the oven to 180°C/350°F/Gas Mark 4.
* Place the almonds on a baking sheet in a single layer. Sprinkle them with the sherry or brandy and mix so that they are coated with alcohol. Scatter over some icing sugar and mix through.
* Put the baking sheet in the oven and cook the almonds for about 5 minutes so they caramelise a little.
* Whip the cream until it forms soft peaks, then mix the fromage frais and lemon curd together and fold them gently into the cream.
* When the jelly is set, pile the citrus cream on top and scatter with almonds.

Mulled Pears with Ginger Cream

These pears poached in mulled wine and served with whipped cream flavoured with
preserved ginger have a festive feel. They are easy to make and can be served hot or
cold, so it's possible to prepare the entire pudding a day or two ahead of time. If you
choose to make the pudding in advance, keep the ginger cream and the pears in their
syrupy liquid in separate airtight containers in the fridge.

Mulled pears
1 bottle red wine
1 orange
100 g caster sugar
4 cloves
1 cinnamon stick
2 pinches of nutmeg (ground or
   freshly grated)
100 ml Madeira or port
4-6 hard pears

Ginger cream
2 knobs stem ginger
1 tbsp syrup from a jar of stem
   ginger
150 ml double cream

*1 hour before
you want to eat*

* Pour the wine into a pan large enough to hold all the pears. Shave a few strips of peel
  from the orange and squeeze out its juice. Add the sugar, cloves, cinnamon, nutmeg,
  Madeira or port and the orange peel and juice. Stir well.
* Peel the pears and add them to the pan. Put a small plate over the pears to hold them
  under the liquid, place over a gentle heat, cover with a lid and allow the pears to
  simmer gently for 30–40 minutes.
* While the pears are cooking make the ginger cream
* Grate the knobs of ginger and mix them with the syrup.
* Pour the cream into a large bowl and whisk until it is starting to become firm.
  You want it to have a soft, floppy consistency so take care not to over whisk it.
* Gently fold the ginger syrup and grated ginger into the cream and place in the fridge
  until required.
* Press one of the pears to check that it's soft, then lift the pears from the liquid and set
  them to one side.
* Fish the cinnamon stick and orange peel out of the wine, then turn the heat up and
  boil rapidly for about 10 minutes or until it has reduced by about half and has a
  syrupy, sticky texture.
* Serve the pears and mulled wine syrup hot or cold, with the ginger cream and some
  brandy snaps on the side.

FOR SPECIAL OCCASIONS WITH FRIENDS AND FAMILY
Five spiced steamed fish with Chinese greens and seaweed rice
Roast chicken with fruit and nut stuffing
Lamb Harira
Roast duck with Seville oranges
Roast guinea fowl (or chicken) with chicory and bacon
Roast lamb with anchovies, rosemary potatoes and winter greens
Layered crab and celeriac
Roast Pork with stuffed baked apples
Rich Beef stew with a french bread and mustard crust
Stuffed fillet of beef
Chowder
Fish stew with aioli
Peppered steaks with Caesar salad
Pot roast carribean pork, roast sweet potatoes and spring greens
Elderflower poached chicken
Pot roast veal with morels
Red spiced poussin
Roast beef with a pepper crust, with garlic new potatoes and green bean and red onion salad
Duck with cherries, roast baby vegetables and spinach
Roast pork loin with a herb crust, and roast tomato salad and potato salad
Salmon parcels with watercress and lemon butter
Braised pork with fennel and tomatoes
Rich shellfish stew
Roast rib of beef
Duck with quinces (or pears) in red wine with roast potatoes and lemon courgettes
Poussin (or chicken) in paper with shallots, mushrooms and potatoes and spinach
Ham and parsley sauce
Pot roast venison (or beef) with root vegetable mash and curly kale
Brill with prawn bisque, citrus onions and new potatoes
Pot roast venison
Boiled Beef and carrots
Venison with pickled walnuts
Baked salmon with saffron leeks
Honey baked ham with mustard leeks

SOCIABLE LUNCHES – OR LIGHTER MEALS FOR SPECIAL OCCASIONS
Upside down chicken pie
Rolled fish fillets with apple stuffing and creamed chicory
Fish with shallot and bacon topping
Fish and potato bake
Italian cauliflower farfalle
Cheese and onion potato bread pizza with rocket, pear and walnut salad
Chicken (or pheasant) wrapped in bacon with Jerusalem artichokes
Spring onion chicken noodle soup
Caldo verde
Spinach, walnut and Roquefort soufflé
Herb leek and lemon risotto
Chicken tortillas with avocado and pomegranate salsa
Roast duck breasts with potato and radish salsa
Chowder
Sea trout baked with asparagus and Serrano ham
Tuna Empanada
Salmon with spinach and spiced rice
Baked omelette with butternut squash and sorrel
Spring vegetable soup with potato and herb dumplings
Braised pork with artichokes and mushrooms
Fish in parma ham with red wine leeks and mustard mash
Goats cheese brushetta with beetroot and rocket salad
Sea trout (or salmon) baked with asparagus and serano ham
Spiced lamb chops with radish and orange salad
Giant sausage roll
Salmon and cucumber tagliatelle
Rolled chicken breasts filled with asparagus and cheese, with new potatoes and salad
Duck salad with bacon and eggs
Chicken red onion bruschetta
Braised chicken with celery and orange
Salmon with lemon horseradish, wild rice salad and beetroot salad
Rosie's coronation chicken
Spinach and smoked trout roulade
Low rise summer soufflé with tomato salad
Sea bream with grated fennel and courgettes
Sweet charred lamb with babaganoush, green and runner beans and potatoes
Baked figs and green bean, potato and walnut salad with smoked duck or bacon

Plaice potato and spinach bake
Chicken with grapes
Glazed chicken with orange and date couscous
Lentil and chorizo stew
Goats cheese and rosemary tortilla with tomato salad
Chilli con carne with corn muffins
Lemon butternut lasagne
Steak, chips and creamed spinach
Lamb and pearl barley stew
Pistachio chicken curry
Kouilibiac – Russian fish pie
Lamb en croute, roasted root vegetables
Baked salmon with watercress dauphinoise
Venison with cranberries and polenta
The London particular – pea and ham soup

WOULD MAKE GOOD STARTERS
Artichoke and pesto tart
Scallop and Jerusalem artichoke bake
Thai fishcakes
Spinach, walnut and roquefort soufflé
French onion soup
Sardine and tomato tart
Goats cheese bruschetta with beetroot and rocket
Smoked salmon, potato pancakes
Baked egg with asparagus and ham
Smoked mackerel salad
New potato, asparagus and egg salad
Haddock with french beans and green sauce
Oatmeal herrings with beetroot salad
Salmon and cucumber tagliatelle
Hoisin chicken wraps with noodle salad
Stilton and watercress penne
Soft goats cheese salad
Duck salad with bacon and eggs
Chilled summer soup
Spiced roast vegetables with seasoned yoghurt
Russian salad with tuna and hot potatoes
Warm salmon potato salad
Spinach and smoked trout roulade
Roast tomato and tapenade tart
Quinoa with aubergine and olive relish
Butter bean and roast pepper soup
Panzanella
Green beans on toast
Fennel nicoise
Baked figs and greent bean, potato and walnut salad
Duck and lentil salad
Glazed chicken with orange and date couscous

Mussel and potato stew
Pheasant and chestnut soup
Mushrooms on toast
Spinach and chickpea soup
Warm haddock and chickpea salad
Swede and lancashire cheese soufflé
Baked field mushrooms wih ham and
   leeks
The London particular

ESPECIALLY GOOD FOR CHILDREN
Guinea fowl or chicken pie
Chicory and bacon pasta
Bobotie – south African shepherd's pie
Red flannel hash with fried eggs
Fish rarebit
Toad in the hole with onion gravy
Herb leek and lemon risotto
Carribean macaroni cheese
Grown up fish fingers and baked beans
Spring onion chicken noodle soup
Egg fried rice with pak choi
Moussaka
Baked eggs with asparagus and ham
Fat pasta ribbons with tomato flageolet
Fish pie
Stuffed baked potatoes
Parmesan chicken gouons with roast
   asparagus, garlic mayonnaise and
   rocket salad
Giant sausage roll
Baked broccoli carbonara
Baked stuffed peppers
Chicken and sweetcorn tortilla salad
Bean burgers
Sausages with peperonata
Sausages with crisp roast vegetables
   and caraway cabbage
Pasta with green vegetables
Fish and potato bake
Root vegetable cakes with spinach and
   fried eggs
Croque monsieur with quick pickled
   onions
Cod with tartar sauce and mushy peas
Chilli con carne with corn muffins
Sausages with root vegetable colcannon
   cakes and onion gravy
Potato crush fish cakes with herb sauce
Cottage pie
Venison (or beef) tagliatelle
Sauasages with fried potatoes and
   apples
Ham and macaroni bake
Romanesque or cauliflower cheese

VEGETARIAN
Caramelised vegetable tart with baked
   celery and broccoli
Spiced chickpea stew
Butternut squash with ricotta
Roast root vegetables with pearl barley
Soup au pistou
Pasta with green vegetables
Spinach Tian
Celeriac and goats cheese bake
Italian Cauliflower farfalle
Artichoke and pesto tart
Polenta with gorgonzola and garlic
   spinach
Root vegetable tagine with couscous
Root vegetable cakes with fried egg and
   spinach
Caldo verde
Flageolet bean crumble
Vegetable cobbler
Caribbean macaroni cheese
Spinach, walnut and roquefort soufflé
Red flannel hash with fried eggs
Herb leek and lemon risotto
Pasta ribbons with tomato and flageolet
   beans
Wild rice, spinach and mushroom loaf
Spring eggs
Goats cheese bruschetta with beetroot
   and rocket
Baked omelette with squash and sorrel
Potato onion and horseradish tart
Spring vegetable soup with potato and
   herb dumplings
Cous cous with pomegranate molasses
Spicy sweetcorn with sesame seeds and
   tomatoes
Stuffed baked potatoes
Sweet potato and goats cheese
   flatbread
New potato asparagus and egg salad
Mexican beans with a polenta topping
Watercress and potato frittata
Spicy bean wraps
Goats cheese gnocchi
Chickpea cakes with tomato salsa
Pearl barley and feta salad
Stilton and watercress penne
Soft goats cheese salad
Root vegetable, caraway and feta salad
Braised lentils with herb cream cheese
Wild rice chilli
Jane's fresh tomato spaghetti
Spiced roast vegetables with seasoned
   yoghurt
Quinoa with aubergine and olive relish
Panzanella
Bean burgers
Fennel nicoise
Bread and butter squash and marrow

Imam bayaldi
Cauliflower and chickpea salad
Courgette and ricotta lasagne
Artichoke and gnocchi bake
Goats cheese and rosemary tortilla
Curried coconut pumpkin
Midweek mushroom curry
Lemon butternut lasagne
Chard and mushroom rice
Spanish pumpkin casserole
Red coleslaw with baked potatoes
Squash and feta pasta
Cheese and onion bread pudding
Mushrooms on toast
Spinach and chickpea soup
Root vegetable and white bean
   minestrone
Romanesque cheese
Leek and chicory gratin
Vegetable curry
Swede and lancashire cheese soufflé
Stilton and celery strudel
Nut bake
Spinach and mushroom pasta
Dahl with coriander and onion roti

WHEN TIME IS OF THE ESSENCE (25 MINS OR UNDER)
(doesn't include SFNs that rely on
leftovers)
Grown up baked beans (20 mins)
Chicken tortillas with avocado and
   pomegranate salsa (20mins)
Spring eggs (25 mins)
Spicy sweetcorn with sesame seeds and
   tomatoes (25 mins)
Japanese noodle soup (20 mins)
Baked egg with asparagus and ham (25
   mins)
Salmon and cucumber tagliatelle
   (20mins)
Tuna Nicoise (25 mins)
Stilton and watercress penne (25 mins)
Soft goats cheese salad (15 mins)
Spiced prawn cous cous (15 mins)
Braised lentils with herb cream cheese
   (25 mins)
Chilled summer soup (25 mins)
Jane's fresh tomato spaghetti (20 mins)
Russian salad with tuna and hot
   potatoes (25 mins)
Sea bream with grated fennel and
   courgette (25 mins)
Baked fig salad (25 mins)
Smoked mussel spaghetti (25mins)
Sardines with tomato bulghur (20 mins)
Mushrooms on toast (25mins)
Romanesque cheese (25 mins)